Wirtschaftsrecht International

Schiedsgerichtsbarkeit in Singapur und Indien

Franz Kaps

Fachmedien Recht und Wirtschaft | dfv Mediengruppe | Frankfurt am Main

Zugl.: Heidelberg, Univ., Diss. iur., 2025

Bibliografische Information Der Deutschen Nationalbibliothek

Die Deutsche Nationalbibliothek verzeichnet diese Publikation in der Deutschen Nationalbibliografie; detaillierte bibliografische Daten sind im Internet über http://dnb.de abrufbar.

ISBN 978-3-8005-1965-1

dfv Mediengruppe

www.ruw.de

Druck: Beltz Grafische Betriebe GmbH, 99947 Bad Langensalza

Printed in Germany

Vorwort

Diese Dissertation ist das Ergebnis einer intensiven wissenschaftlichen Reise, die ohne die Unterstützung und Ermutigung zahlreicher Wegbegleiterinnen und Wegbegleiter nicht möglich gewesen wäre.

Zunächst möchte ich meinem Doktorvater Prof. Dr. Dr. h. c. mult. Burkhard Hess meinen tiefsten Dank aussprechen. Seine langjährige Unterstützung und seine wertvollen Ratschläge haben mich stets motiviert und inspiriert. Er hat mir nicht nur fachlich zur Seite gestanden, sondern auch in schwierigen Momenten stets an mich geglaubt und unterstützt. Seine Expertise und sein Engagement haben maßgeblich zum Erfolg dieser Arbeit beigetragen.

Ein besonderer Dank gilt meiner wunderbaren Frau Liliana und meinen geliebten Kindern Maria Luisa und Francisco. Ihre bedingungslose Unterstützung und Liebe haben mir die Kraft gegeben, diese Promotion zu vollenden. Ohne ihre ständige Ermutigung und ihr Verständnis für die vielen Stunden, die ich in meine Doktorarbeit investiert habe, wäre dieser Erfolg nicht möglich gewesen. Sie haben mir den nötigen Rückhalt gegeben und mich immer wieder daran erinnert, warum ich diesen Weg eingeschlagen habe. Ihre Geduld und ihr Verständnis haben mir zudem geholfen, die Herausforderungen dieser Reise zu meistern.

Ebenso möchte ich meinen Eltern meinen herzlichen Dank aussprechen. Sie haben das Korrekturlesen dieser Arbeit übernommen und die Druckkosten finanziert. Ihre Liebe, ihr Vertrauen und ihre beständige fortwährende Begleitung haben mich in allen Phasen des Promotionsvorhabens unterstützt und gestärkt.

Mit Dankbarkeit blicke ich auf die zahlreichen Begegnungen und Gespräche mit Wegbegleiterinnen und Wegbegleitern in Singapur, Indien, Frankfurt, Heidelberg, Luxemburg und New York City zurück, die mich auf meiner akademischen Reise ermutigt und unterstützt haben. Ihr Zuspruch war in vielerlei Hinsicht bereichernd und hat meinen fachlichen Horizont erweitert

Ein besonderer Dank gilt auch den Mitarbeiterinnen und Mitarbeitern des Max-Planck-Instituts in Luxemburg. Die dortige Arbeitsatmosphäre, die zur Verfügung gestellten Ressourcen sowie der fachliche Austausch haben wesentlich zur Entstehung dieser Dissertation beigetragen.

Gleichfalls danke ich der Universität Heidelberg von Herzen für die Möglichkeit, meine Promotion an einer Institution mit renommierter Forschungstradition und akademischer Exzellenz durchführen zu dürfen. Das inspirierende akademische Umfeld und die kontinuierliche Unterstützung waren von unschätzbarem Wert für mein Dissertationsvorhaben.

Nicht zuletzt danke ich dem Verlag sowie allen beteiligten Mitarbeiterinnen und Mitarbeitern für die professionelle Begleitung bei der Veröffentlichung dieser Arbeit. Ihr Einsatz hat wesentlich dazu beigetragen, dass diese Dissertation in ihrer vorliegenden Form erscheinen konnte.

Ausschließlich aus Gründen der besseren Lesbarkeit und Praktikabilität habe ich in dieser Dissertation überwiegend die männliche Form verwendet. Selbstverständlich sind damit stets Personen jeden Geschlechts gemeint. Diese sprachliche Entscheidung dient allein der stilistischen Vereinfachung und impliziert keinerlei Wertung.

Frankfurt, im Juli 2025 Franz Kaps

Inhaltsverzeichnis

Abkürzungsverzeichnis

AA	Arbitration Act (Singapur)
A. A.	Anderer Ansicht/andere Auffassung
AAA	American Arbitration Association
Acclaim	Acclaim Insurance Brokers Pte Ltd
A. E.	Am Ende
A. F.	Alte Fassung
AIR	All India Reporter
ALD	Andhra Legal Decisions
Aloe Vera	Aloe Vera of America Inc
Alstom	Alstom Technology Ltd
ALT	Andhra Law Times
AMRG	Auzminerals Resource Group Limited
Antig	Antig Investments Pte Ltd
Arbitration Amendment Act	Arbitration and Conciliation (Amendment) Act 2015 (Indien)
Arbitration Ordinance	Arbitration and Conciliation (Amendment) Ordinance 2015 (Indien)
Arb LR	Arbitration Law Reporter
Art.	Artikel
ASA	Association Suisse de l'Arbitrage
Asianic Food	Asianic Food (S) Pte Ltd
Asuransi	PT Asuransi Jasa Indonesia (Persero)
Atlantic	Atlantic & Orient Shipping Corp
Aufl.	Auflage
Ausg.	Ausgabe
Australian	Australian Timber Products Pte Ltd
Balco	Bharat Aluminium Co v Kaiser Aluminium Technical Service Inc
BCL	Butterworths Current Law
Bd.	Band
Begr.	Begründer
BGH	Bundesgerichtshof
Bharat	Bharat Aluminium
Bhatia	Bhatia International v Bulk Trading SA & ANR
Bing.	Bingham's Common Pleas Reports
Bom	Bombay
BomCR	Bombay Cases Reporter
BRIC	Brasilien, Russland, Indien und China
Bulk	Bulk Trading SA
Bzw.	Beziehungsweise
Ca.	Circa
CALLJ	Calcutta Law Journal
Carriers	Front Carriers Ltd

CFR	Cost and Freight
Ch.	Law Journal – Chancery Reports
Chief Justice	Chief Justice of India
Chloro Controls	Chloro Controls (I) P Ltd v Severn Trent Water Purification Inc & Ors
CIF	Cost, Insurance and Freight
Cir.	Circuit
CIV	Civil
Commercial Court Act	Commercial Division and Commercial Appellate Division of High Courts Act 2015
Coop	Coop International Pte Ltd v Ebel SA
Cri	Criminal
Del	Delhi
Dermajaya	Dermajaya Properties Sdn Bhd v Premium Properties Sdn Bhd and another
Dexia	Dexia Bank SA
DIA	Danish Institute of Arbitration
DIAC	Delhi International Arbitration Centre
DIS	Deutsche Institution für Schiedsgerichtsbarkeit e. V.
DLT	Delhi Law Times
Doc.	Document
Engineering	Satyam Venture Engineering Services Ltd
Engl.	Englisch
E. R.	English Reports
Ergänzungen des UNCITRAL Modellgesetzes 2006	UNCITRAL Model Law on International Commercial Arbitration 1985, with amendments as adopted in 2006
f.	folgende
FACT	FICCI Arbitration and Conciliation Tribunal
Ferrostaal	Ferrostaal AG & Anr
ff.	fortfolgende
FICCI	Federation of Indian Chambers of Commerce and Industry
Fn.	Fußnote
FOB	Free On Board
Foreign Award Act	Foreign Awards (Recognition And Enforcement) Act 1961
Front Carriers v Atlantic	Front Carriers Ltd v Atlantic & Orient Shipping Corp
GAFTA	Grain and Feed Trade Association
Gains	Gains Trading Ltd
GE	General Electric Co
Gem.	Gemäß
Hindustan	Hindustan Petroleum Corpn Ltd
Hindustan Petroleum Petroleums	Hindustan Petroleum Corpn Ltd v M/S Pinkcity Midway
Holland Ltd	John Holland Pty Ltd

Hrsg.	Herausgeber
IAA	International Arbitration Act (Singapur)
IBA	International Bar Association
ICA	Indian Council of Arbitration
ICC	International Chamber of Commerce
ICCA	International Council for Commercial Arbitration
ICDR	International Centre for Dispute Resolution
Incoterm	International Commercial Term
Indian Oil	Indian Oil Corp Ltd & Ors v M/S Raja Transport (P) Ltd
Inländische Schiedssprüche	Inländische und internationale nicht handelsrechtliche Schiedssprüche (Indien)
Inländische Schiedsverfahren	Inländische und internationale nicht handelsrechtliche Schiedsverfahren (Indien)
Insigma	Insigma Technology Co Ltd
IPRG	Bundesgesetz über das Internationale Privatrecht
I. S.	Im Sinne
I. S. d.	Im Sinne des
i. S. v.	Im Sinne von
ITA	Institute for Transnational Arbitration
IUA	International Underwriting Association of London
I. V.m.	In Verbindung mit
John Holland	John Holland Pty Ltd v Toyo Engineering Corp
JT	Judgment Today
Kaiser	Kaiser Aluminium Technical Service Inc
Koh Brothers	Koh Brothers Building & Civil Engineering Contractor (Pte) Ltd
Law Commission	Law Commission of India
LCIA	London Court of International Arbitration
Leadenhall	Leadenhall Insurance Brokers Pte Ltd
LKE Europe	LKE Electric Europe A/S
Lloyd's Rep.	Lloyd's Law Reports
LMA	Lloyd's Market Association
LMAA	London Maritime Arbitrators Association
L. R.	Law Reports
LugÜ	Luganer Übereinkommen über die gerichtliche Zuständigkeit und die Anerkennung und Vollstreckung von Entscheidungen in Zivil- und Handelssachen
Magnifica	Magnifica Marina SA
MCIA	Mumbai Centre for Institutional Arbitration
MhLj	Maharashtra Law Journal
Mio.	Million
MOA	Memorandum of Agreement
MP	Madhya Pradesh
Mrd.	Milliarde
MSM	MSM Satellite

MüKo	Münchener Kommentar
National	National Agricultural Co-Op
Navigator	Navigator Investment Services Ltd
Navigator Investment	Navigator Investment Services Ltd v Acclaim Insurance Brokers Pte Ltd
N. F.	Neue Fassung
NJW	Neue Juristische Wochenschrift
No.	Number
Nos.	Numbers
Nr.	Nummer
NTUC	NTUC Income Insurance Cooperative Limited
Odnse	MS Invest Odense A/S
Oil Corp	Indian Oil Corp Ltd & Ors
ONGC	Oil and Natural Gas Corporation Limited
Ori	Orissa
Patel Engineering	SBP & Co v Patel Engineering Ltd & Anr
Patriot	Ooo Patriot
P. C.	Privy Council
Phulchand	Phulchand Exports Ltd v Ooo Patriot
Phulchand Exports	Phulchand Exports Ltd
Pinkcity	Pinkcity Midway Petroleums
Prof.	Professor
PSC	Production Sharing Contract
PT Asuransi v Dexia Bank	PT Asuransi Jasa Indonesia (Persero) v Dexia Bank SA
Raja	M/S Raja Transport(P) Ltd
Raju	P Anand Gajapathi Raju & Ors v P V G Raju (Died) & Ors
Renusagar	Renusagar Power Co Ltd v General Electric Co
Renusagar Power	Renusagar Power Co Ltd
Richter	Richterinnen und Richter
RIW	Recht der internationalen Wirtschaft
Rn.	Randnummer
S.	Seite
SARS	Schwere Akute Respiratorische Syndrom
Satyam	Satyam Computer Services Ltd
Saw Pipes	Oil & Natural Gas Corporation Ltd v Saw Pipes Ltd
SC	Supreme Court
SCALE	Supreme Court Almanac
SCC	Supreme Court Cases
SchiedsG	Arbitration and Conciliation Act 1996 (Indien)
Schiedsrichter	Schiedsrichterinnen und Schiedsrichter
SchiedsVZ	Zeitschrift für Schiedsverfahren
SCMA	Singapore Chamber of Maritime Arbitration
SCR	Supreme Court Reporter
Sec.	Section

Severn	Severn Trent Water Purification
SGCA	Singapore Court of Appeal
SGFC	Singapore Federal Court
SGHC	Singapore High Court
SGS	Société Générale de Surveillance
Shin-Etsu	Shin-Etsu Chemical Co Ltd v M/S Aksh Optifibre Ltd & Anr
Shri Lal Mahal	Shri Lal Mahal Ltd v Progetto Grano Spa
SIAC	Singapore International Arbitration Centre
Silica	Silica Investors Ltd and other appeals
Sim Chay Koon	Sim Chay Koon and others
Sing	Singapore
SLR	Singapore Law Reports
SMS	Short message service
S. o.	Siehe oben
Sog.	Sogenannt
Strandore	Strandore Invest A
Supp.	Supplement
Suppl.	Supplement
Swift	Swift-Fortune Ltd
Swift v Magnifica	Swift-Fortune Ltd v Magnifica Marine SA
Tjong	Tjong Very Sumito
Tomolugen	Tomolugen Holdings Ltd
U. a.	Unter anderem
UKHL	United Kingdom House of Lords
UKPC	United Kingdom Privy Council
U. N.	United Nations
UNCITRAL	United Nations Commission on International Trade Law
UNCITRAL Modellgesetz	UNCITRAL Modellgesetz für die internationale Handelsschiedsgerichtsbarkeit 1985
UNÜ	New Yorker UN-Übereinkommen über die Anerkennung und Vollstreckung ausländischer Schiedssprüche vom 10. Juni 1958
US	United States
USA	Vereinigten Staaten von Amerika
V	Versus
V. a.	Vor allem
Venture	Venture Global Engineering
Venture Global	Venture Global Engineering v Satyam Computer Services Ltd & Anr
Vgl.	Vergleiche
Vgl. o.	Vergleiche oben
Videocon	Videocon Industries Ltd v Union of India & Anr
Vol.	Volume
W. L. R.	Weekly Law Reports

World	World Sport Group
ZPO	Zivilprozessordnung

Literaturverzeichnis

Autor	**Titel**
	In Conversation: An Interview with Honourable Justice of Appeal M Karthigesu, Singapore Law Review 1995, Volume 16, S. 1–22
Agrawal, Divyanshu	Case Comment, India: limiting the jurisdiction of Indian courts over foreign arbitrations – the decision in Reliance Industries, International Arbitration Law Review 2014, S. N43–N46
Agrawal, K. B.	Civil Procedure in India, Alphen aan den Rijn 2012 Zitiert als: Agrawal, K. B., Procedure
Allsop, James	International commercial arbitration – the courts and the rule of law in the Asia Pacific region, Arbitration, 2005, S. 169–175
Anchayil, Anjali	Bhatia International to Videocon Industries and Yograj Infrastructure: Recasting the Foundations of Arbitration Law in India, Arbitration International 2013, Volume 29, Ausgabe 1, S. 105–114
Arvind, T. T.	The "transplant effect" in harmonization, International & Comparative Law Quarterly 2010, S. 65–88
Banerjee, Anil	English Law in India, New Delhi 1984
Bansal, Ashwinie	Bharat's Commentary on the Arbitration & Conciliation Act, 1996, Law, Practice & Procedure, New Delhi 2007, 2 Bände Zitiert als: Bansal, Bharat's Commentary, Bd.
Basu, Durga	Constitutional Law of India, 8. Auflage, Gurgaon 2008
Bell, Gary	The Singapore Legal System in Context – Whither the Concept of the National Legal System?, in: Tan, Kevin (Hrsg.), The Singapore Legal System, 2. Auflage, Singapur 1999, S. 1–25
Berg, Albert van den (Hrsg.)	Yearbook Commercial Arbitration 2002, Volume XXVII, Den Haag 2002
Berger, Klaus	Internationale Wirtschaftsschiedsgerichtsbarkeit, Verfahrens- und materiellrechtliche Grundprobleme im Spiegel moderner Schiedsgesetze und Schiedspraxis, Berlin, New York 1992

Berger, Thierry/Robertson, Mark — Legislative Comment, The new ICC Rules of Arbitration: a brief overview of the main changes, International Arbitration Law Review 2011, S. 145–155

Biswas, Tushar — Introduction to Arbitration in India: The Role of the Judiciary, Alphen aan den Rijn 2014

Biswas, Tushar — Revisiting the matters relating to the appointment of an arbitrator and the role of the Indian judiciary, International Company and Commercial Law Review 2011, S. 165–171

Biswas, Tushar — The doctrine of competence-competence from Indian perspectives, International Arbitration Law Review 2010, S. 42–49

Blackaby, Nigel/Partasides, Constantine/Redfern, Alan/Hunter, Martin — Redfern and Hunter on International Arbitration, 6. Auflage, New York, Oxford 2015
Zitiert als: Blackaby/Partasides/Redfern/Hunter, International Arbitration

Böckstiegel, Karl-Heinz/Kröll, Stefan/Nacimiento, Patricia — Arbitration in Germany: The Model Law in Practice, 2. Auflage, Alphen aan den Rijn 2015
Zitiert als:
Bearbeiter, in: Böckstiegel/Kröll/Nacimiento

Boo, Lawrence — 3. Arbitration, Singapore Academy of Law Annual Review of Singapore Cases 2001, Volume 2, S. 24–35

Boo, Lawrence — 3. Arbitration Law, Singapore Academy of Law Annual Review of Singapore Cases 2006, Volume 7, S. 51–72

Boo, Lawrence — Halsbury's, Law of Singapore, Volume 1 (2), Arbitration, Singapur 2014
Zitiert als:
Boo, Halsbury's

Born, Gary — International Arbitration: Cases and Materials, 2. Auflage, Alphen aan den Rijn 2015
Zitiert als:
Born, Cases and Materials

Born, Gary — International Arbitration: Law and Practice, 2. Auflage, Alphen aan den Rijn 2016
Zitiert als:
Born, Law and Practice

Born, Gary International Commercial Arbitration, 2. Auflage, Alphen aan den Rijn 2014, 3 Bände
Zitiert als:
Born, International Commercial Arbitration, Bd.

Born, Gary International Commercial Arbitration: Commentary and Materials, 2. Auflage, Den Haag, Herndon 2001
Zitiert als:
Born, Commentary and Materials

Born, Gary/Spears, Suzanne International Arbitration and India: "A Truly Excellent Judgment!", Indian Journal of Arbitration Law 2012, Volume I, Ausgabe 1, S. 4–8

Canfield, Jory Growing Pains and Coming-of-Age: The State of International Arbitration in India, Pepperdine Dispute Resolution Law Journal 2014, Volume 14, Ausgabe 3, S. 335–353

Carlevaris, Andrea The Geography of International Arbitration – Places of Arbitration: the Old Ones and the New Ones, in: Brekoulakis, Stavros/Lew, Julian/Mistelis, Loukas (Hrsg.), The Evolution and Future of International Arbitration, Alphen aan den Rijn 2016, S. 331–340

Chan, Andrew/Woodward, Alison Singapore as a place for arbitration: recent developments, Arbitration 2003, S. 10–17

Chan, Darius/Tan, Paul International Arbitration: Internationalist Outlook Leading the Development of Local Jurisprudence, in: Yihan, Goh/Tan, Paul (Hrsg.), Singapore Law, 50 Years in the Making, Singapur 2015, S. 775–797

Chan, Leng Sun Developments in Arbitration Laws, Singapore Academy of Law Journal 2002, Volume 14, S. 49–68

Chan, Leng Sun Injunctions in Aid of Foreign Arbitration: The Singapore Experience, Asian International Arbitration Journal 2007, Volume 3, Ausgabe 2, S. 142–162

Chan, Leng Sun Singapore Law on Arbitral Awards, Singapur 2011

Chan, Sek Keong Application of English Law Act 1993, A New Charter of Justice, in: Yihan, Goh/Tan, Paul (Hrsg.), Singapore Law, 50 Years in the Making, Singapur 2015, S. 26–75

Chang, Daphne/Teo, Liyin Changes in the Supreme Court of Singapore, Singapore Law Review 1993, Volume 14, S. 396–411

Chaterjee, Sujoy Judicial Import of the Model Law: How Far is too Far?, Indian Journal of Arbitration Law 2015, Volume IV, Ausgabe 1, S. 19–25

Chen, Siyuan Evidence and Criminal Procedure: Gradual Development towards Clarity in a Maze of Statutory Enactments, in: Yihan, Goh/Tan, Paul (Hrsg.), Singapore Law, 50 Years in the Making, Singapur 2015, S. 415–471

Chen, Siyuan/Chua, Eunice Civil Procedure in Singapore, Alphen aan den Rijn 2014

Cheng, Teresa/Liu, Joe Enforcement of Foreign Awards in Mainland China: Current Practices and Future Trends, Journal of International Arbitration 2014, Volume 31, Ausgabe 5, S. 651–674

Chew, Leslie Introduction to the Law and Practice of Arbitration in Singapore, Singapur, Hongkong, Malaysia 2010

Chionh, Mavis The Development of the Court System, in: Tan, Kevin (Hrsg.), Essays in Singapore Legal History, Singapur 2005, S. 93–137

Chong, Yee Leong Recognition and Enforcement of the Arbitral Award, in: Menon, Sundaresh/Brock, Denis (Hrsg.), Arbitration in Singapore, A Practical Guide, Singapur 2014, S. 345–375

Choudhary, Tanya Arbitrability of Competition Law Disputes in India, Indian Journal of Arbitration Law 2015, Volume IV, Ausgabe 2, S. 69–86

Chua, Eunice/Leo, Lionel Civil Procedure: Autochthony for Efficiency and Justice, in: Yihan, Goh/Tan, Paul (Hrsg.), Singapore Law, 50 Years in the Making, Singapur 2015, S. 358–414

Constantin, Delphine Indian case law review (2014–2015): anti – arbitration injunctions, International Business Law Journal 2015, S. 409–418

Constantin, Delphine Legislative Comment, India's amended Arbitration Law: what's new for foreign investors?, International Business Law Journal 2016, S. 41–52

Dam, Shubhankar Executive, in: Choudhry, Sujit/Khosla, Madhav/Mehta, Pratap (Hrsg.), The Oxford Handbook of the Indian Constitution, New York, Oxford 2016, S. 307–329

Dang, Minh/Murugaiyan, Siva — Singapore court confuses over arbitration, International Financial Law Review 2001, Ausgabe 9, S. 87–90

Darwazeh, Nadia/Linnane, Rita — Case Comment, Set-aside and enforcement proceedings: the 1996 Indian Arbitration Act under threat, International Arbitration Law Review 2004, S. 81–87

Dewan, Nakul — Arbitration in India: An Unenjoyable Litigating Jamboree!, Asian International Arbitration Journal 2007, Volume 3, Ausgabe 1, S. 99–123

Dundas, Hew — Legislative Comment, The Arbitration (Scotland) Act 2010: converting vision into reality, Arbitration 2010, S. 2–15

Dunning, Graham — Stop – or go? Injunctions and arbitration, Arbitration 2008, S. 254–262

Eisenberg, Theodore/ Kalantry, Sital/ Robinson, Nick — Litigation as a Measure of Well-Being, DePaul Law Review 2013, Volume 62, Ausgabe 2, S. 247–292

Gaillard, Emmanuel — Prima Facie Review of Existence, Validity of Arbitration Agreement, New York Law Journal 2005, S. 3, 7–8

Gaillard, Emmanuel/ Savage, John (Hrsg.) — Fouchard Gaillard Goldman on International Commercial Arbitration, Den Haag 1999
Zitiert als:
Gaillard/Savage, Fouchard Gaillard Goldman

Gandhi, B. M. — V. D. Kulshreshtha's Landmarks in Indian Legal and Constitutional History, 10. Auflage, Lucknow 2013
Zitiert als:
Gandhi, B. M., Kulshreshtha's Landmarks

Gandhi, Mohandas — An Autobiography or The story of my experiments with truth, Ahmedabad 1999
Zitiert als:
Gandhi, Mohandas, An Autobiography

Garner, Bryan (Hrsg.) — Black's Law Dictionary, 10. Auflage, St. Paul 2014
Zitiert als:
Garner, Black's Law Dictionary

Garner, Bryan (Hrsg.) — Black's Law Dictionary, Fifth Pocket Edition, 5. Auflage, St. Paul 2016
Zitiert als:
Garner, Black's Law Dictionary Pocket

Gaya, Javed Judicial ambush of arbitration in India, Law Quarterly Review 2004, S. 571–574

Gupta, Aditya/ Das, Sagnik Case Comment, Reliance industries: Supreme Court of India limits supervisory jurisdiction over foreign seated arbitration, Arbitration 2014, S. 466–469

Gupta, Arpan A New Dawn for India: Reducing Court Intervention in Enforcement of Foreign Awards, Indian Journal of Arbitration Law 2013, Volume II, Ausgabe 2, S. 1–12

Gupta, Nidhi Saving Face or Upholding 'Rule of Law': Reflections on Antrix Corp Ltd. v. Devas Multimedia P. Ltd. (Arbitration Petition No. 20 of 2011, Decided on May 10, 2013), Indian Journal of Arbitration Law 2013, Volume II, Ausgabe 2, S. 1–15

Gupta, Suvrajyoti Maladies of Indian arbitration: a case for a dualist regime, International Arbitration Law Review 2013, S. 69–80

Hamid, Abdul A Chronicle of British Indian Legal History, Jaipur 1991

Hilmer, Sarah Did arbitration fail India or did India fail arbitration?, International Arbitration Law Review 2007, S. 33–37

Ho, Jean Decoding Singapore's International Arbitration Act, Section 12(7), Arbitration International 2008, Volume 24, Ausgabe 4, S. 609–614

Holtzmann, Howard/ Neuhaus, Joseph A Guide To The UNCITRAL Model Law On International Commercial Arbitration: Legislative History and Commentary, Alphen aan den Rijn 1989
Zitiert als:
Holtzmann/Neuhaus, Guide UNCITRAL

Honsell, Heinrich/ Vogt, Nedim/ Schnyder, Anton/Berti, Stephen (Hrsg.) Basler Kommentar, Internationales Privatrecht, 3. Auflage, Basel 2013
Zitiert als:
Bearbeiter, in: Honsell/Vogt/Schnyder/Berti, Basler Kommentar

Howell, David/Duthie, Leigh/Lim, Mark International Arbitration in Singapore – Opting out of the UNCITRAL Model Law, Journal of International Arbitration 2002, Volume 19, Ausgabe 1, S. 39–50

Hoyle, Jonathan — Cohabitation: Do Arbitral Rules and Arbitral Statues Go Together?, "Implied" Opting-Out of the Model Law in Singapore and Australia and What it Might Mean, The International Construction Law Review 2001, S. 692–701

Hsu, Locknie — Section 15 of the Singapore International Arbitration Act – what are the options?, International Arbitration Law Review 1999, S. 17–21

Hwang, Michael — Singapore: amendments to the Singapore International Arbitration Act, International Arbitration Law Review 2002, S. N26–N30

Hwang, Michael/Boo, Lawrence/Han, Yewon — Singapore, in: Bosman, Lise (Hrsg.), ICCA International Handbook on Commercial Arbitration, Band V, Loseblattsammlung, Alphen aan den Rijn, Stand: Dezember 2017, S. Singapore 1–51

Hwang, Michael/Chan, Andrew — Enforcement and Setting Aside of International Arbitral Awards: The Perspective of Common Law Countries, in: Berg, Albert van den (Hrsg.), International Arbitration and National Courts: The Never Ending Story, ICCA Congress Series, Volume 10, S. 145–164

Hwang, Michael/Chan, Andrew — The Role of the Singapore Courts in Relation to International Commercial Arbitration, Journal of International Arbitration 1999, Volume 16, Ausgabe 4, S. 101–114

Hwang, Michael/Chan, Andrew/Selvaraj, Ramesh — Singapore, in: Moser, Michael (Hrsg.), Arbitration in Asia, 2. Auflage, Loseblattsammlung, Huntington, Stand: September 2017, Sing-1–Sing-107

Hwang, Michael/Cheng, Fong Lee — Relevant Considerations in Choosing the Place of Arbitration, Asian International Arbitration Journal 2008, Volume 4, Ausgabe 2, S. 195–220

Hwang, Michael/Lai, Amy — Do egregious errors amount to a breach of public policy?, Arbitration 2005, S. 1–24

Hwang, Michael/Lee, Shaun — Survey of South East Asian Nations on the Application of the New York Convention, Journal of International Arbitration 2008, Volume 25, Ausgabe 6, S. 873–892

Hwang, Michael/Muttath, Rajesh — Enforcement of arbitral awards in Singapore, International Arbitration Law Review 2000, S. 207–214

Hwang, Michael/Muttath, Rajesh — The role of courts in the course of arbitral proceedings: Singapore and other Asian perspectives, Arbitration 2002, S. 223–237

Ibrahim, Ahmad — Singapore, in: Knapp, Viktor (Hrsg.), International Encyclopedia of Comparative Law, National Reports, Volume 1, Boston, Dordrecht, Lancaster, Tübingen 1987, S. 55–62

International Business Publications — Singapore Criminal Laws, Regulations and Procedures Handbook: Strategic Information, Regulations, Procedures, Washington D. C. 2015
Zitiert als:
International Business Publications, Singapore

International Chamber of Commerce — 2015 ICC Dispute Resolution Statistics, ICC Dispute Resolution Bulletin 2016, Ausgabe 1, S. 9–21

Jain, Alok — Yet Another Misad-Venture by Indian Courts in the Satyam Judgment?, Arbitration International 2010, Volume 26, Ausgabe 2, S. 251–280

Jain, Devyani — Judicial Trend of Intervention in Sports Arbitration and its Future in India, Indian Journal of Arbitration Law 2012, Volume I, Ausgabe 1, S. 36–45

Jain, M. P. — Indian Constitutional Law, 7. Auflage, Gurgaon 2014
Zitiert als:
Jain, M. P., Constitution

Jauernig, Othmar/Hess, Burkhard — Zivilprozessrecht, 30. Auflage, München 2011

Jayasimha, Shreyas/Mody, Zia — India, in: Moser, Michael/Choong, John (Hrsg.), Asia Arbitration Handbook, New York, Oxford 2011, S. 843–900

Jenckel, Hans-Wilhelm — Das Rechtssystem der Republik Singapur, Eine Studie zur Rezeption des englischen Rechts im Commonwealth, Bern, Frankfurt am Main, New York 1986

Jenkins, Jane — International Construction Arbitration Law, 2. Auflage, Alphen aan den Rijn 2014

Kachwaha, Sumeet — Enforcement of Arbitration Awards in India, Asian International Arbitration Journal 2008, Volume 4, Ausgabe 1, S. 64–82

Kachwaha, Sumeet The Arbitration Law of India: A Critical Analysis, Asian International Arbitration Journal 2005, Volume 1, Ausgabe 2, S. 105–126

Kachwaha, Sumeet The Indian Arbitration Law: towards a new jurisprudence, International Arbitration Law Review 2007, S. 13–17

Karia, Tejas/Mehra, Karan/Dhawan, Bahaar Judicial Intervention in foreign arbitration: redefined by the Supreme Court of India, The In-House Lawyer, 2012 S. 20–23

Karis, Tejas/Kapoor, Ila/Aggarwal, Ananya Post Amendments: What Plagues Arbitration in India?, Indian Journal of Arbitration Law 2016, Volume V, Ausgabe 1, S. 230–243

Khambata, Darius Arbitration in Asian superpowers: recent developments in Indian arbitration law, Arbitration 2013, S. 441–446

Khanna, Devika Arbitration's recent adventures and misadventures in India, International Arbitration Law Review 2012, S. 203–208

Kimbrough, Philip Singapore, in: Berg, Albert van den (Hrsg.), Yearbook Commercial Arbitration 1986, Volume XI, Deventer 1986, S. 29–52

Klötzel, Thomas Zur Anwendung englischen Rechts in Singapur, RIW 1995, S. 202–204

Kren Kostkiewicz, Jolanta IPRG/LugÜ Kommentar, Bundesgesetz über das Internationale Privatrecht, Lugano-Übereinkommen und weitere Erlasse, Zürich 2015
Zitiert als:
Kren Kostkiewicz, IPRG/LugÜ

Krishan, Ranbir An Overview of the Arbitration and Conciliation Act 1996, Journal of International Arbitration 2004, Volume 21, Ausgabe 3, S. 263–278

Krishan, Ranbir Appointment of an arbitrator in arbitration proceedings under the Indian Arbitration and Conciliation Act 1996, International Arbitration Law Review 2001, S. 90–93

Krishnaprasad, K. V. From Bhatia International to Dozco India: A Response to Vidhu Gupta's 'Stretching the Limits of Statutory Interpretation: Critical Review of Bhatia International v. Bulk Trading', Nalsar Student Law Review 2011, S. 69–81

Kroll, Stefan Setting aside proceedings in Model Law jurisdictions – selected procedural and substantive questions from the case law, International Arbitration Law Review 2005, S. 170–178

Kronke, Herbert/Nacimiento, Patricia/Otto, Dirk/Port, Nicola (Hrsg.) Recognition and Enforcement of Foreign Arbitral Awards: A Global Commentary on the New York Convention, Alphen aan den Rijn 2010
Zitiert als:
Bearbeiter, in: Kronke/Nacimiento/Otto/Port

Krüger, Wolfgang/Rauscher, Thomas Münchener Kommentar zur Zivilprozessordnung, Band 3, §§ 946–1117 ZPO, EGZPO, GVG, EGGVG, UKlaG, Internationales und Europäisches Zivilprozessrecht, 5. Auflage, München 2017
Zitiert als:
Bearbeiter, in: MüKo ZPO

Kumar, Aakanksha Foreign arbitral awards enforcement and the public policy exception – India's move towards becoming an arbitration-friendly jurisdiction, International Arbitration Law Review 2014, S. 76–85

Kwatra, G. K. Arbitration and Conciliation Law of India, 7. Auflage, New Delhi 2008

Lachmann, Jens-Peter Handbuch für die Schiedsgerichtspraxis, 3. Auflage, Köln 2008

Lau, Christopher/Horlach, Christin Party Autonomy – The Turning Point?, Dispute Resolution International 2010, Volume 4, Ausgabe 1, S. 121–130

Law, Jonathan (Hrsg.) A Dictionary of Law, 8. Auflage, New York, Oxford 2015
Zitiert als:
Law, Oxford Dictionary

Lawn, Nicholas/Virjee, Munaf Don't panic at Satyam, Amend your arbitration agreements. The alternatives are far worse, Indian Finance Arbitration 2009, S. 52–53

Lee, Joel The ADR Movement in Singapore, in: Tan, Kevin (Hrsg.), The Singapore Legal System, 2. Auflage, Singapur 1999, S. 414–445

Lee, Michelle Existence of Arbitration Agreements – The Tension between Arbitral and Curial Review, Asian International Arbitration Journal 2014, Volume 10, Ausgabe 2, S. 67–91

Lee, Suet Lin Joyce Much Ado about Errors: The Singapore Perspective, Journal of International Arbitration 1998, Volume 15, Ausgabe 1, S. 95–112

Lew, Julian Commentary on Interim and Conservatory Measures in ICC Arbitration Cases, ICC International Court of Arbitration Bulletin 2000, Volume 11, Ausgabe 1, S. 23–30

Lew, Julian/Mistelis, Loukas/Kröll, Stefan Comparative International Commercial Arbitration, Den Haag 2003

Lewis, Dean The Interpretation and Uniformity of the UNCITRAL Model Law on International Commercial Arbitration: Focusing on Australia, Hong Kong and Singapore, Alphen aan den Rijn 2016

Lim, Charles The Developmental Life Cycle of International Arbitration Legislation – Singapore IAA Case Study, Asian International Arbitration Journal 2011, Volume 7, Ausgabe 1, S. 1–28

Lim, Wei Lee/Yeo, Alvin Singapore, in: Moser, Michael/Choong, John (Hrsg.), Asia Arbitration Handbook, New York, Oxford 2011, S. 671–743

Ly, Filip de Paradigmatic Changes – Uniformity, Diversity, Due Process and Good Administration of Justice: The Next Thirty Years, in: Brekoulakis, Stavros/Lew, Julian/Mistelis, Loukas (Hrsg.), The Evolution and Future of International Arbitration, Alphen aan den Rijn 2016, S. 21–38

Lye, Kah Cheong/Yeo, Chuan Tat/Choo, Zheng Xi Interim Measures in Aid of Foreign Arbitrations, Time for the Deus Ex Machina? Singapore Academy of Law Journal 2009, Volume 21, S. 429–456

Madhavan, M. R. Legislature: Privileges and Process, in: Choudhry, Sujit/Khosla, Madhav/Mehta, Pratap (Hrsg.), The Oxford Handbook of the Indian Constitution, New York, Oxford 2016, S. 270–289

Mahajan, Kartikey Case Comment, Allegations of fraud are no bar to foreign arbitrations, International Arbitration Law Review 2014, S. N9–N11

Mahajan, Kartikey Case Comment, Reversing the clock on "public policy" for foreign awards, International Arbitration Law Review 2013, S. N43–N46

Mahajan, Kartikey Making the case for Post-Award interim relief for Award-Debtor, Indian Journal of Arbitration Law 2014, Volume III, Ausgabe 2, S. 14–22

Mahajan, Kartikey The arbitrability of fraud in India, Arbitration 2015, S. 48–56

Mahajan, Kartikey/Anand, Mallika Case Comment, Heralding a new dawn for arbitration in India: is there reason to be circumspect any more?, Arbitration 2013, S. 28–36

Mahajan, Kartikey/Bhatt, Malak Case Comment, India: extension of arbitration agreement to non-signatories, International Arbitration Law Review 2013, S. N25–N28

Mahajan, Kartikey/Bhatt, Malak Reference of Non-Signatories to Arbitration in Composite Transactions: Did the Indian Supreme Court Get it Right?, Journal of International Arbitration 2013, Volume 30, Ausgabe 6, S. 711–726

Mahajan, Kartikey/Chatterjee, Sujoy The Indian Supreme Court's inconsistency in referring parties to foreign seated arbitrations: need for clarity, International Arbitration Law Review 2015, S. 114–120

Mahajan, Kartikey/Narayan, Vikram The Indian Supreme Court and its public policy seesaw, International Arbitration Law Review 2015, S. 63–73

Mainwaring-Taylor, Christopher/Sullivan, Jeffrey Litigating in the shadow of the New York Convention, Arbitration, 2008, S. 133–138

Malhotra, Indu O. P. Malhotra on The Law & Practice of Arbitration and Conciliation, 3. Auflage, New Delhi 2014
Zitiert als:
Malhotra, Indu, O. P. Malhotra on Arbitration

Malhotra, O. P. Default power of the Chief Justice to appoint arbitrators: Indian Arbitration and Conciliation Act 1996 s. 11, Arbitration 2006, S. 201–206

Malhotra, O. P. Legislative Comment, Default power of the Chief Justice to appoint arbitrators: Indian Arbitration and Conciliation Act 1996 s. 11, Arbitration 2004, S. 177–182

Malhotra, O. P. Opening the Pandora's Box: An Analysis of the Supreme Court's Decision in S. B.P. v. Patel Engineering, Student Bar Review 2007, Volume 19, Ausgabe 2, S. 69–76

Malhotra, O. P. The scope of public policy under the Indian Arbitration and Conciliation Act 1996, Arbitration 2005, S. 36–45

Mangan, Mark/Reed, Lucy/Choong, John A Guide to the SIAC Arbitration Rules, New York, Oxford 2014

Markanda, P. C./Markanda, Naresh/Markanda, Rajesh Law Relating to Arbitration and Conciliation, 8. Auflage, Gurgaon 2012

Megens, Peter Singapore arbitration and the courts: quo vadis?, Arbitration 2012, S. 26–36

Megens, Peter/Finch, Derek Case Comment, Setting aside an award on public policy grounds: AJT v AJU, Arbitration 2011, S. 155–157

Menon, Sundaresh Patron's address, Arbitration 2015, S. 413–426

Merkin, Robert/Hjalmarsson, Johanna Singapore Arbitration Legislation, Annotated, London 2009

Minn, Naing Oo A Survey of National Laws and Practices on Enforcement of Foreign Arbitral Awards in South and South East Asia, in: Berg, Albert van den (Hrsg.), International Arbitration, The Coming of a New Age?, ICCA Congress Series, Volume 17, Alphen aan den Rijn 2013, S. 235–278

Minn, Naing Oo/Foxton, Rachel The Award and Courts – Recent Developments in International Arbitration in Singapore, in: Klausegger, Christian/Klein, Peter/Kremslehner, Florian/Petsche, Alexander/Pitkowitz, Nikolaus/Power, Jenny/Welser, Irene/Zeiler, Gerold (Hrsg.), Austrian Yearbook on International Arbitration 2011, Bern, München, Wien 2011, S. 197–216

Mistelis, Loukas Seat of Arbitration and Indian Arbitration Law, Indian Journal of Arbitration Law 2015, Volume IV, Ausgabe 2, S. 1–13

Mittal, Akaant Arbitrability of oppression and mismanagement claims: a comparative analysis, Journal of Business Law 2016, S. 186–202

Mittal, J. K. Indian Legal History, 10. Auflage, Allahabad 2011

Mody, Zia/Raghenth, B. Case Comment, India: public policy, International Arbitration Law Review 2003, S. N35–N37

Mohta, V. A./Mohta, Anoop Arbitration, Conciliation and Mediation, The Arbitration and Conciliation Act, 1996, 2. Auflage, Noida 2008

Müller, Beate Die Entwicklung des Privatrechts in Singapur, Münster 1999

Nair, Promod Surveying a Decade of the 'New' Law of Arbitration In India, Arbitration International 2007, Volume 23, Ausgabe 4, S. 699–740

Nariman, Fali Application of the New York Convention in India, Journal of International Arbitration 2008, Volume 25, Ausgabe 6, S. 893–898

Nariman, Fali India, in: Bosman, Lise (Hrsg.), ICCA International Handbook on Commercial Arbitration, Band III, Loseblattsammlung, Alphen aan den Rijn, Stand: Dezember 2017, S. India 1–India 70

Nariman, Fali India and International Arbitration, The George Washington International Law Review, Volume 41, Ausgabe 2, 2009–2010, S. 367–379

Nariman, Fali Ten Steps to Salvage Arbitration in India: The First LCIA-India Arbitration Lecture, Arbitration International 2011, Volume 27, Ausgabe 2, S. 115–127

Navarro Jiménez, Seguimundo Comentario sobre el nuevo reglamento de SIAC, Spain Arbitration Review 2013, Ausgabe 18, S. 123–130

Nelson, Jack International Commercial Arbitration in Asia: Hong Kong, Australia and India Compared, Asian International Arbitration Journal 2014, Volume 10, Ausgabe 2, S. 105–136

Neuborne, Burt The Supreme Court of India, International Journal of Constitutional Law 2003, Volume 1, Ausgabe 3, S. 476–510

Newbold, Thomas Political and Statistical Account of the British Settlements in the Straits of Malacca, viz. Pinang, Malacca, and Singapore; with a History of the Malayan States on the Peninsula of Malacca, London 1839

Nicholls, Anthony/ Bloch, Christopher ICC Hybrid Arbitrations Here to Stay: Singapore Courts' Treatment of the ICC Rules Revisions in Articles 1(2) and 6(2), Journal of International Arbitration 2014, Volume 31, Ausgabe 3, S. 393–412

Oommen, Mathew/Tan, Charis The Use of Pre-action Discovery to Aid Arbitration? – A Practitioner's Perspective, Asian International Arbitration Journal 2010, Volume 6, Ausgabe 2, S. 186–200

Panjwani, Pratyush/ Pathak, Harshad Assimilating the Negative Effect of Kompetenz-Kompetenz in India: Need to Revisit the Question of Judicial Intervention?, Indian Journal of Arbitration Law 2013, Volume II, Ausgabe 2, S. 1–28

Paranjape, N. V. Law Relating to Arbitration and Conciliation in India, 7. Auflage, Allahabad 2016

Parekh, Pravin Public Policy as a Ground for Setting Aside the Award, ICA Arbitration Quarterly 2005, Volume XL, Ausgabe 2, S. 11–19

Parthasarathy, Suhrith/ Visalakshi, A. K. Stretching the limits of statutory interpretation: the Indian Arbitration and Conciliation Act 1996, Arbitration 2007, S. 394–399

Paulsson, Jan Arbitration-Friendliness: Promises of Principle and Realities of Practice, Arbitration International, Volume 23, Ausgabe 3, S. 477–498

Perry, Sebastian Is Asia breaking new ground?, Global Arbitration Review 2013, Volume 8, Ausgabe 6, 24.10.2013

Petit, Sherina/Lakhani, Nikhil/Timmers, Leonie India anticipates new arbitration laws, Another positive sign for those looking at business opportunities in India, Norton Rose Fulbright, International arbitration report 2015, Ausgabe 4, S. 22–24

Phang, Andrew From Foundation to Legacy: The Second Charter of Justice, Singapur 2006
Zitiert als:
Phang, Charter

Phang, Andrew Reception of English Law in Singapore: Problems and Proposed Solutions, Singapore Academy of Law Journal 1990, Volume 2, S. 20–40

Phang, Andrew — The Reception of English Law, in: Tan, Kevin (Hrsg.), Essays in Singapore Legal History, Singapur 2005, S. 7–25

Pillay, Mohan — The Singapore Arbitration Regime and the UNCITRAL Model Law, Arbitration International 2004, Volume 20, Ausgabe 4, S. 355–386

Pillay, Mohan — The Singapore Arbitration Regime 2002 –Then, Now and Why, The International Construction Law Review 2003, S. 91–127

Polkinghorne, Michael — More Changes in Singapore: Appearance Rights of Foreign Counsel, Journal of International Arbitration 2005, Volume 22, Ausgabe 1, S. 75–79

Polkinghorne, Michael/Cockayne, James — Case Note (Singapore – John Holland Pty Ltd v. Toyo Engineering Corp (Japan)), Journal of International Arbitration 2001, Volume 18, Ausgabe 6, S. 649–656

Prasad, Aakash — Case Comment, Indtel Technical Services Pvt Ltd v W. S. Atkins Plc, Arbitration 2009, S. 289–291

Prasad, B. M./Mohan, Manish — Mulla the Code of Civil Procedure, 18. Auflage, Gurgaon 2013, 3 Bände
Zitiert als:
Prasad, B. M./Mohan, Mulla Code Procedure, Bd.

Prasad, Piyush/Parolia, Aditya — Case Comment, India: excluding forum conveniens, International Arbitration Law Review 2014, S. N58–N61

Pryles, Michael — Exclusion of the Model Law, International Arbitration Law Review 2001, S. 175–177

Raeschke-Kessler, Hilmar/Lehne, Hans — Aktuelle Rechtsfragen der Schiedsgerichtsbarkeit, Köln 1989

Rai, Sumit — Case Comment, Positive or double negative? A critique of Videocon Industries v Union of India, International Arbitration Law Review 2011, S. 138–143

Rai, Sumit — Proposed Amendments to the Indian Arbitration Act: A Fraction of the Whole?, Journal of International Dispute Settlement 2012, Volume 3, Ausgabe 1, S. 169–204

Rautray, Dharmendra Case Comment, India: Venture Global Engineering v Satyam Computer Services Ltd – foreign awards are open to challenge on the merits as domestic awards – NTPC v Singer Co case revisited, International Arbitration Law Review 2008, S. N29–N31

Rautray, Dharmendra Case Comment, Overruling of Bhatia International and Venture Global – a half measure by Supreme Court of India, International Arbitration Law Review 2012, S. N48–N50

Rautray, Dharmendra India's Supreme Court Places New Hurdles on Enforcement of Foreign Awards: Venture Global and the Cases leading up to it, Dispute Resolution Journal, 2009, Volume 64, Ausgabe 1, S. 80–86

Rautray, Dharmendra Master Guide to Arbitration in India, New Delhi 2008
Zitiert als:
Rautray, Guide Arbitration

Ray, Aloke/Sabharwal, Dipen Competence-Competence: An Indian Trilogy, MEALEY`S International Arbitration Report 2007, Volume 22, S. 26–34

Ray, Ashutosh Case Comment, Bharat Aluminium v Kaiser Aluminium: awakening of the Indian arbitration dream, International Arbitration Law Review 2013, S. 97–103

Ray, Ashutosh Year 2012: Harbinger of Change for Indian Arbitration?, Journal of International Arbitration 2012, Volume 29, Ausgabe 3, S. 345–354

Rebello, Akash Case Comment, Of impossible dreams and recurring nightmares: the set aside of foreign awards in India, Cambridge Student Law Review 2010, S. 274–287

Reddy, Vinay/Nagaraj, V. Arbitrability: The Indian Perspective, Journal of International Arbitration 2002, Volume 19, Ausgabe 2, S. 117–150

Respondek, Andreas Rezeption und Anwendbarkeit des englischen Rechts in Singapur, RIW 1995, S. 28–31

Rewari, Sulabh From Bhatia to Kaiser: Testing the Indian Judiciary's Self-Restraint, Asian International Arbitration Journal 2013, Volume 9, Ausgabe 2, S. 97–146

Reynardson, Tom/Talbot-Garman, Rupert	The consultation paper on amendments to the Indian Arbitration and Conciliation Act 1996 – does it go far enough?, International Arbitration Law Review 2011, S. 90–98
Ritz, Philipp	Pitfalls to Avoid When Drafting Arbitration Clauses in India-Related Contracts, ASA Bulletin 2009, Volume 27, Ausgabe 4, S. 717–733
Robinson, Nick	Judicial Architecture and Capacity, in: Choudhry, Sujit/Khosla, Madhav/Mehta, Pratap (Hrsg.), The Oxford Handbook of the Indian Constitution, New York, Oxford 2016, S. 330–348
Robinson, Nick	Structure Matters: The Impact of Court Structure on the Indian and U. S. Supreme Courts, The American Journal of Comparative Law 2013, Volume 61, S. 173–208
Ross, Alison	A new dawn in Delhi, Global Arbitration Review 2012, Volume 7, Ausgabe 5, 7.11.2012
Rust, Walter	Die Rezeption englischen Wirtschaftsrechts in Singapur und Malaysia unter besonderer Berücksichtigung von Sect. 5 Civil Law Act, Pfaffenweiler 1989
Sabharwal, Dipen/Singh, Aditya	India: From Bhatia to Balco – Where do we go from here?, Global Arbitration Review 2012, Volume 7, Ausgabe 6, 22.10.2012
Sachdeva, Amit	Unlimited jurisdiction of the Indian courts (to intervene) in international arbitrations: an analysis of the Bhatia International case, International Arbitration Law Review 2010, S. 73–79
Saharay, Madhusudan	Textbook on Arbitration & Conciliation with Alternative Dispute Resolution, 3. Auflage, New Delhi 2015
Sathyapalan, Harisankar	Indian judiciary and international arbitration: a BIT of a control?, Arbitration International 2016, S. 1–16
Sattar, Sameer	National Courts and International Arbitration: A Double-edged Sword?, Journal of International Arbitration 2010, Volume 27, Ausgabe 1, S. 51–73
Sau, Ranjit	Indian Economic Growth: Constraints and Prospects, Economic and Political Weekly 1972, Volume 7, Ausgabe 1, S. 368–375

Schäfer, Jan	Der lange Arm der indischen Justiz – Aufhebung von ausländischen Schiedssprüchen bei indischem Nexus, SchiedsVZ 2008, S. 299–300
Schlosser, Peter	Das Recht der internationalen privaten Schiedsgerichtsbarkeit, 2. Auflage, Tübingen 1989
Schütze, Rolf	Schiedsgericht und Schiedsverfahren, 6. Auflage, München 2016 Zitiert als: Schütze, Schiedsgericht
Schütze, Rolf/Hirth, René-Alexander (Hrsg.)	Einführung in das Recht Singapurs, München 2007 Zitiert als: Bearbeiter, in: Schütze/Hirth
Schütze, Rolf/Tscherning, Dieter/Wais, Walter (Hrsg.)	Handbuch des Schiedsverfahrens, Praxis der deutschen und internationalen Schiedsgerichtsbarkeit, 2. Auflage, Berlin, New York 1990 Zitiert als: Bearbeiter, in: Schütze/Tscherning/Wais
Schwab, Karl Heinz/Walter, Gerhard	Schiedsgerichtsbarkeit, 7. Auflage, München 2005
Sen, Aniruddha	The Role of the Court in the Appointment of Arbitrators – an Analysis with Reference to the Supreme Court of India's Decision in S. B.P. v. Patel Engineering, Vindobona Journal of International Commercial Law & Arbitration 2006, S. 45–52
Sethi, Harsh/Gupta, Arpan	International Commercial Arbitration & Its Indian Perspective, New Delhi 2011
Sharma, Ajay	Judicial Intervention In International Commercial Arbitration: Critiquing the Indian Supreme Court's Interpretation of The Arbitration And Conciliation Act, 1996, Indian Journal of Arbitration Law 2014, Volume III, Ausgabe 1, S. 6–30
Sharma, Avinash/Trivedi, Khyati	The Chief Justice's power to appoint arbitrators under the (Indian) Arbitration and Conciliation Act 1996: a brief analysis of synchronised judicial response, International Arbitration Law Review 2010, S. 27–34
Sharma, Raghav	Bhatia International v. Bulk Trading S.A.: Ambushing International Commercial Arbitration Outside India?, Journal of International Arbitration 2009, Volume 26, Ausgabe 3, S. 357–372

Sharma, Raghav Sanctity of foreign awards: recent developments in India, Arbitration 2009, S. 148–157

Sharma, Sidharth Public Policy Under the Indian Arbitration Act: In Defence of the Indian Supreme Court's Judgment in ONGC v. Saw Pipes, Journal of International Arbitration 2009, Volume 26, Ausgabe 1, S. 133–147

Sharma, Sidharth The Chief Justice's Power to Appoint Arbitrators Under the Indian Arbitration Act, Journal of International Arbitration 2006, Volume 23, Ausgabe 5, S. 467–477

Sindhu, Janhavi Fraud, Corruption And Bribery – Dissecting The Jurisdictional Tussle Between Indian Courts And Arbitral Tribunals, Indian Journal of Arbitration Law 2014, Volume III, Ausgabe 2, S. 23–42

Singhania, Ravi Case Comment, India: arbitration – jurisdiction of Indian courts, International Company and Commercial Law Review 2002, S. N93–N95

Singh, Aditya Arbitration and Conciliation Laws in India, Understanding their Evolution and Future Prospects, Saarbrücken 2012
Zitiert als:
Singh, Aditya, Arbitration in India

Singh, Avtar Law of Arbitration & Conciliation, 10. Auflage, Lucknow 2013
Zitiert als:
Singh, Avtar, Arbitration

Singh, Mahendra Outlines of Indian Legal & Constitutional History, 8. Auflage, New Delhi 2006
Zitiert als:
Singh, Mahendra, History

Singh, Mahendra The Federal Scheme, in: Choudhry, Sujit/Khosla, Madhav/Mehta, Pratap (Hrsg.), The Oxford Handbook of the Indian Constitution, New York, Oxford 2016, S. 451–465

Singh, Mohinder/Kumar, Suresh Justice Delivery through Lok Adalats: A Study, Asian Journal of Multidimensional Research 2014, Volume 3, Ausgabe 5, S. 7–14

Singhvi, Abhishek Memoirs of a Personal Journey through Indian Arbitration Law, Indian Journal of Arbitration Law 2015, Volume IV, Ausgabe 2, S. 14–27

Smith, Gordon/Cook, Andrew International commercial arbitration in Asia-Pacific: a comparison of the Australian and Singapore systems, Arbitration 2011, S. 108–115

Somnath, Rathin Case Comment, Enforcement of foreign arbitral awards in India: Lal Mahal reduces the scope for court interference, Arbitration 2014, S. 217–219

Song, Lianbin/Yang, Ling/Chen, Helena Annual review of commercial arbitration in China, Construction Law Journal 2016, S. 3–42

Srikrishna, B. N. Judicial Independence, in: Choudhry, Sujit/Khosla, Madhav/Mehta, Pratap (Hrsg.), The Oxford Handbook of the Indian Constitution, New York, Oxford 2016, S. 349–366

Srinivasan, Badrinath Appeal against the Order of the Chief Justice under Section 11 of the Arbitration and Conciliation Act, 1996: An Empirical Analysis, Indian Journal of Arbitration Law 2012, Volume I, Ausgabe 1, S. 18–35

Stein, Friedrich/Jonas, Martin (Begr.) Bork, Reinhard/Roth, Herbert (Hrsg.), Kommentar zur Zivilprozessordnung, Band 10, §§ 1025–1066, 23. Auflage, Tübingen 2014
Zitiert als:
Bearbeiter, in: Stein/Jonas

Stothard, Paul/Bruce, Stuart/Curran, Sean/Swartz-Zern, Caroline Investment Protection and International Dispute Resolution in Singapore, in: Menon, Sundaresh/Brock, Denis (Hrsg.), Arbitration in Singapore, A Practical Guide, Singapur 2014, S. 575–627

Subramanium, Gopal Writs and Remedies, in: Choudhry, Sujit/Khosla, Madhav/Mehta, Pratap (Hrsg.), The Oxford Handbook of the Indian Constitution, New York, Oxford 2016, S. 614–626.

Sutton, David/Gill, Judith/Gearing, Matthew Russell on Arbitration, 24. Auflage, London 2015

Takahashi, Koji Jurisdiction to Set Aside a Foreign Arbitral Award, in Particular an Award Based on an Illegal Contract: A Reflection on the Indian Supreme Court's Decision in Venture Global Engineering, The American Review of International Arbitration 2008, Volume 19, Ausgabe 1, S. 173–186

Tan, Kevin — A Short Legal and Constitutional History of Singapore, in: Tan, Kevin (Hrsg.), Essays in Singapore Legal History, Singapur 2005, S. 27–72

Tan, Kevin — A Short Legal and Constitutional History of Singapore, in: Tan, Kevin (Hrsg.), The Singapore Legal System, 2. Auflage, Singapur 1999, S. 26–66

Tan, Kevin — Constitutional Law in Singapore, 2. Auflage, Alphen aan den Rijn 2014
Zitiert als:
Tan, Kevin, Constitution

Tan, Kevin — Marshall of Singapore – A Biography, Singapur 2008

Tan, Kevin — Parliament and the Making of Law in Singapore, in: Tan, Kevin (Hrsg.), The Singapore Legal System, 2. Auflage, Singapur 1999, S. 123–159

Tan, Kevin — Singapore, A statist legal laboratory, in: Black, Ann/Bell, Gary (Hrsg.), Law and Legal Institutions of Asia, Melbourne, New York 2011, S. 330–371

Tan, Kevin — The Constitution of Singapore, A Contextual Analysis, Oxford, Portland 2015
Zitiert als:
Tan, Kevin, Constitution Singapore

Tan, Paul — Case Comment, AJU v AJT – nail in Soleimany's coffin?, International Arbitration Law Review 2011, S. 183–188

Tan, Paul — Case Comment, Public policy in Singapore: an unruly horse rears its head – AJT v AJU, International Arbitration Law Review 2010, S. 234–236

Tan, Richard — The emergence of Singapore as a global arbitration hub: reasons for its success, Conference Presentation, Arbitration 2013, S. 436–440

Thadikkaran, Manu — Judicial Intervention in International Commercial Arbitration: Implications and Recent Developments from the Indian Perspective, Journal of International Arbitration 2012, Volume 29, Ausgabe 6, S. 681–690

Tham, Wei Chern — Singapore, Stays of proceedings and arbitrability, Global Arbitration Review 2016, Volume 11, Ausgabe 1, S. 45–48

Tham, Yuet-Ming	Changes to Singapore's arbitral laws and the pitfalls of choosing Singapore as the seat of arbitration, Asian Dispute Review 2003, S. 193–196
Thej, Aravapalli	An adieu to the doctrine of patent illegality: a comment on the Indian Supreme Court's decision in Shri Lal Mahal Ltd v Progetto Grano, International Arbitration Law Review 2014, S. 37–42
Thio, Li-ann	The Constitutional Framework of Powers, in: Tan, Kevin (Hrsg.), The Singapore Legal System, 2. Auflage, Singapur 1999, S. 67–122
Thiruvengadam, Anrun	Tribunals, in: Choudhry, Sujit/Khosla, Madhav/Mehta, Pratap (Hrsg.), The Oxford Handbook of the Indian Constitution, New York, Oxford 2016, S. 412–431
Timothy, Gracious	The final chapter to the public policy saga: the Arbitration Amendment Act 2015?, International Arbitration Law Review 2016, S. 56–64
Vakil, Raeesa	Jurisdiction, in: Choudhry, Sujit/Khosla, Madhav/Mehta, Pratap (Hrsg.), The Oxford Handbook of the Indian Constitution, New York, Oxford 2016, S. 367–385
Verma, Vidhu	Malaysia: State and Civil Society in Transition, Boulder, London 2002
Wadhwa, Anirudh/Krishnan, Anirudh/Bachawat, Bejoy/Bachawat, Ranjan (Hrsg.)	R. S. Bachawat's Law of Arbitration & Conciliation, With Exhaustive Coverage of International Commercial Arbitration & ADR, 5. Auflage, Gurgaon 2010, 2 Bände Zitiert als: Wadhwa/Krishnan/Bachawat/Bachawat, Bachawat's Arbitration, Bd.
Wieczorek, Bernhard/Schütze, Rolf	Zivilprozessordnung und Nebengesetze, 4. Auflage, Berlin, Boston 2014 Bearbeiter, in: Wieczorek/Schütze
Wong, Kok Weng/Sia, Aik Kor	A History of the Singapore Legal Service, in: Tan, Kevin (Hrsg.), Essays in Singapore Legal History, Singapur 2005, S. 73–91
Woon, Walter	The Applicability of English Law in Singapore, in: Tan, Kevin (Hrsg.), The Singapore Legal System, 2. Auflage, Singapur 1999, S. 230–248

Woon, Walter	The Doctrine of Judicial Precedent, in: Tan, Kevin (Hrsg.), The Singapore Legal System, 2. Auflage, Singapur 1999, S. 297–324
Yang, Lih Shyng/Chew, Leslie	Arbitration in Singapore, in: Ali, Shahla/Ginsburg, Tom (Hrsg.), International Commercial Arbitration in Asia, 3. Auflage, Huntington 2013, S. 465–502
Yeo, Alvin	Legislative Comment, Singapore: new enactment – Singapore introduces International Arbitration (Amendment) Bill 2002, International Arbitration Law Review 2002, S. N54–N55
Yeo, Alvin	Recent changes to the law relating to international arbitrations in Singapore, International Arbitration Law Review 2002, S. 71–76
Yeo, Tiong Min	Jurisdiction of the Singapore Courts, in: Tan, Kevin (Hrsg.), The Singapore Legal System, 2. Auflage, Singapur 1999, S. 249–296
Yesilirmak, Ali	Provisional Measures, in: Mistelis, Loukas/Lew, Julian (Hrsg.), Pervasive Problems in International Arbitration, Alphen aan den Rijn 2006, S. 185–200
Yihan, Goh/Tan, Paul	An Empirical Study on the Development of Singapore Law, in: Yihan, Goh/Tan, Paul (Hrsg.), Singapore Law, 50 Years in the Making, Singapur 2015, S. 3–25
Yihan, Goh/Tan, Paul	The Development of Local Jurisprudence, in: Yihan, Goh/Tan, Paul (Hrsg.), Singapore Law, 50 Years in the Making, Singapur 2015, S. 195–250
Yihan, Goh/Tan, Paul	The Next Leap Forward: The Spread of Singapore Law, in: Yihan, Goh/Tan, Paul (Hrsg.), Singapore Law, 50 Years in the Making, Singapur 2015, S. 835–879
Zaiwalla, Sarosh	Commentary on the Indian Supreme Court Judgment in Venture Global Engineering v. Satyam Computers Services Ltd., Journal of International Arbitration 2008, Volume 25, Ausgabe 4, S. 507–512
Zöller, Richard (Begr.)	Geimer, Reinhold/Heßler, Hans-Joachim/Greger, Reinhard/Lückemann, Clemens/Herget, Kurt/Stöber, Kurt/Vollkommer, Max/Feskorn, Christian/Lorenz, Arndt (Bearbeiter), Zivilprozessordnung, 31. Auflage, Köln 2016 Zitiert als: Bearbeiter, in: Zöller

Online Quellen

Autor	**Titel**
Agram Legal Consultants	Government approves introduction of bill to amend the Arbitration and Conciliation Act, 1996, 31.8.2015, verfügbar unter http://www.lexology.com/library/detail.aspx?g=ce7cdaef-3454-4650-87a1-a59a740d040a
Binsy, Susan/Sharma, Neha	New Delhi International Arbitration Centre: Building India into a Global Arbitration Hub, Kluwer Arbitration Blog, 4.5.2018, verfügbar unter http://arbitrationblog.kluwerarbitration.com/2018/05/04/new-delhi-international-arbitration-centre-building-india-global-arbitration-hub/
Boey, Swee Siang/Mahtani, Naresh	International arbitration in Singapore, 28.5.2010, verfügbar unter http://www.lexology.com/library/detail.aspx?g=e78c0d15-facf-4142-9fc9-2e0b4584b83e
Chan, Darius	Singapore Court of Appeal re-affirms commitment to minimal intervention of arbitral awards at the intersection of illegality and public policy, Kluwer Arbitration Blog, 12.9.2011, verfügbar unter: http://kluwerarbitrationblog.com/2011/09/12/singapore-court-of-appeal-re-affirms-commitment-to-minimal-intervention-of-arbitral-awards-at-the-intersection-of-illegality-and-public-policy/
Chugh, Ashish	The Bharat Aluminium Case: The Indian Supreme Court Ushers In a New Era, Kluwer Arbitration Blog, 26.9.2012, verfügbar unter http://kluwerarbitrationblog.com/2012/09/26/the-bharat-aluminium-case-the-indian-supreme-court-ushers-in-a-new-era/
Deepak, Girish	MCIA, India's best foot forward, Kluwer Arbitration Blog, 5.8.2016, verfügbar unter http://kluwerarbitrationblog.com/2016/08/05/mcia-indias-best-foot-forward/
Dewan, Dhruv/Pandey, Mayank	Enforcing foreign awards: Supreme Court widens scope of 'public policy', International Law Office, 22.11.2011, verfügbar unter http://www.internationallawoffice.com/Newsletters/Litigation/India/Amarchand-Mangaldas-Suresh-A-Shroff-Co/Enforcing-foreign-awards-Supreme-Court-widens-scope-of-public-policy

George, Simi — Releasing India's Supreme Court from the Shadow of Delay, A Proposal for Policy Reform, verfügbar unter https://www.hks.harvard.edu/content/download/66823/1240102/version/1/file/SYPA_SimiGeorge_2014.pdf

Herbert Smith — Arbitration e-bulletin, Indian Supreme Court expands public policy definition for enforcement of foreign awards, verfügbar unter http://sites.herbertsmithfreehills.vuturevx.com/33/537/landing-pages/indian-international-arbitration-e-bulletin---article-3.asp

Herbert Smith — Dispute resolution and governing law clauses in India-related commercial contracts, S. 3 ff., verfügbar unter http://hsfnotes.com/arbitration/wp-content/uploads/sites/4/2011/04/2011-Dispute-resolution-and-governing-clauses-in-India-related-commercial-contracts.pdf

Hwang, Michael/Chang, Aloysius — Tomolugen Holdings v. Silica Investors, Supreme Court of Singapore, Court of Appeal, 26 October 2015, A contribution by the ITA Board of Reporters, verfügbar unter http://www.kluwerarbitration.com/document/kli-ka-15-53-001?q=%22Tomolugen%20Holdings%20v%20Silica%22

Koh, Matthew — Singapore Court of Appeal: Prima Facie Standard for Stay in Favour of Arbitration and Arbitrability of Minority Oppression Claims, Kluwer Arbitration Blog, 25.3.2016, verfügbar unter http://kluwerarbitrationblog.com/2016/03/25/singapore-court-of-appeal-affirms-prima-facie-standard-for-stay-in-favour-of-arbitration

Leach, Jonathan/Winter, Henry/Khan, Stephanie — "Something weighty": Chief Justice Menon ex temps the standard required for a court to exercise its discretion to not refer a dispute to arbitration, ARBlog, 9.10.2015, verfügbar unter http://www.hlarbitrationlaw.com/2015/10/something-weighty-chief-justice-menon-ex-temps-the-standard-required-for-a-court-to-exercise-its-discretion-to-not-refer-a-dispute-to-arbitration/

Lee, Bik Wei/Ling, Margaret Singapore Court of Appeal rules stay of proceedings in favour of arbitration, Allen & Gledhill, Legal Bulletin September 2015, 29.9.2015, verfügbar unter http://www.allenandgledhill.com/pages/publications.aspx?list=LBulletinAreas&pub_id=901&view=d

Mahendra, Vikas Arbitration in India: A New Beginning, Kluwer Arbitration Blog, 6.11.2015, verfügbar unter http://kluwerarbitrationblog.com/2015/11/06/arbitration-in-india-a-new-beginning/

Mistelis, Loukas Arbitral Seats: Choices and Competition, Kluwer Arbitration Blog, 26.11.2010, verfügbar unter http://kluwerarbitrationblog.com/2010/11/26/arbitral-seats-choices-and-competition/

Nishith Desai Doing Business in India, verfügbar unter http://www.nishithdesai.com/fileadmin/user_upload/pdfs/Research%20Papers/Doing_Business_in_India.pdf

Pillai, Prakash/Chaudhry, Umer Law Commission's Report Reinforces the Pro-Arbitration Trends in India, Kluwer Arbitration Blog, 9.10.2014, verfügbar unter http://kluwerarbitrationblog.com/2014/10/09/law-commissions-report-reinforces-the-pro-arbitration-trends-in-india/

Pramod, Sanjna Arbitration and Mediation: Shifting Paradigms in India, Kluwer Arbitration Blog, 4.8.2016, verfügbar unter http://kluwerarbitrationblog.com/2016/08/04/arbitration-and-mediation-shifting-paradigms-in-india/

Ray, Aloke/Sabharwal, Dipen India and Arbitration – Arbitration clauses for contracts with Indian parties, Global Arbitration Review, 1.2.2008, verfügbar unter http://globalarbitrationreview.com/article/1027928/india-and-arbitration-arbitration-clauses-for-contracts-with-indian-parties

Robinson, Nick Hard to Reach, Frontline, Volume 27, Ausgabe 3, 30.1.–12.2.2010, verfügbar unter https://www.frontline.in/static/html/fl2703/stories/20100212270304600.htm

Robinson, Nick Too Many Cases, Frontline, Volume 26, Ausgabe 1, 3.–16. Januar 2009, verfügbar unter http://www.frontline.in/static/html/fl2601/stories/20090116260108100.htm

Sabharwal, Dipen	Another setback for Indian arbitration (and foreign investors), White & Case, India, 6.6.2008, verfügbar unter http://www.lexology.com/library/detail.aspx?g=4def9d16-1f37-4e2e-8843-a1faa3f47e93
Singhania & Partners LLP	Solicitors and Advocates, India: Civil Courts System, verfügbar unter http://www.mondaq.com/ac/content.asp?content_id=2808&email_access=on
Singh, Aditya/Sabharwal, Dipen	Arbitration and Conciliation (Amendment) Ordinance, 2015, A contribution by the ITA Board of Reporters, Kluwer Law International, verfügbar unter http://www.kluwerarbitration.com/CommonUI/document.aspx?id=kli-ka-15-49-003
Singh, Kabir/Luttrell, Sam/Krishna, Elan	Third-party funding and arbitration law-making: the race for regulation in the Asia-Pacific, 15.7.2016, Kluwer Arbitration Blog, 14.7.2016, verfügbar unter http://kluwerarbitrationblog.com/2016/07/14/third-party-funding-and-arbitration-law-making-the-race-for-regulation-in-the-asia-pacific/
Uraizee-Sapre, Shafaq/Dembla, Gautam	Now arbitration friendly?, International Financial Law Review, 2010, verfügbar unter http://www.iflr.com/Article/2617832/Now-arbitration-friendly.html
Vivekananda, N.	Interventionist, No More?, Kluwer Arbitration Blog, 30.11.2011, verfügbar unter http://kluwerarbitrationblog.com/2011/11/30/interventionist-no-more/?_ga=1.18170297.1024077138.1455788029
Yeo, Alvin/Yu, Chou Sean	Global Arbitration Review, Singapore, 26.10.2011, verfügbar unter: http://globalarbitrationreview.com/insight/the-asia-pacific-arbitration-review-2012/1036675/singapore

Institutionelle Dokumente

Institution	Titel
International Law Association	London Conference, 2000, Committee on International Commercial Arbitration, Interim Report on Public Policy as a Bar to Enforcement of International Arbitral Awards
International Law Association	New Delhi Conference, 2002, Committee on International Commercial Arbitration, Final Report on Public Policy as a Bar to Enforcement of International Arbitral Awards
Report of the Secretary-General, United Nations General Assembly	Analytical commentary on draft text of a model law on international commercial arbitration, A/CN.9/264, 25.3.1985
UNCITRAL	7. Sitzung, Report of the Working Group on International Contract Practices on the work of its seventh session, A/CN.9/246, 6.–17.2.1984
UNCITRAL	18. Sitzung, Report of the Secretary-General, Analytical Commentary on Draft Text of A Model Law on International Commercial Arbitration, A/CN.9/264, 25.3.1985
UNCITRAL	18. Sitzung, Report of the United Nations Commission on International Trade Law on the work of its eighteenth session, Supplement No. 17, A/40/17, 3.–21.6.1985
UNCITRAL	32. Sitzung, Report of the Secretary General, Settlement of commercial disputes – Possible uniform rules on certain issues concerning settlement of commercial disputes: conciliation, interim measures of protection, written form for arbitration agreement, A/CN.9/WG.II/WP.108, 20–31.3.2000
UNCITRAL Sekretariat	Explanatory note by the UNCITRAL secretariat on the Model Law on International Commercial Arbitration Zitiert als: UNCITRAL Sekretariat, Explanatory note

UNCITRAL Sekretariat	Explanatory Note by the UNCITRAL secretariat on the 1985 Model Law on International Commercial Arbitration as amended in 2006
United Nations General Assembly	61. Sitzung, Resolutions adopted by the General Assembly, on the report of the Sixth Committee, A/61/453, 4.12.2006
World Bank Group	Doing Business 2016, Measures Regulatory Quality and Efficiency, 13. Auflage, verfügbar unter http://www.doingbusiness.org/~/media/WBG/DoingBusiness/Documents/Annual-Reports/English/DB16-Full-Report.pdf
World Bank Group	Doing Business 2017, Equal Opportunity for All, 14. Auflage, Economy Profile 2017, India, verfügbar unter http://www.doingbusiness.org/~/media/wbg/doingbusiness/documents/profiles/country/ind.pdf
World Bank Group	Doing Business 2017, Equal Opportunity for All, 14. Auflage, Economy Profile 2017, Singapore, verfügbar unter http://www.doingbusiness.org/~/media/wbg/doingbusiness/documents/profiles/country/sgp.pdf
World Bank Group	Global Economic Prospects, The Turning of the Tide?, verfügbar unter http://www.worldbank.org/en/publication/global-economic-prospects
World Economic Forum	The Global Competitiveness Report 2016–2017, verfügbar unter http://www3.weforum.org/docs/GCR2016-2017/05FullReport/TheGlobalCompetitivenessReport2016-2017_FINAL.pdf
World Justice Project	Rule of Law Index 2016, verfügbar unter, https://worldjusticeproject.org/sites/default/files/documents/RoLI_Final-Digital_0.pdf

A. Einleitung

I. Die Fragestellung der Arbeit

Das Zusammenspiel von Schiedsgerichten und staatlicher Gerichtsbarkeit ist facettenreich. Es umfasst jede Phase der schiedsgerichtlichen Streitbeilegung von der Durchsetzung der Schiedsvereinbarung bis hin zur Vollstreckung des Schiedsspruchs.[1] So bedarf es für die ordnungsgemäße Durchführung des Schiedsverfahrens partiell einer gerichtlichen Unterstützung.[2] Die gerichtliche Kontrolle des Schiedsverfahrens gewährleistet ein integres Schiedsverfahren[3] und nur die staatlichen Gerichte können die schiedsgerichtlichen Entscheidungen[4] hoheitlich durchsetzen[5]. Die Schiedsgerichte sind daher auf die Mitwirkung der staatlichen Gerichte angewiesen. Das optimale Spannungsverhältnis zwischen Schiedsgerichten und staatlichen Gerichten vergleicht Lord *Mustill* bildlich mit einem Staffellauf:

> *„Ideally, the handling of arbitral disputes should resemble a relay race. In the initial stages, before the arbitrators are seized of the dispute, the baton is in the grasp of the court; for at that stage there is no other organisation which could take steps to prevent the arbitration agreement from being ineffectual. When the arbitrators take charge they take over the baton and retain it until they have made an award. At this point, having no longer a function to fulfil, the arbitrators hand back the baton so that the court can*

1 Artikel (Art.) 8 ff. „UNCITRAL (United Nations Commission on International Trade Law) Modellgesetz"; Art. 2 ff. „New Yorker UN-Übereinkommen über die Anerkennung und Vollstreckung ausländischer Schiedssprüche vom 10. Juni 1958 (UNÜ)".

2 Art. 8, 9, 11 ff., 27 UNCITRAL Modellgesetz; Art. II (3) UNÜ; Lew/Mistelis/Kröll, Comparative International Commercial Arbitration, Rn. 15-1 ff.; Blackaby/Partasides/Redfern/Hunter, International Arbitration, Rn. 7.01 ff.; Born, International Commercial Arbitration, Bd. 2, S. 2056 ff.

3 Art. 13 (3), 16 (3), 34 ff. UNCITRAL Modellgesetz; Art. V UNÜ; Lew/Mistelis/Kröll, Comparative International Commercial Arbitration, Rn. 15-1 ff.; Blackaby/Partasides/Redfern/Hunter, International Arbitration, Rn. 7.02 ff.; Lee, Suet Lin Joyce, Journal of International Arbitration 1998, Vol. 15, Ausg. 1, S. 95; Gaillard/Savage, Fouchard Gaillard Goldman, Rn. 452 ff., 753 ff., 1603 ff., 1694 ff.; Born, Law and Practice, § 2.07 [A], [B], S. 65 ff.; § 7, S. 129 ff.; § 16.03, S. 319 ff.; § 17.04, S. 385 ff.

4 Insbesondere Schiedssprüche und vorläufige Maßnahmen.

5 Art. 17, 35 f. UNCITRAL Modellgesetz; Art. 17 ff. Ergänzungen des UNCITRAL Modellgesetzes 2006; Art. III ff. UNÜ; Lew/Mistelis/Kröll, Comparative International Commercial Arbitration, Rn. 15-1 ff.; Blackaby/Partasides/Redfern/Hunter, International Arbitration, Rn. 7.01 ff.; Born, International Commercial Arbitration, Bd. 2, S. 2446 ff., 3407 ff.; Gaillard/Savage, Fouchard Gaillard Goldman, Rn. 1315 ff., 1558 ff., 1663 ff.

> *in case of need lend its coercive powers to the enforcement of the award.* "[6]

Schiedsverfahren können folglich niemals gänzlich unabhängig von der staatlichen Gerichtsbarkeit durchgeführt werden. Einerseits ist in bestimmten, angemessenen Konstellationen eine gerichtliche Intervention in die schiedsgerichtliche Streitbeilegung notwendig, beziehungsweise die gerichtliche Unterstützung eines Schiedsverfahrens erforderlich. Andererseits können exzessive gerichtliche Eingriffe das Schiedsverfahren beeinträchtigen und das Ziel der Schiedsparteien, ihre Streitigkeit parteiautonom, schnell und flexibel außerhalb der staatlichen Gerichtsbarkeit beizulegen, erschweren.[7] Im Ergebnis muss eine Balance gefunden werden zwischen der gerichtlichen Überwachung und Unterstützung des Schiedsverfahrens und dem Interesse der Schiedsgerichtsbarkeit, gerichtliche Eingriffe in das Schiedsverfahren möglichst zu unterbinden.[8] Dieses widersprüchliche Verhältnis zwischen staatlicher Gerichtsbarkeit und Schiedsverfahren wird auch als „Hassliebe"[9] beschrieben. Die gegenwärtige[10] weltweite Schiedsgesetzgebung trägt diesen Aspekten Rechnung, indem sie gerichtliche Interventionen und Kontrollen auf ein Minimum begrenzt, aber zugleich gerichtliche Unterstützung gewährleistet.[11]

Vor diesem Hintergrund soll die Singapurer Schiedsrechtsordnung der indischen Schiedsrechtsordnung gegenübergestellt werden. Die Vergleichbarkeit der Singapurer und der indischen Schiedsrechtsordnung ergibt sich aus den konvergierenden Rahmenbedingungen. Beide Länder sind kulturell miteinander verbunden, beide Rechtssysteme beruhen auf dem englischen Common Law, Gerichtsentscheidungen von englischen und anderen Common Law Rechtsordnungen werden in beiden Staaten von den Gerichten in der

---

6 Lord Mustill, Comments and Conclusions, in: ICC Publication (Hrsg.), Conservatory Provisional Measures in International Arbitration: 9th Joint Colloquium, 1993, S. 118. Zitiert in Blackaby/Partasides/Redfern/Hunter, International Arbitration, Rn. 7.07.

7 Lew/Mistelis/Kröll, Comparative International Commercial Arbitration, Rn. 15-1 ff.; Lee, Suet Lin Joyce, Journal of International Arbitration 1998, Vol. 15, Ausg. 1, S. 95; Blackaby/Partasides/Redfern/Hunter, International Arbitration, Rn. 7.01 ff.

8 Lew/Mistelis/Kröll, Comparative International Commercial Arbitration, Rn. 15-1 ff.; Blackaby/Partasides/Redfern/Hunter, International Arbitration, Rn. 7.01 ff.

9 Lee, Suet Lin Joyce, Journal of International Arbitration 1998, Vol. 15, Ausg. 1, S. 95.

10 Im letzten Jahrhundert entwickelte sich die Haltung der meisten Ländern gegenüber der Schiedsgerichtsbarkeit von einer skeptischen und von intensiver gerichtlicher Kontrolle geprägten Einstellung zu einer positiven Haltung gegenüber der schiedsgerichtlichen Streitbeilegung. Gerichte achten gegenwärtig die Parteiautonomie und versucht schonend in Schiedsverfahren einzugreifen, Lew/Mistelis/Kröll, Comparative International Commercial Arbitration, Rn. 15-5 ff.

11 Art. 5 UNCITRAL Modellgesetz; Art. 8, 9, 11 ff., Art. 27 UNCITRAL Modellgesetz; Art. 17 ff. Ergänzungen des UNCITRAL Modellgesetzes 2006; Art. 2 (3) UNÜ; Lew/Mistelis/Kröll, Comparative International Commercial Arbitration, Rn. 15-1 ff.

Urteilsfindung berücksichtigt. Die Schiedsgesetzgebung in Singapur und die in Indien basiert auf dem „UNCITRAL[12] Modellgesetz für die internationale Handelsschiedsgerichtsbarkeit 1985 (UNCITRAL Modellgesetz)".[13]

Die vorliegende Arbeit untersucht die Gemeinsamkeiten und Unterschiede der Singapurer und der indischen schiedsgerichtlichen Rechtsordnung. Es werden die zentralen Fragen erörtert, ob im Wechselspiel zwischen Schiedsverfahren und indischen Gerichten die Gerichtsverfahren der weltgrößten Demokratie zu langwierig sind und ob die indischen Gerichte gegenüber der Schiedsgerichtsbarkeit eine schiedsunfreundliche Einstellung einnehmen und regelmäßig in Schiedsverfahren intervenieren.[14] Im Gegensatz hierzu soll beim Stadtstaat Singapur die Frage beleuchtet werden, ob es zutrifft, dass Singapur ein schiedsfreundlicher Schiedsort mit einem effektiven Gerichtssystem ist, der versucht, Schiedsverfahren nach Möglichkeit zu unterstützen und die gerichtlichen Interventionen in Schiedsverfahren auf ein Minimum zu reduzieren.[15]

---

12 UNCITRAL steht für „United Nations Commission on International Trade Law".

13 Engl. UNCITRAL Model Law on International Commercial Arbitration (1985).

14 Ritz, ASA Bulletin 2009, Vol. 27, Ausg. 4, S. 717 (724 ff.); Nelson, Asian International Arbitration Journal 2014, Vol. 10, Ausg. 2, S. 105 (112 ff.); Gupta, Nidhi, Indian Journal of Arbitration Law 2013, Vol. II, Ausg. 2, S. 1; Born, International Commercial Arbitration, S. 198 (Bd. 1), 1628 ff. (Bd. 2), 2996 ff. (Bd. 3); Canfield, Pepperdine Dispute Resolution Law Journal 2014, Vol. 14, Ausg. 3, S. 335 ff.; Vivekananda N., Interventionist, No More?, Kluwer Arbitration Blog, 30.11.2011, verfügbar unter http://kluwerarbitrationblog.com/2011/11/30/interventionist-no-more/?_ga=1.18170297.1024077138.1455788029 (zuletzt abgerufen am 28.4.2021); Shafaq Uraizee-Sapre/Gautam Dembla, Now arbitration friendly?, International Financial Law Review, 2010, verfügbar unter http://www.iflr.com/Article/2617832/Now-arbitration-friendly.html (zuletzt abgerufen am 28.4.2021); Biswas, S. xi. Zu den langwierigen Gerichtsverfahren, siehe Investitionsschiedsspruch *White Industries Australia Limited v The Republic of India*, Schiedsspruch vom 30.11.2011, verfügbar unter http://www.italaw.com/sites/default/files/case-documents/ita0906.pdf (zuletzt abgerufen am 28.4.2021). Zur Schiedsunfreundlichkeit, Karis/Kapoor/Aggarwal, Indian Journal of Arbitration Law 2016, Vol. V, Ausg. 1, S. 230 ff.; Anchayil, Arbitration International 2013, Vol. 29, Ausg. 1, S. 105 (113); Mahajan, Indian Journal of Arbitration Law 2014, Vol. III, Ausg. 2, S. 14.

15 Minn/Foxton, in: Klausegger/Klein/Kremslehner/Petsche/Pitkowitz (Hrsg.), Austrian Yearbook on International Arbitration 2011, S. 197 (201 ff.); Chan, Darius/Tan, Paul, in: Yihan/Tan, Paul (Hrsg.), Singapore Law, 50 Years in the Making, S. 775 (778); Born, Law and Practice, § 1.06 [E] [2] S. 29 f.; Hwang/Chan, Andrew/Selvaraj, in: Moser (Hrsg.), Arbitration in Asia, Sing-74. Zur Schiedsfreundlichkeit, Navarro Jiménez, Spain Arbitration Review, 2013, Ausg. 18, S. 123; Ly, in: Brekoulakis/Lew/Mistelis (Hrsg.), The Evolution and Future of International Arbitration, S. 21 (33); SIAC, Resources, Articles, verfügbar unter http://www.siac.org.sg/index.php?option=com_content&view=article&id=150&Itemid=63 (zuletzt abgerufen am 28.4.2021); Boey Swee Siang/Naresh Mahtani, International arbitration in Singapore, verfügbar unter http://www.lexology.com/library/detail.aspx?g=e78c0d15-facf-4142-9fc9-2e0b4584b83e (zuletzt abgerufen am 28.4.2021).

Nach einer Einführung in die Singapurer und die indische Rechtsordnung untersucht die vorliegende Dissertation die Schiedsgesetzgebung und die Rechtsprechung sowohl in Singapur als auch in Indien auf ihre Schiedsfreundlichkeit hin.

Die Schiedsfreundlichkeit der beiden Rechtsordnungen wird am internationalen Standard der Schiedsgerichtsbarkeit gemessen. Als internationale Richtschnur des Schiedsgerichtswesens werden das UNCITRAL Modellgesetz, die Rechtsordnungen der international wichtigen Schiedszentren in England, Frankreich, Hongkong, der Schweiz und den Vereinigten Staaten von Amerika (USA),[16] das „New Yorker UN-Übereinkommen über die Anerkennung und Vollstreckung ausländischer Schiedssprüche vom 10. Juni 1958 (UNÜ)“ und die einschlägige Literatur herangezogen.

Nach der internationalen Norm der Schiedsgerichtsbarkeit zeichnet sich die Schiedsfreundlichkeit einer Rechtsordnung durch eine schnelle, die Parteiautonomie respektierende, schiedsgerichtliche Streitbeilegung aus. Außerdem begünstigt eine minimale gerichtliche Kontrolle und die gerichtliche Unterstützung und Förderung des privaten Schiedsverfahrens die Schiedsfreundlichkeit einer Rechtsordnung.[17]

1. Schiedsverfahren in Singapur – ein Überblick

Singapur ist seit Jahrzehnten ein wichtiger Wirtschaftsstandort in Asien und entwickelte sich in den letzten Jahren zudem zu einem weltweit führenden Schiedsort.[18] Die Schiedsgesetzgebung ist in Singapur für inländische

16 Loukas Mistelis/Paul Friedland, 2010 International Arbitration Survey: Choices in International Arbitration, S. 1 ff., verfügbar unter http://www.arbitration.qmul.ac.uk/docs/123290.pdf (zuletzt abgerufen am 28.4.2021); Born, International Commercial Arbitration, Bd. 2, S. 2064; ICC, 2015 ICC Dispute Resolution Statistics, ICC Dispute Resolution Bulletin 2016, Ausg. 1, S. 9 (16).

17 Paulsson, Arbitration International, Vol. 23, Ausg. 3, S. 477 (478 ff.); Carlevaris, in: Brekoulakis/Lew/Mistelis (Hrsg.), The Evolution and Future of International Arbitration, S. 331 (334 ff.); Hwang/Cheng, Fong Lee, Asian International Arbitration Journal 2008, Vol. 4, Ausg. 2, S. 195 (199 ff.); Art. 5 ff. Sekretariat, Explanatory note, Rn. 14 ff.; Section (Sec.) 1 ff. englischer „Arbitration Act 1996“; Art. 1505 ff. französischer „Code de procédure civile“; Sec. 2 ff. amerikanisches „Federal Arbitration Act (Title 9, US Code)“; Art. 176 ff. Schweizer „Bundesgesetz über das Internationale Privatrecht“; Sec. 3 ff. Hongkonger „Arbitration Ordinance“; Art. 2 ff. UNÜ; Born, Cases and Materials, S. 28 ff.; Blackaby/Partasides/Redfern/Hunter, International Arbitration, Rn. 1.02 ff.; Gaillard/Savage, Fouchard Gaillard Goldman, Rn. 9 ff.; Lew/Mistelis/Kröll, Comparative International Commercial Arbitration, Rn. 1-8 ff.; Born, International Commercial Arbitration, Bd. 1, S. 63 ff.

18 Chan, Leng Sun, Singapore Law on Arbitral Awards, S. vii; Carlevaris, in: Brekoulakis/Lew/Mistelis (Hrsg.), The Evolution and Future of International Arbitration, S. 331 (333); ICC, 2015 ICC Dispute Resolution Statistics, ICC Dispute Resolution

Schiedsverfahren im „Arbitration Act 2001[19], Chapter 10 (AA)“ und für internationale Schiedsverfahren im „International Arbitration Act 1994[20], Chapter 143A (IAA)“ kodifiziert.

Zuvor eröffnete der „Arbitration Act 1953“ gerichtliche Eingriffe in die Singapurer Schiedsverfahren.[21] Auch die Gerichte traten der Schiedsgerichtsbarkeit anfänglich nicht sonderlich aufgeschlossen entgegen. Dies zeigte sich 1988 exemplarisch in der bekannten *Turner (East Asia) Pte Ltd v Builders Federal (Hong Kong) Ltd & Another*[22]-Entscheidung des „High Courts“. Der High Court entschied, dass es ausländischen Anwälten nicht gestattet sei, Parteien in Schiedsverfahren mit Sitz in Singapur zu vertreten, weil eine solche anwaltliche Vertretung gegen den „Singapore Legal Profession Act 1966“ verstoße:

> „*The primary object of the Act is to protect the public from claims to legal services by unauthorized persons. Parties who prefer to have their disputes resolved through arbitration rather than by court proceedings are no less members of the public. Their common law right to retain whomsoever (from the category of unauthorized persons) they desire or prefer for their legal services in arbitration proceedings in Singapore has, in my view, been taken away by the Act.* […] *...it means that only those with practicing certificates may practice law in arbitration proceedings.*
>
> *For the above reasons, I am of the view that* [the New York firm’s] *representation of the respondents at the arbitration proceedings in Singapore will contravene Sect. 29 (1) and/or Sect.* 30 (1) of the Act [Legal Profession Act]. “[23]

Auf Grund dieses Urteils unterzog der Singapurer Gesetzgeber den Legal Profession Act im Jahre 1992 einer Schiedsverfahren fördernden Reform,

---

Bulletin 2016, Ausg. 1, S. 9 (16); Kabir Singh/Sam Luttrell/Elan Krishna, Third-party funding and arbitration law-making: the race for regulation in the Asia-Pacific, 14.7.2016, Kluwer Arbitration Blog, verfügbar unter http://kluwerarbitrationblog.com/2016/07/14/third-party-funding-and-arbitration-law-making-the-race-for-regulation-in-the-asia-pacific/ (zuletzt abgerufen am 28.4.2021); Loukas Mistelis/Paul Friedland, 2010 International Arbitration Survey: Choices in International Arbitration, S. 2 ff., verfügbar unter http://www.arbitration.qmul.ac.uk/docs/123290.pdf (zuletzt abgerufen am 28.4.2021); Loukas Mistelis, Arbitral Seats: Choices and Competition, Kluwer Arbitration Blog, 26.11.2010, verfügbar unter http://kluwerarbitrationblog.com/2010/11/26/arbitral-seats-choices-and-competition/ (zuletzt abgerufen am 28.4.2021); Schütze, in Wieczorek/Schütze, § 1025 Rn. 92.

19 Den AA verabschiedete das Parlament im Jahr 2001 und er trat am 1.3.2002 in Kraft.

20 Den IAA verabschiedete das Parlament im Jahr 1994 und er trat am 27.1.1995 in Kraft.

21 Pillay, The International Construction Law Review 2003, S. 91 (92 ff.).

22 [1988] SGHC 28, 30.3.1988.

23 Rn. 34 f.

die es ausländischen Anwälten fortan gestattete, in Singapurer Schiedsverfahren aufzutreten.[24]

Im IAA kodifizierte der Gesetzgeber die *lex arbitri* für internationale Schiedsverfahren und rezipierte das international anerkannte, liberal ausgestaltete UNCITRAL Modellgesetz.[25] Das auf inländische Schiedsverfahren zugeschnittene AA verbindet Bestimmungen des UNCITRAL Modellgesetzes mit Vorschriften des englischen „Arbitration Acts 1996".[26] Inländische Schiedsverfahren unterstehen im Vergleich zu internationalen Schiedsverfahren einer intensiveren gerichtlichen Kontrolle.[27]

Obschon einige Rechtsunsicherheit hervorrufende und schiedsunfreundliche Urteile ergingen, gelang es den Singapurer Gerichten in den letzten 20 Jahren, eine schiedsfreundliche Einstellung zu entwickeln und die Schiedsgerichtsbarkeit als gleichberechtigte Streitbeilegung neben der staatlichen Gerichtsbarkeit zu etablieren, wodurch die staatlichen Gerichte entlastet wurden. Dies bringt der „Court of Appeal" in seinem Urteil *Tjong Very Sumito and Others v Antig Investments Pte Ltd*[28] wie folgt zum Ausdruck:

---

24 Sec. 34A (aktuell Sec. 35) Legal Profession Act; Prof. S. Jayakumar, Minister for Law, Parliamentary Debates, Official Reports, 27.2.1992, Vol. 59, Column (Rn.) 425 ff., verfügbar unter https://sprs.parl.gov.sg/search/report.jsp?currentPubID=00069662-ZZ (zuletzt abgerufen am 28.4.2021); Hwang/Chan, Andrew/Selvaraj, in: Moser (Hrsg.), Arbitration in Asia, Sing-5 f.; Polkinghorne, Journal of International Arbitration 2005, Vol. 22, Ausg. 1, S. 75; Schütze, in Wieczorek/Schütze, § 1025 Rn. 92.

25 Lee, Suet Lin Joyce, Journal of International Arbitration 1998, Vol. 15, Ausg. 1, S. 95 (104 ff.); Lim, Charles, Asian International Arbitration Journal 2011, Vol. 7, Ausg. 1, S. 1 (5); Howell/Duthie/Lim, Mark, Journal of International Arbitration 2002, Vol. 19, Ausg. 1, S. 39; Born, Cases and Materials, S. 99; Gaillard/Savage, Fouchard Gaillard Goldman, Rn. 153, S. 70.

26 Chan, Leng Sun, Singapore Law on Arbitral Awards, S. 3; Howell/Duthie/Lim, Mark, Journal of International Arbitration 2002, Vol. 19, Ausg. 1, S. 39 (40); Associate Prof. Ho Peng Kee (Minister of State for Law), Parliamentary Debates, Official Reports, 5.10.2001, Vol. 73, Column 2213 ff., verfügbar unter http://sprs.parl.gov.sg/search/topic.jsp?currentTopicID=00068180-ZZ&currentPubID=00069892-ZZ&topicKey=00069892-ZZ.00068180-ZZ_1%2Bid016_20011005_S0004_T00041-bill%2B (zuletzt abgerufen am 28.4.2021); Attorney-General's Chambers, Review of Arbitration Laws, LRRD No. 3/2001, S. vii, verfügbar unter https://www.agc.gov.sg/DATA/0/Docs/PublicationFiles/Review_Of_Arbitration_LawsMar_2001.pdf (zuletzt abgerufen am 28.4.2021); Pillay, The International Construction Law Review 2003, S. 91 (110 ff.).

27 Merkin/Hjalmarsson, S. 2; Chew, S. 10; Pillay, The International Construction Law Review 2003, S. 91 (110 ff.); Prof. Ho Peng Kee (Minister of State for Law), Parliamentary Debates, Official Reports, 5.10.2001, Vol. 73, Column 2213 ff., verfügbar unter http://sprs.parl.gov.sg/search/topic.jsp?currentTopicID=00068180-ZZ&currentPubID=00069892-ZZ&topicKey=00069892-ZZ.00068180-ZZ_1%2Bid016_20011005_S0004_T00041-bill%2B (zuletzt abgerufen am 28.4.2021).

28 [2009] 4 SLR 732; [2009] SGCA 41, 26.8.2009.

„There was a time when arbitration was viewed disdainfully as an inferior process of justice. Those days are now well behind us. An unequivocal judicial policy of facilitating and promoting arbitration has firmly taken root in Singapore. It is now openly acknowledged that arbitration, and other forms of alternative dispute resolution such as mediation, help to effectively unclog the arteries of judicial administration as well as offer parties realistic choices on how they want to resolve their disputes at a pace they are comfortable with. More fundamentally, the need to respect party autonomy (manifested by their contractual bargain) in deciding both the method of dispute resolution (and the procedural rules to be applied) as well as the substantive law to govern the contract, has been accepted as the cornerstone underlying judicial non-intervention in arbitration. In essence, a court ought to give effect to the parties' contractual choice as to the manner of dispute resolution unless it offends the law.“[29]

2. Schiedsverfahren in Indien – ein Überblick

Der alte „Arbitration Act 1940“ gestattete den staatlichen Gerichten Eingriffe in das Schiedsverfahren innerhalb und außerhalb Indiens.[30] Die lange Dauer der Gerichtsverfahren und die gerichtlichen Interventionen in jeder Phase des Schiedsverfahrens bremsten in der Folge die Entwicklung einer effektiven schiedsgerichtlichen Streitbeilegung.[31] Unter dem Arbitration Act 1940 beschrieb der „Supreme Court“ im Jahr 1981 in seinem Urteil *Guru Nanak Foundation v Rattan Singh & Sons*[32] diese Schiedsfeindlichkeit der indischen Rechtsordnung und die damit vertane Chance, eine effiziente schiedsgerichtliche Streitbeilegung neben dem trägen und kostspieligen Gerichtsystem zu etablieren, zutreffend:

„Interminable, time consuming, complex and expensive court procedures impelled jurists to search for an alternative forum, less formal, more effective and speedy for resolution of disputes avoiding procedural claptrap and this led them to Arbitration Act, 1940 (‚Act' for short). However, the way in which the proceedings under the Act are conducted and without an exception challenged in Courts, has made lawyers laugh and legal philosophers weep. Experience shows and law reports bear ample testimony

29 Rn. 28.

30 Biswas, S. xi, 9; Hilmer, International Arbitration Law Review 2007, S. 33 (34); Government of India, Law Commission of India, 246. Report, Amendments to the Arbitration and Conciliation Act 1996, 5.8.2014, S. 14.

31 Vgl. Kapitel: Einleitung; Indien; Schiedsgerichtsbarkeit; Entstehungsgeschichte (A.III.7.b)aa)).

32 1981 AIR 2075; 1982 SCR (1) 842; 1981 SCC (4) 634; 1981 SCALE (3) 1543, 29.9.1981.

> *that the proceedings under the Act have become highly technical accompanied by unending prolixity, at every stage providing a legal trap to the unwary. Informal forum chosen by the parties for expeditious disposal of their disputes has by the decisions of the Courts been clothed with ‚legalese' of unforeseeable complexity.“*

Mit der Verabschiedung des „Arbitration and Conciliation Acts 1996 (SchiedsG)“ verfolgte das indische Parlament das Ziel, eine schiedsfreundlichere Gesetzgebung in Indien zu etablieren. Das SchiedsG beruht auf dem den „internationalen Goldstandard“[33] der Schiedsgerichtsbarkeit verkörpernden UNCITRAL Modellgesetz 1985.[34] Mit dem SchiedsG wollte der indische Gesetzgeber die Parteiautonomie in Schiedsverfahren stärken, die gerichtliche Kontrolle des Schiedsverfahrens minimieren und Schiedsverfahren durch gerichtliche Hilfestellungen unterstützen.[35] Was die gerichtliche Überprüfung des Schiedsverfahrens anbelangt, führte der Supreme Court in der Rechtssache *Konkan Railway Corpn Ltd & Ors v M/S Mehul Construction Co*[36] im Jahr 2000 aus, dass eine schiedsfreundliche Schiedsgesetzgebung nach der wirtschaftlichen Öffnung und Liberalisierung Indiens für eine wirtschaftliche Entwicklung unabdingbar sei und bestätigte die dem SchiedsG im Gegensatz zum Arbitration Act 1940 zu Grunde liegende schiedsfreundliche gesetzgeberische Intention, gerichtliche Interventionen in das Schiedsverfahren auf ein Minimum zu beschränken:

> *„To attract the confidence of International Mercantile community and the growing volume of Indias trade and commercial relationship with the rest of the world after the new liberalisation policy of the Government, Indian Parliament was persuaded to enact the Arbitration and Conciliation Act of 1996 in Uncitral model and, therefore, in interpreting any provisions of the 1996 Act Courts must not ignore the objects and purpose of the enactment of 1996. A bare comparison of different provisions of the Arbitration Act of 1940 with the provisions of the Arbitration and Conciliation Act 1996 would unequivocally indicate that 1996*

---

33 Lim, Charles, Asian International Arbitration Journal 2011, Vol. 7, Ausg. 1, S. 1 (5); Born, Cases and Materials, S. 99; Emmanuel Gaillard/John Savage (Hrsg.), Fouchard Gaillard Goldman, Rn. 153, S. 70.

34 Siehe Preamble SchiedsG.

35 Biswas, S. 9 ff.; Ministry of Justice and Law, Proposed Amendments to the Arbitration & Conciliation Act, 1996, A Consultation Paper, S. 1, verfügbar unter http://lawmin.nic.in/la/consultationpaper.pdf (zuletzt abgerufen am 28.4.2021); Sethi/Gupta, Arpan, S. 8; Government of India, Law Commission of India, 246. Report, Amendments to the Arbitration and Conciliation Act 1996, 5.8.2014, S. 3 f., 14; Law Commission of India, 176. Report, The Arbitration and Conciliation (Amendment) Bill, 2001, Consultation Paper on Review of Working of the Arbitration and Conciliation Act, 1996, 12.9.2001, S. 238.

36 AIR 2000 SC 2821; (2000) 7 SCC 201, 21.8.2000.

Act limits intervention of Court with an arbitral process to the minimum and it is certainly not the legislative intent that each and every order passed by an authority under the Act would be a subject matter of judicial scrutiny of a Court of Law. "

Die *Bhatia International v Bulk Trading SA & ANR (Bhatia)*[37]-Entscheidung aus dem Jahr 2002 beendete die schiedsfreundliche Einstellung des Supreme Courts. In diesem Urteil erweiterte das oberste indische Gericht den Anwendungsbereich von Teil I SchiedsG, entgegen dem eindeutigen Wortlaut von Section (Sec.) 2 (2) a. F. SchiedsG, auf Schiedsverfahren mit ausländischem Sitz:

„*...Part I is to apply also to international commercial arbitrations which take place out of India, unless the parties by agreement, express or implied exclude it or any of its provisions.* "[38]

Diese Ausdehnung des Geltungsbereiches des SchiedsG verlieh den indischen Gerichten *inter alia* die Kompetenz, im Ausland ergangene Schiedssprüche aufheben zu können.[39]

Dies kam dem indischen Staat im Jahr 2011 teuer zu stehen. Denn in der Rechtssache *White Industries Australia Limited v The Republic of India*[40] verurteilte ein Investitionsschiedsgericht mit Sitz in Singapur den Staat Indien zur Zahlung von Schadensersatz für die Nichtvollstreckung eines ausländischen Schiedsspruchs. Dem lag zu Grunde, dass unter der *Bhatia*-Präzedenzentscheidung – die eine Aufhebung eines im Ausland ergangenen Schiedsspruchs ermöglichte – parallel zu einer bereits beantragten Aufhebung des ausländischen Schiedsspruchs[41] fünf Tage später ein Voll-

37 Appeal (civil) 6527 of 2001; (2002) 4 SCC 105; AIR 2002 SC 1432, 13.3.2002.

38 Appeal (civil) 6527 of 2001, Rn. 35.

39 In der Entscheidung *Venture Global Engineering v Satyam Computer Services Ltd & Anr* (AIR 2008 SC 1061; Appeal [civil] 309 of 2008, 10.1.2008) folgte der Supreme Court dem *Bhatia*-Urteil und entschied, dass indische Gerichte auch ausländische Schiedssprüche aufheben können, weil die Aufhebung (Sec. 34 SchiedsG) von Schiedsverfahren in Teil I SchiedsG geregelt ist. Zudem konnten die indischen Gerichte für ausländische Schiedsverfahren Schiedsrichter (im Folgenden wird der Begriff „Schiedsrichter" geschlechtsneutral verwendet und bezieht sich gleichermaßen auf Schiedsrichterinnen und Schiedsrichter) bestellen, einstweilige Maßnahmen anordnen, Schiedsgerichte bei der Beweisaufnahme unterstützen und bei Zuständigkeitsentscheidungen des Schiedsgerichts intervenieren, siehe Kapitel: Indien; Anwendungsbereich der Schiedsgesetzgebung; Gerichtliche Entscheidungen nach Bhatia (C. I. 1. c)) und Kapitel: Indien; Anwendungsbereich der Schiedsgesetzgebung; Bharat Aluminium v Kaiser Aluminium (Balco); Bewertung (C. I. 1. b)bb)).

40 Schiedsspruch vom 30.11.2011, verfügbar unter http://www.italaw.com/sites/default/files/case-documents/ita0906.pdf (zuletzt abgerufen am 28.4.2021).

41 Kalkutta High Court, *White Industries Australia Limited v Coal India Limited*, CALLJ 2004 (2) 197, 7.5.2004.

streckungsantrag eingereicht worden war. Das Vollstreckungsverfahren des ausländischen Schiedsspruchs wurde bis zur Entscheidung des Aufhebungsverfahrens ausgesetzt. Auf Grund des über neun Jahre andauernden Aufhebungsverfahrens sprach das Investitionsschiedsgericht dem Kläger Schadensersatz in Höhe von 4,08 Millionen (Mio.) australische Dollar zu.

Die die Schiedsverfahren wieder fördernde Entscheidung *Bharat Aluminium Co v Kaiser Aluminium Technical Service Inc (Balco)*[42] des Supreme Courts verwarf das *Bhatia*-Urteil im Jahr 2012 und begrenzte die gerichtliche Kontrolle von Schiedsverfahren im Einklang mit dem Wortlaut von Sec. 2 (2) a. F. SchiedsG auf Schiedsverfahren mit Sitz in Indien:

> „*...we are of the considered opinion that the Arbitration Act, 1996 has accepted the territoriality principle which has been adopted in the UNCITRAL Model Law. Section 2(2) makes a declaration that Part I of the Arbitration Act, 1996 shall apply to all arbitrations which take place within India. We are of the considered opinion that Part I of the Arbitration Act, 1996 would have no application to International Commercial Arbitration held outside India.*“[43]

Die Schiedsgerichtsbarkeit fand seit der Verabschiedung des SchiedsG 1996 in Indien eine schiedsfreundliche Legislatur vor. Aber die *Bhatia*-Rechtsprechung zeigt exemplarisch, dass es dem indischen Supreme Court an einer konstant Schiedsverfahren unterstützenden Einstellung fehlte. Um die Rahmenbedingungen für die Schiedsgerichtsbarkeit zu verbessern, unterzog der indische Gesetzgeber das SchiedsG im Jahr 2015 einer Schiedsverfahren fördernden Gesetzesreform.

3. Ziel der vorliegenden Arbeit

Nach einer historischen Herleitung des Rechtssystems in Singapur und in Indien und einer Einführung in die Singapurer und die indische Rechtsordnung (A.II./A.III.) wird diese Dissertation die relevantesten Berührungspunkte zwischen staatlichen Gerichten und Schiedsverfahren erörtern. Dazu zählen die höchstrichterliche Rechtsprechung und die einschlägige Schiedsgesetzgebung hinsichtlich des anwendbaren Rechts (B. I./C. I.), der Kompetenz-Kompetenz des Schiedsgerichts (B.II./C.II.), der Unabhängigkeit der Schiedsvereinbarung vom Hauptvertrag (B.III./C.III.), der Aussetzung des gerichtlichen Verfahrens zu Gunsten der schiedsgerichtlichen Streitbeilegung bzw. der Verweisung einer gerichtlichen Streitigkeit an das Schiedsverfahren (B.IV./C.IV.), der Schiedsrichterbestellung (B. V./C. V.), einstweiliger Maßnahmen (B.VI./C.VI.), der Aufhebung von Schiedssprüchen (B.VII./C.VII.) und der Vollstreckung von Schiedssprüchen (B.VIII./C.VIII.). Schlussend-

42 (2012) 9 SCC 552; 2012 (3) Arb LR 515 (SC); Civil Appeal No. 7019 of 2005, 9.6.2012.
43 Civil Appeal No. 7019 of 2005, Rn. 198.

lich werden diese Berührungspunkte der staatlichen Gerichte mit Schiedsverfahren in der Singapurer und indischen Rechtsordnung bezüglich ihrer schiedsfreundlichen Ausgestaltung miteinander verglichen (D) und ein Gesamtergebnis erarbeitet (E).

Die vorliegende Arbeit wird dabei die Rechtsordnung in Singapur und Indien in Bezug auf ihre Schiedsfreundlichkeit begutachten. Es wird untersucht werden, in welchem Umfang die Singapurer und die indischen Gerichtsentscheidungen die von ihrem Gesetzgeber vorgegebenen Schranken des UNCITRAL Modellgesetzes[44] und des UNÜ achten. Der Fokus wird auf der Einstellung der staatlichen Gerichte gegenüber inländischen und internationalen Schiedsverfahren liegen. Diese Fokussierung beruht auf dem Stellenwert, den gerichtliche Entscheidungen und die richterliche Rechtsfortbildung in den im Common Law verwurzelten Rechtsordnungen Singapurs und Indiens haben. Die schiedsfördernde bzw. ablehnende Haltung einer Rechtsordnung kommt zudem am deutlichsten in der dynamischen gerichtlichen Auslegung der Schiedsgesetzgebung zum Vorschein.

Ferner werden die schiedsgesetzlichen Rahmenbedingungen und Gesetzesanpassungen in den Rechtsordnungen der beiden Staaten unter dem Gesichtspunkt der Schiedsfreundlichkeit untersucht.

Die Gründe für eine gewogene bzw. ablehnende Geisteshaltung der Singapurer und der indischen Rechtsordnung gegenüber inländischen und internationalen Schiedsverfahren sollen analysiert und herausgearbeitet werden.

Darüber hinaus wird die Effektivität der Gerichtssysteme untersucht, weil bei der gerichtlichen Kontrolle und Unterstützung des schiedsgerichtlichen Streitbeilegungsmechanismus nur ein funktionierender Gerichtsapparat eine schnelle schiedsgerichtliche Streitbeilegung gewährleisten kann.

4. Methodik

In dieser Dissertation liegt das Hauptaugenmerk auf den wegweisenden gerichtlichen Entscheidungen. Dabei soll insbesondere die sich in ihnen manifestierende Einstellung der staatlichen Gerichte gegenüber der Schiedsgerichtsbarkeit betrachtet werden. Insbesondere wird die höchstrichterliche Rechtsprechung in Singapur und in Indien, die für die nachgeordneten Instanzen Bindungswirkung entfaltet, untersucht. Im Subkontinent Indien kann auf Grund der Fülle von Entscheidungen der High Courts nur auf die Entwicklung der Rechtsprechung des Supreme Courts eingegangen werden.

---

44 Nur im auf inländische Schiedsverfahren anwendbaren Singapurer Arbitration Act rezipierte der Singapurer Gesetzgeber neben dem UNCITRAL Modellgesetz auch Bestimmungen des englischen Arbitration Acts 1996. Der Singapurer International Arbitration Act und das indische SchiedsG beruhen auf dem UNCITRAL Modellgesetz.

Im Stadtstaat Singapur wird den Entscheidungen des Court of Appeals als letzter Rechtsmittelinstanz ein besonderer Stellenwert beigemessen. Die Entscheidungen des Singapurer High Courts werden jedoch auch in die Beurteilung der Schiedsfreundlichkeit bzw. -unfreundlichkeit der Gerichte mit einfließen. Für die Bewertung, wie schiedsfreundlich die Schiedsrechtsordnungen in Singapur und Indien sind, werden ferner die Gesetzgebungsgeschichte, die gegenwärtige Schiedsgesetzgebung und die gerichtliche Verfahrensdauer in den beiden Ländern herangezogen. Am Ende der Arbeit steht eine differenzierende Gesamtsicht, die die Komplexität des Zusammenspiels von Gesetzgeber, staatlicher Gerichtsbarkeit und den Interessen der Schiedsgerichtsbarkeit würdigt.

II. Singapur

1. Geschichtlicher Überblick

a) Britische und indische Prägung

Das heutige Staatsgebiet des Insel- und Stadtstaates Singapurs (Deutsch Löwenstadt[45])[46] hat eine wechselhafte Geschichte. Es stand zunächst Jahrhunderte lang unter indischem und chinesischem Einfluss.[47] Im 14. Jahrhundert gehörte Singapur zum Herrschaftsgebiet des javanischen Königreichs „Majapahit" und unterlag in der Folge dem islamischen Einflussbereich.[48] In dieser Periode war das angewendete Recht vermutlich eine Mischung aus einer hinduistisch geprägten Gesetzgebung und einem Gewohnheitsrecht. Seit dem 15. Jahrhundert dominierte das *Adat*-Gewohnheitsrecht die Rechtskultur in Singapur.[49]

aa) Britische Kolonie unter Verwaltung der „East India Company" in Indien

Die moderne Geschichte Singapurs beginnt mit dem britischen Gründungsvater *Stamford Raffles*. Um der holländischen Handelsdominanz im ostasiatischen Raum entgegenzuwirken, überzeugte er den General-Gouverneur

45 Engl. Lion City.
46 Woon, in: Tan, Kevin (Hrsg.), The Singapore Legal System, S. 230 (231); Jenckel, S. 3 Fn. 1; Turnbull, S. 21.
47 Jenckel, S. 3.
48 Jenckel, S. 3; Tan, Kevin, in: Black/Bell (Hrsg.), Law and Legal Institutions of Asia, S. 330; Turnbull, S. 20 ff.
49 Tan, Kevin, in: Black/Bell (Hrsg.), Law and Legal Institutions of Asia, S. 330 (331); Bell, in: Tan, Kevin (Hrsg.), The Singapore Legal System, S. 1 (11).

(engl. Governor-General)[50] von Bengalen (Indien), in den von Holländern noch nicht besetzten Häfen britische Handelsposten zu errichten.[51] Sodann erwarb *Raffles* 1819 vom „Temenggong"[52] und vom „Sultan von Jahores" das Recht, auf der Singapurer Insel in einem kleinen Fischerdorf und Piratenaußenposten[53] mit nicht mehr als 150 Einwohnern[54] einen Handelsposten der britischen „East India Company" (Ostindien-Kompanie) errichten zu dürfen.[55] Die Herrschaft des Sultans über die Insel Singapur blieb dabei bestehen.[56] Der neu geschaffene Handelsstützpunkt in Singapur unterstand der Verwaltung des im „Fort William" im indischen Kalkutta residierenden General-Gouverneurs von Bengalen.[57] Zu diesem Zeitpunkt war der Einfluss der Briten auf die Einwohner Singapurs mangels Kontrolle über das singapurische Territorium begrenzt. Der erste Gerichtsapparat Singapurs unterstellte Streitigkeiten, abhängig von der ethnischen Abstammung der Streitparteien, drei verschiedenen Streitbeilegungsmechanismen:

1. Die ursprünglichen Einwohner Singapurs unterfielen der Gerichtsbarkeit des Sultans bzw. des Temenggongs.[58]
2. Für die verschiedenen aus Asien eingewanderten Volksgruppen[59] schlichteten die jeweiligen Führer, die sog. „Kapitan", Streitigkeiten nach ihren jeweiligen Bräuchen.[60] Gegen die Entscheidung ihres Kapitan konnten die

---

50 Der General-Gouverneur war oberster Verwaltungsbeamter der „East India Company" in Indien.

51 Tan, Kevin, in: Black/Bell (Hrsg.), Law and Legal Institutions of Asia, S. 330 (331); Chionh, in: Tan, Kevin (Hrsg.), Essays in Singapore Legal History, S. 93 (94); Tan, Kevin, in: Tan, Kevin (Hrsg.), The Singapore Legal System, S. 26 (28 f.).

52 Ein Vasall des Sultans. Der Temenggong lebte auf der Singapurer Insel, er stand den Einwohnern Singapurs vor und vertrat den Sultan von Johore, Müller, S. 7.

53 Tan, Kevin, in: Black/Bell (Hrsg.), Law and Legal Institutions of Asia, S. 330 (331); Chionh, in: Tan, Kevin (Hrsg.), Essays in Singapore Legal History, S. 93 (94); Müller, S. 7.

54 Phang, in: Tan, Kevin (Hrsg.), Essays in Singapore Legal History, S. 7 (8); Müller, S. 7; Newbold, S. 377.

55 Tan, Kevin, in: Tan, Kevin (Hrsg.), Essays in Singapore Legal History, S. 27 (30); Jenckel, S. 4; Tan, Kevin, in: Black/Bell (Hrsg.), Law and Legal Institutions of Asia, S. 330 (331); Müller, S. 7 f.; Tan, Kevin, in: Black/Bell (Hrsg.), Law and Legal Institutions of Asia, S. 330 (331); Chionh, in: Tan, Kevin (Hrsg.), Essays in Singapore Legal History, S. 93 (94 f.); Tan, Kevin, Constitution, Rn. 49; Tan, Kevin, Constitution Singapore, S. 12.

56 Jenckel, S. 10; Tan, Kevin, in: Tan, Kevin (Hrsg.), Essays in Singapore Legal History, S. 27 (30 f.); Müller, S. 7 f.

57 Jenckel, S. 5; Tan, Kevin, in: Black/Bell (Hrsg.), Law and Legal Institutions of Asia, S. 330 (331 f.).

58 Jenckel, S. 11.

59 Die meisten Einwanderer waren Chinesen. Aber es wanderten auch Inder, Javaner, Bugis und Araber in das heutige Staatsgebiet Singapurs ein, siehe Jenckel, S. 12 Fn. 2.

60 Jenckel, S. 11.

Volksgruppen eine Berufung zu einem Spruchkörper, bestehend aus dem britischen Resident[61] in Singapur und dem Temenggong, einlegen[62].[63]

3. Für die in Singapur lebenden Europäer war der 1726 gegründete Supreme Court im indischen Kalkutta[64] zuständig.[65]

1824 wies das britische Parlament Singapur der East India Company zu und der Sultan und der Temenggong traten das singapurische Territorium an die East India Company ab, sodass diese die vollständige Kontrolle über Singapur übernahm.[66] Die „Second Charter of Justice 1826" entzog Singapur der Verwaltung der „Presidency" (Präsidentschaft) aus dem indischen Bengalen und legte Singapur mit Malakka und Penang zur „Presidency of the Straits Settlements" zusammen. Die Bezeichnung „Straits Settlements"[67] umfasste Singapur, Malakka und Penang.[68] Die Gesetzgebungskompetenz für die Präsidentschaft oblag dem „Supreme Government" aus dem indischen Bengalen und dem britischen Parlament.[69] Die Presidency erhielt ein eigenes Gerichtssystem, das das oben beschriebene dreigeteilte Gerichtssystem vereinheitlichte und alle Streitigkeiten dem bereits zuvor in Penang (unter

---

61 Dem obersten Verwaltungsbeamten des britischen Handelspostens.

62 Diese entschieden die Streitigkeiten nach dem jeweiligen auf die Bevölkerungsgruppe anwendbaren Recht, Jenckel, S. 12.

63 Jenckel, S. 11 f. Die Rafflesche Verordnung 1823 strukturierte diesen zweistufigen Streitbeilegungsmechanismus durch die Einführung des „Magistrates' Courts" in einen dreistufigen Gerichtsaufbau mit dem Magistrates' Court auf der mittleren Ebene um, Jenckel, S. 13 ff. Die von Raffle erlassene Verordnung und der hierdurch geschaffene Magistrates' Court waren aber rechtswidrig, Wong/Sia, in: Tan, Kevin (Hrsg.), Essays in Singapore Legal History, S. 73 (75); Tan, Kevin, in: Black/Bell (Hrsg.), Law and Legal Institutions of Asia, S. 330 (332); Tan, Kevin, in: Tan, Kevin (Hrsg.), Essays in Singapore Legal History, S. 27 (30); Chionh, in: Tan, Kevin (Hrsg.), Essays in Singapore Legal History, S. 93 (96 f.).

64 Der Gouverneur von Bengalen aus Kalkutta verwaltete auch den Singapurer Handelsstützpunkt für die East India Company.

65 Jenckel, S. 12; Tan, Kevin, in: Black/Bell (Hrsg.), Law and Legal Institutions of Asia, S. 330 (333); Tan, Kevin, in: Tan, Kevin (Hrsg.), The Singapore Legal System, S. 26 (29 f.).

66 Tan, Kevin, in: Black/Bell (Hrsg.), Law and Legal Institutions of Asia, S. 330 (333); Müller, S. 32; Tan, Kevin, Constitution, Rn. 50; Tan, Kevin, Constitution Singapore, S. 12; Tan, Kevin, in: Tan, Kevin (Hrsg.), The Singapore Legal System, S. 26 (30).

67 Auf Deutsch: Siedlungen an der Meerenge.

68 Müller, S. 33; Jenckel, S. 16; Chionh, in: Tan, Kevin (Hrsg.), Essays in Singapore Legal History, S. 93 (98); Pillay, The International Construction Law Review 2003, S. 91 (92); Woon, in: Tan, Kevin (Hrsg.), The Singapore Legal System, S. 230 (232); Rust, S. 33; Turnbull, S. 53.

69 Tan, Kevin, in: Tan, Kevin (Hrsg.), Essays in Singapore Legal History, S. 27 (33); Tan, Kevin, in: Black/Bell (Hrsg.), Law and Legal Institutions of Asia, S. 330 (335); Tan, Kevin, in: Tan, Kevin (Hrsg.), The Singapore Legal System, S. 26 (32).

britischer Herrschaft auch „Prince of Wales Island[70]" genannt) geschaffenen „Recorder's Court" zuwies.[71] Dieses Gericht trug fortan den Namen „Court of Judicature of Prince of Wales Island, Singapore and Malacca"[72] und bestand aus einem Berufsrichter[73] (im Folgenden wird der Begriff „Richter" geschlechtsneutral verwendet und bezieht sich gleichermaßen auf Richterinnen und Richter), dem sog. „Recorder", und zwei Laienrichtern.[74] Bei den Laienrichtern handelte es sich um den Gouverneur oder den Präsidenten und einen „Resident Councillor" aus den Straits Settlements.[75] Durch die „Second Charter of Justice"[76] wurde das englische Recht 1826 in Singapur eingeführt[77].[78] Die Entscheidung *Regina v Willans*[79] bestätigte die Rezeption

---

70 Die Engländer übernahmen die Insel Penang am Geburtstag des Prinzen von Wales und benannten sie eine Zeitlang nach diesem, Müller, S. 5.

71 Jenckel, S. 16; Tan, Kevin, in: Black/Bell (Hrsg.), Law and Legal Institutions of Asia, S. 330 (334 f.); Tan, Kevin, in: Tan, Kevin (Hrsg.), Essays in Singapore Legal History, S. 27 (32 f.); Müller, S. 34; Tan, Kevin, in: Tan, Kevin (Hrsg.), The Singapore Legal System, S. 26 (31).

72 Auch als „Court of Judicature for the Straits Settlements" bezeichnet.

73 Erforderlich war, dass der Richter ein „Barrister" in England oder Irland war und mindestens fünf Jahre Berufserfahrung hatte, siehe Tan, Kevin, in: Black/Bell (Hrsg.), Law and Legal Institutions of Asia, S. 330 (335); Tan, Kevin, in: Tan, Kevin (Hrsg.), Essays in Singapore Legal History, S. 27 (33).

74 Müller, S. 34 f.; Jenckel, S. 16; Tan, Kevin, in: Black/Bell (Hrsg.), Law and Legal Institutions of Asia, S. 330 (335); Tan, Kevin, in: Tan, Kevin (Hrsg.), Essays in Singapore Legal History, S. 27 (33); Chionh, in: Tan, Kevin (Hrsg.), Essays in Singapore Legal History, S. 93 (98); Tan, Kevin, in: Tan, Kevin (Hrsg.), The Singapore Legal System, S. 26 (31).

75 Müller, S. 35; Tan, Kevin, in: Tan, Kevin (Hrsg.), Essays in Singapore Legal History, S. 27 (33); Chionh, in: Tan, Kevin (Hrsg.), Essays in Singapore Legal History, S. 93 (98).

76 Diese Charter wurde als „Second Charter of Justice" bezeichnet, weil sie der „First Charter of Justice" für Penang aus dem Jahr 1807 nachgebildet war, siehe Müller, S. 29 f., 34; Tan, Kevin, in: Black/Bell (Hrsg.), Law and Legal Institutions of Asia, S. 330 (334).

77 Das englische Recht musste jedoch lokalen Umständen angemessen Rechnung tragen, Jenckel, S. 49 ff. Von der Rezeption war entsprechend das Familien- und Erbrecht ausgenommen, da das englische Recht den Besonderheiten der verschieden, in Singapur lebenden, asiatischen Volksgruppen nicht gerecht wurde, Jenckel, S. 43, 49 ff.

78 Tan, Kevin, in: Black/Bell (Hrsg.), Law and Legal Institutions of Asia, S. 330 (336 f.); Chionh, in: Tan, Kevin (Hrsg.), Essays in Singapore Legal History, S. 93 (98 f.); Phang, Charter, S. 8 ff. Das englische Recht sollte bereits nach den Raffleschen Verordnungen anwendbar sein, es bestehen jedoch berechtigte Zweifel, ob diese Verordnungen wirksam waren, sodass erst durch die Second Charter of Justice die Anwendung des englischen Rechts erstmals legitimiert wurde; Chionh, in: Tan, Kevin (Hrsg.), Essays in Singapore Legal History, S. 93 (96 f.); Phang, Singapore Academy of Law Journal 1990, Vol. 2, S. 20 (22 ff.); Phang, Charter, S. 4; Tan, Kevin, in: Black/Bell (Hrsg.), Law and Legal Institutions of Asia, S. 330 (332).

79 (1858) 3 Kyshe 15, siehe Tan, Kevin, in: Black/Bell (Hrsg.), Law and Legal Institutions of Asia, S. 330 (337); Chionh, in: Tan, Kevin (Hrsg.), Essays in Singapore Legal

des englischen Rechts durch die „Justice and Right"-Klausel, begrenzte sie aber statisch auf das britische Recht von 1826.[80] Das Gericht folgte in seiner Entscheidung der seit dem Jahr 1726 in den indischen „Presidency Towns"[81] praktizierten Auslegung der Justice and Right-Klausel.[82] Die lokalen Religionen und Gebräuche der Einwohner mussten nach der Second Charter of Justice bei der Anwendung des englischen Rechts berücksichtigt werden.[83] Die Gerichte der Straits Settlements[84] fühlten sich an das englische ungeschriebene Common Law gebunden und folgten den englischen Rechtsmittelgerichten.[85] Darüber hinaus war der „Privy Council" (Kronrat) in London, dessen Richter abwechselnd im „House of Lords " und im Privy Council saßen, das oberste Rechtsmittelgericht für die Straits Settlements. Der Privy Council folgte auf Grund seiner Zusammensetzung den Entscheidungen des englischen House of Lords.[86] Die Gerichte im Straits Settlements waren mit in England ausgebildeten Rechtsexperten besetzt.[87] Der Einfluss des englischen Common Laws bestand somit auch nach 1826 in Singapur fort. 1830, nur vier Jahre nach seiner Gründung, wurde die „Presidency of the Straits Settlements" aufgehoben und in drei „Residencies"[88] umgewandelt, die wieder der Verwaltung des General-Gouverneurs im indischen Bengalen unterstanden.[89]

History, S. 93 (98 f.); Müller, S. 27, 35 ff.; Phang, in: Tan, Kevin (Hrsg.), Essays in Singapore Legal History, S. 7 (9); Woon, in: Tan, Kevin (Hrsg.), The Singapore Legal System, S. 230 (235). Die *Regina v Willans*-Entscheidung bestätigte der High Court in der Rechtssache *State of Johor and Another v Tunku Alam Shah ibni Tunku Abdul Rahman and Others* ([2005] 4 SLR 380; [2005] SGHC 156, 31.8.2005).

80 Tan, Kevin, in: Black/Bell (Hrsg.), Law and Legal Institutions of Asia, S. 330 (336 f.); Phang, Charter, S. 8 ff.; Jenckel, S. 43; Woon, in: Tan, Kevin (Hrsg.), The Singapore Legal System, S. 230 (235 f.); Rust, S. 43 ff.

81 Hierzu zählten Bombay, Kalkutta und Madras.

82 Jenckel, S. 43.

83 Chionh, in: Tan, Kevin (Hrsg.), Essays in Singapore Legal History, S. 93 (99); Tan, Kevin, in: Black/Bell (Hrsg.), Law and Legal Institutions of Asia, S. 330 (341); Privy Council, *Yeap Cheah Neo and others v Ong Cheng Neo and others*, [1875] UKPC 64; (1875) L. R. 6 P. C. 381, 28.7. 1875; Woon, in: Tan, Kevin (Hrsg.), The Singapore Legal System, S. 230 (235 f.); Yihan/Tan, Paul, in: Yihan/Tan, Paul (Hrsg.), Singapore Law, 50 Years in the Making, S. 3 (11).

84 Dieses setzt sich aus Singapur, Penang und Malakka zusammen, siehe S. 14.

85 Müller, S. 41 ff.; Jenckel, S. 45 f.

86 Müller, S. 44, 121; Jenckel, S. 114 ff.

87 Jenckel, S. 38 ff.

88 Singapur, Malakka und Penang.

89 Tan, Kevin, in: Black/Bell (Hrsg.), Law and Legal Institutions of Asia, S. 330 (335); Tan, Kevin, in: Tan, Kevin (Hrsg.), Essays in Singapore Legal History, S. 27 (34); Jenckel, S. 16 f.; Wong/Sia, in: Tan, Kevin (Hrsg.), Essays in Singapore Legal History, S. 73 (77); Chionh, in: Tan, Kevin (Hrsg.), Essays in Singapore Legal History, S. 93 (100); Müller, S. 37; Tan, Kevin, in: Tan, Kevin (Hrsg.), The Singapore Legal System, S. 26 (33).

Durch den „Charter Act 1833“ entstand eine zentrale Verwaltung aller von der East India Company administrierten Gebiete[90]. Der Charter Act übertrug der East India Company erstmals eine eigenständige Gesetzgebungskompetenz für die gesamten britisch-indischen Gebiete. Der „Governor-General of India in Council“ (General-Gouverneur unter Beratung [durch den Rat]) war befugt, für das gesamte von der East India Company kontrollierte Gebiet, das auch Singapur umfasste, die sog. „Indian Acts“ zu erlassen.[91] Die vom englischen Parlament verabschiedeten Gesetze waren nur dann auf das von der East India Company kontrollierte Gebiet anwendbar, wenn das britische Parlament einem verabschiedeten Gesetz explizit für das britisch-indische Territorium Geltung verlieh (sog. „Imperial Acts“).[92]

Seit der Etablierung des britischen Handelspostens 1819 entwickelte sich Singapur rasch zu einem wichtigen Handelsknotenpunkt in der Region,[93] es war ein bedeutender Umschlagplatz für die Rohstoffe von der malaiischen Halbinsel und aus Indonesien. Schon 1827 lagen die auf der kleinen Insel Singapur erwirtschafteten Gewinne der East India Company über denen in den anderen Gebieten[94] der Straits Settlements.[95] Mit dem wirtschaftlichen Aufschwung stieg die Bevölkerung Singapurs durch chinesische, malaysische und indische Einwanderer rasant an.[96] Das 1826 geschaffene Gerichtssystem der Straits Settlements blieb nach der Angliederung der Straits Settlements an Indien bestehen, war aber mit dieser florierenden Entwicklung Singapurs überfordert und hielt selten Gericht in Singapur, was zu Unmut in der singapurischen Bevölkerung führte.[97] Diese Missstände behob die britische Krone 1855 mit der „Third Charter of Justice“. Die Charter strukturierte den Court of Judicature of Prince of Wales Island, Singapore and Malacca in einen zwei Kammern-Spruchkörper um. Eine der Kammern war für Penang und die andere für Singapur und Malakka zuständig. Den beiden Kam-

90 Hierzu gehörte auch Singapur.

91 Müller, S. 38; Jenckel, S. 139; Phang, Charter, S. 56; Tan, Kevin, in: Black/Bell (Hrsg.), Law and Legal Institutions of Asia, S. 330 (344); Tan, Kevin, Constitution Singapore, S. 13.

92 Phang, Charter, S. 56 Fn. 190; Jenckel, S. 82; Woon, in: Tan, Kevin (Hrsg.), The Singapore Legal System, S. 230 (238); Rust, S. 44 f.

93 Chionh, in: Tan, Kevin (Hrsg.), Essays in Singapore Legal History, S. 93 (100 ff.).

94 Malakka und Penang.

95 Jenckel, S. 18.

96 Müller, S. 10, 32, 39, 49; Woon, in: Tan, Kevin (Hrsg.), The Singapore Legal System, S. 230 (232); Turnbull, S. 46.

97 Müller, S. 37 ff.; Chionh, in: Tan, Kevin (Hrsg.), Essays in Singapore Legal History, S. 93 (100 ff.); Jenckel, S. 18.

mern saß ein Berufsrichter vor[98].[99] Hierdurch war das Gerichtssystem den schnellen wirtschaftlichen Entwicklungen und dem Bevölkerungswachstum Singapurs wieder gewachsen und Singapur erhielt das ersehnte eigene Gericht.[100] Die Abschaffung der East India Company 1858 und der Transfer des indischen Territoriums und der Straits Settlements an die britische Krone hatten keinen spürbaren Einfluss auf die Straits Settlements.[101] Verwaltet wurden die Straits Settlements weiterhin vom indischen Kalkutta aus.[102] Während der indischen Verwaltung der Straits Settlements von 1834–1867 ergingen etwa 1.000 Gesetze, u.a. der indische „Wills Act 1838“[103] und der „Indian Companies Act 1866“[104].[105]

bb) Selbständige britische Kolonie

1867 wurden die Straits Settlements aus dem Einflussbereich von Britisch-Indien herausgelöst und als Kolonie verselbstständigt.[106] Sie erhielten ein von Indien unabhängiges Regierungs- und Rechtssystem. An der Spitze der Exekutive stand der Gouverneur, der wiederum direkt dem „Secretary of State for the Colonies“ in England unterstand. Nach der Selbstständigkeit war der „Legislative Council of the Colony“ befugt, Gesetze für die Straits Settlements Gebiete[107] zu erlassen. Diese Gesetze werden als „Straits Settlements

98 Neben dem Berufsrichter bestand jede Kammer aus dem „Governor“ und dem „Resident Councillor“.

99 Wong/Sia, in: Tan, Kevin (Hrsg.), Essays in Singapore Legal History, S. 73 (78); Müller, S. 39 f.; Chionh, in: Tan, Kevin (Hrsg.), Essays in Singapore Legal History, S. 93 (103 f.); Jenckel, S. 18; Tan, Kevin, in: Tan, Kevin (Hrsg.), The Singapore Legal System, S. 26 (35).

100 Müller, S. 40; Chionh, in: Tan, Kevin (Hrsg.), Essays in Singapore Legal History, S. 93 (103).

101 Chionh, in: Tan, Kevin (Hrsg.), Essays in Singapore Legal History, S. 93 (104); Müller, S. 49; Tan, Kevin, in: Tan, Kevin (Hrsg.), Essays in Singapore Legal History, S. 27 (36); Tan, Kevin, in: Black/Bell (Hrsg.), Law and Legal Institutions of Asia, S. 330 (345).

102 Chionh, in: Tan, Kevin (Hrsg.), Essays in Singapore Legal History, S. 93 (104).

103 Dieser beruhte auf dem englischen Wills Act 1837; Tan, Kevin, in: Black/Bell (Hrsg.), Law and Legal Institutions of Asia, S. 330 (345).

104 Es beruhte auf dem englischen Companies Act 1862.

105 Müller, S. 50.

106 Tan, Kevin, in: Black/Bell (Hrsg.), Law and Legal Institutions of Asia, S. 330 (345); Jenckel, S. 19; Wong/Sia, in: Tan, Kevin (Hrsg.), Essays in Singapore Legal History, S. 73 (79); Müller, S. 48; Tan, Kevin, in: Tan, Kevin (Hrsg.), Essays in Singapore Legal History, S. 27 (35 ff.); Müller, S. 49; Chionh, in: Tan, Kevin (Hrsg.), Essays in Singapore Legal History, S. 93 (104); Tan, Kevin, Constitution, Rn. 2, 51; Tan, Kevin, Constitution Singapore, S. 13; Tan, Kevin, in: Tan, Kevin (Hrsg.), The Singapore Legal System, S. 26 (34 f.); Rust, S. 33; Turnbull, S. 89.

107 Singapur, Malakka und Penang.

Acts bzw. Ordinances"[108] bezeichnet.[109] Die unter der indischen Verwaltung der Straits Settlements ergangene Gesetzgebung, die Indian Acts, blieben in Kraft.[110] Das 1855 durch die Third Charter of Justice geschaffene zweikammerige Gerichtssystem wurde erneut reformiert. Der Court of Judicature of Prince of Wales Island, Singapore and Malacca wurde 1868 in den „Supreme Court of the Straits Settlements" umbenannt[111] und umfasste fortan drei Kammern. Jeweils eine Kammer war für Singapur, Malakka und Penang zuständig.[112] Diese Kammern bestanden zum ersten Mal vollständig aus Berufsrichtern.[113] Die grundlegendste Veränderung war die Abschaffung des von der Exekutive ausgeübten Laienrichteramtes. Hierdurch entstand erstmals ein von der Verwaltung unabhängiges Gericht in den Straits Settlements.[114] Der Supreme Court of the Straits Settlements war die erste gerichtliche Instanz im Gebiet der Straits Settlements. Auf zweiter Stufe stand den Parteien ein Rechtsmittelverfahren vor dem Privy Council in London offen.[115]

Durch die Loslösung von Britisch-Indien entstand 1867 erstmals ein von Indien unabhängiges Rechtssystem,[116] dennoch blieb eine enge Zusammengehörigkeit zwischen der singapurischen und der indischen Rechtsordnung bestehen. So übernahm Singapur 1871 den indischen „Criminal Code" und den indischen „Criminal Procedural Code"[117] in das singapurische Recht.[118]

---

108 Zwischen Act und Ordinance besteht nur ein terminologischer Unterschied, die Bezeichnung Act war bis 1868 gebräuchlich, danach wurde der Begriff Ordinance verwendet und nach 1945 war wiederum der Begriff Act gebräuchlich, siehe Jenckel, S. 19 Fn. 2.; Tan, Kevin, in: Tan, Kevin (Hrsg.), The Singapore Legal System, S. 26 (62, Fn. 85).

109 Jenckel, S. 19; Müller, S. 53; Wong/Sia, in: Tan, Kevin (Hrsg.), Essays in Singapore Legal History, S. 73 (80).

110 Müller, S. 53 f.

111 Dies geschah durch die Rechtsverordnung („Ordinance") No. V von 1868, die sog. Supreme Court Ordinance.

112 Jenckel, S. 20; Müller, S. 58 f.; Chionh, in: Tan, Kevin (Hrsg.), Essays in Singapore Legal History, S. 93 (104 f.); Tan, Kevin, in: Tan, Kevin (Hrsg.), The Singapore Legal System, S. 26 (36).

113 Jenckel, S. 20; Müller, S. 59; Chionh, in: Tan, Kevin (Hrsg.), Essays in Singapore Legal History, S. 93 (104 f.); Wong/Sia, in: Tan, Kevin (Hrsg.), Essays in Singapore Legal History, S. 73 (80).

114 Jenckel, S. 20; Chionh, in: Tan, Kevin (Hrsg.), Essays in Singapore Legal History, S. 93 (104 f.); Müller, S. 58.

115 Schütze, in: Schütze/Hirth, S. 1 f.; Jenckel, S. 20.

116 Schütze, in: Schütze/Hirth, S. 1 f.

117 1900 wurde der „Criminal Procedural Code" reformiert, er basierte jedoch weiterhin auf dem indischen „Criminal Procedural Code", Wong/Sia, in: Tan, Kevin (Hrsg.), Essays in Singapore Legal History, S. 73 (80 f.).

118 Wong/Sia, in: Tan, Kevin (Hrsg.), Essays in Singapore Legal History, S. 73 (80); Phang, in: Tan, Kevin (Hrsg.), Essays in Singapore Legal History, S. 7.

Der Wills Act beruht noch heute auf einem Indian Act aus der Zeit der indischen Regierungskontrolle über Singapur.[119]

1873 entstand innerhalb des Supreme Courts ein Court of Appeal für Zivilsachen. Dadurch wandelte sich das zweistufige in ein dreistufiges Gerichtssystem.[120] Erst 1934 entstand der „Court of Criminal Appeal". Der Supreme Court umfasste einen High Court mit jeweils einer Kammer in Singapur, Penang und Malakka, den Court of Appeal für zivilrechtliche Verfahren und den Court of Criminal Appeal.[121] Der Court of Appeal war innerhalb des Supreme Courts das oberste Gericht, ihm nachgeordnet war der High Court. Seit 1878 orientierte sich die Rechtsprechung des Supreme Courts der Straits Settlements am englischen High Court.[122] Ab 1878 rezipierte Singapur mit der „Civil Law Ordinance"[123] zu Gunsten der singapurischen Kaufleute das zum jeweiligen Anwendungszeitpunkt gültige englische Handelsrecht, vorbehaltlich lokaler Gebräuche und eigener Gesetzgebung, in seine Rechtsordnung.[124] Nach dem Vorbild der Gerichtsreformen in Burma und Indien wurden 1907 in Malakka, Penang und Singapur zwei weitere, nachgeordnete gerichtliche Instanzen unter dem Supreme Court ins Leben gerufen.[125] Der „District Court" hatte jeweils eine Abteilung für Zivil- und Strafsachen. Unterhalb des District Courts entstanden die für Bagatell-Strafsachen zuständigen sog. „Magistrates' oder Police Courts".[126] Ferner übten die „Coroner" in Fällen unnatürlichen Todes sowie Friedensrichter in Bagatellsachen richterliche Funktionen aus.[127] Hieraus ergab sich folgender gerichtlicher Instanzenzug:

119 Siehe Wills Act 1838; Jenckel, S. 139.

120 Jenckel, S. 20 f.; Chionh, in: Tan, Kevin (Hrsg.), Essays in Singapore Legal History, S. 93 (105 f.); Müller, S. 43.

121 Jenckel, S. 21; Woon, in: Tan, Kevin (Hrsg.), The Singapore Legal System, S. 297 (307).

122 Jenckel, S. 21; Chionh, in: Tan, Kevin (Hrsg.), Essays in Singapore Legal History, S. 93 (106); Schütze, in: Schütze/Hirth, S. 2.

123 Diese Ordinance erließ der englische „Legislative Council".

124 Wong/Sia, in: Tan, Kevin (Hrsg.), Essays in Singapore Legal History, S. 73 (81); Müller, S. 61 ff.; Schütze, in: Schütze/Hirth, S. 3; Respondek, RIW 1995, S. 28 (29); Klötzel, RIW 1995, S. 202.

125 Müller, S. 60 f.; Jenckel, S. 21.

126 Jenckel, S. 21; Chionh, in: Tan, Kevin (Hrsg.), Essays in Singapore Legal History, S. 93 (107).

127 Jenckel, S. 20 f.

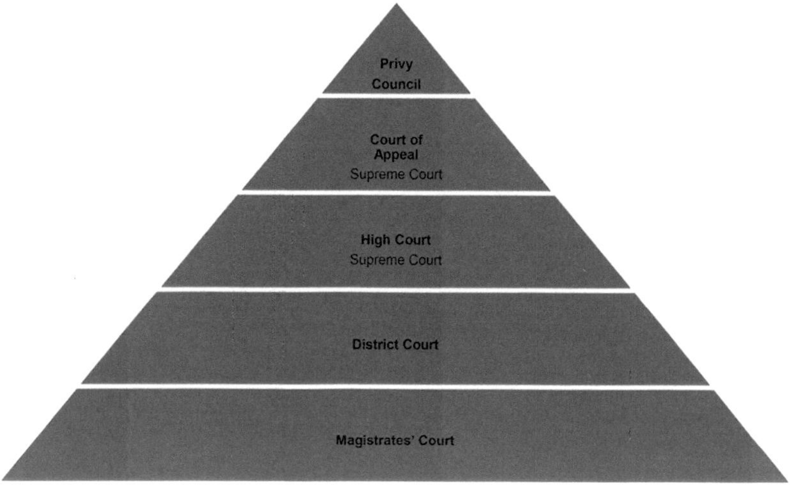

cc) Japanische Besetzung

Während der japanischen Besetzung (1942–1945) behielten die Japaner die District, Magistrates' und Coroners' Courts bei. Den Supreme Court ersetzte ein Gericht mit dem Namen „Syonan[128] Koto-Hoin[129]". Dieses Gericht glich in Aufbau und Struktur dem alten Supreme Court.[130] Die Richterämter dieser Gerichte wurden an Japaner und kooperationswillige Singapurer vergeben.[131] Das in Singapur zu dieser Zeit bestehende Recht blieb anwendbar und wurde durch die japanische Militärverwaltung nur geringfügig modifiziert.[132] Nach dem Ende des 2. Weltkrieges lösten die Briten die Straits Settlements auf und Singapur wurde eine Kronkolonie.[133] Die von den Japanern eingeführten Rechtsakte hoben die Briten auf und der Singapurer

---

128 Singapur erhielt den Namen Syonan.

129 Supreme Court.

130 Wong/Sia, in: Tan, Kevin (Hrsg.), Essays in Singapore Legal History, S. 73 (84); Chionh, in: Tan, Kevin (Hrsg.), Essays in Singapore Legal History, S. 93 (108); Jenckel, S. 22; Tan, Kevin, in: Tan, Kevin (Hrsg.), The Singapore Legal System, S. 26 (40).

131 Jenckel, S. 22.

132 Chionh, in: Tan, Kevin (Hrsg.), Essays in Singapore Legal History, S. 93 (108); Tan, Kevin, Constitution, Rn. 4; Tan, Kevin, in: Tan, Kevin (Hrsg.), The Singapore Legal System, S. 26 (40).

133 Chionh, in: Tan, Kevin (Hrsg.), Essays in Singapore Legal History, S. 93 (109 f.); Tan, Kevin, in: Tan, Kevin (Hrsg.), Essays in Singapore Legal History, S. 27 (42 f.); Müller, S. 81 ff.; Jenckel, S. 23.

Rechtsordnung wurde wieder vollumfänglich Wirkung verliehen.[134] Penang und Malakka wurden nach dem 2. Weltkrieg Teil der „Malayan Union“.[135]

dd) Weg zur Unabhängigkeit

Seit dem Ende des 2. Weltkrieges war Singapur eine eigenständige britische Kolonie und bekam ab 1958 das Recht zur Selbstverwaltung[136] übertragen.[137] Singapur etablierte nach dem Ende des 2. Weltkrieges wieder den vor 1942 bestehenden kolonialen Gerichtsapparat.[138] An die Spitze des Singapurer Gerichtssystems trat der Supreme Court von Singapur.[139] Die letzte Berufungsinstanz war – wie bereits vor dem 2. Weltkrieg – der in London ansässige Privy Council.[140] Die beiden übrigen Kammern des Supreme Courts der Straits Settlements in Malakka und Penang wurden zum „Supreme Court of the Malayan Union“.[141]

Singapur schloss sich 1963 der „Föderation Malaya“[142] an, die hierdurch zur „Föderation Malaysia“[143] wurde.[144] Als Teil der Föderation Malaysia löste sich Singapur erstmals seit über 140 Jahren von der britischen Herrschaft. Die zwischenzeitliche Angliederung an Malaysia führte wiederum zu einer

---

134 Müller, S. 71; Tan, Kevin, in: Tan, Kevin (Hrsg.), The Singapore Legal System, S. 26 (40). *Tan* verweist auf Bartholomew, Introduction to The Table of Written Laws of Singapore, 1819–1971, Malay Law Review 1972, S. li.

135 Wong/Sia, in: Tan, Kevin (Hrsg.), Essays in Singapore Legal History, S. 73 (85); Müller, S. 80; Tan, Kevin, in: Black/Bell (Hrsg.), Law and Legal Institutions of Asia, S. 330 (347); Tan, Kevin, Constitution Singapore, S. 16; Woon, in: Tan, Kevin (Hrsg.), The Singapore Legal System, S. 230 (233).

136 Großbritannien bestimmte lediglich Fragen der Landesverteidigung, der Außenpolitik und teilweise der inneren Sicherheit, siehe Jenckel, S. 24; Müller, S. 87, 94; Tan, Kevin, Constitution, Rn. 53.

137 Jenckel, S. 23 f.; Chionh, in: Tan, Kevin (Hrsg.), Essays in Singapore Legal History, S. 93 (110 f.); Tan, Kevin, in: Tan, Kevin (Hrsg.), Essays in Singapore Legal History, S. 27 (43 ff.); Tan, Kevin, Constitution Singapore, S. 16 ff.; Tan, Kevin, in: Tan, Kevin (Hrsg.), The Singapore Legal System, S. 26 (41 ff.).

138 Chionh, in: Tan, Kevin (Hrsg.), Essays in Singapore Legal History, S. 93 (111); Tan, Kevin, Constitution Singapore, S. 17.

139 Dieser übernahm die Aufgaben des „Supreme Court of the Straits Settlements“, Müller, S. 85; Tan, Kevin, Constitution Singapore, S. 17.

140 Tan, Kevin, Constitution Singapore, S. 17.

141 Tan, Kevin, Marshall of Singapore – A Biography, S. 144 Fn. 9; Jenckel, S. 23.

142 Die Malayan Union wurde 1948 zur Föderation Malaya, Verma, S. 29.

143 Neben Singapur wurden der Föderation Malaya Nordborneo (Sabah) und Sarawak hinzugefügt.

144 Chionh, in: Tan, Kevin (Hrsg.), Essays in Singapore Legal History, S. 93 (112); Müller, S. 102; Jenckel, S. 25; Tan, Kevin, Constitution, Rn. 54; Tan, Kevin, Constitution Singapore, S. 21; Woon, in: Tan, Kevin (Hrsg.), The Singapore Legal System, S. 230 (233); Rust, S. 34.

Umgestaltung des Gerichtssystems. Es entstanden drei gleichberechtigte High Courts in Malaya, Borneo und Singapur[145]. Das oberste Berufungsgericht[146] von Malaysia war der „Federal Court of Malaysia“.[147] Die letzte Berufungsinstanz war der Privy Council in England.[148] Die vor dem Beitritt zur Föderation von Malaysia ergangenen Singapurer Gesetze blieben in Kraft und wurden durch die Gesetzgebung[149] des malaysischen Parlaments ergänzt.[150]

ee) Unabhängigkeit

Nach der Abspaltung von Malaysia wurde Singapur in seiner heutigen Form am 9. August 1965 ein souveräner Staat[151].[152] 15 Jahre lang bestand die Verfassung Singapurs aus folgenden Dokumenten:

1. „Constitution of the State of Singapore 1963“
2. „Federal Constitution of Malaysia 1963“
3. „Republic of Singapore Independence Act 1965“

1980 erschien eine abgestimmte Zusammenfassung dieser drei Dokumente zusammen mit den zwischenzeitlich erfolgten Verfassungsänderungen.[153] Die in der Malaysischen Föderation ergangenen Gesetze blieben im unabhängigen Singapur in Kraft.[154] Nach der Abspaltung von Malaysia musste Singapur seine Kräfte zunächst bündeln, um sich als kleiner Inselstaat poli-

---

145 Der High Court in Singapur war für alle Verfahren in Singapur zuständig. Entsprechendes galt für die anderen beiden High Courts.

146 Der Supreme Court in Singapur wurde aufgelöst. Der High Court in Singapur blieb jedoch bestehen.

147 Jenckel, S. 25 f.; Chionh, in: Tan, Kevin (Hrsg.), Essays in Singapore Legal History, S. 93 (113); Tan, Kevin, in: Tan, Kevin (Hrsg.), Essays in Singapore Legal History, S. 27 (55); Müller, S. 104; Tan, Kevin, Constitution, Rn. 21; Tan, Kevin, in: Tan, Kevin (Hrsg.), The Singapore Legal System, S. 26 (51).

148 Woon, in: Tan, Kevin (Hrsg.), The Singapore Legal System, S. 297 (300 f.); Tan, Kevin, Constitution Singapore, S. 148.

149 Diese Gesetzgebung unterschied sich nicht wesentlich von der singapurischen Gesetzgebung, da beide Rechtsordnungen den gleichen Ursprung hatten.

150 Müller, S. 104 f.

151 Erstmals hatte Singapur alle Kompetenzen eines unabhängigen Staates, inklusive der Verteidigungs- und Außenpolitik, siehe Jenckel, S. 26.

152 Ibrahim, in: Knapp (Hrsg.), International Encyclopedia of Comparative Law, National Reports, Vol. 1, S. 55; Müller, S. 106; Jenckel, S. 26; Tan, Kevin, Constitution, Rn. 54; Tan, Kevin, in: Tan, Kevin (Hrsg.), The Singapore Legal System, S. 26 (46); Woon, in: Tan, Kevin (Hrsg.), The Singapore Legal System, S. 230 (233).

153 Jenckel, S. 26 f.; Tan, Kevin, in: Black/Bell (Hrsg.), Law and Legal Institutions of Asia, S. 330 (343); Müller, S. 107; Tan, Kevin, Constitution, Rn. 17; Tan, Kevin, Constitution Singapore, S. 30; Tan, Kevin, in: Tan, Kevin (Hrsg.), The Singapore Legal System, S. 26 (47 f.).

154 Müller, S. 115.

tisch und wirtschaftlich etablieren zu können. Entsprechend war Singapur *ad interim* nicht in der Lage, einen vollständig selbstständigen Gerichtsapparat zu erschaffen und somit bestand ein weitgehender Gleichlauf zwischen der Rechtsordnung Singapurs und Malaysias.[155] Dies kam auch in der Gerichtsstruktur des souveränen Singapurs zum Ausdruck. In den ersten vier Jahren seines Bestehens blieb das Gerichtssystem aus der Zeit des Zusammenschlusses mit Malaysia erhalten. Berufungen gegen Urteile des High Courts von Singapur entschied weiterhin der Federal Court von Malaysia.[156] In den letzten Jahrzehnten entwickelten sich die beiden Rechtsordnungen jedoch unabhängig voneinander weiter.[157] Im Jahre 1969 löste sich Singapur von dem malaysischen Gerichtsapparat.[158] An die Stelle des Federal Courts of Malaysia trat der Supreme Court von Singapur, der neben dem High Court auch den Court of Appeal und den Court of Criminal Appeal umfasste.[159] Die Erschaffung eines eigenen Supreme Courts war für Singapur ein erster Schritt hin zur Entwicklung eines eigenen singapurischen Rechtsystems. Eine Stufe über dem Supreme Court von Singapur war der britische Privy Council mit Sitz in London als letztinstanzliches Berufungsgericht bis 1994 zuständig.[160] 1970 regelte der Singapurer Gesetzgeber im „Subordinate Courts Act"[161] die Verfassung der District, Magistrates', Juvenile und Coroners' Courts.[162] 1993 verschmolz die Legislative den Court of Appeal und den Court of Criminal Appeal zu einem, sowohl für zivil- als auch strafrechtliche Berufungsverfahren zuständigen Court of Appeal.[163] Die enge

155 Chionh, in: Tan, Kevin (Hrsg.), Essays in Singapore Legal History, S. 93 (113 ff.); Müller, S. 106 ff., 118 f.

156 Tan, Kevin, in: Tan, Kevin (Hrsg.), Essays in Singapore Legal History, S. 27 (55); Müller, S. 118 f.; Tan, Kevin, in: Tan, Kevin (Hrsg.), The Singapore Legal System, S. 26 (51); Tan, Kevin, Constitution, Rn. 21 f. Letztinstanzlich war der Privy Council zuständig, Tan, Kevin, Constitution Singapore, S. 32; Woon, in: Tan, Kevin (Hrsg.), The Singapore Legal System, S. 297 (308).

157 Schütze, in: Schütze/Hirth, S. 2; Müller, S. 118 f.; Tan, Kevin, in: Tan, Kevin (Hrsg.), Essays in Singapore Legal History, S. 27 (55 ff.).

158 Tan, Kevin, Constitution, Rn. 24; Jenckel, S. 28; Müller, S. 119.

159 Jenckel, S. 28; Wong/Sia, in: Tan, Kevin (Hrsg.), Essays in Singapore Legal History, S. 73 (88); Müller, S. 119.

160 Chionh, in: Tan, Kevin (Hrsg.), Essays in Singapore Legal History, S. 93 (114); Tan, Kevin, in: Tan, Kevin (Hrsg.), Essays in Singapore Legal History, S. 27 (55); Müller, S. 119 f. Tan, Kevin, Constitution, Rn. 22, 24, 46.

161 Der Subordinate Courts Act 1970 wurde 2014 in State Courts Act 1970 umbenannt, siehe Subordinate Courts (Amendment) Act 2014.

162 Chionh, in: Tan, Kevin (Hrsg.), Essays in Singapore Legal History, S. 93 (114).

163 Chionh, in: Tan, Kevin (Hrsg.), Essays in Singapore Legal History, S. 93 (116); Müller, S. 130 f.; Chang, Daphne/Liyin, Singapore Law Review 1993, Vol. 14, S. 396 (397).

Verbindung zum britischen „Common Wealth“ führte zu einer weitgehenden Rezeption des englischen Rechts in Singapur.[164]

ff) Lösung vom englischen Recht und vom Privy Council

In den 90er Jahren begann die Singapurer Rechtsordnung sich vom englischen Rechtskreis zu lösen. Durch den „Judicial Committee (Repeal) Act 1994“ schaffte das Parlament den Privy Council als oberstes Rechtsmittelgericht ab. Die andauernde Rezeption des englischen Rechts beendet der Gesetzgeber mit dem „Application of English Law Act 1993“, um den Entwicklungen des souveränen Staates Singapur besser gerecht zu werden.[165] Die Abschaffung der Privy Council Berufungsebene begründete das Singapurer Parlament mit den unterschiedlichen rechtlichen, wirtschaftlichen, sozialen und politischen Entwicklungen der beiden Länder seit dem Beitritt Englands zur Europäischen Union.[166] Der Court of Appeal war fortan nicht mehr an seine eigenen, zuvor ergangenen Entscheidungen und auch nicht an Präzedenzentscheidungen des Privy Councils gebunden.[167] Durch die Abschaffung des Privy Councils und die Abkehr von der permanenten Rezeption des englischen Rechts entwickelte sich erstmals ein eigenständiges singapurisches Rechtssystem. Trotz der Abkopplung von seiner englischen Mutterrechtsordnung, bleibt das singapurische Recht durch die britisch geprägte Ausgestaltung der Gesetzgebung und des Gerichtssystems eine stark vom Common Law beeinflusste Rechtsordnung. Singapur gehört folglich weiter zum Common Law-Rechtskreis.[168]

---

164 Phang, in: Tan, Kevin (Hrsg.), Essays in Singapore Legal History, S. 7 ff.; mit weiteren Nachweisen, Schütze, in: Schütze/Hirth, S. 2.

165 Schütze, in: Schütze/Hirth, S. 2; Chionh, in: Tan, Kevin (Hrsg.), Essays in Singapore Legal History, S. 93 (116 f.); Müller, S. 120 ff.; Phang, in: Tan, Kevin (Hrsg.), Essays in Singapore Legal History, S. 7 ff.; Tan, Kevin, Constitution, Rn. 24, 46; Woon, in: Tan, Kevin (Hrsg.), The Singapore Legal System, S. 230 (238 ff.); Woon, in: Tan, Kevin (Hrsg.), The Singapore Legal System, S. 297 (301). Zur vor 1993 bestehenden engen Verbundenheit mit dem englischen Recht ausführlich, Rust, S. 68 ff.

166 Müller, S. 128. Zur sich abzeichnenden Auseinanderentwicklung des singapurischen und des englischen Rechts auf Grund des Beitritts des Vereinigten Königreiches zur Europäischen Union, Rust, S. 113 ff.

167 Chionh, in: Tan, Kevin (Hrsg.), Essays in Singapore Legal History, S. 93 (113 ff.).

168 Schütze, in: Schütze/Hirth, S. 2; Bell, in: Tan, Kevin (Hrsg.), The Singapore Legal System, S. 1 ff.; Woon, in: Tan, Kevin (Hrsg.), The Singapore Legal System, S. 230 (238 ff.); Yihan/Tan, Paul, in: Yihan/Tan, Paul (Hrsg.), Singapore Law, 50 Years in the Making, S. 3 ff.

gg) Entwicklung des effektiven Gerichtswesens

Schon früh etablierte Singapur alternative Streitbeilegungsmechanismen neben den staatlichen Gerichten, um den zunehmenden Streitigkeiten im Zusammenhang mit der ansteigenden Anzahl von Gesetzen und Verordnungen und der expandierenden Verwaltung Rechnung zu tragen. Es entstanden keine weiteren spezialisierten Gerichte, sondern alternative Streitbeilegungsspruchkörper im Bereich des Arbeits-, Miet-, Steuer-, Bau- und Enteignungsrechts.[169] Diese Entwicklung mag auch die Offenheit Singapurs für die Schiedsgerichtsbarkeit begründen.

Die Erhöhung der Prozesskosten führte alleine zu keiner signifikanten Verringerung der anhängigen Verfahren. In den 90er Jahren führte das Parlament deshalb eine effektive „Case Management" Reform der singapurischen Gerichte durch, die die Grundlage für die Erschaffung eines der effizientesten Gerichtssysteme weltweit war, mit einer geringen Anzahl rechtshängiger Verfahren beim Supreme Court und bei den „State Courts".[170] Das „Case Management" umfasst u. a. sog. „Pre-Trial Conferences", in denen sich die Parteien schon vor Beginn des Gerichtsverfahrens über die Zahl der Zeugen oder der Sachverständigen einigen können.[171] Zudem besitzt Singapur einen modernen „Technology Court", durch den Zeugen im Ausland in Videositzungen einfach vernommen werden können und es wurde ein papierloses Gerichtsverfahren eingeführt. Mit Hilfe des sog. „Electronic Filing Systems" können Klagen elektronisch eingereicht und zugestellt werden und auf die Gerichtsakten kann digital zugegriffen werden („eLitigation").[172] Das „Elec-

---

169 Jenckel, S. 130 ff.

170 Chionh, in: Tan, Kevin (Hrsg.), Essays in Singapore Legal History, S. 93 (117 f.); Chen, Siyuan/Chua, S. 65 ff.; Müller, S. 172; Chang, Daphne/Liyin, Singapore Law Review 1993, Vol. 14, S. 396 (405 ff.); Chua/Leo, in: Yihan/Tan, Paul (Hrsg.), Singapore Law, 50 Years in the Making, S. 358 (368 ff.).

171 In Conversation: An Interview with Honourable Justice of Appeal M Karthigesu, Singapore Law Review, Vol. 16, 1995, S. 1 (17); Müller, S. 172; Chua/Leo, in: Yihan/Tan, Paul (Hrsg.), Singapore Law, 50 Years in the Making, S. 358 (372 f.).

172 Supreme Court, Services, Court Service, Technology Courts Booking, verfügbar unter http://www.supremecourt.gov.sg/services/services-for-the-legal-profession/elitigation (zuletzt abgerufen am 28.4.2021); Supreme Court, Services, Service for the Legal Profession, eLitigation, verfügbar unter http://www.supremecourt.gov.sg/services/services-for-the-legal-profession (zuletzt abgerufen am 28.4.2021); Supreme Court, Rules, Court Processes, Civil Proceedings, Pre-Trial Matters, Service of Documents and Stages up to Trial, verfügbar unter http://www.supremecourt.gov.sg/rules/court-processes/civil-proceedings/pre-trial-matters/service-of-documents-and-stages-up-to-close-of-pleadings (zuletzt abgerufen am 28.4.2021); Chionh, in: Tan, Kevin (Hrsg.), Essays in Singapore Legal History, S. 93 (119); Chua/Leo, in: Yihan/Paul, Tan (Hrsg.), Singapore Law, S. 358 (377, 399). Für weitere Informationen siehe eLitigation, About eLitigation, verfügbar unter https://www.elitigation.sg/home.aspx (zuletzt abgerufen am 28.4.2021).

tronic Filing System" ermöglicht der Judikative die genaue Kontrolle des Verfahrensverlaufs und automatisierte Benachrichtigungen erinnern die Gerichte an die Einhaltung von Fristen.[173] Die meisten Singapurer Anwaltskanzleien nutzen das eLitigation System, das ihnen durch die elektronische Vereinbarung von Verhandlungsterminen, durch digitalisierte Formulare und elektronische Benachrichtigungen[174] hilft, ihre Gerichtsverfahren effizient zu organisieren.[175] In Singapur steht den Parteien vor dem Subordinate Court auch ein gerichtliches Mediationsverfahren zur Verfügung (sog. „Court Dispute Resolution").[176] Singapur ernennt als Richter seine besten Praktiker und Verwaltungsjuristen und das Richteramt ist durch die weltweit höchste Vergütung für die besten Juristen attraktiv. All diese Entwicklungen führten dazu, dass sich die Singapurer Gerichte 50 Jahre nach der Unabhängigkeit den Ruf effektiver und neutraler Verfahren und qualitativ hochwertiger Urteile erworben haben.[177]

b) Common Law Rechtssystem

Das singapurische Recht beruht im Wesentlichen auf englischem Recht.[178] Dies kommt auch in der Schiedsgesetzgebung zum Ausdruck, denn die alten Singapurer Schiedsgesetze[179] rezipierten die englische Schiedslegisla-

---

173 Chua/Leo, in: Yihan/Paul, Tan (Hrsg.), Singapore Law, S. 358 (377).

174 Durch SMS und E-Mail.

175 eLitigation, verfügbar unter https://www.elitigation.sg/home.aspx (zuletzt abgerufen am 28.4.2021).

176 Chionh, in: Tan, Kevin (Hrsg.), Essays in Singapore Legal History, S. 93 (118); Chua/Leo, in: Yihan/Tan, Paul (Hrsg.), Singapore Law, 50 Years in the Making, S. 358 (386 ff.); Lee, Joel, in: Tan, Kevin (Hrsg.), The Singapore Legal System, S. 414 (432); State Courts, FAQ, Civil Justice Division. Court Dispute Resolution, verfügbar unter http://www.ifaq.gov.sg/STATECOURTS/apps/fcd_faqmain.aspx?qst=hRhkP9BzcBImsx2T-BbssMsxu7lqt6UJK70a1wAEVmyccgTHgophcaVURnEmqVusmPj-0KKX5T7jClLEaOYxCHlmyr%2FLJEZwpFStAp635uyfks79lsO22rVYfPZCesOt-kI6j9BqevPqkGD%2FzMrqxen4Wycnh0HghxwnQEViprI2Tj%2BgHMtMtR6B6y-VuvZpYSZ83SbnQe7qbO1Ah%2FxBigps%2FkyljJjeX2czUzOc1BJh0aE%3D (zuletzt abgerufen am 28.4.2021); The State Courts Centre for Dispute Resolution, Serving the Society with Quality Dispute Resolution Services, verfügbar unter http://www.lawgazette.com.sg/2016-01/1508.htm (zuletzt abgerufen am 28.4.2021); State Courts, Overview of Alternative Dispute Resolution, https://www.statecourts.gov.sg/Mediation_ADR/Pages/Overview-of-Alternative-Dispute-Resolution.aspx, verfügbar unter (zuletzt abgerufen am 28.4.2021).

177 Tan, Kevin, in: Black/Bell (Hrsg.), Law and Legal Institutions of Asia, S. 330 (355); Schütze/Hirth, in: Schütze/Hirth, Vorwort.

178 Chew, S. 8; Jenckel, S. 81, 144; Mangan/Reed/Choong, S. 7; Respondek, RIW 1995, S. 28; Phang, Singapore Academy of Law Journal 1990, Vol. 2, S. 20 ff.; Yihan/Tan, Paul, in: Yihan/Tan, Paul (Hrsg.), Singapore Law, 50 Years in the Making, S. 3 ff.

179 Arbitration Ordinance 1890, Arbitration Ordinance 1809 und Arbitration Act 1953. Siehe ausführlich Kapitel: Geschichte der Schiedsgerichtsbarkeit (A.II.8.a)).

tion.[180] Der für inländische Schiedsverfahren vorgesehene Arbitration Act 2001 übernahm gleichfalls Bestimmungen des englischen „Arbitration Acts 1996".[181]

Nach der „Stichtag Rezeption" des englischen Rechts durch die Second Charter of Justice 1826 waren darauffolgende Entwicklungen des englischen Common Laws nur unter der Voraussetzung anwendbar, dass die singapurischen Gerichte sie für anwendbar erklärten.[182] Nicht englisch geprägt war das Familien- und Erbrecht, hier kam das „persönliche Recht"[183] der Hindus, Muslime und Chinesen zur Anwendung.[184] Vor der Einführung der „Women's Charter 1961" bestimmte sich das Eherecht der Chinesen, Moslems, Hindus, Sikhs und Christen nach den jeweiligen religiösen Vorschriften.[185]

Mit der Einführung der Women's Charter 1961[186] ersetzte Singapur das chinesische und hinduistische Eherecht weitgehend durch ein englisch ausgestaltetes Eherecht.[187] Einzig das muslimische Recht klammerte das Parlament in der Women's Charter aus.[188]

---

180 Mangan/Reed/Choong, S. 21, 26; Court of Appeal, *Lum Chang Building Contractors Pte Ltd v Anderson Land Pte Ltd*, [2000] 2 SLR 261; [2000] SGCA 18, 5.4.2000, Rn. 22 ff.; Associate Prof. Ho Peng Kee (Minister of State for Law) und Associate Prof. Chin Tet Yung, Parliamentary Debates, Official Reports, 5.10.2001, Vol. 73, Column 2214, verfügbar unter http://sprs.parl.gov.sg/search/topic.jsp?currentTopicID=00068180-ZZ&currentPubID=00069892-ZZ&topicKey=00069892-ZZ.00068180-ZZ_1%2Bid016_20011005_S0004_T00041-bill%2B (zuletzt abgerufen am 28.4.2021); Kimbrough, in: Berg (Hrsg.), Yearbook Commercial Arbitration 1986, Vol. XI, S. 29; Chan, Leng Sun, Singapore Academy of Law Journal 2002, Vol. 14, S. 49; Jenckel, S. 135 f.; Chew, S. 8.

181 Associate Prof. Ho Peng Kee (Minister of State for Law), Parliamentary Debates, Official Reports, 5.10.2001, Vol. 73, Column 2213 f., verfügbar unter http://sprs.parl.gov.sg/search/topic.jsp?currentTopicID=00068180-ZZ&currentPubID=00069892-ZZ&topicKey=00069892-ZZ.00068180-ZZ_1%2Bid016_20011005_S0004_T00041-bill%2B (zuletzt abgerufen am 28.4.2021); Attorney-General's Chambers, Law Reform and Revision Division, Review of Arbitration Laws, LRRD No. 3/2001, März 2001, S. vii; Howell/Duthie/Lim, Mark, Journal of International Arbitration 2002, Vol. 19, S. 39.

182 Tan, Kevin, in: Black/Bell (Hrsg.), Law and Legal Institutions of Asia, S. 330 (337).

183 Engl. personal law. Differenziert wurde nach Religion bei den Hindus und Moslems und nach der Rasse bei den Chinesen.

184 Jenckel, S. 83 ff.; Ibrahim, in: Knapp (Hrsg.), International Encyclopedia of Comparative Law, National Reports, Vol. 1, S. 55 (57).

185 Müller, S. 94 f.; vgl. auch Sec. 181 (1) Women's Charter: „Nothing in this Act shall affect the validity of any marriage solemnized under any law, religion, custom or usage prior to 15th September 1961."

186 Als auch den daraufhin folgenden Reformen der Women's Charter.

187 Jenckel, S. 85 ff.; Müller, S. 95.

188 Siehe Sec. 3 Women's Charter; Jenckel, S. 104 ff.; Müller, S. 95.

Durch die lokale Singapurer Legislatur ersetzte der Singapurer Gesetzgeber das durch die Second Charter of Justice bis zum Stichtag 1826 eingeführte englische Recht[189].[190] Bei der Kodifizierung der singapurischen Gesetzgebung rezipierte die Legislative zumeist englisches Recht[191], orientierte sich aber teilweise auch am indischen[192] und australischen Recht[193].[194] Dies zeigt, dass Indien und Singapur nicht nur kontinental, ethnisch und durch ihre Common Law Prägung miteinander verbandelt sind, sondern auch durch rezipierte Rechtsakte.

Die enge Verbundenheit Singapurs mit dem englischen Recht ergibt sich auch aus der Tatsache, dass die Richter am Supreme Court bis 1954 ausschließlich englischer Abstammung waren.[195] Ferner hatte Singapur das aktuelle englische Handelsrecht in das singapurische Recht übernommen.[196]

Im Jahr 1993 verabschiedete das singapurische Parlament den „Application of English Law Act", der die Anwendbarkeit des englischen Rechts in Singapur verbindlich festgelegte. Demnach soll das bis zum 12. November 1993 in Singapur geltende englische Common Law, sofern es Teil des Singapurer Rechts geworden war, anwendbar bleiben.[197] Das englische Common Law kann allerdings modifiziert werden, um den lokalen Anforderungen des modernen Singapurs zu entsprechen.[198] Der Application of English Law Act übernimmt auch heute weiterhin bestimmte englische Gesetze[199],

189 Siehe Kapitel: Britische Kolonie unter Verwaltung der „East India Company" in Indien (A.II.1.a)aa)).

190 Tan, Kevin, in: Black/Bell (Hrsg.), Law and Legal Institutions of Asia, S. 330 (344 ff.); Ibrahim, in: Knapp (Hrsg.), International Encyclopedia of Comparative Law, National Reports, Vol. 1, S. 55 (57 ff.).

191 Application of English Law Act; Jenckel, S. 81. Siehe auch beispielsweise den Copyright Act 1987, Jenckel, S. 144; Chew, S. 8.

192 Beispiele hierfür sind der indische „Penal Code" oder der indische „Evidence Act", Yihan/Tan, Paul, in: Yihan/Tan, Paul (Hrsg.), Singapore Law, 50 Years in the Making, S. 195 (227, 234); International Business Publications, Singapore, S. 39; Chen, Siyuan, in: Yihan/Tan, Paul (Hrsg.), Singapore Law, 50 Years in the Making, S. 415 (416); Yihan/Tan, Paul, in: Yihan/Tan, Paul (Hrsg.), Singapore Law, 50 Years in the Making, S. 835 (859 f.).

193 Der „Companies Act" beruht auf englischem und australischem Recht.

194 Phang, in: Tan, Kevin (Hrsg.), Essays in Singapore Legal History, S. 7; Ibrahim, in: Knapp (Hrsg.), International Encyclopedia of Comparative Law, National Reports, Vol. 1, S. 55 (57).

195 Jenckel, S. 82 f., 121.

196 Jenckel, S. 57 ff.; Hirth, in: Schütze/Hirth, S. 14; Phang, in: Tan, Kevin (Hrsg.), Essays in Singapore Legal History, S. 7 (13 ff.).

197 Sec. 3 i. V. m. First Schedule Application of English Law Act.

198 Sec. 3 Application of English Law Act.

199 Insbesondere Handelsgesetze, aber auch ausgewählte „Imperial Acts", ausführlich hierzu Klötzel, RIW 1995, S. 202 (203 f.).

darüber hinaus findet keine Rezeption der englischen Rechtsakte mehr statt.[200] Teilweise übernahm die Singapurer Legislative auch englische Rechtsakte als singapurische Gesetzesakte (sog. „Re-Enactment“)[201].[202] Obwohl Singapur 140 Jahre eine britische Kolonie mit der korrespondierenden Common Law Prägung war, werden gesetzliche Veränderungen in Singapur durch parlamentarische Gesetze und nicht durch Richterrecht herbeigeführt.[203] Unterm Strich entfernte sich die singapurische Gesetzgebung immer weiter von der englischen Mutterrechtsordnung, um ihren veränderten wirtschaftlichen und kulturellen Eigenarten Rechnung zu tragen.[204] Obschon das Singapurer Recht seine eigene rechtliche Identität entwickelte, beruhen seine Grundpfeiler auf englischem Recht.

2. Wichtigste Daten

Singapur ist mit seinen 707 Quadratkilometern[205] eine kleine „Insel-Republik“ an der südlichen Spitze der Malaiischen Halbinsel.[206] Der Stadtstadt Singapur ist geographisch sowohl für asiatische als auch für australische Schiedsparteien günstig gelegen und leicht zu erreichen. Singapur ist etwas nördlich vom Äquator situiert und dementsprechend eine Insel mit tropischem Klima.[207] Es ist eines der wohlhabendsten[208] und am dichtesten besiedelten[209] Länder weltweit. 2016 umfasste die Bevölkerung in Singapur 5,6 Mio. Einwohner. Hiervon sind 3,9 Mio. sog. „Singapur Residents“.[210]

200 Sec. 3 ff. i. V. m. First Schedule Application of English Law Act.

201 Hierzu zählt das „Carriage of Goods by Sea Act“, der „Frustrated Contract Act“, der „Defamation Act“ und der „Contributory Negligence and Personal Injuries Act“.

202 Jenckel, S. 81; Respondek, RIW 1995, S. 28 (31).

203 Klötzel, RIW 1995, S. 202; Tan, Kevin, in: Black/Bell (Hrsg.), Law and Legal Institutions of Asia, S. 330 (355); Jenckel, S. 59; Schütze, in: Schütze/Hirth, S. 6 ff.

204 Vgl. Tan, Kevin, in: Black/Bell (Hrsg.), Law and Legal Institutions of Asia, S. 330 (366); Jenckel, S. 59, 188; Singapore Law, verfügbar unter http://www.singaporelaw.sg/sglaw/ (zuletzt abgerufen am 28.4.2021); Singapore Jurisdiction & Law, verfügbar unter http://www.singaporelaw.sg/sglaw/singapore-legal-system/singapore-jurisdiction-law (zuletzt abgerufen am 28.4.2021); Respondek, RIW 1995, S. 28; Klötzel, RIW 1995, S. 202 (204); Chan, Sek Keong, in: Yihan/Tan, Paul (Hrsg.), Singapore Law, 50 Years in the Making, S. 26 (27 ff.).

205 Land area, Data, The World Bank, verfügbar unter http://data.worldbank.org/indicator/AG.LND.TOTL.K2 (zuletzt abgerufen am 28.4.2021).

206 Tan, Kevin, in: Black/Bell (Hrsg.), Law and Legal Institutions of Asia, S. 330; Klötzel, RIW 1995, S. 202.

207 Tan, Kevin, in: Black/Bell (Hrsg.), Law and Legal Institutions of Asia, S. 330; Mangan/Reed/Choong, S. 7; Tan, Kevin, Constitution, Rn. 47.

208 Tan, Kevin, Constitution Singapore, S. 1.

209 Tan, Kevin, Constitution, Rn. 55; Turnbull, S. 370.

210 Singapore Department of Statistics, Publications, Population Trends, Population Trends 2016, S. 3, verfügbar unter http://www.singstat.gov.sg/docs/default-source/

„Residents“ sind Einwohner mit unbegrenztem Bleiberecht und Staatsbürger Singapurs.[211] 2016 bestand die ethnische Zusammensetzung der Residents zu 74 % aus Residents mit chinesischer Abstammung, zu 13 % aus Residents mit malaysischer Abstammung, zu 9 % aus Residents mit indischer Abstammung und zu 3 % aus einer anderen, zuvor nicht genannten Volksgruppe.[212] Neben den Residents lebten 2016 1,7 Mio. Ausländer ohne permanenten Aufenthaltsstatus[213] in Singapur.[214] Korrespondierend mit der ethnischen Zusammensetzung der Bevölkerung gibt es vier offizielle Sprachen in Singapur: Englisch, Malaysisch, Mandarin und Tamil, wobei Englisch als „Lingua Franca“ in offiziellen Angelegenheiten vorherrscht[215].[216] Auch die Gerichtssprache ist Englisch.[217] Singapur ist eine freie Marktwirtschaft und bietet Unternehmen steuerrechtliche Vorteile, politische Stabilität und eine moderne Infrastruktur.[218] Der Stadtstaat Singapur besitzt keine Bodenschätze, seine Lebensgrundlage beruht daher auf den persönlichen Fähigkeiten seiner Einwohner[219]. Die Wirtschaft des Industriestaates[220] Singapur basiert

default-document-libra-ry/publications/publications_and_papers/population_and_population_structure/population2016.pdf (zuletzt abgerufen am 28.4.2021).

211 Singapore Department of Statistics, Publications, Population Trends, Population Trends 2016, S. 3, verfügbar unter http://www.singstat.gov.sg/docs/default-source/default-document-libra-ry/publications/publications_and_papers/population_and_population_structure/population2016.pdf (zuletzt abgerufen am 28.4.2021).

212 Singapore Department of Statistics, Publications, Population Trends, Population Trends 2016, S. 5, verfügbar unter http://www.singstat.gov.sg/docs/default-source/default-document-libra-ry/publications/publications_and_papers/population_and_population_structure/population2016.pdf (zuletzt abgerufen am 28.4.2021).

213 Sog. „Non-Residents“.

214 Singapore Department of Statistics, Publications, Population Trends, Population Trends 2016, S. 3, verfügbar unter http://www.singstat.gov.sg/docs/default-source/default-document-libra-ry/publications/publications_and_papers/population_and_population_structure/population2016.pdf (zuletzt abgerufen am 28.4.2021).

215 Eigentlich ist gem. Art. 153A der Singapurer Verfassung „Malay“ die Amtssprache in Singapur. In offiziellen Angelegenheiten ist aber die englische Sprache vorherrschend. Auch die Unterrichtssprache in der Schule ist Englisch.

216 Lim, Wei Lee/Yeo, Alvin, in: Moser/Choong (Hrsg.), Asia Arbitration Handbook, S. 671 (672); Müller, S. 178 ff.; Mangan/Reed/Choong, S. 7; Tan, Kevin, Constitution, Rn. 58; vgl. auch Art. 153A der Singapurer Verfassung.

217 Müller, S. 180; Mangan/Reed/Choong, S. 7.

218 Lim, Wei Lee/Yeo, Alvin, in: Moser/Choong (Hrsg.), Asia Arbitration Handbook, S. 671 (672); Mangan/Reed/Choong, S. 8 f.; Klötzel, RIW 1995, S. 202.

219 Turnbull, S. 375.

220 The Organisation for Economic Co-operation and Development, Strong Performers and Successful Reformers in Education: Lessons from PISA for the United States, 17.5.2011, Chapter 7: Singapore: Rapid Improvement Followed by Strong Performance, S. 159, verfügbar unter https://www.oecd.org/pisa/46623978.pdf (zuletzt abgerufen am 28.4.2021); The World Economic Forum, The 10 countries best prepared for the new digital economy, 6.7.2016, verfügbar unter https://www.weforum.org/

auf dem Zwischenhandel, seinem für den weltweiten Handel bedeutenden Hafen, auf der Produktion von hochwertigen Gütern und auf seinem von Finanz- und Rechtsdienstleistungen geprägten Dienstleistungssektor.[221] Der „Doing Business“ Bericht der Weltbank zeichnete Singapur mit Rang 2 von 190 bewerteten Ländern aus.[222] Im Stadtstaat Singapur herrscht demnach für Unternehmen ein äußerst wirtschaftsfreundliches Klima. Dies wird durch das wirtschaftliche Wachstum in Singapur bestätigt. Singapur konnte sein Bruttoinlandsprodukt seit seiner Unabhängigkeit durchschnittlich um 7,7% pro Jahr steigern.[223] Im Jahr 2017 wuchs das Bruttoinlandsprodukt in Singapur noch um 3,6%.[224] Singapur entwickelte sich ferner in den letzten 25 Jahren zu einem wichtigen Schiedsort und zählt neben Hongkong zu den beliebtesten Schiedssitzen in Asien.[225] Die Singapurer bezeichnen ihre

---

agenda/2016/07/countries-best-prepared-for-the-new-digital-economy/ (zuletzt abgerufen am 28.4.2021); United Nations Development Programme, Human Development Report 2016, Human Development for Everyone, S. 98 ff., verfügbar unter http://hdr.undp.org/sites/default/files/2016_human_development_report.pdf (zuletzt abgerufen am 28.4.2021).

221 The Monetary Authority of Singapore, The Singapore Economy, verfügbar unter http://www.sgs.gov.sg/The-SGS-Market/The-Singapore-Economy.aspx (zuletzt abgerufen am 28.4.2021); Tan, Kevin, in: Black/Bell (Hrsg.), Law and Legal Institutions of Asia, S. 330; Carlevaris, in: Brekoulakis/Lew/Mistelis (Hrsg.), The Evolution and Future of International Arbitration, S. 331 (333); Mangan/Reed/Choong, S. 3; International Business Publications, Singapore, S. 24 ff.; Turnbull, S. 367, 375.

222 World Bank Group, Doing Business 2017, Equal Opportunity for All, 14. Aufl., S. 7, verfügbar unter http://www.doingbusiness.org/~/media/WBG/DoingBusiness/Documents/Annual-Reports/English/DB17-Report.pdf (zuletzt abgerufen am 28.4.2021). Zudem zeichnete das Weltwirtschaftsforum Singapur 2016–2017 gleichfalls mit Platz 2 von 138 bewerteten Ländern aus, The World Economic Forum, The Global Competitiveness Report 2016–2017, S. 7, verfügbar unter http://www3.weforum.org/docs/GCR2016-2017/05FullReport/TheGlobalCompetitivenessReport2016-2017_FINAL.pdf (zuletzt abgerufen am 28.4.2021). Kritisch zu den Doing Business Reports der Weltbank, Kern, Juristenzeitung 2009, S. 498 ff.

223 The World Bank, Singapore, Overview, verfügbar unter http://www.worldbank.org/en/country/singapore/overview (zuletzt abgerufen am 28.4.2021).

224 The World Bank, Data, GDP growth (annual %), Singapore, verfügbar unter https://data.worldbank.org/indicator/NY.GDP.MKTP.KD.ZG?locations=SG (zuletzt abgerufen am 28.4.2021).

225 Carlevaris, in: Brekoulakis/Lew/Mistelis (Hrsg.), The Evolution and Future of International Arbitration, S. 331 (333); ICC, 2015 ICC Dispute Resolution Statistics, ICC Dispute Resolution Bulletin 2016, Ausg. 1, S. 9 (16); Kabir Singh/Sam Luttrell/Elan Krishna/, Third-party funding and arbitration law-making: the race for regulation in the Asia-Pacific, Kluwer Arbitration Blog, 14.7.2016, verfügbar unter http://kluwerarbitrationblog.com/2016/07/14/third-party-funding-and-arbitration-law-making-the-race-for-regulation-in-the-asia-pacific/ (zuletzt abgerufen am 28.4.2021); Schütze, in: Wieczorek/Schütze, § 1025 Rn. 92; Loukas Mistelis/Paul Friedland, 2010 International Arbitration Survey: Choices in International Arbitration, S. 2 ff., verfügbar unter http://www.arbitration.qmul.ac.uk/docs/123290.pdf (zuletzt abgerufen am 28.4.2021);

Schiedsgesetzgebung selbst als „Rolls Royce“ der internationalen Schiedslegislation.[226]

3. Politische und institutionelle Struktur Singapurs

Singapur ist ein Stadtstaat und eine unabhängige Republik. Als frühere britische Kolonie übernahm Singapur nach seiner Unabhängigkeit am 9. August 1965 das „Westminster“ Parlamentsmodell. Der Regierungschef ist der vom Parlament aus seinen Reihen gewählte „Prime Minister“, der die politische Richtung in seinem Kabinett[227] vorgibt.[228] Das Parlament wird alle fünf Jahre neu gewählt.[229] Es besteht gegenwärtig aus 93 Abgeordneten.[230] Staatsoberhaupt ist der Präsident. Er hat eine repräsentative Funktion und wird auf sechs Jahre von den Staatsbürgern direkt gewählt.[231] Eine Gesetzesinitiative kann von der Regierung oder von Parlamentariern ausgehen.[232] Ein Gesetz entsteht, indem ein Gesetzesentwurf in drei Lesungen vom Parlament verabschiedet wird und der Präsident dem Gesetz zustimmt.[233]

Loukas Mistelis, Arbitral Seats: Choices and Competition, Kluwer Arbitration Blog, 26.11.2010, verfügbar unter http://kluwerarbitrationblog.com/2010/11/26/arbitral-seats-choices-and-competition/ (zuletzt abgerufen am 28.4.2021); International Business Publications, Singapore, S. 39.

226 Kabir Singh/Sam Luttrell/Elan Krishna/July 14, 2016, Third-party funding and arbitration law-making: the race for regulation in the Asia-Pacific, 15.7.2016, Kluwer Arbitration Blog, verfügbar unter http://kluwerarbitrationblog.com/2016/07/14/third-party-funding-and-arbitration-law-making-the-race-for-regulation-in-the-asia-pacific/ (zuletzt abgerufen am 28.4.2021).

227 Das Kabinett besteht aus dem Prime Minister und den Ministern.

228 Lim, Wei Lee/Yeo, Alvin, in: Moser/Choong (Hrsg.), Asia Arbitration Handbook, S. 671 (672); Tan, Kevin, Constitution, Rn. 84, 278 ff.; Tan, Kevin, Constitution Singapore, S. 107 ff.

229 Art. 65 (4) der Singapurer Verfassung; Tan, Kevin, Constitution, Rn. 173; Hirth, in: Schütze/Hirth, S. 11.

230 Auch zur Zusammensetzung des Parlaments, Parliament of Singapore, Members of Parliament, https://www.parliament.gov.sg/members-parliament (zuletzt abgerufen am 28.4.2021).

231 Art. 17 ff. der Singapurer Verfassung; Tan, Kevin, Constitution, Rn. 88 ff.; Tan, Kevin, Constitution Singapore, S. 123 ff.

232 Tan, Kevin, in: Black/Bell (Hrsg.), Law and Legal Institutions of Asia, S. 330 (348); Tan, Kevin, Constitution, Rn. 197; Tan, Kevin, Constitution Singapore, S. 96 f.; Tan, Kevin, in: Tan, Kevin (Hrsg.), The Singapore Legal System, S. 123 (140 f.).

233 Ausführlich zu den drei Lesungen der Gesetzesvorlage und zur Zustimmung durch den Präsidenten, Tan, Kevin, Constitution, Rn. 197 ff.; Tan, Kevin, Constitution Singapore, S. 100 ff.; Tan, Kevin, in: Tan, Kevin (Hrsg.), The Singapore Legal System, S. 123 (141 ff.).

4. Gerichtliche Entscheidungen

Durch die britische Kolonialzeit bedingt, beruht das singapurische Rechtssystem schwerpunktmäßig auf dem britischen Common Law[234]. Daher orientieren sich die Gerichte an Gerichtsentscheidungen aus den „Common Wealth“ Rechtsordnungen, wobei den Entscheidungen der englischen Gerichte von den singapurischen Gerichten besondere Bedeutung beigemessen wird und diese folglich primär für die gerichtliche Rechtsfortbildung zu Rate gezogen werden.[235] Darüber hinaus beachten die singapurischen Gerichte Entscheidungen aus Indien, Australien, Kanada und Malaysia.[236] Die singapurischen Gerichte weichen jedoch von der Common Law Rechtsprechung ab, um der singapurischen Gesetzgebung und den lokalen Besonderheiten Rechnung zu tragen.[237] Wie in anderen Common Law Ländern entwickeln Urteile höherer gerichtlicher Instanzen Präzedenzwirkung für die unteren Instanzen bei einer vergleichbaren Rechtsfrage. Diese Bindungswirkung wird als *Judicial Precedent* oder *stare decisis* bezeichnet. Dabei entfaltet aber nur die sog. *ratio decidendi*, der Teil des Urteils, in dem eine konkrete rechtliche Würdigung des zugrunde liegenden Sachverhalts stattfindet, Präzedenzwirkung. Im singapurischen Gerichtssystem bindet der Court of Appeal als oberste Gerichtsinstanz Singapurs mit seinen Entscheidungen den High Court und letzterer bindet wiederum die ihm nachgeordneten Instanzen. Die Präzedenzwirkung des in London ansässigen Privy Councils hob

---

234 Vgl. o.

235 Singapore Jurisdiction & Law, verfügbar unter http://www.singaporelaw.sg/sglaw/singapore-legal-system/singapore-jurisdiction-law (zuletzt abgerufen am 28.4.2021); Lim, Wei Lee/Yeo, Alvin, in: Moser/Choong (Hrsg.), Asia Arbitration Handbook, S. 671 (673); Tan, Kevin, in: Black/Bell (Hrsg.), Law and Legal Institutions of Asia, S. 330 (356); Jenckel, S. 175, 188; Woon, in: Tan, Kevin (Hrsg.), The Singapore Legal System, S. 230 ff.; Yihan/Tan, Paul, in: Yihan/Tan, Paul (Hrsg.), Singapore Law, 50 Years in the Making, S. 195 (222 ff.); Chua/Leo, in: Yihan/Tan, Paul (Hrsg.), Singapore Law, 50 Years in the Making S. 358 (364 ff.).

236 Tan, Kevin, in: Black/Bell (Hrsg.), Law and Legal Institutions of Asia, S. 330 (356); Lim, Wei Lee/Yeo, Alvin, in: Moser/Choong (Hrsg.), Asia Arbitration Handbook, S. 671 (673); Yihan/Tan, Paul, in: Yihan/Tan, Paul (Hrsg.), Singapore Law, 50 Years in the Making, S. 195 (223 ff.); Chua/Leo, in: Yihan/Tan, Paul (Hrsg.), Singapore Law, 50 Years in the Making, S. 358 (364 ff.); Ibrahim, in: Knapp (Hrsg.), International Encyclopedia of Comparative Law, National Reports, Vol. 1, S. 55 (57).

237 Lim, Wei Lee/Yeo, Alvin, in: Moser/Choong (Hrsg.), Asia Arbitration Handbook, S. 671 (673); Singapore Jurisdiction & Law, verfügbar unter http://www.singaporelaw.sg/sglaw/singapore-legal-system/singapore-jurisdiction-law (zuletzt abgerufen am 28.4.2021); Jenckel, S. 175, 183, 188; Tan, Kevin, in: Black/Bell (Hrsg.), Law and Legal Institutions of Asia, S. 330 (356); Chionh, in: Tan, Kevin (Hrsg.), Essays in Singapore Legal History, S. 93 (116 f.).

der Court of Appeal im Juli 1994 in seinem „Practice Statement“[238] auf und stellte in diesem klar, dass mit dem Ausscheiden des Privy Councils aus dem singapurischen Rechtsystem der Court of Appeal von nun an weder an seine vorherigen, eigenen Entscheidungen noch an die Urteile des Privy Councils gebunden ist.[239] Der High Court bleibt hingegen an die vor 1994 ergangenen Entscheidungen des Privy Councils und an Urteile des Court of Appeals gebunden[240].[241]

5. Gerichte

Nach der Unabhängigkeit Singapurs blieben die Gerichtssysteme von Singapur und Malaysia zunächst miteinander verbunden. Erst 1969 gründete Singapur einen eigenständigen „Supreme Court“. Als Richter werden in Singapur nur die besten Juristen des Landes rekrutiert.[242] Die kontinuierliche juristische und technische Weiterbildung der Richter erfolgt am modernen „Singapore Judicial College“.[243] Das Singapurer Gerichtssystem zeichnet sich durch seinen unabhängigen Gerichtsapparat aus.[244]

a) Supreme Court

Der Supreme Court besteht aus dem „High Court“ und dem „Court of Appeal“. Er ist sowohl für zivilrechtliche als auch strafrechtliche Verfahren zuständig.[245] Im Januar 2015 erweiterte Singapur den High Court für internationale Handelsstreitigkeiten mit dem „Singapore International Com-

238 The Singapore Court of Appeal’s Practical Statement (Judicial Precedent), [1994] 2 SLR 689; [1994] SGCA 148.

239 Tan, Kevin, in: Black/Bell (Hrsg.), Law and Legal Institutions of Asia, S. 330 (338 f.); Müller, S. 132 ff.

240 Der High Court ist auch an Urteile anderer Gerichte gebunden, die für Singapur vor dessen Unabhängigkeit zuständig waren, Tan, Kevin, in: Black/Bell (Hrsg.), Law and Legal Institutions of Asia, S. 330 (339).

241 Tan, Kevin, in: Black/Bell (Hrsg.), Law and Legal Institutions of Asia, S. 330 (338 f.). Siehe ausführlich zur Rechtslage mit dem Privy Council als oberster Berufungsinstanz, Jenckel, S. 161 ff.

242 Tan, Kevin, in: Black/Bell (Hrsg.), Law and Legal Institutions of Asia, S. 330 (355).

243 Singapore Judicial College, Home, verfügbar unter http://www.supremecourt.gov.sg/sjc/ (zuletzt abgerufen am 28.4.2021); Singapore Judicial College, About Us, Message from the Chief Justice, verfügbar unter http://www.supremecourt.gov.sg/sjc/about-us/message-from-the-chief-justice (zuletzt abgerufen am 28.4.2021); Supreme Court Singapore, About Us, The Supreme Court, Role of Supreme Court, http://www.supremecourt.gov.sg/about-us/the-supreme-court/role-of-supreme-court (zuletzt abgerufen am 28.4.2021).

244 Mangan/Reed/Choong, S. 7.

245 Sec. 3 „Supreme Court of Judicature Act“; Supreme Court Singapore, About Us, The Supreme Court, Structure of the Courts, verfügbar unter http://www.supremecourt.

mercial Court (SICC)"[246].[247] Der Supreme Court setzt sich aus dem „Chief Justice", den „Judges of Appeal", den „Justices", den „Judicial Commissioners" und den „International Judges"[248] zusammen.[249] Der Chief Justice sowie die Richter des Supreme Courts werden vom Präsidenten nach einer Beratung mit dem Prime Minister ernannt.[250] Ein Richter kann vom Präsidenten nur auf Grund von Fehlverhalten oder Unfähigkeit, die bei einer Untersuchung von einem *ad hoc* Tribunal festgestellt werden, seines Amtes enthoben werden.[251] Insgesamt hat der Supreme Court 19 Richter[252] und

gov.sg/about-us/the-supreme-court/structure-of-the-courts (zuletzt abgerufen am 28.4.2021).

246 Dieser stellt einen Senat (engl. Division) des High Courts dar.

247 Supreme Court Singapore, About Us, The Supreme Court, Role of Supreme Court, http://www.supremecourt.gov.sg/about-us/the-supreme-court/role-of-supreme-court (zuletzt abgerufen am 28.4.2021). Supreme Court Singapore, About Us, The Supreme Court, Structure of the Courts, verfügbar unter http://www.supremecourt.gov.sg/about-us/the-supreme-court/structure-of-the-courts (zuletzt abgerufen am 28.4.2021). Singapore International Commercial Court, About the SICC, verfügbar unter http://www.sicc.gov.sg/About.aspx?id=22 (zuletzt abgerufen am 28.4.2021). Für ausführliche Informationen zum Singapore International Commercial Court, Singapore International Commercial Court, verfügbar unter http://www.sicc.gov.sg/Judges.aspx?id=30#14 (zuletzt abgerufen am 28.4.2021).

248 Hierbei handelt es sich um Richter des Singapore International Commercial Courts. Diese Richter sind auf Handelsstreitigkeiten spezialisiert und stammen aus Ländern, die durch die kontinentaleuropäische Rechtstradition und durch das Common Law geprägt sind, Singapore International Commercial Court, About the SICC, Establishment of the SICC, verfügbar unter http://www.sicc.gov.sg/About.aspx?id=22 (zuletzt abgerufen am 28.4.2021); Supreme Court Singapore, About Us, The Supreme Court, Supreme Court Jurisdiction, verfügbar unter http://www.supremecourt.gov.sg/about-us/the-supreme-court/supreme-court-jurisdiction (zuletzt abgerufen am 28.4.2021).

249 Supreme Court Singapore, About Us, The Supreme Court Bench, verfügbar unter http://www.supremecourt.gov.sg/about-us/the-supreme-court-bench/justices (zuletzt abgerufen am 28.4.2021); Chen, Siyuan/Chua, S. 79 f.

250 Art. 95 der Singapurer Verfassung; Tan, Kevin, Constitution Singapore, S. 155; Ibrahim, in: Knapp (Hrsg.), International Encyclopedia of Comparative Law, National Reports, Vol. 1, S. 55 (56); Tan, Kevin, Constitution, Rn. 366; Thio, in: Tan, Kevin (Hrsg.), The Singapore Legal System, S. 67 (92).

251 Art. 98 der Singapurer Verfassung; Thio, in: Tan, Kevin (Hrsg.), The Singapore Legal System, S. 67 (92). Ibrahim, in: Knapp (Hrsg.), International Encyclopedia of Comparative Law, National Reports, Vol. 1, S. 55 (56).

252 Inklusive dem Chief Justice.

12 Judicial Commissioner[253].[254] Der Supreme Court unterhält Listen über die Spezialisierung seiner Richter, hiermit versucht das Gericht, der zunehmenden Komplexität von Handelsstreitigkeiten – auch für Schiedsverfahren – Rechnung zu tragen.[255]

aa) Court of Appeal

Der Court of Appeal ist für Berufungsverfahren[256] gegen Entscheidungen des High Courts in Zivil- und Strafrechtssachen zuständig.[257] Mit der Abschaffung des Privy Councils machte der Gesetzgeber den Court of Appeal 1994 zur obersten Rechtsmittelinstanz in Singapur.[258] Der Court of Appeal besteht aus dem Vorsitzenden Chief Justice und Richtern des Court of Appeals[259], auf Anfrage des Chief Justice können auch Richter des High Courts, Judicial Commissioners und International Judges[260] für Verfahren vor dem Court of Appeal abgeordnet werden.[261] Ein Senat des obersten Ge-

253 Ein „Judicial Commissioner" wird für eine bestimmte Zeit (sechs Monate bis zu drei Jahren) ernannt und darf die gleichen Aufgaben übernehmen wie die Richter des Supreme Courts, siehe Supreme Court Singapore, About Us, The Supreme Court Bench, Judicial Commissioners, verfügbar unter http://www.supremecourt.gov.sg/about-us/the-supreme-court-bench/judges-judicial-commissioners-and-registrars (zuletzt abgerufen am 28.4.2021); Tan, Kevin, in: Black/Bell (Hrsg.), Law and Legal Institutions of Asia, S. 330 (353); Chen, Siyuan/Chua, S. 80.

254 Supreme Court Singapore, About Us, The Supreme Court Bench, Justices, verfügbar unter http://www.supremecourt.gov.sg/about-us/the-supreme-court-bench/justices (zuletzt abgerufen am 28.4.2021).

255 Für die Schiedsgerichtsbarkeit umfasst diese Liste aktuell folgende Richter: Judith Prakash JA, Belinda Ang J, Quentin Loh J, Vinodh Coomaraswamy J, Chua Lee Ming J und Kannan Ramesh J., Supreme Court Singapore, About Us, The Supreme Court, Structure of the Courts, verfügbar unter http://www.supremecourt.gov.sg/about-us/the-supreme-court/structure-of-the-courts (zuletzt abgerufen am 28.4.2021).

256 „Appeal" wurde mit Berufung übersetzt und wird auch in Zukunft so übersetzt. Denn nach Sec. 37 (1) Supreme Court of Judicature Act findet eine erneute Anhörung der Rechtssache vor dem Court of Appeal statt. Zudem wird im Supreme Court of Judicature Act zwischen Revision (engl. revision) und Berufung (engl. appeal) differenziert, siehe Sec. 23 ff. Supreme Court of Judicature Act.

257 Sec. 29 A Supreme Court of Judicature Act; Supreme Court Singapore, About Us, The Supreme Court, Supreme Court Jurisdiction, verfügbar unter http://www.supremecourt.gov.sg/about-us/the-supreme-court/supreme-court-jurisdiction (zuletzt abgerufen am 28.4.2021).

258 Siehe Kapitel: Lösung vom englischen Recht und dem Privy Council (A.II.1.a)ff)).

259 Engl. Judges of Appeal.

260 Die International Judges können vom Chief Justice für ein dem Singapore International Commercial Court entspringendes Berufungsverfahren zum Court of Appeal abgeordnet werden.

261 Sec. 29 (3) Supreme Court of Judicature Act; Supreme Court Singapore, About Us, The Supreme Court, Structure of the Courts, verfügbar unter http://www.supreme-

richts Singapurs ist im Regelfall mit drei Richtern besetzt. In wichtigen Verfahren kann der Senat auch in der Besetzung von fünf Richtern oder einer höheren ungeraden Anzahl an Richtern entscheiden.[262] Berufungsverfahren gegen Beschlüsse (engl. order[263]) werden in der Besetzung von zwei Richtern entschieden.[264] Lediglich erfahrene Juristen haben die Qualifikation für das Richteramt.[265] Der Court of Appeal besitzt die Kompetenz, erstinstanzliche und zweitinstanzliche Entscheidungen des High Courts[266] zu überprüfen.[267] Teilweise ist die Zulassung der Berufung (engl. leave) durch den High Court bzw. den Court of Appeal für die Einlegung einer Berufung erforderlich.[268] Der Court of Appeal ist befugt, in der Berufung Rechtssachen neu zu verhandeln[269].[270] Der Court of Appeal besitzt die Befugnis, Urteile des High Courts aufzuheben, zu ändern oder zur erneuten Verhandlung an den High Court zurückzuverweisen.[271] Die Entscheidungen des Court of Appeals binden im Rahmen der vertikalen Präzedenzfallbindung die nachgeordneten Gerichte.[272] *Obiter dicta* Entscheidungen entfalten hingegen keine strikte Bindungswirkung.[273]

---

court.gov.sg/about-us/the-supreme-court/structure-of-the-courts (zuletzt abgerufen am 28.4.2021).

262 Sec. 30 Supreme Court of Judicature Act; Chionh, in: Tan, Kevin (Hrsg.), Essays in Singapore Legal History, S. 93 (121 f.); Supreme Court Singapore, About Us, The Supreme Court, Singapore Judicial System, verfügbar unter http://www.supremecourt.gov.sg/about-us/the-supreme-court/singapore-judicial-system (zuletzt abgerufen am 28.4.2021); Tan, Kevin, Constitution, Rn. 343.

263 Dies umfasst auch einstweilige Beschlüsse (engl. interlocutory order).

264 Sec. 30 (2) Supreme Court of Judicature Act.

265 Art. 96 der Singapurer Verfassung; Supreme Court Singapore, About Us/the Supreme Court Bench, Justices, verfügbar unter http://www.supremecourt.gov.sg/about-us/the-supreme-court-bench/justices (zuletzt abgerufen am 28.4.2021).

266 In Strafverfahren besteht die Berufungszuständigkeit des Court of Appeals nur gegen erstinstanzliche Entscheidungen des High Courts, siehe Sec. 29A (2) Supreme Court of Judicature Act; Chen, Siyuan/Chua, S. 79.

267 Sec. 29A Supreme Court of Judicature Act.

268 Sec. 34 Supreme Court of Judicature Act.

269 Der Court of Appeal ist keine reine Revisionsinstanz.

270 Sec. 37, 44 und 55 Supreme Court of Judicature Act.

271 Sec. 37 ff. Supreme Court of Judicature Act.

272 Tan, Kevin, in: Black/Bell (Hrsg.), Law and Legal Institutions of Asia, S. 330 (338 f.); Tan, Kevin, Constitution, Rn. 345; Tan, Kevin, Constitution Singapore, S. 152; Woon, in: Tan, Kevin (Hrsg.), The Singapore Legal System, S. 297 (301 ff.).

273 International Business Publications, Singapore, S. 34; Singapore Law, Laws of Singapore, Overview, The Singapore Legal System, verfügbar unter http://www.singaporelaw.sg/sglaw/laws-of-singapore/overview/chapter-1 (zuletzt abgerufen am 28.4.2021).

bb) High Court

Der High Court ist erstinstanzlich für Zivil- und Strafverfahren zuständig, er ist auch Berufungs- und Revisionsinstanz.[274] Der High Court besteht aus dem Chief Justice und den Richtern des High Courts[275].[276] Der High Court ist erstinstanzlich für Verfahren zuständig, sofern die mit der Klage geltend gemachte Summe 250.000 Singapur-Dollar übersteigt[277]. Ergänzend ist der High Court ausschließlich für seerechtliche Streitigkeiten[278], Konkursverfahren und die Zulassung von Anwälten zuständig[279].[280] Die High Court-Verfahren entscheidet ein Einzelrichter.[281] Im Berufungsverfahren

274 Sec. 15 ff. Supreme Court of Judicature Act; Supreme Court Singapore, About Us, The Supreme Court, Singapore Judicial System, verfügbar unter http://www.supremecourt.gov.sg/about-us/the-supreme-court/singapore-judicial-system (zuletzt abgerufen am 28.4.2021); Jenckel, S. 121, 125.

275 Bei Bedarf können die Richter des Court of Appeals den High Court unterstützen, Sec. 10 (3) Supreme Court of Judicature Act.

276 Sec. 9 Supreme Court of Judicature Act.

277 Darüber hinaus ist der High Court ab einem Streitwert von mehr als 5 Mio. Singapur-Dollar (ca. 3,3 Mio. Euro) für erbrechtliche Rechtsstreitigkeiten bzw. 1,5 Mio. Singapur-Dollar (ca. 990.000 Euro) für Familienverfahren zuständig.

278 Engl. admiralty matters.

279 Ferner besitzt er originäre Zuständigkeit für strafrechtliche Verfahren, bei denen dem Angeklagten die Todesstrafe droht oder eine Gefängnisstrafe von mehr als 10 Jahren.

280 Für die detaillierten Zuständigkeiten, ausführlich Supreme Court Singapore, About Us, The Supreme Court, Singapore Judicial System, verfügbar unter http://www.supremecourt.gov.sg/about-us/the-supreme-court/singapore-judicial-system (zuletzt abgerufen am 28.4.2021); Supreme Court Singapore, About Us, The Supreme Court, Structure of the Courts, verfügbar unter http://www.supremecourt.gov.sg/about-us/the-supreme-court/structure-of-the-courts (zuletzt abgerufen am 28.4.2021); Supreme Court Singapore, About Us, The Supreme Court, Supreme Court Jurisdiction, verfügbar unter http://www.supremecourt.gov.sg/about-us/the-supreme-court/supreme-court-jurisdiction (zuletzt abgerufen am 28.4.2021); Chionh, in: Tan, Kevin (Hrsg.), Essays in Singapore Legal History, S. 93 (122 f.); Müller, S. 140 ff.; Tan, Kevin, in: Black/Bell (Hrsg.), Law and Legal Institutions of Asia, S. 330 (351); Jenckel, S. 125.

281 Soweit gesetzlich nichts anderes bestimmt ist, entscheidet ein Einzelrichter, Supreme Court Singapore, About Us, The Supreme Court, Supreme Court Jurisdiction, verfügbar unter http://www.supremecourt.gov.sg/about-us/the-supreme-court/supreme-court-jurisdiction (zuletzt abgerufen am 28.4.2021); Supreme Court Singapore, About Us, The Supreme Court, Structure of the Courts, verfügbar unter http://www.supremecourt.gov.sg/about-us/the-supreme-court/structure-of-the-courts (zuletzt abgerufen am 28.4.2021). Sec. 10 (1) und 21 (2) Supreme Court of Judicature Act; Müller, S. 141.

wird die Rechtssache neu verhandelt[282].[283] Gegen Entscheidungen des High Courts kann Berufung zum Court of Appeal eingelegt werden.[284]

b) Constitutional Tribunal

Das Constitutional Tribunal wird auf *ad hoc* Basis konstituiert und beantwortet dem Präsidenten verbindlich verfassungsrechtliche Fragen.[285]

c) State Courts

Zu den „State Courts“[286] gehören die „District Courts“, die „Magistrates' Courts“, die „Juvenile Courts“, die „Coroners' Courts“ und die „Small Claims Tribunals“.[287] Die State Courts sind erstinstanzlich zuständig.[288]

d) Syariah Courts

Für eherechtliche Streitigkeiten nach dem „Administration of Muslim Law Act“ unter Muslimen ist der „Syariah Court“ und auf der Berufungsebene ist der „Appeal Board“ des Syariah Courts zuständig.[289]

---

282 In der Praxis sind jedoch nur neu entstandene Beweise zulässig, siehe Müller, S. 141.
283 Sec. 22 Supreme Court of Judicature Act.
284 Sec. 32A ff. Supreme Court of Judicature Act.
285 Art. 100 der Singapurer Verfassung; Tan, Kevin, Constitution Singapore, S. 153; Tan, Kevin, in: Black/Bell (Hrsg.), Law and Legal Institutions of Asia, S. 330 (352, 362); Tan, Kevin, Constitution, Rn. 350; Yeo, Tiong Min, in: Tan, Kevin (Hrsg.), The Singapore Legal System, S. 249 (270).
286 Die State Courts wurden früher als Subordinate Courts bezeichnet. Das Parlament benannte sie 2014 in State Courts um, Sec. 3 (1) „State Courts Act 1970“; Tan, Kevin, Constitution, Rn. 351; Tan, Kevin, Constitution Singapore, S. 153.
287 Sec. 3 State Courts Act 1970. Tan, Kevin, Constitution Singapore, S. 153 f.; Jenckel, S. 127 f.; Müller, S. 145. Detaillierte Ausführungen, Müller, S. 145 ff.; Tan, Kevin, in: Black/Bell (Hrsg.), Law and Legal Institutions of Asia, S. 330 (351); Chionh, in: Tan, Kevin (Hrsg.), Essays in Singapore Legal History, S. 93 (123 f.); International Business Publications, Singapore, S. 31 f.; Yeo, in: Tan, Kevin (Hrsg.), The Singapore Legal System, S. 249 (270 ff.).
288 Müller, S. 145; siehe auch Sec. 3 State Courts Act 1970; Yeo, Tiong Min, in: Tan, Kevin (Hrsg.), The Singapore Legal System, S. 249 (268 ff.).
289 Tan, Kevin, Constitution Singapore, S. 154 f.; Müller, S. 151 ff.; Jenckel, S. 128 ff.; Yeo, in: Tan, Kevin (Hrsg.), The Singapore Legal System, S. 249 (278).

e) Instanzenzug

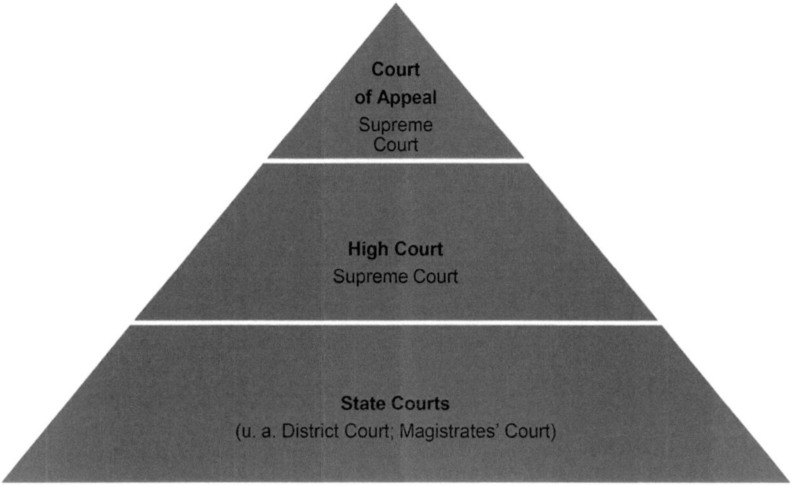

Für alle zivilrechtlichen Gerichtsverfahren in Singapur sind als Verfahrensregeln die „Rules of Court“ anwendbar.[290] Das zivilrechtliche Verfahrensrecht in Singapur ist englisch geprägt.[291]

6. Verfahrenszahlen

Im Rahmen der Entwicklung Singapurs zu einem bedeutenden Finanz- und Wirtschaftszentrum haben sich die Verfahrenszeit und die Effektivität der Gerichte seit den 90er Jahren weiter verbessert.[292]

a) Supreme Court

Nachfolgende Tabelle vergleicht die Entwicklung von zivilrechtlichen und strafrechtlichen Gerichtsverfahren vor dem Court of Appeal und dem High Court des Supreme Courts innerhalb einer Zeitspanne von fünf Jahren miteinander (2007 und fünf Jahre später 2012).

---

290 Sec. 2 Rules of Court 1996; Müller, S. 154.

291 Müller, S. 154 ff.

292 Yang, Lih Shyng/Chew, in: Ali/Ginsburg (Hrsg.), International Commercial Arbitration in Asia, S. 465 (467); vgl. auch Kapitel: Entwicklung des effektiven Gerichtswesens (A.II.1.a)gg)).

2007[293]

	Neue Verfahren	Erlassene Entscheidungen	Erledigte Verfahren	Verfahren pro 100.000 Einwohner[294]
Court of Appeal	252	246	98 %	5,5
High Court	13.857	13.778	99 %	302

2012[295]

	Neue Verfahren	Erlassene Entscheidungen	Erledigte Verfahren	Verfahren pro 100.000 Einwohner[296]
Court of Appeal	281	255	91 %	5,3
High Court	14.953	14.015	94 %	281

Sowohl 2007 als auch 2012 begannen alle Zivilverfahren zeitnah, spätestens vier Wochen nach Klageerhebung.[297] Die vor dem Court of Appeal anhängig gemachten Verfahren sind in diesen fünf Jahren im Verhältnis zur Bevölkerung Singapurs um 4 %, die vor dem High Court um 7 % rückläufig. Die Verfahrensanzahl erhöhten sich in diesem Zeitraum dennoch, vor dem Court of Appeal um 29 Verfahren (12 %) und vor dem High Court um 1.096

293 Supreme Court Singapore, Annual Report 2007, Timeliness of Justice, verfügbar unter http://www.supremecourt.gov.sg/data/AnnualReport/AnnualRpt2007/timeliness.html (zuletzt abgerufen am 28.4.2021).

294 2007 hatte Singapur 4,5886 Mio. Einwohner, siehe Singapore Department of Statistics, Publications, Population Trends, Population Trends 2016, S. 39, verfügbar unter http://www.singstat.gov.sg/docs/default-source/default-document-libra-ry/publications/publications_and_papers/population_and_population_structure/population2016.pdf (zuletzt abgerufen am 28.4.2021).

295 Siehe Supreme Court Singapore, Annual Report 2012, Timeliness of Justice, S. 53, verfügbar unter http://www.supremecourt.gov.sg/data/AnnualReport/AnnualRpt2012/ (zuletzt abgerufen am 28.4.2021).

296 2012 beheimatete Singapur 5,3124 Mio. Einwohner, siehe Singapore Department of Statistics, Publications, Population Trends, Population Trends 2016, S. 3, verfügbar unter http://www.singstat.gov.sg/docs/default-source/default-document-libra-ry/publications/publications_and_papers/population_and_population_structure/population2016.pdf (zuletzt abgerufen am 28.4.2021).

297 Supreme Court Singapore, Annual Report 2007, Timeliness of Justice, verfügbar unter http://app.supremecourt.gov.sg/data/doc/ManagePage/44/AnnualRpt2007/timeliness.html (zuletzt abgerufen am 28.4.2021); Court Singapore, Annual Report 2012, Timeliness of Justice, S. 56 f., verfügbar unter http://www.supremecourt.gov.sg/data/AnnualReport/AnnualRpt2012/ (zuletzt abgerufen am 28.4.2021).

Gerichtsverfahren (8%). Die Anzahl an abgeschlossenen Verfahren weist über diesen Zeitraum mit 98% bzw. 91% für Court of Appeal Verfahren und 99% bzw. 94% für High Court Gerichtsverfahren eine gute Erledigungsquote auf. Durch den Anstieg der Verfahrenszahlen nahm die Erledigungsquote allerdings ab. Insgesamt demonstrieren die Erledigungszahlen die Effektivität des Supreme Courts.

b) Untere Instanzen

Nachfolgend werden die Statistiken über die Anzahl der Verfahren[298] der dem Supreme Court nachgeordneten Gerichte (State Courts[299]) innerhalb eines Zeitfensters von fünf Jahren (2007–2012) miteinander verglichen.

2007[300]

	Neue Verfahren	Verfahren pro 100.000 Einwohner[301]
Untere Instanzen	399.020	8.696

2012[302]

	Neue Verfahren	Verfahren pro 100.000 Einwohner[303]
Untere Instanzen	352.763	6.640

In dem fünfjährigen Zeitraum zwischen 2007 und 2012 nahmen die Verfahren von 399.020 auf 352.763 ab, dies entspricht 13%. Die Anzahl an Ge-

298 Zivilrechtliche und strafrechtliche Verfahren.

299 Bis 2014 wurden diese als Subordinate Courts bezeichnet, Tan, Kevin, Constitution, Rn. 351.

300 State Courts, Resources, The Next Phase of Justice, Annual Report 2007, verfügbar unter https://www.statecourts.gov.sg/Resources/Documents/AnnualReport2007.pdf (zuletzt abgerufen am 28.4.2021), S. 104.

301 2007 beheimatete Singapur 4,5886 Mio. Einwohner, siehe Singapore Department of Statistics, Publications, Population Trends, Population Trends 2016, S. 39, verfügbar unter http://www.singstat.gov.sg/docs/default-source/default-document-libra-ry/publications/publications_and_papers/population_and_population_structure/population2016.pdf (zuletzt abgerufen am 28.4.2021).

302 State Courts, Resources, Upholding Justice, Serving Society, Inspiring Trust, Annual Report 2012, S. 35 f., verfügbar unter https://www.statecourts.gov.sg/Resources/Documents/AnnualReport2012.pdf (zuletzt abgerufen am 28.4.2021).

303 2012 hatte Singapur 5,3124 Mio. Einwohner, siehe Singapore Department of Statistics, Publications, Population Trends, Population Trends 2016, S. 3, verfügbar unter http://www.singstat.gov.sg/docs/default-source/default-document-libra-ry/publications/publications_and_papers/population_and_population_structure/population2016.pdf (zuletzt abgerufen am 28.4.2021).

richtsverfahren verringerte sich in Singapur in diesen fünf Jahren, im Verhältnis zu je 100.000 Einwohnern, um 2.056 (31 %) Gerichtsverfahren. Nach dem von Singapur durchgeführten „Court User Survey“ von 2013 gaben 9 von 10 Beklagten an ein faires Verfahren gehabt zu haben. 98 % der Beklagten waren mit der Dienstleistung der Gerichte zufrieden.[304] Somit weisen die Verfahren der unteren Instanzen Zufriedenheit der beteiligten Parteien und rückläufige Verfahrenszahlen auf.

7. Qualität der Gerichtsverfahren

Der „Doing Business“ Bericht der Weltbank untersucht die gerichtliche Durchsetzung von inländischen Handelsverträgen. In ihrem Bericht beurteilte die Weltbank die Singapurer Gerichtsverfahren als einen besonders wirkungsvollen Streitbeilegungsmechanismus und verlieh Singapur den ersten Platz unter 189 bewerteten Ländern. Die Verfahrensdauer der Singapurer Gerichtsverfahren und die Verfahrenskosten liegen erheblich unter dem Durchschnitt der ostasiatischen und der Pazifik Anrainerstaaten. In ihrem „Doing Business“ Bericht erachtet die Weltbank die Qualität der Singapurer gerichtlichen und außergerichtlichen Streitbeilegung als weltweit führend. Der Bericht der Weltbank bewertete auch die automatisierten Singapurer Gerichtsverfahren mit voller Punktzahl und lobte das elektronische „Case Management“. Die Weltbank kam demzufolge zu dem Schluss, dass das Singapurer Gerichtssystem wegen der geringen Verfahrensdauer, seinem effektiven „Case Management“, seinen elektronischen und automatisierten Gerichtsverfahren, seinen spezialisierten Gerichten, seinen niedrigen Verfahrenskosten und der Qualität der gerichtlichen und der alternativen Streitbeilegung das weltweit effektivste Gerichtssystem ist.[305]

304 State Courts, Resources, Renewing Our Commitment to Justice, Annual Report 2013, Our Commitment to Justice, Court User's Surveys 2013, verfügbar unter https://www.statecourts.gov.sg/Resources/Documents/Annual%20Report%202013%20(Full%20length%20-%20HTML).pdf (zuletzt abgerufen am 28.4.2021).

305 World Bank Group, Doing Business 2016, Measures Regulatory Quality and Efficiency, 13. Aufl., S. 5 ff., verfügbar unter http://www.doingbusiness.org/~/media/WBG/DoingBusiness/Documents/Annual-Reports/English/DB16-Full-Report.pdf (zuletzt abgerufen am 28.4.2021). Hinsichtlich der Durchsetzung von Handelsstreitigkeiten in Singapur, World Bank Group, Doing Business 2017, Equal Opportunity for All, 14. Aufl., Economy Profile 2017, Singapore, S. 83 ff. verfügbar unter http://www.doingbusiness.org/~/media/wbg/doingbusiness/documents/profiles/country/sgp.pdf (zuletzt abgerufen am 28.4.2021). Kritisch zu den Doing Business Reports der Weltbank, Kern, Juristenzeitung 2009, S. 498 ff.

Auch das Weltwirtschaftsforum zeichnete die Effizienz des Singapurer Streitbeilegungsregimes mit Rang 1 von 138 beurteilten Ländern aus.[306]

Das „World Justice Project" bewertete die Singapurer Zivilgerichtsbarkeit in seinem „Rule of Law Index 2016" mit der Position 4 bei 113 untersuchten Rechtsordnungen gleichfalls sehr positiv[307].[308]

Dies zeigt, dass die zivile Gerichtsbarkeit in Singapur gut funktioniert, modern ausgestaltet ist und unabhängig und effektiv Recht spricht.[309]

8. Schiedsgerichtsbarkeit

a) Geschichte der Schiedsgerichtsbarkeit

Schon seit Anfang des 19. Jahrhunderts gibt es Belege für Schiedsverfahren in den Straits Settlements[310]. 1809 trat mit der „Arbitration Ordinance" die erste Schiedsgesetzgebung in den Straits Settlements in Kraft. Die „Arbitration Ordinance 1890" ersetzte die ebenfalls englisch geprägte Arbitration Ordinance aus dem Jahre 1809. 1953 unterzog der Gesetzgeber die

---

306 Das Weltwirtschaftsforum untersuchte jedoch nur die Effizienz der Streitbeilegung für Unternehmen, The World Economic Forum, The Global Competitiveness Report 2016–2017, S. 319, verfügbar unter http://www3.weforum.org/docs/GCR2016-2017/05FullReport/TheGlobalCompetitivenessReport2016-2017_FINAL.pdf (zuletzt abgerufen am 28.4.2021).

307 Die Zivilgerichtsbarkeit schnitt nach dem „Rule of Law Index" gegenüber den Ostasiatischen- und Pazifik Anrainerstaaten überdurchschnittlich gut ab, World Justice Project, Rule of Law Index 2016, S. 134, verfügbar unter https://worldjusticeproject.org/sites/default/files/documents/RoLI_Final-Digital_0.pdf (zuletzt abgerufen am 28.4.2021).

308 World Justice Project, Rule of Law Index 2016, S. 40 f., verfügbar unter https://worldjusticeproject.org/sites/default/files/documents/RoLI_Final-Digital_0.pdf (zuletzt abgerufen am 28.4.2021).

309 Vgl. World Justice Project, Rule of Law Index 2016, S. 40 f., 134, verfügbar unter https://worldjusticeproject.org/sites/default/files/documents/RoLI_Final-Digital_0.pdf (zuletzt abgerufen am 28.4.2021); World Bank Group, Doing Business 2016, Measures Regulatory Quality and Efficiency, 13. Aufl., S. 5 ff., verfügbar unter http://www.doingbusiness.org/~/media/WBG/DoingBusiness/Documents/Annual-Reports/English/DB16-Full-Report.pdf (zuletzt abgerufen am 28.4.2021); The World Economic Forum, The Global Competitiveness Report 2016–2017, S. 319, verfügbar unter http://www3.weforum.org/docs/GCR2016-2017/05FullReport/TheGlobalCompetitivenessReport2016-2017_FINAL.pdf (zuletzt abgerufen am 28.4.2021). Hinsichtlich der Durchsetzung von Handelsstreitigkeiten in Singapur, World Bank Group, Doing Business 2017, Equal Opportunity for All, 14. Aufl., Economy Profile 2017, Singapore, S. 83 ff. verfügbar unter http://www.doingbusiness.org/~/media/wbg/doingbusiness/documents/profiles/country/sgp.pdf (zuletzt abgerufen am 28.4.2021).

310 Singapur war vor seiner Unabhängigkeit zusammen mit Penang und Malakka Teil des Straits Settlements, vgl. ausführlich Kapitel: Geschichtlicher Überblick (A.II.1.).

Arbitration Ordinance einer Gesetzgebungsreform und benannte sie nach der Unabhängigkeit Singapurs in den „Arbitration Act“ um.[311] Der Arbitration Act 1953 beruhte auf dem englischen „Arbitration Act“ aus dem Jahre 1950.[312] 1969, 1970, 1980 und 1985 unterzog das Parlament den Arbitration Act 1953 einer Gesetzesreform.[313] Singapur ist seit 1986 Vertragsstaat des „New Yorker UN-Übereinkommen über die Anerkennung und Vollstreckung ausländischer Schiedssprüche vom 10. Juni 1958 (UNÜ)“[314] und setzte es im „Arbitration (Foreign Awards) Act“[315] in das Singapurer Recht um.[316] Um Singapur als Sitz für internationale Schiedsverfahren zu etablieren, wurde der von gerichtlichen Interventionsmöglichkeiten geprägte Arbitration Act 1953 durch den liberalen „International Arbitration Act (IAA)“ ersetzt.[317] Der Gesetzgeber kodifizierte das Schiedsrecht für internationale Schiedsverfahren im IAA 1994[318] und die Schiedsgesetzgebung für inländische Schiedsverfahren im „Arbitration Act (AA) 2001“[319].[320]

In Singapur werden die meisten Schiedsverfahren unter der Verwaltung einer Schiedsinstitution und nicht *ad hoc* durchgeführt.[321] Die meisten Schiedsverfahren werden von dem „Singapore International Arbitration Centre (SIAC)“ unter den „SIAC-Regeln“ verwaltet. Zudem ist es auch möglich,

---

311 Mangan/Reed/Choong, S. 26; Hwang/Chan, Andrew/Selvaraj, in: Moser (Hrsg.), Arbitration in Asia, Sing-3 f.; Court of Appeal, *Lum Chang Building Contractors Pte Ltd v Anderson Land Pte Ltd*, [2000] 2 SLR 261; [2000] SGCA 18, 5.4.2000, Rn. 22 ff.; Pillay, The International Construction Law Review 2003, S. 91 f.; Chan, Leng Sun, Singapore Academy of Law Journal 2002, Vol. 14, S. 49. Kimbrough, in: Berg (Hrsg.), Yearbook Commercial Arbitration 1986, Vol. XI, S. 29.

312 Kimbrough, in: Berg (Hrsg.), Yearbook Commercial Arbitration 1986, Vol. XI, S. 29; Chan, Leng Sun, Singapore Academy of Law Journal 2002, Vol. 14, S. 49; Jenckel, S. 135 f.

313 Chan, Leng Sun, Singapore Academy of Law Journal 2002, Vol. 14, S. 49; Kimbrough, in: Berg (Hrsg.), Yearbook Commercial Arbitration 1986, Vol. XI, S. 29.

314 Status, Convention on the Recognition and Enforcement of Foreign Arbitral Awards (New York, 1958), verfügbar unter http://www.uncitral.org/uncitral/en/uncitral_texts/arbitration/NYConvention_status.html (zuletzt abgerufen am 28.4.2021).

315 Der Arbitration (Foreign Awards) Act trat 1986 in Kraft, Yang, Lih Shyng/Chew, in: Ali/Ginsburg (Hrsg.), International Commercial Arbitration in Asia, S. 465.

316 Hwang/Chan, Andrew/Selvaraj, in: Moser (Hrsg.), Arbitration in Asia, Sing-4.

317 Pillay, The International Construction Law Review 2003, S. 91 (92 ff.).

318 Der IAA trat am 27.1.1995 in Kraft.

319 Der AA trat am 1.3.2002 in Kraft.

320 Chew, S. 8 ff.; Yang, Lih Shyng/Chew, in: Ali/Ginsburg (Hrsg.), International Commercial Arbitration in Asia, S. 465 (466 ff.); Pillay, The International Construction Law Review 2003, S. 91 (96 ff.). Durch die Einführung des IAA differenziert das Singapurer Schiedsrecht erstmals zwischen internationalen und inländischen Schiedsverfahren.

321 Lim, Wei Lee/Yeo, Alvin, in: Moser/Choong (Hrsg.), Asia Arbitration Handbook, S. 671 (674).

ein Schiedsverfahren nach den „UNCITRAL Arbitration Rules“ der Verwaltung des SIAC zu unterstellen.[322] In den modernen ADR[323]-Räumlichkeiten des Maxwell Chambers[324] befinden sich neben dem Sitz vom SIAC und dem „Singapore Chamber of Maritime Arbitration (SCMA)“ auch Büroräume der internationalen Schiedsinstitutionen „International Chamber of Commerce (ICC)“[325] und „International Centre for Dispute Resolution (ICDR)“.[326] Darüber hinaus schloss der „Permanent Court of Arbitration“ 2007 ein „Host Country Agreement“ mit Singapur ab.[327]

b) Rechtliche Rahmenbedingungen der Schiedsgerichtsbarkeit

Singapur setzte das UNÜ durch den „Arbitration (Foreign Awards) Act“ in das Singapurer Recht um.[328] Im geltenden Schiedsrecht integrierte die Legislative das UNÜ in Teil III („Part III Foreign Awards“) des International Arbitration Acts 1995[329] (IAA). Die schiedsgerichtliche Streitbeilegung ist aktuell im Arbitration Act 2001[330] (AA) für inländische und im IAA für ausländische Schiedsverfahren geregelt.[331] Das auf dem UNCITRAL Modellgesetz beruhende IAA schuf der Gesetzgeber 1995, um die veraltete Schiedsgesetzgebung zu modernisieren und Singapur zu einem führenden

---

322 Siehe hinsichtlich der UNCITRAL Arbitration Rules, SIAC, Frequently Asked Questions, Frage 16, verfügbar unter http://www.siac.org.sg/faqs (zuletzt abgerufen am 28.4.2021); Lim, Wei Lee/Yeo, Alvin, in: Moser/Choong (Hrsg.), Asia Arbitration Handbook, S. 671 (674).

323 Alternative Dispute Resolution.

324 Chiam See Tong, Parliamentary Debates, Official Reports, 19.10.2009, Vol. 86, Column 1637, verfügbar unter http://sprs.parl.gov.sg/search/topic.jsp?currentTopicID=00003591-WA&currentPubID=00004793-WA&topicKey=00004793-WA.00003591-WA_1%2B%2B (zuletzt abgerufen am 28.4.2021); Maxwell Chambers, About, verfügbar unter http://www.maxwell-chambers.com/profile (zuletzt abgerufen am 28.4.2021); Mangan/Reed/Choong, S. 4.

325 Seit 2017 nimmt dieses Büro „Case Management“-Aufgaben wahr, ICC, Singapore Ministry of Law and ICC sign MOU to boost arbitration, verfügbar unter https://iccwbo.org/media-wall/news-speeches/singapore-ministry-law-international-chamber-commerce-sign-mou-boost-arbitration/ (zuletzt abgerufen am 28.4.2021).

326 Maxwell Chambers, Offices, verfügbar unter http://www.maxwell-chambers.com/partners/office (zuletzt abgerufen am 28.4.2021).

327 Tan, Kevin, in: Black/Bell (Hrsg.), Law and Legal Institutions of Asia, S. 330 (367); Mangan/Reed/Choong, S. 10.

328 Vgl. Kapitel: Geschichte der Schiedsgerichtsbarkeit (A.II.8.a)).

329 Der IAA trat am 27.1.1995 in Kraft.

330 Den AA verabschiedete das Parlament im Jahr 2001 und er trat am 1.3.2002 in Kraft.

331 Darüber hinaus regelt der Arbitration (International Investment Disputes) Act die Behandlung von Schiedssprüchen des „International Centre for Settlement of Investment Disputes“, Chan, Leng Sun, Singapore Law on Arbitral Awards, S. 1. Die Investitions-Schiedsgerichtsbarkeit in Singapur ist jedoch nicht Teil dieser Bearbeitung und wird in dieser Bearbeitung deshalb nicht näher erörtert.

Schiedsort in Asien zu machen.[332] Die Legislative wählte ein zweigleisiges Schiedsrecht, weil sie das für internationale Schiedsverfahren entworfene UNCITRAL Model Law 1985, das minimale gerichtliche Interventionen vorsieht, für inländische Schiedsverfahren zwischen zwei singapurischen Parteien für ungeeignet erachtete. Im für inländische Schiedsverfahren geschaffenen AA sollte eine stärkere Kontrollmöglichkeit durch die staatlichen Gerichte gewährleistet werden.[333] Die stärkere gerichtliche Kontrolle in inländischen Schiedsverfahren des AA dient dem Schutz von wirtschaftlich schwächeren inländischen Parteien.[334] Nach einer Konsultation mit Singapurer Schiedsverfahrensexperten überarbeitete der Gesetzgeber 2001[335] den AA[336] und den IAA mit dem Ziel, das Schiedsverfahrensrecht für internationale und nationale Schiedsverfahren zu harmonisieren, Rechtssicherheit zu schaffen, die Attraktivität des Schiedsortes Singapur weiter zu forcieren und die Singapurer Schiedsgesetzgebung den zukünftigen Entwicklungen und Erfordernissen der Schiedsgerichtsbarkeit anzupassen.[337] Als ehemalige britische Kronkolonie ist das singapurische Rechtssystem eng mit der englischen Rechtsordnung verbunden. Folglich basierte der Arbitration Act 1953, wie viele andere Gesetze in Singapur, noch immer auf englischem Recht.[338]

---

332 Associate Prof. Ho Peng Kee (Singapore Parliamentary Secretary to the Minister for Law), Parliamentary Debates, Official Reports, 31.10.1994, Vol. 63, Column 625 ff., verfügbar unter http://sprs.parl.gov.sg/search/report.jsp?currentPubID=00069725-ZZ (zuletzt abgerufen am 28.4.2021); Chew, S. 8.

333 Associate Prof. Ho Peng Kee (Minister of State for Law), Parliamentary Debates, Official Reports, 5.10.2001, Vol. 73, Column 2213 ff., verfügbar unter http://sprs.parl.gov.sg/search/topic.jsp?currentTopicID=00068180-ZZ&currentPubID=00069892-ZZ&topicKey=00069892-ZZ. 00068180-ZZ_1%2Bid016_20011005_S0004_T00041-bill%2B (zuletzt abgerufen am 28.4.2021); Howell/Duthie/Lim, Mark, Journal of International Arbitration 2002, Vol. 19, S. 39 f.; Merkin/Hjalmarsson, S. 2; Lim, Charles, Asian International Arbitration Journal 2011, Vol. 7, Ausg. 1, S. 1 (11).

334 Merkin/Hjalmarsson, S. 2; Chew, S. 10.

335 Den AA verabschiedete das Parlament im Jahr 2001 und er trat am 1.3.2002 in Kraft.

336 Das Singapurer Parlament verabschiedete ein komplett neues AA.

337 Associate Prof. Ho Peng Kee (Minister of State for Law) und Associate Prof. Chin Tet Yung, Parliamentary Debates, Official Reports, 5.10.2001, Vol. 73, Column 2213 ff., verfügbar unter http://sprs.parl.gov.sg/search/topic.jsp?currentTopicID=00068180-ZZ&currentPubID=00069892-ZZ&topicKey=00069892-ZZ. 00068180-ZZ_1%2Bid016_20011005_S0004_T00041-bill%2B (zuletzt abgerufen am 28.4.2021); Associate Prof. Ho Peng Kee (Minister of State for Law) und Associate Prof. Chin Tet Yung, Parliamentary Debates, Official Reports, 5.10.2001, Vol. 73, Column 2223 ff., verfügbar unter http://sprs.parl.gov.sg/search/topic.jsp?currentTopicID=00068181-ZZ&currentPubID=00069892-ZZ&topicKey=00069892-ZZ. 00068181-ZZ_1%2Bid017_20011005_S0004_T00091-bill%2B (zuletzt abgerufen am 28.4.2021); Chan, Leng Sun, Singapore Law on Arbitral Awards, S. 3.

338 Vgl. Kapitel: Geschichtlicher Überblick (A.II.1.).

Bei der erforderlichen Modernisierung[339] der inländischen Schiedsgesetzgebung (AA) im Jahre 2001 ließ sich der singapurische Gesetzgeber sowohl von Bestimmungen des englischen Arbitration Acts 1996 als auch von dem, im Singapurer IAA umgesetzten, UNCITRAL Modellgesetz inspirieren. Es besteht somit aus einer Verschmelzung von Vorschriften des UNCITRAL Modellgesetzes mit Vorschriften des englischen Schiedsrechts.[340] Das Singapurer Parlament passte die Schiedslegislation in seinen Reformen des IAA in den Jahren 1995, 2001, 2002, 2005, 2009, 2012 und 2016 nach einer Konsultation mit der lokalen und internationalen Schiedsbranche den Bedürfnissen der modernen Schiedsgerichtsbarkeit an und beseitigte bestehende Rechtsunklarheiten. Ferner sollte durch eine stetige, schnelle und flexible Anpassung der Schiedsgesetzgebung ein schiedsfreundliches Klima für Schiedsverfahren mit möglichst geringer gerichtlicher Intervention geschaffen werden, um Singapur zu einem attraktiven Schiedsort zu formen.[341]

aa) International Arbitration Act (IAA)

Der International Arbitration Act (IAA) ist in vier Teile untergliedert. Der erste Teil gibt lediglich den Namen des IAA wieder. Im zweiten Teil des IAA wird das in Singapur geltende Schiedsrecht behandelt. Hierfür übernahm der Gesetzgeber das UNCITRAL Modellgesetz mit vereinzelten Modifikationen. In Teil III wird das UNÜ in das Schiedsrecht von Singapur umgesetzt. Teil IV enthält Ergänzungsvorschriften.[342]

---

339 Der Arbitration Act 1953 war veraltet und wurde den Anforderungen des modernen Handels in Singapur nicht mehr gerecht.

340 Chew, S. 8 f.

341 Associate Prof. Ho Peng Kee (Senior Minister of State for Law), Parliamentary Debates, Official Reports, 1.10.2002, Vol. 75, Column 1107 ff., verfügbar unter http://sprs.parl.gov.sg/search/topic.jsp?currentTopicID=00068650-ZZ&currentPubID=00069920-ZZ&topicKey=00069920-ZZ.00068650-ZZ_1%2Bid022_20021001_S0003_T00071-bill%2B (zuletzt abgerufen am 28.4.2021); Shanmugam (Minister for Law), Christopher de Souza und Chiam See Tong, Parliamentary Debates, Official Reports, 19.10.2009, Vol. 86, Column 1627 ff., verfügbar unter http://sprs.parl.gov.sg/search/topic.jsp?currentTopicID=00003591-WA&currentPubID=00004793-WA&topicKey=00004793-WA.00003591-WA_1%2B%2B (zuletzt abgerufen am 28.4.2021); Shanmugam (Minister for Law), Patrick Tay Teck Guan, Pritam Singh, Lina Chiam und Hri Kumar Nair, Parliamentary Debates, Official Reports, 9.4.2012, Vol. 89, verfügbar unter http://sprs.parl.gov.sg/search/topic.jsp?currentTopicID=00077287-WA&currentPubID=00077335-WA&topicKey=00077335-WA.00077287-WA_5%2Bid-92b4e92e-6efb-4fcd-bd99-4c99467b63e0%2B (zuletzt abgerufen am 28.4.2021).

342 Chan, Leng Sun, Singapore Law on Arbitral Awards, S. 2; Hwang/Chan, Andrew/Selvaraj, in: Moser (Hrsg.), Arbitration in Asia, Sing-7.

(1) Anwendungsbereich

Nach Sec. 5 IAA findet der IAA Anwendung, wenn der Schiedssitz in Singapur gelegen ist, sofern:

1. Mindestens eine der Parteien der Schiedsvereinbarung zum Zeitpunkt des Abschlusses dieser Vereinbarung ihre Niederlassung nicht in Singapur hat, oder
2. einer der folgenden Orte außerhalb des Staates liegt, in dem die Parteien ihre Niederlassung haben:
   a. der Ort des schiedsrichterlichen Verfahrens,
   b. jeder Ort, an dem ein wesentlicher Teil der Pflichten aus der Handelsbeziehung zu erfüllen ist, oder der Ort, mit dem der Gegenstand des Streites die engste Verbindung aufweist, oder
3. die Parteien ausdrücklich vereinbart haben, dass der Gegenstand der Schiedsvereinbarung Beziehungen zu mehr als einem Land aufweist (künstlicher Auslandsbezug).

Bei mehr als einer Niederlassung einer Partei ist diejenige maßgebend, die mit der Schiedsvereinbarung die engste Verbindung aufweist. Für eine Partei ohne Niederlassung wird an ihren gewöhnlichen Aufenthalt angeknüpft.

Diese Voraussetzungen für den räumlich-persönlichen Anwendungsbereich entsprechen denen des UNCITRAL Modellgesetzes. Darüber hinaus erweiterte der Gesetzgeber den Anwendungsbereich des IAA gegenüber dem UNCITRAL Modellgesetz. Der IAA findet auch auf zwei ausländische Parteien gleicher Nationalität Anwendung, um auch für inländische Schiedsverfahren zwischen zwei ausländischen Parteien derselben Staatsangehörigkeit die Streitbeilegung in Singapur zu ermöglichen. Zudem erlaubt der IAA den Parteien eines inländischen Singapurer Schiedsverfahrens zu vereinbaren, dass der IAA auf ihr inländisches Schiedsverfahren anwendbar sein soll.[343] Dementsprechend können zwei singapurische Parteien aus dem von mehr gerichtlicher Kontrolle geprägten AA herausoptieren und dem IAA in ihrem Schiedsverfahren Geltung verleihen.

(2) Abweichungen vom UNCITRAL Modellgesetz

Nach Sec. 3 (1) IAA findet Kapitel VIII UNCITRAL Modellgesetz, welches die Anerkennung und Vollstreckung von Schiedssprüchen regelt, auf Singapurer Schiedsverfahren keine Anwendung. Hierdurch soll eine Überlappung des UNÜ mit dem UNCITRAL Modellgesetz zu Gunsten des UNÜ verhindert und Rechtssicherheit und normative Klarheit erreicht werden.[344]

343 Sec. 5 (1) IAA.

344 Chan, Leng Sun, Singapore Law on Arbitral Awards, S. 6; Lim, Wei Lee/Yeo, Alvin, in: Moser/Choong (Hrsg.), Asia Arbitration Handbook, S. 671 (676).

Gem. Sec. 3 (1) IAA haben vom UNCITRAL Modellgesetz abweichende Bestimmungen des IAA gegenüber dem UNCITRAL Modellgesetz Vorrang.

bb) Arbitration Act (AA)

Bis zum Jahre 2002 basierte das Schiedsverfahrensrecht für ausländische Schiedsverfahren in Singapur schwerpunktmäßig auf dem englischen „Arbitration Act 1950“.[345] Im Rahmen der Gesetzesreform glich der Gesetzgeber die Bestimmungen des AA denen des IAA an. Entsprechend übernahm die Legislative viele Vorschriften des UNCITRAL Modellgesetzes auch im AA.[346] Innerhalb des AA blieb es gleichwohl bei einer stärkeren Überwachung und Kontrolle von inländischen Schiedsverfahren nach dem Vorbild des englischen „Arbitration Acts 1996“.[347] Die erhöhte Überwachung von inländischen Schiedssprüchen in Singapur beruht auf dem Umstand, dass ein großer Teil dieser Schiedsverfahren Baustreitigkeiten betrifft, bei denen die Schiedsrichter (im Folgenden wird der Begriff „Schiedsrichter“ geschlechtsneutral verwendet und bezieht sich gleichermaßen auf Schiedsrichterinnen und Schiedsrichter) meist keine juristische Ausbildung haben und außerdem auf der Tatsache, dass in inländischen Schiedsverfahren meist singapurisches Recht Anwendung findet.[348] Des Weiteren sollten singapurische Verbraucher und kleine Betriebe vor unbilligen[349] Vertragsbestimmungen geschützt werden, sodass die staatlichen Gerichte zu deren Schutz in inlän-

---

345 Den AA verabschiedete das Parlament im Jahr 2001 und er trat am 1.3.2002 in Kraft.

346 Siehe Howell/Duthie/Lim, Mark, Journal of International Arbitration 2002, Vol. 19, S. 39; Associate Prof. Ho Peng Kee (Minister of State for Law), Parliamentary Debates, Official Reports, 5.10.2001, Vol. 73, Column 2213 f., verfügbar unter http://sprs.parl.gov.sg/search/topic.jsp?currentTopicID=00068180-ZZ&currentPubID=00069892-ZZ&topicKey=00069892-ZZ. 00068180-ZZ_1%2Bid016_20011005_S0004_T00041-bill%2B (zuletzt abgerufen am 28.4.2021); Attorney-General's Chambers, Law Reform and Revision Division, Review of Arbitration Laws, LRRD No. 3/2001, März 2001, S. vii (https://www.agc.gov.sg/DATA/0/Docs/PublicationFiles/Review_Of_Arbitration_LawsMar_2001.pdf); Pillay, The International Construction Law Review 2003, S. 91 (110).

347 Chan, Leng Sun, Singapore Law on Arbitral Awards, S. 3; Associate Prof. Ho Peng Kee (Minister of State for Law), Parliamentary Debates, Official Reports, 5.10.2001, Vol. 73, Column 2214, verfügbar unter http://sprs.parl.gov.sg/search/topic.jsp?currentTopicID=00068180-ZZ&currentPubID=00069892-ZZ&topicKey=00069892-ZZ. 00068180-ZZ_1%2Bid016_20011005_S0004_T00041-bill%2B (zuletzt abgerufen am 28.4.2021); Attorney-General's Chambers, Law Reform and Revision Division, Review of Arbitration Laws, LRRD No. 3/2001, März 2001, S. vii.; Pillay, The International Construction Law Review 2003, S. 91 (110).

348 Chew, S. 10; Lim, Charles, Asian International Arbitration Journal 2011, Vol. 7, Ausg. 1, S. 1 (9).

349 Engl. unreasonable.

dische Schiedsverfahren eingreifen können.[350] Der Anwendungsbereich des AA wird in Sec. 3 auf Schiedsverfahren mit Sitz in Singapur beschränkt und zusätzlich negativ gegenüber internationalen Schiedsverfahren gem. Teil II des International Arbitration Acts (IAA) abgegrenzt.[351] Folglich ist der AA immer dann anwendbar, wenn der IAA nicht anwendbar ist. Die Parteien können bei einem internationalen Schiedsverfahren den AA aber für anwendbar erklären.[352] Der AA respektiert die Parteiautonomie der Schiedsparteien und gestattet ihnen, die Normen des AA durch die Vorschriften einer Schiedsinstitution abzubedingen und ein ausländisches materielles Recht als anwendbares Recht für das Schiedsverfahren zu vereinbaren.[353]

c) Zuständigkeiten der Singapurer Gerichte für Schiedsverfahren

Die Singapurer Gerichte sind nach der Schiedsgesetzgebung (AA und IAA) Singapurs insbesondere zu den folgenden in das Schiedsverfahren eingreifenden oder das Schiedsverfahren fördernden Handlungen berufen:

- Kontrolle der „Kompetenz-Kompetenz" des Schiedsgerichts und Kontrolle der Unabhängigkeit der Schiedsvereinbarung (Sec. 3 IAA i. V. m. Artikel [Art.] 16 UNCITRAL Modellgesetz; Sec. 21 AA)
- Kontrolle der Unzuständigkeitserklärung des Schiedsgerichts (Sec. 10 IAA; Sec. 21 f. AA)
- Kontrolle der Zuständigkeitsentscheidung des Schiedsgerichts (Sec. 10 IAA; Sec. 21 f. AA)
- Aussetzung einer gerichtlich rechtsanhängigen Rechtsstreitigkeit zu Gunsten des vereinbarten Schiedsverfahrens (Sec. 6 IAA; Sec. 6 AA)
- Einstweiliger Rechtsschutz (Sec. 12A i. V. m. 12 IAA; Sec. 31 i. V. m. 28 AA).
- Gerichtliche Unterstützung bei der Beweisaufnahme (Sec. 12A i. V. m. 12 IAA; Sec. 31 i. V. m. 28 AA)
- Aufhebungsverfahren (Sec. 3 [1] IAA i. V. m. Art. 34 UNICTRAL Modellgesetz; Sec. 24 IAA; Sec. 48 AA)
- Berufung gegen Rechtsfragen des Schiedsspruchs (Sec. 49 AA)
- Vollstreckung von ausländischen Schiedssprüchen (Sec. 29 ff. IAA)

350 Merkin/Hjalmarsson, S. 2; Chew, S. 10.

351 Schütze, in: Schütze/Hirth, S. 79; vgl. zudem Sec. 5 (4) IAA.

352 Sec. 15 (1) IAA; Sec. 3 AA; Mangan/Reed/Choong, S. 20, 27; Chan, Leng Sun, Singapore Academy of Law Journal 2002, Vol. 14, S. 49 ff.; Pillay, The International Construction Law Review 2003, S. 91 (109).

353 Schütze, in: Schütze/Hirth, S. 79 f.; Chan, Leng Sun, Singapore Academy of Law Journal 2002, Vol. 14, S. 49 (50); vgl. auch Sec. 23 und 32 AA.

9. Schiedsfreundliches Klima in Singapur

Die Regierung und die Rechtsprechung in Singapur verfolgen das Ziel, Singapur zu einem der weltweit führenden, internationalen Schiedsorte zu machen. Von gesetzgeberischer Seite wird die im IAA und AA normierte Schiedsgesetzgebung den Anforderungen der modernen Schiedsverfahren angepasst.[354] Das von der singapurischen Regierung 1990 gegründete „Singapore International Arbitration Centre (SIAC)“ förderte die Schiedsgerichtsbarkeit in Singapur ungemein und stieg in den letzten Jahren zu einer der weltweit führenden Schiedsinstitutionen auf.[355] Die staatlichen Gerichte in Singapur haben eine schiedsfreundliche und unterstützende Einstellung entwickelt und greifen minimalistisch in das parteiautonome Schiedsverfahren ein.[356] Die geschichtliche Entwicklung der Schiedsgerichtsbarkeit und deren gegenwärtiger Stellenwert beschrieb der Court of Appeal trefflich im Urteil *Tjong Very Sumito and Others v Antig Investments Pte Ltd*[357]:

> *„There was a time when arbitration was viewed disdainfully as an inferior process of justice. Those days are now well behind us. An unequivocal judicial policy of facilitating and promoting arbitration has firmly taken root in Singapore. It is now openly acknowledged that arbitration, and other forms of alternative dispute resolution such as mediation, help to effectively unclog the arteries of judicial administration as well as offer parties realistic choices on how they want to resolve their disputes at a pace they are comfortable with. More fundamentally, the need to respect party autonomy (manifested by their contractual bargain) in deciding both the method of dispute resolution (and the procedural rules to be applied) as well as the substantive law to govern the contract, has been accepted as the cornerstone underlying judicial non-intervention in arbitration. In essence, a court ought to give effect to the parties' contractual choice as to the manner of dispute resolution unless it offends the law.*
>
> [...]

---

354 Mangan/Reed/Choong, S. 2 ff.; Lim, Wei Lee/Yeo, Alvin, in: Moser/Choong (Hrsg.), Asia Arbitration Handbook, S. 671 (673 f.); vgl. auch Hwang/Chan, Andrew/Selvaraj, in: Moser (Hrsg.), Arbitration in Asia, Sing-5 ff., Sing-74; Pillay, The International Construction Law Review 2003, S. 91 (94 f.).

355 Lim, Wei Lee/Yeo, Alvin, in: Moser/Choong (Hrsg.), Asia Arbitration Handbook, S. 671 (674); Mangan/Reed/Choong, S. 3 ff.; Yang, Lih Shyng/Chew, in: Ali/Ginsburg (Hrsg.), International Commercial Arbitration in Asia, S. 465 (468); SIAC, About Us, Our Vision, Mission & Core Values, verfügbar unter http://www.siac.org.sg/2014-11-03-13-33-43/why-siac/our-vision-mission-core-values (zuletzt abgerufen am 28.4.2021).

356 Lim, Wei Lee/Yeo, Alvin, in: Moser/Choong (Hrsg.), Asia Arbitration Handbook, S. 671 (673 f.); Mangan/Reed/Choong, S. 4 ff.

357 [2009] 4 SLR 732; [2009] SGCA 41, 26.8.2009.

> *Courts should therefore be slow to find reasons to assume jurisdiction over a matter that the parties have agreed to refer to arbitration. It must also be remembered that the whole thrust of the IAA is geared towards minimising court involvement in matters that the parties have agreed to submit to arbitration.* "[358]

Um Singapur als international anerkannten Schiedsort zu etablieren, ist eine schiedsfreundliche Rechtsordnung erforderlich. Dies brachte der High Court in der *Re An Arbitration Between Hainan Machinery Import and Export Corp and Donald & McArthy Pte Ltd*[359]-Entscheidung zum Ausdruck:

> „*As a nation which itself aspires to be an international arbitration centre, Singapore must recognise foreign awards if it expects its own awards to be recognised abroad.* "[360]

III. Indien

1. Geschichtlicher Überblick

a) Die britische Prägung Indiens

Auf die vedische[361] und hinduistische Epoche folgte ab 1526 eine von muslimischer Mogulherrschaft geprägte Zeit in Indien[362].[363] Die britische „East India Company" etablierte ihren ersten indischen Handelsposten 1612 in Surat[364].[365] Im Laufe des 17. Jahrhunderts folgten weitere Handelsposten u. a. in Madras[366], Bombay[367] und Kalkutta.[368] Die „Charter 1600" verlieh

---

358 Rn. 28 f.
359 [1995] SGHC 232, 28.6., 5.7., 19.7. und 29.9.1995.
360 Rn. 45.
361 Engl. Vedic period.
362 Nach *Mittal* eroberten muslimische Eroberer bereits ab dem 8. Jahrhundert Teile Indiens und besetzten Indien ab dem 16. Jahrhundert dauerhaft, Mittal, J. K., S. 1. *Gandhi* spricht von ersten Ansiedelungen von Muslimen ab dem 8. Jahrhundert und größeren muslimischen Eroberungen ab dem 10. Jahrhundert. Die ersten muslimischen Eroberer etalierten ab dem 12. Jahrhundert Sultanate in Indien. Im 16. Jahrhundert wurde das Mogulreich gegründet, Gandhi, B. M., Kulshreshtha's Landmarks, S. 18 ff.
363 Mittal, J. K., S. 1; Gandhi, B. M., Kulshreshtha's Landmarks, S. 4 ff.
364 Surat liegt heute im Bundesstaat Gujarat. Ab 1687 wurde der Handelsposten von Surat nach Bombay verlegt und Surat verlor an Bedeutung, Gandhi, B. M., Kulshreshtha's Landmarks, S. 45, Singh, Mahendra, History, S. 4 ff.
365 Gandhi, B. M., Kulshreshtha's Landmarks, S. 44; Singh, Mahendra, History, S. 3, Hamid, S. 5 f.
366 Heutzutage „Chennai".
367 Bombay heißt seit 1995 offiziell „Mumbai".
368 Mittal, J. K., S. 3; Gandhi, B. M., Kulshreshtha's Landmarks, S. 45 ff.; Hamid, S. 8 ff.; Singh, Mahendra, History, S. 4 ff.

der East India Company das Exklusivrecht, mit Indien[369] Handel betreiben zu dürfen und stattete die East India Company mit der Kompetenz aus, Gesetze für Handelsgeschäfte und ihre Mitarbeiter zu erlassen.[370] Die erlassenen Regelungen durften allerdings nicht gegen englisches Recht und gegen Gewohnheitsrecht verstoßen.[371] In der „Charter 1661“ übertrug die britische Krone dem „Gouverneur und dem Rat“[372] (engl. governor and council) das Recht, Gerichtsverfahren in den Handelsposten abzuhalten. Die Zuständigkeit dieser Gerichtsbarkeit war auf Personen, die der East India Company angehörten als auch auf unter ihrer Herrschaft lebende Personen beschränkt. Die Gerichtsverfahren waren nach englischem Recht durchzuführen.[373] Im 17. Jahrhundert führten die rechtlichen und regionalen Unterschiede in den Handelsposten Bombay, Madras und Kalkutta zur Entwicklung von unterschiedlichen Gerichtssystemen. Gemeinsam war diesen Gerichtsapparaten, dass sie das Richteramt überwiegend von Mitarbeitern der East India Company begleiten ließen und in diesen Verfahren meist englisches Recht Anwendung fand.[374] An der Verwaltungsspitze des Handelspostens stand der Präsident oder ein Gouverneur. Die Verwaltungsaufgaben übernahm der Rat[375].[376] In der „Royal Charter 1726“ etablierte die britische Krone mit den zivilgerichtlichen „Mayor's Courts“[377] in Bombay, Madras und Kalkutta[378] erstmals königliche Gerichte britischer Prägung.[379] Gegen Entscheidungen des königlichen Mayor's Courts konnten die Parteien in der ersten Berufungsinstanz vor den Gouverneur und den Rat[380] ziehen. Durch die Insti-

369 Das exklusive Handelsrecht umfasste Asien, Afrika und Amerika.

370 Der East India Company stand somit ein mit kommunalen Körperschaften vergleichbares Selbstverwaltungsrecht zu.

371 Gandhi, B. M., Kulshreshtha's Landmarks, S. 38 ff.; Banerjee, S. 7, 92; Mittal, J. K., S. 8; Singh, Mahendra, History, S. 1 f.

372 Der Rat bestand überwiegend aus erfahrenen Kaufleuten der East India Company, siehe Gandhi, B. M., Kulshreshtha's Landmarks, S. 43.

373 Mittal, J. K., S. 10; Gandhi, B. M., Kulshreshtha's Landmarks, S. 41 ff.

374 Singh, Mahendra, History, S. 3 ff.; Gandhi, B. M., Kulshreshtha's Landmarks, S. 41 ff.; Hamid, S. 8 ff.

375 Der Rat (engl. council) bestand aus Kaufleuten der East India Company, den Vorsitz hatte der Gouverneur oder der Präsident der Presidency.

376 Mittal, J. K., S. 13; Gandhi, B. M., Kulshreshtha's Landmarks, S. 43.

377 Dieser setzte sich aus dem Mayor („Bürgermeister“) und den „Aldermen“ („Stadträten“) zusammen. Der Mayor und 7 von 9 Aldermen mussten in England geborene britische Staatsangehörige sein, es wurde allerdings nie ein indischer Aldermen berufen. Der Mayor's Court bestand aus dem Mayor einer der Handelsposten und zwei bzw. drei Stadträten. Gandhi, B. M., Kulshreshtha's Landmarks, S. 70; Singh, Mahendra, History, S. 16, Hamid, S. 27 f.

378 Die Zuständigkeit war auf die „Presidency Towns“ Bombay, Madras und Kalkutta begrenzt, Singh, Mahendra, History, S. 16 ff.; Hamid, S. 27.

379 Mittal, J. K., S. 29; Singh, Mahendra, History, S. 16 ff.

380 Dieses Gericht war auch für Strafverfahren zuständig.

tutionalisierung des Mayor's Courts durch die britische Krone stand den Parteien aber zum ersten Mal ein zweites Berufungsverfahren zum ausschließlich mit englischen Richtern besetzten „Privy Council"[381] in London offen.[382] Die englische Krone schuf mit dem Mayor's Court ein von der East India Company unabhängiges Gericht. Die Charter 1726 führte ferner erstmalig englisches Recht in Indien ein[383]. Hierzu zählten sowohl das englische Common Law als auch das kodifizierte Recht bis zum Jahre 1726[384].[385] Korrespondierend zu den lokalen Erfordernissen ergänzten und modifizierten jedoch das muslimische und hinduistische Recht als auch das lokale Brauchtum das englische Recht.[386] Mit der Charter 1726 delegierte die britische Krone die Gesetzgebungskompetenz[387] an den Gouverneur und den Rat[388] in den „Presidency Towns" Bombay, Madras und Kalkutta.[389]

---

381 Der Privy Council wird auch als „King in Council" bezeichnet, Gandhi, B. M., Kulshreshtha's Landmarks, S. 70 f., 211 f. Der Berufungsmechanismus funktionierte folgendermaßen. Das „Judicial Committee" des Privy Councils führte das Berufungsverfahren durch und gab sodann dem König („His Majesty in Council") eine Empfehlung, wie die Rechtsstreitigkeit zu entscheiden ist und Letzterer traf als „King in Council" die Entscheidung über die Berufung als sog. „Order in Council", siehe Banerjee, S. 226 f.; Jenckel, S. 114 f.; Müller, S. 120. In der Praxis hielt sich der König an die Empfehlung, entsprechend kann von einem verbindlichen Berufungsverfahren vor dem Judicial Committee des Privy Councils gesprochen werden, Mittal, J. K., S. 177; Hamid, S. 140. Ab 1833 („Judicial Committee Act") wurde die Berufungszuständigkeit vom King-in-Council zum Judicial Committee des Privy Councils transferiert, das fortan ausschließlich für Berufungen aus den britischen Kolonien zuständig war. Durch diese Reform fungierte der Privy Council als richtiges Berufungsgericht, Mittal, J. K., S. 183; Singh, Mahendra, History, S. 102; Hamid, S. 139; Jenckel, S. 114; Müller, S. 120 ff. Trotz des dargelegten systematischen Unterschieds werden die Begriffen Privy Council und King-in-Council als Synonyme verwendet, siehe Mittal, J. K., S. 53, 81 f., 176; Gandhi, B. M., Kulshreshtha's Landmarks, S. 70; Singh, Mahendra, History, S. 100 ff. Meist wird der Begriff Privy Council verwendet, siehe Mittal, J. K., S. 175 ff.; Gandhi, B. M., Kulshreshtha's Landmarks, S. 70 f., 211. Im Folgenden wird deshalb der Begriff Privy Council primär verwendet werden.

382 Mittal, J. K., S. 29 ff., 179; Gandhi, B. M., Kulshreshtha's Landmarks, S. 70, 216; Banerjee, S. 11 ff., 225; Singh, Mahendra, History, S. 17 f., 100; Hamid, S. 28, 141.

383 Kein späterer Rechtsakt rezipierte das gesamte englische Recht in Indien, Mittal, J. K., S. 230 ff.

384 Diese Rezeption berücksichtigte keine indischen Gebräuche und Traditionen.

385 Gandhi, B. M., Kulshreshtha's Landmarks, S. 73; Banerjee, S. 11; Mittal, J. K., S. 230 ff.; Singh, Mahendra, History, S. 17 f.

386 Mittal, J. K., S. 233; Banerjee, S. 12 f.

387 Die verabschiedeten Gesetze galten erstmals auch für indische Einwohner der Handelsposten und durften nicht gegen englisches Recht verstoßen.

388 Zuvor wurden gesetzliche Bestimmungen in England von dem Court of Directors der East India Company erlassen.

389 Gandhi, B. M., Kulshreshtha's Landmarks, S. 69 ff.; Banerjee, S. 11, 92 ff.; Singh, Mahendra, History, S. 17 f.

aa) Gerichte in Kalkutta, Madras und Bombay

Mit der „Charter 1774“[390] schuf die britische Krone den königlichen „Supreme Court of Judicature“ im bengalischen Kalkutta. Der Supreme Court ersetzte den Mayor's Court in Kalkutta. Er bestand aus vier im englischen Recht ausgebildeten Berufsrichtern[391].[392] Durch den Erlass der „königlichen Charter 1798“[393] ersetzte die britische Krone in Madras und Bombay die Mayor's Courts durch die „Recorder Courts“.[394] Der Recorder Court bestand aus dem Mayor, drei Stadträten[395] und dem in englischem Recht ausgebildeten „Recorder“[396]. Die Recorder Courts entsprachen dem Supreme Court in Kalkutta. Mit dem Erlass von zwei königlichen Chartern[397] strukturierten die Briten die Recorder Courts bereits 1801 in Madras und 1824 in Bombay in die mit juristisch ausgebildeten Berufsrichtern besetzten Supreme Courts um.[398] Die sachliche Zuständigkeit der Supreme Courts und der Recorder Courts umfasste zivilrechtliche, strafrechtliche, seerechtliche[399] und kirchenrechtliche[400] Streitigkeiten. Das anwendbare Recht für die Supreme Courts in den drei „Presidency Towns“[401] war das englische Recht des Jahres 1726 sowie neuere Rechtsakte, die der britischen Gesetzgeber für Indien für anwendbar erklärte und die lokale indische Gesetzgebung.[402] Neben dem englischen Recht waren Bestimmungen des muslimischen und hinduistischen Rechts im Erb- und Vertragsrecht als auch für die Rechts-

---

390 Der „Regulation Act 1773“ gestattete den Erlass der Charter.

391 Dem Präsidenten des Gerichts („Chief Justice“) und drei Richtern. Die Anzahl der Richter wurde später auf zwei reduziert. Die Richter mussten Juristen („Barrister“) in Irland oder England gewesen sein und mindestens fünf Jahre Berufserfahrung haben. Die britische Krone entsandte die Richter.

392 Singh, Mahendra, History, S. 35 f.; Gandhi, B. M., Kulshreshtha's Landmarks, S. 112 f.

393 1797 autorisierte das britische Parlament die britische Krone zum Erlass dieser Charter.

394 Mittal, J. K., S. 80; Gandhi, B. M., Kulshreshtha's Landmarks, S. 79 f.; Singh, Mahendra, History, S. 50.

395 Engl. aldermen.

396 Als Qualifikation war es erforderlich, dass der Recorder fünf Jahre Berufserfahrung als Barrister hatte.

397 Zu diesen ermächtige das britische Parlament die britische Krone.

398 Singh, Mahendra, History, S. 50 f.; Gandhi, B. M., Kulshreshtha's Landmarks, S. 79 f., 144 ff.; Mittal, J. K., S. 80 ff.

399 Engl. admiralty jurisdiction.

400 Engl. ecclesiastical.

401 Kalkutta, Madras, Bombay.

402 Gandhi, B. M., Kulshreshtha's Landmarks, S. 144 ff.; Mittal, J. K., S. 80 ff.

nachfolge anwendbar[403].[404] Gegen Urteile des Supreme Courts und des Recorder Courts war die Berufung zum Privy Council statthaft.[405] Parallel zu dem königlichen Supreme Court etablierte die East India Company ein muslimisch geprägtes Adalats-Gerichtssystem[406].[407]

bb) Gesetzgebungskompetenz

Vor dem „Charter Act 1833“ war die Rechtsordnung in Indien fragmentiert. Die Gerichte wandten in den von der East India Company kontrollierten Gebieten neben dem englischen Recht und dem religiösen Recht die von den Gouverneuren in den jeweiligen Handelsposten erlassenen unterschiedlichen gesetzlichen Bestimmungen an.[408] 1833[409] übertrug das britische Parlament dem „Governor-General in Council“ (General-Gouverneur unter Beratung [durch den Rat]) mit Sitz im Fort Williams[410] in Bengalen die Kompetenz, Gesetze für ganz Indien zu erlassen. Anschließend war es möglich, einheitliche gesetzliche Regelungen für das gesamte indische Territorium zu erlassen.[411] Diese erstmalige einheitliche Gesetzgebungskompetenz nutzten der Governor-General in Council um ein Strafverfahrensgesetz, ein Strafgesetzbuch und ein Zivilverfahrensgesetz zu schaffen, das jeweils alle Einwohner erfasste und sie unabhängig von ihrer Kaste oder Religion gleich behandelte[412].[413] Der „Government of India Act 1858“ transferierte das von der East India Company kontrollierte Indien an die britische Krone.[414] Dieser

403 Bei diesen Streitigkeiten kam bei muslimischen Verfahren muslimisches Recht zur Anwendung, bei hinduistischen Verfahren hinduistisches Recht, gemischte Verfahren entschieden die Gerichte nach dem Recht des Beklagten.

404 Gandhi, B.M., Kulshreshtha's Landmarks, S. 140, 148; Banerjee, S. 25, 108; Mittal, J.K., S. 81 ff.; Singh, Mahendra, History, S. 50.

405 Mittal, J.K., S. 53, 80 ff., 179 f.; Gandhi, B.M., Kulshreshtha's Landmarks, S. 113, 144, 212; Singh, Mahendra, History, S. 37,100 f., 141.

406 Das Adalats-Gerichtssystem bestand aus drei Instanzen und umfasste zivilrechtliche und strafrechtliche Streitigkeiten, vgl. hierzu ausführlich Mann, S. 145 ff.

407 Singh, Mahendra, History, S. 25 ff.; Gandhi, B.M., Kulshreshtha's Landmarks, S. 116 f., 329; Banerjee, S. 58 f.; Mittal, J.K., S. 129 ff.

408 Banerjee, S. 52, 104 f.; Singh, Mahendra, History, S. 106 ff; vgl. auch oben.

409 Durch den Charter Act 1833.

410 Im heutigen Kalkutta.

411 Mittal, J.K., S. 289 ff.; Gandhi, B.M., Kulshreshtha's Landmarks, S. 188, 264, 286 ff., 337; Banerjee, S. 112 ff.; Singh, Mahendra, History, S. 109; Hamid, S. 123 f., 127 f.

412 Darüber hinaus schuf der indische Gesetzgeber den „Indian Limitation Act 1859“, den „Indian Succession Act 1865“, den „Indian Evidence Act 1872“ und den „Indian Contract Act 1872“.

413 Singh, Mahendra, History, S. 112; Gandhi, B.M., Kulshreshtha's Landmarks, S. 188, 296 ff., 337 f.; Banerjee, S. 179.

414 Gandhi, B.M., Kulshreshtha's Landmarks, S. 112, 143, 188; Banerjee, S. 5; Hamid, S. 122 f.

Vorgang erleichterte die weitere Vereinheitlichungen der gesetzlichen Bestimmungen.[415]

cc) High Court

Der „High Court Act 1861" ersetzte die Supreme Courts in den Presidencies Bombay, Madras und Kalkutta durch „High Courts"[416].[417] Anschließend wurden weitere High Courts in Indien etabliert.[418] Die High Courts waren die oberste Berufungsinstanz in Indien. Das von den muslimischen Herrschern übernommene, muslimisch geprägte Adalats-Gerichtssystem mit seinen verschiedenen Instanzen in Straf- und Zivilrechtsverfahren unterstand fortan den High Courts als Berufungsinstanz[419].[420] High Courts waren für zivilrechtliche Verfahren, Steuersachen[421], Seerechtsverfahren[422], Erbrechtssachen[423] und Strafverfahren originär zuständig. Hinzu kam eine Berufungszuständigkeit für Zivil- und Strafsachen.[424] Den Parteien stand gegen Entscheidungen des High Courts die Berufung zum Privy Council in England offen.[425] Die Richter der High Courts waren erfahrene Juristen und Angestellte des öffentlichen Dienstes. Ein Drittel der Richter musste zunächst in England ausgebildet[426] sein[427].[428] In seiner originären zivilrechtlichen Zuständigkeit entsprach das von den High Courts angewandte Recht der Rechtsanwendung der Supreme Courts in den „Presidency Towns". Auf außerhalb der „Presidency Towns" entspringende zivilrechtliche Berufungs-

---

415 Gandhi, B. M., Kulshreshtha's Landmarks, S. 188; Hamid, S. 152 f.

416 Dies geschah durch „Letters Patents".

417 Gandhi, B. M., Kulshreshtha's Landmarks, S. 188 ff.; Mittal, J. K., S. 154 ff.; Singh, Mahendra, History, S. 51, 92 f.; Hamid, S. 156.

418 Gandhi, B. M., Kulshreshtha's Landmarks, S. 190 ff.; Mittal, J. K., S. 159; Banerjee, S. 238; Singh, Mahendra, History, S. 95 f.

419 Hierdurch sollten sich widersprechende Entscheidungen des Adalat-Gerichtssystems und des Supreme Courts vermieden werden.

420 Mittal, J. K., S. 153 f.; Singh, Mahendra, History, S. 92, 52 ff.; Hamid, S. 143, 156; Gandhi, B. M., Kulshreshtha's Landmarks, S. 188 ff.

421 Engl. revenue. Diese Zuständigkeit wurde dem High Court 1915 wieder entzogen.

422 Engl. admiralty jurisdiction.

423 Engl. testamentary, interstate and probate jurisdiction.

424 Singh, Mahendra, History, S. 94 ff.; Hamid, S. 157 ff.

425 Gandhi, B. M., Kulshreshtha's Landmarks, S. 189; Mittal, J. K., S. 186; Singh, Mahendra, History, S. 101 f.

426 Barrister oder „Advocates".

427 Der High Court bestand zunächst aus dem Chief Justice und aus bis zu 15 weiteren Richtern. 1915 erhöhte sich die Anzahl der Richter auf 20. Mindestens jeweils 1/3 der Richter mussten englische Juristen sein. Ab 1935 wurde diese 1/3 Quote beseitigt, zudem konnten auch indische Juristen das Amt des Chief Justice ausüben.

428 Mittal, J. K., S. 155, 161, 163; Banerjee, S. 240 f.; Singh, Mahendra, History, S. 93, 96; Hamid, S. 157, 164; Gandhi, B. M., Kulshreshtha's Landmarks, S. 194.

verfahren war neben dem englisch geprägten „equity, justice and good conscience"-Rechtsprinzip[429] das auf die vorausgehende Instanz anwendbare Recht einschlägig[430].[431] Insbesondere durch die Besetzung der High Courts mit im englischen Common Law ausgebildeten Juristen[432] blieb es bei der Dominanz des englischen Rechts in Indien.[433]

dd) Federal Court

Mit dem „Government of India Act 1935" führte das britische Parlament eine föderale Struktur in Indien ein und konstituierte den „Federal Court"[434]. Mit dem Federal Court in Delhi schuf der Gesetzgeber eine neue oberste indische Berufungsinstanz gegen alle Urteile der High Courts.[435] Der Federal Court hatte eine originäre, eine beratende und eine Berufungszuständigkeit.[436] Der englische König berief den „Chief Justice"[437] und bis zu sechs weitere Richter[438].[439] Gegen Entscheidungen des Federal Courts konnte wiederum Berufung zum Privy Council in England eingelegt werden.[440] Nach der Unabhängigkeit Indiens vom britischen Empire am 15. August 1947 konnte der in England ansässige Privy Council ab 1948 nur noch vom Federal Court angerufen werden.[441] Die Berufung zum Privy Council schaffte der indische Gesetzgeber im Rahmen der Ausarbeitung der Verfassung in der „Constituent Assembly" durch den „Privy Council Jurisdiction Act 1949" ab.[442] Im unabhängigen Indien ersetzte der neu gegründete „Supreme Court of India" den Federal Court als das letztinstanzliche Gericht Indiens.[443]

429 Gandhi, B.M., Kulshreshtha's Landmarks, S. 325.

430 Für die besondere originäre Zuständigkeit des High Courts war auf das in einem hypothetischen erstinstanzlichen Verfahren anwendbare Recht abzustellen.

431 Mittal, J.K., S. 158 ff.; Singh, Mahendra, History, S. 95.

432 Vgl. o.

433 Banerjee, S. 240 f.; Mittal, J.K., S. 155 ff.; Singh, Mahendra, History, S. 93 ff.

434 Er wurde 1937 eröffnet.

435 Gandhi, B.M., Kulshreshtha's Landmarks, S. 220 f.; Mittal, J.K., S. 193 ff.

436 Gandhi, B.M., Kulshreshtha's Landmarks, S. 222 ff.; Mittal, J.K., S. 188, 194 ff.

437 Präsident des Gerichts.

438 Alle Richter des Federal Courts mussten erfahrene Juristen sein.

439 Gandhi, B.M., Kulshreshtha's Landmarks, S. 221; Mittal, J.K., S. 194.

440 Mittal, J.K., S. 188, 196; Singh, Mahendra, History, S. 103; Hamid, S. 143.

441 Gandhi, B.M., Kulshreshtha's Landmarks, S. 214 f., 225; Hamid, S. 143 f. Die zuvor zulässige direkte Berufung gegen eine High Court Entscheidung zum Privy Council war nicht mehr statthaft, Gandhi, B.M., Kulshreshtha's Landmarks, S. 215, 225, 230; Hamid, S. 143 f.

442 Gandhi, B.M., Kulshreshtha's Landmarks, S. 226; Mittal, J.K., S. 189, 196; Singh, Mahendra, History, S. 103; Hamid, S. 144.

443 Hamid, S. 168; Gandhi, B.M., Kulshreshtha's Landmarks, S. 226 ff.; Singh, Mahendra, History, S. 103.

ee) Common Law Rechtssystem

Zu Beginn der britischen Besetzung von Indien wendete die East India Company auf Inder das jeweilige religiöse Recht und auf Engländer englisches Recht an.[444] Die „Charter 1727“ etablierte nicht nur die mit Engländern besetzten Mayor's Courts, sie führte auch das englische Recht in Indien ein. Die vor allem mit dem englischen Common Law vertrauten britischen Richter der indischen Gerichte wendeten auf die vor ihnen anhängigen Verfahren britische Rechtsakte und Common Law an, sofern dies mit den lokalen Gegebenheiten in Indien vereinbar war.[445] Ab 1871 mussten die königlichen Gerichte in Indien[446] auf muslimische und hinduistische Verfahren im Erb- und Vertragsrecht als auch in Rechtsnachfolge-Streitigkeiten muslimisches bzw. hinduistisches Recht anwenden. Auf gemischte Verfahren fand das Recht des Beklagten Anwendung. Alle anderen Bereiche unterstanden dem englischen Recht. Durch die mit dem Common Law vertrauten englischen Richter überlagerte das englische Recht immer mehr die indischen Gebräuche und das indische Recht.[447] Die Gerichte in Indien wendeten das britische Common Law aber nur auf Verfahren an, wenn dies den Umständen in Indien nicht zuwiderlief.[448] Dies führte im Ergebnis dazu, dass den besonderen Verhältnissen und Bedürfnissen Indiens durch eine verständnisvolle Auslegung Rechnung getragen werden konnte. Die „Law Commission“, die seit 1833 für die Ausarbeitung von Gesetzen für den gesamten indischen Subkontinent betraut war, war überwiegend mit englischen Juristen besetzt[449].[450] Es ist daher nicht überraschend, dass der „Penal Code 1860“ und der „Criminal Procedere Code 1861“ das drakonische, muslimisch geprägte, indische Strafrecht durch englische Rechtsakte[451] ersetzte.[452] Diese Strafgesetzgebung war die erste einheitliche, englisch geprägte, gesetzliche Regelung, die auf alle Einwohner Indiens gleichermaßen anwendbar war.[453]

---

444 Gandhi, B.M., Kulshreshtha's Landmarks, S. 329, 339; Mittal, J.K., S. 336.

445 Mittal, J.K., S. 230 ff.; Banerjee, S. 12 f.; vgl. auch oben.

446 Der Supreme Court in Kalkutta und der Recorder Court und später der Supreme Court in Madras und Bombay.

447 Gandhi, B.M., Kulshreshtha's Landmarks, S. 328 ff., 482 ff.; vgl. auch oben.

448 Gandhi, B.M., Kulshreshtha's Landmarks, S. 325, 333 ff.; vgl. o.

449 Ab der Unabhängigkeit änderte sich die Zusammensetzung der Law Commission, fortan war sie von indischen Juristen besetzt, siehe Gandhi, B.M., Kulshreshtha's Landmarks, S. 300 ff.

450 Gandhi, B.M., Kulshreshtha's Landmarks, S. 293 ff.; vgl. auch oben.

451 Der Penal Code war zudem vom französischen Strafgesetzbuch als auch vom „Code of Louisiana“ geprägt. Die wesentliche Grundlage des Penal Codes blieb jedoch englisches Recht mit Abweichungen, um den Umständen in Indien Rechnung zu tragen, Mittal, J.K., S. 326 f.; Banerjee, S. 174, 177.

452 Gandhi, B.M., Kulshreshtha's Landmarks, S. 188, 253 ff., 329, 337; Banerjee, S. 55 ff., 179 ff.

453 Gandhi, B.M., Kulshreshtha's Landmarks, S. 188, 337 f.; vgl. o.

Der Siegeszug des englischen Rechts in Indien hängt auch damit zusammen, dass die englisch besetzten Gerichte Schwierigkeiten hatten, das indische Recht durch dessen Aufspaltung nach Religionszugehörigkeit richtig zu ermitteln, zudem wurden Mängel des indischen Rechts durch englische Rechtsprinzipien substituiert.[454] Trotz der weitgehenden, flächendeckenden Einführung des englischen Rechts in Indien überlebte eine zeitgemäße Form des Hindu-Rechts und des muslimischen Rechts im religiös geprägten Familien- und Erbrecht.[455] Mit der Zeit entstanden verschiedene, englisch geprägte, einheitliche Gesetze für Britisch-Indien, die teilweise Ausnahmebestimmungen für Hindus, Muslime und Buddhisten enthielten. Hierzu zählten *inter alia*: Der „Indian Succession Act 1885", der „Transfer of Property Act 1882", der „Easement Act 1882", der „Penal Code 1860", der „Code of Criminal Procedure 1861", der „Indian Contract Act 1872", der „Sales of Goods Act 1930", der „Partnership Act 1932", der „Indian Evidence Act 1872", der „Civil Procedure Code 1908", der „Indian Companies Act 1862" und der „Land Acquisition Act 1894".[456] Nach der Unabhängigkeit Indiens blieb gem. Art. 372 der indischen Verfassung das zuvor geltende Recht bestehen und umfasste nicht nur gesetzliche Bestimmungen, sondern auch das von den indischen Gerichten angewendete Common Law sowie die hinduistische und muslimische Gesetzgebung.[457]

Von 1726 bis 1949 spielte der englische Privy Council mit über 2.500 Urteilen eine tragende Rolle in der Entwicklung des indischen Rechts- und Gerichtssystems. Noch im heutigen Indien werden die Entscheidungen des Privy Councils von der indischen Gerichtsbarkeit respektiert.[458] Vorkons-

---

454 Gandhi, B. M., Kulshreshtha's Landmarks, S. 333 ff., 482 ff.

455 Gandhi, B. M., Kulshreshtha's Landmarks, S. 340 ff., 339 ff., 482 ff.; Mittal, J. K., S. 330 f., 351 ff., 361 ff.; Banerjee, S. 183 f. Siehe auch beispielsweise der „Indian Succession Act 1925", der „Hindu Succession Act 1956" und der „Muslim Personal Law (Shariat) Application Act 1937".

456 Banerjee, S. 183 ff.; Gandhi, B. M., Kulshreshtha's Landmarks, S. 337 f.; Mittal, J. K., S. 329 ff.; Jayasimha/Mody, in: Moser/Choong (Hrsg.), Asia Arbitration Handbook, S. 843 (844 f.).

457 Gandhi, B. M., Kulshreshtha's Landmarks, S. 344; Mittal, J. K., S. 230; Basu, S. 474.

458 Gandhi, B. M., Kulshreshtha's Landmarks, S. 216 f.; Supreme Court of India, Practice & Procedure, A Handbook of Information, S. 9, verfügbar unter http://supremecourtofindia.nic.in/handbook3rdedition.pdf (zuletzt abgerufen am 28.4.2021). Der Privy Council verhandelte 286 Berufungsverfahren von den Mayor's Courts und den Supreme Courts, Hamid, S. 141. In den 60 Jahren von 1774 bis 1833 entschied der Privy Council ca. 300 indische Berufungsverfahren, Mittal, J. K., S. 181. Hinsichtlich des respektvollen Umgangs mit Entscheidungen des Privy Councils, Supreme Court, *Chief Controlling Revenue v Maharashtra Sugar Mills Ltd,* 1950 AIR 218; 1950 SCR 536, 27.5.1950; Supreme Court, *State of Gujarat v Vora Fiddali Badruddin*, 1964 AIR 1043; 1964 SCR (6) 461, 30.1.1964.

titutionelle Entscheidungen[459] des Privy Councils sind für die indischen High Courts immer noch bindend, sofern in einem vergleichbaren Fall keine Entscheidung des indischen Supreme Courts vorliegt.[460] *Ergo* ist nur der Supreme Court in seiner Urteilsfindung frei und nicht an Entscheidungen des Privy Councils gebunden.[461] Durch den Privy Council war die Rechtsprechung Indiens eng mit dem englischen Common Law verbunden und hieraus folgte, dass viele indische Gesetze auf englischen Rechtsprinzipien fußen.[462] Auch heute noch beziehen die indischen Gerichte Entscheidungen aus England, anderen Common Law Ländern und den Vereinigten Staaten in ihre Gerichtsentscheidungen mit ein.[463]

b) Bewertung

Als britische Kolonie ist Indien über 300 Jahre stark von der englischen Rechtsordnung beeinflusst worden. Während dieser Zeit prägten die britisch ausgestalteten Gerichte und die auf englischem Recht beruhende Gesetzgebung die indische Rechtsordnung dauerhaft. Dies spiegelt sich auch in der Schiedsgerichtsgesetzgebung Indiens wider, sowohl der „Indian Arbitration Act 1899“ als auch der „Arbitration Act 1940“ basieren auf dem englischen „Arbitration Act“.[464] Bis heute beruhen einige indische Gesetze auf der korrespondierenden englischen Gesetzgebung.[465] Indien zählt daher wie andere ehemalige britische Kolonien zum Rechtskreis des Common Law.

---

459 Entscheidungen, die vor dem Inkrafttreten der indischen Verfassung („Constitution of India 1949“) am 26. Januar 1950 ergingen.

460 Bombay High Court, *State of Bombay v Chhaganlal Gangaram Lavar,* AIR 1955 Bom 1; (1954) 56 BOMLR 1084; ILR 1955 Bom 203, 15.7.1954; Supreme Court, *State of Gujarat v Vora Fiddali Badruddin*, 1964 AIR 1043; 1964 SCR (6) 461, 30.1.1964; Gandhi, B.M., Kulshreshtha's Landmarks, S. 216.

461 Vgl. Supreme Court, *Shrinivas Krishnarao Kango v Narayan Devji Kango And Others*, 1954 AIR 379; 1955 SCR 1, 23.3.1954.

462 Mittal, J.K., S. 189 f.; Hamid, S. 30.

463 Supreme Court, Constitutional Bench, 13 Richter, *Kesavananda Bharati Sripadagalvaru and Ors v State of Kerala and Anr*, Writ Petition (civil) 135 of 1970; AIR 1973 SC 1461, 24.4.1973; Jayasimha/Mody, in: Moser/Choong (Hrsg.), Asia Arbitration Handbook, S. 843 (844 f.).

464 Paranjape, S. 2 f.; Sethi/Gupta, Arpan, S. 7; Government of India, Law Commission of India, 246. Report, Amendments to the Arbitration and Conciliation Act 1996, 5.8.2014, S. 1.

465 Vgl. o.

2. Wichtigste Daten

Indien ist ein föderaler Staat, er besteht aus 29 Bundestaaten und 7 „Union Territories“ [466].[467] Indien ist ein Subkontinent und hat eine Fläche von 2.973.190 Quadratkilometern.[468] 2017 hatte Indien eine Bevölkerung von 1,3 Milliarden (Mrd.) Menschen.[469] Ein Sechstel der Weltbevölkerung von 7,6 Mrd. Menschen[470] lebt somit in Indien. Das Schwellenland[471] Indien transformiert seine Wirtschaft mehr und mehr von einer ursprünglichen „Agrar-Ökonomie“ in eine „Service- und Industrie-Wirtschaft“. Entsprechend entwickelte sich Indien zu einem weltweit wichtigen Zentrum für Informationstechnologie und Dienstleistungen. Seine günstigen Arbeitskräfte machen Indien darüber hinaus attraktiv für arbeitsintensive Industrieproduktionen.[472] Die indische Wirtschaft ist in den vergangenen Jahren kontinuierlich gewachsen,[473] Zudem zählt Indien zu den BRIC-Staaten, einer Vereinigung

466 Die Union Territories unterstehen der Verwaltung durch den indischen Präsidenten. Letzterer ernennt einen Verwalter für die Union Territories, Jain, M. P., Constitution, S. 482; Art. 239 ff. der indischen Verfassung.

467 Art. 1 der indischen Verfassung; Jain, M. P., Constitution, S. 19; Government of India, web directory, States & Union Territories, verfügbar unter http://goidirectory.nic.in/state.php (zuletzt abgerufen am 28.4.2021); Singh, Mahendra, in: Choudhry/Khosla/Mehta, The Oxford Handbook of the Indian Constitution, S. 451 ff.

468 The World Bank, Data, Land area (sq. km), India, verfügbar unter http://data.worldbank.org/indicator/AG.LND.TOTL.K2 (zuletzt abgerufen am 28.4.2021).

469 Population Reference Bureau, 2017 World Population Data Sheet, S. 2, verfügbar unter https://www.prb.org/wp-content/uploads/2017/08/WPDS-2017.pd (zuletzt abgerufen am 28.4.2021).

470 Stiftung Weltbevölkerung, Die Weltbevölkerungsuhr, verfügbar unter http://www.weltbevoelkerung.de/meta/whats-your-number.html (zuletzt abgerufen am 28.4.2021).

471 The World Economic Forum, The Global Competitiveness Report 2016–2017, S. 8, verfügbar unter http://www3.weforum.org/docs/GCR2016-2017/05FullReport/TheGlobalCompetitivenessReport2016-2017_FINAL.pdf (zuletzt abgerufen am 28.4.2021); The Organisation for Economic Co-operation and Development, OECD Economic Surveys India, Februar 2017, S. 13 ff., verfügbar unter http://www.oecd.org/eco/surveys/INDIA-2017-OECD-economic-survey-overview.pdf (zuletzt abgerufen am 28.4.2021).

472 Nishith Desai, Doing Business in India, S. 1, verfügbar unter http://www.nishithdesai.com/fileadmin/user_upload/pdfs/Research%20Papers/Doing_Business_in_India.pdf (zuletzt abgerufen am 28.4.2021); India in Business, Ministry of External Affairs, Govt. of India, Investment and Technology Promotion Division, India At A Glance, Economic Profile, http://indiainbusiness.nic.in/newdesign/index.php?param=indiaataglance/153 (zuletzt abgerufen am 28.4.2021); Sau, Economic and Political Weekly 1972, Vol. 7, Ausg. 1, S. 368 (373).

473 The World Bank, Data, GDP growth (annual %), India, verfügbar unter http://data.worldbank.org/indicator/NY.GDP.MKTP.KD.ZG?end=2015&locations=IN&name_desc=false&start=1990 (zuletzt abgerufen am 28.4.2021).

aufstrebender Wirtschaftsnationen.[474] Seit der Öffnung und Liberalisierung der indischen Wirtschaft Anfang der 90er Jahre ist Indien zu einem der weltweit attraktivsten Ziele für ausländische Investoren geworden.[475] Die gegenwärtige Regierung *Modi* [476] (seit 2014) versucht durch wirtschaftsfreundliche Rahmenbedingungen Investitionen in Indien zu fördern und die weitere wirtschaftliche Entwicklung zu stimulieren.[477] Allein die Tatsache, dass Indien ein Sechstel der Weltbevölkerung besitzt und diese Bevölkerung bis 2050 auf 1,7 Mrd. Einwohner steigen soll[478], macht deutlich, dass Indien eine entscheidende Rolle im internationalen Handel einnehmen wird. Bei der Bewertung der Rahmenbedingungen für Unternehmen durch den „Doing Business“ Bericht der Weltbank belegte Indien mit Rang 130 von den 190 untersuchten Ländern einen Platz im hinteren Drittel.[479] Dies zeigt, dass Indien noch viel Arbeit vor sich hat, um zu einem attraktiven Wirtschaftsstandort zu werden. Der Subkontinent Indien zählt bisher nicht zu den von Schiedsparteien präferierten Schiedsorten.[480]

474 The World Economic Forum, The Global Competitiveness Report 2016–2017, S. 8, verfügbar unter http://www3.weforum.org/docs/GCR2016-2017/05FullReport/TheGlobal CompetitivenessReport2016-2017_FINAL.pdf (zuletzt abgerufen am 28.4.2021).

475 Sathyapalan, Arbitration International 2016, S. 1 (7).

476 *Narendra Modi* ist seit 26.5.2014 der Premierminister von Indien.

477 Nishith Desai, Doing Business in India, S. 1, verfügbar unter http://www.nishithdesai.com/fileadmin/user_upload/pdfs/Research%20Papers/Doing_Business_in_India.pdf (zuletzt abgerufen am 28.4.2021).

478 Population Reference Bureau, 2016 World Population Data Sheet, S. 2, verfügbar unter http://www.prb.org/pdf16/prb-wpds2016-web-2016.pdf (zuletzt abgerufen am 28.4.2021).

479 World Bank Group, Doing Business 2017, Equal Opportunity for All, 14. Aufl., S. 7, verfügbar unter http://www.doingbusiness.org/~/media/WBG/DoingBusiness/Documents/Annual-Reports/English/DB17-Report.pdf (zuletzt abgerufen am 28.4.2021). Das Weltwirtschaftsforum bewertete Indien 2016–2017 hingegen mit Platz 39 von 138 beurteilten Ländern (um 16 Positionen verbessert) verheißungsvoller, The World Economic Forum, The Global Competitiveness Report 2016–2017, S. 7, 202, verfügbar unter http://www3.weforum.org/docs/GCR2016-2017/05FullReport/TheGlobalCompetitivenessReport2016-2017_FINAL.pdf (zuletzt abgerufen am 28.4.2021). Kritisch zu den Doing Business Reports der Weltbank, Kern, Juristenzeitung 2009, S. 498 ff.

480 Carlevaris, in: Brekoulakis/Lew/Mistelis (Hrsg.), The Evolution and Future of International Arbitration, S. 331 (333); ICC, 2015 ICC Dispute Resolution Statistics, ICC Dispute Resolution Bulletin 2016, Ausg. 1, S. 9 (16) Loukas Mistelis/Paul Friedland, 2010 International Arbitration Survey: Choices in International Arbitration, S. 2 ff., verfügbar unter http://www.arbitration.qmul.ac.uk/docs/123290.pdf (zuletzt abgerufen am 28.4.2021).

3. Politische und institutionelle Struktur Indiens

Indien ist die weltweit größte Demokratie. Die indische Verfassung ist nach der Unabhängigkeit vom Vereinigten Königreich am 26. Januar 1950 in Kraft getreten. Die Präambel der Verfassung charakterisiert Indien als unabhängige, sozialistische und säkulare demokratische Republik. Indien ist ein föderaler Staat mit zentralstaatlichen Elementen. Es ist eine von Parteienvielfalt geprägte, repräsentative Demokratie, die das Westminster Modell übernahm. Das indische Parlament besteht aus der „Rajya Sabha" (Oberhaus), in der die Bundesstaaten Indiens ihre Interessen vertreten und der „Lok Sabha" (Unterhaus), letztere besteht aus vom indischen Volk gewählten Repräsentanten.[481] Die Abgeordneten der Lok Sabha werden alle fünf Jahre gewählt.[482] Gesetzesinitiativen können von der Regierung oder einem Parlamentsmitglied ins Parlament eingebracht und nach drei Lesungen von beiden Parlamentskammern verabschiedet werden.[483] In Kraft tritt ein Gesetz erst nach der Zustimmung des Präsidenten.[484] Die Verfassung sieht den Präsidenten als oberstes Exekutivorgan in Indien vor. Der „Council of Ministers", angeführt vom Prime Minister, berät den Präsidenten bei seinen Amtsgeschäften und der Präsident hat entsprechend zu handeln.[485] Tatsächlich ruht die Exekutivgewalt daher in den Händen des Council of Ministers mit dem Prime Minister an dessen Spitze.[486] Die Gewaltenteilung zwischen Legislative, Exekutive und Judikative ist in der indischen Verfassung ver-

---

481 Madhavan, in: Choudhry/Khosla/Mehta, The Oxford Handbook of the Indian Constitution, S. 270 ff. Jayasimha/Mody, in: Moser/Choong (Hrsg.), Asia Arbitration Handbook, S. 843 (844); India.gov.in, national portal of india, My Government, Indian Parliament, verfügbar unter https://india.gov.in/my-government/ (zuletzt abgerufen am 28.4.2021); Jain, M. P., Constitution, S. 24 ff.

482 Indian Parliament, Our Parliament, verfügbar unter http://164.100.47.132/LssNew/our%20parliament/Our%20Parliament.pdf (zuletzt abgerufen am 28.4.2021).

483 Indian Parliament, How A Bill Becomes An Act, verfügbar unter http://164.100.47.132/LssNew/our%20parliament/How%20a%20bill%20become%20an%20act.pdf (zuletzt abgerufen am 28.4.2021); Art. 83 (2) der indischen Verfassung.

484 Indian Parliament, How A Bill Becomes An Act, verfügbar unter http://164.100.47.132/LssNew/our%20parliament/How%20a%20bill%20become%20an%20act.pdf (zuletzt abgerufen am 28.4.2021); Art. 111 der indischen Verfassung.

485 Jayasimha/Mody, in: Moser/Choong (Hrsg.), Asia Arbitration Handbook, S. 843 (844); India.gov.in, national portal of india, My Government, Constitution of India, verfügbar unter https://india.gov.in/my-government/constitution-india (zuletzt abgerufen am 28.4.2021); Art. 53, 74 der indischen Verfassung; Dam, in: Choudhry/Khosla/Mehta, The Oxford Handbook of the Indian Constitution, S. 307 (316 ff.).

486 India.gov.in, national portal of india, My Government, Constitution of India, verfügbar unter https://india.gov.in/my-government/constitution-india (zuletzt abgerufen am 28.4.2021); Jain, M. P., Constitution, S. 122 f.

brieft, sodass die indischen Gerichte unabhängig von den anderen Staatsgewalten operieren können.[487]

4. Gerichte

In Indien gibt es einen Supreme Court, 18 High Courts[488] und 12.800 Gerichte nachgeordneter Instanzen[489], letztere umfassen u. a. die District Courts.[490] Die Fortbildung der Richter übernehmen die „National Judicial Academy" und die für die jeweiligen Bundestaaten zuständigen „State Judicial Academies".[491]

a) Supreme Court

Der Supreme Court besitzt in Indien ein hohes Ansehen und wird als „Guardian of the Constitution" bezeichnet [492] Der Supreme Court wurde zwei Tage nach der Unabhängigkeit Indiens am 28. Januar 1950 in Delhi[493] eröffnet.[494] Bei seiner Gründung bestand das Gericht aus einem „Chief Justice of India (im Folgenden Chief Justice) "[495] und sieben Richtern.[496] Auf Grund der ständig ansteigenden Verfahren vor dem Supreme Court wurde die An-

---

487 Agrawal, K. B., Procedure, S. 37.

488 Indian Courts, Indian Judiciary, verfügbar unter http://indiancourts.nic.in/ (zuletzt abgerufen am 28.4.2021).

489 Hilmer, International Arbitration Law Review 2007, S. 33; vgl. Thiruvengadam, in: Choudhry/Khosla/Mehta, The Oxford Handbook of the Indian Constitution, S. 412 (413).

490 Indian Courts, District Courts, http://indiancourts.nic.in/districtcourt.html (zuletzt abgerufen am 28.4.2021).

491 National Judicial Academy, About us, The Institution, verfügbar unter http://www.nja.nic.in/the-institution.html (zuletzt abgerufen am 28.4.2021); Delhi Judicial Academy, About Us, Our Vision, verfügbar unter http://judicialacademy.nic.in/index.php?option=article&id=1&ItemId=5 (zuletzt abgerufen am 28.4.2021); Tamil Nadu State Judicial Academy, Objectives, verfügbar unter http://www.tnsja.tn.nic.in/objectives.html (zuletzt abgerufen am 28.4.2021); Maharashtra Judicial Academy and Indian Mediation Centre and Training Institute, Aim and Objectives, verfügbar unter http://mja.gov.in/1037/Aim-and-Objectives (zuletzt abgerufen am 28.4.2021); West Bengal State Judicial Academy, About Us, Objective and Vision, verfügbar unter http://www.wbja.nic.in/pages/display/115-objectivevision (zuletzt abgerufen am 28.4.2021).

492 Mittal, J. K., S. 198.

493 Gem. Art. 130 der indischen Verfassung ist der Sitz des Supreme Courts in Delhi.

494 Supreme Court of India, History, verfügbar unter https://www.supremecourtofindia.nic.in/history (zuletzt abgerufen am 28.4.2021).

495 Zum „Chief Justice of India" wird bei einer Neubesetzung der erfahrenste Richter des Supreme Courts ernannt, siehe Gandhi, B. M., Kulshreshtha's Landmarks, S. 231.

496 Art. 124 der indischen Verfassung.

zahl der Richter mehrmals erhöht[497]. Momentan besteht der oberste Gerichtshof Indiens aus dem Chief Justice und 30 Richtern. Auf Grund des hohen Verfahrensaufkommens besteht ein Senat (engl. bench) aus zwei[498] oder drei Richtern.[499] Bei unterschiedlichen Auffassungen innerhalb des Supreme Courts oder bei grundlegenden Entscheidungen können größere Senate, die sog. „Constitutional Bench“, von fünf oder mehr Richtern gebildet werden.[500] Es gibt keine vorgesehene Anzahl von Senaten beim Supreme Court, die jeweils entscheidenden Senate werden vom Chief Justice festgelegt und ergeben sich nach der Verfügbarkeit der Richter. Dabei kann die Anzahl der Richter eines Senats erhöht oder verringert werden. Den Senaten sind spezielle Sachgebiete zugewiesen.[501] Ein Einzelrichter[502] ist im Zivilrecht insbesondere für Anträge auf Zulassung der Berufung[503] zuständig und erledigt diese Anhörungen während einer kurzen sog. „Lunch Session“[504].[505]

Die Richter des obersten indischen Gerichts werden vom indischen Präsidenten berufen.[506] Zur Qualifikation als Richter ist erforderlich, dass er indischer Staatsbürger ist und zuvor für mindestens fünf Jahre Richter an einem High Court bzw. 10 Jahre Anwalt an einem High Court war oder dass er oder sie nach der Einschätzung des Präsidenten ein bedeutender Jurist oder eine bedeutende Juristin ist.[507] Die Richter können wegen Fehlverhal-

---

497 Neben dem Chief Justice stieg die Anzahl an Richtern von 7 Richtern 1950 auf 10 Richter 1956, 13 Richter 1960, 17 Richter 1977, 25 Richter 1986, Supreme Court of India, History, verfügbar unter https://www.supremecourtofindia.nic.in/history (zuletzt abgerufen am 28.4.2021); Mittal, J.K., S. 197.

498 Im Regelfall besteht ein Senat aus zwei Richtern, siehe Order VI Nr. 1 „Supreme Court Rules 2013“.

499 Supreme Court, Constitutional Bench, 5 Richter, *Union of India & Anr v Raghubir Singh (Dead) By Lrs Etc*, AIR 1989 SC 1933; [1989] 3 SCR 316, 16.5.1989.

500 Art. 145 (3) der indischen Verfassung; Supreme Court of India, History, verfügbar unter https://www.supremecourtofindia.nic.in/history (zuletzt abgerufen am 28.4.2021); Jain, M.P., Constitution, S. 288 f.; Agrawal, K.B., Procedure, S. 40; Baxi, in: Choudhry/Khosla/Mehta, The Oxford Handbook of the Indian Constitution, S. 94 (97). Die größte Constitutional Bench umfasste 13 Richter, Robinson, The American Journal of Comparative Law 2013, Vol. 61, S. 173 (191); Neuborne, International Journal of Constitutional Law 2003, Vol. 1, Ausg. 3, S. 476 (480 i. V. m. Fn. 24).

501 Agrawal, K.B., Procedure, S. 40; Neuborne, International Journal of Constitutional Law 2003, Vol. 1, Ausg. 3, S. 476 (480 f.); Order VI „Supreme Court Rules 2013“.

502 „Chamber Judge“.

503 „Special leave petitions“ und „leave to appeal“.

504 Anhörung zur Mittagszeit.

505 Agrawal, K.B., Procedure, S. 40; Order V Nr. 2, XXI Nr. 1, XXII Nr. 1 Supreme Court Rules 2013“.

506 Art. 124 (2) der indischen Verfassung; Gandhi, B.M., Kulshreshtha's Landmarks, S. 231; Hamid, S. 170; Srikrishna, in: Choudhry/Khosla/Mehta, The Oxford Handbook of the Indian Constitution, S. 349 (352).

507 Art. 124 (3) der indischen Verfassung.

ten oder wegen Unfähigkeit der Ausübung des Richteramtes mittels einer zweidrittel Mehrheit[508] beider Kammern des Parlaments durch den Präsidenten aus ihrem Amt entlassen werden.[509] Ist ein Richter aus seinem Amt ausgeschieden, ist es ihm oder ihr nicht gestattet, vor staatlichen Gerichten oder Behörden anwaltlich aufzutreten. Hierdurch sollen die Unabhängigkeit und die Neutralität des obersten Gerichtshofs gewahrt bleiben.[510] Ehemalige Richter des Supreme Courts sind allerdings häufig als Schiedsrichter tätig.[511] Verfahrenssprache ist trotz einer Vielzahl von offiziellen Amtssprachen ausschließlich Englisch.[512]

Der Chief Justice of India verdient 100.000 Rupien (ca. 1.340 Euro) im Monat. Das monatliche Salär eines Richters des Supreme Courts beträgt 90.000 Rupien (ca. 1.200 Euro). Der indische Staat stellt allen Richtern des obersten Gerichtshofs neben ihrem Monatseinkommen eine steuerfreie Aufwandsentschädigung[513], einen Dienstwagen und eine kostenlose, möblierte Unterkunft zur Verfügung.[514] Die Vergütung der obersten indischen Richter ist im Vergleich zu der Anwaltsvergütung gering. Ein vor dem Supreme Court auftretender Anwalt kann für eine einzige Verhandlung ein Honorar von 400.000 Rupien (ca. 5.090 Euro) bis zu 10.000 US-Dollar (ca. 8.247 Euro) verdienen.[515]

aa) Zuständigkeiten

(1) Originäre Zuständigkeit

Die ausschließliche originäre Zuständigkeit des Supreme Courts umfasst föderale Streitigkeiten zwischen dem indischen Staat[516] und den Bundes-

---

508 Erforderlich ist die zweidrittel Mehrheit der anwesenden Abgeordneten.

509 Art. 124 (4) der indischen Verfassung; Gandhi, B. M., Kulshreshtha's Landmarks, S. 232; Hamid, S. 169.

510 Supreme Court of India, History, verfügbar unter https://www.supremecourtofindia.nic.in/history (zuletzt abgerufen am 28.4.2021).

511 Delhi International Arbitration Centre (DIAC), DIAC Panel of Arbitrators, verfügbar unter http://www.dacdelhi.org/topics.aspx?mid=20 (zuletzt abgerufen am 28.4.2021); Indian Council of Arbitration (ICA), Arbitrators, Judges, verfügbar unter http://www.icaindia.co.in/htm/1302/Judges.pdf (zuletzt abgerufen am 28.4.2021).

512 Art. 348 (1) der indischen Verfassung.

513 Chief Justice 20.000 Rupien (ca. 270 Euro), Richter 15.000 Rupien (ca. 200 Euro).

514 Ministry of Law and Justice, Department of Justice, Act and Rules Governing the Service Conditions of Supreme Court Judges (As on 5th April, 2016), verfügbar unter http://doj.gov.in/sites/default/files/SC.pdf (zuletzt abgerufen am 28.4.2021).

515 Robinson, in: Choudhry/Khosla/Mehta, The Oxford Handbook of the Indian Constitution, S. 330 (348). *Robinson* beziffert das Anwaltshonorar auf 10.000 US-Dollar, Robinson, The American Journal of Comparative Law 2013, Vol. 61, S. 173 (183 f.).

516 Der Supreme Court ist auch für Streitigkeiten zwischen dem indischen Staat und einem oder mehreren Bundesstaaten gegen einen oder mehrere Bundesstaaten zuständig.

staaten sowie zwischen den Bundestaaten.[517] Auch Streitigkeiten bei der Wahl des Präsidenten oder des Vize-Präsidenten fallen in die ausschließliche Zuständigkeit des obersten Bundesgerichts.[518] Des Weiteren ist es für die Durchsetzung der Grundrechte in Indien zuständig.[519] Bis zur Gesetzgebungsreform des Schiedsgesetzes aus dem Jahr 2015 war der Chief Justice des Supreme Courts bei internationalen Handelsschiedsverfahren für die Bestellung von Schiedsrichtern zuständig.[520] Die Novelle der Schiedsgesetzgebung übertrug diese Bestellungskompetenz dem Supreme Court.[521]

(2) Berufungszuständigkeit

Art. 137 der indischen Verfassung eröffnet dem Supreme Court die Kompetenz, eigene Urteile und eigene Beschlüsse[522] zu überprüfen.[523] Für die Berufung zum Supreme Court[524] ist eine Zulassung[525] des betreffenden High Courts notwendig.[526] Nach Art. 132 (1) und 133 (1) der indischen Verfassung ist die Berufung gegen eine gerichtliche Entscheidung[527] zuzulassen, wenn es sich entweder um eine zentrale juristische Frage hinsichtlich der Auslegung der indischen Verfassung oder um eine Rechtsfrage von grundsätzlicher Bedeutung[528] handelt.[529] Der Supreme Court kann die vom High

517 Siehe Art. 131 der indischen Verfassung; Agrawal, K. B., Procedure, S. 76; Vakil, in: Choudhry/Khosla/Mehta, The Oxford Handbook of the Indian Constitution, S. 367 (375).

518 Art. 71 der indischen Verfassung; Agrawal, K. B., Procedure, S. 76 f.; Gandhi, B. M., Kulshreshtha's Landmarks, S. 243.

519 Art. 32 der indischen Verfassung. Es handelt sich hierbei um eine konkurrierende Zuständigkeit, die High Courts sind gem. Art. 226 der indischen Verfassung ebenfalls für die Durchsetzung der Grundrechte zuständig, siehe Agrawal, K. B., Procedure, S. 77.

520 Sec. 11 (12) (b) a. F. SchiedsG; Supreme Court of India, Court, Jurisdiction, verfügbar unter http://supremecourtofindia.nic.in/history.htm (zuletzt abgerufen am 28.4.2021).

521 Sec. 11 SchiedsG n. F.

522 Engl. order. U. a. die Nichtverweisung an das schiedsgerichtliche Verfahren (Sec. 37 [1] [a], 50 [1] [a] SchiedsG), der einstweilige gerichtliche Rechtsschutz (Sec. 9, 37 [1] [b] SchiedsG), die gerichtliche Unterstützung bei der Beweisaufnahme (Sec. 27 SchiedsG), die Entscheidung über die Aufhebung (Sec. 37 [1] [c] SchiedsG) und die Nichtvollstreckung (Sec. 50 [1] [b] SchiedsG) eines Schiedsspruchs erfolgt durch Beschluss.

523 Basu, S. 301 f.

524 Die Berufungszuständigkeit ist in Art. 132–136 der indischen Verfassung geregelt.

525 Engl. certificate.

526 Art. 132 (1), 133 (1) der indischen Verfassung; Vakil, in: Choudhry/Khosla/Mehta, The Oxford Handbook of the Indian Constitution, S. 367 ff.

527 Hierzu zählen: Ein Urteil (engl. judgement), ein vollstreckbarer Titel (engl. decree) und ein bindender Beschluss (engl. final order).

528 Art. 133 (1) (a) der indischen Verfassung.

529 In Ermangelung einer anderslautenden gesetzlichen Regelung kann gem. Art. 133 (3) der indischen Verfassung gegen eine zivilrechtliche Entscheidung eines Einzelrichters des High Courts keine Berufung zum Supreme Court eingelegt werden.

Court zugelassene Berufung zurückweisen, sofern er der Auffassung ist, dass der High Court die Berufung zu Unrecht zugelassen hat.[530] Nimmt der oberste Gerichtshof Indiens die Berufung an, ist er bei dem Berufungsverfahren nicht auf die für die Zulassung der Berufung ausschlaggebende Frage beschränkt, es kann vielmehr eine umfassende Überprüfung der vorangegangenen Entscheidungen stattfinden.[531] Es steht ferner auch im Ermessen des Supreme Courts, eine sog. „Special Leave" (besondere Zulassung) zur Berufung gegen eine Entscheidung[532] eines indischen Gerichts oder Tribunals zuzulassen.[533]

(3) Beratende Zuständigkeit

Dem Supreme Court ist zudem eine beratende Zuständigkeit für Rechtsfragen eröffnet, die ihm gem. Art. 143 der indischen Verfassung vom Präsidenten von Indien vorgelegt werden.[534] Die Rechtsauffassung des Supreme Courts ist weder für den Präsidenten noch die indischen Gerichte bindend, faktisch entsteht jedoch eine gewisse Bindungswirkung.[535]

bb) Rechtliche Wirkung der Supreme Court Entscheidungen

Nach Art. 141 der indischen Verfassung sind die Urteile des Supreme Courts für alle Gerichte innerhalb Indiens bindend.[536] Der Supreme Court ist hinge-

---

530 Agrawal, K. B., Procedure, S. 78.

531 Supreme Court, *Addagada Raghavamma And Anr v Addagada Chenchamma And Anr*, 1964 AIR 136; 1964 SCR (2) 933, 9.4.1963; Art. 137 der indischen Verfassung.

532 Hierzu zählen ein Urteil (engl. judgement), ein vollstreckbarer Titel (engl. decree), eine gerichtliche Bestimmung (engl. determination), eine Verurteilung (engl. sentence) und ein Beschluss (engl. order).

533 Art. 136 der indischen Verfassung; Baxi, in: Choudhry/Khosla/Mehta, The Oxford Handbook of the Indian Constitution, S. 94 (97). Streitigkeiten mit Bezug zu den indischen Streitkräften („Armed Forces") sind von dieser „Special Leave" gem. Art. 136 (2) der indischen Verfassung ausgeschlossen.

534 Supreme Court of India, Court, Jurisdiction, verfügbar unter http://supremecourtofindia.nic.in/jurisdiction.htm (zuletzt abgerufen am 28.4.2021). Für weitere beratende Zuständigkeiten, siehe Supreme Court of India, Practice & Procedure, A Handbook of Information, S. 15, verfügbar unter http://supremecourtofindia.nic.in/handbook3rdedition.pdf (zuletzt abgerufen am 28.4.2021); Vakil, in: Choudhry/Khosla/Mehta, The Oxford Handbook of the Indian Constitution, S. 367 (367; 374).

535 Agrawal, K. B., Procedure, S. 77; Gandhi, B. M., Kulshreshtha's Landmarks, S. 237 f.; Supreme Court, Constitutional Bench, 5 Richter, (2001) 4 SCC 448; Appeal (civil) 6213 of 1997, 25.4.2001; Jain, M. P., Constitution, S. 290; Vakil, in: Choudhry/Khosla/Mehta, The Oxford Handbook of the Indian Constitution, S. 367 (374).

536 Agrawal, K. B., Procedure, S. 79; Gandhi, B. M., Kulshreshtha's Landmarks, S. 245 f.; Jain, M. P., Constitution, S. 286 ff.; Vakil, in: Choudhry/Khosla/Mehta, The Oxford Handbook of the Indian Constitution, S. 367 (378).

gen nicht an seine eigenen Entscheidungen gebunden, sondern ist frei, seine Rechtsprechung jederzeit zu ändern.[537] Ein Senat des obersten indischen Gerichts bleibt allerdings an die Entscheidung eines gleich großen oder größeren Senats gebunden. Der Supreme Court kann von der vorherigen Rechtsprechung nur abweichen, sofern die neue höchstrichterliche Entscheidung von einem größeren Senat bzw. einer größeren Constitutional Bench ergeht. Ein kleiner Senat kann bei einer von der bisherigen Rechtsprechung abweichenden Rechtsaufassung beim Chief Justice beantragen, dass die Rechtssache an einen größeren Senat oder an eine Constitutional Bench[538] verwiesen wird.[539] Bei der Zusammensetzung der Senate und der Einberufung einer Constitutional Bench hat der Chief Justice einen Ermessensspielraum.[540] Indische Gerichte folgen dem Präjudizsystem des Common Law, Bindungswirkung entfaltet die sog. *ratio decidendi*[541] der Entscheidung des Supreme Courts und nicht die gesamten Urteilsgründe.[542] Zudem sind *obiter dicta* des Supreme Courts für alle nachgeordneten gerichtlichen Instanzen bindend[543].[544] Die nachgeordneten Gerichte müssen bei zwei unterschiedlichen

537 Supreme Court, *The Bengal Immunity Company v The State of Bihar And Others*, AIR 1955 SC 661; (1955) 2 SCR 603, 628; Appeal (civil) 159 of 1953, 6.9.1955; Gandhi, B. M., Kulshreshtha's Landmarks, S. 246 f., 345; Jain, M. P., Constitution, S. 290.

538 Diese Constitutional Bench muss gegenüber der bisherigen höchstrichterlichen Rechtsprechung des Supreme Courts mit einer höheren Anzahl an Richter besetzt sein.

539 Supreme Court, *Central Board of Dawoodi Bohra v State of Maharashtra & Anr*, Writ Petition (civil) 740 of 1986; (2005) 2 SCC 673; AIR 2005 SC 752, 17.12.2004; Gandhi, B. M., Kulshreshtha's Landmarks, S. 247; Order VI Supreme Court Rules 2013; Supreme Court, Constitutional Bench, 5 Richter, *Union of India & Anr v Raghubir Singh (Dead) By Lrs Etc*, AIR 1989 SC 1933; [1989] 3 SCR 316, 16.5.1989; Supreme Court, *Union of India & Ors v Godfrey Philips India Ltd Etc*, AIR 1986 SC 806, 30.9.1985; Supreme Court, Constitutional Bench, 5 Richter, *Supreme Court Advocates-on-Record – Association and another v Union of India*, (2016) 5 SCC 1; Writ Petition (Civil) No. 13 of 2015, 16.10.2015; Jain, M. P., Constitution, S. 288 ff.; Robinson, in: Choudhry/Khosla/Mehta, The Oxford Handbook of the Indian Constitution, S. 330 (338).

540 Supreme Court, *Central Board of Dawoodi Bohra v State Of Maharashtra & Anr*, Writ Petition (civil) 740 of 1986; (2005) 2 SCC 673; AIR 2005 SC 752, 17.12.2004; Supreme Court, Constitutional Bench, 5 Richter, *Union of India & Anr v Raghubir Singh (Dead) By Lrs Etc,* AIR 1989 SC 1933; [1989] 3 SCR 316, 16.5.1989.

541 Tragende Entscheidungsgründe, die die nachgeordneten Instanzen bindend. Sie entsprechen der tragenden juristischen Begründung einer Gerichtsentscheidung im deutschen Recht.

542 Gandhi, B. M., Kulshreshtha's Landmarks, S. 246; Mittal, J. K., S. 204; Jain, M. P., Constitution, S. 286.

543 Es besteht aber keine absolute Bindungswirkung, siehe Mittal, J. K., S. 204; Basu, S. 474.

544 Supreme Court, *CIT v Messrs Vazir Sultan & Sons,* 1959 AIR 814; 1959 SCR Suppl. (2) 375, 20.3.1959; Orissa High Court, *Nalu Sahu And Anr v The State*, AIR 1965 Ori 7, 3.3.1964; Gandhi, B. M., Kulshreshtha's Landmarks, S. 246; Jain, M. P., Constitution, S. 287.

Entscheidungen des Supreme Courts derjenigen Entscheidung folgen, die der jeweils größere Senat erlassen hat.[545]

b) High Court

Neben dem Chief Justice des High Courts variiert die Anzahl von Richtern an den High Courts.[546] Die Anzahl der Richter orientiert sich an den Verfahrenszahlen und am Zuständigkeitsgebiet des jeweiligen High Courts.[547] Der Präsident ernennt die Richter und den Chief Justice.[548] Der High Court ist unterteilt in Einzelrichter und Senate, den „Divisional Judges Benches (Division Bench)“, die aus zwei Richtern bestehen und den „Full Benches“, die aus drei oder mehr Richtern bestehen. Die Konstituierung der Senate obliegt dem Chief Justice des jeweiligen High Courts. Den Senaten ist die Zuständigkeit für spezifische Rechtsmaterien zugeteilt. Besonders eilbedürftige Rechtssachen werden von den Richtern in der sog. „Lunch Session“ verhandelt.[549] Die High Courts sind das oberste bundesstaatliche Gericht. In Indien gibt es gegenwärtig 18 High Courts.[550] Die Richter des High Courts können wie die Richter des Supreme Courts aus ihrem Amt entlassen werden. Einzig indische Staatsbürger mit jeweils 10-jähriger Erfahrung als Anwalt an einem High Court oder als Richter können Richter am High Court werden. [551] Nach Art. 226 der indischen Verfassung hat der High Court eine „Write“-Zuständigkeit zum Schutz der Grundrechte[552] und für jeden anderen Zweck[553].[554]

545 Vgl. *Central Board of Dawoodi Bohra v State of Maharashtra & Anr*, Writ Petition (civil) 740 of 1986; (2005) 2 SCC 673; 2005 SCC (Cri) 546; AIR 2005 SC 752, 17.12.2004; Supreme Court, Constitutional Bench, 5 Richter, *Union of India & Anr v Raghubir Singh (Dead) By Lrs Etc*, AIR 1989 SC 1933; [1989] 3 SCR 316, 16.5.1989; Supreme Court, Constitutional Bench, 5 Richter, *Bharat Petroleum Corporation Ltd v Mumbai Shramik Sangha And Ors,* Appeal (civil) 6213 of 1997, 25.4.2011.

546 Art. 216 der indischen Verfassung.

547 Agrawal, K. B., Procedure, S. 40; Jain, M. P., Constitution, S. 380.

548 Art. 216 f. der indischen Verfassung.

549 Agrawal, K. B., Procedure, S. 40; Jain, M. P., Constitution, S. 380.

550 Indian Courts, Indian Judiciary, verfügbar unter http://indiancourts.nic.in/ (zuletzt abgerufen am 28.4.2021).

551 Art. 217 der indischen Verfassung; Indian Courts, Indian Judiciary, High Courts, verfügbar unter http://indiancourts.nic.in/ (zuletzt abgerufen am 28.4.2021).

552 Beim Grundrechtsschutz handelt es sich um eine konkurrierende Zuständigkeit, die der High Court zusammen mit dem Supreme Court ausübt, siehe Art. 226 (4), 32 der indischen Verfassung.

553 Insbesondere bei Rechtsverletzungen.

554 Basu, S. 377 ff.; Jain, M. P., Constitution, S. 403 ff.; Hamid, S. 168; Indian Courts, Indian Judiciary, verfügbar unter http://indiancourts.nic.in/ (zuletzt abgerufen am 28.4.2021).

Zudem überwacht der High Court alle Gerichte in seinem territorialen Zuständigkeitsbereich.[555]

Das monatliche Gehalt eines Chief Justice des High Courts beträgt 90.000 Rupien (ca. 1.200 Euro) und das monatliche Salär eines High Court Richters beträgt 80.000 Rupien (ca. 1.070 Euro). Neben dem monatlichen Salär erhalten die Richter eine steuerfreie Aufwandsentschädigung[556], einen Dienstwagen und eine kostenlose möblierte Wohnung.[557]

Die Zuständigkeit des Chief Justice eines High Courts für die Schiedsrichterbestellung inländischer Schiedsverfahren (inländische und internationale nicht handelsrechtliche Schiedsverfahren[558]) übertrug die Schiedsgesetzgebungsreform im Jahr 2015 dem High Court.[559] Nach der Reform der indischen Schiedslegislation im Jahr 2015 ist der High Court ferner für alle Gerichtsverfahren mit Bezug zu internationalen Handelsschiedsverfahren erstinstanzlich zuständig.[560]

c) District Court

Hierarchisch den High Courts untergeordnet sind die „District Courts".[561] Den District Courts sind wiederum verschiedene Gerichte nachgeordnet[562].

---

555 Art. 227 der indischen Verfassung; Indian Courts, Indian Judiciary, High Courts, verfügbar unter http://indiancourts.nic.in/ (zuletzt abgerufen am 28.4.2021); Hamid, S. 168.

556 Diese beträgt für den Chief Justice 15.000 Rupien (ca. 200 Euro) und 12.000 Rupien (ca. 160 Euro) für die anderen Richter des High Courts.

557 Ministry of Law and Justice, Department of Justice, Acts and Rules, Salaries-Service Conditions, The Act and Rules Governing the Service Conditions of High Court Judges (As modified upto 5th April, 2016) verfügbar unter http://doj.gov.in/sites/default/files/HC.pdf (zuletzt abgerufen am 28.4.2021). Zu der im Verhältnis zu den Anwaltshonoraren geringen Vergütung der Richter, vgl. Kapitel: Supreme Court (A.III.4.a)).

558 Der Begriff inländische Schiedssprüche wird verwendet, da die Anzahl der internationalen Nichthandelsschiedsverfahren gering ist.

559 Sec. 11 (12) (b) a. F. SchiedsG und Sec. 11 SchiedsG n. F.

560 Sec. 2 (1) (e) (ii) SchiedsG n. F.

561 Siehe Sec. 3 „Code of Civil Procedure 1908"; Art. 235 der indischen Verfassung; India Courts, District Courts, verfügbar unter http://indiancourts.nic.in/districtcourt.html (zuletzt abgerufen am 28.4.2021); Robinson, in: Choudhry/Khosla/Mehta, The Oxford Handbook of the Indian Constitution, S. 330 (333 f.).

562 Sec. 3 Code of Civil Procedure 1908; Jayasimha/Mody, in: Moser/Choong (Hrsg.), Asia Arbitration Handbook, S. 843 (845); Agrawal, K. B., Procedure, S. 41; Singhania & Partners LLP, Solicitors and Advocates, India: Civil Courts System, verfügbar unter http://www.mondaq.com/ac/content.asp?content_id=2808&email_access=on (zuletzt abgerufen am 28.4.2021); India Courts, District Courts, verfügbar unter http://indiancourts.nic.in/districtcourt.html (zuletzt abgerufen am 28.4.2021); Agrawal, K. B., Procedure, S. 37; Hamid, S. 170 f.; Robinson, in: Choudhry/Khosla/Mehta, The Oxford Handbook of the Indian Constitution, S. 330 (333 ff.). Nishith Desai, Do-

Letztere sind für Schiedsverfahren nicht zuständig.[563] Die District Courts bestehen aus einem oder mehreren Richtern.[564] Der District Court konnte nach Sec. 2 (1) (e) a. F. SchiedsG im Rahmen seiner originären Zuständigkeit für alle Schiedsverfahren erstinstanzlich zuständig sein.[565] Nach der Novelle des SchiedsG aus dem Jahr 2015 kann der District Court nach Sec. 2 (1) (e) SchiedsG n. F. lediglich für inländische Schiedsverfahren[566] in erster Instanz zuständig sein.[567]

d) Instanzenzug

In Indien gibt es folgende Gerichtsinstanzen:

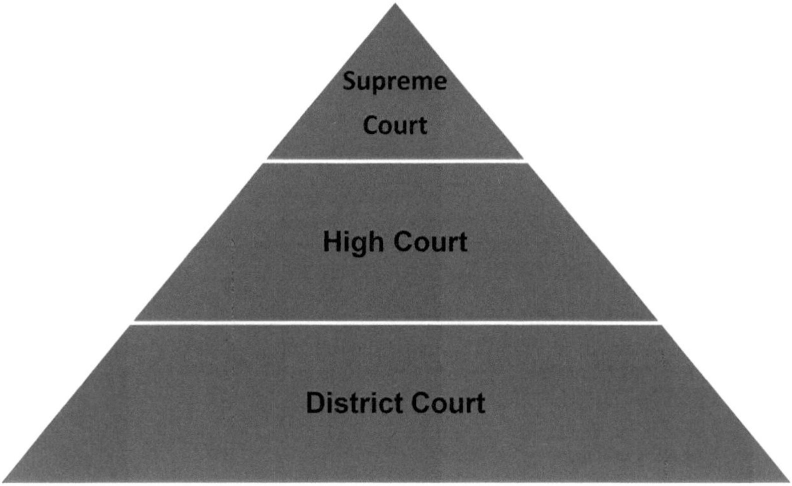

ing Business in India, S. 4, verfügbar unter http://www.nishithdesai.com/fileadmin/user_upload/pdfs/Research%20Papers/Doing_Business_in_India.pdf (zuletzt abgerufen am 28.4.2021). Dem District Court ist in zivilrechtlichen Verfahren der „Court of Civil Judge“ nachgeordnet und diesem ist wiederum der „Civil Judge“ nachrangig, Indian Courts, District Courts, verfügbar unter http://indiancourts.nic.in/districtcourt.html# (zuletzt abgerufen am 28.4.2021).

563 Die dem District Court untergeordneten Gerichte haben allerdings auf Antrag einer Partei gem. Sec. 8 SchiedsG von einer Schiedsvereinbarung erfasste Streitigkeiten an das Schiedsverfahren zu verweisen.

564 Agrawal, K. B., Procedure, S. 41.

565 Law Commission of India, 176. Report, The Arbitration and Conciliation (Amendment) Bill, 2001, 12.9.2001, S. 19 f.

566 Inländische und internationale nicht handelsrechtliche Schiedsverfahren.

567 Für die Schiedsrichterbestellung ist gem. Sec. 11 SchiedsG n. F. der High Court bzw. der Supreme Court ausschließlich zuständig.

5. Verfahrenszahlen

Die strukturellen Probleme des indischen Gerichtssystems sollen durch einen Vergleich der Verfahrensstatistiken (zivilrechtliche und strafrechtliche Klagen) in den Jahren 2007 und 2012 (fünf Jahreszeitraum) veranschaulicht werden:

2007[568]

	Eingereichte Verfahren	Erlassene Entscheidungen	Erledigte Verfahren	Anhängige Verfahren Ende 2007	Verfahren pro 100.000 Einwohner[569]
Supreme Court	69.103	61.957	90%	46.926	6,1
High Court	1.568.475	1.450.996	93%	3.743.060	139
Untere Instanzen	15.164.847	14.913.900	98%	25.418.165	1.340

2012[570]

	Eingereichte Verfahren	Erlassene Entscheidungen	Erledigte Verfahren	Anhängige Verfahren Ende 2012	Verfahren pro 100.000 Einwohner[571]
Supreme Court	76.917	68.744	89%	66.692	6,1
High Court	1.913.761	1.791.391	94%	4.436.915	152
Untere Instanzen	18.120.280	18.156.554	100%	26.951.461	1.438

568 Supreme Court of India, Court News, 2007 Vol. II Issue No. 1, 2, 3 & 4, 2008 Vol. III Issue No. 1, verfügbar unter http://supremecourtofindia.nic.in/courtnews.htm (zuletzt abgerufen am 28.4.2021).

569 Indien hatte 2007 1,1319 Mrd. Einwohner, siehe Population Reference Bureau, 2007 World Population, Data Sheet, S. 9, verfügbar unter http://www.prb.org/pdf07/07wpds_eng.pdf (zuletzt abgerufen am 28.4.2021).

570 Supreme Court of India, Court News, 2012 Vol. III Issue Nos. 1, 2, 3 & 4 und 2013 Vol. VIII Issue No. 1, verfügbar unter http://supremecourtofindia.nic.in/courtnews.htm (zuletzt abgerufen am 28.4.2021).

571 Indien beheimatete 2012 1,2597 Mrd. Einwohner, siehe Population Reference Bureau, 2012 World Population, Data Sheet, S. 8, verfügbar unter http://www.prb.org/pdf12/2012-population-data-sheet_eng.pdf (zuletzt abgerufen am 28.4.2021).

Vor dem „Supreme Court of India" wurden im Jahr 2012 76.917 Verfahren eingereicht. Im selben Jahr wurden 1.913.761 Verfahren vor den High Courts und 18.120.280 Klagen bei den Gerichten der unteren Instanzen anhängig gemacht. Allein diese hohe Verfahrensanzahl macht deutlich, dass es schwierig ist, dieses hohe Pensum an Verfahren zeitnah zu bewältigen.

In dem hier untersuchten fünfjährigen Zeitfenster[572] ist die Zahl der aufgestauten Zivilrechts- und Strafrechtsverfahren beträchtlich angestiegen. In lediglich fünf Jahren schwoll die Anzahl der sich am Ende des Kalenderjahres angestauten Gerichtsverfahren vor dem Supreme Court um 19.766 (42%) Verfahren an. Die vor den High Courts angestauten Verfahren erhöhten sich um 693.855 Gerichtsverfahren (19%). Bei den, dem High Court nachgeordneten Gerichten, nahm die Zahl der angestauten Verfahren um 1.533.296 (6%) zu. Die Statistik zeigt, dass es den indischen Gerichten auf keiner Ebenen gelungen ist, den Rückstau von Gerichtsverfahren zu stoppen oder die Anzahl der rechtshängigen Verfahren nachhaltig abzubauen. Dies hängt v.a. mit dem stetigen Anstieg von Verfahren vor staatlichen Gerichten zusammen. Von 2008 bis 2012 erhöhte sich die Anzahl der neu eingereichten Verfahren vor dem Supreme Court um 7.814 Verfahren (11%), vor den High Courts wuchs die Zahl der neuen Gerichtsverfahren um 345.286 (22%) und vor den unteren Instanzen stieg die Zahl der neu initiierten Verfahren um 2.955.433 (19%) an. Auch die Anzahl der Gerichtsverfahren im Verhältnis zu je 100.000 Einwohnern ist stetig gestiegen. Vor dem Supreme Court nahmen die Verfahren in diesen fünf Jahren pro 100.000 Einwohner marginal um 0,015% zu, vor dem High Court erhöhte sich die Verfahrensanzahl um 13 Verfahren (9,6%) und vor den unteren Instanzen um 98 Verfahren (7,4%) je 100.000 Einwohner. Das permanente Anwachsen von rechtshängigen Verfahren demonstriert die Überlastung des indischen Gerichtssystems, auch verursacht durch das fortlaufende Bevölkerungswachstum und den wirtschaftlichen Aufschwung. Die geringe Anzahl an Richtern[573] in Indien ist mit der hohen Anzahl an Verfahren überfordert. Im Verhältnis zu seiner Einwohnerzahl entfallen in Indien auf eine Millionen Einwohner 12–13 Richter, in hochentwickelten Ländern gibt es hingegen 40–100 Richter pro eine Million Einwohner.[574] Die Unterbesetzung der indischen Gerichte, das steigende Bildungsniveau der

---

572 Von Ende des Jahres 2007 bis Ende des Jahres 2012.

573 Zur Unterbesetzung der indischen Gerichte, Robinson, in: Choudhry/Khosla/Mehta, The Oxford Handbook of the Indian Constitution, S. 330 (336).

574 Singh, Mohinder/Kumar, Suresh, Asian Journal of Multidimensional Research 2014, Vol. 3, Ausg. 5, S. 7 (8). Mit leicht abweichenden Zahlen, Kachwaha, International Arbitration Law Review 2007, S. 13; Dewan, Nakul, Asian International Arbitration Journal 2007, Vol. 3, Ausg. 1, S. 99 (122); vgl. Robinson, Too Many Cases, Frontline, Vol. 26, Ausg. 1, 3.–16. Januar 2009, verfügbar unter http://www.frontline.in/static/html/fl2601/stories/20090116260108100.htm (zuletzt abgerufen am 28.4.2021).

indischen Staatsbürger und das Wirtschafts[575]- und Bevölkerungswachstum wird die Zahl der Gerichtsverfahren in Zukunft weiter ansteigen lassen[576].[577]

Der „Doing Business“ Bericht der Weltbank untersucht die gerichtliche Durchsetzung von inländischen Handelsstreitigkeiten und kam zu der Konklusion, dass in Indien sowohl die Dauer eines Gerichtsverfahrens als auch die Verfahrenskosten erheblich über dem Durchschnitt in Südostasien liegen. Die Qualität der gerichtlichen und alternativen Streitbeilegung in Mumbai und Delhi bewertete der Bericht mit 7,5 von möglichen 18 Punkten als unterdurchschnittlich. Entsprechend belegt die Durchsetzung von Handelsstreitigkeiten in Indien die ungenügende Position 172 von 190 untersuchen Gerichtssystemen. Der Doing Business Bericht offenbart schonungslos die unzureichende Qualität des indischen Gerichtsapparats: Es existiere kein effektives Verfahrensmanagement, die Automatisierung des Verfahrensablaufs sei verbesserungsbedürftig, die Verfahren dauerten zu lange und seien zu kostspielig.[578] Auch nach dem „Rule of Law Index 2016“ des „World Justice Project“ befindet sich die indische Zivilgerichtsbarkeit mit Platz 93 von 113 untersuchten Ländern im hinteren Drittel der bewerteten nationalen Zivilgerichte.[579]

575 Zum weiteren Anstieg der Verfahrensanzahlen durch weiteres wirtschaftliches Wachstum, Robinson, in: Choudhry/Khosla/Mehta, The Oxford Handbook of the Indian Constitution, S. 330 (336).

576 Seit der Unabhängigkeit Indiens wuchsen die Verfahrenszahlen kontinuierlich an, Thiruvengadam, in: Choudhry/Khosla/Mehta, The Oxford Handbook of the Indian Constitution, S. 412 (413 f.); vgl. Nick Robinson, Hard to Reach, Frontline, Vol. 27, Ausg. 3, 30.1.–12.2.2010, verfügbar unter https://www.frontline.in/static/html/fl2703/stories/20100212270304600.htm (zuletzt abgerufen am 28.4.2021); vgl. Robinson, The American Journal of Comparative Law 2013, Vol. 61, S. 173 (180 f.).

577 Chief Justice Shri K. G. Balakrishnan, Address by Hon’ble Shri K. G. Balakrishnan, Chief Justice of India, at the Joint Conference of Chief Ministers and Chief Justices, at Vigyan Bhawan, 8. 4.2007, verfügbar unter http://www.supremecourtofindia.nic.in/speeches/speeches_2007/8.4.2007.pdf (zuletzt abgerufen am 28.4.2021); Eisenberg/Kalantry/Robinson, DePaul Law Review 2013, Vol. 62, Ausg. 2, S. 247 (289 ff.).

578 World Bank Group, Doing Business 2017, Equal Opportunity for All, 14. Aufl., Economy Profile 2017, India, S. 124 ff., verfügbar unter http://www.doingbusiness.org/~/media/wbg/doingbusiness/documents/profiles/country/ind.pdf (zuletzt abgerufen am 28.4.2021). Kritisch zu den Doing Business Reports der Weltbank, Kern, Juristenzeitung 2009, S. 498 ff.

579 World Justice Project, Rule of Law Index 2016, S. 40 f., verfügbar unter https://worldjusticeproject.org/sites/default/files/documents/RoLI_Final-Digital_0.pdf (zuletzt abgerufen am 28.4.2021). Das Weltwirtschaftsforum bewertete 2016–2017 die Beilegung von Unternehmensstreitigkeiten mit Platz 16 von 138 untersuchten Ländern positiver, The World Economic Forum, The Global Competitiveness Report 2016–2017, S. 203, verfügbar unter http://www3.weforum.org/docs/GCR2016-2017/05FullReport/TheGlobalCompetitivenessReport2016-2017_FINAL.pdf (zuletzt abgerufen am 28.4.2021).

In diesem Kontext ist es von entscheidendem Vorteil, dass ein Schiedsverfahren meist schneller und günstiger ist als ein Verfahren vor den indischen Gerichten, weil die Anzahl von gerichtlichen Interventionsmöglichkeiten und Berufungen in Schiedsverfahren begrenzt ist.[580]

6. Strukturelle Probleme der indischen Gerichte

Die „Law Commission of India" (Im Folgenden Law Commission) kritisierte in ihrem 120., 245., 246. und 253. Report die durch die zu geringe Anzahl an Richtern verursachte Überlastung des indischen Gerichtssystems.[581] Im 245. Report weist die Law Commission darauf hin, dass die unterbesetzten indischen Gerichte die aufgestauten Verfahren nicht abbauen und neue eingereichte Gerichtsverfahren nicht schnell genug entscheiden können.[582] Mit einem Gerichtssystem, das zu kollabieren drohe, verletze der indische Staat seine rechtsstaatlichen Verpflichtungen einer effektiven gerichtlichen Streitbeilegung und verstoße gegen den in der indischen Verfassung verankerten Justizgewährungsanspruch[583].[584] Schon 1987 postulierte die indische Law Commission in ihrem 120. Report, das Verhältnis der Richter zu je einer Millionen Einwohner von 10,5 auf mindestens 50 zu erhöhen.[585]

580 Parliament of India, Rajya Sabha, Department Related Parliamentary Standing Committee on Personnel, Public Grievance, Law and Justice, Ninth Report on the Arbitration and Conciliation (Amendment) Bill, 2003, in: Ministry of Law and Justice, Government of India, Proposed Amendments to the Arbitration & Conciliation Act, 1996, A Consultation Paper, Annex V, S. 138, verfügbar unter http://lawmin.nic.in/la/consultationpaper.pdf (zuletzt abgerufen am 28.4.2021). 2017/05FullReport/TheGlobalCompetitivenessReport2016-2017_FINAL.pdf (zuletzt abgerufen am 28.4.2021).

581 Law Commission of India, 120. Report, Manpower Planning in Judiciary: A Blueprint, Juli 1987, S. 1 ff.; Government of India, Law Commission of India, 245. Report, Arrear and Backlog: Creating Additional Judicial (wo)manpower, 7.7.2014, S. 44 ff.; Government of India, Law Commission of India, 246. Report, Amendments to the Arbitration and Conciliation Act 1996, 5.8.2014, S. 1, 8, 15 f.; Government of India, Law Commission of India, 253. Report, Commercial Division and Commercial Appellate Division of High Courts and Commercial Courts Bill, 2015, 29.1.2015, S. 16 ff.

582 Zu der Unterbesetzung der indischen Gerichte und den angestauten Verfahren, siehe auch Robinson, in: Choudhry/Khosla/Mehta, The Oxford Handbook of the Indian Constitution, S. 330 (336). Zu den aufgestauten Verfahren und Verzögerungen, Subramanium, in: Choudhry/Khosla/Mehta, The Oxford Handbook of the Indian Constitution, S. 614 (626); Thiruvengadam, in: Choudhry/Khosla/Mehta, The Oxford Handbook of the Indian Constitution, S. 412 ff.; Eisenberg/Kalantry/Robinson, DePaul Law Review 2013, Vol. 62, Ausg. 2, S. 247 (248 ff.).

583 Engl. access to justice.

584 Government of India, Law Commission of India, 245. Report, Arrear and Backlog: Creating Additional Judicial (wo)manpower, S. 1.

585 Law Commission of India, 120. Report, Manpower Planning in Judiciary: A Blueprint, Juli 1987, S. 3.

Dieser Empfehlung ist der indische Staat nicht gefolgt. Im Jahr 2001 ordnete das oberste indische Gericht daher im *All India Judges Association And v Union of India*[586]-Urteil an, dass die Anzahl der Richterstellen von 10,5–13 Richtern im Verhältnis zu einer Million Bürger auf 50 Richter aufzustocken sei. Ein unabhängiges und effektives Gerichtssystem stelle einen Grundpfeiler der indischen Verfassung dar und sei essentiell, um die hohe Anzahl an zurückgestauten Verfahren[587] abzubauen und für die indische Bevölkerung einen effektiven Rechtsschutz zu verbürgen.[588]

Der 245. und der 253. Report der Law Commission erneuerte 2014 bzw. 2015 diese Forderung nach einer erheblichen Aufstockung der Richterstellen an den indischen Gerichten, um die große Zahl an rechtshängigen Gerichtsverfahren reduzieren zu können[589] und zügige Gerichtsverfahren zu gewährleisten.[590]

Auch der Supreme Court monierte 2012 im Urteil *Imtiyaz Ahmad v State of UP & Ors*[591] die lange Verfahrensdauer in Indien und verwies darauf, dass der Justizgewährungsanspruch schnelle Gerichtsverfahren gebiete. Um dem Justizgewährungsanspruch[592] Rechnung zu tragen, fordert das oberste indische Gericht, dass in Indien zusätzliche Gerichte geschaffen werden müssen, um die Verzögerungen in indischen Gerichtsverfahren[593] zu eliminieren und ein schnelles und kostengünstigeres Gerichtssystem zu etablieren.[594]

Im Bezug zur Schiedsgerichtsbarkeit merkt die Law Commission in ihrem 246. Bericht an, dass sich die Schiedsverfahren zwei Jahrzehnte nach dem Inkrafttreten des SchiedsG 1996 hinsichtlich der hohen Kosten und der lan-

586 3 Richter, AIR 2002 SC 1752; (2002) 4 SCC 247, 8.2.2001.

587 Zu den zurückgestauten Verfahren siehe auch, Subramanium, in: Choudhry/Khosla/Mehta, The Oxford Handbook of the Indian Constitution, S. 614 (626); Thiruvengadam, in: Choudhry/Khosla/Mehta, The Oxford Handbook of the Indian Constitution, S. 412 ff.; Eisenberg/Kalantry/Robinson, DePaul Law Review 2013, Vol. 62, Ausg. 2, S. 247 (248 ff.).

588 Rn. 24.

589 Vgl. zu der geringen Richteranzahl und der hohen Anzahl an Gerichtsverfahren, Kapitel: Strukturelle Probleme der indischen Gerichte (A.III.6.).

590 Government of India, Law Commission of India, 245. Report, Arrear and Backlog: Creating Additional Judicial (wo)manpower, 7.7.2014, S. 44 ff.; Government of India, Law Commission of India, 253. Report, Commercial Division and Commercial Appellate Division of High Courts and Commercial Courts Bill, 2015, 29.1.2015, S. 16 ff.

591 AIR SC 2012 642; Criminal Appeal Nos. 254–262 of 2012, 1.2.2012.

592 Engl. access to justice.

593 Zu den Verfahrensverzögerungen, siehe auch Subramanium, in: Choudhry/Khosla/Mehta, The Oxford Handbook of the Indian Constitution, S. 614 (626); Thiruvengadam, in: Choudhry/Khosla/Mehta, The Oxford Handbook of the Indian Constitution, S. 412 ff.; Eisenberg/Kalantry/Robinson, DePaul Law Review 2013, Vol. 62, Ausg. 2, S. 247 (248 ff.).

594 Rn. 61.

gen Verfahrensdauer[595] den indischen Gerichtsverfahren angeglichen hätten und dies zu einer Rechtslage geführt habe, die mit der Situation unter dem Schiedsgesetz des Jahres 1940 vergleichbar sei. Bei Verfahren, in denen die indischen Gerichte Schiedsverfahren unterstützen oder kontrollieren sollen, besteht nach der Law Commission die Gefahr, im ineffizienten und überlasteten indischen Gerichtssystem lange Zeit rechtshängig zu sein[596]. Solche Verzögerungen widersprächen dem Charakter der Schiedsgerichtsbarkeit als schnellem Streitbeilegungsmechanismus. Die Law Commission sieht in den vom Delhi High Court eingeführten auf Schiedsverfahren spezialisierten Senaten, durch die die Verfahrensdauern verkürzt werden konnten, ein Vorbild für die Umstrukturierung des indischen Gerichtssystems. Die Verzögerungen in Gerichtsverfahren mit Schiedsbezug führt die Law Commission auf die fehlenden auf Schiedsverfahren spezialisierten Kammern bzw. Senate im indischen Gerichtssystem zurück.[597]

Das fehlende Vertrauen der Parteien und der oberen indischen Gerichte in die nachgeordnete Gerichtsbarkeit führe ferner zu einem sich kontinuierlich erhöhenden Aufkommen von Berufungsverfahren.[598]

a) Kostensanktionen

Das SchiedsG 1996 a.F. enthielt keine Kostenregelung für Gerichtsverfahren im Zusammenhang mit Schiedsverfahren. Nach Sec. 35 „Civil Procedure Code 1908“ steht die Verfahrenskostenverteilung unter den Parteien im Ermessen des entscheidenden Gerichts. Wenn es die Kosten allerdings nicht der unterlegenen Partei auferlegt, unterliegt das Gericht einer Begründungspflicht.[599] Aus Sec. 35 Civil Procedure Code 1908 lässt sich daher entneh-

595 Siehe auch Law Commission of India, 176. Report, The Arbitration and Conciliation (Amendment) Bill, 2001, 12.9.2001, S. 16, 67 f., 124.

596 Siehe auch Subramanium, in: Choudhry/Khosla/Mehta, The Oxford Handbook of the Indian Constitution, S. 614 (626); Thiruvengadam, in: Choudhry/Khosla/Mehta, The Oxford Handbook of the Indian Constitution, S. 412 ff.; Eisenberg/Kalantry/Robinson, DePaul Law Review 2013, Vol. 62, Ausg. 2, S. 247 (248 ff.).

597 Government of India, Law Commission of India, 246. Report, Amendments to the Arbitration and Conciliation Act 1996, 5.8.2014, S. 1, 8, 15 f.

598 Robinson, in: Choudhry/Khosla/Mehta, The Oxford Handbook of the Indian Constitution, S. 330 (331 f.). Zum fehlenden Vertrauen in die nachgeordneten Gerichtsinstanzen, Nick Robinson, Too Many Cases, Frontline, Vol. 26, Ausg. 1, 3.–16. Januar 2009, verfügbar unter http://www.frontline.in/static/html/fl2601/stories/20090116260108100.htm (zuletzt abgerufen am 28.4.2021).

599 Nach Sec. 35A Civil Procedure Code können schikanöse, unrichtige erstinstanzliche Klagen und Klageerwiderungen sanktioniert werden. Die Höhe der Sanktion ist aber auf 3.000 Rupien (ca. 40 Euro) begrenzt. Auf Berufungs- und Revisionsverfahren ist Sec. 35A Civil Procedure Code 1908 nicht anwendbar. Bei Verzögerungen eines Gerichtsverfahrens kann das Gericht gem. Sec. 35B Civil Procedure Code der betrof-

men, dass die Verfahrenskosten grundsätzlich von der unterlegenen Partei zu tragen sind. Dies spiegelt aber nicht die Praxis der gerichtlich ausgesprochenen Verfahrenskostenverteilung wider.[600] Der Supreme Court monierte in der Rechtssache *Salem Advocate Bar Association, Tamil Nadu v Union of India*[601], dass die Verfahrenskosten nach gerichtlichem Ermessen festgesetzt werden. Die Gerichte würden erfahrungsgemäß entscheiden, dass nicht die unterlegene Partei die tatsächlichen Verfahrenskosten zu bezahlen habe, sondern dass beide Parteien ihre Verfahrenskosten selbst tragen müssten, obschon dies nicht Sec. 35 (2) Civil Procedure Code 1908 entspreche. Nach dem obersten indischen Gericht bewirke dies, dass skrupellose Parteien ohne Kostenrisiko unbegründete Gerichtsverfahren initiierten bzw. nicht substantiierte Klageerwiderungen einreichten.

Die Law Commission ist in ihrem 253. Report ebenfalls zu dem Ergebnis gekommen, dass der im Gerichtsverfahren nicht obsiegenden Partei selten die tatsächlichen Verfahrenskosten der obsiegenden Partei auferlegt werden. Die nicht sanktionierten Verzögerungstaktiken der Parteien führten im Zusammenspiel mit der Bezahlung der Anwälte auf Honorarbasis zu häufigen Vertagungen der Gerichtsverfahren. Diese Vertagungspraxis führe zu einer überlangen Dauer von Gerichtsverfahren.[602]

Die fehlenden Kostenanreize lassen sich auch empirisch belegen. In einer Studie von Berufungsverfahren[603] vor dem Supreme Court stellte *Srinivasan* fest, dass das oberste Gericht Indiens nur in 1,2 Prozent der Verfahren der unterlegenen Partei die Kosten des Verfahrens auferlegte.[604]

Die gerichtliche Praxis, der unterlegenen Partei nicht die tatsächlichen Kosten der obsiegenden Partei aufzuerlegen, wird auch in der Literatur mit dem Argument kritisiert, dass mangels Kostenauferlegung renitente Parteien aus

fenen Partei seine angemessenen Kosten gegenüber der das Gerichtsverfahren verschleppenden Partei zusprechen.

600 Prasad, B. M./Mohan, Mulla Code Procedure, Bd. 1, Sec. 35, S. 547; Supreme Court, *Salem Advocate Bar Association, Tamil Nadu v Union of India*, Writ Petition (civil) 496 of 2002, 2.8.2005; Supreme Court, *Ashok Kumar Mittal v Ram Kumar Gupta & Anr*, (2009) 2 SCC 656; Special Leave Petition [Civil] Nos. 30991–30992/20089, 9.1.2009.

601 Writ Petition (civil) 496 of 2002, 2.8.2005.

602 Government of India, Law Commission of India, 253. Report, Commercial Division and Commercial Appellate Division of High Courts and Commercial Courts Bill, 2015, 29.1.2015, S. 25; Baxi, in: Choudhry/Khosla/Mehta, The Oxford Handbook of the Indian Constitution, S. 94 (97).

603 *Srinivasan* untersuchte 83 Berufungsverfahren für die Bestellung von Schiedsrichtern (Sec. 11 SchiedsG).

604 Srinivasan, Indian Journal of Arbitration Law 2012, Vol. I, Ausg. 1, S. 18 (30).

strategischen Gründen unbegründete Gerichtsverfahren eingelegt hätten[605] und dass die Kostenentscheidungen des Supreme Courts nicht den hohen tatsächlichen Kosten entsprechen würden, die bei den komplexen Verfahren vor dem obersten indischen Gerichtshof anfielen.[606]

2014 konkludierte der Supreme Court in der Rechtssache *Subrata Roy Sahara v Uoi & Ors*[607], dass das indische Gerichtssystem unter der hohen Anzahl an ungerechtfertigten Klagen leide. Es sei daher erforderlich, Kläger von ihrer Besessenheit, sinnlose und unüberlegte Ansprüche geltend zu machen, abzuhalten. Dies begründete das oberste indische Gericht mit dem Argument, dass ansonsten der Beklagte unter den unbegründeten Gerichtsverfahren leiden müsse. Als Lösungsansatz für dieses Problem forderte der oberste Gerichtshof vom Gesetzgeber, dass die unterlegene Partei die Kosten für ein solches, sinnloses Gerichtsverfahren tragen müsse.[608]

Dieser Forderung ist der indische Gesetzgeber nachgekommen, die Verfahrenskosten in Schiedsverfahren und Gerichtsverfahren sind nach der Schiedsrechtsreform aus dem Jahre 2015 gem. Sec. 31A SchiedsG n.F. der unterlegenen Partei aufzuerlegen,[609] um Schiedsverfahren und das Gerichtssystem mittels wirtschaftlicher Anreize von unbegründeten Verfahren zu entlasten.[610] Die Kostenbestimmungen des Civil Procedure Codes 1908 klammerte der Gesetzgeber in Sec. 31A (1) SchiedsG aus.[611] Verzögerungstaktiken und unangemessenes Verhalten der Parteien können somit durch den neuen Sec. 31A SchiedsG auf Kostenebene sanktioniert werden.[612] Par-

605 Aditya Singh/Dipen Sabharwal, Arbitration and Conciliation (Amendment) Ordinance, 2015, A contribution by the ITA Board of Reporters, Kluwer Law International, verfügbar unter http://www.kluwerarbitration.com/CommonUI/document.aspx?id=kli-ka-15-49-003 (zuletzt abgerufen am 28.4.2021).

606 Srinivasan, Indian Journal of Arbitration Law 2012, Vol. I, Ausg. 1, S. 18 (30 f.).

607 Writ Petition (Criminal) No. 57 of 2014; (2014) 8 SCC 470, 6.5.2014.

608 Supreme Court, *Subrata Roy Sahara v Uoi & Ors*, Writ Petition (Criminal) No. 57 of 2014; (2014) 8 SCC 470, 6.5.2014, Rn. 150. Zustimmend 253. Report der Law Commission, Government of India, Law Commission of India, 253. Report, Commercial Division and Commercial Appellate Division of High Courts and Commercial Courts Bill, 2015, 29.1.2015, S. 25 f.

609 Sec. 31A SchiedsG n. F. Diese Rechtslage entspricht dem Wortlaut von Sec. 35 ff. Code of Civil Procedure 1908.

610 Government of India, Law Commission of India, 246. Report, Amendments to the Arbitration and Conciliation Act 1996, 5.8.2014, S. 34 f., 40 f.

611 Aditya Singh/Dipen Sabharwal, Arbitration and Conciliation (Amendment) Ordinance, 2015, A contribution by the ITA Board of Reporters, Kluwer Law International, verfügbar unter http://www.kluwerarbitration.com/CommonUI/document.aspx?id=kli-ka-15-49-003 (zuletzt abgerufen am 28.4.2021).

612 Aditya Singh/Dipen Sabharwal, Arbitration and Conciliation (Amendment) Ordinance, 2015, A contribution by the ITA Board of Reporters, Kluwer Law Interna-

allel zum Schiedsverfahren rechtshängig gemachte, unbegründete Gerichtsverfahren können durch die Gesetzesänderungen reduziert werden.

b) Reform des Gerichtssystems

Bereits im Jahr 2003 regte die Law Commission in ihrem 188. Report im Zuge der Liberalisierung und der fortschreitenden Globalisierung Indiens die Einführung von spezialisierten Handelsgerichten an, um dem schnell wachsenden Handel eine effektive und schnelle gerichtliche Streitbeilegung zu ermöglichen und investorenfreundliche Rahmenbedingungen[613] zu kreieren.[614] Ein auf dem 188. Report basierender Gesetzesentwurf ist 2009 nicht in Kraft getreten. [615] Im 253. Report der indischen Law Commission wurde 2015 vorgeschlagen, einen „Commercial Court" und eine „Commercial Division" in den High Courts zu etablieren, um durch eine schnelle und kostengünstige Beilegung von Handelsstreitigkeiten die weitere wirtschaftliche Entwicklung zu fördern, ausländische Investitionen anzuziehen und Indien hierdurch zu einem attraktiveren Handelsplatz zu machen.[616] Die Einführung der Handelsgerichtsbarkeit für Verfahren mit einem hohen Streitwert war nach der Law Commission notwendig, weil mangels einer ausreichenden Anzahl an Richtern die High Courts vollkommen überlastet seien und es daher zu langen Verzögerungen der Gerichtsverfahren komme.[617]

Im Dezember 2015[618] verabschiedete das indische Parlament den „Commercial Courts, Commercial Division and Commercial Appellate Division of

---

tional, verfügbar unter http://www.kluwerarbitration.com/CommonUI/document.aspx?id=kli-ka-15-49-003 (zuletzt abgerufen am 28.4.2021).

613 Die Law Commission weist darauf hin, dass amerikanische und englische Gerichte sich für zuständig erklärten, weil sie das indische Gerichtssystem als kollabiert ansahen.

614 Law Commission of India, 188. Report, Proposals for Constitution of Hi-Tech Fast – Track Commercial Divisions in High Courts, 15.12.2003, S. 2 ff.

615 Government of India, Law Commission of India, 253. Report, Commercial Division and Commercial Appellate Division of High Courts and Commercial Courts Bill, 2015, 29.1.2015, S. 3 ff.

616 Government of India, Law Commission of India, 253. Report, Commercial Division and Commercial Appellate Division of High Courts and Commercial Courts Bill, 2015, 29.1.2015, S. 52. Sathyapalan, Arbitration International 2016, S. 1 (15 f.).

617 Government of India, Law Commission of India, 253. Report, Commercial Division and Commercial Appellate Division of High Courts and Commercial Courts Bill, 2015, 29.1.2015, S. 16 ff.; vgl. o.

618 Bereits am 23. Oktober 2015 führte der indische Präsident mit der „Commercial Courts, Commercial Division and Commercial Appellate Division of High Courts Ordinance 2015" spezialisierte Handelsgerichte in das indische Gerichtssystem ein.

High Courts Act 2015 (Commercial Court Act)".[619] Durch den Commercial Court Act sollen in Indien Commercial Courts und Commercial High Courts für handelsrechtliche Verfahren mit einem Streitwert von mindestens einem „Crore" (10 Mio.) Rupien (ca. 135.000 Euro) geschaffen werden[620]. Auf der Ebene der District Courts wurden Commercial Courts eingerichtet.[621] Als Richter für die Commercial Courts sollen auf Handelsstreitigkeiten spezialisierte Richter berufen werden.[622] In jedem High Court sollen spezialisierte Senate für Handelsstreitigkeiten etabliert werden, die von mit Handelsstreitigkeiten vertrauten Richtern besetzt werden sollen.[623] Nach Sec. 10 (1) Commercial Court Act ist ein spezialisierter Handelssenat des High Courts[624] für internationale[625] schiedsrechtliche Handelsstreitigkeiten mit einem Streitwert von mindestens einem Crore Rupie zuständig. Nicht internationale schiedsrechtliche Handelsstreitigkeiten, die die Streitwertgrenze des Commercial Court Acts erfüllen[626] und für die der High Court originär zuständig ist, werden ebenfalls von der „Commercial Division" des zuständigen High Courts entschieden.[627] Soweit es sich um keine internationale Handelsstreitigkeit handelt, sind auf der Ebene der District Courts die Commercial Courts für Gerichtsverfahren unter dem SchiedsG mit einem Streitwert von mindestens einem Crore Rupien zuständig.[628] Für die Berufung gegen eine Entscheidung des Commercial Courts oder eines Handelssenats des High Courts ist der Berufungssenat für Handelsstreitigkeiten des High Courts[629] zuständig.[630] Im Commercial Court Act regelte der indische Gesetzgeber „Case Management"-Bestimmungen[631], die Zulässigkeit von elektronischen und von Audio- und Video-Beweisen in „Disclosure"-Verfahren[632], Kosten-

---

619 Der indische Präsident erteilte dem Gesetz am 31.12.2015 seine Zustimmung. Das Gesetz gilt aber rückwirkend als bereits am 23.10.2015 (Datum der präsidialen Verordnung, Fn. 618) in Kraft getreten.

620 Sec. 2 (1) (c), 2 (g) (i), 6, 12 Commercial Court Act. Die Law Commission war der Auffassung, dass es, ohne eine Begrenzung der Zuständigkeit auf hohe Streitwerte, wegen der hohen Anzahl an anhängigen Verfahren unmöglich sei, eine effektive Handelsgerichtsbarkeit zu etablieren, Government of India, Law Commission of India, 253. Report, Commercial Division and Commercial Appellate Division of High Courts and Commercial Courts Bill, 2015, 29.1.2015, S. 13.

621 Sec. 6 und 3 (1) Commercial Court Act.

622 Sec. 3 Commercial Court Act.

623 Sec. 4 f. Commercial Court Act.

624 Engl. Commercial Division of a High Court.

625 Zur Definition „internationale Handelsstreitigkeit", siehe Sec. 2 (1) (f) SchiedsG.

626 Die Streitwertgrenze liegt bei mindestens einem Crore Rupien, vgl. o.

627 Sec. 10 (2) Commercial Court Act.

628 Sec. 10 (3) Commercial Court Act.

629 Engl. Commercial Appellate Division.

630 Sec. 10 und 13 Commercial Court Act.

631 Rule 1, 3 Order XV Commercial Courts Act.

632 Rule 6 (2) Order XI Schedule Commercial Court Act.

sanktionen bei unbegründeten Klagen oder Widerklagen[633] und statuiert eine Pflicht zur Urteilsverkündung innerhalb von 90 Tagen nach der letzten mündlichen Verhandlung[634], abweichend vom Code of Civil Procedure 1908.[635] Der „Doing Business“ Bericht der Weltbank aus dem Jahr 2016 bewertete das Verfahrensmanagement der Gerichte in Delhi und Mumbai mit 0.5 von 6 möglichen Punkten.[636] Die Einführung eines effektiveren „Case Managements“ war folglich überfällig. Die „Case Management“-Vorschriften gewährleisten, dass innerhalb von vier Wochen, nachdem alle klagerelevanten Unterlagen gerichtlich anhängig gemacht wurden, das Handelsgericht eine „Case Management“-Verhandlung durchführen muss und binnen sechs Monaten nach der „Case Management“-Verhandlung alle Verhandlungstermine stattgefunden haben müssen.[637] Die Gesetzesreform soll bewirken, dass das Urteil eines Handelsgerichts innerhalb von zehn Monaten, nachdem alle klagerelevanten Unterlagen eingereicht wurden, verkündet wird. Berufungen in Handelsstreitigkeiten muss der High Court innerhalb von sechs Monaten entscheiden.[638] Sollten diese Fristen von den indischen Handelsgerichten eingehalten werden, hat der Gesetzgeber die überlangen Verfahrensdauern der indischen Gerichtsbarkeit für Handelsgerichtsverfahren mit hohen Streitwerten[639] durch eine angemessene Verfahrenshöchstdauer wirkungsvoll behoben. Der Commercial Court Act wird auf viele Schiedsverfahren unter dem SchiedsG anwendbar sein, da es sich bei Schiedsstreitigkeiten meist um Handelsstreitigkeiten[640] mit einem hohen Streitwert handelt[641]. Die Law Commission empfahl in ihrem 253. Report die Gründung einer Ausbildungsstätte für die Fort- und Weiterbildung der Richter der Handelskammern und

633 Durch Sec. 2 und 3 Schedule Commercial Court Act i. V. m. Sec. 16 Commercial Court Act wurde Sec. 35 und Sec. 35A (2) Code of Civil Procedure 1908 modifiziert.

634 Nach Rule 11 Order XV-A Schedule Commercial Court Act i. V. m. Sec. 16 Commercial Court Act wurde die Order XX Code of Civil Procedure 1908 entsprechend für die handelsrechtlichen Gerichtsverfahren geändert.

635 Sec. 16 Commercial Court Act.

636 World Bank Group, Doing Business 2017, Equal Opportunity for All, 14. Aufl., Economy Profile 2017, India, S. 131 f., verfügbar unter http://www.doingbusiness.org/~/media/wbg/doingbusiness/documents/profiles/country/ind.pdf (zuletzt abgerufen am 28.4.2021). Kritisch zu den Doing Business Reports der Weltbank, Kern, Juristenzeitung 2009, S. 498 ff.

637 Rule 1, 3 Order XV Schedule Commercial Courts Act.

638 Sec. 14 Commercial Court Act.

639 Der Streitwert muss mindestens ein Crore Rupie betragen.

640 Eine Handelsstreitigkeit definierte der indische Gesetzgeber weit, siehe Sec. 2 (1) (c) Commercial Courts Act.

641 Vgl. ICC, 2015 ICC Dispute Resolution Statistics, ICC Dispute Resolution Bulletin 2016, Ausg. 1, S. 9 (17).

der Handelssenate.[642] Dieser Empfehlung ist der Gesetzgeber bisher nicht nachgekommen.[643]

Die Reform der Schiedsgesetzgebung aus dem Jahre 2015 folgte dem Vorschlang des 246. Reports der Law Commission und übertrug den High Courts die erstinstanzliche Zuständigkeit für internationale Handelsschiedsverfahren gem. Sec. 2 (1) (e) (ii) und Sec. 47 SchiedsG n. F.[644] Diese erstinstanzliche Zuständigkeit des High Courts soll dazu führen, dass mit Handelsstreitigkeiten vertraute Richter diese Verfahren entscheiden und somit ein investorenfreundlicheres Klima geschaffen wird.[645] Vor der Gesetzesreform konnten alle gerichtlichen Verfahren mit Schiedsverfahrensbezug erstinstanzlich vor den District Courts anhängig sein.[646] Die Zuständigkeit der überlasteten District Courts verzögerte diese Verfahren.[647] Die Richter der District Courts waren zudem mit den internationalen Schiedsverfahren nur unzureichend vertraut. Es kam demzufolge zu mangelhaften Entscheidungen, gegen die kostenintensive und langwierige Berufungsverfahren eingelegt werden mussten.[648] Ein Grund für die Gesetzesänderung war ferner der gegen den Staat Indien ergangene Schiedsspruch *White Industries Australia Limited v The Republic of India*[649]. In diesem Investitionsschiedsverfahren entschied das Schiedsgericht, dass Indien wegen überlanger gerichtlicher Verfahrensdauer bei der Vollstreckung eines ausländischen Schiedsspruchs über 4 Mio. australische Dollar Schadensersatz zahlen musste. Die Gesetzesreform sollte eine potentielle Haftung des Staates Indiens für erneute überlange gerichtliche Verfahrensdauern verhindern.[650] Die erstinstanzliche

642 Government of India, Law Commission of India, 253. Report, Commercial Division and Commercial Appellate Division of High Courts and Commercial Courts Bill, 2015, 29.1.2015, S. 33, 41, 54, 57, 60, 72.

643 Siehe Sec. 20 Commercial Courts Act. Die Bundestaaten dürfen aber gem. Sec. 20 Commercial Courts Act Fortbildungseinrichtungen für ernannte Richter schaffen.

644 Government of India, Law Commission of India, 246. Report, Amendments to the Arbitration and Conciliation Act 1996, 5.8.2014, S. 17, 37 f., 57.

645 Government of India, Law Commission of India, 246. Report, Amendments to the Arbitration and Conciliation Act 1996, 5.8.2014, S. 17.

646 Aditya Singh/Dipen Sabharwal, Arbitration and Conciliation (Amendment) Ordinance, 2015, A contribution by the ITA Board of Reporters, Kluwer Law International, verfügbar unter http://www.kluwerarbitration.com/CommonUI/document.aspx?id=kli-ka-15-49-003 (zuletzt abgerufen am 28.4.2021).

647 Ein Verfahren vor dem District Court kann 6–10 Jahre dauern.

648 Aditya Singh/Dipen Sabharwal, Arbitration and Conciliation (Amendment) Ordinance, 2015, A contribution by the ITA Board of Reporters, Kluwer Law International, verfügbar unter http://www.kluwerarbitration.com/CommonUI/document.aspx?id=kli-ka-15-49-003 (zuletzt abgerufen am 28.4.2021).

649 Schiedsspruch vom 30.11.2011, verfügbar unter http://www.italaw.com/sites/default/files/case-documents/ita0906.pdf (zuletzt abgerufen am 28.4.2021).

650 Government of India, Law Commission of India, 246. Report, Amendments to the Arbitration and Conciliation Act 1996, 5.8.2014, S. 17 f.

Zuständigkeit der High Courts für internationale Handelsschiedsverfahren erhöht die Qualität der gerichtlichen Entscheidungen.[651] Bei hohen Streitwerten können die High Courts ihre Gerichtsverfahren mit Schiedsbezug nach Bestimmungen des Commercial Court Acts zudem schneller und effektiver entscheiden. Entscheidend wird aber sein, ob die Gerichte in schiedsfördernder Weise von diesen Gesetzesreformen Gebrauch machen und genannte Verfahren effizient aburteilen.

7. Schiedsgerichtsbarkeit

a) Entwicklung der Schiedsgerichtsbarkeit seit der Kolonialzeit

Im 19. Jahrhundert ordnete die East India Company im Rahmen der ihr von der britischen Regierung übertragenen Gesetzeskompetenzen in sog. „Regulations" an, wann eine gerichtlich anhängige Streitigkeit an ein Schiedsgericht verwiesen werden konnte. Detaillierte Bestimmungen über den prozessualen Ablauf des Schiedsverfahrens[652] enthielten diese Regulations nicht.[653] Das erste umfassende indische Schiedsgesetz war der „Indian Arbitration Act 1899". Er basierte auf dem englischen „Arbitration Act" aus dem Jahre 1889. Der Indian Arbitration Act 1899 war auf die „Presidency Towns" von Kalkutta, Bombay und Madras begrenzt und eröffnete den Parteien die Möglichkeit, ihre gegenwärtigen oder zukünftigen Streitigkeiten der Schiedsgerichtsbarkeit zu unterwerfen.[654] Der „Arbitration Act 1940" ersetzte den Indian Arbitration Act 1899, der wiederum auf dem englischen „Arbitration Act 1934" beruhte.[655] Die Entscheidungen der indischen Ge-

651 Aditya Singh/Dipen Sabharwal, Arbitration and Conciliation (Amendment) Ordinance, 2015, A contribution by the ITA Board of Reporters, Kluwer Law International, verfügbar unter http://www.kluwerarbitration.com/CommonUI/document.aspx?id=kli-ka-15-49-003 (zuletzt abgerufen am 28.4.2021).

652 Diese Regulations normierten die Eingriffskompetenz der staatlichen Gerichte in das Schiedsverfahren, sie enthielten Bestimmungen, um ein faires Verfahren zu gewährleisten und sahen ein Verfahren für die Zeugenvernehmungen vor.

653 Markanda/Markanda/Markanda, S. 2 f.; Parliament of India, Rajya Sabha, Department Related Parliamentary Standing Committee on Personnel, Public Grievance, Law and Justice, Ninth Report on the Arbitration and Conciliation (Amendment) Bill, 2003, in: Ministry of Law and Justice, Government of India, Proposed Amendments to the Arbitration & Conciliation Act, 1996, A Consultation Paper, Annex V, S. 139, verfügbar unter http://lawmin.nic.in/la/consultationpaper.pdf (zuletzt abgerufen am 28.4.2021); Sethi/Gupta, Arpan, S. 7.

654 Sethi/Gupta, Arpan, S. 7, Markanda/Markanda/Markanda, S. 5.

655 Paranjape, S. 2 f.; Government of India, Law Commission of India, 246. Report, Amendments to the Arbitration and Conciliation Act 1996, 5.8.2014, S. 1.

richte unter dem alten indischen Arbitration Act 1940 waren in erheblichem Ausmaß von der englischen Rechtsprechung geprägt.[656]

b) Schiedsverfahrensgesetz (SchiedsG) 1996

Das indische Schiedswesen ist im „Arbitration and Conciliation Act 1996" kodifiziert. Dieses Gesetz wird im Folgenden mit Schiedsgesetz (SchiedsG[657]) übersetzt. Die nachfolgenden Erläuterungen behandeln lediglich das Schiedsverfahren im 1. Teil des SchiedsG und die Vollstreckung ausländischer Schiedssprüche nach dem „New Yorker UN-Übereinkommen über die Anerkennung und Vollstreckung ausländischer Schiedssprüche vom 10. Juni 1958 (UNÜ)" aus dem 2. Teil des SchiedsG.[658]

aa) Entstehungsgeschichte

Nach der Unabhängigkeit Indiens führten die langen und kostspieligen Gerichtverfahren zum Anstieg von Handelsschiedsverfahren. Die Zunahme von Schiedsverfahren brachte aber gleichzeitig die Schwächen und Unzulänglichkeiten des Arbitration Acts 1940 zu Tage.[659] Unter dem Schiedsgesetz aus dem Jahre 1940 kontrollierten staatliche Gerichte Schiedsverfahren in beachtlichem Maße und es war den Gerichten gestattet, in jeder Phase in das Schiedsverfahren einzugreifen.[660] Der Arbitration Act 1940 war für inländische Schiedsverfahren bestimmt und von Misstrauen gegenüber der Streitbeilegung durch Schiedsverfahren geprägt.[661] Ein autonomes Schiedsverfahren ohne gerichtliche Interventionen konnte nicht stattfinden. Indien war und ist bekannt für seine zermürbenden und langwierigen Gerichtsprozesse. Unter dem Arbitration Act 1940 bestanden ausländische Investoren daher

---

656 Jayasimha/Mody, in: Moser/Choong (Hrsg.), Asia Arbitration Handbook, S. 843 (844 f.).

657 Im Folgenden als SchiedsG abgekürzt.

658 Auf die Vollstreckung von Schiedssprüchen nach dem Genfer Übereinkommen wird nicht näher eingegangen. Die Schlichtung in Teil III des SchiedsG ist von dieser Bearbeitung ausgeklammert.

659 Parliament of India, Rajya Sabha, Department Related Parliamentary Standing Committee on Personnel, Public Grievance, Law and Justice, Ninth Report on the Arbitration and Conciliation (Amendment) Bill, 2003, in: Ministry of Law and Justice, Government of India, Proposed Amendments to the Arbitration & Conciliation Act, 1996, A Consultation Paper, Annex V, S. 139, verfügbar unter http://lawmin.nic.in/la/consultationpaper.pdf (zuletzt abgerufen am 28.4.2021); Hilmer, International Arbitration Law Review 2007, S. 33 (34).

660 Hilmer, International Arbitration Law Review 2007, S. 33 (34); Government of India, Law Commission of India, 246. Report, Amendments to the Arbitration and Conciliation Act 1996, 5.8.2014, S. 14.

661 Government of India, Law Commission of India, 246. Report, Amendments to the Arbitration and Conciliation Act 1996, 5.8.2014, S. 1.

auf eine Streitbeilegung außerhalb Indiens.[662] Nach der wirtschaftlichen Öffnung Indiens im Jahre 1991 erforderten der Anstieg des internationalen Handelsvolumens und der sich stetig erhöhende Zufluss von ausländischen Direktinvestitionen einen wirksamen Streitbeilegungsmechanismus.[663] Zutreffend stellte der Supreme Court im Urteil *Guru Nanak Foundation v Rattan Singh & Sons*[664] mit Ironie fest, dass die Art, wie staatliche Gerichte unter dem Arbitration Act 1940 in das Schiedsverfahren eingriffen:

„*... has made Lawyers laugh and legal philosophers weep.*"

Diese Ausgangslage erforderte eine grundlegende Reform der Schiedsgerichtsbarkeit. Die Reformen führten zum SchiedsG 1996, das am 25. Januar 1996 in Kraft trat[665].[666] Das SchiedsG konsolidierte die drei bestehenden Gesetzgebungen zur Schiedsgerichtsbarkeit, das Schiedsgesetz, den Arbitration (Protocol and Convention) Act 1937 und den Foreign Awards (Recognition and Enforcement) Act 1961 in einem Gesetz.[667] Das SchiedsG 1996 rezipierte das UNCITRAL Modellgesetz 1985[668] und ist auf inländi-

---

662 Parliament of India, Rajya Sabha, Department Related Parliamentary Standing Committee on Personnel, Public Grievance, Law and Justice, Ninth Report on the Arbitration and Conciliation (Amendment) Bill, 2003, in: Ministry of Law and Justice, Government of India, Proposed Amendments to the Arbitration & Conciliation Act, 1996, A Consultation Paper, Annex V, S. 139, verfügbar unter http://lawmin.nic.in/la/consultationpaper.pdf (zuletzt abgerufen am 28.4.2021).

663 Sethi/Gupta, Arpan, S. 7; Government of India, Law Commission of India, 246. Report, Amendments to the Arbitration and Conciliation Act 1996, 5.8.2014, S. 2, 8; Parliament of India, Rajya Sabha, Department Related Parliamentary Standing Committee on Personnel, Public Grievance, Law and Justice, Ninth Report on the Arbitration and Conciliation (Amendment) Bill, 2003, in: Ministry of Law and Justice, Government of India, Proposed Amendments to the Arbitration & Conciliation Act, 1996, A Consultation Paper, Annex V, S. 139, verfügbar unter http://lawmin.nic.in/la/consultationpaper.pdf (zuletzt abgerufen am 28.4.2021); Hilmer, International Arbitration Law Review 2007, S. 33 (34); Paranjape, S. 3.

664 1981 AIR 2075; 1982 SCR (1) 842; 1981 SCC (4) 634, 29.9.1981.

665 Das SchiedsG verabschiedete das Parlament im August 1996 und der Präsident erteilte am 22.8.1996 die Zustimmung (engl. assent) zu dem Gesetz. Das SchiedsG galt aber rückwirkend seit dem 25.1.1996 (Tag der ersten präsidialen Verordnung) als in Kraft getreten, siehe Mohta/Mohta, S. 9; Malhotra, Indu, O. P. Malhotra on Arbitration, Sec. 1, S. 40.

666 Sec. 1 (3) SchiedsG.

667 Singh, Avtar, Arbitration, S. 2; Sethi/Gupta, Arpan, S. 8; Government of India, Law Commission of India, 246. Report, Amendments to the Arbitration and Conciliation Act 1996, 5.8.2014, S. 2 f.

668 Im Unterschied zum UNCITRAL Modellgesetz (vgl. Art. 1 [1]) ist das SchiedsG nicht nur auf internationale Schiedsverfahren anwendbar.

sche und ausländische Schiedsverfahren anwendbar[669].[670] Die Einführung des SchiedsG sollte die gerichtlichen Interventionen in Schiedsverfahren reduzieren, die Verfahrensdauern verkürzen, Verfahrenskosten verringern, die Parteiautonomie stärken und die Anzahl der angestauten Gerichtsverfahren reduzieren. Die Schiedsverfahren sollen durch die staatlichen Gerichte unterstützt werden.[671]

Der Supreme Court urteilte im Sinne der gesetzlichen Neuerungen des SchiedsG 1996:

> „*The legislative intent underlying the 1996 Act is to minimize the supervisory rules of courts in arbitral process and nominate/ appoint the Arbitrator without wasting time, leaving all contentious issues to be urged and agitated before the Arbitral Tribunal itself.*"[672]

Die mit dem SchiedsG verfolgten Ziele des indischen Gesetzgebers geben den Gerichten eine Auslegungshilfe für die betreffenden Vorschriften an die Hand.[673] Der gesetzgeberische Wille ist insbesondere bei mehrdeutigen Vorschriften heranzuziehen.[674] Der dem Schiedsgesetz zugrundeliegende Leit-

---

669 Durch die Anwendbarkeit des SchiedsG auf inländische und ausländische Schiedsverfahren, weicht das SchiedsG vom ausschließlich für internationale Schiedsverfahren vorgesehenen UNCITRAL Modellgesetz ab.

670 Law Commission of India, 176. Report, The Arbitration and Conciliation (Amendment) Bill, 2001, 12.9.2001, S. 5 f.; Paranjape, S. 16.

671 Parliament of India, Rajya Sabha, Department Related Parliamentary Standing Committee on Personnel, Public Grievance, Law and Justice, Ninth Report on the Arbitration and Conciliation (Amendment) Bill, 2003, in: Ministry of Law and Justice, Government of India, Proposed Amendments to the Arbitration & Conciliation Act, 1996, A Consultation Paper, Annex V, S. 140, verfügbar unter http://lawmin.nic.in/la/consultationpaper.pdf (zuletzt abgerufen am 28.4.2021); Ministry of Law and Justice, Government of India, Proposed Amendments to the Arbitration & Conciliation Act, 1996, A Consultation Paper, S. 1 f., verfügbar unter http://lawmin.nic.in/la/consultationpaper.pdf (zuletzt abgerufen am 28.4.2021); Paranjape, S. 16; Mohta/Mohta, S. 8 f.; Sethi/Gupta, Arpan, S. 8; Malhotra, Indu, O. P. Malhotra on Arbitration, Sec. 1, S. 33 ff.; Government of India, Law Commission of India, 246. Report, Amendments to the Arbitration and Conciliation Act 1996, 5.8.2014, S. 3 f.; Shri Ramakant Khalap, Minister of State of the Department Legal Affairs, Legislative Department and Department of Justice, Rajya Sabha, The Arbitration and Conciliation Bill, 1995, S. 295, 22.7.1996, verfügbar unter http://rsdebate.nic.in/bit stream/123456789/156970/1/PD_178_22071996_9_p290_p312_18.pdf#search=Arbitration (zuletzt abgerufen am 28.4.2021).

672 Supreme Court, *Food Corporation of India v Indian Council of Arbitration & Ors, etc etc*, Appeal (civil) 4655–4809 of 2003, 17.7.2003.

673 Supreme Court, *Bharat Singh v Management of New Delhi*, 1986 AIR 842; 1986 SCR (2) 169, 4.4.1986; Supreme Court, *Doypack Systems Pvt Ltd Etc v Union of India & Ors*, 1988 AIR 782; 1988 SCR (2) 962, 12.2.1988.

674 Siehe Supreme Court, *Doypack Systems Pvt Ltd Etc v Union of India & Ors*, 1988 AIR 782; 1988 SCR (2) 962, 12.2.1988; Supreme Court, *Regional Provident Fund*

gedanke, die Parteiautonomie zu achten und die staatlichen Gerichte möglichst nicht in das Schiedsverfahren eingreifen zu lassen, bringt Sec. 5 [675] SchiedsG klar zum Ausdruck:[676]

> „*Notwithstanding anything contained in any other law for the time being in force, in matter governed by this Part, no judicial authority shall intervene except where so provided in this Part.*"

In diesem Sinne kann es Indien mittels eines effektiven und kostengünstigen Streitbeilegungsmechanismus wie der Schiedsgerichtsbarkeit gelingen, die staatlichen Gerichte zu entlasten und Indien für Kaufleute, Unternehmer und Investoren mittels wirksamer Schiedsverfahren attraktiver zu machen.

bb) Internationale Handelsschiedsverfahren

Die Unterscheidung zwischen internationalen Handelsschiedsverfahren und inländischen Schiedsverfahren als auch internationalen Nichthandelsschiedsverfahren (im Folgenden inländische Schiedsverfahren[677]) ist insbesondere von Bedeutung bei der Bestellung von Schiedsrichtern (Sec. 11 SchiedsG), der materiellen Rechtswahl (Sec. 28 [1] SchiedsG)[678], der Zuständigkeit der Gerichte (Sec. 2 [1] [e], 47 SchiedsG n. F.)[679] und der Aufhebung von Schiedssprüchen (Sec. 34 [2a] SchiedsG)[680]. Gem. Sec. 2 (1) (f) SchiedsG charakterisieren folgende Merkmale ein internationales Handelsschiedsverfahren:

1. Handelsstreitigkeit nach indischem Recht
2. Zumindest eine Partei muss:

---

v Shri T S Hariharan, 1971 AIR 1519; 1971 SCR 305, 1.4.1971; Supreme Court, *State of Haryana & Anr v Chanan Mal Etc*, 1976 AIR 1654; 1976 SCR (3) 688, 18.3.1976; Supreme Court, *In Re: The Kerala Education Bill v Unknown*, 1959 1 SCR 995, 22.5.1958.

675 Die amtliche Überschrift von Sec. 5 Schiedsgesetz 1996 lautet „Extent of judicial intervention".

676 Hilmer, International Arbitration Law Review 2007, S. 33 (35).

677 Der Begriff inländische Schiedsverfahren umfasst inländische Schiedsverfahren und internationale Nichthandelsschiedsverfahren. Der Terminus inländische Schiedsverfahren wird verwendet, da die Anzahl der internationalen Nichthandelsschiedsverfahren gering ist.

678 Nach Sec. 28 (1) (a) SchiedsG können inländische Schiedsverfahren nur nach indischem Recht entschieden werden, internationale Handelsschiedsverfahren hingegen steht die Vereinbarung eines ausländischen Rechts offen.

679 Gem. Sec. 2 (1) (e) SchiedsG n. F. ist der High Court für internationale Handelsschiedsverfahren erstinstanzlich zuständig. Für alle anderen Schiedsverfahren bestimmt sich die Zuständigkeit der Gerichte unter Rückgriff auf die jeweiligen einschlägigen Zuständigkeitsnormen.

680 Internationale Handelsschiedssprüche unterfallen beim Aufhebungsgrund der öffentlichen Ordnung einer schonenderen gerichtlichen Kontrolle.

a. eine nicht indische Staatangehörigkeit haben oder ihren gewöhnlichen Aufenthalt außerhalb von Indien haben, oder
b. eine juristische Person sein, die außerhalb Indiens gegründet wurde, oder
c. eine Vereinigung[681] oder eine Personenvereinigung[682] sein, deren zentrale Geschäftsführung außerhalb Indiens gesteuert wird[683], oder
d. die Regierung eines ausländischen Staates sein.

Indien traf hierdurch eine vom UNCITRAL Modellgesetz abweichende Regelung für das Kriterium der Internationalität eines Schiedsverfahrens.[684] Abweichend von Art. 1 III UNCITRAL Modellgesetz liegt gem. Sec. 2 (1) (f) SchiedsG ein internationales Schiedsverfahren auch vor, wenn eine juristische Person außerhalb von Indien gegründet wurde, bzw. die Geschäftsführung einer Vereinigung bzw. Personenvereinigung einer Partei von außerhalb Indiens gesteuert wird. Oder eine Partei ein ausländischer Staat ist.

cc) Zuständigkeiten der indischen Gerichte für Schiedsverfahren

Für die Untersuchung des Zusammenspiels von Schiedsverfahren und staatlichen Gerichtsverfahren werden nachfolgend die wichtigsten Zuständigkeiten der staatlichen Gerichte unter dem SchiedsG aufgezeigt:

- Kontrolle der „Kompetenz-Kompetenz" des Schiedsgerichts und Kontrolle der Unabhängigkeit der Schiedsvereinbarung (Sec. 16 SchiedsG)
- Kontrolle der Unzuständigkeitserklärung des Schiedsgerichts (Sec. 16 SchiedsG)
- Verweisung einer gerichtlich rechtsanhängigen Rechtsstreitigkeit an das vereinbarte Schiedsverfahren (Sec. 8 und 45 SchiedsG)
- Bestellung von Schiedsrichtern (Sec. 11 SchiedsG)
- Einstweiliger Rechtsschutz (Sec. 9 SchiedsG)
- Gerichtliche Unterstützung bei der Beweisaufnahme (Sec. 27 SchiedsG)
- Aufhebungsverfahren (Sec. 34 SchiedsG)
- Vollstreckung von ausländischen Schiedssprüchen (Sec. 48)

dd) Reformvorschläge zum SchiedsG 1996

Im 176. Report regte die Law Commission im Jahr 2001 an, die gerichtlichen Interventionen und Verzögerungen weiter zu reduzieren.[685] 2003

681 Engl. association.
682 Engl. body of individuals.
683 Seit der Gesetzesreform des Jahres 2015 umfasst Sec. 2 (1) (f) (iii) SchiedsG n. F. keine Unternehmen (engl. company) mehr.
684 Vgl. Art. 3 UNCITRAL Modellgesetz.
685 Law Commission of India, 176. Report, The Arbitration and Conciliation (Amendment) Bill, 2001, 12.9.2001, S. 11, 16.

sollte nach diesem Vorschlag der Law Commission das SchiedsG geändert werden.[686] In diesem Kontext stellte das „Department Related Parliamentary Standing Committee on Personnel, Public Grievance, Law and Justice“ der Rajya Sabha in seinem 9. Report zu den geplanten Gesetzesänderungen des SchiedsG fest, dass: die gerichtliche Auslegung des SchiedsG weder dem Geist noch dem Wortlaut des UNCITRAL Modellgesetzes entsprach.[687] Befürchtungen, die dem indischen Parlament vorgelegte Gesetzesanpassung würde zusätzliche gerichtliche Interventionen und Verzögerungen bewirken, führten jedoch dazu, dass das Parlament[688] die Gesetzesreform nicht beschloss.[689] Auch ein Gesetzesentwurf aus dem Jahre 2010 führte zu keiner gesetzlichen Änderung.[690] 2014 regte die Law Commission in ihrem 246. Report erneut eine Reform des SchiedsG an.[691] Dieser Report sieht vor, institutionelle Schiedsgerichtsbarkeit in Indien zu etablieren, um die mit den *ad hoc*-Schiedsverfahren einhergehende, verstärkte gerichtliche Kontrolle der Schiedsverfahren zu verringern. Die vorgeschlagene Gesetzesreform sieht eine angemessene Balance zwischen gerichtlicher Kontrolle und gerichtlicher Unterstützung des Schiedsverfahrens vor. Die Verzögerungen bei

686 Ministry of Law and Justice, Government of India, Proposed Amendments to the Arbitration & Conciliation Act, 1996, A Consultation Paper, S. 1, verfügbar unter http://lawmin.nic.in/la/consultationpaper.pdf (zuletzt abgerufen am 28.4.2021); Government of India, Law Commission of India, 246. Report, Amendments to the Arbitration and Conciliation Act 1996, 5.8.2014, S.5; Paranjape, S.3.

687 Parliament of India, Rajya Sabha, Department Related Parliamentary Standing Committee on Personnel, Public Grievance, Law and Justice, Ninth Report on the Arbitration and Conciliation (Amendment) Bill, 2003, in: Ministry of Law and Justice, Government of India, Proposed Amendments to the Arbitration & Conciliation Act, 1996, A Consultation Paper, Annex V, S. 140, verfügbar unter http://lawmin.nic.in/la/consultationpaper.pdf (zuletzt abgerufen am 28.4.2021).

688 Die zweite Kammer die sog. „Rajya Sabha“, entspricht dem Bundesrat in Deutschland, lehnte die Verabschiedung ab.

689 Government of India, Law Commission of India, 246. Report, Amendments to the Arbitration and Conciliation Act 1996, 5.8.2014, S.IV, 5f.; Parliament of India, Rajya Sabha, Department Related Parliamentary Standing Committee on Personnel, Public Grievance, Law and Justice, Ninth Report on the Arbitration and Conciliation (Amendment) Bill, 2003, in: Ministry of Law and Justice, Government of India, Proposed Amendments to the Arbitration & Conciliation Act, 1996, A Consultation Paper, Annex V, S. 141 ff., verfügbar unter http://lawmin.nic.in/la/consultationpaper.pdf (zuletzt abgerufen am 28.4.2021).

690 Nicholas Peacock/Vikas Mahendra, Law Commission of India proposes wide-ranging changes to the country's arbitration regime, verfügbar unter http://hsfnotes.com/arbitration/2014/09/25/law-commission-of-india-proposes-wide-ranging-changes-to-the-countrys-arbitration-regime/ (zuletzt abgerufen am 28.4.2021); Government of India, Law Commission of India, 246. Report, Amendments to the Arbitration and Conciliation Act 1996, 5.8.2014, S.iv f., 6f.

691 Government of India, Law Commission of India, 246. Report, Amendments to the Arbitration and Conciliation Act 1996, 5.8.2014, S.IV f., 8ff.

der schiedsgerichtlichen Streitbeilegung durch die Eingriffe des überlasteten indischen Gerichtssystems[692] in Schiedsverfahren sollten nach dem 246. Report beseitigt werden.[693]

ee) Arbitration Amendment

In *White Industries Australia Limited v The Republic of India*[694], sprach ein Investitionsschiedsgericht dem australischen Kapitalanleger *White Industries* wegen der überlangen Verfahrensdauer bei der Vollstreckung eines ausländischen Schiedsspruchs in Indien Schadensersatz zu. Der *White Industries Australia Limited v The Republic of India*-Schiedsspruch beschleunigte die Gesetzesreform des SchiedsG.[695] Auf Grundlage des 246. Reports der Law Commission brachte die indische Regierung im August 2015 einen Gesetzesentwurf in das indische Parlament ein. Die Verabschiedung der reformierten indischen Schiedsgesetzgebung durch das Parlament verzögerte sich.[696] Am 23.10.2015 ordnete der indische Präsident deshalb durch die „Arbitration and Conciliation (Amendment) Ordinance 2015 (Arbitration Ordinance)" eine sofortige Novelle der Schiedsgesetzgebung an.[697] Die Arbitration Ordinance war ab der nächsten Sitzung beider Kammern des Parlaments für sechs Wochen gültig.[698] Das indische Parlament verab-

---

692 Zum überlasteten Gerichtssystem siehe auch, Subramanium, in: Choudhry/Khosla/Mehta, The Oxford Handbook of the Indian Constitution, S. 614 (626); Thiruvengadam, in: Choudhry/Khosla/Mehta, The Oxford Handbook of the Indian Constitution, S. 412 ff.; Eisenberg/Kalantry/Robinson, DePaul Law Review 2013, Vol. 62, Ausg. 2, S. 247 (248 ff.).

693 Government of India, Law Commission of India, 246. Report, Amendments to the Arbitration and Conciliation Act 1996, 5.8.2014, S. 8 ff. Zu den angestauten Verfahren, den Verfahrensverzögerungen und der Überforderung des indischen Gerichtssystems siehe auch, Subramanium, in: Choudhry/Khosla/Mehta, The Oxford Handbook of the Indian Constitution, S. 614 (626); Thiruvengadam, in: Choudhry/Khosla/Mehta, The Oxford Handbook of the Indian Constitution, S. 412 ff.; Eisenberg/Kalantry/Robinson, DePaul Law Review 2013, Vol. 62, Ausg. 2, S. 247 (248 ff.).

694 Schiedsspruch vom 30.11.2011, verfügbar unter http://www.italaw.com/sites/default/files/case-documents/ita0906.pdf (zuletzt abgerufen am 28.4.2021).

695 Sathyapalan, Arbitration International 2016, S. 1 (16); Government of India, Law Commission of India, 246. Report, Amendments to the Arbitration and Conciliation Act 1996, 5.8.2014, S. 17 f.

696 Sathyapalan, Arbitration International 2016, S. 1 (15); Press Information Bureau, Government of India, Cabinet, verfügbar unter http://pib.nic.in/newsite/PrintRelease.aspx?relid=126356 (zuletzt abgerufen am 28.4.2021).

697 Siehe Sec. 1 (2) Arbitration Ordinance.

698 Art. 123 der indischen Verfassung. Dem Präsidenten obliegt die Kompetenz präsidiale Verordnungen zu erlassen nur während der Sitzungspause des Parlaments, Art. 123 (1) der indischen Verfassung. Siehe auch Vikas Mahendra, Arbitration in India: A New Beginning, Kluwer Arbitration Blog, 6.11.2015, verfügbar unter http://kluwerarbitra-

schiedete die Gesetzesänderung des SchiedsG im „Arbitration and Conciliation (Amendment) Act 2015 (Arbitration Amendment Act)“ sodann im Dezember 2015.[699] Der Arbitration Amendment Act wurde rückwirkend zum 23.10.2015[700] in Kraft gesetzt.[701] Die reformierte Schiedsgesetzgebung ist auf alle Schiedsverfahren anwendbar, deren Schiedsklageschrift dem Beklagten nach dem 22.10.2015 zugestellt wurde.[702] Die Parteien können ferner vereinbaren, dass das modernisierte SchiedsG auf laufende Schiedsverfahren Anwendung finden soll.[703] Mit der Gesetzesnovelle will die Regierung *Modi*[704] die rechtlichen Voraussetzungen für die weitere wirtschaftliche Entwicklung und für ausländische Investitionen schaffen und die Attraktivität des Schiedsortes Indien vorantreiben.[705] Durch das novellierte SchiedsG sollen die gesetzlichen Hürden für das Eingreifen der indischen Gerichte in allen Phasen des Schiedsverfahrens erhöht und Verzögerungen eliminiert werden.[706]

8. Schiedsinstitutionen in Indien

Das SchiedsG nimmt gegenüber *ad hoc* und institutionellen Schiedsverfahren eine neutrale Position ein.[707] In Indien gibt es eine Vielzahl von Schiedsinstitutionen, dennoch werden die meisten Schiedsverfahren *ad hoc* durch-

---

tionblog.com/2015/11/06/arbitration-in-india-a-new-beginning/ (zuletzt abgerufen am 28.4.2021).

699 Siehe Arbitration Amendment Act.

700 Datum des Inkrafttretens der Arbitration Ordinance, Sec. 1 (2) Arbitration Ordinance.

701 Sec. 1 (2) Arbitration Amendment Act.

702 Sec. 26 Arbitration Amendment Act i. V. m. Sec. 1 (2) Arbitration Amendment Act und Sec. 26 SchiedsG.

703 Sec. 26 Arbitration Amendment Act.

704 *Narendra Modi* ist seit 26.5.2014 der Premierminister von Indien.

705 Press Information Bureau, Government of India, Cabinet, verfügbar unter http://pib.nic.in/newsite/PrintRelease.aspx?relid=126356 (zuletzt abgerufen am 28.4.2021); The Hindu, Ordinance route for quick arbitration reforms, 31.12.2014, verfügbar unter http://www.thehindu.com/news/national/ordinance-to-amend-law-on-arbitration/article6739783.ece (zuletzt abgerufen am 28.4.2021); Agram Legal Consultants, Government approves introduction of bill to amend the Arbitration and Conciliation Act, 1996, 31.8.2015, verfügbar unter http://www.lexology.com/library/detail.aspx?g=ce7cdaef-3454-4650-87a1-a59a740d040a (zuletzt abgerufen am 28.4.2021); Petit/Lakhani/Timmers, India anticipates new arbitration laws, Norton Rose Fulbright, International arbitration report 2015, Ausg. 4, S. 22 ff.; Sathyapalan, Arbitration International 2016, S. 1 (15 f.).

706 Government of India, Law Commission of India, 246. Report, Amendments to the Arbitration and Conciliation Act 1996, 5.8.2014, S. 8, 13 ff., 15 ff., 37 ff.; Sathyapalan, Arbitration International 2016, S. 1 (15 f.).

707 Government of India, Law Commission of India, 246. Report, Amendments to the Arbitration and Conciliation Act 1996, 5.8.2014, S. 9.

geführt.[708] Die 1927 gegründete, größte indische Wirtschaftsorganisation „Federation of Indian Chambers of Commerce and Industry (FICCI)“ schuf 1952 das „FICCI Arbitration and Conciliation Tribunal (FACT)“ mit dem Ziel, nationale und internationale Streitigkeiten durch Schiedsverfahren beizulegen. Das FACT operiert als Schiedsinstitution und administriert die Schiedsverfahren.[709] Bereits 1965 führte eine gemeinsame Initiative der indischen Regierung und von Wirtschaftsorganisationen zur Gründung des „Indian Council of Arbitration (ICA)“. Der ICA administriert jährlich 400 Schiedsverfahren.[710] 2009 gründete der international renommierte englische „London Court of International Arbitration (LCIA)“ mit dem „LCIA India“ eine indische Schiedsinstitution. Der LCIA India bot durch auf Indien zugeschnittene Schiedsregeln dasselbe Servicespektrum an wie der London Court of International Arbitration. Die zu geringe Anzahl an LCIA India-Schiedsverfahren führte im Juni 2016 zur Schließung des LCIA India[711].[712] Ebenfalls 2009 wurde das „Delhi International Arbitration Centre (DIAC)“ vom Delhi High Court in New Delhi gegründet, um Parteien eine effektive schiedsgerichtliche Streitbeilegung zu ermöglichen.[713] Die vielen SIAC-Schiedsverfahren mit indischer Beteiligung bewogen das SIAC im Jahr 2013 dazu, ein Büro im indischen Mumbai zu eröffnen. Das Büro in Mumbai soll indische Parteien von den Vorzügen eines SIAC-Schiedsverfahrens in Singapur überzeugen und die Stellung von SIAC als eine von indischen Schiedsparteien präferierte Schiedsinstitutionen erhalten. Das SIAC Büro in Indien administriert jedoch keine Schiedsverfahren, dies geschieht am Hauptsitz in Singapur.[714] 2016 wurde mit dem „Mumbai Centre for International Arbitration (MCIA)“ eine moderne indische Schiedsinstitution ins

---

708 Jayasimha/Mody, in: Moser/Choong (Hrsg.), Asia Arbitration Handbook, S. 843 (847); Government of India, Law Commission of India, 246. Report, Amendments to the Arbitration and Conciliation Act 1996, 5.8.2014, S. 9; Paranjape, S. 11; Sanjna Pramod, Arbitration and Mediation: Shifting Paradigms in India, 4.8.2016, verfügbar unter http://kluwerarbitrationblog.com/2016/08/04/arbitration-and-mediation-shifting-paradigms-in-india/ (zuletzt abgerufen am 28.4.2021).

709 FICCI Arbitration and Conciliation Tribunal, About FACT, verfügbar unter http://www.ficci-arbitration.com/htm/about.htm (zuletzt abgerufen am 28.4.2021).

710 Indian Council of Arbitration, About US, verfügbar unter http://www.icaindia.co.in/htm/about-us.html (zuletzt abgerufen am 28.4.2021).

711 Bereits initiierte und vereinbarte LCIA India Schiedsverfahren werden von der LCIA in London administriert.

712 LCIA India, verfügbar unter http://www.lcia-india.org/ (zuletzt abgerufen am 28.4.2021).

713 Delhi International Arbitration Centre, About Us, verfügbar unter http://www.dac-delhi.org/topics.aspx?mid=1 (zuletzt abgerufen am 28.4.2021). Auch der Punjab und Haryana High Court gründete eine Schiedsinstitution, weitere Informationen verfügbar unter https://highcourtchd.gov.in/?trs=adr_rules (zuletzt abgerufen am 28.4.2021).

714 SIAC, About Us, SIAC Mumbai Office, verfügbar unter http://siac.org.sg/2014-11-03-13-33-43/about-us/siac-mumbai-office (zuletzt abgerufen am 28.4.2021).

Leben gerufen.[715] Um institutionelle Schiedsgerichtsverfahren in Indien zu verbreiten und zu fördern, brachte der 246. Report der Law Commission die Gründung einer „Arbitration Commission of India“ ins Spiel.[716] Auf Grund des Vorschlags des 246. Reports gründete die indische Legislative[717] im Jahre 2018 mit dem „New Delhi International Arbitration Centre (NDIAC)“ eine neue Schiedsinstitution.[718] Es bleibt abzuwarten, ob sich das New Delhi International Arbitration Centre auf dem indischen Schiedsverfahrensmarkt etablieren kann.

IV. Vergleichbarkeit von Singapur und Indien

Die Rechtsordnungen Singapurs und Indiens sind nicht nur durch ihre britische Prägung in der Kolonialzeit eng miteinander verbunden. Singapur wurde in dieser britischen Kolonialzeit über 40 Jahre vom indischen Handelsposten in Bengalen regiert. Die Singapurer Bevölkerung ist zu 9% indischer Abstammung und mit Tamil ist eine indische Sprache als offizielle Sprache in Singapur anerkannt. Zudem rezipierte Singapur indische Rechtsakte und indische Gerichtsentscheidungen werden von den Singapurer Gerichten berücksichtigt. Dies zeigt, dass die Rechtsordnungen in Indien und Singapur eine Vielzahl an Schnittmengen aufweisen. Die Rechtsordnungen in Singapur und Indien basieren auf englischem Recht und beide Länder haben mit dem UNCITRAL Modellgesetz ein modernes Schiedsrecht kodifiziert. Es wird daher untersucht werden, warum trotz einer gemeinsamen geschichtlichen und rechtlichen Entwicklung der beiden Länder und der Rezeption des UNCITRAL Modellgesetzes die Singapurer Rechtsordnung für ihre Schiedsfreundlichkeit, die indische Rechtsordnung hingegen für ihre Schiedsunfreundlichkeit bekannt geworden ist.[719]

---

715 Girish Deepak, MCIA, India's best foot forward, Kluwer Arbitration Blog, 5.8.2016, verfügbar unter http://kluwerarbitrationblog.com/2016/08/05/mcia-indias-best-foot-forward/ (zuletzt abgerufen am 28.4.2021); MCIA, verfügbar unter http://mcia.org.in/ (zuletzt abgerufen am 28.4.2021).

716 Government of India, Law Commission of India, 246. Report, Amendments to the Arbitration and Conciliation Act 1996, 5.8.2014, S. 10.

717 „New Delhi International Arbitration Centre Bill 2018“.

718 Binsy Susan/Neha Sharma, New Delhi International Arbitration Centre: Building India into a Global Arbitration Hub, Kluwer Arbitration Blog, 4.5.2018, verfügbar unter http://arbitrationblog.kluwerarbitration.com/2018/05/04/new-delhi-international-arbitration-centre-building-india-global-arbitration-hub/ (zuletzt abgerufen am 28.4.2021).

719 Vgl. Kapitel: Einleitung (A. I.).

B. Singapur

I. Anwendbares Recht

1. Anwendungsbereich des Verfahrensrechts

Der auf internationale Schiedsverfahren zugeschnittene International Arbitration Act (IAA) gesteht den staatlichen Gerichten im Vergleich zu dem für inländische Schiedsverfahren vorgesehenen Arbitration Act (AA) weniger Interventionsmöglichkeiten zu.[720] Der IAA erklärt in Sec. 3 (1) IAA das „UNCITRAL[721] Modellgesetz 1985 (UNCITRAL Modellgesetz)“[722] für anwendbar. Dementsprechend besteht die Singapurer internationale Schiedsgesetzgebung im Kern aus den Bestimmungen des UNCITRAL Modellgesetzes, sofern der Gesetzgeber nicht im IAA eine abweichende Regelung getroffen hat.[723]

Der geographische Anwendungsbereich des auf internationale Schiedsverfahren anwendbaren IAA und des für inländische[724] Schiedsverfahren einschlägigen AA ist auf Schiedsverfahren mit Sitz in Singapur beschränkt.[725]

Der räumlich-persönliche Anwendungsbereich des IAA erfasst grundsätzlich Schiedsverfahren mit zumindest einer ausländischen Partei.[726] Der

---

720 Siehe Ausführungen im Folgenden. Vgl. Associate Prof. Ho Peng Kee (Singapore Parliamentary Secretary to the Minister for Law), Parliamentary Debates, Official Reports, 31.10.1994, Vol. 63, Column 625 ff., verfügbar unter http://sprs.parl.gov.sg/search/report.jsp?currentPubID=00069725-ZZ (zuletzt abgerufen am 28.4.2021); Howell/Duthie/Lim, Mark, Journal of International Arbitration 2002, Vol. 19, Ausg. 1, S. 39 f.; Merkin/Hjalmarsson, S. 2; Court of Appeal, *NCC International AB v Alliance Concrete Singapore Pte Ltd*, [2008] 2 SLR 565; [2008] SGCA 5, 26.2.2008.

721 Steht für „United Nations Commission on International Trade Law“.

722 Die „United Nations Commission on International Trade Law (UNCITRAL)“ verfolgte mit der Verabschiedung des UNCITRAL Modellgesetzes das Ziel, die internationale Handelsschiedsgesetzgebung zu harmonisieren und diese dem internationalen Standard der Handelsschiedsgerichtsbarkeit anzupassen, UNCITRAL Sekretariat, Explanatory note, Rn. 1 ff.; Seiler, in: Thomas/Putzo, Vorbemerkung Buch 10 Rn. 1 f.; Schütze, in: Wieczorek/Schütze, § 1025 Rn. 3 f.

723 Die Anerkennungs- und Vollstreckungsbestimmungen des UNCITRAL Modellgesetzes substituierte der Gesetzgeber durch die Vorschriften des UNÜ für ausländische Schiedssprüche. Aber auch in anderen Vorschriften wich die Legislative von den Bestimmungen des UNCITRAL Modellgesetzes ab, siehe Sec. 3 ff. IAA.

724 Schiedsverfahren zwischen zwei Singapurer Parteien. Bei Auslandsbezug handelt es sich um ein internationales Schiedsverfahren, das dem IAA unterfällt.

725 Sec. 3 IAA i. V. m. Art. 1 (2) UNCITRAL Modellgesetz und Sec. 3 AA. Der AA wird in Sec. 3 AA negativ vom IAA abgegrenzt und erfasst alle Schiedsverfahren, die nicht vom zweiten Teil des IAA erfasst werden. Dies wird auch im IAA in Sec. 5 (4) bestätigt.

726 Sec. 5 IAA. Siehe ausführlich zu den Anknüpfungsmomenten von Sec. 5 IAA, Kapitel: Einleitung; Anwendungsbereich (A.II.8.b)aa)(1)).

räumlich-persönliche Geltungsbereich des IAA stimmt hierdurch weitgehend mit dem UNCITRAL Modellgesetz überein.[727] Der AA ist auf Schiedsverfahren anwendbar, sofern Teil II IAA keine Anwendung findet.[728]

a) Parteivereinbarung

Der Anwendungsbereich des IAA und des AA ist flexibel ausgestaltet. Er erlaubt es den Parteien, von der einen Schiedsgesetzgebung in die andere mittels Vereinbarung hineinzuoptieren.[729] Dadurch sind Parteien in der Lage, ein Schiedsverfahren unter den schiedsgesetzlichen Rahmenbedingungen durchzuführen, die von ihnen bevorzugt werden. Der Parteiautonomie, einem der Grundpfeiler der Schiedsgerichtsbarkeit, wird auf diese Weise vollumfänglich Rechnung getragen. Diese Wahlmöglichkeit ist insbesondere für inländische Singapurer Schiedsverfahren von Relevanz, denn die Parteien dieser Verfahren können vom auf ihr Schiedsverfahren anwendbaren AA in den durch weniger gerichtliche Interventionen geprägten IAA i. V. m. dem UNCITRAL Modellgesetz wechseln.

aa) Vereinbarung des AA

Sec. 15 IAA a. F. entnahmen die Singapurer Gerichte eine konkludente Abbedingungsmöglichkeit des IAA und des UNCITRAL Modellgesetzes.

Der alte Sec. 15 IAA besagte:

> „*If the parties to an arbitration agreement have (whether in the arbitration agreement or in any other document in writing) agreed that any dispute that has arisen or may arise between them is to be settled or resolved otherwise than in accordance with this Part* [Part II] *or the Model Law, this Part* [Part II] *and the Model Law shall not apply in relation to the settlement or resolution of that dispute.*“[730]

---

727 Vgl. Sec. 5 IAA und Art. 1 (3) UNCITRAL Modellgesetz. Siehe ausführlich hierzu Kapitel: Einleitung; International Arbitration Act (A.II.8.b)aa)(1)).

728 Sec. 3 AA und Sec. 5 (4) IAA.

729 Sec. 5 (1) IAA und Sec. 15 IAA, Court of Appeal, *Navigator Investment Services Ltd v Acclaim Insurance Brokers Pte Ltd,* [2009] SGCA 45, 29.9.2009; High Court, *Dermajaya Properties Sdn Bhd v Premium Properties Sdn Bhd and another*, [2002] SGHC 53, 20.3.2002.

730 Howell/Duthie/Lim, Mark, Journal of International Arbitration 2002, Vol. 19, Ausg. 1, S. 39 (44).

(1) Coop International v Ebel

Unter Sec. 15 IAA a. F. merkte der High Court im Verfahren *Coop International Pte Ltd v Ebel SA (Coop)*[731] *obiter dicta* an, dass die Vereinbarung eines Schiedsprozesses, der zwingenden Vorschriften des UNCITRAL Modellgesetzes widerspreche, indirekt dazu führe, dass die Schiedsparteien den zweiten Teil des IAA und das UNCITRAL Modellgesetz konkludent abbedungen hätten. Auf ihr Schiedsverfahren sei demzufolge der AA anwendbar. Einer expliziten Vereinbarung, in der die Parteien an Stelle des auf internationale Schiedsverfahren ausgerichteten IAA in das für inländische Schiedsverfahren bestimmte AA optieren, bedürfe es nicht. Entsprechend entschied der High Court für den hypothetischen Fall, bei dem die Parteien ein Schiedsverfahren mit Sitz in Singapur unter den Schiedsregeln der Handelskammer in Genf[732] vereinbart hätten, dass die Unvereinbarkeit der Schiedsregeln der Handelskammer in Genf mit dem UNCITRAL Modellgesetz zu einem konkludenten Ausschluss des UNCITRAL Modellgesetzes als auch von Teil II IAA und zur Wahl des AA führe.[733]

Grundsätzlich können die Schiedsparteien im Rahmen der Parteiautonomie vereinbaren, dass ihr Schiedsverfahren nach der Schiedsordnung einer Schiedsinstitution durchgeführt wird. Sie verdrängen hierdurch das auf das Schiedsverfahren anwendbare, dispositive staatliche Recht.[734] Das zwingend auf das Schiedsverfahren anwendbare Recht können die Parteien indessen nicht durch die gewählte institutionelle Schiedsordnung abbedingen.[735]

Die Rechtsaufassung des High Courts konterkariert den Willen der Parteien eines internationalen Schiedsverfahrens, die durch die Vereinbarung von institutionellen Schiedsregeln, die auf ihr Schiedsverfahren angewandt werden sollen, lediglich von der Gestaltungsfreiheit innerhalb der internationalen

---

731 [1998] SGHC 425, 27.1. und 4.3.1998. In dem Verfahren hatte der High Court darüber zu entscheiden, ob die Streitigkeit zwischen den Parteien auszusetzen war. Im Ergebnis lehnte es der High Court ab, dass die Streitigkeit zu Gunsten eines schiedsgerichtlichen Verfahrens ausgesetzt werden muss, da es sich um eine Streitigkeit handelte, die nicht im Zusammenhang mit dem, die Schiedsklausel enthaltenden, Vertrag stand. Der Vertrag enthielt eine Schiedsklausel für ein Schiedsverfahren in der Schweiz, unter den Schiedsregeln der Handelskammer in Genf.

732 Engl. Geneva Rules.

733 High Court, *Coop International Pte Ltd v Ebel SA,* [1998] SGHC 425, 27.1. und 4.3.1998. Zustimmend, Pillay, The International Construction Law Review 2003, S. 91 (117).

734 Born, International Commercial Arbitration, Bd. 2, S. 1625; Art. 1509 f. französischer Code de procédure civile; Art. 182 Schweizer Bundesgesetz über das Internationale Privatrecht; Sec. 4 englischer Arbitration Act 1996.

735 Blackaby/Partasides/Redfern/Hunter, International Arbitration, Rn. 3.64; UNCITRAL Sekretariat, Explanatory note, Rn. 13; Sec. 4 englischer Arbitration Act 1996; Born, International Commercial Arbitration, Bd. 2, S. 1609 ff.

Schiedsgesetzgebung Gebrauch machen wollen.[736] Die Parteien intendieren nicht konkludent und indirekt dazu, mittels der Wahl der Schiedsregeln einer Schiedsinstitution von dem durch weniger gerichtliche Interventionen geprägten IAA in das mehr gerichtliche Kontrolle zulassende AA[737] hineinzuoptieren. Vielmehr wollen die Parteien durch die Vereinbarung der institutionellen Schiedsregeln weitgehend von dem abdingbaren nationalen Schiedsrecht am Sitz des Schiedsverfahrens zu Gunsten eines frei bestimmten, institutionellen Verfahrensrechts abweichen.

(2) John Holland v Toyo Engineering

In *John Holland Pty Ltd v Toyo Engineering Corp (John Holland)*[738] hatte der High Court darüber zu urteilen, ob ein Schiedsspruch der ICC zwischen dem australischen Kläger und dem japanischen Beklagten in Singapur aufgehoben werden kann.

John Holland Pty Ltd war die Subunternehmerin von *Toyo Engineering Corp* für die Nachrüstung einer Erdölraffinerie[739] in Australien. Der Subunternehmervertrag enthielt eine Schiedsklausel, die zur Streitbeilegung ein Schiedsverfahren in Singapur nach Singapurer Recht unter der ICC-Schiedsgerichtsordnung vorsah. Bei dem Schiedsverfahren zwischen den Parteien handelte es sich um ein internationales Schiedsverfahren nach dem IAA. *John Holland Pty Ltd* plädierte im Verfahren vor dem High Court, dass durch die Unvereinbarkeit der ICC-Schiedsgerichtsordnung mit dem UNCITRAL Modellgesetz die Parteien sowohl das UNCITRAL Modellgesetz als auch den IAA abbedungen hätten und deshalb Sec. 17 AA auf das Aufhebungsverfahren anwendbar sei. Der High Court setze sich mit der *Coop*-Rechtsprechung auseinander und entschied, dass die Schiedsparteien durch die Vereinbarung von der Schiedsgesetzgebung widersprechenden institutionellen Schiedsregeln, im Sinne eines Schiedsverfahrens „à la carte", entweder nur Teil II IAA oder einzig das UNCITRAL Modellgesetz abwählen können oder dass sie Teil II IAA und das UNCITRAL Modellgesetz zusammen abbedingen können. Der High Court stellte darüber hinaus klar,

736 Vgl. Art. 19 UNCITRAL Modellgesetz; Chew, S. 24 f.; vgl. auch Howell/Duthie/Lim, Mark, Journal of International Arbitration 2002, Vol. 19, Ausg. 1, S. 39 (43 ff.).

737 Associate Prof. Ho Peng Kee (Singapore Parliamentary Secretary to the Minister for Law), Parliamentary Debates, Official Reports, 31.10.1994, Vol. 63, Column 625 ff., verfügbar unter http://sprs.parl.gov.sg/search/report.jsp?currentPubID=00069725-ZZ (zuletzt abgerufen am 28.4.2021); Howell/Duthie/Lim, Mark, Journal of International Arbitration 2002, Vol. 19, Ausg. 1, S. 39 (40); Merkin/Hjalmarsson, S. 2; Lim, Charles, Asian International Arbitration Journal 2011, Vol. 7, Ausg. 1, S. 1 (11).

738 *John Holland Pty Ltd (formerly known as John Holland Construction & Engineering Pty Ltd) v Toyo Engineering Corp (Japan),* [2001] SGHC 48, 14.3. 2001.

739 Engl. oil-refining facility.

dass die Parteien eines internationalen Schiedsverfahrens durch den Ausschluss des IAA das eigentlich für inländische Schiedsverfahren geschaffene AA für anwendbar erklären würden. Nach Ansicht des High Courts hatten die Parteien *in casu* nur das, mit vertraglich vereinbarten institutionellen Schiedsregeln auf einer Ebene stehende, UNCITRAL Modellgesetz durch die ICC-Schiedsgerichtsordnung abbedungen. Teil II IAA bliebe hingegen auf das Schiedsverfahren anwendbar. Der High Court erachtete demnach Sec. 24 IAA und nicht Sec. 17 AA für die Aufhebung des Schiedsspruchs als maßgeblich. Das Gericht wies aber die Aufhebung des Schiedsspruchs unter Sec. 24 IAA[740] zurück.[741]

Der *John Holland*-Entscheidung muss entgegengehalten werden, dass es sich bei dem UNCITRAL Modellgesetz nicht um ein Schiedsregelwerk handelt, das mit einer vertraglich vereinbarten, institutionellen Schiedsordnung vergleichbar ist.[742] Schon seinem Titel und den Art. 1 ff. UNCITRAL Modellgesetz lässt sich entnehmen, dass es sich bei dem UNCITRAL Modellgesetz um eine verbindliche Vorlage für ein Schiedsgesetz handelt.[743] Das UNCITRAL Modellgesetz gesteht den Schiedsparteien freilich weitgehende Freiheit zu, ihr Schiedsverfahren nach ihren Vorstellungen und Bedürfnissen auszugestalten. Dies zeigen Art. 19 und Art. 2 (e) UNCITRAL Modellgesetz und die parteiautonomen Abweichungsmöglichkeiten in den Art. 3 (1), 10 (1), 10 (2), 11 (2), 11 (3), 13 (1), 13 (2), 17, 19 (1), 20 (1), 21, 22 (1), 23 (2), 24 (1), 25, 26 (1) UNCITRAL Modellgesetz.[744] Andererseits sind Art. 11 (3), 13 (3), 14 (1), 16 (3), 27 und 34 UNCITRAL Modellgesetz als zwingende Normen nicht abdingbar.[745] Das UNCITRAL Modellgesetz gibt

---

740 Die Aufhebungsgründe von Art. 34 UNCITRAL Modellgesetz waren abbedungen worden (s. o.).

741 Rn. 13 ff.

742 Howell/Duthie/Lim, Mark, Journal of International Arbitration 2002, Vol. 19, Ausg. 1, S. 39 (48 ff.); Boo, Singapore Academy of Law Annual Review of Singapore Cases 2001, Vol. 2, S. 24 (S. 29 f.); Lim, Charles, Asian International Arbitration Journal 2011, Vol. 7, Ausg. 1, S. 1 (14 f.); Tham, Wei Chern, Asian Dispute Review 2003, S. 193 (194).

743 Das UNCITRAL Modellgesetz soll nationales Schiedsrecht harmonisieren, UNCITRAL Sekretariat, Explanatory note, Rn. 2 ff.; Howell/Duthie/Lim, Mark, Journal of International Arbitration 2002, Vol. 19, Ausg. 1, S. 39 (48).

744 Zu den Abweichungsmöglichkeiten, Born, International Commercial Arbitration, Bd. 2, S. 1609 Fn. 477. Howell/Duthie/Lim, Mark, Journal of International Arbitration 2002, Vol. 19, Ausg. 1, S. 39 (42 ff.); Polkinghorne/Cockayne, Journal of International Arbitration 2001, Vol. 18, Ausg. 6, S. 649 f.

745 Born, International Commercial Arbitration, Bd. 2, S. 1568 f., 1612. Es ist internationaler Konsens, dass Schiedsgesetzgebungen einen zwingenden Kern vorsehen, der auf alle Schiedsverfahren mit Sitz in ihrem Territorium angewendet werden muss, Born, International Commercial Arbitration, Bd. 2, S. 1589; UNCITRAL Sekretariat, Explanatory note, Rn. 13; Art. 1509 f. französischer Code de procédure civile; Art. 182

folglich bei einer Rezeption ins nationale Schiedsrecht den Rechtsrahmen für Schiedsverfahren mit Sitz in diesem Staat verbindlich vor, lässt aber in begrenztem Maße Abweichungen zu.[746] Eine vollständige Abbedingung des UNCITRAL Modellgesetzes durch die Vereinbarung der Schiedsregeln einer Schiedsinstitution sieht das UNCITRAL Modellgesetz nicht vor. Vielmehr geht das UNCITRAL Modellgesetz von einem das Schiedsverfahren ummantelnden Gerüst aus staatlichem Schiedsrecht aus, von dem durch Parteivereinbarung abgewichen werden kann, sofern dies das UNCITRAL Modellgesetz zulässt.[747]

Die Singapurer Rechtslage mit ihrer dual ausgestalteten Schiedsgesetzgebung stellt es den Parteien anheim, von dem für internationale Schiedsverfahren vorgesehenen IAA und UNCITRAL Modellgesetz in das für inländische Schiedsverfahren ausgestaltete AA zu wechseln. Bei der Abwahl des UNCITRAL Modellgesetzes ist jedoch zu berücksichtigen, dass durch die Vereinbarung von institutionellen Schiedsregeln die Schiedsparteien nur vom dispositiven Grundmodell des UNCITRAL Modellgesetzes abweichende Regelungen treffen können.[748] Eine parteiautonome Abbedingung der zwingenden Normen des UNCITRAL Modellgesetzes und des IAA findet hierdurch nicht statt.[749]

Der Wortlaut von Sec. 15 IAA a. F. sah nur die Option vor, den IAA und das UNCITRAL Modellgesetz zusammen abzuwählen. Mit seiner Entscheidung, lediglich das UNCITRAL Modellgesetz als abbedungen anzusehen, setzte sich der High Court über den gesetzgeberischen Willen hinweg.[750] Diese legislative Intention verdeutlicht die im Jahr 2001 eingeführte Sec. 15 (1) IAA n. F. In Sec. 15 (1) IAA n. F. stellte der Gesetzgeber nochmals klar, dass der Ausschluss des UNCITRAL Modellgesetzes oder des IAA zu ihrer

---

Schweizer Bundesgesetz über das Internationale Privatrecht; Sec. 4 englischer Arbitration Act 1996; Sec. 15A Singapurer IAA.

746 Pryles, International Arbitration Law Review 2001, S. 175 (177); Blackaby/Partasides/Redfern/Hunter, International Arbitration, Rn. 3.53 ff.; Born, International Commercial Arbitration, Bd. 2, S. 1568 f.; Howell/Duthie/Lim, Mark, Journal of International Arbitration 2002, Vol. 19, Ausg. 1, S. 39 (42 ff.).

747 UNCITRAL Sekretariat, Explanatory note, Rn. 13 und 30 ff.; Report of the Secretary-General, United Nations General Assembly, Analytical commentary on draft text of a model law on international commercial arbitration, A/CN.9/264, 25.3.1985, Art. 19, S. 44 f.; Born, International Commercial Arbitration, Bd. 2, S. 1567 ff., 1585 f., 1602 ff.; Pillay, Arbitration International 2004, Vol. 20, Ausg. 4, S. 355 (380); Holtzmann/Neuhaus, Guide UNCITRAL, S. 564 ff.; Howell/Duthie/Lim, Mark, Journal of International Arbitration 2002, Vol. 19, Ausg. 1, S. 39 (42 ff.).

748 Howell/Duthie/Lim, Mark, Journal of International Arbitration 2002, Vol. 19, Ausg. 1, S. 39 (42 ff.); Pillay, Arbitration International 2004, Vol. 20, Ausg. 4, S. 355 (380 f.).

749 Boo, Halsbury's, S. 16; Chew, S. 25; Pillay, Arbitration International 2004, Vol. 20, Ausg. 4, S. 355 (380 f.); Sec. 15A IAA.

750 Vgl. Yeo, Alvin, International Arbitration Law Review 2002, S. 71 (73).

kumulativen Abbedingung führt.[751] Der IAA und das UNCITRAL Modellgesetz können nicht isoliert voneinander anwendbar sein. Das UNCITRAL Modellgesetz wird durch Sec. 3 IAA für internationale Schiedsverfahren für anwendbar erklärt. Ohne das UNCITRAL Modellgesetz ist der IAA zudem weitgehend inhaltslos, da die Bestimmungen des IAA lediglich das UNCITRAL Modellgesetz modifizieren, welches den Kern der Singapurer internationalen Schiedslegislation bildet.[752]

(3) Fazit

Die rechtswissenschaftliche Literatur kritisiert an den Urteilen *Coop* und *John Holland*, dass die Vereinbarung von auf das Schiedsverfahren anwendbaren institutionellen Schiedsregeln nicht den konkludenten Ausschluss des UNCITRAL Modellgesetzes bewirken könne. Die Urteile führten hierdurch ferner zu Rechtsunsicherheiten.[753] Die Schiedsgerichtsbranche und international tätige Rechtsanwälte kritisierten die Entscheidungen *Coop* und *John Holland* ebenfalls und erachteten Singapur nicht mehr als geeignetes Schiedszentrum für die Beilegung von internationalen Schiedsverfahren.[754] Im November 2001 reagierte der Singapurer Gesetzgeber auf diese Kritik und reformierte Sec. 15 IAA a. F.[755] Nach Sec. 15 (2) IAA n. F. reicht die Ver-

---

751 So auch, High Court, *Dermajaya Properties Sdn Bhd v Premium Properties Sdn Bhd and another*, [2002] SGHC 53, 20.3.2002.

752 Vgl. High Court, *Dermajaya Properties Sdn Bhd v Premium Properties Sdn Bhd and another*, [2002] SGHC 53, 20.3.2002; Tham, Wei Chern, Asian Dispute Review 2003, S. 193 (194); Howell/Duthie/Lim, Mark, Journal of International Arbitration 2002, Vol. 19, Ausg. 1, S. 39 ff.; Hwang, International Arbitration Law Review 2002, S. N26 (N27).

753 Howell/Duthie/Lim, Mark, Journal of International Arbitration 2002, Vol. 19, Ausg. 1, S. 39 (45 ff.). Zur Rechtsunsicherheit durch die beiden Urteile, Hoyle, The International Construction Law Review 2001, S. 692 (699 ff.). Zur Rechtsunsicherheit durch die *John Holland*-Entscheidung, Polkinghorne/Cockayne, Journal of International Arbitration 2001, Vol. 18, Ausg. 6, S. 649 (654 f.). Zur Abbedingung des UNCITRAL Modellgesetzes, Lim, Charles, Asian International Arbitration Journal 2011, Vol. 7, Ausg. 1, S. 1 (13 ff.); Boo, Singapore Academy of Law Annual Review of Singapore Cases 2001, Vol. 2, S. 24 (S. 29 f.); Boo, Halsbury's, S. 23 Fn. 18. Kritisch zur Abbedingung des UNCITRAL Modellgesetzes im *John Holland*-Urteil, Hwang, International Arbitration Law Review 2002, S. N26 (N27); Dang/Murugaiyan, International Financial Law Review 2001, S. 87 (89). Differenziert zu der *Coop*-Entscheidung, Hsu, International Arbitration Law Review 1999, S. 17 (21). Kritik an dem *John Holland*-Urteil, Smith/Cook, Arbitration 2011, S. 108 (113); Yeo, Alvin, International Arbitration Law Review 2002, S. 71 (73). Differenziert zu den beiden Entscheidung, Pillay, Arbitration International 2004, Vol. 20, Ausg. 4, S. 355 (378).

754 Chew, S. 27 f.; Dang/Murugaiyan, International Financial Law Review 2001, S. 87 ff.

755 Act 38 of 2001, International Arbitration (Amendment) Act 2001, in Kraft getreten am 1.11.2001; Berg (Hrsg.), Singapore, Yearbook Commercial Arbitration 2002,

einbarung einer institutionellen Schiedsgerichtsordnung nicht aus, um den zweiten Teil des IAA oder das UNCITRAL Modellgesetz abzuwählen und dadurch in indirekter Weise in den AA hinein zu wechseln. Die Gesetzesreform beendete auch die „à la carte“ Auswahl der staatlichen Schiedsgesetzgebungen unter der *John Holland*-Rechtsprechung. Aus Sec. 15 IAA n. F. lässt sich entnehmen, dass Teil II IAA und das UNCITRAL Modellgesetz nur gemeinsam[756] und ausdrücklich abbedungen werden können und dass sodann der AA auf das Schiedsverfahren Anwendung findet. Die Gesetzesreform des Jahres 2001 ließ jedoch die Frage offen, inwieweit institutionelle Schiedsverfahrensregeln anwendbar bleiben, die dem Teil II IAA und dem UNCITRAL Modellgesetz widersprechen.[757]

(4) Dermajaya Properties v Premium Properties

In *Dermajaya Properties Sdn Bhd v Premium Properties Sdn Bhd and another (Dermajaya)*[758] hatte der High Court – im Rahmen der Kontrolle einer schiedsgerichtlich angeordneten Prozesskostensicherheit – darüber zu entscheiden, ob die Parteien den IAA abbedungen haben.

Die bruneiische Klägerin *Dermajaya Properties Sdn Bhd* erwarb von den malaysischen Beklagten eine Kapitaleinlage[759] an einem malaysischen Unternehmen. Der Kaufvertrag enthielt eine Schiedsklausel, nach der Streitigkeiten in einem Schiedsverfahren gem. den UNCITRAL Rules in Singapur beigelegt werden sollten. Der Einzelschiedsrichter[760] entschied in einem „vorläufigen Schiedsspruch“, dass die Klägerin den Beklagten Prozesskostensicherheit gewähren müsse. Die Klägerin legte gegen diesen Schiedsspruch im Februar 2002 Berufung beim High Court ein und trug vor, dass der Einzelschiedsrichter für die Anordnung von Prozesskostensicherheit nicht zuständig gewesen sei.

Vol. XXVII, S. 386 (388 f.); Associate Prof. Ho Peng Kee, Singapore Parliamentary Debates, Official Reports, 5.10.2001, Vol. 73, Column 2223, verfügbar unter http://sprs.parl.gov.sg/search/topic.jsp?currentTopicID=00068181-ZZ&currentPubID=00069892-ZZ&topicKey=00069892-ZZ.00068181-ZZ_1%2Bid017_20011005_S0004_T00091-bill%2B (zuletzt abgerufen am 28.4.2021); Lim, Charles, Asian International Arbitration Journal 2011, Vol. 7, Ausg. 1, S. 1 (15); Howell/Duthie/Lim, Mark, Journal of International Arbitration 2002, Vol. 19, Ausg. 1, S. 39 (49 f.); Smith/Cook, Arbitration 2011, S. 108 (113); Tham, Wei Chern, Asian Dispute Review 2003, S. 193 (196); Hwang, International Arbitration Law Review 2002, S. N26 (N30); Pillay, The International Construction Law Review 2003, S. 91 (117 f.).

756 Die Abbedingung von Teil II IAA oder dem UNCITRAL Modellgesetz führt zum Ausschluss beider Statuten.

757 Pillay, The International Construction Law Review 2003, S. 91 (119).

758 [2002] SGHC 53, 20.3.2002.

759 Engl. paid-up capital.

760 Die Schiedsklausel sah einen Einzelschiedsrichter vor.

Die UNCITRAL Rules gestatten es dem Schiedsgericht nicht, einer Partei Sicherheiten für ihre Prozesskosten zuzusprechen. Nach dem AA kann das Schiedsgericht gleichfalls keine Prozesskostensicherheit anordnen. Sec. 12 IAA räumt dem Schiedstribunal hingegen die Kompetenz ein, Sicherheiten für die Prozesskosten einer Partei anzuordnen.

Die Klägerin machte geltend, dass die Parteien durch die Vereinbarungen der, mit dem UNCITRAL Modellgesetz im Widerspruch stehenden, UNCITRAL Rules konkludent Teil II des IAA und das UNCITRAL Modellgesetz abbedungen hätten. Die Beklagten trugen vor, dass die Parteien nicht konkludent den IAA abbedingen können. Der High Court leitete aus der reformierten Sec. 15 IAA n. F. auch für Sec. 15 IAA a. F. den gesetzgeberischen Willen ab, dass, wenn die Schiedsparteien das UNCITRAL Modellgesetz oder Teil II IAA für ein Schiedsverfahren ausdrücklich ausgeschlossen haben, sowohl das UNCITRAL Modellgesetz als auch Teil II IAA nicht anwendbar seien.

Der High Court entschied allerdings im März 2002, dass die Parteien den IAA und das UNCITRAL Modellgesetz nicht ausdrücklich ausgeschlossen hätten, da die Vereinbarung einer dem IAA oder dem UNCITRAL Modellgesetz widersprechenden institutionellen Schiedsordnung hierfür nicht ausreiche. Das Gericht schlussfolgerte, dass die vereinbarten Schiedsregeln, die mit dem UNCITRAL Modellgesetz unvereinbar seien, nicht nur hinsichtlich der den zwingenden Bestimmungen des UNCITRAL Modellgesetzes widersprechenden Bestimmungen unwirksam seien, sondern gänzlich auf das Schiedsverfahren unanwendbar seien. Es handele sich bei dem UNCITRAL Modellgesetz um die „zwingende" Schiedsgesetzgebung, die auf alle internationalen Schiedsverfahren mit Sitz in Singapur angewendet werden müsse. Das Gericht urteilte daher, dass die UNCITRAL Rules in diesem Fall nicht auf das Schiedsverfahren anwendbar seien und wies die Berufung zurück.[761]

Das Urteil des High Courts räumte der *lex arbitri*[762] in einer der Parteiautonomie widersprechenden Weise den Vorrang gegenüber der von den Parteien vereinbarten institutionellen Schiedsverfahrensordnung ein.[763] Dabei übersah der High Court, dass institutionelle Schiedsordnungen für sich nicht in Anspruch nehmen, das auf das Schiedsverfahren anwendbare staatliche Schiedsrecht gänzlich zu substituieren. Lediglich die dispositiven Schieds-

---

761 Rn. 67 ff.

762 Schiedsgesetzgebung.

763 *Chew* kritisiert diese Verletzung der Parteiautonomie und erachtet das Urteil als schiedsfeindlich, Chew, S. 29. Nach *Boo* irrte der High Court im Urteil *Dermajaya*, als er die UNCITRAL Rules als unvereinbar mit dem IAA ansah, Boo, Halsbury's, S. 23 Fn. 19, S. 16 Fn. 7 f.

gesetzesnormen sollen durch die Schiedsordnung abbedungen werden. Zwingendes Schiedsrecht bleibt auf das Schiedsverfahren anwendbar.[764]

Die Literatur kritisiert im Hinblick auf das *Dermajaya*-Urteil die Verletzung der Parteiautonomie.[765] Die praktische Auswirkung der *Dermajaya*-Entscheidung war, dass Anwälte ihren Mandanten rieten, den Schiedsort Singapur zu meiden.[766]

Das Parlament reagierte innerhalb von wenigen Monaten[767] im Interesse des Schiedsortes Singapur auf die durch das *Dermajaya*-Urteil ausgelöste Rechtsunsicherheit und führte im Oktober 2002 Sec. 15A (1) in den IAA ein.[768] In Sec. 15A (1) IAA hob der Gesetzgeber hervor, dass die von den Parteien vereinbarten Schiedsregeln auf das Schiedsverfahren anwendbar sind[769], soweit sie nicht gegen zwingende Vorschriften des UNCITRAL Modellgesetzes oder Teil II des IAA verstoßen.[770] Mit der Gesetzesänderung bezweckte die Legislative, Singapurs Status quo als attraktiven Schiedsort

---

764 Vgl. Chew, S. 31; Tham, Wei Chern, Asian Dispute Review 2003, S. 193 (195 f.). Siehe Regel 1.1 SIAC Rules 2013; Regel 27 SIAC Rules 2016; Regel 2 SCMA Arbitration Rules 2015; Art. 1 (5) Swiss Rules 2012; Art. 14.5, 20.5, 20.7, 29.2 LCIA Arbitration Rules 2014; AAA, International Centre for Dispute Resolution, International Dispute Resolution Procedures 2014, Art. 1 (2) International Arbitration Rules; vgl. zudem Ausführungen zum Urteil *John Holland*, Kapitel: Anwendungsbereich des Verfahrensrechts; John Holland v Toyo Engineering (B. I. 1. a)aa)(2)).

765 Chan Andrew/Woodward, Arbitration 2003, S. 10 (14); Pillay, Arbitration International 2004, Vol. 20, Ausg. 4, S. 355 (382). Kritisch zu dem Urteil, Smith/Cook, Arbitration 2011, S. 108 (113); Dundas, Arbitration 2010, S. 2 (11).

766 Associate Prof. Ho Peng Kee (Senior Minister of State for Law), Parliamentary Debates, Official Reports, 1.10.2002, Vol. 75, Column 1107 ff., verfügbar unter http://sprs.parl.gov.sg/search/topic.jsp?currentTopicID=00068650-ZZ&currentPubID=00069920-ZZ&topicKey=00069920-ZZ. 00068650-ZZ_1%2Bid022_20021001_S0003_T00071-bill%2B (zuletzt abgerufen am 28.4.2021); Chew, S. 29 f.; Lim, Charles, Asian International Arbitration Journal 2011, Vol. 7, Ausg. 1, S. 1 (16); Chan, Andrew/Woodward, Arbitration 2003, S. 10 (14 ff.); Yeo, Alvin, International Arbitration Law Review 2002, S. N54; Pillay, Arbitration International 2004, Vol. 20, Ausg. 4, S. 355 (382); Pillay, The International Construction Law Review 2003, S. 91 (120).

767 Das Urteil *Dermajaya* erging am 20.3.2002, die 1. Lesung der Gesetzesänderung fand am 27.8.2002 statt (Pillay, The International Construction Law Review 2003, S. 91 [120]) und das Gesetz ist am 31.12.2002 in Kraft getreten.

768 Act 28 of 2002, International Arbitration (Amendment) Act 2002, in Kraft getreten am 25.10.2002; Lim, Charles, Asian International Arbitration Journal 2011, Vol. 7, Ausg. 1, S. 1 (16); Tham, Wei Chern, Asian Dispute Review 2003, S. 193 (195).

769 Zur Achtung der Parteiautonomie, Smith/Cook, Arbitration 2011, S. 108 (113). Chan, Andrew/Woodward, Arbitration 2003, S. 10 (15.); Pillay, Arbitration International 2004, Vol. 20, Ausg. 4, S. 355 (382).

770 Sec. 15A (2) IAA. Sec. 15A (2) IAA besagt, dass Sec. 15A (3)–(6) IAA festlegen, welche Bestimmungen des UNCITRAL Modellgesetzes und von Teil II des IAA unabdingbar sind.

zu erhalten.[771] Diese Rechtslage korrespondiert mit den Schiedsregeln der Singapurer Schiedsinstitutionen „SIAC“ und „Singapore Chamber of Maritime Arbitration (SCMA)“ und mit den international anerkannten Schiedsregeln der „AAA[772] International Arbitration Rules“, der „Swiss Rules“ sowie der „LCIA[773] Arbitration Rules“. Diese Schiedsregeln sehen vor, dass die Parteien durch die Vereinbarung einer institutionellen Schiedsordnung nicht von den zwingenden Normen des auf das Schiedsverfahren anwendbaren nationalen Schiedsrechts abweichen können.[774] Die Schiedsordnungen zollen hierdurch der primären Regelungsbefugnis der nationalen Schiedsgesetzgebungen Respekt. Sie bringen zum Ausdruck, dass die Vereinbarung von institutionellen Schiedsregeln nicht *per se* zur vollständigen Abbedingung des nationalen, auf das Schiedsverfahren anwendbaren, Schiedsrechts führen kann, sondern vielmehr lediglich das *ius dispositivum* des nationalen Schiedsrechts abbedungen wird.

(5) Bewertung

Die Entscheidungen des High Courts in *Coop* und *John Holland* führten zu erheblicher Rechtsunsicherheit bei der Frage, ob die Parteien durch die Vereinbarung von institutionellen Schiedsregeln konkludent den Anwendungsbereich des IAA und des UNCITRAL Modellgesetzes ganz oder teilweise zu Gunsten des AA abbedungen haben. Mit der Einführung des neuen Sec. 15 IAA beseitigte der Gesetzgeber die durch die High Court Rechtsprechung geschaffene Rechtsunklarheit. Für ein Herausoptieren aus dem IAA und dem UNCITRAL Modellgesetz in den AA bedarf es nun einer ausdrücklichen Vereinbarung. Eine konkludente Abwahl mittels der Vereinbarung einer mit dem UNCITRAL Modellgesetz bzw. mit dem IAA unvereinbaren institutionellen Schiedsgerichtsordnung ist nicht mehr möglich. Durch diese Gesetzesanpassung entsprach Singapur dem Anforderungsprofil der internationalen Schiedsgerichtsbarkeit.

---

771 Associate Prof. Ho Peng Kee (Senior Minister of State for Law), Parliamentary Debates, Official Reports, 1.10.2002, Vol. 75, Column 1107 ff. verfügbar unter http://sprs.parl.gov.sg/search/topic.jsp?currentTopicID=00068650-ZZ&currentPubID=00069920-ZZ&topicKey=00069920-ZZ. 00068650-ZZ_1%2Bid022_20021001_S0003_T00071-bill%2B (zuletzt abgerufen am 28.4.2021); Chew, S. 29 f.; Berg (Hrsg.), Singapore, Yearbook Commercial Arbitration 2002, Vol. XXVII, S. 386 (388 ff.); Lim, Charles, Asian International Arbitration Journal 2011, Vol. 7, Ausg. 1, S. 1 (16); Smith/Cook, Arbitration 2011, S. 108 (113); Chan, Andrew/Woodward, Arbitration 2003, S. 10 (14 ff.).

772 „American Arbitration Association“.

773 „London Court of International Arbitration“.

774 Regel 1.1 SIAC Rules 2013; Regel 27 SIAC Rules 2016; Regel 2 SCMA Arbitration Rules 2015; Art. 1 (5) Swiss Rules 2012; Art. 14.5, 20.5, 20.7, 29.2. LCIA Arbitration Rules 2014; AAA, International Centre for Dispute Resolution, International Dispute Resolution Procedures 2014, Art. 1 (2) International Arbitration Rules.

Nach der *Dermajaya*-Rechtsprechung konnte eine der Singapurer Schiedsgesetzgebung widersprechende institutionelle Schiedsordnung zu deren Ausschluss führen. Die verursachte Rechtsunklarheit, ob die vereinbarten Schiedsregeln anwendbar bleiben, beeinträchtige die Attraktivität des Schiedsortes Singapur. Im neu geschaffenen Sec. 15A IAA stellte der Gesetzgeber deshalb klar, dass lediglich die mit zwingenden Vorschriften von Teil II IAA und dem UNCITRAL Modellgesetz nicht in Einklang zu bringende Bestimmungen einer institutionellen Schiedsordnung unwirksam sind.

Das durch die *Coop-*, *John Holland*- und die *Dermajaya*-Rechtsprechung zu Tage getretene für Schiedsverfahren hinderliche Klima behob der Gesetzgeber innerhalb von wenigen Monaten. Dies zeigt, dass die flexible Legislative des Stadtstaates Singapur die Schiedsrechtsordnung zügig den Notwendigkeiten des Schiedswesens angleicht.

bb) Vereinbarung des IAA

(1) Navigator Investment v Acclaim Insurance Brokers

Im Urteil *Navigator Investment Services Ltd v Acclaim Insurance Brokers Pte Ltd (Navigator Investment)*[775] entschied der Court of Appeal, dass die Schiedsparteien in inländischen Schiedsverfahren durch ihre Wahl der SIAC-Schiedsordnung indirekt den IAA für anwendbar erklärt haben.

In dieser Rechtssache schloss *Acclaim Insurance Brokers Pte Ltd (Acclaim)* 2004 mit *Navigator Investment Services Ltd (Navigator)* einen Vertriebsvertrag[776], nach dem *Acclaim* die Anlageprodukte[777] von *Navigator* vertreiben und hierfür eine Vertriebsprovision erhalten sollte. Der Vertriebsvertrag enthielt eine SIAC-Schiedsklausel, nach der Streitigkeiten nach der aktuellen SIAC-Schiedsordnung von einem Schiedsgericht zu entscheiden waren. *Herr Wong*, seit 2006 Abteilungsleiter bei *Acclaim,* organisierte im Juli 2007 den Transfer von 26 Mio. Singapur-Dollar an Anlagewerten von *Acclaims* Konten bei *Navigator* zu *Leadenhall Insurance Brokers Pte Ltd (Leadenhall)*. *Acclaim* behauptete, *Herr Wong* und sein Vater hätten ein finanzielles Interesse am Transfer der Vermögenswerte zu *Leadenhall* gehabt. Am 14. Dezember 2007 klagte Herr *Wong* vor dem High Court gegen *Acclaim* auf ausstehende Provisionen[778]. *Acclaim* beantragte am 17. Dezember 2007

---

775 [2009] SGCA 45, 29.9.2009. In dieser Entscheidung folgte der Court of Appeal der Entscheidung des Court of Appeals in der Rechtssache *NCC International AB v Alliance Concrete Singapore Pte Ltd* ([2008] 2 SLR 565; [2008] SGCA 5, 26.2.2008).

776 Engl. distribution agreement.

777 Engl. investment products.

778 Engl. unpaid commissions.

vorgerichtliche[779] „Discovery“ und „Interrogatories“[780] von *Navigator* (Discovery-Verfahren), um gegen die Verantwortlichen des Betruges beim Anlagetransfer zu Lasten von *Acclaim* vorgehen zu können. *Navigator* machte im Januar 2008 gegenüber *Acclaim* zwei weitere Verfahren anhängig.

Navigator legte zudem im April 2008 Schiedsklage beim SIAC ein. Im Schiedsverfahren beantragte *Navigator* die Feststellung, dass sie gegenüber *Acclaim* nicht hafte. Der Schiedsrichter setzte das Schiedsverfahren aus, bis die Parteien weitere Anträge stellen. *Navigator* beantragte im von *Acclaim* initiierten Discovery-Verfahren vergeblich die Aussetzung des Verfahrens zu Gunsten des vereinbarten Schiedsverfahrens. Die Berufung von *Navigator* richtete sich gegen die Nichtaussetzung des Discovery-Verfahrens durch den High Court unter Sec. 6 IAA. Auf das Schiedsverfahren war die SIAC-Schiedsordnung aus dem Jahr 2007 anwendbar, deren Regel 32 besagte, dass auf ein unter der SIAC-Schiedsordnung durchgeführtes Schiedsverfahren mit Sitz in Singapur der IAA als *lex arbitri* anzuwenden ist.[781] Der Court of Appeal hatte zu entscheiden, ob der AA oder der IAA auf das Schiedsverfahren anwendbar war.[782] Das oberste Singapurer Gericht urteilte, dass die Parteien mittels der Wahl der SIAC-Schiedsordnung in ihrer Schiedsklausel durch Regel 32 der SIAC-Schiedsordnung 2007 den IAA als das für sie maßgebende Schiedsrecht gem. Sec. 5 (1) IAA vereinbart hätten.[783] Bei der Aussetzungsentscheidung gem. Sec. 6 IAA wog der Court of Appeal das Ziel, den Schiedsort Singapur zu fördern und die Vertraulichkeit des Schiedsverfahrens zu schützen gegen das Interesse, prozessuale und materielle Gerechtigkeit in den Singapurer Gerichtsverfahren zu verbürgen, gegeneinander ab. Der Court of Appeal wies die Berufung zurück und entschied in seiner Abwägung, dass vorgerichtliche Discovery und Interrogatories im vorliegenden Sachverhalt auch für Parteien einer Schiedsvereinbarung eröffnet seien.[784]

Das Gericht urteilte ferner, dass die Wahlmöglichkeit zwischen dem IAA und dem AA die für die Parteiautonomie erforderliche Flexibilität gewährleiste. Die Schiedsparteien sollten in der Lage sein, das auf ihr Schiedsverfahren anwendbare Schiedsrecht (IAA oder AA) selbst zu bestimmen.[785]

Obwohl Sec. 5 (1) IAA für die Anwendbarkeit des IAA auf inländische Schiedsverfahren fordert, dass die Parteien schriftlich in den IAA wechseln,

779 Engl. pre-action.
780 Schriftliche Beweisfragen.
781 Regel 32 SIAC Rules 2007.
782 Hiervon war abhängig, ob Sec. 6 AA oder Sec. 6 IAA für die Aussetzung des Verfahrens einschlägig war.
783 Rn. 31 ff.
784 Rn. 63 ff.
785 Rn. 31 ff.

reichte es dem Court of Appeal aus, dass die Parteien indirekt durch die Vereinbarung der SIAC-Schiedsordnung, auf Grund von Regel 32 der SIAC-Schiedsordnung 2007, den IAA für ihr Schiedsverfahren für anwendbar erklärt hatten.

Das *Navigator Investment*-Urteil unterstützt das Interesse der Schiedsgerichtsbarkeit, möglichst geringen Interventionen durch die Gerichte ausgesetzt zu sein. Andererseits ist dieses Urteil nicht mit dem Wortlaut von Sec. 5 IAA vereinbar, der fordert, dass die Parteien schriftlich aus dem AA heraus optieren müssen. Die indirekte Wahl des IAA mittels der Vereinbarung eines SIAC-Schiedsverfahrens, dessen Regel 32 der SIAC-Schiedsordnung 2007 den IAA für anwendbar erklärt, stellt eine schriftliche Vereinbarung dar. Hierdurch erfolgt aber lediglich konkludent eine mittelbare Abwahl des AA durch die Verweisung auf die SIAC-Schiedsordnung. Der reformierte Sec. 15 IAA[786] regelt die umgekehrte Konstellation des aus dem IAA und dem UNCITRAL Modellgesetz in den AA Hineinoptierens. Die Ratio von Sec. 15 (2) IAA n. F., dass die Vereinbarung der Schiedsregeln einer Schiedsinstitution nicht ausreichen, um dadurch mittelbar vom internationalen[787] in das inländische Schiedsrecht[788] zu wechseln, wird auch auf die umgekehrte Konstellation anwendbar sein.[789] Von einem gesetzlichen Verbot einer indirekten Abwahl des AA zu Gunsten des IAA sah der Singapurer Gesetzgeber vermutlich ab, da die aktuelle SIAC-Schiedsordnung 2016 als auch die SIAC-Schiedsordnung 2013 und 2010 keine mit Regel 32 der SIAC-Schiedsordnung 2007 vergleichbare Bestimmung mehr enthalten.[790]

786 Act 38/2001, International Arbitration (Amendment) Act 2001, in Kraft getreten am 1.11.2001. Der alte Sec. 15 IAA besagte: „If the parties to an arbitration agreement have (whether in the arbitration agreement or in any other document in writing) agreed that any dispute that has arisen or may arise between them is to be settled or resolved otherwise than in accordance with this Part or the Model Law, this Part and the Model Law shall not apply in relation to the settlement or resolution of that dispute.“ Siehe Howell/Duthie/Lim, Mark, Journal of International Arbitration 2002, Vol. 19, Ausg. 1, S. 39 (44).

787 IAA und UNCITRAL Modellgesetz.

788 AA.

789 Der Gesetzgeber stellte in Sec. 15 (2) IAA n. F. nochmals klar, dass ein konkludentes Herausoptieren aus dem IAA nicht zulässig ist, Associate Prof. Ho Peng Kee, Singapore Parliamentary Debates, Official Reports, 5.10.2001, Vol. 73, Column 2223, verfügbar unter http://sprs.parl.gov.sg/search/topic.jsp?currentTopicID=00068181-ZZ&currentPubID=00069892-ZZ&topicKey=00069892-ZZ.00068181-ZZ_1%2Bid017_20011005_S0004_T00091-bill%2B (zuletzt abgerufen am 28.4.2021); High Court, *Dermajaya Properties Sdn Bhd v Premium Properties Sdn Bhd and another*, [2002] SGHC 53, 20.3.2002, Rn. 66 f.

790 Einzig Regel 22.1 i. V. m. 1.2 der SCMA Arbitration Rules 2015 enthält noch immer eine indirekte Wahl des IAA, wenn der Schiedssitz in Singapur gelegen ist. SCMA administrierte aber von 2009–2016 bisher 173 Schiedsverfahren, davon waren lediglich 23 inländische Schiedsverfahren (SCMA Case Summary, verfügbar unter http://www.

(2) Bewertung

Die Reform der SIAC-Schiedsordnung[791] machte das Urteil *Navigator Investment* des Court of Appeals obsolet und passte den Schiedsort Singapur dem globalen Standard der institutionellen Schiedsregeln an[792]. Zwei Singapurer Schiedsparteien können nur durch schriftliche Vereinbarung den IAA für anwendbar erklären. Inländische Schiedsparteien bedürfen eines besonderen Schutzes.[793] Es ist deshalb folgerichtig, ihnen diesen lediglich bei schriftlichem Konsens zu entziehen. Diese zusätzliche Anforderung an das Abbedingen des AA stellt keine schiedsunfreundliche Regelung dar. Denn den Parteien bleibt es anheimgestellt, ein von weniger gerichtlicher Kontrolle geprägtes Schiedsverfahren unter dem IAA[794] für ihr inländisches Schiedsverfahren schriftlich zu vereinbaren.

---

scma.org.sg/pdf/casesummary.pdf [zuletzt abgerufen am 28.4.2021]). SIAC verwaltete von 2005–2015 1.882 Schiedsverfahren (Statistics, verfügbar unter http://siac.org.sg/2014-11-03-13-33-43/facts-figures/statistics [zuletzt abgerufen am 28.4.2021]). Dieser Vergleich zeigt, dass die Anzahl von SCMA Schiedsverfahren zu vernachlässigen ist. Dies mag auch der Grund sein, dass der Singapurer Gesetzgeber im AA keinen Gleichklang mit Sec. 15 IAA normierte. Freilich bleibt es für die geringe Anzahl von inländischen SCMA Schiedsverfahren trotzdem bei der Rechtsunsicherheit, ob die Parteien den AA abbedungen haben. Diese Rechtsunklarheit können juristisch beratene Parteien durch eine explizite, schriftliche, verfahrensrechtliche Rechtswahl einfach beseitigen. Zudem ist davon auszugehen, dass Singapurer Schiedsparteien aus der Schifffahrtsbranche bei Abschluss einer Schiedsklausel durch mit dem Singapurer Schiedsrecht vertraute Anwälte beraten werden.

791 Zu den SCMA Arbitration Rules 2015 siehe Fn 790.

792 Keine der international führenden Schiedsinstitutionen (ICC, LCIA, AAA [International Dispute Resolution Procedures, International Arbitration Rules], Swiss Rules) enthält eine prozessuale Rechtswahl in ihrer Schiedsordnung.

793 Merkin/Hjalmarsson, S. 2; Associate Prof. Ho Peng Kee (Singapore Parliamentary Secretary to the Minister for Law), Parliamentary Debates, Official Reports, 31.10.1994, Vol. 63, Column 625 ff., verfügbar unter http://sprs.parl.gov.sg/search/report.jsp?currentPubID=00069725-ZZ (zuletzt abgerufen am 28.4.2021); Howell/Duthie/Lim, Mark, Journal of International Arbitration 2002, Vol. 19, Ausg. 1, S. 39 f.; Merkin/Hjalmarsson, S. 2; Lim, Charles, Asian International Arbitration Journal 2011, Vol. 7, Ausg. 1, S. 1 (11).

794 Associate Prof. Ho Peng Kee (Singapore Parliamentary Secretary to the Minister for Law), Parliamentary Debates, Official Reports, 31.10.1994, Vol. 63, Column 625 ff., verfügbar unter http://sprs.parl.gov.sg/search/report.jsp?currentPubID=00069725-ZZ (zuletzt abgerufen am 28.4.2021); Howell/Duthie/Lim, Mark, Journal of International Arbitration 2002, Vol. 19, Ausg. 1, S. 39 f.; Merkin/Hjalmarsson, S. 2; Lim, Charles, Asian International Arbitration Journal 2011, Vol. 7, Ausg. 1, S. 1 (11).

b) Erweiterung des geographischen Anwendungsbereichs

Der Anwendungsbereich des IAA und des AA ist auf Schiedsverfahren mit Sitz in Singapur begrenzt.[795] Entsprechend urteilte der High Court im Verfahren *Coop International Pte Ltd v Ebel SA (Coop)*[796]:

> „*No doubt the scheme of the IAA which incorporates the Model Law is intended to apply to arbitrations in Singapore. When parties choose a place of arbitration in a foreign country, I do not think that Parliament ever intended the IAA and the Model Law to apply to that foreign arbitration such that the parties must expressly opt out of those procedures pursuant to s 15. Comity of nations and reciprocity dictate that a foreign country's own substantive laws and procedures governing the conduct of arbitration within their own territory must be respected.*"[797]

Der Singapurer Gesetzgeber erweiterte jedoch 2010 den Geltungsbereich des IAA ausnahmsweise auf vorläufige gerichtliche Maßnahmen für Parteien eines Schiedsverfahrens mit ausländischem Sitz.[798] Die Möglichkeit, einstweilige gerichtliche Maßnahmen auch für die Parteien eines Schiedsverfahrens mit Sitz im Ausland zu erlassen, korrespondiert mit den Ergänzungen des UNCITRAL Modellgesetzes 2006[799], die der Gesetzgeber aber nicht in das Singapurer Recht übernahm. Den einstweiligen gerichtlichen Rechtsschutz führte der Gesetzgeber ein, weil zuvor der Court of Appeal im Berufungsverfahren *Swift-Fortune Ltd v Magnifica Marine SA II*[800] den Singapurer Gerichten die Kompetenz absprach, vorläufige Maßnahmen für Schiedsverfahren mit ausländischem Sitz anzuordnen. Dies sollte die Schiedsfreundlichkeit der Singapurer Schiedsgesetzgebung stärken.[801] Im Rahmen des „Comitas" versucht Singapur *inter alia* bei der Vollstreckung von ausländischen Schiedssprüchen großzügig zu sein, um andererseits die Vollstreckung von Singapurer Schiedssprüchen im Ausland zu gewährleis-

---

795 Siehe Kapitel: Anwendungsbereich des Verfahrensrechts (B. I. 1.).

796 [1998] SGHC 425, 27.1.und 4.3.1998; siehe Kapitel: Coop International v Ebel (B. I. 1. a)aa)(1)).

797 Rn. 131.

798 Sec. 12A IAA. Des Weiteren können seit 2012 durch Schiedsgerichte mit ausländischem Sitz angeordnete einstweilige Maßnahmen in Singapur vollstreckt werden, siehe hierzu Kapitel: Einstweiliger Rechtsschutz durch Schiedsgerichte; Ausländische Schiedsverfahren (B. VI. 2. b)).

799 UNCITRAL Model Law on International Commercial Arbitration, 1985, With amendments as adopted in 2006; Art. 17 J.

800 Court of Appeal, [2007] 1 SLR 629; [2006] SGCA 42, 1.12.2006.

801 Shanmugam (Minister for Law), Parliamentary Debates, Official Reports, 19.10.2009, Vol. 86, Column 1627 ff., verfügbar unter http://sprs.parl.gov.sg/search/topic.jsp?currentTopicID=00003591-WA&currentPubID=00004793-WA&topicKey=00004793-WA.00003591-WA_1%2B%2B (zuletzt abgerufen am 28.4.2021).

ten. Das Ziel dabei ist, den Schiedsort Singapur attraktiver zu machen.[802] Dies kommt auch in der Gestattung von vorläufigen gerichtlichen Maßnahmen zum Ausdruck, die lediglich ausländische Schiedsverfahren begünstigen. *De lege ferenda* wäre es hilfreich, neben dieser schiedsortunabhängigen Ausnahme des IAA Anwendungsbereichs, als zweite Ausnahme auch Schiedsverfahren mit ausländischem Sitz eine gerichtliche Beweisaufnahme zu eröffnen.[803] Die Gerichte könnten hierdurch auch am Schiedsverfahren unbeteiligte Dritte dazu verpflichten, sich am Schiedsverfahren zu beteiligen[804] und verhindern, dass Parteien versuchen, die Beweisaufnahme des Schiedsgerichts zu torpedieren[805]. Mangels hoheitlicher Zwangsmittel ist das Schiedsgericht bei der Beweiserhebung auf die Mitwirkung der Gerichte angewiesen.[806] Diesen lückenhaften Rechtsschutz für Schiedsparteien behoben auch die Ergänzungen des UNCITRAL Modellgesetzes 2006 nicht.[807] Durch eine gerichtliche Beweisaufnahme für Schiedsverfahren mit extraterritorialem Sitz können umständliche Rechtshilfeersuchen der Gerichte am Sitz des Schiedsverfahrens an den ausländischen Staat, in dem sich der

---

802 High Court, *Re An Arbitration Between Hainan Machinery Import and Export Corp and Donald & McArthy Pte Ltd*, [1995] SGHC 232, 28.6., 5.7., 19.7. und 29.9.1995.

803 In Singapur ist die gerichtliche Unterstützung bei der Beweisaufnahme für Schiedsverfahren mit singapurischem Sitz durch Sec. 3 (1) IAA i. V. m. Art. 27 UNCITRAL Modellgesetz kodifiziert. Für Schiedsverfahren mit ausländischem Sitz sind die Singapurer Gerichte für Beweisaufnahmen gem. Sec. 3 (1) IAA i. V. m. Art. 1 (2), 27 UNCITRAL Modellgesetz nicht zuständig. Durch einstweilige gerichtliche Maßnahmen können Beweise gem. Sec. 12A i. V. m. Sec. 12 (1) IAA nur in begrenztem Maße gesichert werden.

804 Das Schiedsgericht kann die Beteiligung von Zeugen (Dritten) am Schiedsverfahren nicht „erzwingen", Schütze, Schiedsgericht, Rn. 450; Born, International Commercial Arbitration, Bd. 2, S. 2321 ff.; 2445 ff.; Born, Law and Practice, § 9.01, S. 185 ff.; Lew/Mistelis/Kröll, Comparative International Commercial Arbitration, Rn. 15-38 ff.; Blackaby/Partasides/Redfern/Hunter, International Arbitration, Rn. 7.18 ff.; Gaillard/Savage, Fouchard Gaillard Goldman, Rn. 1336 f.

805 Born, Law and Practice, § 9.01 S. 185 ff., § 9.01 [E], S. 195; Born, International Commercial Arbitration, Bd. 2, S. 2388 f., 2448; Blackaby/Partasides/Redfern/Hunter, International Arbitration, Rn. 7.01, 7.19 ff.

806 Schütze, Schiedsgericht, Rn. 442, 450; Born, International Commercial Arbitration, Bd. 2, S. 2323, 2389 ff.; Gaillard/Savage, Fouchard Gaillard Goldman, Rn. 1334 ff.; Lew/Mistelis/Kröll, Comparative International Commercial Arbitration, Rn. 15-38 ff.

807 Die Unterstützung der staatlichen Gerichte bei der Beweisaufnahme ist nach wie vor auf Schiedsverfahren mit Sitz im jeweiligen Staat begrenzt, Art. 1 (2) i. V. m. Art. 27 Ergänzungen des UNCITRAL Modellgesetzes 2006. Eine Ausnahme des Anwendungsbereichs für eine Beweisaufnahme unter Art. 27 UNCITRAL Modellgesetz wurde erörtert, im Ergebnis aber abgelehnt, UNCITRAL, 18. Sitzung, Report of the Secretary-General, Analytical Commentary on Draft Text of A Model Law on International Commercial Arbitration, A/CN.9/264, 25.3.1985, Art. 27, S. 59 f.; Holtzmann/Neuhaus, Guide UNCITRAL, S. 35.

Beweis befindet, vermieden werden.[808] Eine gerichtliche Unterstützung bei der Beweisaufnahme für Schiedsverfahren mit Sitz im Ausland würde es Schiedsgerichten demzufolge auch in schwierigen Beweiskonstellationen ermöglichen, ein schnelles und effektives Schiedsverfahren durchzuführen. Singapur könnte durch die Einführung einer solchen gerichtlichen Beweisaufnahme in den IAA eine moderne gerichtliche Unterstützung von Schiedsgerichten mit ausländischem Sitz etablieren. Dies würde Singapurs guten Ruf als Schiedsverfahren unterstützende Rechtsordnung bestätigen.[809] Durch die Kodifizierung einer gerichtlichen Beweisaufnahme im IAA n. F. für Schiedsverfahren mit Sitz im Ausland würden andere Rechtsordnungen herausgefordert, diese Regelungslücke in ihrer Schiedsgesetzgebung ebenfalls durch die Einführung einer gerichtlichen Beweiserhebung für Schiedsverfahren im Ausland zu schließen[810]. Von dieser Dynamik würden wiederum die Singapurer Schiedsverfahren durch die Unterstützung von ausländischen Gerichten bei der Beweiserhebung profitieren.

c) Schlussbetrachtung

Der weite Anwendungsbereich[811] des gegenüber dem AA von weniger Interventionsmöglichkeiten der Gerichte geprägten IAA[812] bringt die gesetzgebe-

808 Singapur ratifizierte das Haager Übereinkommen über die Beweisaufnahme im Ausland in Zivil- und Handelssachen vom 18.3.1970, entsprechend kann das Haager Übereinkommen auch bei der Beweiserhebung im Ausland zu Gunsten von Schiedsverfahren angewendet werden. Hierfür beantragt das Schiedsgericht bei dem zuständigen Gericht im Sitzstaat des Schiedsverfahrens ein Rechtshilfeersuchen. Letzteres wird über eine zentrale Behörde daraufhin an die zuständige Behörde des die Beweisaufnahme durchführenden Staates weitergeleitet, vgl. Schütze, Schiedsgericht, Rn. 476 f.; Born, International Commercial Arbitration, Bd. 2, S. 2423. Dem Schiedstribunal steht daher unter dem Haager Übereinkommen keine mit einem direkten Kontakt zwischen dem Schiedsgericht und dem ausländischen Gericht vergleichbare, schnelle Unterstützungshandlung bei der Beweisaufnahme zur Verfügung.

809 Das englische Schiedsrecht gestattet seinen Gerichten Beweisersuche für Schiedsgerichte mit Sitz außerhalb seines Territoriums (Sec. 2 [3], 43 f. Arbitration Act 1996). US-amerikanische Gerichte kamen von Schiedsverfahren mit ausländischem Sitz gestellten Beweisersuchen meist gem. Sec. 7 Federal Arbitration Act (Title 9, US Code) nach, andererseits ist die amerikanische Rechtsprechung unter 28 US Code § 1782 in dieser Frage gespalten, Born, International Commercial Arbitration, Bd. 2, S. 2409 ff. Die Schiedsgesetzgebung in Frankreich, Hongkong und der Schweiz sehen die gerichtliche Beweisaufnahme für Schiedsverfahren mit Sitz im Ausland nicht vor.

810 U. a. Frankreich, Schweiz und Hongkong, vgl. Fn. 809.

811 Siehe Sec. 5 IAA; Kapitel: Anwendungsbereich des Verfahrensrechts (B. I. 1.) und Kapitel: Einleitung; International Arbitration Act (IAA); Anwendungsbereich (A.II.8.b) aa)(1)).

812 Associate Prof. Ho Peng Kee (Singapore Parliamentary Secretary to the Minister for Law), Parliamentary Debates, Official Reports, 31.10.1994, Vol. 63, Column 625 ff., verfügbar unter http://sprs.parl.gov.sg/search/report.jsp?currentPubID=00069725-ZZ

rische Intention zum Ausdruck, einen schiedsfreundlichen gesetzlichen Rahmen für internationale und ausländische Schiedsverfahren zu schaffen. Der AA ist indessen auf inländische Schiedsverfahren anwendbar, um u. a. in von Nichtjuristen durchgeführten Bau-Schiedsverfahren[813] und zum Schutz der schwächeren Partei[814] durch ein höheres Maß an gerichtlicher Kontrolle ein rechtmäßiges und faires Schiedsverfahren zu gewährleisten.[815] Die Parteien dürfen sowohl aus dem IAA als auch dem AA in das jeweilige andere Gesetz wechseln. In der Praxis werden die Parteien wohl lediglich die Anwendung des IAA an Stelle des AA vereinbaren. Dass Schiedsparteien eines internationalen Schiedsverfahrens freiwillig ein Schiedsverfahren der erhöhten gerichtlichen Kontrolle des AA unterwerfen, ist nicht anzunehmen. Neben der Schiedsverfahren fördernden Ausnahme vom auf Singapur beschränkten Geltungsbereich des IAA bei vorläufigen gerichtlichen Maßnahmen für die Parteien eines ausländischen Schiedsverfahrens, würde eine zweite schiedsortunabhängige Ausnahme zur Unterstützung von ausländischen Schiedsverfahren bei der Beweisaufnahme die Schiedsfreundlichkeit des IAA auf eine neue Ebene heben. Singapur würde dadurch als Vorreiter[816] für die internationale Entwicklung der Schiedslegislation neue Maßstäbe setzen.

(zuletzt abgerufen am 28.4.2021); Howell/Duthie/Lim, Mark, Journal of International Arbitration 2002, Vol. 19, Ausg. 1, S. 39 f.; Merkin/Hjalmarsson, S. 2; Lim, Charles, Asian International Arbitration Journal 2011, Vol. 7, Ausg. 1, S. 1 (11).

813 Lim, Charles, Asian International Arbitration Journal 2011, Vol. 7, Ausg. 1, S. 1 (9); Chew, S. 10; Jenkins, S. 139 f. Siehe auch Kapitel: Einleitung; Arbitration Act (AA) (A.II.8.b)bb)).

814 Merkin/Hjalmarsson, S. 2; Chew, S. 10; Lim, Charles, Asian International Arbitration Journal 2011, Vol. 7, Ausg. 1, S. 1 (9 f.). Siehe auch Kapitel: Einleitung; Arbitration Act (AA) (A.II.8.b)bb)).

815 Zur stärkeren gerichtlichen Überwachung des Schiedsverfahrens unter dem AA, Associate Prof. Ho Peng Kee (Parliamentary Secretary to the Minister for Law), Parliamentary Debates, Official Reports, 31.10.1994, Vol. 63, Column 625, verfügbar unter http://sprs.parl.gov.sg/search/topic.jsp?currentTopicID=00064401-ZZ&currentPubID=00069725-ZZ&topicKey=00069725-ZZ.00064401-ZZ_1%2Bid027_19941031_S0004_T00101-bill%2B (zuletzt abgerufen am 28.4.2021).

816 Singapur intendiert, zur internationalen Drehschreibe für die internationale Handelsschiedsgerichtsbarkeit zu werden, siehe Shanmugam (Minister for Law), Patrick Tay Teck Guan, Pritam Singh, Parliamentary Debates, Official Reports, 9.4.2012, Vol. 89, verfügbar unter http://sprs.parl.gov.sg/search/topic.jsp?currentTopicID=00077287-WA&currentPubID=00077335-WA&topicKey=00077335-WA.00077287-WA_5%2Bid-92b4e92e-6efb-4fcd-bd99-4c99467b63e0%2B (zuletzt abgerufen am 28.4.2021); High Court, *Re An Arbitration Between Hainan Machinery Import and Export Corp and Donald & McArthy Pte Ltd,* 28.6., 5.7., 19.7. und 29.9.1995.

2. Anwendbares materielles Recht

In internationalen[817] und inländischen[818] Schiedsverfahren können die Parteien das materielle Recht ihrer Wahl vereinbaren. Die Schiedsparteien können zudem das Schiedsgericht ermächtigen *ex aequo et bono* oder als „Amiable Compositeur" zu entscheiden.[819]

II. Kompetenz-Kompetenz

Die „Kompetenz-Kompetenz" gestattet dem Schiedsgericht, über seine eigene Zuständigkeit einschließlich aller Einreden bezüglich des Bestehens oder der Gültigkeit der Schiedsvereinbarung zu entscheiden.[820]

In der Entscheidung *Ian Leonard Jackman v Culifrance Furniture Pte Ltd*[821] erkannte der High Court 1992 die Kompetenz-Kompetenz des Schiedsgerichts noch nicht an. Das Gericht urteilte, dass, sofern ein Gericht über die Zuständigkeit eines Schiedsrichters oder die Wirksamkeit der Schiedsvereinbarung bereits entschieden hat, diese Rechtsfragen nicht mehr vom Schiedsrichter entschieden werden können.[822]

Durch die Einführung des IAA (1995)[823] i. V. m. dem UNCITRAL Modellgesetz und dem AA (2002)[824] erkannte der Gesetzgeber die Kompetenz-Kompetenz der Schiedsgerichte an. Nach Sec. 3 (1) IAA i. V. m. Art. 16 (1) UNCITRAL Modellgesetz bzw. Sec. 21 (1) AA wird dem Schiedsgericht die Kompetenz-Kompetenz, über seine Zuständigkeit und über alle Einreden bezüglich des Bestehens oder der Gültigkeit der Schiedsvereinbarung zu entscheiden, eingeräumt.

1. PT Asuransi Jasa Indonesia v Dexia Bank

In der Rechtssache *PT Asuransi Jasa Indonesia (Persero) v Dexia Bank SA (PT Asuransi v Dexia Bank II)*[825] hatte *PT Asuransi Jasa Indonesia (Per-*

---

817 Sec. 3 (1) IAA i. V. m. Art. 28 UNCITRAL Modellgesetz.

818 Sec. 32 AA.

819 Sec. 3 (1) IAA i. V. m. Art. 28 (3) UNCITRAL Modellgesetz; Sec. 32 (3) AA. Siehe auch zu Sec. 32 (3) AA, Merkin/Hjalmarsson, S. 152.

820 Art. 16 (1) UNCITRAL Modellgesetz.

821 Nicht veröffentlichte Gerichtsentscheidung, *Ian Leonard Jackman v Culifrance Furniture Pte Ltd*, Suit 1590 of 1991, 30.9.1992, siehe Chew, S. 45 Fn. 40.

822 Die Entscheidung erging unter dem alten Arbitration Act 1953.

823 Den IAA verabschiedete das Parlament im Jahr 1994 und er trat am 27.1.1995 in Kraft.

824 Den AA verabschiedete das Parlament im Jahr 2001 und er trat am 1.3.2002 in Kraft.

825 [2007] 1 SLR 597; [2006] SGCA 41, 1.12.2006.

sero) [*Asuransi]* 2005 vor dem Court of Appeal in einem Aufhebungsverfahren[826] geltend gemacht, dass der Schiedsspruch II von der Schiedsvereinbarung nicht erfasst werde[827].

Hintergrund der Entscheidung war, dass sich das indonesische Staatsunternehmen *Asuransi* für Inhaberpapiere gegenüber der *Dexia Bank SA (Dexia)* verbürgt hatte. Es fand eine Umstrukturierung der Inhaberpapiere statt[828], an der *Dexia* nicht teilnahm. *Dexia* klagte stattdessen im Schiedsverfahren I gegen den Aussteller der Inhaberpapiere und gegen *Asuransi* 8,6 Mio. US-Dollar erfolgreich ein. Das Schiedsgericht I erachtete die Umstrukturierung der Inhaberpapiere als unwirksam. *Asuransi* initiierte gegen *Dexia* ein zweites Schiedsverfahren (Schiedsverfahren II), in dem es beantragte, festzustellen, dass die Restrukturierung der Inhaberpapiere für *Dexia* wirksam sei. Das Schiedsgericht II hatte zunächst über seine eigene Zuständigkeit zu urteilen. Das Schiedsgericht erklärte sich für unzuständig. Das Schiedsverfahren II sei rechtsmissbräuchlich, da *Asuransi* seine Rechtsauffassung im Schiedsverfahren I hätte vorbringen müssen. Der High Court (Oktober 2005) und der Court of Appeal (Dezember 2006) wiesen den Aufhebungsantrag zurück. In seinem Urteil bestätigte der Court of Appeal die Kompetenz-Kompetenz des Schiedsgerichts:

> „*Under Art 16(1) of the Model Law, an arbitral tribunal has the power to rule on its own jurisdiction, and by implication, to rule on the underlying issues of fact or law that are relevant to determining whether it has jurisdiction.*“[829]

Der High Court erkannte das in Art. 16 (1) UNCITRAL Modellgesetz verankerte Rechtsprinzip der Kompetenz-Kompetenz im Urteil *Aloe Vera of America Inc v Asianic Food (S) Pte Ltd and another*[830] ebenfalls an.[831]

Die Kompetent-Kompetenz wird in Singapur sowohl von der Schiedsgesetzgebung als auch von der staatlichen Gerichtsbarkeit in Schiedsverfahren fördernder Weise respektiert.

826 Gem. Art. 34 UNCITRAL Modellgesetz.
827 Art. 34 (2) (iii) UNCITRAL Modellgesetz.
828 Die Mehrheit der Schuldscheininhaber billigte 2000 die Umstrukturierung.
829 Rn. 45.
830 [2006] 3 SLR 174; [2006] SGHC 78, 1.2., 2.2., 10.2. und 10.5.2006. Für eine ausführliche Darstellung der Entscheidung, siehe Kapitel: Materielle Vollstreckungsversagungsgründe; Aloe Vera of America v Asianic Food (B.VIII.2.b)bb)).
831 Rn. 47. Zustimmend, Chew, S. 46.

2. Zuständigkeitsentscheidung

Vor der Gesetzesreform aus dem Jahre 2012 konnte nur die positive Zuständigkeitsentscheidung des Schiedsgerichts vom High Court überprüft werden.[832]

In der Entscheidung *PT Asuransi v Dexia Bank II*[833] folgte der Court of Appeal der Rechtsauffassung des von ihm in der Person von Associate Professor *Lawrence Boo*, dem Stellvertretenden Vorsitzenden von SIAC, bestimmten *amicus curiae*. Der Court of Appeal urteilte, dass lediglich die positive Zuständigkeitsentscheidung des Schiedsgerichts einer gerichtlichen Kontrolle unterliege.[834]

Die Kontrolle der positiven Zuständigkeitsentscheidung durch den High Court ist in der aktuellen Singapurer Schiedsgesetzgebung in Sec. 10 (3) IAA und Sec. 21 (9) i. V. m. Sec. 2 AA normiert.

3. Unzuständigkeitsentscheidung

Vor der Gesetzesnovelle von Sec. 10 IAA und Sec. 21 AA im Jahr 2012 konnte gem. Art. 16 UNCITRAL Modellgesetz und Sec. 21 AA a. F. die Unzuständigkeitsentscheidung eines Schiedsgerichtes nicht gerichtlich überprüft werden.[835]

Diese Rechtslage bestätigte auch der Court of Appeal im Urteil *PT Asuransi v Dexia Bank II*[836]. Die Unzuständigkeitsentscheidung des Schiedsgerichts sei verbindlich und könne von den Gerichten nicht überprüft werden. Die Entscheidung des Schiedsgerichts über seine eigene Unzuständigkeit stelle nach dem obersten Singapurer Gericht zudem keinen Schiedsspruch im Sinne von Sec. 2 (1) IAA dar und könne daher nicht nach Sec. 3 (1) IAA i. V. m. Art. 34 UNCITRAL Modellgesetz bzw. Sec. 24 IAA aufgehoben werden.[837]

---

832 Sec. 3 (1) IAA i. V. m. Art. 16 (3) UNCITRAL Modellgesetz und Sec. 21 (9) AA a. F. Der High Court war in Sec. 8 IAA a. F. als das nach Art. 6, 16 (3) UNCITRAL Modellgesetz zuständige Gericht ausgewiesen. Der High Court ist auch gem. Sec. 21 (9) und Sec. 2 AA das zuständig Gericht.

833 [2007] 1 SLR 597; [2006] SGCA 41, 1.12.2006. Für den dem Verfahren zu Grunde liegenden Tatbestand, siehe Kapitel: Kompetenz-Kompetenz; PT Asuransi Jasa Indonesia v Dexia Bank (B.II.1.).

834 Rn. 68.

835 Sec. 3 (1) IAA i. V. m. Art. 16 (3) UNCITRAL Modellgesetz und Sec. 21 (9) und (10) AA.

836 [2007] 1 SLR 597; [2006] SGCA 41, 1.12.2006.

837 Rn. 55 ff.

Die Literatur teilt die Rechtsauffassung des Court of Appeals zu Art. 16 (3) UNCITRAL Modellgesetz und Sec. 2 (1) IAA.[838] Die Unzuständigkeitsentscheidung des Schiedsgerichts stellte nach der alten gesetzlichen als auch gerichtlichen Rechtslage in Singapur eine bindende und nicht aufhebbare Entscheidung des Schiedsgerichts dar. Der Court of Appeal begründet dies damit, dass das Schiedsgericht nicht gerichtlich „gezwungen" werden könne, das Schiedsverfahren durchzuführen.[839] Die mangels gerichtlicher Kontrolle entstandene Rechtsschutzlücke für die Schiedsparteien unter der alten Schiedsgesetzgebung wurde zu Recht kritisiert.[840] Von *Born* wird zur Überbrückung der Rechtsschutzlücke vertreten, dass Art. 34 UNCITRAL Modellgesetz analog auch auf einen, zu Unrecht die Zuständigkeit des Schiedsgerichts verneinenden, Prozessschiedsspruch anwendbar sei.[841] Richtig erkennt *Born,* dass den Parteien eine Rechtsschutzmöglichkeit gegen die unrechtmäßige Unzuständigkeitsentscheidung des Schiedsgerichts zustehen muss. Ansonsten laufen die Parteien Gefahr, dass nach der abgelehnten Zuständigkeit eines Schiedsgerichts ein angerufenes Gericht

---

838 Lim, Charles, Asian International Arbitration Journal 2011, Vol. 7, Ausg. 1, S. 1 (20); Boo, Halsbury's, S. 43 f. Fn. 7, S. 115 f. Fn. 5; Merkin/Hjalmarsson, S. 94, 116.

839 Court of Appeal, *PT Asuransi Jasa Indonesia (Persero) v Dexia Bank SA*, [2007] 1 SLR 597; [2006] SGCA 41, 1.12.2006. Sie auch UNCITRAL, 18. Sitzung, Report of the United Nations Commission on International Trade Law on the work of its eighteenth session, Supplement No. 17, A/40/17, 3.–21.6.1985, Rn. 163.

840 Chan, Leng Sun, Singapore Law on Arbitral Awards, S. 16; Law Reform Committee, Singapore Academy of Law, Report of the Law Reform Committee on the Right to Judicial Review of Negative Jurisdictional Rulings, Januar 2011, S. 4 ff., verfügbar unter http://www.sal.org.sg/Lists/Law%20Reform%20Committee%20Reports/Attachments/33/LRC%20on%20Right%20to%20Judicial%20Review%20of%20Negative%20Jurisdictional%20Rulings.pdf (zuletzt abgerufen am 28.4.2021).

841 Born, International Commercial Arbitration, Bd. 1, S. 1098 ff. Der Bundesgerichtshof (BGH) gestattet die Anwendung des auf Art. 34 UNCITRAL Modellgesetz beruhenden § 1059 Zivilprozessordnung (ZPO), BGH, III ZB 44/01, SchiedsVZ 2003, S. 39 f., 6.6.2002. Laut *Born* soll Art. 34 (2) (a) (iv) UNCITRAL Modellgesetz entsprechend auf die negative Zuständigkeitsentscheidung anwendbar sein, Born, International Commercial Arbitration, Bd. 1, S. 1104. Es liegt allerdings keine für eine Analogie erforderliche planwidrige Regelungslücke vor, weil UNCITRAL eine, auch prozessuale Entscheidungen umfassende, Definition eines Schiedsspruchs in Erwägung zog, im Endeffekt dann aber verwarf, UNCITRAL, 7. Sitzung, Report of the Working Group on International Contract Practices on the work of its seventh session, A/CN.9/246, 6.–17.2.1984, S. 211. Siehe zudem den Wortlaut von Art. 16 (3) und Art. 34 UNCITRAL Modellgesetz. Zu § 1040 ZPO (beruht auf Art. 16 UNCITRAL Modellgesetz) wird eine analoge oder direkte Anfechtbarkeit eines Prozessschiedsspruchs im Aufhebungsverfahren vertreten, Seiler, in: Thomas/Putzo, § 1040 Rn. 9; Münch, in: MüKo ZPO, § 1040 ZPO Rn. 29 f.; Geimer, in: Zöller, § 1040 Rn. 10; Huber/Bach, in: Böckstiegel/Kröll/Nacimiento (Hrsg.), S. 222.

die Streitigkeit nicht mehr an die Schiedsgerichtsbarkeit verweist.[842] Auch birgt die Konstituierung eines zweiten Schiedsgerichts die Gefahr einer Aufhebung oder Nichtvollstreckung des Schiedsspruchs wegen sich widersprechender Entscheidungen der Schiedsgerichte[843].[844] Gegen die Auffassung von *Born* spricht aber zunächst die fehlende planwidrige Regelungslücke. UNCITRAL zog im UNCITRAL Modellgesetz 1985 eine, auch prozessuale Entscheidungen umfassende, Definition eines Schiedsspruchs in Erwägung, verwarf eine solche Definition aber im Endeffekt.[845] Die Schiedsgesetzgebung u.a. in Frankreich[846], England[847] und der Schweiz[848] sieht zudem die

---

842 Sec. 34 (5) Hongkonger Arbitration Ordinance besagt beispielsweise, dass wenn sich das Schiedsgericht für unzuständig erklärt, das angerufene, zuständige staatliche Gericht die Rechtsstreitigkeit entscheiden muss und eine Verweisung an das schiedsgerichtliche Verfahren ausgeschlossen ist. A. A. BGH, III ZB 44/01, SchiedsVZ 2003, S. 39 (40), 6.6.2002. Der BGH ist der Auffassung, dass bei der die Zuständigkeit verneinenden Entscheidung des Schiedsgerichts keine Rechtsschutzlücke bestehe, weil nach einer Unzuständigkeitsentscheidung die Streitigkeit vor den zuständigen gesetzlichen Richter gebracht werde. Diese Rechtsauffassung des BGH ist aber lediglich zutreffend, wenn das Schiedsgericht sich zu Recht für unzuständig erklärt. Wenn sich das Schiedstribunal zu Unrecht für unzuständig erklärt, wird den Parteien ohne Rechtsschutzmöglichkeit die vereinbarte Streitbeilegung durch ein Schiedsverfahren entzogen. Ferner können hierdurch Streitigkeiten trotz wirksamer Schiedsvereinbarung von dem staatlichen Gericht im Heimatland einer Partei entschieden werden und die Streitbelegung vor einem neutralen und mit Experten für die betreffende Rechtsstreitigkeit besetzten Schiedsgericht verhindert werden, siehe auch Born, International Commercial Arbitration, Bd. 1, S. 1104, 1236 f. Shanmugam (Minister for Law), Patrick Tay Teck Guan, Parliamentary Debates, Official Reports, 9.4.2012, Vol. 89, verfügbar unter http://sprs.parl.gov.sg/search/topic.jsp?currentTopicID=00077287-WA&currentPubID=00077335-WA&topicKey=00077335-WA.00077287-WA_5%2Bid-92b4e92e-6efb-4fcd-bd99-4c99467b63e0%2B (zuletzt abgerufen am 28.4.2021). Teilweise wird vertreten, dass die Verneinung der schiedsgerichtlichen Zuständigkeit zu einem „Verbrauch" der Schiedsvereinbarung führe, mit der Folge, dass die staatlichen Gerichte zuständig seien, Wais, in: Schütze/Tscherning/Wais (Hrsg.), S. 70; Raeschke-Kessler/Lehne, S. 35.

843 Das erste Schiedsgericht erklärt sich für unzuständig, das zweite angerufene Schiedsgericht erklärt sich für zuständig und erlässt einen Schiedsspruch.

844 Vgl. Law Reform Committee, Singapore Academy of Law, Report of the Law Reform Committee on Right to Judicial Review of Negative Jurisdictional Rulings, Januar 2011, S. 7, verfügbar unter http://www.sal.org.sg/Lists/Law%20Reform%20Committee%20Reports/Attachments/33/LRC%20on%20Right%20to%20Judicial%20Review%20of%20Negative%20Jurisdictional%20Rulings.pdf (zuletzt abgerufen am 28.4.2021).

845 UNCITRAL, 7. Sitzung, Report of the Working Group on International Contract Practices on the work of its seventh session, A/CN.9/246, 6.–17.2.1984, S. 211.

846 Art. 1520 (1) Code de procédure civile.

847 Sec. 67 Arbitration Act 1996; Sutton/Gill/Gearing, Russell on Arbitration, Rn. 5-064 f., 8-064; Born, International Commercial Arbitration, Bd. 1, S. 1213 f.

848 Art. 190 (2) (b) Bundesgesetz über das Internationale Privatrecht.

Aufhebung einer Unzuständigkeitsentscheidung des Schiedsgerichts vor. Das UNCITRAL Modellgesetz hätte deshalb die Kontrolle der negativen Zuständigkeitsentscheidung bei dessen Überarbeitung im Jahre 2006 aufnehmen können.[849]

Der Singapurer Legaldefinition eines Schiedsspruchs gem. Sec. 2 (1) IAA und Sec. 2 (1) AA lässt sich ferner entnehmen, dass prozessuale Entscheidungen des Schiedsgerichts keinen Schiedsspruch darstellen. Bei der Unzuständigkeitsentscheidung des Schiedsgerichts handelt es sich in Singapur demnach nicht um einen Schiedsspruch. Die Rechtsauffassung von *Born* widerspricht folglich der Singapurer Schiedsgesetzgebung.

Ohne eine gerichtliche Überprüfungsmöglichkeit führt eine unzutreffende Unzuständigkeitsentscheidung des Schiedsgerichts dazu, dass die Schiedsparteien ihres vereinbarten neutralen Schiedsverfahrens beraubt werden. Die Parteien müssen ihre Ansprüche dann vor staatlichen Gerichten durchsetzen, obwohl sie sich in ihrer Schiedsvereinbarung auf eine schiedsgerichtliche Streitbeilegung im gewählten Forumstaat verständigt haben.[850] Um diese Schwäche von Art. 16 (3) UNCITRAL Modellgesetz zu beseitigen, führte der Gesetzgeber im Jahr 2012 eine vom UNCITRAL Modellgesetz abweichende Regelung in den IAA ein.[851] Die Legislative übertrug dem High Court gem. Sec. 10 (3) IAA und Sec. 21 (9) i. V. m. Sec. 2 AA auch die Kontrolle der Unzuständigkeitsentscheidung des Schiedsgerichts. Der singapurische Gesetzgeber schloss hierdurch den beschriebenen lückenhaften Rechtsschutz für die Schiedsparteien.[852] Die Gesetzesänderung befürwortete auch die nationale und internationale Schiedsgerichtsbranche.[853] Sie erfolgte, um

---

849 Spätestens bei der Überarbeitung des UNCITRAL Modellgesetzes 2006 hätte die gerichtliche Kontrolle der Unzuständigkeitsentscheidung des Schiedsgerichts in das UNCITRAL Modellgesetz eingefügt werden können. Auch die Schiedsgesetzgebung Indiens beruht auf dem UNCITRAL Modellgesetz, der indische Gesetzgeber fügte aber vom Modellgesetz abweichend die Kontrolle der Unzuständigkeitsscheidung des Schiedsgerichts in das SchiedsG 1996 ein (siehe Kapitel: Indien; Kompetenz-Kompetenz [C.II.1.]).

850 Siehe Law Reform Committee, Singapore Academy of Law, Report of the Law Reform Committee on Right to Judicial Review of Negative Jurisdictional Rulings, Januar 2011, S. 5, verfügbar unter http://www.sal.org.sg/Lists/Law%20Reform%20Committee%20Reports/Attachments/33/LRC%20on%20Right%20to%20Judicial%20Review%20of%20Negative%20Jurisdictional%20Rulings.pdf (zuletzt abgerufen am 28.4.2021); vgl. auch Art. 1052 (5) Wetboek van Burgerlijke Rechtsvordering, Sec. 34 (5) Hongkong Arbitration Ordinance.

851 Dies ist gem. Sec. 3 (1) IAA möglich.

852 Die meisten Schiedsrechtsordnungen gestatten die gerichtliche Kontrolle sowohl der Zuständigkeits- als auch der Unzuständigkeitsentscheidung, Born, International Commercial Arbitration, Bd. 1, S. 1101 f., 1124 f., 1236 f.

853 Shanmugam (Minister for Law), Parliamentary Debates, Official Reports, 9.4.2012, Vol. 89, verfügbar unter http://sprs.parl.gov.sg/search/topic.jsp?current-

der internationalen Schiedsgerichtsbranche die Schiedsverfahren fördernde Haltung der Singapurer Legislativen zu signalisieren.[854] Ziel der Gesetzesnovelle war, dem Schiedsort Singapur seine führende Rolle zu erhalten.[855]

4. Berufung gegen gerichtliche Kontrolle

Nach Sec. 10 (3) IAA und Sec. 21 (9) AA kann die Zuständigkeits- bzw. Unzuständigkeits-Entscheidung des Schiedsgerichts zunächst innerhalb von 30 Tagen vom High Court überprüft werden. Gegen die Entscheidung des High Courts kann mit dessen Zulassung[856] eine Berufung beim Court of Appeal eingelegt werden.[857] Durch den zweistufigen gerichtlichen Kontrollmechanismus weichen Sec. 10 IAA und Sec. 21 f. AA von Art. 16 (3) UNCITRAL Modellgesetz ab, der eine einstufige, finale gerichtliche Kontrollinstanz gegen die Zuständigkeitsentscheidung des Schiedsgerichts vorsieht.

Ein unter diesem Aspekt vom High Court und Court of Appeal schiedsfreundlich entschiedenes Gerichtsverfahren ist *Insigma Technology Co Ltd v Alstom Technology Ltd*[858]. In diesem Verfahren focht *Insigma Technology Co Ltd (Insigma)* die Zuständigkeitsentscheidung eines SIAC-Schiedsgerichts an. Die Schiedsparteien hatten einen Lizenzvertrag abgeschlossen. Nach der im Lizenzvertrag enthaltenen Schiedsklausel sollten Streitigkeiten in einem vom SIAC durchzuführenden Schiedsverfahren unter der ICC-Schiedsge-

---

TopicID=00077287-WA&currentPubID=00077335-WA&topicKey=00077335-WA.00077287-WA_5%2Bid-92b4e92e-6efb-4fcd-bd99-4c99467b63e0%2B (zuletzt abgerufen am 28.4.2021); Law Reform Committee, Singapore Academy of Law, Report of the Law Reform Committee on Right to Judicial Review of Negative Jurisdictional Rulings, S. 6 f., verfügbar unter http://www.sal.org.sg/Lists/Law%20Reform%20Committee%20Reports/Attachments/33/LRC%20on%20Right%20to%20Judicial%20Review%20of%20Negative%20Jurisdictional%20Rulings.pdf (zuletzt abgerufen am 28.4.2021).

854 Shanmugam (Minister for Law), Parliamentary Debates, Official Reports, 9.4.2012, Vol. 89, verfügbar unter http://sprs.parl.gov.sg/search/topic.jsp?currentTopicID=00077287-WA&currentPubID=00077335-WA&topicKey=00077335-WA.00077287-WA_5%2Bid-92b4e92e-6efb-4fcd-bd99-4c99467b63e0%2B (zuletzt abgerufen am 28.4.2021).

855 Shanmugam (Minister for Law), Patrick Tay Teck Guan, Pritam Singh und Lina Chiam, Parliamentary Debates, Official Reports, 9.4.2012, Vol. 89, verfügbar unter http://sprs.parl.gov.sg/search/topic.jsp?currentTopicID=00077287-WA&currentPubID=00077335-WA&topicKey=00077335-WA.00077287-WA_5%2Bid-92b4e92e-6efb-4fcd-bd99-4c99467b63e0%2B (zuletzt abgerufen am 28.4.2021).

856 Engl. leave.

857 Sec. 10 (4) IAA, Sec. 21A (1) AA.

858 High Court, [2009] 1 SLR 23; [2008] SGHC 134, 14.8.2008; Court of Appeal, *Insigma Technology Co Ltd v Alstom Technology Ltd*, [2009] 3 SLR 936; [2009] SGCA 24, 2.6.2009.

richtsordnung beigelegt werden.[859] *Alstom Technology Ltd (Alstom)* legte 2006 angesichts eines Verstoßes gegen den Lizenzvertrag[860] Schiedsklage bei der ICC ein. Die Schiedsbeklagte *Insigma* wandte dagegen ein, dass das Schiedsverfahren vom SIAC nach den ICC-Schiedsgerichtsordnung administriert werden sollte und machte mehrere Gegenansprüche geltend. Daraufhin initiierte die Schiedsklägerin *Alstom* ein Schiedsverfahren unter Administration vom SIAC und ein Schiedsgericht konstituierte sich. Das Schiedsverfahren sollte nach der ICC-Schiedsgerichtsordnung durchgeführt werden und das SIAC erklärte sich bereit, die Funktionen der ICC-Organe zu übernehmen. Die Schiedsbeklagte erhob nun die Einrede, dass die Schiedsvereinbarung zu unbestimmt und deshalb unwirksam sei. Das Schiedsgericht entschied im Rahmen seiner Kompetenz-Kompetenz, dass es für die vorliegende Streitigkeit zuständig sei. Der Schiedsvereinbarung sei zu entnehmen, dass das Schiedsverfahren vom SIAC administriert und nach der ICC-Schiedsgerichtsordnung durchgeführt werden sollte.

2008 beantragte die Schiedsbeklagte vor dem High Court[861] gem. Art. 16 (3) UNCITRAL Modellgesetz die Überprüfung der Zuständigkeitsentscheidung des Schiedsgerichts. Der High Court[862] hielt die hybride „ICC-SIAC"-Schiedsvereinbarung aufrecht. Er erachtete das von den Parteien vereinbarte Schiedsverfahren als ein zulässiges „hybrides" *ad-hoc*-Schiedsverfahren nach der ICC-Schiedsgerichtsordnung, in dem die Organe des SIAC die Funktionen und Aufgaben der ICC-Organe übernehmen:

> *„In my view, the present case is not one where reference to two different sets of arbitration rules may lead to inconsistencies ren-*

---

859 „Any dispute arising out of or in connection with this Agreement, including any question regarding its existence, validity or termination, shall be referred to executive representatives of the Parties for settlement through friendly consultations between the Parties. In case no agreement can be reached through consultation within 40 days from either Party's notice to the other for commencement of such consultations, the dispute may be submitted to arbitration for settlement by either Party. Any and all such disputes shall be finally resolved by arbitration before the Singapore International Arbitration Centre in accordance with the Rules of Arbitration of the International Chamber of Commerce then in effect and the proceedings shall take place in Singapore and the official language shall be English. The tribunal shall consist of three arbitrator(s) to be appointed in accordance with the Rules which are hereby incorporated by reference into this clause. The arbitration award shall be final and binding on both Parties. Both Parties shall perform the award accordingly." Siehe Rn. 3.

860 *Alstom* machte Lizenzgebühren und Schadensersatz geltend.

861 Unter der alten Rechtslage war der High Court gem. Sec. 3 (1) IAA, Art. 16 (3), 6 UNCITRAL Modellgesetz i. V. m. Sec. 8, 10 IAA a. F. für die Kontrolle der Zuständigkeitsentscheidung zuständig. Nach der aktuellen Gesetzesfassung ergibt sich diese Zuständigkeit aus Sec. 10 IAA.

862 *Insigma Technology Co Ltd v Alstom Technology Ltd*, [2009] 1 SLR 23; [2008] SGHC 134, 14.8.2008.

> *dering the arbitration inoperative. Here, only the ICC Rules have been designated, and the SIAC as administering body has confirmed that it would be able to follow the ICC Rules, substituting the appropriate corresponding actors to perform the functions of the ICC Secretariat, Secretary-General, and Court. This adaptation would be within the degree of flexibility allowed by the ICC Rules since the ICC Rules recognise the autonomy of the parties as a guiding principle.* "[863]

Der High Court bestätigte die schiedsgerichtliche Zuständigkeitsentscheidung im August 2008. Im Berufungsverfahren folgte der Court of Appeal im Juni 2009 der Rechtsauffassung des High Courts und wies die Berufung zurück.[864]

Es ist zu begrüßen, dass die Rechtsprechung die Gestaltungsfreiheit der Schiedsparteien akzeptierte. In ihrer Schiedsvereinbarung hatten die Parteien ein „hybrides" Schiedsverfahren unter der Verwaltung vom SIAC nach der ICC-Schiedsgerichtsordnung vereinbart. Es sollte für die Parteien zulässig sein, ein „gemischtes" Schiedsverfahren durchzuführen, soweit ein solches Schiedsverfahren nicht nach einer der beiden Schiedsordnungen ausgeschlossen ist. Die in den Urteilen zum Ausdruck gebrachte Achtung der Parteiautonomie lobt das Schrifttum zutreffend und beurteilt die Entscheidungen als schiedsfreundlich.[865]

III. Unabhängigkeit der Schiedsvereinbarung

Eine Schiedsvereinbarung kann als Schiedsklausel in einem Hauptvertrag enthalten sein oder als selbständige Schiedsabrede vereinbart werden.[866]

---

863 Rn. 28.

864 Court of Appeal, *Insigma Technology Co Ltd v Alstom Technology Ltd*, [2009] 3 SLR 936; [2009] SGCA 24, 2.6.2009, Rn. 29 ff.

865 Mangan/Reed/Choong, S. 4 ff.; Lau/Horlach, Dispute Resolution International 2010, Vol. 4, Ausg. 1, S. 121 (122). Der Schiedsspruch des hybriden Schiedsverfahrens konnte jedoch nicht in der Volksrepublik China vollstreckt werden, Song/Yang, Ling/Chen, Helena, Construction Law Journal 2016, S. 3 (37); Cheng, Teresa/Liu, Journal of International Arbitration 2014, Vol. 31, Ausg. 5, S. 651 (658 ff.); Nicholls/Bloch, Journal of International Arbitration 2014, Vol. 31, Ausg. 3, S. 393 (396). Der ICC änderte seine Schiedsregeln als Reaktion auf das Urteil *Insigma Technology Co Ltd v Alstom Technology Ltd* 2012. Es ist nur noch dem ICC-Gerichtshof gestattet, ein ICC-Schiedsverfahren zu administrieren, Berger, Thierry/Robertson, International Arbitration Law Review 2011, S. 145 (146); Nicholls/Bloch, Journal of International Arbitration 2014, Vol. 31, Ausg. 3, S. 393 (393 f.); siehe Art. 1 (2) ICC-Schiedsgerichtsordnung 2012 und 2017.

866 Art. 16 UNCITRAL Modellgesetz. Siehe für Singapur, Sec. 2A (2) IAA; Sec. 4 (2) AA.

1. Rechtsprechung vor Einführung des IAA und des AA

In der Entscheidung *New India Assurance Co Ltd v Lewis*[867] erkannte der damals für Singapur als oberste gerichtliche Instanz zuständige „Federal Court of Malaysia“[868] im Jahr 1967 eine Schiedsklausel nicht als eine vom Hauptvertrag rechtlich unabhängige Vereinbarung an. Auch noch im Jahr 1997 achtete der Singapurer High Court im Urteil *Lim Kitt Ping Lynnette v People's Insurance Co Ltd and another*[869] das Rechtsprinzip der separaten Gültigkeitsbeurteilung der Schiedsvereinbarung vom Hauptvertrag nicht. In diesem Verfahren ging es um die Gültigkeit einer Schiedsklausel in einem unwirksamen Versicherungsvertrag.[870] Die Singapurer Gerichte lehnten demzufolge vor der Einführung des IAA und des AA die rechtliche Unabhängigkeit der Schiedsklauseln von dem sie enthaltenden Hauptvertrag ab.

2. Einführung des IAA und des AA

Für internationale Schiedsverfahren ergibt sich aus Sec. 3 (1) IAA i. V. m. Art. 16 (1) UNCITRAL Modellgesetz, dass die Schiedsklausel als eine vom Hauptvertrag rechtlich unabhängige Vereinbarung anzusehen ist. Gleiches gilt gem. Sec. 21 (2) AA auch für inländische Schiedsverfahren.

In der Rechtssache *Government of the Republic of the Philippines v Philippine International Air Terminals Co, Inc*[871] urteilte der High Court im November 2006, dass die Schiedsklausel eine vom Hauptvertrag rechtlich separate Vereinbarung darstelle.

Zwischen der *Government of the Republic of the Philippines (Philippines)* und der *Philippine International Air Terminals Co Inc* war in diesem Verfahren strittig, ob mehrere Konzessionsvereinbarungen für den Bau und den Betrieb des Terminal III am „Ninoy Aquino International Airport“ in Manila wirksam waren[872]. Eine der Konzessionsvereinbarungen enthielt eine

---

867 [1966] SGFC 13, 18.10.1966.

868 Siehe zur damaligen Zuständigkeit Kapitel: Einleitung; Unabhängigkeit (A.II.1.ee)).

869 [1997] SGHC 122, 11.2., 12.2. und 12.5.1997. Im nicht veröffentlichten Urteil *Ian Leonard Jackman v Culifrance Furniture Pte Ltd* (Suit 1590 of 1991) erkannte der High Court die Unabhängigkeit der Schiedsvereinbarung ebenfalls nicht an, siehe Chew, S. 44 Fn. 36, S. 45 Fn. 40.

870 Nach einem Autounfall machte der Versicherer geltend, dass die Versicherungsprämie nicht nach der im Versicherungsvertrag bestimmten Frist entrichtet wurde und kündigte den Versicherungsvertrag.

871 [2007] 1 SLR 278; [2006] SGHC 206, 17.11.2006.

872 Der philippinische Supreme Court hatte vor Beginn des Schiedsverfahrens entschieden, dass die Konzessionsvereinbarung wegen Verstößen gegen die philippinische Verfassung, die philippinischen Gesetze und die philippinische öffentliche Ordnung unwirksam sei.

ICC-Schiedsklausel, sodass ein ICC-Schiedsgericht diese Streitigkeit entschied. Das Schiedsgericht hatte seinen Sitz in Singapur und erließ einen Teilschiedsspruch[873], dessen Aufhebung *Philippines* gem. Sec. 24 IAA und Art. 34 UNCITRAL Modellgesetz im Jahr 2005 beantragte. *Philippines* trug im Aufhebungsverfahren vor, dass das Schiedstribunal zu Unrecht das Rechtsprinzip der „Unabhängigkeit der Schiedsvereinbarung" angewandt habe. Im Teilschiedsspruch beurteilte das Schiedsgericht die Wirksamkeit der Schiedsvereinbarung, unabhängig von der Gültigkeit des sie enthaltenden Hauptvertrages. Der High Court stimmte der Rechtsauffassung des Schiedsgerichts zu und wies den Aufhebungsantrag zurück.[874]

3. Bewertung

Durch die Einführung der unabhängigen Beurteilung der Wirksamkeit von Schiedsklausel und Hauptvertrag entsprechen die Schiedsgesetzgebung und die Rechtsprechung dem globalen Standard der Schiedsgerichtsbarkeit gem. Art. 16 (1) UNCITRAL Modellgesetz.[875]

IV. Aussetzung des Gerichtsverfahrens

1. Aussetzung nach dem IAA

In internationalen Streitigkeiten, die Gegenstand einer Schiedsvereinbarung sind, müssen die Gerichte nach Sec. 6 (1) und (2) IAA ein bei ihnen rechtshängiges Verfahren auf Antrag einer Schiedspartei zwingend aussetzen.[876] Bei der Frage, ob das gerichtliche Verfahren auszusetzen ist, erlaubt

873 Im Teilschiedsspruch entschied das Schiedsgericht, dass das Singapurer Recht auf das Schiedsverfahren und auf die Schiedsvereinbarung anzuwenden sei und wandte dabei das Rechtsprinzip der Unabhängigkeit der Schiedsvereinbarung vom Hauptvertrag an. *Philippines* machte geltend, dass dem Schiedsgericht einzig die Rechtsfragen des anwendbaren Schiedsrechts und des auf die Schiedsvereinbarung anwendbaren Rechts zur Entscheidung vorgelegt wurden.

874 Rn. 25 ff.

875 Vgl. auch Art. 178 (3) Schweizer Bundesgesetz über das Internationale Privatrecht; Art. 1447 (1) französischer Code de procédure civile; Sec. 6 (2) englischer Arbitration Act 1996; Sec. 34 (1) Hongkonger Arbitration Ordinance; Born, International Commercial Arbitration, Bd. 1, S. 349 ff.; Blackaby/Partasides/Redfern/Hunter, International Arbitration, Rn. 2.101 ff.; Schlosser, in Stein/Jonas, § 1040 ZPO Rn. 5, 11.

876 Siehe Sec. 6 (2) IAA, da diese Bestimmung das englische Wort „shall" verwendet. Dieser zwingende Charakter von Sec. 6 (2) wird auch von der singapurischen Jurisprudenz anerkannt, High Court, *Coop International Pte Ltd v Ebel SA*, [1998] SGHC 425, 27.1. und 4.3.1998; High Court, *Dalian Hualiang Enterprise Group Co Ltd and Another v Louis Dreyfus Asia Pte Ltd*, [2005] 4 SLR 646; [2005] SGHC 161, 7.9.2005; High Court, *Mancon (BVI) Investment Holding Co Ltd v Heng Holdings SEA (Pte)*

Sec. 6 (2) IAA den Gerichten, die Schiedsvereinbarung auf ihre Nichtigkeit[877], Unwirksamkeit[878] und Undurchführbarkeit[879] zu kontrollieren. Eine Verweisung an das Schiedsgericht ist im Unterschied zu Art. 8 (1) UNCITRAL Modellgesetz nicht vorgesehen.[880]

a) Zwingende Aussetzung

Schon vor dem Inkrafttreten des IAA urteilte der High Court 1992 im Verfahren *The Dai Yun Shan*[881], dass die Gerichte ihr Verfahren beim Vorliegen einer Schiedsklausel obligatorisch auszusetzen haben.

In der Entscheidung *Tjong Very Sumito and others v Antig Investments Pte Ltd*[882] hatte der Court of Appeal darüber zu befinden, ob ein gerichtliches Verfahren bei Bestehen einer Schiedsvereinbarung gem. Sec. 6 IAA zwingend ausgesetzt werden muss.

Dem Tatbestand dieses Urteils ist zu entnehmen, dass *Tjong Very Sumito (Tjong)* an *Antig Investments Pte Ltd (Antig)* einen Teil eines Unternehmens veräußert hatte. Der Kaufvertrag enthielt eine Schiedsklausel für ein SIAC-Schiedsverfahren in Singapur. *Tjong* beantragte im Mai 2008 beim zuständigen Gericht eine einstweilige Maßnahme zu erlassen, die es *Antig* untersagen sollte, einen Teil des Kaufpreises an eine andere Partei zu zahlen. *Tjong* machte zudem Schadensersatz geltend. *Antig* beantragte im Juni 2008 auf Grund der Schiedsvereinbarung die Aussetzung der Gerichtsverfahren. Der „Assistant Registrar"[883] lehnte den Antrag im August 2008 ab. Im No-

Ltd and others, [1999] SGHC 324, 15.11 und 28.12.1999; High Court, *Sembawang Engineers and Constructors Pte Ltd v Covec (Singapore) Pte Ltd*, [2008] SGHC 229, 10.12.2008; High Court, *Car & Cars Pte Ltd v Volkswagen AG and another*, [2009] SGHC 233, 19.10.2009.

877 Eine Schiedsvereinbarung ist nichtig (engl. null and void), sofern zwischen den Parteien keine rechtswirksame Schiedsvereinbarung besteht, siehe High Court, *Sembawang Engineers and Constructors Pte Ltd v Covec (Singapore) Pte Ltd*, [2008] SGHC 229, 10.12.2008.

878 Unwirksam sind Schiedsvereinbarungen, die nicht mehr fortbestehen, High Court, *Sembawang Engineers and Constructors Pte Ltd v Covec (Singapore) Pte Ltd*, [2008] SGHC 229, 10.12.2008.

879 Hierunter ist eine Schiedsvereinbarung zu verstehen, der eine Partei auf Grund von externen Faktoren nicht nachkommen kann, High Court, *Sembawang Engineers and Constructors Pte Ltd v Covec (Singapore) Pte Ltd*, [2008] SGHC 229, 10.12.2008.

880 Durch Sec. 6 IAA durchbrach der IAA die generelle Rezeption des UNCITRAL Modellgesetzes und ersetzt Art. 8 (1) UNCITRAL Modellgesetz gem. Sec. 3 (1) IAA.

881 [1992] SGHC 51, 2.3.1992.

882 [2009] 4 SLR 732; [2009] SGCA 41, 26.8.2009.

883 Der Assistant Registrar übernimmt die gleichen Aufgaben wie ein Registrar (Sec. 2 Supreme Court of Judicature Act). Ein Registrar übernimmt am Supreme Court richterliche Funktionen (Sec. 2 Supreme Court of Judicature Act) – gewisse nicht öffent-

vember 2008 setzte der High Court die Verfahren zu Gunsten eines schiedsgerichtlichen Verfahrens im ersten Berufungsverfahren gem. Sec. 6 (2) IAA aus. Der Court of Appeal erachtete die zweite Berufung als unbegründet. Er urteilte im August 2009, dass sich aus Sec. 6 IAA der Vorrang der Schiedsvereinbarung entnehmen lasse. Ein gerichtliches Verfahren müsse deshalb ausgesetzt werden, sofern der Antragsteller nachweise, dass die anhängige Streitigkeit von der Schiedsvereinbarung erfasst sei und es sich in der Schiedsvereinbarung um dieselben Parteien handle. Etwas anderes gelte nur, wenn der Antragsgegner des Aussetzungsantrags nachweise, dass die Schiedsvereinbarung nichtig, unwirksam oder undurchführbar sei.[884]

Das Court of Appeal Urteil *Tjong Very Sumito and others v Antig Investments Pte Ltd* begrüßten Stimmen in der Literatur zutreffend als schiedsfördernd.[885] Das Urteil verpflichtete die Gerichte das Gerichtsverfahren zu Gunsten des wirksam vereinbarten Schiedsverfahrens auszusetzten.

Bereits vor und nach dem Urteil des Court of Appeals erachtete der Singapurer High Court die Aussetzung nach Sec. 6 IAA als zwingend.[886]

b) Kontrollmaßstab der Schiedsvereinbarung

Im Verfahren *Tomolugen Holdings Ltd and another v Silica Investors Ltd and other appeals*[887] hatte der Court of Appeal im Jahr 2015 zu entscheiden, in welcher Intensität eine Schiedsvereinbarung unter Sec. 6 IAA gerichtlich kontrolliert werden darf.

---

liche (engl. heard in chamber) Zivilverfahren werden von ihm erledigt, Order 32 Rule 9 und Order 69A Rule 3 „Supreme Court of Judicature Act, Rules of Court 1996". Es besteht eine Berufungsmöglichkeit gegen eine Entscheidung des Registrars zum High Court, Order 56 Rule 1 Supreme Court of Judicature Act, Rules of Court 1996. Siehe auch Fn. 1074, S. 169.

884 Rn. 22.

885 Mangan/Reed/Choong, S. 4; Hwang/Boo/Han, in: Bosman (Hrsg.), ICCA International Handbook on Commercial Arbitration, Bd. V, S. Singapore 1 (Singapore 16 Fn. 46); Lim, Charles, Asian International Arbitration Journal 2011, Vol. 7, Ausg. 1, S. 1 (19); Lee, Michelle, Asian International Arbitration Journal 2014, Vol. 10, Ausg. 2, S. 67 (86).

886 High Court, *Coop International Pte Ltd v Ebel SA,* [1998] SGHC 425, 27.1. und 4.3.1998; High Court, *Mancon (BVI) Investment Holding Co Ltd v Heng Holdings SEA (Pte) Ltd and others,* [1999] SGHC 324, 15.11. und 28.12.1999; High Court, *Dalian Hualiang Enterprise Group Co Ltd and Another v Louis Dreyfus Asia Pte Ltd,* [2005] 4 SLR 646; [2005] SGHC 161, 7.9.2005; High Court, *Sembawang Engineers and Constructors Pte Ltd v Covec (Singapore) Pte Ltd,* [2008] SGHC 229, 10.12.2008; High Court, *Car & Cars Pte Ltd v Volkswagen AG and another*, [2009] SGHC 233, 19.10.2009.

887 [2015] SGCA 57, 26.10.2015.

Bereits seit dem Jahre 2013 unterzog der High Court Schiedsvereinbarungen nach Sec. 6 IAA einer begrenzten *prima-facie*-Überprüfung.[888]

Hintergrund des Verfahrens war, dass die Klägerin *Silica Investors Ltd (Silica)* mit der zweiten Beklagten (*Lionsgate Holdings Pte Ltd*) den Erwerb von 4,2 Prozent der Aktien des Bergbauunternehmens *Auzminerals Resource Group Limited (AMRG)*[889] vereinbart hatte. Die zweite Beklagte ist ein Tochterunternehmen der ersten Beklagten *Tomolugen Holdings Ltd (Tomolugen)*. *Tomolugen* ist der Mehrheitsaktionär (55 Prozent) von *AMRG*. In einer Schiedsklausel unterwarf der Aktienkaufvertrag alle Streitigkeiten einem SIAC-Schiedsverfahren. Gleichwohl initiierte *Silica* ein gerichtliches Verfahren und begründete dies mit *AMRG* Geschäften zu ihren Lasten als Minderheitsaktionär gem. Sec. 216 „Companies Act 1967“[890]. Die Kla-

---

888 High Court, *The "Titan Unity"*, [2013] SGHCR 28, 19.12.2013; High Court, *Malini Ventura v Knight Capital Pte Ltd and others*, [2015] SGHC 225, 27.8.2015.

889 *AMRG* ist die achte Beklagte im Verfahren.

890 Personal remedies in cases of oppression or injustice

216. (1) Any member or holder of a debenture of a company or, in the case of a declared company under Part IX, the Minister may apply to the Court for an order under this section on the ground

(a) that the affairs of the company are being conducted or the powers of the directors are being exercised in a manner oppressive to one or more of the members or holders of debentures including himself or in disregard of his or their interests as members, shareholders or holders of debentures of the company; or

(b) that some act of the company has been done or is threatened or that some resolution of the members, holders of debentures or any class of them has been passed or is proposed which unfairly discriminates against or is otherwise prejudicial to one or more of the members or holders of debentures (including himself).

(2) If on such application the Court is of the opinion that either of such grounds is established the Court may, with a view to bringing to an end or remedying the matters complained of, make such order as it thinks fit and, without prejudice to the generality of the foregoing, the order may –

(a) direct or prohibit any act or cancel or vary any transaction or resolution;

(b) regulate the conduct of the affairs of the company in future;

(c) authorise civil proceedings to be brought in the name of or on behalf of the company by such person or persons and on such terms as the Court may direct;

(d) provide for the purchase of the shares or debentures of the company by other members or holders of debentures of the company or by the company itself;

(e) in the case of a purchase of shares by the company provide for a reduction accordingly of the company's capital; or

(f) provide that the company be wound up.

(3) Where an order that the company be wound up is made pursuant to subsection (2) (f), the provisions of this Act relating to winding up of a company shall, with such adaptations as are necessary, apply as if the order had been made upon an application duly made to the Court by the company.

(4) Where an order under this section makes any alteration in or addition to any company's constitution, then, notwithstanding anything in any other provision of this Act,

ge richtete sich neben der ersten und der zweiten Beklagten gegen sechs weitere Beklagte[891]. Die zweite Beklagte beantragte, dass die Streitigkeit gem. Sec. 6 IAA ausgesetzt werden solle, weil der gerichtlich rechtshängige Streitgegenstand von der im Aktienkaufvertrag enthaltenen Schiedsklausel erfasst sei. Die verbleibenden Beklagten beantragten im Rahmen des dem Gericht zustehenden „Case Management“ ebenfalls die Aussetzung des Verfahrens bis zur Entscheidung im Schiedsverfahren. Im Mai 2014 lehnte der High Court die Aussetzung des Verfahrens ab. Der High Court erachtete die Schiedsklausel – mangels Schiedsfähigkeit der Streitigkeit – als unwirksam.

Im Berufungsverfahren erkannte der Court of Appeal das Spannungsverhältnis zwischen dem Kontrollmaßstab der Schiedsvereinbarung gem. Sec. 6 IAA und dem Umfang der Kompetenz-Kompetenz des Schiedsgerichts. Die „Travaux Préparatoires“ des UNCITRAL Modellgesetzes, die Analyse von Gerichtsentscheidungen aus England, Kanada und Hongkong und die *amicus curiae*-Rechtsauffassung von Prof. *Boo* bewogen das oberste Singapurer Gericht bei der Ausbalancierung zwischen der gerichtlichen und der schiedsgerichtlichen Überprüfung der Schiedsvereinbarung dazu, zu Gunsten der schiedsgerichtlichen Kompetenz-Kompetenz zu entscheiden. Der Court of Appeal urteilte, dass die Gerichte unter Sec. 6 IAA die Schiedsvereinbarung keiner umfassenden Kontrolle unterziehen dürften, sondern vielmehr lediglich *prima facie* festzustellen hätten, ob eine wirksame Schiedsvereinbarung bestehe und ob der gerichtlich rechtshängige Streitgegenstand von der Schiedsvereinbarung erfasst werde. Die umfassende Entscheidung über die Zuständigkeit sollte dem zu konstituierenden Schiedsgericht überlassen werden.[892]

---

but subject to the provisions of the order, the company concerned shall not have power, without the leave of the Court, to make any further alteration in or addition to the constitution inconsistent with the provisions of the order; but subject to the foregoing provisions of this subsection the alterations or additions made by the order shall be of the same effect as if duly made by resolution of the company.

(5) A copy of any order made under this section shall be lodged by the applicant with the Registrar within 14 days after the making of the order.

(6) Any person who fails to comply with subsection (5) shall be guilty of an offence and shall be liable on conviction to a fine not exceeding $ 1,000 and also to a default penalty.

(7) This section shall apply to a person who is not a member of a company but to whom shares in the company have been transmitted by operation of law as it applies to members of a company; and references to a member or members shall be construed accordingly.

891 Insgesamt gab es acht Beklagte. Der dritte bis siebente Beklagte sind Aktionäre, gegenwärtige oder frühere Geschäftsführer der zweiten Beklagten, von *AMRG* bzw. *Solar Silicon Resources Group Pte Ltd* (ein Tochterunternehmen von *AMRG*, das australische Bergbau Lizenzen und Genehmigungen besitzt). Der achte Beklagte ist *AMRG*.

892 Rn. 25 ff.

Bei der Kontrolle der Schiedsvereinbarung kam der Court of Appeal zu dem Schluss, dass der sog. „Minority Oppression Claim“ gem. Sec. 216 Companies Act schiedsfähig sei. Rechtsfolgen, die vom Schiedsgericht unter Sec. 216 Companies Act nicht angeordneten werden können[893], könnten von den Gerichten durchgesetzt werden.[894]

Der Court of Appeal entschied unter dem *prima facie*-Kontrollmaßstab, dass lediglich der Streitgegenstand bezüglich der Mitwirkung im *AMRG*-Management von der Schiedsvereinbarung erfasst und auszusetzen sei. Die anderen Klageanträge des „Minority Oppression Claims“ seien nicht von der Schiedsvereinbarung erfasst. Im Rahmen des dem Gericht zustehenden „Case Management“ urteilte der Court of Appeal, dass sofern *Silica* ein Schiedsverfahren initiiere, die anderen Anträge gleichwohl auszusetzen seien, bis das Schiedsgericht den Managementstreit entschieden habe. Eine Aussetzung habe zu erfolgen, um parallele Verfahren bei den sich überschneidenden Streitgegenständen zu vermeiden.[895]

Das Schrifttum beurteilte die reduzierte Kontrollintensität in dieser Entscheidung als Schiedsverfahren unterstützend.[896] Gelobt wird an dem Urteil die Bestätigung der Kompetenz-Kompetenz und die dadurch verringerte Interventionskompetenz der staatlichen Gerichtsbarkeit.[897] Zudem steigere dieses Urteil die Attraktivität des Schiedsstandortes Singapur.[898]

---

893 U. a. die Abwicklung eines Unternehmens.

894 Rn. 71 ff.

895 Rn. 104 ff.

896 Michael Hwang/Aloysius Chang, Tomolugen Holdings v. Silica Investors, Supreme Court of Singapore, Court of Appeal, 26 October 2015, A contribution by the ITA Board of Reporters, verfügbar unter http://www.kluwerarbitration.com/document/kli-ka-15-53-001?q=%22Tomolugen%20Holdings%20v%20Silica%22 (zuletzt abgerufen am 28.4.2021); Tham, Wei Chern, Global Arbitration Review 2016, Vol. 11, Ausg. 1, S. 45 (47 f.); Matthew Koh, Singapore Court of Appeal: Prima Facie Standard for Stay in Favour of Arbitration and Arbitrability of Minority Oppression Claims, Kluwer Arbitration Blog, 25.3.2016, verfügbar unter http://kluwerarbitrationblog.com/2016/03/25/singapore-court-of-appeal-affirms-prima-facie-standard-for-stay-in-favour-of-arbitration/ (zuletzt abgerufen am 28.4.2021). *Mittal* kritisiert an dem Court of Appeal Urteil, dass es die gut begründete High Court Entscheidung hinsichtlich der Schiedsfähigkeit verwarf, Mittal, J. K., Akaant, Journal of Business Law 2016, S. 186 (196 ff.).

897 Tham, Wei Chern, Global Arbitration Review 2016, Vol. 11, Ausg. 1, S. 45 (47 f.); Matthew Koh, Singapore Court of Appeal: Prima Facie Standard for Stay in Favour of Arbitration and Arbitrability of Minority Oppression Claims, Kluwer Arbitration Blog, 25.3.2016, verfügbar unter http://kluwerarbitrationblog.com/2016/03/25/singapore-court-of-appeal-affirms-prima-facie-standard-for-stay-in-favour-of-arbitration/ (zuletzt abgerufen am 28.4.2021).

898 Tham, Wei Chern, Global Arbitration Review 2016, Vol. 11, Ausg. 1, S. 45 (47 f.); Matthew Koh, Singapore Court of Appeal: Prima Facie Standard for Stay in Favour of Arbitration and Arbitrability of Minority Oppression Claims, Kluwer Arbitration Blog, 25.3.2016, verfügbar unter http://kluwerarbitrationblog.com/2016/03/25/singa-

Das Urteil *Tomolugen Holdings Ltd and another v Silica Investors Ltd and other appeals* führt zu einer Schiedsverfahren fördernden, zeitgemäßen Reduzierung der gerichtlichen Kontrolle von Schiedsvereinbarungen unter Sec. 6 IAA gegenüber dem intensiveren Überprüfungsmaßstab in Art. 8 (1) UNCITRAL Modellgesetz und Art. II (3) UNÜ. Der Court of Appeal gesteht dem Schiedsgericht in diesem Urteil die primäre Entscheidungskompetenz über die Gültigkeit der Schiedsvereinbarung zu. Hierdurch werden die Kompetenz-Kompetenz des Schiedsgerichts und die Integrität der Schiedsvereinbarung geachtet. Das Urteil zeigt exemplarisch die moderne und flexible gerichtliche Anpassung der Singapurer Schiedsgesetzgebung an die Bedürfnisse einer effektiven schiedsgerichtlichen Streitbeilegung.

c) Bewertung

Die Singapurer Gerichte erkennen die in Sec. 6 (2) IAA zwingend vorgesehene Aussetzung des Gerichtsverfahrens zu Gunsten eines Schiedsverfahrens an. Nach dem Wortlaut von Sec. 6 (2) IAA können die Gerichte allerdings die Wirksamkeit der Schiedsvereinbarung überprüfen und nur wenn das Gericht die Schiedsvereinbarung als gültig ansieht, muss es die Streitigkeit zu Gunsten eines Schiedsverfahrens aussetzen. Die zwingende Aussetzungspflicht und Kontrollmöglichkeit der Schiedsvereinbarung steht im Einklang mit Art. 8 (1) UNCITRAL Modellgesetz und Art. II (3) UNÜ und spiegelt folglich den internationalen Schiedsgerichtsstandard[899] wider. Die Gerichte reduzierten den gerichtlichen Überprüfungsmaßstab der Schiedsvereinbarung unter Sec. 6 IAA jedoch auf eine *prima facie*-Kontrolle. Es gelang der Rechtsprechung dadurch, die Singapurer Schiedsrechtsordnung zu unterstützen und über die internationale Norm der Schiedsgerichtsbarkeit hinaus schiedsfreundlich weiter zu entwickeln.[900]

2. Aussetzung nach dem AA

Erfasst eine Schiedsvereinbarung einen bei einem Gericht rechtshängigen Streitgegenstand und wird von einer Partei deshalb die Aussetzung[901] des

pore-court-of-appeal-affirms-prima-facie-standard-for-stay-in-favour-of-arbitration/ (zuletzt abgerufen am 28.4.2021).

899 Siehe auch Sec. 9 (4) englischer Arbitration Act 1996; Sec. 3 US Federal Arbitration Act (Title 9, US Code); Sec. 20 (1), (5) Hongkonger Arbitration Ordinance; Art. 1448 (1) französischer Code de procédure civile; Art. 7 Schweizer Bundesgesetz über das Internationale Privatrecht.

900 Vgl. Art. 8 (1) UNCITRAL Modellgesetz und Art. II (3) UNÜ.

901 Wie im IAA sieht Sec. 6 AA die Aussetzung des gerichtlichen Verfahrens vor. Sec. 6 (2) (a) AA spricht von Verweisung (engl. referred), hierbei handelt es sich je-

Gerichtsverfahrens beantragt[902], darf das Gericht die Schiedsvereinbarung auf ihre Wirksamkeit unter Sec. 6 (2) (a) AA überprüfen. Sec. 6 (2) AA räumt den Gerichten – im Unterschied zum IAA – einen Ermessensspielraum[903] bei der Aussetzungsentscheidung ein.

a) Gerichtliches Ermessen

Im Verfahren *Australian Timber Products Pte Ltd v Koh Brothers Building & Civil Engineering Contractor (Pte) Ltd*[904] hatte der High Court zu beurteilen, ob ein Versäumnisurteil gegen eine Partei aufzuheben ist, die zwar die Aussetzung des gerichtlichen Verfahrens für das vereinbarte Schiedsverfahren beantragte, aber die Klage ansonsten nicht erwiderte.

Australian Timber Products Pte Ltd (Australian) war die Subunternehmerin von *Koh Brothers Building & Civil Engineering Contractor (Pte) Ltd (Koh Brothers)* für ein Bauwerk in Singapur. Die Parteien waren sich über die Höhe der Vergütung für die von *Australian* erledigten Arbeiten uneinig. *Australian* legte deshalb gegen *Koh Brothers* Klage beim District Court ein. Im Februar 2004 beantragte *Koh Brothers* die Aussetzung des gerichtlichen Verfahrens nach Sec. 6 (1) AA. Strittig war zwischen den Parteien, ob die zwischen ihnen bestehende Schiedsvereinbarung ihre Vergütungsstreitigkeit erfasse. Mangels Klageerwiderung erging gegen *Koh Brothers* ein Versäumnisurteil. Im Berufungsverfahren hob der District Court das Versäumnisurteil im Mai 2004 wieder auf. Die Berufung gegen die Aufhebung des Versäumnisurteils war Gegenstand des zweiten Berufungsverfahrens vor dem High Court. Der High Court hielt das Versäumnisurteil im Oktober 2004 aufrecht, weil ein Aussetzungsantrag gem. Sec. 6 AA die Berufungsbeklagte *Koh Brothers* nicht von der Pflicht, sich gegen die Klage zu verteidigen, befreie. Der High Court stellte in seinem Urteil klar, dass eine Aussetzung des gerichtlichen Verfahrens nach Sec. 6 (2) AA im Ermessen des zuständigen Gerichts stehe. Ein Gerichtsverfahren müsse unter Sec. 6 (2) AA nicht – wie unter dem IAA – zwingend ausgesetzt werden.[905]

Das Urteil *Australian Timber Products Pte Ltd v Koh Brothers Building & Civil Engineering Contractor (Pte) Ltd* entspricht der gefestigten Rechtsprechung der Singapurer Gerichte, die den zuständigen Gerichten bei der Aus-

---

doch um eine Konkretisierung des gerichtlichen Ermessens in Sec. 6 (2) AA und nicht um den Regelfall von Sec. 6 (2) AA.

902 Sec. 6 (1) AA.

903 Dies wird durch die Verwendung des englischen Wortes „may" in Sec. 6 AA zum Ausdruck gebracht. Merkin/Hjalmarsson, S. 131; High Court, *Australian Timber Products Pte Ltd v Koh Brothers Building & Civil Engineering Contractor (Pte) Ltd*, [2004] SGHC 243, 8.7. und 29.10.2004; Boo, Halsbury's, S. 47.

904 [2004] SGHC 243, 8.7. und 29.10.2004.

905 Rn. 11.

setzungsentscheidung gem. Sec. 6 AA ebenfalls einen Ermessensspielraum einräumte.[906]

Das gerichtliche Ermessen unter Sec. 6 AA widerspricht der im internationalen Vergleich als zwingend angesehenen gerichtlichen Verweisung, Aussetzung bzw. Klageabweisung eines Gerichtsverfahrens, dessen Streitgegenstand von einer wirksamen Schiedsvereinbarung erfasst wird[907].

b) Prüfungsmaßstab der Schiedsvereinbarung

Im Verfahren *Sim Chay Koon and others v NTUC Income Insurance Cooperative Limited*[908] hatte der Court of Appeal über den Maßstab der Schiedsvereinbarungskontrolle gem. Sec. 6 AA zu entscheiden.

Das Verfahren vor dem obersten Singapurer Gericht betraf einen von den Berufungsklägern[909] *Sim Chay Koon and others* behaupteten Verstoß gegen ihre Arbeitsverträge und die unzulässigen Kündigungen ihrer Arbeitsverhältnisse durch die Beklagte *NTUC Income Insurance Cooperative Limited (NTUC)*. Ihre Streitigkeiten hatten die Parteien einem SIAC-Schiedsverfahren unterworfen. *NTUC* beantragte die Aussetzung des gerichtlichen Verfahrens gem. Sec. 6 AA. Der High Court setzte das Gerichtsverfahren dementsprechend im Februar 2015 aus.

Im Verfahren vor dem Court of Appeal trugen *Sim Chay Koon and others* vor, dass das gerichtliche Ermessen in Sec. 6 AA der Aufrechterhaltung der Schiedsvereinbarung und der damit verbundenen Aussetzung der rechtshängigen Streitigkeit zu Gunsten des vereinbarten Schiedsverfahrens entgegenstehe. Dies begründeten die Berufungskläger mit den hohen Kosten eines Schiedsverfahrens, mit der fehlenden Schiedsfähigkeit der arbeitsrechtli-

---

906 High Court, *Dalian Hualiang Enterprise Group Co Ltd and Another v Louis Dreyfus Asia Pte Ltd,* [2005] SGHC 161, 7.9.2005; High Court, *Sembawang Engineers and Constructors Pte Ltd v Covec (Singapore) Pte Ltd*, [2008] SGHC 229, 10.12.2008; High Court, *Car & Cars Pte Ltd v Volkswagen AG and another*, [2009] SGHC 233, 19.10.2009; High Court, *Petroprod Ltd (in official liquidation in the Cayman Islands and in compulsory liquidation in Singapore) v Larsen Oil and Gas Pte Ltd*, [2010] SGHC 186, 30.6.2010; Court of Appeal, *Larsen Oil and Gas Pte Ltd v Petroprod Ltd (in official liquidation in the Cayman Islands and in compulsory liquidation in Singapore)*, [2011] SGCA 21, 11.5.2011.

907 Sec. 9 (4) englischer Arbitration Act 1996; Sec. 3 US Federal Arbitration Act (Title 9, US Code); Sec. 20 (1), (5) Hongkonger Arbitration Ordinance; Art. 1448 (1) französischer Code de procédure civile; Art. 7 Schweizer Bundesgesetz über das Internationale Privatrecht; Art. 8 UNCITRAL Modellgesetz. Zur universellen Anerkennung der zwingenden Aussetzung bzw. Klageabweisung, Born, International Commercial Arbitration, Bd. 1, S. 1278 ff.

908 [2015] SGCA 46, 20.8.2015.

909 Vier Kläger initiierten das Gerichtsverfahren selbst und vertraten im Verfahren weitere 34 betroffene Parteien (engl. representation action).

chen Streitigkeiten und mit einer besseren Beachtung des rechtlichen Gehörs vor den staatlichen Gerichten.

Nach dem Court of Appeal dürften die Gerichte eine Schiedsvereinbarung unter Sec. 6 AA einzig einer *prima facie*-Überprüfung unterziehen, weil eine umfassendere Kontrolle der Schiedsvereinbarung nicht mit der „Kompetenz-Kompetenz“[910] des Schiedsgerichts zu vereinbaren sei. Das Gericht urteilte, dass eine wirksame Schiedsvereinbarung vorliege. Dem Klägervortrag entgegnete es, dass gewichtige Gründe vorliegen müssen, um unter dem gerichtlichen Ermessen in Sec. 6 AA zu dem Ergebnis zu gelangen, dass, obschon die Parteien eine wirksame Schiedsvereinbarung abgeschlossen haben, der Streitgegenstand nicht auszusetzen sei. Ein gewichtiger Grund sei *in casu* nicht gegeben, sodass der Court of Appeal die Berufung im August 2015 zurückwies und die Aussetzung des Gerichtsverfahrens aufrechterhielt.[911]

An dem Urteil lobt die Literatur die reduzierte gerichtliche Interventionskompetenz bei der Aussetzungsentscheidung, durch die der Court of Appeal seine schiedsfreundliche Haltung zum Ausdruck bringe.[912]

Im Urteil *Sim Chay Koon and others v NTUC Income Insurance Cooperative Limited* wich das oberste Singapurer Gericht von der umfassenderen Überprüfungskompetenz gem. Art. 8 (1) UNCITRAL Modellgesetz ab und reduzierte den Prüfungsmaßstab der gerichtlichen Kontrolle unter Sec. 6 AA. Der Court of Appeal gewährleistet hierdurch die Aussetzung eines gerichtlichen Verfahrens für das vereinbarte Schiedsverfahren und stärkt die Kompetenz-Kompetenz des Schiedsgerichts. Dieses Urteil demonstriert, wie die Singapurer Gerichte die Schiedslegislation durch progressive Rechtsfortbildung Schiedsverfahren fördernd weiterentwickeln.

c) Bewertung

Die höchstrichterliche Entscheidung *Sim Chay Koon and others v NTUC Income Insurance Cooperative Limited* beschränkt die gerichtliche Kon-

910 Sec. 21 (1) AA.

911 Rn. 4 ff.

912 Jonathan Leach/Henry Winter/Stephanie Khan, “Something weighty“: Chief Justice Menon ex temps the standard required for a court to exercise its discretion to not refer a dispute to arbitration, ARBlog, 9.10,2015, verfügbar unter http://www.hlarbitrationlaw.com/2015/10/something-weighty-chief-justice-menon-ex-temps-the-standard-required-for-a-court-to-exercise-its-discretion-to-not-refer-a-dispute-to-arbitration/ (zuletzt abgerufen am 28.4.2021); Lee Bik Wei/Margaret Joan Ling, Singapore Court of Appeal rules stay of proceedings in favour of arbitration, Allen & Gledhill, Legal Bulletin September 2015, 29.9.2015, verfügbar unter http://www.allenandgledhill.com/pages/publications.aspx?list=LBulletinAreas&pub_id=901&view=d (zuletzt abgerufen am 28.4.2021).

trolle der Schiedsvereinbarung gem. Sec. 6 AA auf eine Schiedsverfahren unterstützende *prima facie*-Überprüfung. Aber selbst wenn ein Gericht eine Schiedsvereinbarung für wirksam erachtet, steht es nach Sec. 6 AA im Ermessen des Gerichts, ob es das Gerichtsverfahren für ein inländisches Schiedsverfahren aussetzt. Im Rahmen dieses Ermessens können die Gerichte die Integrität des Schiedsverfahrens verletzen, indem sie Verfahren nicht zu Gunsten des vereinbarten inländischen Schiedsverfahrens aussetzen. Das Ermessen bei der Aussetzungsentscheidung i. S. v. Sec. 6 AA weicht außerdem vom international anerkannten[913] zwingenden Charakter der Aussetzung gem. Art. 8 (1) UNCITRAL Modellgesetz ab. Die Singapurer Rechtsordnung ist auf Grund des gerichtlichen Ermessens unter Sec. 6 AA bei der Aussetzungsentscheidung als schiedsunfreundlich zu bewerten.

V. Schiedsrichterbestellung

Die Zusammensetzung des Schiedsgerichts ist in Singapur in den Sec. 9 f. IAA, Sec. 3 (1) IAA i. V. m. Art. 10 f. UNCITRAL Modellgesetz und Sec. 12 f. AA geregelt. Die Schiedsrichterbestellung soll vorrangig nach dem von den Parteien vereinbarten Verfahren erfolgen.[914] Für eine parteiautonome Schiedsrichterbestellung gibt es zwei Möglichkeiten. Die Parteien vereinbaren entweder ausdrücklich ein Bestellungsverfahren oder die auf das Schiedsverfahren anwendbare institutionelle Schiedsordnung führt konkludent zur Wahl der institutionellen Bestellungsregelungen.[915]

Ein oder mehrere Schiedsrichter werden, wenn keine Bestellung durch die Parteien[916] oder durch einen zur Bestellung ermächtigten Dritten erfolgt, durch den Präsidenten des Gerichtshofs des international anerkannten

913 Sec. 9 (4) englischer Arbitration Act 1996; Sec. 3 US Federal Arbitration Act (Title 9, US Code); Sec. 20 (1), (5) Hongkonger Arbitration Ordinance; Art. 1448 (1) französischer Code de procédure civile; Art. 7 Schweizer Bundesgesetz über das Internationale Privatrecht. Zur universellen Anerkennung der zwingenden Aussetzung bzw. Klageabweisung, Born, International Commercial Arbitration, Bd. 1, S. 1278 ff.; siehe auch Kapitel: Aussetzung des Gerichtsverfahrens; Aussetzung nach dem IAA; Bewertung (B.IV.1.c)).

914 Sec. 3 (1) i. V. m. Art. 11 (2) UNCITRAL Modellgesetz und Sec. 13 (2) AA.

915 UNCITRAL Sekretariat, Explanatory note, Rn. 22; Born, Law and Practice, § 7.01, S. 129 ff.; Born, International Commercial Arbitration, Bd. 2, S. 1642 ff.; Art. 2 (e), 11 (2) UNCITRAL Modellgesetz.

916 Das dispositive Grundmodell für die Schiedsrichtbestellung besagt in Sec. 9A IAA und Sec. 13 (3) AA, dass ein aus drei Schiedsrichtern bestehendes Schiedsgericht durch die Bestellung jeweils eines Schiedsrichters durch jede Partei und die einvernehmliche Bestellung des Vorsitzenden des Schiedsgerichts erfolgen soll. Bei einem Einzelschiedsrichter müssen die Parteien sich auf einen Einzelschiedsrichter einigen (Sec. 3 [1] i. V. m. Art. 11 [3] [b] UNCITRAL Modellgesetz; Sec. 13 [3] [b] AA).

SIAC[917] oder durch eine, vom Chief Justice des Supreme Courts bestimmte Person bestellt. Diese Delegation der Schiedsrichterbestellung soll den High Court entlasten.[918] Zu den vom Chief Justice designierten Personen zählen die Mitglieder des SIAC-Gerichtshofs *Dr. Michael Pryles, Cavinder Bull SC* und *John Savage.*[919] Zuvor gehörten der frühere stellvertretende Vorsitzende[920] des SIAC und augenblickliche Chief Justice *Sundaresh Menon* und *Prof. Lawrence Boo* während seiner Zeit als stellvertretender SIAC Vorsitzender zu den bestimmten Personen.[921] Die vom Chief Justice ausgewählten Persönlichkeiten verbindet als leitende Funktionsträger des SIAC und als Mitglieder des SIAC-Gerichtshofs eine fundierte Kenntnis und langjährige Erfahrung mit der Materie der Schiedsgerichtsbarkeit. Der gegenwärtige Präsident des SIAC-Gerichtshofs, *Gary Born*, gilt als eine Koryphäe auf dem Gebiet der Schiedsgerichtsbarkeit.[922] Der Präsident des SIAC-Gerichtshofs und die vom Chief Justice berufenen Personen sind zweifelsfrei mit der Schiedsrichterbestellung bestens vertraut und in der Lage für eine qualifizierte Schiedsrichterbestellung zu sorgen. Diese Art der Schiedsrichterbestellung ist vorbildlich und zeigt die Akzeptanz der Schiedsverfahren in Singapur. Schiedsverfahren werden als ein rechtsprechungsäquivalentes Verfahren angesehen. Die Delegation der Schiedsrichterbestellung

917 Dies ergibt sich aus Art. 11 (3), (4) UNCITRAL Modellgesetz i. V. m. Sec. 8 (2) IAA und Sec. 13 (5), (8) AA. Gem. Sec. 8 (2) IAA a. F. und Sec. 13 (8) AA a. F. erfolgte die Schiedsrichterbestellung früher durch den Vorsitzenden des SIAC. Dies entsprach der Schiedsrichterbestellung in SIAC-Schiedsverfahren vor der Einführung der SIAC Rules 2013 (vgl. Regeln 6 ff. SIAC Rules 2010). Durch die Änderung der SIAC Rules im Jahre 2013 ist nunmehr der SIAC Präsident (Präsident bedeutet Präsident des SIAC-Schiedsgerichtshofs [Regel 1.3 SIAC Rules 2013/2016]) nach Regeln 6 ff. SIAC Rules 2016 bzw. Regeln 9 ff. SIAC Rules 2016 mit der Bestellung von Schiedsrichtern betraut. 2016 passte der Gesetzgeber Sec. 8 (2) IAA und Sec. 13 (8) AA kongruent an (Statutes Miscellaneous Amendments Act 2016). Seit 2016 ist der Präsident des SIAC-Gerichtshofs für die Schiedsrichterbestellung zuständig. Durch die Bestellung von Schiedsrichtern durch den Präsidenten des Gerichtshofs wird der Sachverstand des SIAC bei der Schiedsrichterbestellung weiter erhöht.

918 Associate Prof. Ho Peng Kee (Minister of State for Law), Parliamentary Debates, Official Reports, 5.10.2001, Vol. 73, Column 2216, verfügbar unter http://sprs.parl.gov.sg/search/topic.jsp?currentTopicID=00068180-ZZ&currentPubID=00069892-ZZ&topicKey=00069892-ZZ.00068180-ZZ_1%2Bid016_20011005_S0004_T00041-bill%2B unter (zuletzt abgerufen am 28.4.2021).

919 Mangan/Reed/Choong, S. 32 Fn. 111; SIAC, About Us, Court of Arbitration, verfügbar unter http://www.siac.org.sg/2014-11-03-13-33-43/about-us/court-of-arbitration (zuletzt abgerufen am 28.4.2021).

920 Der stellvertretende Vorsitzende nahm nach Regel 1.2 SIAC Rules 2007 und Regel 1.3 SIAC-Rule 2010 die gleichen Aufgaben wie der SIAC Vorsitzende wahr.

921 Mangan/Reed/Choong, S. 32 Fn. 111; Government Gazette Notification No. 923 vom 9.4.2009 und No. 1653 vom 2.7.2004.

922 SIAC, About Us, Court of Arbitration, verfügbar unter http://www.siac.org.sg/2014-11-03-13-33-43/about-us/court-of-arbitration (zuletzt abgerufen am 28.4.2021).

entspricht nicht der in Art. 11 UNCITRAL Modellgesetz vorgesehenen gerichtlichen Schiedsrichterbestellung durch das, in Art. 6 UNCITRAL Modellgesetz vom implementierenden Staat für zuständig erklärte Gericht oder die für zuständig befundene Behörde. Die in Singapur praktizierte Delegation der Schiedsrichterbestellung an Spezialisten der Schiedsszene ist gleichwohl einer gerichtlichen Bestellung vorzugswürdig[923] und ist deshalb als Schiedsverfahren unterstützend zu erachten.

VI. Einstweilige Maßnahmen

Der Parteiautonomie wird in der Singapurer Schiedsgesetzgebung bei Maßnahmen des einstweiligen[924] Rechtsschutzes Vorrang eingeräumt. Für die Parteien eines Schiedsverfahrens soll vorläufiger Rechtsschutz primär durch die Schiedsgerichte, Schiedsinstitutionen oder andere Institutionen sowie durch von den Schiedsparteien ernannte Personen erfolgen. Dies bringt der Gesetzgeber in Sec. 12A (7) IAA und Sec. 31 (2) AA zum Ausdruck, indem er klarstellt, dass eine von den Gerichten angeordnete vorläufige Maßnahme unwirksam wird, sofern vorläufiger Rechtsschutz durch das Schiedsgericht, eine Institution oder eine von den Parteien ernannte Person erlassen wird.[925]

923 Staatliche Richter haben meist, insbesondere bei der Bestellung eines ausländischen Schiedsrichters, nicht die erforderliche Erfahrung, siehe Born, International Commercial Arbitration, Bd. 2, S. 1712 f. Die staatlichen Gerichte bestellen meist lokal verwurzelte Rechtsanwälte und pensionierte Richter mit begrenzter Expertise der internationalen Schiedsgerichtsbarkeit, Born, Law and Practice, § 7.01 [C] [2] [vi], S. 137. Da staatliche Gerichte folglich nicht die erforderliche Expertise haben, einen passenden Schiedsrichter für ein internationales Schiedsverfahren zu bestellen, sollte die Schiedsrichterbestellung an eine Schiedsinstitution oder an eine andere Ernennungsstelle übertragen werden, Blackaby/Partasides/Redfern/Hunter, International Arbitration, Rn. 4.35; Born, Law and Practice, § 7.01 [C] [2], S. 136 f.

924 Einstweilige und vorläufige Maßnahmen bzw. einstweiliger und vorläufiger Rechtsschutz werden als Synonyme verwandt, siehe §§ 1033, 1041 ZPO und Art. 9, 17 Deutsche Institution für Schiedsgerichtsbarkeit (DIS) Übersetzung des UNCITRAL Modellgesetzes, DIS, Materialien, UNCITRAL Modellgesetz für die internationale Handelsschiedsgerichtsbarkeit 85, verfügbar unter http://www.disarb.org/en/51/materials/uncitral-modellgesetz-f%C3%BCr-die-internationale-handelsschiedsgerichtsbarkeit-85-id31 (zuletzt abgerufen am 28.4.2021).

925 Shanmugam (Minister for Law), Parliamentary Debates, Official Reports, 19.10.2009, Vol. 86, Column 1629, verfügbar unter http://sprs.parl.gov.sg/search/topic.jsp?currentTopicID=00003591-WA&currentPubID=00004793-WA&topicKey=00004793-WA.00003591-WA_1%2B%2B (zuletzt abgerufen am 28.4.2021); Ministry of Law, International Arbitration (Amendment) Bill, Ministry of Law's Responses to Public Feedback Received, 12A (7) Automatic Lapsing of Court Order, S. 6 f., verfügbar unter https://www.mlaw.gov.sg/content/dam/minlaw/corp/assets/documents/linkclick1e3a.pdf (zuletzt abgerufen am 28.4.2021).

In Sec. 12A (6) IAA geht der Gesetzgeber noch einen Schritt weiter und gestattet dem High Court den Erlass von einstweiligen Maßnahmen nur, wenn das Schiedsgericht, eine Institution oder eine ernannte Person kein effektives Eilverfahren gewährleisten können.[926] Das Singapurer Schiedsrecht räumt dadurch in schiedsfreundlicher Weise dem schiedsgerichtlichen einstweiligem Rechtsschutz den Vorzug ein.[927]

1. Rechtsprechung zu Sec. 12 IAA a. F.

Unter der alten Sec. 12 IAA a. F. war sich die Singapurer Rechtsprechung nicht einig, ob nach Sec. 12 IAA a. F. einstweilige gerichtliche Maßnahmen zu Gunsten von Schiedsverfahren, die ihren Sitz im Ausland haben, angeordnet werden konnten.

Sec. 12 IAA a. F. besagte:

> ***„Powers of arbitral tribunal***
>
> *12. — (1) Without prejudice to the powers set out in any other provision of this Act and in the Model Law, an arbitral tribunal shall have powers to make orders or give directions to any party for —...*
>
> [Der Katalog an vom Schiedsgericht anzuordnenden Maßnahmen entspricht der aktuellen Version von Sec. 12 (1) IAA.]
>
> *(7) The High Court or a Judge thereof shall have, for the purpose of and in relation to an arbitration to which this Part* [Part II] applies, *the same power of making orders in respect of any of the matters set out in subsection (1) as it has for the purpose of and in relation to an action or matter in the court.* “[928]

926 Shanmugam (Minister for Law), Parliamentary Debates, Official Reports, 19.10.2009, Vol. 86, Column 1628, verfügbar unter http://sprs.parl.gov.sg/search/topic.jsp?currentTopicID=00003591-WA&currentPubID=00004793-WA&topicKey=00004793-WA.00003591-WA_1%2B%2B (zuletzt abgerufen am 28.4.2021). So auch schon zu Sec. 12 (7) IAA a. F., Court of Appeal, *NCC International AB v Alliance Concrete Singapore Pte Ltd,* [2008] 2 SLR 565; [2008] SGCA 5, 26.2.2008.

927 Zur Vorzugswürdigkeit des Vorrangs des schiedsgerichtlichen einstweiligen Rechtsschutzes, Lew/Mistelis/Kröll, Comparative International Commercial Arbitration, Rn. 23-120 ff.; Born, International Commercial Arbitration, Bd. 2, S. 2553; Blackaby/Partasides/Redfern/Hunter, International Arbitration, Rn. 7.13 ff. Der Vorrang des schiedsgerichtlichen einstweiligen Rechtsschutzes spiegelt sich auch in Sec. 44 (4), (5), (6) englischer Arbitration Act 1996, Art. 1449 (1) französischer Code de procédure civile, Art. 183 Schweizer Bundesgesetz über das Internationale Privatrecht und Art. 28 ICC-Schiedsgerichtsordnung wider.

928 Merkin/Hjalmarsson, S. 32 f.

a) Swift-Fortune v Magnifica Marine I

Im März 2005 hatte der High Court in der Rechtssache *Swift-Fortune Ltd v Magnifica Marine SA (Swift v Magnifica I)*[929] darüber zu urteilen, ob die Singapurer Gerichte gem. Sec. 12 IAA a. F. befugt waren, einstweilige gerichtliche Maßnahmen für Schiedsverfahren mit ausländischem Sitz zu erlassen.

In dieser Rechtssache verkaufte das panamaische Unternehmen *Magnifica Marina SA (Magnifica)* das Schiff „Capaz Ducking" an das liberische Unternehmen *Swift-Fortune Ltd (Swift)* für 9,5 Mio. US-Dollar. Den Verkauf vereinbarten die Parteien in einem sog. „Memorandum of Agreement (MOA)". Der Kaufpreis war nach Übergabe des Schiffs fällig. Die Übereignung des Schiffs und die Zahlung des Kaufpreises sollten in Singapur stattfinden und die Übergabe des Schiffs in China erfolgen. Nach der im MOA enthaltenen Schiedsklausel war London der Sitz des Schiedsverfahrens. Als Übergabetermin bestimmten die Parteien den 6. Dezember 2004. Im MOA vereinbarten die Parteien, dass *Swift* bei einer verspäteten Übergabe Schadensersatz verlangen kann. Die Übergabe des Schiffs Capaz Ducking verzögerte sich. *Swift* stimmte einem verspäteten Übergabetermin unter dem Vorbehalt zu, dass hierdurch ihr Verzugsschadensersatzanspruch bestehen bleibe. Das Schiff erreichte den Hafen von Jingtang in China im Februar 2005. Einen Tag vor dem letztendlich vereinbarten Übergabetermin, dem 9. März 2005, machte die Klägerin *Swift* ihr einstweiliges Rechtsschutzersuchen in Singapur anhängig. *Inter alia* ersuchte *Swift* einstweiligen Rechtsschutz in der Form einer „Mareva Injunction" gegen die Beklagte *Magnifica,* nach dem Letztere ihr Vermögen in Höhe von mindestens 2,5 Mio. US-Dollar in Singapur belassen müsse.[930] Die Klägerin machte geltend, dass Eilbedürftigkeit bestehe, weil nach der Zahlung des Kaufpreises das Geld Singapur verlassen werde. Für die Schadensersatzansprüche der Klägerin gegen die Beklagte sei dann kein Vermögen mehr in Singapur vorhanden, in das die Klägerin ihre schiedsgerichtlich durchgesetzten Schadensersatzansprüche vollstrecken könne. Der High Court erließ zunächst die beantragte einstweilige Maßnahme und untersagte es *Magnifica,* während des Londoner Schiedsverfahrens, ihr Vermögen aus Singapur zu entfernen. Im April 2005 beantragte die Beklagte, dass der High Court die erlassene vorläufige Maßnahme aufhebt, weil das Singapurer Gericht für den Erlass der Mareva Injunction unzuständig gewesen sei. Der High Court hob die vorläufige gerichtliche Maßnahme gegen *Magnifica* antragsgemäß auf. Das Gericht entschied, dass die Singapurer Gerichte zum Erlass einstweiliger Maßnahmen für Schiedsverfahren mit Sitz im Ausland nicht zuständig seien. Dies begründete der High

929 High Court, [2006] 2 SLR 323; [2006] SGHC 36, 1.3.2006.

930 *Swift* verlangte von *Magnifica* 2–2,5 Mio. US-Dollar Verzugsschadensersatz.

Court damit, dass es sich bei Sec. 12 (7) IAA a. F. nicht um eine Bestimmung mit rein deklaratorischem Charakter handle. Die Kompetenz, den privaten Streitbeilegungsmechanismus der Schiedsgerichtsbarkeit durch Maßnahmen der staatlichen Gerichte zu unterstützen und zu fördern – u. a. durch Beweisaufnahmen und einstweilige Maßnahmen – müsse den Gerichten ausdrücklich gesetzlich verliehen werden. Das Singapurer Recht sei jedoch auf das Territorium Singapurs beschränkt. Die extraterritoriale Anwendung des Singapurer Rechts müsse vom Gesetzgeber ausdrücklich geregelt werden. Auch in analoger Anwendung könne Art. 9 UNCITRAL Modellgesetz nicht zu einem extraterritorialen Anwendungsbereich von Sec. 12 (7) a. F. IAA führen. Denn eine solche Analogie würde dem gesetzgeberischen Willen widersprechen, einstweilige gerichtliche Maßnahmen i. S. d. Sec. 12 (7) IAA auf Schiedsverfahren mit Sitz in Singapur zu beschränken.[931]

b) Front Carriers v Atlantic & Orient Shipping

Im Juli desselben Jahres (2005) hatte der High Court im Verfahren *Front Carriers Ltd v Atlantic & Orient Shipping Corp (Front Carriers v Atlantic)*[932] gleichfalls darüber zu entscheiden, ob eine vorläufige gerichtliche Maßnahme in Form einer Mareva Injunction gem. Sec. 12 (7) IAA a. F. auch für ein Schiedsverfahren mit Sitz im Ausland angeordnet werden kann.

Im Verfahren war strittig, ob das liberische Unternehmen *Front Carriers Ltd (Carriers)* mit einem auf den Westindischen Inseln inkorporierten Unternehmen, *Atlantic & Orient Shipping Corp (Atlantic)*, die „Charter“[933] eines Containerschiffs der Panamax-Klasse für 31.500 US-Dollar am Tag vereinbart hatte. Nach Auffassung von *Carriers* war der Charter-Vertrag für *Carriers* durch einen Londoner Broker und für *Atlantic* durch Herrn *Lee Heng Juan* im März 2005 abgeschlossen worden. *Lee Heng Juan* bestritt den Vertragsabschluss mit *Carriers* und wies darauf hin, dass ihm die erforderliche Vertretungsmacht für *Atlantic* gefehlt habe. Das Arbeitsverhältnis von *Lee Heng Juan* und *Atlantic* war seit Januar oder Februar 2005 beendet gewesen und er hatte als „Executive Director“ bei *Amstec* eine neue Anstellung gefunden. Am 11.8.2005 informierte *Amstec Carriers* über die Unwirksamkeit der Chartervereinbarung zwischen *Carriers* und *Atlantic* wegen der unwirksamen Vertretung durch *Lee Heng Juan*. Die Versuche von *Carriers*, Kontakt mit *Atlantic* aufzunehmen, blieben erfolglos. Vor diesem Hintergrund ersuchte *Carriers* den High Court am 22.8.2005, eine einstweilige Maßnahme gem. Sec. 12 IAA a. F. in der Form einer Mareva Injunction gegen *Atlantic* anzuordnen. Zudem initiierte *Carriers* gegen *Atlantic* ein Schiedsver-

931 Rn. 42 ff.

932 High Court, [2006] 3 SLR 854; [2006] SGHC 127, 19.7.2006.

933 Anmietung.

fahren mit Sitz in London. Am 26.8.2005 verbot der High Court *Atlantic* in einer *ex parte* erlassenen Mareva Injunction, einen Teil ihres Vermögens aus Singapur zu entfernen. *Atlantic* beantragte beim High Court die Aufhebung der einstweiligen gerichtlichen Mareva Injunction wegen der Unzuständigkeit der Singapurer Gerichte für eine solche Maßnahme zu Gunsten eines Schiedsverfahrens mit ausländischem Sitz (London). Der High Court wich in seinem Urteil von der in der Entscheidung *Swift v Magnifica I*[934] ein paar Monate zuvor geäußerten, Rechtsauffassung ab. Der High Court urteilte, dass Sec. 12 (7) IAA a. F. es den Singapurer Gerichten gestatte, vorläufige Maßnahmen für Schiedsverfahren mit einem ausländischen Sitz anzuordnen. Dies begründete das Gericht in Anlehnung an den extraterritorialen Anwendungsbereich von Art. 9 (i. V. m. Art. 1 [2]) UNCITRAL Modellgesetz. Rezipienten des UNCITRAL Modellgesetzes seien eher bereit, ein internationales Schiedsverfahren mit ausländischem Sitz zu unterstützen. Sec. 12 (7) IAA a. F. sei vom Gesetzgeber ausreichend weit formuliert worden, damit die Singapurer Gerichte auch einstweilige Maßnahmen für Schiedsverfahren mit ausländischem Sitz gewähren können.[935] Der High Court erachtete die Mareva Injunction jedoch im Ergebnis als unbegründet und hob sie auf.

c) Swift-Fortune v Magnifica Marine II

Die beiden sich widersprechenden Urteile[936] *Swift v Magnifica I* und *Front Carriers v Atlantic* führten bezüglich der Frage, ob die Singapurer Gerichte nach Sec. 12 (7) IAA a. F. befugt waren, einstweilige Maßnahmen für Schiedsverfahren mit ausländischem Sitz anzuordnen, zu Rechtsunsicherheit. Es ist daher zu begrüßen, dass sich der Court of Appeal im Berufungsverfahren *Swift-Fortune Ltd v Magnifica Marine SA (Swift v Magnifica II)*[937] im Dezember 2006 der Klärung dieser strittigen Rechtsfrage widmete. Das Gericht setzte sich mit den gegensätzlichen Entscheidungen des High Courts in den Urteilen *Swift v Magnifica I* und *Front Carriers v Atlantic* ausführlich auseinander und kam zu der Bewertung, dass Art. 9 UNCITRAL Modellgesetz lediglich zum Ausdruck bringe, dass vorläufige Maßnahmen der staatlichen Gerichte mit einem Schiedsverfahren vereinbar seien. Art. 9 UNCITRAL Modellgesetz habe darüber hinaus keine Auswirkung auf Sec. 12 (7) IAA a. F. Der Court of Appeal folgte dem *Swift v Magnifica I*-Urteil des High Courts und entschied, dass der Gesetzgeber den Anwendungsbereich

934 High Court, [2006] 2 SLR 323; [2006] SGHC 36, 1.3. 2006.

935 Rn. 16 ff.

936 Die unterschiedlichen Urteile in *Swift-Fortune Ltd v Magnifica Marine* und *Front Carriers Ltd v Atlantic & Orient Shipping Corp* entschieden mit der Schiedsgerichtsbarkeit bestens vertraute Richter des High Courts, Lim, Charles, Asian International Arbitration Journal 2011, Vol. 7, Ausg. 1, S. 1 (22).

937 [2007] 1 SLR 629; [2006] SGCA 42, 1.12.2006.

von Sec. 12 (7) IAA a. F. auf Schiedsverfahren mit Sitz in Singapur begrenzt habe. Ansonsten wären auch die anderen gerichtlichen Unterstützungshandlungen in Sec. 12 (1) IAA für Schiedsverfahren mit extraterritorialem Sitz anwendbar. Ferner könne nicht davon ausgegangen werden, dass das Parlament die Singapurer Gerichte in Sec. 12 (7) IAA a. F. universell ermächtigt habe, einstweilige Maßnahmen für jedwedes Schiedsverfahren mit ausländischem Sitz zu erlassen, unabhängig davon, ob es sich bei dem Sitzstaat um einen Rezipienten des UNCITRAL Modellgesetzes oder um einen Vertragsstaat des UNÜ handle.[938]

Diese Rechtsprechung des Court of Appeals entsprach dem Wortlaut von Sec. 12 IAA a. F., dessen Anwendungsbereich keine Schiedsverfahren mit extraterritorialem Schiedssitz erfasste.[939] Die Fachliteratur kritisierte die Beschränkung von 12 IAA a. F. auf Schiedsverfahren mit Singapurer Sitz im Urteil *Swift v Magnifica II* dennoch als schiedsunfreundlich[940] und forderte eine Gesetzesänderung[941].

d) Gesetzesanpassung

Der Singapurer Gesetzgeber reagierte auf diese Kritik an der höchstrichterlichen *Swift v Magnifica II*-Rechtsprechung und erließ im Oktober 2009[942] mit Sec. 12A IAA eine Bestimmung, die es den Singapurer Gerichten erlaubt, einstweilige gerichtliche Maßnahmen auch für Schiedsverfahren mit Sitz im Ausland anzuordnen[943].[944] Der Gesetzgeber berücksichtigte bei der

938 Rn. 33 ff.

939 *Ho* ist hingegen der Auffassung, dass sich aus den Gesetzgebungsmaterialien nicht eindeutig ergebe, dass der Anwendungsbereich von Sec. 12 IAA a. F. auf Schiedsverfahren mit Sitz in Singapur beschränkt sei. Er ist der Auffassung, dass der Singapurer Gesetzgeber bei der Verabschiedung des IAA den Anwendungsbereich von Sec. 12 IAA a. F. nicht auf Schiedsverfahren mit Sitz in Singapur beschränken wollte, Ho, Arbitration International 2008, Vol. 24, Ausg. 4, S. 609 (612 f.).

940 Zur Schiedsunfreundlichkeit, Boo, Singapore Academy of Law Annual Review of Singapore Cases 2006, Vol.7, S. 51 (59 f.); Lye/Yeo, Chuan Tat/Choo, Singapore Academy of Law Journal 2009, Vol. 21, S. 429 (433 ff.). Zur Kritik in der Literatur, Lim, Charles, Asian International Arbitration Journal 2011, Vol. 7, Ausg. 1, S. 1 (23); Menon, Arbitration 2015, S. 413 (416 f.).

941 Lye/Yeo, Chuan Tat/Choo, Singapore Academy of Law Journal 2009, Vol. 21, S. 429 (440 ff.); Ho, Arbitration International 2008, Vol. 24, Ausg. 4, S. 609 (612 ff.); Chan, Leng Sun, Asian International Arbitration Journal 2007, Vol. 3, Ausg. 2, S. 142 (162).

942 Diese Gesetzesänderung trat am 1.1.2010 in Kraft.

943 Sec. 12A (1) (b) IAA gestattet den Erlass von vorläufigen Maßnahmen unabhängig vom Sitz des Schiedsverfahrens.

944 Shanmugam (Minister for Law), Parliamentary Debates, Official Reports, 19.10.2009, Vol. 86, Column 1627, verfügbar unter http://sprs.parl.gov.sg/search/topic.jsp?currentTopicID=00003591-WA&currentPubID=00004793-WA&topicKey=00004793-WA.00003591-WA_1%2B%2B (zuletzt abgerufen am 28.4.2021); International Arbi-

Einführung von Sec. 12A IAA das Ergebnis eines Konsultationsprozesses lokaler und internationaler Schiedsexperten sowie die Ergänzungen des UNCITRAL Modellgesetzes 2006.[945] Mit der Gesetzesänderung verfolgte die Legislative das Ziel, den IAA schiedsfreundlich und effektiv zu modernisieren, um Singapurs Position als einen der weltweit führenden Schiedsorte auszubauen.[946] Durch die Gesetzesreform brachte der Gesetzgeber seine Unterstützung für internationale Schiedsverfahren zum Ausdruck. Denn mit der Einführung von einstweiligen gerichtlichen Maßnahmen zu Gunsten von Schiedsverfahren mit extraterritorialem Sitz förderte das Parlament ausschließlich ausländische Schiedsverfahren. Ein Bedarf für gerichtlich angeordnete vorläufige Maßnahmen zur Sicherung von Beweisen und von vollstreckbarem Vermögen besteht insbesondere bei Eilbedürftigkeit[947] oder gegenüber Dritten.[948] Das Schiedsgericht kann nur für und gegen die Parteien des Schiedsverfahrens einstweiligen Rechtsschutz anordnen, nicht jedoch gegenüber Dritten. Selbst gegenüber den Schiedsparteien kann das Schiedsgericht die angeordneten vorläufigen Maßnahmen nicht hoheitlich vollstrecken, sondern es kann allenfalls im Schiedsspruch oder in der Kostenentscheidung Zuwiderhandlungen der Parteien nachteilig berücksichtigen.[949]

---

tration (Amendment) Bill, Explanatory Statement, S. 8, verfügbar unter https://www.mlaw.gov.sg/content/dam/minlaw/corp/assets/documents/linkclick83db.pdf (zuletzt abgerufen am 28.4.2021); Oommen/Tan, Charis, Asian International Arbitration Journal 2010, Vol. 6, Ausg. 2, S. 186 (200); Hwang/Boo/Han, in: Bosman (Hrsg.), ICCA International Handbook on Commercial Arbitration, Bd. V, S. Singapore 1 (Singapore 27 i. V. m. Fn. 118); Mangan/Reed/Choong, S. 2 f.

945 Shanmugam (Minister for Law), Parliamentary Debates, Official Reports, 19.10.2009, Vol. 86, Column 1627, verfügbar unter http://sprs.parl.gov.sg/search/topic.jsp?currentTopicID=00003591-WA&currentPubID=00004793-WA&topicKey=00004793-WA.00003591-WA_1%2B%2B (zuletzt abgerufen am 28.4.2021).

946 Shanmugam (Minister for Law), Parliamentary Debates, Official Reports, 19.10.2009, Vol. 86, Column 1629 ff., verfügbar unter http://sprs.parl.gov.sg/search/topic.jsp?currentTopicID=00003591-WA&currentPubID=00004793-WA&topicKey=00004793-WA.00003591-WA_1%2B%2B (zuletzt abgerufen am 28.4.2021); vgl. auch Menon, Arbitration 2015, S. 413 (416 f.); Chan, Leng Sun, Asian International Arbitration Journal 2007, Vol. 3, Ausg. 2, S. 142 (162).

947 Insbesondere, wenn sich das Schiedsgericht noch nicht konstituiert hat.

948 Lew/Mistelis/Kröll, Comparative International Commercial Arbitration, Rn. 23-1 f., Rn. 23-100 ff.; Blackaby/Partasides/Redfern/Hunter, International Arbitration, Rn. 7.13 ff.; Gaillard/Savage, Fouchard Gaillard Goldman, Rn. 1302 ff.; Born, International Commercial Arbitration, Bd. 2, S. 2426 ff. Vgl. auch zur Notwendigkeit von einstweiligen gerichtlichen Maßnahmen bei Dringlichkeit, Sec. 42 (3) englischer Arbitration Act 1996.

949 UNCITRAL, 32. Sitzung, Report of the Secretary General, Settlement of commercial disputes – Possible uniform rules on certain issues concerning settlement of commercial disputes: conciliation, interim measures of protection, written form for arbitration agreement, A/CN.9/WG.II/WP.108, 20–31.3.2000, S. 18; Yesilirmak, in: Lew/Mistelis (Hrsg.), Pervasive Problems in International Arbitration, S. 185 (196 f.); Lew, ICC

Sec. 12A IAA kann in der Zukunft andere Gesetzgeber dazu bewegen, gleichfalls einstweilige gerichtliche Maßnahmen für Schiedsverfahren mit ausländischem Sitz zu gestatten, wodurch wiederum die Schiedsverfahren in Singapur profitieren würden. Andererseits können einstweilige gerichtliche Maßnahmen für extraterritoriale Schiedsverfahren zu Nachteilen für ausländisches Kapital und für die Niederlassungen ausländischer Unternehmen führen und hiermit die Attraktivität Singapurs in diesen Sektoren schmälern.[950] Die „Monetary Authority of Singapore"[951] hatte hingegen nichts gegen Sec. 12A IAA einzuwenden und betonte, dass dieser sicherstelle, dass das in Singapur angelegte Vermögen einer rechtmäßigen Quelle entspringe.[952] Die meisten Schiedsrechtsordnungen gewähren nur gerichtlichen einstweiligen Rechtsschutz für Schiedsverfahren mit Sitz in ihrem Staatsterritorium. Sofern sich das zu sichernde Vermögen oder die für das Schiedsverfahren essentiellen Beweise nicht im „Sitzstaat" befinden, gewähren, auf den Sitzstaat beschränkte, vorläufige gerichtliche Maßnahmen keinen effek-

---

International Court of Arbitration Bulletin 2000, Vol. 11, Ausg. 1, S. 23 (24); Lew/Mistelis/Kröll, Comparative International Commercial Arbitration, Rn. 23-83; Born, International Commercial Arbitration, Bd. 2, S. 2448; Born, Commentary and Materials, S. 971 f.

950 Nach *de Souza* wurde in der öffentlichen Debatte zu Sec. 12A IAA vertreten, dass hierdurch die Attraktivität, ausländisches Kapital in Singapur anzulegen, geschmälert werden könne. *De Souza* selbst sieht ausländische Kapitalanlagen in Singapur als nicht gefährdet an und ist der Auffassung, dass die Singapurer Gesetzgebung Transparenz, Kooperation und die Einhaltung von internationalem Rechts gewähren müsse, um ein legitimer Finanzplatz von Weltrang zu bleiben, Christopher de Souza, Parliamentary Debates, Official Reports, 19.10.2009, Vol. 86, Column 1633 f., verfügbar unter http://sprs.parl.gov.sg/search/topic.jsp?currentTopicID=00003591-WA&currentPubID=00004793-WA&topicKey=00004793-WA.00003591-WA_1%2B%2B (zuletzt abgerufen am 28.4.2021). Zu den möglichen Gefahren für die Vermögensverwaltung in Singapur, Lye/Yeo, Chuan Tat/Choo, Singapore Academy of Law Journal 2009, Vol. 21, S. 429 (432 f.); Ministry of Law, International Arbitration (Amendment) Bill, Ministry of Law's Responses to Public Feedback Received, Disagreement with section 12A, Feedback received, S. 8 f., verfügbar unter https://www.mlaw.gov.sg/content/dam/minlaw/corp/assets/documents/linkclick1e3a.pdf (zuletzt abgerufen am 28.4.2021); Lim, Charles, Asian International Arbitration Journal 2011, Vol. 7, Ausg. 1, S. 1 (23).

951 Zentralbank von Singapur.

952 Siehe hierzu Christopher de Souza, Parliamentary Debates, Official Reports, 19.10.2009, Vol. 86, Column 1634, verfügbar unter http://sprs.parl.gov.sg/search/topic.jsp?currentTopicID=00003591-WA&currentPubID=00004793-WA&topicKey=00004793-WA.00003591-WA_1%2B%2B (zuletzt abgerufen am 28.4.2021); vgl. auch Minn/Foxton, in: Klausegger/Klein/Kremslehner/Petsche/Pitkowitz/Power/Welser/Zeiler (Hrsg.), Austrian Yearbook on International Arbitration 2011, S. 197 (203); Ministry of Law, International Arbitration (Amendment) Bill, Ministry of Law's Responses to Public, Feedback Received, Disagreement with section 12A, Ministry of Law's response, S. 8, verfügbar unter https://www.mlaw.gov.sg/content/dam/minlaw/corp/assets/documents/linkclick1e3a.pdf (zuletzt abgerufen am 28.4.2021).

tiven Rechtsschutz.[953] Sec. 12A steht ferner mit Art. 17 J, 9 i. V. m. Art. 1 (2) Ergänzungen des UNCITRAL Modellgesetzes 2006[954] im Einklang, das ebenfalls vorläufige gerichtliche Maßnahmen für Schiedsverfahren mit extraterritorialem Sitz vorsieht. Auch das englische[955] und das Hongkonger[956] Schiedsrecht gestatten einstweilige gerichtliche Maßnahmen für Schiedsverfahren mit Sitz im Ausland. Darüber hinaus ordnen US-amerikanische, englische, Hongkonger und Schweizer Gerichte einstweilige Maßnahmen zu Gunsten von Schiedsverfahren mit ausländischem Sitz an.[957] Aus der Perspektive der Schiedsfreundlichkeit fördert Sec. 12A IAA die internationale Schiedsgerichtsbarkeit.[958] Sec. 12A IAA entspricht dem Schiedsverfahren unterstützenden UNCITRAL Modellgesetzes 2006 und den schiedsfreundlichen Rechtsordnungen in England, Hongkong, der Schweiz und den USA.

2. Einstweiliger Rechtsschutz durch Schiedsgerichte

a) Inländische Schiedsverfahren

Die von einem Schiedsgericht erlassenen Maßnahmen des einstweiligen Rechtsschutzes[959] in Schiedsverfahren mit Sitz in Singapur werden gem. Sec. 12 (6) IAA und Sec. 28 (4) AA wie gerichtliche Beschlüsse vollstreckt. Erforderlich ist allerdings, dass der High Court der Vollstreckung der vom Schiedstribunal angeordneten vorläufigen Maßnahmen zustimmt[960]. Die Vollstreckbarkeit von schiedsgerichtlich angeordneten einstweiligen Maß-

953 Born, International Commercial Arbitration, Bd. 2, S. 2555 ff.; Born, Law and Practice, § 11.04, S. 224 f. Die Vollstreckung von gerichtlichem einstweiligem Rechtsschutz in einem anderen Staat ist problematisch, siehe Born, International Commercial Arbitration, Bd. 2, S. 2560 f.; Born, Law and Practice, § 11.04, S. 224 f.

954 Auch das UNCITRAL Modellgesetz 1985 ließ bereits einstweilige gerichtliche Maßnahmen für Schiedsverfahren mit ausländischem Sitz zu, siehe Art. 9 i. V. m. 1 (2) UNCITRAL Modellgesetz 1985.

955 Sec. 43 f. i. V. m. Sec. 2 (3) Arbitration Act 1996.

956 Sec. 45, 21 i. V. m. Sec. 5 (2) Arbitration Ordinance.

957 Born, Law and Practice, § 11.04, S. 224 f.; Born, International Commercial Arbitration, Bd. 2, S. 2555 ff.

958 Zumal davon auszugehen ist, dass die Singapurer Gerichte das ihnen gem. Sec. 12A (3) zugestandene Ermessen bei der Anordnung von einstweiligen gerichtlichen Maßnahmen zu Gunsten eines Schiedsverfahrens mit Sitz im Ausland in angemessener und neutraler Weise anwenden werden, vgl. Christopher de Souza, Parliamentary Debates, Official Reports, 19.10.2009, Vol. 86, Column 1634, verfügbar unter http://sprs.parl.gov.sg/search/topic.jsp?currentTopicID=00003591-WA&currentPubID=00004793-WA&topicKey=00004793-WA.00003591-WA_1%2B%2B (zuletzt abgerufen am 28.4.2021).

959 Diese vorläufigen Maßnahmen ergehen nach Sec. 12 (1) IAA und Sec. 28 (2) AA als Beschluss (engl. order) oder als Verfügung (engl. direction).

960 Engl. leave.

nahmen gewährt das Schiedsrecht seit Inkrafttreten des IAA im Jahre 1995[961] und des AA im Jahre 2002[962]. Die Ergänzungen des UNCITRAL Modellgesetzes 2006 sehen dagegen erstmals die Vollstreckung von durch ein Schiedsgericht erlassenen vorläufigen Maßnahmen vor.[963] In den internationalen Schiedszentren in England[964], Hongkong[965] und der Schweiz[966] werden gleichermaßen von Schiedsgerichten angeordnete einstweilige Maßnahmen wie eine Gerichtsentscheidung vollstreckt. Die Schiedsgesetzgebung Frankreichs[967] und der USA[968] sieht hingegen die Vollstreckung von schiedsgerichtlich erlassenem einstweiligem Rechtsschutz nicht vor. Die schiedsgerichtlich angeordneten vorläufigen Maßnahmen können, entgegen der Auffassung von *Born*[969], nicht als finaler Schiedsspruch nach den allgemeinen Vollstreckungsvorschriften durchgesetzt werden.[970] Die Vollstreckung der durch das Schiedsgericht angeordneten vorläufigen Maßnahmen ist deshalb für die Effektivität des schiedsgerichtlichen einstweiligen Rechtsschutzes unerlässlich.[971] Infolgedessen ist die Vollstreckung von schiedsgerichtlich angeordnetem einstweiligen Rechtsschutz in Singapur schiedsfreundlich und Singapur den internationalen Schiedszentren Frankreich und USA einen Schritt voraus.

---

961 Den IAA verabschiedete das Parlament im Jahr 1994 und er trat am 27.1.1995 in Kraft.

962 Den AA verabschiedete das Parlament im Jahr 2001 und er trat am 1.3.2002 in Kraft.

963 Siehe Art. 17 H Ergänzungen des UNCITRAL Modellgesetzes 2006.

964 Sec. 42 Arbitration Act 1996.

965 Sec. 61 Hongkonger Arbitration Ordinance.

966 Art. 183 Bundesgesetz über das Internationale Privatrecht (IPRG); Kren Kostkiewicz, IPRG/LugÜ, Art. 183 IPRG Rn. 7; Mabillard, in: Honsell/Vogt/Schnyder/Berti, Basler Kommentar, Art. 183 IPRG Rn. 16.

967 Viertes Buch französischer Code de procédure civile.

968 Federal Arbitration Act (Title 9, US Code). Teilweise vollstrecken die amerikanischen Gerichte aber schiedsgerichtlich angeordnete einstweilige Maßnahme, siehe Born, International Commercial Arbitration, Bd. 2, S. 2513 f; Born, Law and Practice, § 11.02 [B], S. 218.

969 Born, International Commercial Arbitration, Bd. 2, S. 2515 f.; Born, Law and Practice, § 11.02 [B], S. 218.

970 Blackaby/Partasides/Redfern/Hunter, International Arbitration, Rn. 7.19; Lew/Mistelis/Kröll, Comparative International Commercial Arbitration, Rn. 23-84 ff.; Lachmann, S. 499 f. Die Ergänzungen des UNCITRAL Modellgesetzes 2006 unterscheiden zwischen der Vollstreckung von durch das Schiedsgericht angeordneten einstweiligen Maßnahmen gem. Art. 17 H Ergänzungen des UNCITRAL Modellgesetzes 2006 (Vollstreckung *sui generis*) und der Vollstreckung von Schiedssprüchen gem. Art. 35 Ergänzungen des UNCITRAL Modellgesetzes 2006. In Art. 17 (2) Ergänzungen des UNCITRAL Modellgesetzes 2006 wird fernerhin eine einstweilige Maßnahme, unabhängig von ihrer Form, als vorübergehende Maßnahme definiert.

971 Vgl. Lew/Mistelis/Kröll, Comparative International Commercial Arbitration, Rn. 23-82 ff.; Born, Cases and Materials, S. 896 f.; Born, Law and Practice, § 11.02, S. 217 ff.

b) Ausländische Schiedsverfahren

Seit 2012 können in Singapur von Schiedsgerichten mit extraterritorialem Schiedssitz angeordnete vorläufige Maßnahmen wie ausländische Schiedssprüche vollstreckt werden.[972] Der Gesetzgeber erweiterte hierfür die Legaldefinition eines Schiedsspruchs in Sec. 27 (1) IAA. Sec. 27 (1), 29 (1), 19 IAA gestattet nunmehr auch den durch ausländische Schiedsgerichte[973] erlassenen einstweiligen Maßnahmen i. S. d. Sec. 12 (1) (c)–(i) IAA die Vollstreckung in Singapur. Nach einem Beratungsverfahren mit nationalen und internationalen Schiedsrechtsexperten bezweckte der Gesetzgeber, mit der Eröffnung der Vollstreckung solcher einstweiliger Maßnahmen, dem schiedsfreundlichem Ruf Singapurs zu entsprechen.[974] Wie auf die Vollstreckung ausländischer Schiedssprüche finden auf die Vollstreckung schiedsgerichtlich angeordneter einstweiliger Maßnahmen die Vollstreckungsversagungsgründe von Sec. 31 IAA (Art. 5 UNÜ) Anwendung.[975] Dieses Singapurer Vollstreckungsregime gewährt den Parteien eines Schiedsverfahrens mit ausländischem Sitz effektiven Rechtschutz. Nur die Hongkonger Schiedslegislation eröffnet die Vollstreckung von durch ausländische Schiedsgerichte angeordnete vorläufige Maßnahmen.[976] Die Schiedsgesetzgebung der international bedeutenden Schiedsorte Englands[977], Frankreichs[978], der Schweiz[979] und der USA[980] gestatten keine Vollstreckung solcher vorläufigen Maßnahmen. Die Vollstreckbarkeit von einstweiligen Maßnahmen, die durch ausländische Schiedsgerichte erlassenen werden, ist als Schiedsverfahren fördernd anzusehen,[981] weil sie auch den Parteien eines Schiedsverfahrens mit ausländischem Sitz effektiven Rechtsschutz gewährt. Singapur weist folglich durch die Gesetzesnovelle von 2012 gegenüber den

---

972 International Arbitration (Amendment) Act 2012, in Kraft getreten am 1.6.2012.

973 Schiedsverfahren mit Sitz im Ausland.

974 Shanmugam (Minister for Law), Patrick Tay Teck Guan, Official Reports, 9.4.2012, Vol. 89, verfügbar unter http://sprs.parl.gov.sg/search/topic.jsp?currentTopicID=00077287-WA&currentPubID=00077335-WA&topicKey=00077335-WA.00077287-WA_5%2Bid-92b4e92e-6efb-4fcd-bd99-4c99467b63e0%2B (zuletzt abgerufen am 28.4.2021).

975 Die Vollstreckung einer solchen einstweiligen Maßnahme bedarf der Zustimmung (engl. leave) des High Courts, Sec. 27 (1), 29 (1), 19 IAA.

976 Sec. 61 i. V. m. Sec. 5 (2) Arbitration Ordinance.

977 Siehe Sec. 42 i. V. m. Sec. 2 Arbitration Act 1996.

978 4. Buch Code de procédure civile.

979 12. Kapitel, Bundesgesetz über das Internationale Privatrecht.

980 Federal Arbitration Act, (Title 9, US Code).

981 Nach *Lew/Mistelis/Kröll* und *Born* ist die extraterritoriale Vollstreckung von schiedsgerichtlich erlassenen einstweiligen Maßnahmen wünschenswert, Lew/Mistelis/Kröll, Comparative International Commercial Arbitration, Rn. 23-95 f.; Born, International Commercial Arbitration, Bd. 2, S. 2516 f.

bedeutendsten internationalen Schiedszentren schiedsfreundlichere gesetzliche Rahmenbedingungen auf.

c) Bewertung

Die Singapurer Gesetzgebung bringt durch die umfassende Vollstreckung einstweiliger Maßnahmen, die in- und ausländische Schiedsgerichte anordnen, der Schiedsgerichtsbarkeit das erforderliche Vertrauen entgegen. Die Vollstreckung schiedsgerichtlicher vorläufiger Maßnahmen verhalf Schiedsverfahren zudem zu einem effektiven und mit staatlichen Gerichten äquivalenten Streitbeilegungsmechanismus.

3. Einstweiliger Rechtsschutz durch Emergency Arbitrator

Um den Schiedsort Singapur sowie die Schiedsinstitution SIAC zu fördern, stellte die Legislative 2012[982], als erster Gesetzgeber weltweit, in Sec. 2 (1) IAA und Sec. 2 (1) AA den durch die SIAC-Schiedsordnung 2010[983] eingeführten „Emergency Arbitrator“ („Notfallschiedsrichter“) einem Schiedsgericht gleich. Die vom Emergency Arbitrator angeordneten vorläufigen Maßnahmen[984] können nach der neuen Legaldefinition eines Schiedsgerichts in Sec. 2 (1) IAA n. F. und Sec. 2 (1) AA n. F. unter Sec. 12 (6) IAA bzw. Sec. 28 (4) AA vollstreckt werden.[985] Der Emergency Arbitrator kann den Schiedsparteien hierdurch effektive einstweilige Maßnahmen gewähren, wenn das Schiedsgericht sich noch nicht konstituieren konnte. Dies respektiert den Willen der Schiedsparteien, ihre Streitigkeit exklusiv der Schiedsgerichtsbarkeit zu unterwerfen. Mit dieser schiedsfreundlichen[986] Gesetzesreform schloss der Gesetzgeber eine weitere Rechtsschutzlücke für die Schiedsparteien. Einzig die Hongkonger[987] Schiedsgesetzgebung gestattet gleichfalls die Vollstreckung von durch den Emergency Arbitrator angeordneten vorläufigen Maßnahmen. Singapur besitzt demzufolge im Ver-

982 International Arbitration (Amendment) Act 2012, in Kraft getreten am 1.6.2012.

983 Das SIAC war eine der ersten Schiedsinstitutionen, die einen Emergency Arbitrator einführte.

984 Sec. 12 i. V. m. Sec. 2 (1) IAA und Sec. 28 i. V. m. Sec. 2 (1) AA.

985 Shanmugam (Minister for Law) und Patrick Tay Teck Guan, Official Reports, 9.4.2012, Vol. 89, verfügbar unter http://sprs.parl.gov.sg/search/topic.jsp?currentTopicID=00077287-WA&currentPubID=00077335-WA&topicKey=00077335-WA.00077287-WA_5%2Bid-92b4e92e-6efb-4fcd-bd99-4c99467b63e0%2B (zuletzt abgerufen am 28.4.2021).

986 *Born* erachtet die Gleichstellung von Schiedsgericht und Emergency Arbitrator und die Vollstreckbarkeit von durch den Emergency Arbitrator angeordnetem einstweiligen Rechtsschutz als erstrebenswert, Born, International Commercial Arbitration, Bd. 2, S. 2521 f.

987 Sec. 22 B Arbitration Ordinance.

gleich zu den Schiedszentren in England, Frankreich, der Schweiz und den USA eine schiedsfreundlichere Gesetzgebung. Im Ergebnis ist festzuhalten, dass dem Singapurer Gesetzgeber die bezweckte Schiedsverfahren fördernde Anpassung der Schiedsgesetzgebung an die Bedürfnisse von modernen Schiedsverfahren gelungen ist.[988]

VII. Aufhebungsverfahren

Internationale und inländische Schiedssprüche können in Singapur gem. Sec. 3 (1) IAA i. V. m. Art. 34 UNCITRAL Modellgesetz und Sec. 24 IAA bzw. Sec. 48 AA bei tatbestandlicher Erfüllung eines der abschließend[989] enumerierten Gründe aufgehoben werden. Der Wortlaut von Sec. 48 AA korrespondiert mit Art. 34 UNCITRAL Modellgesetz.

1. Formelle Aufhebungsgründe

Eine schiedsunfreundliche Rechtsprechung existiert zu den formellen Aufhebungsgründen von Sec. 3 (1) IAA i. V. m. Art. 34 (2) (a) UNCITRAL Modellgesetz und Sec. 48 (1) (a) AA bislang nicht.[990]

2. Materielle Aufhebungsgründe

Sec. 3 (1) IAA i. V. m. Art. 34 (2) (b) UNCITRAL Modellgesetz und Sec. 48 (1) (b) AA enthalten die materiellen Aufhebungsgründe der fehlenden Schiedsfähigkeit[991] und der Verletzung der öffentlichen Ordnung.

a) Öffentliche Ordnung

Ein Schiedsspruch kann nach Sec. 3 (1) IAA i. V. m. Art. 34 (2) (b) (ii) UNCITRAL Modellgesetz bzw. Sec. 48 (1) (b) (ii) AA aufgehoben werden, wenn der High Court von Amts wegen feststellt, dass der Schiedsspruch gegen die öffentliche Ordnung (*ordre public*) verstößt. Der unbestimmte Rechtsbegriff

---

988 Shanmugam (Minister for Law) und Patrick Tay Teck Guan, Official Reports, 9.4.2012, Vol. 89, verfügbar unter http://sprs.parl.gov.sg/search/topic.jsp?currentTopicID=00077287-WA&currentPubID=00077335-WA&topicKey=00077335-WA.00077287-WA_5%2Bid-92b4e92e-6efb-4fcd-bd99-4c99467b63e0%2B (zuletzt abgerufen am 28.4.2021); Mangan/Reed/Choong, S. 3.

989 Siehe Sec. 3 (1) IAA i. V. m. Art. 34 (1) UNCITRAL Modellgesetz und Sec. 47 AA.

990 Chan, Leng Sun, Singapore Law on Arbitral Awards, S. 152 ff.; Boo, Halsbury's, S. 152 f., 158 ff.; Merkin/Hjalmarsson, S. 116 f., 164 f.

991 Siehe zur Schiedsfähigkeit in Singapur, Chan, Leng Sun, Singapore Law on Arbitral Awards, S. 177 ff. Merkin/Hjalmarsson, S. 74 f., 117; vgl. Chew, S. 109.

der öffentlichen Ordnung bedarf der Auslegung bzw. Konkretisierung[992], um ihm Konturen zu verleihen[993]. Richter *Burrough* verglich die Auslegung der öffentlichen Ordnung in der Entscheidung *Richardson v Mellish*[994] 1824 mit einem nicht zu bändigenden Pferd:

> „...*it* [public policy] *is a very unruly horse, and when once you get astride it you never know where it will carry you.*“

Der Aufhebungsgrund des *ordre public* verändert sich mit der gesellschaftlichen Entwicklung eines Landes dynamisch und die Rechtsprechung gibt ihm die erforderliche Kontur.[995] Im Folgenden werden deshalb die Singapurer Grundsatzentscheidungen zur öffentlichen Ordnung erörtert.

aa) PT Asuransi Jasa Indonesia v Dexia Bank

Der High Court hatte in der Rechtssache *PT Asuransi Jasa Indonesia (Persero) v Dexia Bank SA* (*PT Asuransi v Dexia Bank I)*[996] zunächst darüber zu urteilen, ob ein Schiedsspruch wegen eines Verstoßes gegen die öffentliche Ordnung unter Sec. 3 (1) IAA i. V. m. Art. 34 (2) (b) (ii) UNCITRAL Modellgesetz aufzuheben ist. Der Court of Appeal setzte sich im anschließenden Berufungsverfahren mit derselben Rechtsfrage auseinander.[997]

Der Aufhebungskläger *PT Asuransi Jasa Indonesia (Persero) [Asuransi]* machte gegen den Schiedsspruch II vor dem High Court geltend, dass der Schiedsspruch die öffentliche Ordnung in Singapur verletze. Der Schiedsspruch II habe den Schiedsspruch I überprüft, korrigiert und abgeändert und hierdurch gegen die in Sec. 19B IAA kodifizierte Rechtskraft des Schiedsspruchs verstoßen. Dem Aufhebungskläger zufolge machte die Verletzung von Sec. 19B IAA den Schiedsspruch II unvereinbar mit der öffentlichen Ordnung in Singapur. Der High Court urteilte, dass ein Verstoß gegen die einfachgesetzliche Vorschrift von Sec. 19B IAA für eine Verletzung der öffentlichen Ordnung in Singapur nicht ausreiche. Die öffentliche Ordnung könne zwar in einer einfachgesetzlichen Vorschrift normiert sein, jedoch

---

992 Vgl. Wiedemann, NJW 2014, S. 2407 ff.

993 Vgl. Blackaby/Partasides/Redfern/Hunter, International Arbitration, Rn. 10.81 ff.; Born, International Commercial Arbitration, Bd. 3, S. 3312 ff.

994 Court of Common Pleas, 130 E. R. 294; (1824) 2 Bing. 229; (1824) 2 Bingham 229, 2.7.1824.

995 Eine Legaldefinition des Terminus der öffentlichen Ordnung existiert in der Singapurer Schiedsgesetzgebung nicht.

996 [2006] 1 SLR 197; [2005] SGHC 197, 20.10.2005. Für den Tatbestand der Entscheidung, siehe Kapitel: Kompetenz-Kompetenz; PT Asuransi Jasa Indonesia v Dexia Bank (B.II.1.).

997 *PT Asuransi Jasa Indonesia (Persero) v Dexia Bank SA*, [2007] 1 SLR 597; [2006] SGCA 41, 1.12.2006. Für den Tatbestand der Entscheidung, siehe Kapitel: Kompetenz-Kompetenz; PT Asuransi Jasa Indonesia v Dexia Bank (B.II.1.).

zähle nicht jede gesetzliche Bestimmung zur öffentlichen Ordnung. Ein Verstoß des Schiedsspruchs gegen das einfache Recht Singapurs führe mithin nicht *ipso jure* zu einer Verletzung der öffentlichen Ordnung. In einem internationalen Schiedsverfahren führe weder eine falsche Rechtsanwendung noch sich widersprechende Schiedssprüche zu einem Verstoß gegen die öffentliche Ordnung Singapurs.[998] Im Oktober 2005 wies der High Court die Aufhebungsklage folglich ab.

Nach dem internationalen Standard der Schiedsgerichtsbarkeit ist der unbestimmte Begriff der öffentlichen Ordnung eng auszulegen und Schiedssprüche können nur ausnahmsweise aufgehoben werden. Eine falsche Rechtsanwendung des nationalen Rechts des Aufhebungsstaates durch das Schiedsgericht reicht demnach nicht für eine Verletzung der öffentlichen Ordnung aus. Erforderlich ist vielmehr, dass der Schiedsspruch eindeutig gegen die fundamentalen Gerechtigkeitsvorstellungen oder das elementare zwingende Recht[999] des Aufhebungsstaates verstößt[1000].[1001] Die enge Konkretisierung des Begriffs der öffentlichen Ordnung durch den High Court spiegelt somit den internationalen Schiedsgerichtsstandard wider.

Im Berufungsverfahren *PT Asuransi Jasa Indonesia (Persero) v Dexia Bank SA (PT Asuransi v Dexia Bank II)*[1002] vor dem Court of Appeal trug der Aufhebungskläger *Asuransi* vor, dass die Entscheidung des High Courts hinsichtlich des Verstoßes gegen Sec. 19B (1) IAA unzutreffend gewesen sei. Dies begründete der Aufhebungskläger insbesondere mit dem Urteil *Oil & Natural Gas Corporation Ltd v Saw Pipes Ltd (Saw Pipes)*[1003] des indischen Supreme Courts. Im *Saw Pipes*-Urteil entschied der Supreme Court, dass ein Schiedsspruch, der gegen eine Bestimmung des indischen SchiedsG

998 Rn. 29.

999 Eine Verletzung des abdingbaren einfachen Rechts des Aufhebungsstaates ist nicht ausreichend, Born, International Commercial Arbitration, Bd. 3, S. 3312 ff.; Born, Law and Practice, § 16.03 [B] [7], S. 333.

1000 Unterschiedlich wird beurteilt, ob der dem Schiedsspruch zu Grunde liegende materielle Anspruch oder die Durchsetzung des Schiedsspruchs gegen die öffentliche Ordnung des Aufhebungsstaates verstoßen muss. *Born* befürwortet, dass der im Schiedsspruch geltend gemachte Anspruch gegen die öffentliche Ordnung verstoßen muss, Born, International Commercial Arbitration, Bd. 3, S. 3318 f. Erforderlich ist nach *Born* zudem, dass die konkrete Rechtsanwendung in einem Schiedsspruch die öffentliche Ordnung verletzt. Ein abstrakter Verstoß eines im Schiedsspruch angewandten Gesetzes gegen die öffentliche Ordnung ist deshalb nicht ausreichend, Born, International Commercial Arbitration, Bd. 3, S. 3320; vgl. auch BGH, KZR 43/71, NJW 1972, S. 2180 (2181).

1001 Born, International Commercial Arbitration, Bd. 3, S. 3178 f., 3312 ff.; Born, Law and Practice, § 16.03 [B] [7], S. 333 f.; Blackaby/Partasides/Redfern/Hunter, International Arbitration, Rn. 10.81 ff.

1002 [2007] 1 SLR 597; [2006] SGCA 41, 1.12.2006.

1003 AIR 2003 SC 2629; (2003) 5 SCC 705; Appeal (civil) 7419 2001 of 518, 17.4.2003.

verstoße, offensichtlich rechtswidrig (engl. patently illegal) und deshalb nicht mit der indischen öffentlichen Ordnung zu vereinbaren sei. Nach dem Aufhebungskläger müsse ein Verstoß gegen Singapurer Recht (u. a. durch eine falsche Rechtsanwendung) auch in Singapur zu einer Verletzung der öffentlichen Ordnung und zur Aufhebung des Schiedsspruchs führen.[1004] Der Court of Appeal erachtete die *Saw Pipes*-Rechtsprechung des indischen Supreme Courts als nicht auf die internationale Singapurer Schiedsgesetzgebung anwendbar. Unter dem IAA sollten gerichtliche Interventionen in Schiedsverfahren minimiert werden und der Privatautonomie des Schiedsverfahrens hierdurch der notwendige Handlungsspielraum zugestanden werden. Die falsche Rechtsanwendung oder ein Tatsachenfehler des Schiedsgerichts sei verbindlich für die Schiedsparteien und eröffne den Parteien keine Aufhebung des Schiedsspruchs gem. Sec. 24 IAA oder Art. 34 UNCITRAL Modellgesetz. Um eine Kohärenz innerhalb des IAA i. V. m. dem UNCITRAL Modellgesetz zu gewährleisten, können Rechts- und Tatsachenfehler nur dann zur Aufhebung des Schiedsspruchs führen, sofern der Schiedsspruch i. S. d. Art. 34 (2) (a) (iii) UNCITRAL Modellgesetz eine Streitigkeit betreffe, die nicht vom Anwendungsbereich der Schiedsvereinbarung erfasst werde. Letzteres war nach dem Court of Appeal nicht der Fall.[1005]

Das oberste Singapurer Gericht leitete seine enge Auslegung der öffentlichen Ordnung aus einer Gesamtschau neuseeländischer[1006], englischer[1007] und amerikanischer[1008] Gerichtsentscheidungen und den „Travaux Préparatoires“[1009] des UNCITRAL Modellgesetzes ab. Nach dem Court of Appeal verletzen Schiedssprüche die öffentliche Ordnung in Singapur, die das Gewissen erschüttern und die klar dem Gemeinwohl schaden. Zudem verletzten Schiedssprüche die öffentliche Ordnung, die gegen das Anstandsgefühl eines umfänglich informierten Bürgers oder die gegen die grundlegendsten Moral- und Gerechtigkeitsvorstellungen in Singapur verstoßen:

> *„Although the concept of public policy of the State is not defined in the Act or the Model Law, the general consensus of judicial*

1004 Rn. 56.

1005 Rn. 56 f.

1006 Christchurch High Court, *Downer Connect Ltd v Pot Hole People Ltd*, CIV 2003-409-2878; [2004] BCL 586; BC200469167, 19.5.2004.

1007 Court of Appeal, *Deutsche Schachtbau-Und Tiefbohrgesellschaft mbH v R'as al-Khaimah National Oil Co*, [1987] 2 All E.R. 769; [1987] 2 Lloyd's Rep. 246; [1987] 3 W.L.R. 1023, 24.3.1987.

1008 U.S. Court of Appeals, Second Circuit, *Parsons & Whittemore Overseas Co v Societe Generale De L'industrie Du Papier (RAKTA)*, 508 F.2d 969 (2d Cir. 1974), 23.12.1974.

1009 UNCITRAL, 18. Sitzung, Report of the United Nations Commission on International Trade Law on the work of its eighteenth session, Supplement No. 17, A/40/17, 3.–21.6.1985, Rn. 297.

and expert opinion is that public policy under the Act encompasses a narrow scope. In our view, it should only operate in instances where the upholding of an arbitral award would ‚shock the conscience' (see Downer Connect ([58] supra) at [136]), or is ‚clearly injurious to the public good or ... wholly offensive to the ordinary reasonable and fully informed member of the public' (see Deutsche Schachbau v Shell International Petroleum Co Ltd [1987] 2 Lloyds' Rep 246 at 254, per Sir John Donaldson MR), or where it violates the forum's most basic notion of morality and justice: see Parsons & Whittemore Overseas Co Inc v Societe Generale de L'Industrie du Papier (RAKTA) 508 F 2d, 969 (2nd Cir, 1974) at 974. This would be consistent with the concept of public policy that can be ascertained from the preparatory materials to the Model Law. As was highlighted in the Commission Report (A/40/17), at para 297... "[1010]

Der Court of Appeal widersprach der Rechtsauffassung des indischen Supreme Courts in dessen Entscheidung *Saw Pipes* und urteilte, dass eine fehlerhafte Rechtsanwendung des Singapurer Schiedsrechts nicht zu einem Verstoß gegen die öffentliche Ordnung in Singapur führen könne. Dies begründete das oberste Gericht Singapurs mit der im IAA zum Ausdruck gebrachten gesetzgeberischen Wertung, dass die Gerichte nach Möglichkeit nicht in das Schiedsverfahren eingreifen sollten. Im Ergebnis folgte der Court of Appeal der Entscheidung des High Courts und wies die Berufung im Dezember 2006 zurück.[1011]

Die Literatur lobt die enge Auslegung der öffentlichen Ordnung durch den Court of Appeal, da diese mit der internationalen Norm der Schiedsgerichtsbarkeit übereinstimme.[1012] Sie erachtet die *PT Asuransi v Dexia Bank II*-Entscheidung als positiv, weil der Court of Appeal der weit gefassten Konkretisierung der öffentlichen Ordnung des indischen Supreme Courts im Urteil *Saw Pipes* nicht folgte.[1013] Dies fördere den Schiedsort Singapur.[1014]

1010 Rn. 59.

1011 Rn. 57 ff.

1012 Born, International Commercial Arbitration, Bd. 3, S. 3315 i. V. m. Fn. 839, S. 3321 i. V. m. Fn. 876, S. 3669 i. V. m. Fn. 1382; Thej, International Arbitration Law Review 2014, S. 37 (38 f.); Minn, in: Berg (Hrsg.), International Arbitration, The Coming of a New Age?, S. 235 (268 f.); Hwang/Lee, Shaun, Journal of International Arbitration 2008, Vol. 25, Ausg. 6, S. 873 (881 ff. i. V. m. Fn. 42 und 84); Timothy, International Arbitration Law Review 2016, S. 56 (58 f.); Chan, Darius/Tan, Paul, in: Yihan/Tan, Paul (Hrsg.), Singapore Law, 50 Years in the Making, S. 775 (796).

1013 Chew, 119 ff.; Arvind, International & Comparative Law Quarterly 2010, S. 65 (81 f.).

1014 Minn, in: Berg (Hrsg.), International Arbitration, The Coming of a New Age?, S. 235 (268 f.); Chew, S. 86 f., 119 ff. Zur Schiedsfreundlichkeit der Entscheidung, Menon, Arbitration 2015, S. 413 (417 i. V. m. Fn. 20). Zur engen Auslegung der öffentlichen Ordnung, Born, International Commercial Arbitration, Bd. 3, S. 3315 i. V. m. Fn. 839,

Der Court of Appeal und der High Court brachten zum Ausdruck, dass die Privatautonomie von Schiedsverfahren durch schonende gerichtliche Eingriffe in die Integrität des Schiedsverfahrens gewährleistet werden soll. Dies entspricht dem internationalen Standard der Schiedsgerichtsbarkeit nach dem der Aufhebungsgrund der öffentlichen Ordnung eng auszulegen ist.[1015] Auf Grund der restriktiven Auslegung der öffentliche Ordnung sind die Urteile *PT Asuransi v Dexia Bank* des Court of Appeals und des High Courts als schiedsfreundlich zu charakterisieren.

bb) AJT v AJU/AJU v AJT

Der High Court und der Court of Appeal hatten im Verfahren *AJT v AJU*[1016] bzw. *AJU v AJT*[1017] zu entscheiden, ob die Gerichte den materiellen Inhalt eines Schiedsspruchs unter dem Aufhebungsgrund der öffentlichen Ordnung i.S.v. Sec.3 (1) IAA i.V.m. Art.34 (2) (b) (ii) UNCITRAL Modellgesetz überprüfen dürfen.

Im dem Aufhebungsprozess zu Grunde liegenden Sachverhalt initiierte das auf den Virgin Islands inkorporierte Unternehmen *AJT* 2006 gegen *AJU* ein vom SIAC administriertes Schiedsverfahren mit Sitz in Singapur. *AJU* hatte mit einem Unternehmen, das mit dem Alleinaktionär von *AJT* assoziiert war, einen Vertrag abgeschlossen. Das Unternehmen trat die vertraglichen Ansprüche an *AJT* ab. Dieser Vertrag enthielt eine Schiedsklausel zu Gunsten eines vom SIAC administrierten Schiedsverfahrens nach den „UNCITRAL Arbitration Rules“. Der Vertrag gestattete *AJT* die Ausrichtung eines jährlich stattfindenden Tennisturniers im thailändischen Bangkok. Nach dem Beginn des Schiedsverfahrens stellte das thailändische Unternehmen *AJU* in Thailand eine Strafanzeige gegen den Alleinaktionär von *AJT* und zwei mit Letzterem assoziierte Unternehmen. In der Strafanzeige behauptete *AJU*, der Vertragsschluss beruhe auf einem von den Beschuldigten begangenem Betrug. Die Strafverfolgungsbehörde in Thailand ermittelte gegen die Beschuldigten wegen gemeinschaftlich begangenen Betrugs, gemeinschaftlich begangener Urkundenfälschung und wegen Gebrauchs einer unechten Urkunde. Nach thailändischem Strafrecht ist Betrug ein Antragsdelikt, die Herstellung und der Gebrauch einer unechten Urkunde sind hingegen Offizialdelikte.

S.3321 i.V.m. Fn.876, S.3669 i.V.m. Fn.1382; Thej, International Arbitration Law Review 2014, S.37 (38f.); Timothy, International Arbitration Law Review 2016, S.56 (58f.).

1015 Born, International Commercial Arbitration, Bd.3, S.S.3178f., 3312ff.; Born, Law and Practice, §16.03 [B] [7], S.333; Blackaby/Partasides/Redfern/Hunter, International Arbitration, Rn.10.83f.

1016 High Court, [2010] SGHC 201, 16.7.2010.

1017 Court of Appeal, [2011] SGCA 41, 22.8.2011.

Während des strafrechtlichen Ermittlungsverfahrens schlossen die Schiedsparteien und die Beschuldigten einen Vergleich, nach dem das Strafverfahren und das Schiedsverfahren zu beenden waren. *AJU* sollte zudem 470.000 US-Dollar an *AJT* zahlen. Auf den Vergleich war Singapurer Recht anwendbar. Daraufhin zog *AJU* seine Strafanzeige zurück und zahlte die vereinbarte Summe an *AJT*. Die thailändische Staatsanwaltschaft stellte das Strafverfahren ein. *AJT* weigerte sich dennoch, seine Schiedsklage zurückzunehmen. *AJU* beantragte vor dem Schiedsgericht, dass das Schiedsverfahren auf Grund des Vergleichs zu beenden sei. *AJT* machte andererseits geltend, dass die Vereinbarung wegen Nötigung, unzulässiger Beeinflussung und Rechtswidrigkeit unwirksam sei. Die Parteien verständigten sich darauf, dass das Schiedsgericht über die Wirksamkeit des Vergleichs entscheiden sollte. Das Schiedstribunal befand in einem vorläufigen Schiedsspruch, dass diese Vereinbarung aus dem Jahr 2008 wirksam und durchsetzbar sei.

Im Verfahren *AJT v AJU*[1018] vor dem High Court beantragte *AJT* die Aufhebung des vorläufigen Schiedsspruchs gem. Art. 34 (2) (b) (ii) UNCITRAL Modellgesetz. Der High Court urteilte, dass das Schiedsgericht in seinem Schiedsspruch die Wirksamkeit des Vergleichs nicht schlüssig begründet habe. In einem angemessenen Fall stehe es den Gerichten in einem Aufhebungsverfahren im Rahmen ihrer „Kontrollzuständigkeit" auch zu, die dem Schiedsspruch zugrunde liegenden Tatsachen zu überprüfen und über die Rechtswidrigkeit einer Vereinbarung zu entscheiden. Dies begründete der High Court mit einer Abwägung zwischen der Finalität eines Schiedsspruchs und dem öffentlichen Interesse, dass ein Schiedsverfahren von den Parteien nicht zur Rechtsbeugung missbraucht werden dürfe:

> *„Thus, on the facts of this present case, while the Tribunal determined that the Concluding Agreement was not illegal, this was not conclusive. In an appropriate case, the court, in exercising its supervisory jurisdiction, may examine the facts of the case and decide the issue of illegality. While there is a need to uphold the public interest in ensuring the finality of arbitral awards, the court must also safeguard the countervailing public interest in ensuring that its processes are not abused by litigants.*"[1019]

Der High Court urteilte im Juli 2010, dass Vereinbarungen mit dem Ziel, strafrechtliche Offizialdelikte zu unterdrücken, gegen die öffentliche Ordnung Singapurs verstießen. Solche Vereinbarungen würden das öffentliche Interesse an einer gerechten Strafverfolgung erschüttern. Unschuldige können hierdurch erpresst werden und schuldige Straftäter sich der Strafverfolgung durch eine Entschädigung an die Opfer entziehen. Eine solche Partei-

---

1018 [2010] SGHC 201, 16.7.2010.
1019 Rn. 24.

vereinbarung verstoße entsprechend gegen die Grundsätze des Strafrechts sowie gegen die Strafrechtspflege.[1020] Der High Court hob den vorläufigen Schiedsspruch daher auf. Das Urteil des High Courts basiert auf der Erwägung, dass das öffentliche Interesse an einer gerechten und effektiven Strafrechtspflege die materielle Kontrolle eines Schiedsspruchs rechtfertige.

Diese Argumentation des High Courts ist nachvollziehbar. Durch den Vergleich aus dem Jahr 2008 sollen nicht nur Bagatelldelikte der Strafverfolgung entzogen werden. Andererseits besteht ein berechtigtes Interesse der internationalen Schiedsgerichtsbarkeit daran, dass die Gerichte lediglich bei unhaltbaren Verletzungen von elementaren Rechtgrundsätzen einen Schiedsspruch aufheben dürfen.[1021] In Schiedsverfahren soll grundsätzlich eine „révision au fond" des Schiedsspruchs durch das für das Aufhebungsverfahren zuständige Gericht vermieden werden.[1022] Die Literatur rügt an dem Urteil des High Courts, dass es durch die Überprüfungsmöglichkeit des Schiedsspruchs zu gerichtlichen Interventionen in Schiedsverfahren komme.[1023] Dieser Kritik ist zuzustimmen, weil die materielle Kontrolle des Schiedsspruchs eine im Aufhebungsverfahren unzulässige „révision au fond" darstellt.

Im Berufungsverfahren *AJU v AJT*[1024] hatte der Court of Appeal zu beurteilen, ob der High Court den materiellen Inhalt des vorläufigen Schiedsspruchs überprüfen durfte. Der Court of Appeal entschied, dass im IAA durch Sec. 19B (1) IAA zum Ausdruck gebracht werde, dass internationale Schiedssprüche verbindlich seien und nur in engen Grenzen einer gerichtlichen Kontrolle im Aufhebungsverfahren offen stünden. Die dem Schiedsverfahren zu Grunde gelegten Tatsachen dürften von den Gerichten im Aufhebungsverfahren einzig bei Betrug oder einer Verletzung der „Natural Justice" überprüft werden:

> *„In our view, the Judge was not entitled to reject the Tribunal's findings and substitute his own findings for them. On the facts of this case, s 19B(1) of the IAA calls for the court to give deference to the factual findings of the Tribunal. The policy of the IAA is to treat IAA awards in the same way as it treats foreign arbi-*

1020 Rn. 33.

1021 Born, International Commercial Arbitration, Bd. 3, S. 3312 ff.; Born, Law and Practice, § 16.03 [B] [7], S. 333; Blackaby/Partasides/Redfern/Hunter, International Arbitration, Rn. 10.83 f.

1022 Born, International Commercial Arbitration, Bd. 3, S. 3325 f.; Born, Law and Practice, § 16.03 [B] [7], S. 333; Berger, Klaus, S. 473 f.

1023 Tan, Paul, International Arbitration Law Review 2010, S. 234 ff.; Megens/Finch, Arbitration 2011, S. 155 (156 ff.); Megens, Arbitration 2012, S. 26 (33 ff.); A.A. Lewis, 106 f.

1024 [2011] SGCA 41, 29.11. 2010 und 22.8.2011.

tral awards where public policy objections to arbitral awards are concerned, even though, in the case of IAA awards, the seat of the arbitration is Singapore and the governing law of the arbitration is Singapore law. Arbitration under the IAA is international arbitration, and not domestic arbitration. That is why s 19B(1) provides that an IAA award is final and binding on the parties, subject only to narrow grounds for curial intervention. This means that findings of fact made in an IAA award are binding on the parties and cannot be reopened except where there is fraud, breach of natural justice or some other recognised vitiating factor. "[1025]

Der Court of Appeal[1026] folgte der Rechtsaufassung desselben Gerichts im Urteil *PT Asuransi v Dexia Bank II.* Er war gleichfalls der Ansicht, dass Rechts- und Tatsachenfehler des Schiedsgerichts *per se* nicht die öffentlichen Ordnung verletzten würden und deshalb im Aufhebungsverfahren nach Art. 34 (2) (b) (ii) UNCITRAL Modellgesetz nicht angefochten werden können.[1027] Das oberste Gericht Singapurs urteilte entsprechend, dass der High Court die Entscheidung des Schiedsgerichts bezüglich des Vergleiches nicht habe überprüfen dürfen und diese Vereinbarung nicht gegen die öffentliche Ordnung Singapurs gem. Art. 34 (2) (b) (ii) UNCITRAL Modellgesetz verstoße.[1028] Der Court of Appeal wies die Aufhebungsklage im August 2011 ab.

Der Court of Appeal begrenzte die materielle Überprüfungskompetenz der Gerichte in Aufhebungsverfahren. Lediglich ein Schiedsspruch, der gravierende Unvereinbarkeiten mit der öffentlichen Ordnung Singapurs offenbare, dürfe aufgehoben werden. Das oberste Singapurer Gericht stellte klar, dass den Gerichten in Aufhebungsverfahren nach Art. 34 (2) (b) (ii) UNCITRAL Modellgesetz keine „révision au fond" des Schiedsspruchs zustehe.[1029] Der Court of Appeal verlieh hiermit der öffentlichen Ordnung unter Art. 34 (2) (b) (ii) UNCITRAL Modellgesetz die notwendige enge Struktur[1030] und stellte sicher, dass Schiedsverfahren vor gerichtlichen Interventionen in den materiellen Inhalt des Schiedsspruchs geschützt werden.

1025 Rn. 65.

1026 *AJU v AJT*, [2011] SGCA 41, 22.8.2011.

1027 Rn. 66 ff. Der Court of Appeal stellte jedoch klar, dass eine falsche Rechtsanwendung durch das Schiedsgericht die öffentliche Ordnung verletzen könne, sofern der Verstoß gegen die öffentliche Ordnung Singapurs die notwendige Erheblichkeitsschwelle erreiche. Die falsche Tatsachenermittlung durch das Schiedsgericht könne allerdings zu keinem Verstoß gegen die öffentliche Ordnung i. S. v. Art. 34 (2) (b) (ii) UNCITRAL Modellgesetz führen, Rn. 67 ff.

1028 Rn. 75.

1029 Rn. 65 ff.

1030 Born, International Commercial Arbitration, Bd. 3, S. 3178 f., 3312 ff.; Born, Law and Practice, § 16.03 [B] [7], S. 333; Blackaby/Partasides/Redfern/Hunter, International Arbitration, Rn. 10.81 ff.

Im Schrifttum stößt das Urteil des obersten Gerichts Singapurs auf Zustimmung und wird als schiedsfreundlich[1031] angesehen, weil es den Erfordernissen des internationalen Handels entspreche[1032] und die Integrität des Schiedsverfahrens achte[1033].[1034] Die Literatur würdigt ferner, dass der Court of Appeal im Urteil *AJU v AJT* Interventionen der Gerichte in das Schiedsverfahren begrenzt habe[1035] und das Urteil damit den Schiedsort Singapur fördere[1036]. Dem Urteil *AJU v AJT* wird von *Megens* andererseits in unzutreffender Weise vorgehalten, dass durch das Urteil die Gefahr bestehen bleibe, dass die Singapurer Gerichte in Schiedsverfahren intervenieren.[1037]

b) Bewertung

Nach dem globalen Standard des Schiedsgerichtswesens sollen Schiedssprüche nur in engen Grenzen unter dem Aufhebungsgrund der öffentlichen

1031 Tan, Paul, International Arbitration Law Review 2011, S. 183 f.; Tan, Richard, Arbitration 2013, S. 436 (438 i. V. m. Fn. 10).

1032 Alvin Yeo/Chou Sean Yu, Global Arbitration Review, Singapore, 26.10.2011, verfügbar unter: http://globalarbitrationreview.com/insight/the-asia-pacific-arbitration-review-2012/1036675/singapore (zuletzt abgerufen am 28.4.2021).

1033 Darius Chan, Singapore Court of Appeal re-affirms commitment to minimal intervention of arbitral awards at the intersection of illegality and public policy, Kluwer Arbitration Blog, 12.9.2011, verfügbar unter: http://kluwerarbitrationblog.com/2011/09/12/singapore-court-of-appeal-re-affirms-commitment-to-minimal-intervention-of-arbitral-awards-at-the-intersection-of-illegality-and-public-policy/ (zuletzt abgerufen am 28.4.2021).

1034 Chong, in: Menon/Brock (Hrsg.), Arbitration in Singapore, A Practical Guide, S. 345 (370); Darius Chan, Singapore Court of Appeal re-affirms commitment to minimal intervention of arbitral awards at the intersection of illegality and public policy, Kluwer Arbitration Blog, 12.9.2011, verfügbar unter: http://kluwerarbitrationblog.com/2011/09/12/singapore-court-of-appeal-re-affirms-commitment-to-minimal-intervention-of-arbitral-awards-at-the-intersection-of-illegality-and-public-policy/ (zuletzt abgerufen am 28.4.2021). Zur restriktiven Auslegung der öffentlichen Ordnung, Born, International Commercial Arbitration, Bd. 3, S. 3316 i. V. m. Fn. 847, S. 3329 f. i. V. m. Fn. 930; Megens, Arbitration 2012, S. 26 (35 f.).

1035 Stothard/Bruce/Curran/Swartz-Zern, in: Menon/Brock (Hrsg.), Arbitration in Singapore, A Practical Guide, S. 575 (620 i. V. m. Fn. 198); Hwang/Boo/Han, in: Bosman (Hrsg.), ICCA International Handbook on Commercial Arbitration, Bd. V, S. Singapore 1 (Singapore 45 i. V. m. Fn. 227); Darius Chan, Singapore Court of Appeal re-affirms commitment to minimal intervention of arbitral awards at the intersection of illegality and public policy, Kluwer Arbitration Blog, 12.9.2011, verfügbar unter: http://kluwerarbitrationblog.com/2011/09/12/singapore-court-of-appeal-re-affirms-commitment-to-minimal-intervention-of-arbitral-awards-at-the-intersection-of-illegality-and-public-policy/ (zuletzt abgerufen am 28.4.2021).

1036 Minn, in: Berg (Hrsg.), International Arbitration, The Coming of a New Age?, S. 235 (267 ff.); Tan, Richard, Arbitration 2013, S. 436 (438 i. V. m. Fn. 10).

1037 Megens, Arbitration 2012, S. 26 (35 f.); Lewis, S. 125.

Ordnung angefochten werden können. Eine materielle Nachkontrolle des Schiedsspruchs auf seine Richtigkeit i. S. einer „révision au fond“ ist nicht zulässig.[1038] Der Court of Appeal verlieh dem Begriff der öffentlichen Ordnung gem. Sec. 3 (1) IAA i. V. m. Art. 34 (2) (b) (ii) UNCITRAL Modellgesetz in seiner Rechtsprechung das erforderliche restriktive Gewand. Einzig die materielle Kontrolle des Schiedsspruchs in der High Court Entscheidung *AJT v AJU* ist als schiedsunfreundlich zu bewerten. Im Berufungsverfahren revidierte der Court of Appeal erfreulicher Weise die Rechtsauffassung des High Courts im Urteil *AJU v AJT* und entschied höchstrichterlich, dass eine „révision au fond“ eines Schiedsspruchs nicht erlaubt sei. In Konklusion ist die Rechtsprechung zur öffentlichen Ordnung gem. Art. 34 (2) (b) (ii) UNCITRAL Modellgesetz als schiedsfreundlich zu bewerten. Die Entscheidung *AJT v AJU* des High Courts zeigt aber, dass auch in der schiedsfördernden Rechtsordnung Singapurs mitunter schiedsunfreundliche Entscheidungen getroffen werden. Im Urteil *Enderby Town Football Club Ltd v The Football Association Ltd*[1039] ist der englische Court of Appeal 1970 dem Vergleich der öffentlichen Ordnung mit einem ungebändigtem Pferd in der Entscheidung *Richardson v Mellish*[1040] entgegengetreten. Der englische Court of Appeal war stattdessen der Auffassung, dass ein gutes Gericht die öffentliche Ordnung durch eine korrekte Rechtsanwendung kontrollieren könne:

> *„So unruly is the horse, it is said [per Burrough J. in Richardson v. Mellish (1824) 2 Bing. 229, 252], that no judge should ever try to mount it lest it run away with him. I disagree. With a good man in the saddle, the unruly horse can be kept in control. It can jump over obstacles. It can leap the fences put up by fictions and come down on the side of justice…“*

Die Singapurer Gerichte haben sich auf den Sattel der als nicht zu bändigendes Pferd beschriebenen öffentlichen Ordnung geschwungen. Es gelang ihnen, die bei der Konkretisierung des *ordre public* immanenten schiedsunfreundlichen Hindernisse sicher zu überspringen und den Aufhebungsgrund der öffentlichen Ordnung durch ihre restriktive Auslegung zu bändigen.

1038 Born, International Commercial Arbitration, Bd. 3, S. 3325 f.; Born, Law and Practice, § 16.03 [B] [7], S. 333; Berger, Klaus, S. 473 f.

1039 [1971] Ch. 591; [1971] 1 All E. R. 215, 12.10.1970.

1040 Court of Common Pleas, 130 E. R. 294; (1824) 2 Bing. 229; (1824) 2 Bingham 229; 130 E. R. 294, 2.7.1824.

3. Zusätzliche Aufhebungsgründe

a) Betrug, Korruption und „Natural Justice“

Neben den im UNCITRAM Modellgesetz vorgesehenen Aufhebungsgründen erfassen Sec. 24 IAA und Sec. 48 (1) (a) (vi–vii) AA noch die zusätzlichen „Common Law“-Aufhebungsgründe[1041] Betrug, Korruption und „Natural Justice“[1042]. Der Schiedsspruch kann hiernach aufgehoben werden, wenn er auf Betrug oder Korruption beruht oder gegen die Natural Justice verstößt. Eine Verletzung der Natural Justice überschneidet sich mit dem Aufhebungsgrund von Art. 34 (2) (a) (ii) UNCITRAL Modellgesetz und Sec. 48 (1) (a) (iii) AA[1043] und beinhaltet ein umfassendes rechtliches Gehör, die Gleichbehandlung der beiden Schiedsparteien und das Verbot von irrationalen oder willkürlichen Schiedssprüchen.[1044] Betrug und Korruption sind als Annullierungsgründe international akzeptiert, obwohl sie nicht als Aufhebungsgründe im UNCITRAL Modellgesetz geregelt sind.[1045] Der Aufhebungsgrund der Verletzung der Natural Justice ist auch Teil der Schiedsgesetzgebung der ehemaligen britischen Kolonien und UNCITRAL Modellgesetz-Länder Australien[1046], Neuseeland[1047] und Zimbabwe[1048].[1049] Der zusätzliche Annullierungsgrund der Natural Justice ist im internationa-

1041 Pillay, The International Construction Law Review 2003, S. 91 (102).

1042 Natürliche Gerechtigkeit.

1043 Siehe auch Chan, Leng Sun, Singapore Law on Arbitral Awards, S. 199 und Merkin/Hjalmarsson, S. 62.

1044 Court of Appeal, *Soh Beng Tee & Co Pte Ltd v Fairmount Development Pte Ltd*, [2007] 3 SLR 86; [2007] SGCA 28, 9.5.2007; High Court, *Sobati General Trading LLC v PT Multistrada Arahsarana*, [2009] SGHC 245, 28.10.2009; High Court, *Front Row Investment Holdings (Singapore) Pte Ltd v Daimler South East Asia Pte Ltd*, [2010] SGHC 80, 15.3.2010.

1045 Lew/Mistelis/Kröll, Comparative International Commercial Arbitration, Rn. 25-40; Born, Law and Practice, § 16.03 [B] [9], S. 335 f.; Born, International Commercial Arbitration, Bd. 3, S. 3318 ff.; Sec. 10 (a) (1) US Federal Arbitration Act (Title 9, US Code); Sec. 68 (2) (g) englischer Arbitration Act 1996; Sec. 4 (2) (g) Schedule 2 Hongkonger Arbitration Ordinance. Betrug und Korruption sind vom Aufhebungsgrund der öffentlichen Ordnung im UNCITRAL Modellgesetz umfasst, UNCITRAL, 18. Sitzung, Report of the United Nations Commission on International Trade Law on the work of its eighteenth session, A/40/17, 3.–21.6.1985, Rn. 297 ff. Betrug wird traditionell vom Begriff der öffentlichen Ordnung im Common Law erfasst, Chew, S. 117. Vgl. auch Art. 52 (1) (c) International Centre for Settlement of Investment Disputes (ICSID) Convention.

1046 Sec. 19 International Arbitration Act 1974.

1047 Schedule 1 Sec. 34 (6) (b) Arbitration Act 1996.

1048 Art. 34 (5) (b) Arbitration Act 1996.

1049 International Law Association, London Conference, 2000, Committee on International Commercial Arbitration, Interim Report on Public Policy as a Bar to Enforcement of International Arbitral Awards, S. 26.

len Vergleich der Schiedsgesetzgebung gleichwohl unüblich[1050]. Der unbestimmte Rechtbegriff der Natural Justice birgt ferner die Gefahr, dass die Verbindlichkeit des Schiedsspruchs in schiedsunfreundlicher Weise von den Gerichten untergraben wird.

b) Berufungsverfahren für Rechtsfragen

Bei inländischen Schiedsverfahren können die Parteien zudem eine Berufung gem. Sec. 49 AA hinsichtlich einer im Schiedsspruch entschiedenen Rechtsfrage einlegen. Der High Court kann in einem solchen Berufungsverfahren den Schiedsspruch bestätigen, abändern, aufheben und an das Schiedsgericht zurückverweisen.[1051] Diese Berufungsmöglichkeit kann allerdings abbedungen werden und die tatbestandlichen Voraussetzungen einer Berufung sind restriktiv formuliert. Die zusätzliche Berufungsmöglichkeit ist dennoch als schiedsunfreundlich zu bewerten, weil die Gerichte in der Berufung den materiellen Inhalt des Schiedsspruchs nachkontrollieren können. Dies ist mit dem Verbot einer „révision au fond" nicht zu vereinbaren.[1052]

4. Schlussbetrachtung

Die Aufhebungsgründe Betrug und Korruption sowie Natural Justice gehen über die Vorgaben des UNCITRAL Modellgesetzes hinaus. Diese Annullierungsgründe und das Berufungsverfahren für Schiedssprüche eines inländischen Schiedsverfahrens stellen eine Erweiterung der Aufhebungsgründe dar. Die Annullierung eines durch Betrug oder Korruption beeinflussten Schiedsspruchs entspricht gleichwohl dem internationalen Standard der Schiedsgerichtsbarkeit. Obschon die Schiedsgesetzgebung ehemaliger britischer Kolonien den zusätzlichen Aufhebungsgrund der Natural Justice teilweise ebenfalls vorsehen und die Berufungsmöglichkeit auf Schiedssprüche inländischer Schiedsverfahren beschränkt ist, sind diese zusätzlichen Aufhebungsmöglichkeiten als Schiedsverfahren beeinträchtigend zu bewerten. Im Gleichklang mit der internationalen Norm der Schiedsgerichtsbarkeit verliehen die Singapurer Gerichte der öffentlichen Ordnung schiedsfreundliche enge Konturen. Im Ergebnis überwiegt wegen der restriktiven gerichtlichen Auslegung der öffentlichen Ordnung der Schiedsverfahren unterstützende Charakter der Singapurer Schiedsrechtsordnung.

1050 Der Aufhebungsgrund ist im UNCITRAL Modellgesetz nicht enthalten.

1051 Sec. 49 (8) AA.

1052 Sec. 49 AA entspricht Sec. 69 englischer Arbitration Act 1996. Dennoch widerspricht es dem internationalen Schiedsgerichtstandard, eine materielle Nachprüfung des Schiedsspruchs zuzulassen, Born, International Commercial Arbitration, Bd. 3, S. 3325 f.; Born, Law and Practice, § 16.03 [B] [7], S. 333; Berger, Klaus, S. 473 f.

VIII. Anerkennung und Vollstreckung

1. Inländische Schiedssprüche

Nach Sec. 19 IAA und Sec. 46 AA werden inländische Schiedssprüche mit Zustimmung[1053] des High Courts[1054] wie eine äquivalente gerichtliche Entscheidung in Singapur vollstreckt. Schiedssprüche sind zudem gem. Sec. 19B (1) IAA und Sec. 44 (1) AA vom zuständigen Gericht anzuerkennen.

2. Ausländische Schiedssprüche

Das New Yorker UN-Übereinkommen über die Anerkennung und Vollstreckung ausländischer Schiedssprüche vom 10. Juni 1958 (UNÜ)[1055] setzte die Legislative in Teil III (Sec. 27 ff. IAA) des IAA in die Singapurer Schiedsgesetzgebung um.[1056] Nach Sec. 29 IAA sind die Vollstreckungsbestimmungen von Teil III IAA ferner entsprechend auf die Anerkennung von ausländischen Schiedssprüchen anwendbar. Die Vollstreckungsversagungsgründe in Sec. 31 IAA entsprechen Art. V UNÜ. Ausländische Schiedssprüche werden nach Sec. 29 (1) und 19 IAA mit Zustimmung des High Courts wie Gerichtsentscheidungen in Singapur vollstreckt[1057].

a) Formelle Vollstreckungsversagungsgründe

Die verfahrensrechtlichen Versagungsgründe des UNÜ übernahm der Gesetzgeber inhaltsgleich in Sec. 31 (2) IAA[1058]. Sie werden von den Singapurer Gerichten in Konformität mit Art. V (1) UNÜ angewendet.[1059]

b) Materielle Vollstreckungsversagungsgründe

Die materiellen Vollstreckungsverweigerungsgründe erstrecken sich auf die fehlende Schiedsfähigkeit[1060] der schiedsgerichtlich entschiedenen Streitigkeit und auf die Verletzung der öffentlichen Ordnung (*ordre public*) Sin-

1053 Engl. leave.
1054 Sec. 19 IAA; Sec. 31 i. V. m. 2 AA.
1055 Die vorliegende Arbeit beschränkt sich auf die Vollstreckung von Schiedssprüchen unter dem UNÜ.
1056 In Singapur können unter dem UNÜ nur Schiedssprüche anerkannt oder vollstreckt werden, die auf dem Territorium eines anderen Vertragsstaates des UNÜ ergingen (Territorialitätsvorbehalt), Sec. 27 ff. IAA.
1057 Vgl. inländische Schiedssprüche.
1058 Die Nichtvollstreckungsgründe formulierte der Gesetzgeber teilweise etwas abweichend.
1059 Chew, S. 102 ff.; Merkin/Hjalmarsson, S. 72 ff.; Boo, Halsbury's, S. 172 ff.
1060 Zur Schiedsfähigkeit von Schiedsstreitigkeiten, siehe Chan, Leng Sun, Singapore Law on Arbitral Awards, S. 257 f.; Boo, Halsbury's, S. 179; Chew, S. 109.

gapurs.[1061] Sie sind in Sec. 31 (4) IAA geregelt und entsprechen Art. V (2) UNÜ.[1062] Das Vorliegen eines materiellen Nichtvollstreckungsgrundes ist vom zuständigen Gericht von Amts wegen zu überprüfen.[1063] Es ist Aufgabe der Rechtsprechung dem unbestimmten Rechtsbegriff des *ordre public* ein klares Profil zu verleihen und ihn den gesellschaftlichen Entwicklungen anzupassen. Auf Grund seiner unklaren Konturen verglich Richter *Burrough* den Terminus der öffentlichen Ordnung mit einem nicht zu bändigenden Pferd, das durch die Rechtsprechung gezähmt werden müsse.[1064] Im Folgenden werden die Singapurer Leitentscheidungen, die sich mit dem Vollstreckungsverweigerungsgrund der Verletzung der öffentlichen Ordnung befassen, untersucht.[1065]

aa) Re An Arbitration Between Hainan Machinery and Donald & McArthy

Der High Court hatte 1995 im Verfahren *Re An Arbitration Between Hainan Machinery Import and Export Corp and Donald & McArthy Pte Ltd*[1066] über die Reichweite der öffentlichen Ordnung bei der Vollstreckung eines ausländischen Schiedsspruchs unter Sec. 31 (4) (b) IAA zu entscheiden.

Die Klägeren war ein chinesisches Unternehmen, die Beklagte ein Unternehmen aus Singapur. Zwischen den Parteien kam es zu Meinungsverschiedenheiten und die Klägerin initiierte im Einklang mit der vereinbarten Schiedsklausel ein Schiedsverfahren mit Sitz in China. Die Beklagte war der Auffassung, dass das Schiedsgericht unzuständig sei und verweigerte die Teilnahme am Schiedsverfahren. Im April 1994 entschied das Schiedstribunal zu Gunsten der Klägerin.

Im Oktober 1994 wurde der Schiedsspruch in Singapur für vollstreckbar erklärt. Der Assistant Registrar[1067] lehnte die von der Beklagten beantragte Aufhebung der Vollstreckbarerklärung ab. Die Beklagte legte anschließend Berufung beim High Court ein. Vor dem High Court machte die Beklagte geltend, dass die Vollstreckung des Schiedsspruchs gegen die öffentliche Ordnung verstoße. Der High Court urteilte, dass die öffentliche Ordnung in Singapur eng auszulegen sei. Eine im Sinne des internationalen „Comitas-Gedankens" großzügige Vollstreckung von ausländischen Schiedssprüchen erleichtere in der Zukunft auch die Vollstreckung Singapurer

1061 Sec. 31 (4) IAA.
1062 In der sprachlichen Ausgestaltung bestehen kleine Unterschiede.
1063 Sec. 31 (4) IAA.
1064 Vgl. Kapitel: Singapur; Aufhebungsverfahren; Öffentliche Ordnung (B.VII.2.a)).
1065 Der Singapurer Gesetzgeber definierte den Vollstreckungsversagungsgrund der öffentlichen Ordnung nicht.
1066 [1995] SGHC 232, 28.6., 5.7., 19.7. und 29.9.1995.
1067 Siehe ausführliche Darstellung Fn. 1074, S. 169 und Fn. 883, S. 129 f.

Schiedssprüche im Ausland. Nur ausnahmsweise dürfe ein ausländischer Schiedsspruch nicht vollstreckt werden. Dies sei erforderlich, um den internationalen Schiedsort Singapur zu etablieren:

> „*As the plaintiffs submitted, the principle of comity of nations requires that the awards of foreign arbitration tribunals be given due deference and be enforced unless exceptional circumstances exist. As a nation which itself aspires to be an international arbitration centre, Singapore must recognise foreign awards if it expects its own awards to be recognised abroad.*“[1068]

Der High Court hielt deshalb die Vollstreckbarerklärung des Schiedsspruchs aufrecht und wies die Berufung zurück.

Es entspricht dem internationalen Standard unter dem UNÜ, dass der Vollstreckungsversagungsgrund der öffentlichen Ordnung restriktiv ausgelegt wird. Ein Schiedsspruch soll im Zusammenhang mit dem sog. „Pro-Enforcement Bias“ lediglich ausnahmsweise nicht vollstreckt werden. Eine Kontrolle des Schiedsspruchs i. S. einer „révision au fond“ durch das Vollstreckungsgericht ist unzulässig. Für eine Verletzung des *ordre public* des Vollstreckungsstaates ist es erforderlich, dass der ausländische Schiedsspruch[1069] gegen die fundamentalsten, zwingenden Normen bzw. die elementaren Gerechtigkeitsvorstellungen des Vollstreckungsstaates in gravierender Weise verstößt.[1070] Grundsätzlich sollen die Schiedssprüche unter dem UNÜ frei zirkulieren und in jedem UNÜ Vertragsstaat vollstreckt werden.

Durch sein klares Bekenntnis zur Vollstreckung von ausländischen Schiedssprüchen und durch die enge Auslegung des Vollstreckungsverweigerungsgrundes der öffentlichen Ordnung besteht zwischen dem High Court Urteil und der Norm des Schiedsgerichtswesens Einklang. Die Entscheidung des High Courts zeigt exemplarisch die schiedsfreundliche Einstellung der

---

1068 Rn. 45.

1069 Erforderlich ist, dass die im Schiedsspruch entschiedene, konkrete Rechtsfrage gegen die öffentliche Ordnung verstößt, Born, International Commercial Arbitration, Bd. 3, S. 3690; vgl. auch BGH, KZR 43/71, NJW 1972, S. 2180 (2181), 31.5.1972; Schlosser, in: Stein/Jonas, Anhang zu § 1061 ZPO Rn. 321 ff.

1070 Blackaby/Partasides/Redfern/Hunter, International Arbitration, Rn. 11.60 f., 11.105 ff.; Born, Law and Practice, § 17.03, S. 383, § 17.05 [H], S. 407 ff.; Gaillard/Savage, Fouchard Gaillard Goldman, Rn. 1711 ff.; Born, International Commercial Arbitration, Bd. 3, S. 3646 ff.; Born, Cases and Materials, S. 1198, 1250 ff.; Lew/Mistelis/Kröll, Comparative International Commercial Arbitration, Rn. 26-111 ff.; International Law Association, London Conference, 2000, Committee on International Commercial Arbitration, Interim Report on Public Policy as a Bar to Enforcement of International Arbitral Awards, S. 13 ff.; International Law Association, New Delhi Conference, 2002, Committee on International Commercial Arbitration, Final Report on Public Policy as a Bar to Enforcement of International Arbitral Awards, S. 2 ff.; Schlosser, in: Stein/Jonas, Anhang zu § 1061 ZPO Rn. 316 ff.

Singapurer Gerichte. Die Gerichte sollen auch in Zukunft ausländische Schiedssprüche großzügig vollstrecken, um den Schiedsort Singapur weiter zu stärken.

Die Literatur hebt gleichfalls hervor, dass die Entscheidung das Schiedsverfahren fördernde „Pro-Enforcement Bias" widerspiegele.[1071]

bb) Aloe Vera of America v Asianic Food

In der Entscheidung *Aloe Vera of America Inc v Asianic Food (S) Pte Ltd and another*[1072] hatte der High Court einen Antrag auf Vollstreckbarerklärung eines ausländischen Schiedsspruchs gem. Sec. 31 IAA unter dem Gesichtspunkt der öffentlichen Ordnung zu beurteilen.

Das texanische Unternehmen *Aloe Vera of America Inc (Aloe Vera)* schloss mit der singapurischen ersten Beklagten *Asianic Food (S) Pte Ltd (Asianic Food)* eine Vereinbarung über den Vertrieb von Aloe Vera Produkten. Der zweite Beklagte, Herr *Chiew*, hatte *Asianic Food* für den Vertragsschluss mit *Aloe Vera* und den anschließenden Vertrieb der *Aloe Vera*-Produkte gegründet. Herr *Chiew* unterschrieb diese Vereinbarung als Manager der ersten Beklagten *Asianic Food*, war aber laut der Vereinbarung nicht Vertragspartner. Als Streitbeilegungsmechanismus sah die Vereinbarung eine Schiedsklausel vor. Auf das vereinbarte Schiedsverfahren war das Recht des US-Bundesstaates Arizona anwendbar. Nach der Kündigung der Vereinbarung reichte die Klägerin *Aloe Vera* Schiedsklage ein. Der zweite Beklagte Herr *Chiew* war der Auffassung, dass er nicht von der Schiedsvereinbarung erfasst sei. Das AAA[1073]-Schiedsgericht war allerdings der Ansicht, die Schiedsvereinbarung erfasse auch Herrn *Chiew*. Dieser nahm dennoch nicht am Schiedsverfahren teil. Gleichwohl erließ das Schiedsgericht einen Schiedsspruch gegen die erste und den zweiten Beklagten.

Im Juni 2004 wurde der ausländische Schiedsspruch antragsgemäß in Singapur für vollstreckbar erklärt. Im Juli 2004 beantragte Herr *Chiew*, die

---

1071 Born, International Commercial Arbitration, S. 107 i. V. m. Fn. 735 (Bd. 1), S. 3414 i. V. m. Fn. 100 (Bd. 3), S. 3417 i. V. m. Fn. 121 (Bd. 3); Hwang/Chan, Andrew, Journal of International Arbitration 1999, Vol. 16, Ausg. 4, S. 101 (105 ff.); Minn/Foxton, in: Klausegger/Klein/Kremslehner/Petsche/Pitkowitz/Power/Welser/Zeiler (Hrsg.), Austrian Yearbook on International Arbitration 2011, S. 197 (199 i. V. m. Fn. 10); Hwang/Lai, Arbitration 2005, S. 1 (16); Hwang/Chan, Andrew, in: Berg (Hrsg.), International Arbitration and National Courts: The Never Ending Story, S. 145 (148, 156 i. V. m. Fn. 56); Hwang/Muttath, International Arbitration Law Review 2000, S. 207 (214 i. V. m. Fn. 96); Chan, Andrew/Woodward, Arbitration 2003, S. 10 i. V. m. Fn. 4; Hwang/Muttath, Arbitration 2002, S. 223 (224 f.); Chew, S. 86 f., 116 f.

1072 [2006] 3 SLR 174; [2006] SGHC 78, 10.5.2006.

1073 „American Arbitration Association".

Vollstreckbarerklärung aufzuheben. Der zuständige Assistant Registrar[1074] lehnte den Antrag im November 2005 ab. Im Berufungsverfahren vor dem High Court trug Herr *Chiew* vor, dass die Vollstreckbarerklärung hätte verweigert werden müssen. Die Vollstreckung des Schiedsspruchs gegen den Nichtunterzeichner der Schiedsvereinbarung Herrn *Chiew* verletze gem. Sec. 31 (4) (b) IAA die öffentliche Ordnung in Singapur. Unter Bezugnahme auf ein Hongkonger[1075]-Urteil und seine frühere Entscheidung *Re An Arbitration Between Hainan Machinery Import and Export Corp and Donald & McArthy Pte Ltd*[1076] urteilte der High Court, dass eine Verletzung der öffentlichen Ordnung in Singapurer nur vorliege, sofern der Schiedsspruch die wesentlichen in Singapur vorherrschenden Moral- und Gerechtigkeitsvorstellungen verletze. Der High Court kam zu dem Schluss, der internationale „Comitas-Gedanken" erfordere es, dass ein ausländischer Schiedsspruch in Singapur respektiert und vollstreckt werden müsse, wenn keine außergewöhnlichen Umstände vorlägen:

> *„Such an award must be enforced unless it offends against our basic notions of justice and morality. In Re An Arbitration Between Hainan Machinery Import and Export Corp and Donald & McArthy Pte Ltd [1995] 3 SLR(R) 354 at [45], I held that the principle of comity of nations requires that the awards of foreign arbitration tribunals be given due deference and be enforced unless exceptional circumstances exist. I have not changed my mind since then."*[1077]

In concreto war der High Court nicht der Auffassung, dass die Vollstreckung des Schiedsspruchs gegen Herrn *Chiew* die wesentlichen Moral- und Gerechtigkeitsvorstellungen in Singapur verletze und mithin nicht gegen die öffentliche Ordnung in Singapur verstoße. Das Gericht urteilte zunächst, dass Herr *Chiew*, als der die Vereinbarung unterzeichnende Manager der ersten Beklagten *Asianic Food,* kein Nichtunterzeichner der Vereinbarung

---

1074 Der Assistant Registrar übernimmt die gleichen Aufgaben wie ein Registrar (Sec. 2 Supreme Court of Judicature Act). Ein Registrar übernimmt am Supreme Court (Sec. 2 Supreme Court of Judicature Act) richterliche Funktionen – gewisse nicht öffentliche (engl. heard in chamber) Zivilverfahren werden von dem Registrar erledigt, Order 32 Rule 9 und Order 69A Rule 3 Supreme Court of Judicature Act, Rules of Court 1996. Der Registrar ist insbesondere für die Vollstreckung zuständig (Sec. 63 f. Supreme Court of Judicature Act 1969). Diese Vollstreckungszuständigkeit umfasst auch die Kompetenz des Registrars, ausländische Schiedssprüche unter dem UNÜ in Singapur zu vollstrecken, Order 69A Rule 3 Supreme Court of Judicature Act, Rules of Court 1996. Schließlich besteht eine Berufungsmöglichkeit gegen eine Entscheidung des Registrars zum High Court, Order 56 Rule 1 Supreme Court of Judicature Act, Rules of Court 1996. Siehe auch Fn. 883, S. 129 f.

1075 Hongkong Court of Final Appeal, [1999] 2 HKC 205, 9.2.1999.

1076 [1995] 3 SLR(R) 354, 28.6., 5.7.,19.7. und 29.9.1995, Rn. 45.

1077 Rn. 75.

sei. Der High Court wies zudem darauf hin, dass das Singapurer Recht eine Haftung einer Nichtvertragspartei bei einer Vertragsverletzung kenne und einer nicht im Vertrag erwähnten Partei dennoch die Vertragserfüllung obliegen könne. Ob ein Singapurer Gericht auf Grundlage des im Schiedsverfahren ermittelten Tatbestandes zu derselben Entscheidung wie das Schiedsgericht gekommen wäre, ist nach dem High Court unerheblich. Der zweite Beklagte Herr *Chiew* hätte ferner jederzeit im Schiedsverfahren die Möglichkeit gehabt, seinen Standpunkt zu materiellen Rechtsfragen vorzutragen. Denn Herr *Chiew* wusste seit Einlegung der Schiedsklage, dass *Aloe Vera* die erste (*Asianic Food*) und den zweiten Beklagten (*Chiew*) zusammen verklagte. Gleichwohl rügte Herr *Chiew* lediglich die Unzuständigkeit des Schiedsgerichts, nahm sodann nicht am Schiedsverfahren teil und rief nicht die für die Überwachung und Kontrolle des Schiedsverfahrens zuständigen Gerichte in Arizona an. Der Schiedsspruch verstoße daher, trotz der Nichtteilnahme von Herr *Chiew* am Schiedsverfahren, nicht gegen die öffentliche Ordnung in Singapur. Der High Court verlangt demzufolge regelmäßig eine Einlassung des Schiedsbeklagten vor dem Schiedsgericht. Nach dem High Court gelte dies auch für Konstellationen, in denen die Existenz bzw. die Wirksamkeit der Schiedsvereinbarung vom Schiedsbeklagten nach den international anerkannten Nichtvollstreckungsgründen gem. Art. V (1) (a) bzw. (c) UNÜ[1078] – in Singapur umgesetzt in Sec. 31 (2) (a), (b) bzw. (d) IAA – bestritten werde. Mangels eines glaubhaften Nachweises eines dieser Vollstreckungsversagungsgründe führe auch das vorgetragene Fehlen bzw. die vorgetragene Unwirksamkeit einer Schiedsvereinbarung nicht *per se*, zur Nichtvollstreckung eines ausländischen Schiedsspruchs in Singapur. Der High Court wies die Berufung demzufolge im Mai 2006 zurück.

Der High Court legte die öffentliche Ordnung entsprechend dem internationalen Schiedsgerichtsstandard restriktiv aus.[1079] Lediglich ausnahmsweise dürfen die Singapurer Gerichte einen ausländischen Schiedsspruch nicht vollstrecken.

1078 Born, Law and Practice, § 17.01, S. 375 ff.; Blackaby/Partasides/Redfern/Hunter, International Arbitration, Rn. 11.40 ff., 11.63 ff.

1079 Blackaby/Partasides/Redfern/Hunter, International Arbitration, Rn. 11.111 ff.; Born, Law and Practice, § 17.03, S. 383, § 17.05 [H], S. 407 ff.; Gaillard/Savage, Fouchard Gaillard Goldman, Rn. 1711 ff.; Born, International Commercial Arbitration, Bd. 3, S. 3649 ff.; Born, Cases and Materials, S. 1198, 1250 ff.; Lew/Mistelis/Kröll, Comparative International Commercial Arbitration, Rn. 26-114 ff.; International Law Association, New Delhi Conference, 2002, Committee on International Commercial Arbitration, Final Report on Public Policy as a Bar to Enforcement of International Arbitral Awards, S. 2 ff.

In der Literatur wird das Urteil als Schiedsverfahren fördernd und als vollstreckungsfreundlich[1080] bewertet, weil es den Schiedsspruch aufrechterhielt.[1081]

cc) Strandore Invest v Soh Kim Wat

Im Rechtsstreit *Strandore Invest A/S and others v Soh Kim Wat*[1082] hatte der High Court im Jahr 2010 über die Vollstreckung eines dänischen Schiedsspruchs in Singapur zu entscheiden.

Die Klägerinnen *Strandore Invest A/S (Strandore), MS Invest Odense A/S (Odense)* und *LKE Electric Europe A/S (LKE Europe)* stellten im Januar 2010 einen Antrag auf Vollstreckbarerklärung des Schiedsspruchs gegen den Beklagten Herrn *Soh Kim Wat. Strandore, Odense* und *LKE Europe* waren Aktionäre des malaysischen Unternehmens *LKE Electric. Soh Kim Wat* ist und war Vorstandsvorsitzender und ebenfalls Aktionär von *LKE Electric. Soh Kim Wat* vereinbarte 2003/2004 mit *Strandore, Odense* und *LKE Europe* den Erwerb von deren Aktienpaketen an *LKE Electric*. Alle Aktienkaufverträge enthielten eine Schiedsklausel, die Dänemark als Sitz des Schiedsverfahrens bestimmte. Nach der Klausel sollte das Schiedsverfahren nach der Schiedsordnung von „Copenhagen Arbitration" durchgeführt werden. *Soh Kim Wat* zahlte lediglich einen geringen Teil des Kaufpreises. *Strandore, Odense* und *LKE Europe* legten daraufhin 2006 beim „Danish Institute of Arbitration (DIA)" Schiedsklage ein. Das DIA konnte die Schiedsklage nicht an die im Kaufvertrag angegebene Adresse von *Soh Kim Wat* in Singapur zustellen. Daraufhin stellte das DIA die Schiedsklage an die malaysische Geschäftsadresse von *Soh Kim Wat* zu. Letzterer monierte in einem Schreiben an das DIA *inter alia* die Schiedsklage sei fehlerhaft erhoben und zugestellt worden. Mangels Schiedsrichterbenennung durch *Soh Kim Wat* ernannte das DIA das in der DIA-Schiedsgerichtsordnung 2006[1083] vorgesehene drei Personenschiedsgericht. Das konstituierte Schiedsgericht erachtete sich als unzuständig, weil im Rahmen der Schiedsrichterbestellung eine DIA-Benachrichtigung dem Schiedsbeklagten nicht wirksam zugegangen sei. Die Schiedsinstitution DIA startete daraufhin ein zweites Schiedsverfahren. *Soh Kim Wat* benannte trotz Aufforderung und Nachfrist keinen Schiedsrichter für das zweite DIA-Schiedsverfahren. Er war der Ansicht, dass sowohl die Schiedsrichterbestellung als auch das DIA-Schiedsverfah-

---

1080 Engl. pro-enforcement.

1081 Minn, in: Berg (Hrsg.), International Arbitration, The Coming of a New Age?, S. 235 (264 i. V. m. Fn. 139). Zu „Pro-Enforcement", Born, International Commercial Arbitration, Bd. 3, S. 3412 i. V. m. Fn. 85, S. 3414 i. V. m. Fn. 100; Hwang/Lee, Shaun, Journal of International Arbitration 2008, Vol. 25, Ausg. 6, S. 873 (877 f.); Chew, S. 86 f.

1082 [2010] SGHC 151, 14.5.2010.

1083 Rules of Arbitration Procedure of the Danish Institute of Arbitration.

ren an sich unwirksam seien. Ergänzend machte der Schiedsbeklagte geltend, die Schiedsklausel sei nie gegen ihn durchsetzbar gewesen. Das DIA bestellte im zweiten Schiedsverfahren dieselben drei Schiedsrichter wie im ersten Schiedsverfahren. Das Schiedsgericht forderte den Schiedsbeklagten auf, eine Klageerwiderung einzureichen. *Soh Kim Wat* beanstandete daraufhin gegenüber dem Schiedstribunal erneut aus den oben genannten Gründen das DIA-Schiedsverfahren. Der Schiedsbeklagte ließ auch eine Nachfrist zur Klageerwiderung verstreichen. Das Schiedsgericht lud den Beklagten sodann zum Termin der mündlichen Verhandlung. *Soh Kim Wat* protestierte erneut gegen das Schiedsverfahren mit einer E-Mail an den Vorsitzenden des Schiedsgerichts. *Soh Kim Wat* reichte jedoch keine Klageerwiderung ein und nahm am Schiedsverfahren nicht teil. Im zweiten Schiedsverfahren gab das Schiedsgericht der Klage der Schiedsklägerinnen gegen *Soh Kim Wat* 2008 statt. Das Aufhebungsverfahren des Schiedsbeklagten scheiterte 2009 vor den dänischen Gerichten.

Die Schiedsklägerinnen beantragten im Januar 2010 die Vollstreckbarerklärung des Schiedsspruchs in Singapur[1084]. *Soh Kim Wat* beantragte die Aussetzung des Vollstreckungsverfahrens und rügte, dass die Vollstreckung des Schiedsspruchs gegen die öffentliche Ordnung Singapurs verstoße. Der High Court übertrug hinsichtlich des geltend gemachten Verstoßes gegen die öffentliche Ordnung Singapurs die enge Auslegung des Court of Appeals im Urteil *PT Asuransi v Dexia Bank II* auf die Vollstreckung von ausländischen Schiedssprüchen. In der Entscheidung *PT Asuransi v Dexia Bank II* hatte der Court of Appeal für Aufhebungsverfahren einen Verstoß gegen die öffentlichen Ordnung auf Schiedssprüche beschränkt, die das Gewissen erschüttern[1085], die klar dem Gemeinwohl schaden[1086] oder gegen das Anstandsgefühl eines umfänglich informierten Bürgers verstoßen[1087] als auch auf Schiedssprüche, die die grundlegendsten Moral- und Gerechtigkeitsvorstellungen in Singapur verletzen[1088]. Der High Court entschied, dass die von *Soh Kim Wat* vorgetragenen Argumente zur fehlenden Durchsetzbarkeit der Aktienkaufverträge im zweiten Schiedsverfahren hätten vorgebracht werden müssen. Der verspätete Vortrag dieser Gesichtspunkte im Vollstreckungsverfahren stelle eine unzulässige Rechtsausübung dar und könne nicht mehr berücksichtigt werden.[1089] Das Gericht erklärte den ausländischen Schiedsspruch entsprechen im Mai 2010 für in Singapur vollstreckbar.

1084 *Strandore, Odense* und *LKE Europe* bekamen zudem eine später beantragte „Mareva Injunction" zugesprochen.
1085 Engl. shock the conscience.
1086 Engl. clearly injurious to the public good.
1087 Engl. wholly offensive to the ordinary reasonable and fully informed member of the public.
1088 Engl. forum's most basic notion of morality and justice.
1089 Rn. 21 ff.

Der High Court übertrug die enge, für Aufhebungsverfahren gem. Art. 34 UNCITRAL Modellgesetz geschaffene, Konkretisierung der öffentlichen Ordnung des Court of Appeals in der Rechtssache *PT Asuransi v Dexia Bank II* auf Vollstreckungsverfahren. Die Übernahme der engen Auslegung der öffentlichen Ordnung bei der Vollstreckung ausländischer Schiedssprüche ist zu begrüßen. Sie führt zu einer, im Einklang mit der internationalen Norm der Schiedsgerichtsbarkeit stehenden, restriktiven gerichtlichen Konkretisierung der öffentlichen Ordnung in Singapur. Darüber hinaus führt dies zu einem Gleichklang des Begriffs der öffentlichen Ordnung in Aufhebungs- und Vollstreckungsverfahren. Die enge „Pro-Enforcement" Auslegung der öffentlichen Ordnung durch den High Court schließt eine „révision au fond" des Schiedsspruchs aus. Dies entspricht der internationalen Praxis der Schiedsgerichtsbarkeit[1090] und mithin ist das Urteil *Strandore Invest A/S and others v Soh Kim Wat*[1091] als schiedsfreundlich einzuordnen.

Der High Court stellte ferner klar, dass Parteien am Schiedsverfahren partizipieren müssen und Rechts- und Tatsachenvorträge, die bereits im Schiedsverfahren hätten vorgetragen werden können, unter dem Gesichtspunkt der öffentlichen Ordnung Singapurs eine unzulässige Rechtsausübung darstellen und nicht zur Vollstreckungsverweigerung des Schiedsspruchs führen. Durch die Rechtsfigur der unzulässigen Rechtsausübung hat der High Court die Verbindlichkeit des Schiedsspruchs gestärkt und späteren Anfechtungen im Vollstreckungsverfahren einen Riegel vorgeschoben. Auch dieser Aspekt des Urteils *Strandore Invest A/S and others v Soh Kim Wat* ist als Schiedsverfahren unterstützend zu bewerten.

c) Bewertung

Die formellen und materiellen Vollstreckungsversagungsgründe legt die Singapurer Rechtsordnung eng aus. Bereits im Urteil *Re An Arbitration Between Hainan Machinery Import and Export Corp and Donald & McArthy Pte Ltd* konkretisierte der High Court die öffentliche Ordnung für die Vollstreckung von ausländischen Schiedssprüchen restriktiv. Durch eine großzügige Vollstreckung von ausländischen Schiedssprüchen in Singapur bezweckte das Gericht auch die Vollstreckung von in Singapur erlassenen Schiedssprüchen im Ausland zu erleichtern und so den Schiedsort Singapur

1090 Born, Law and Practice, § 17.05 [H] [3], S. 409; Gaillard/Savage, Fouchard Gaillard Goldman, Rn. 1711 ff.; Born, International Commercial Arbitration, Bd. 3, S. 3649 ff.; Born, Cases and Materials, S. 1198; Lew/Mistelis/Kröll, Comparative International Commercial Arbitration, Rn. 26-66, 26-114 ff.; International Law Association, New Delhi Conference, 2002, Committee on International Commercial Arbitration, Final Report on Public Policy as a Bar to Enforcement of International Arbitral Awards, S. 2 ff.

1091 [2010] SGHC 151, 14.5.2010.

zu fördern. Diese schiedsfreundliche restriktive Auslegung behielt der High Court im Urteil *Aloe Vera of America Inc v Asianic Food (S) Pte Ltd and another* bei. Der High Court fasste den Begriff der öffentlichen Ordnung in der Entscheidung *Strandore Invest A/S and others v Soh Kim Wat* nochmals enger als in den zuvor ergangenen Urteilen. Die Singapurer Rechtsprechung war demzufolge in der Lage, den mit einem widerspenstigen Pferd verglichenen Terminus der öffentlichen Ordnung zu zähmen.[1092] Aus der Gesamtschau der Rechtsprechung und der Rezeption des UNÜ in das Singapurer Recht ergibt sich, dass die Singapurer Rechtsordnung ein den Anforderungen für die Anerkennung und Vollstreckung ausländischer Schiedssprüche maßgeschneidertes Gewand anfertigen konnte.

1092 Vgl. Kapitel: Aufhebungsverfahren; Öffentliche Ordnung (B.VII.2.a)) und Kapitel: Anerkennung und Vollstreckung; Materielle Vollstreckungsversagungsgründe (B.VIII.2.b)).

C. Indien

I. Anwendbares Recht

1. Anwendungsbereich der Schiedsgesetzgebung

Der erste Teil[1093] des indischen „Arbitration and Conciliation Acts (SchiedsG)“ ist nach Sec. 2 (2) SchiedsG räumlich auf Schiedsverfahren anwendbar, die ihren Sitz im indischen Hoheitsgebiet haben.[1094] Der sachliche Anwendungsbereich[1095] von Teil I SchiedsG unterscheidet bei der Schiedsrichterbestellung, bei der zulässigen materiellen Rechtswahl und bei der gerichtlichen Zuständigkeit zwischen internationalen Handelsschiedsverfahren und den übrigen Schiedsverfahren (im Folgenden inländische Schiedsverfahren)[1096].[1097] Nach dem Wortlaut von Sec. 2 (2) SchiedsG a. F. war Teil I SchiedsG lediglich anwendbar, wenn das Schiedsverfahren seinen Sitz in Indien hatte:

> „*This Part* [Part I] *shall apply where the place of arbitration is in India.*“

Das SchiedsG 1996 rezipierte das „‚United Nations Commission on International Trade Law (UNCITRAL)‘ Modellgesetz 1985 (UNCITRAL Modellgesetz)“[1098] in die indische Schiedsgesetzgebung.[1099] In Sec. 2 (2) SchiedsG a. F. war die Legislative aber vom UNCITRAL Modellgesetz abgewichen. Das UNCITRAL Modellgesetz begrenzt seinen Geltungsbereich in Art. 1 (2) auf das Hoheitsgebiet des Sitzstaates des Schiedsverfahrens. Art. 1 (2) UNCITRAL Modellgesetz sieht aber schiedsortunabhängige Ausnahmen hiervon für die gerichtliche Verweisung einer rechtshängigen Streitigkeit an das

---

1093 Teil I SchiedsG enthält Bestimmungen über das Schiedsverfahren, die Aufhebung von Schiedssprüchen und die Vollstreckung von inländischen Schiedssprüchen. Teil II SchiedsG regelt die Vollstreckung ausländischer Schiedssprüche und Teil III SchiedsG die Schlichtung.

1094 Der räumliche Anwendungsbereich von Teil II SchiedsG erfasst die Vollstreckung von in Vertragsstaaten des New Yorker UN-Übereinkommen über die Anerkennung und Vollstreckung ausländischer Schiedssprüche vom 10. Juni 1958 (UNÜ) ergangenen Schiedssprüchen.

1095 Sachlich ist Teil I SchiedsG von Natur aus auf Schiedsverfahren begrenzt, vgl. Sec. 2 (5) SchiedsG.

1096 Siehe Fn. 677 auf S. 91.

1097 Siehe Sec. 11, Sec. 28 und Sec. 2 (1) (e) SchiedsG n. F. Internationale Handelsschiedsverfahren definierte der Gesetzgeber in Sec. 2 (1) (f) SchiedsG legal. Ausführlich hierzu Kapitel: Einleitung; Internationale Handelsschiedsverfahren (A.III.7.b)bb)).

1098 Zu den mit dem UNCITRAL Modellgesetz verfolgten Zielen, siehe Kapitel: Singapur; Anwendungsbereich des Verfahrensrechts (B.I.1.).

1099 Siehe Kapitel: Einleitung; Schiedsverfahrensgesetz (SchiedsG) 1996; Entstehungsgeschichte (A.III.7.b)aa)).

Schiedsverfahren (Art. 8), für vorläufige gerichtliche Maßnahmen (Art. 9) und für die Anerkennung und Vollstreckung von Schiedssprüchen (Art. 35 und 36) vor[1100]:

> *„The provisions of this Law, except articles 8, 9, 35 and 36, apply only if the place of arbitration is in the territory of this State."*

Nach dem Wortlaut von Sec. 2 (2) SchiedsG a. F. war der Anwendungsbereich von Teil I SchiedsG im Unterschied zum UNCITRAL Modellgesetz auf Indien beschränkt, ohne Ausnahmen von diesem strikten Territorialitätsprinzip zuzulassen. Im „Arbitration and Conciliation (Amendment) Act 2015 (Arbitration Amendment Act)" glich der Gesetzgeber den Geltungsbereich von Teil I SchiedsG an das UNCITRAL Modellgesetz an. Sec. 2 (2) SchiedsG n. F. überträgt den indischen Gerichten die Kompetenz, auch Schiedsverfahren mit ausländischem Sitz durch einstweilige gerichtliche Maßnahmen (Sec. 9 SchiedsG) und bei der Beweisaufnahme (Sec. 27 SchiedsG) zu unterstützen.

a) Gerichtliche Entscheidungen vor Bhatia

Vor dem Urteil *Bhatia International v Bulk Trading SA & ANR (Bhatia)*[1101] des Supreme Courts war die indische Rechtsprechung bezüglich der Reichweite des räumlichen Anwendungsbereiches von Teil I SchiedsG a. F. gespalten. Teilweise erachteten die High Courts den territorialen Anwendungsbereich des SchiedsG a. F. als weit genug, um auch Schiedsverfahren mit ausländischem Sitz zu erfassen.[1102] Andererseits gab es mehrere High Court Urteile und eine Entscheidung des Supreme Courts, die den räumlichen Anwendungsbereich des SchiedsG auf Schiedsverfahren mit Sitz in Indien beschränkten.[1103]

1100 Die Ergänzungen des UNCITRAL Modellgesetzes 2006 sehen in Art. 1 (2) als weitere Ausnahme die Vollstreckung einstweiliger schiedsgerichtlicher Maßnahmen vor.

1101 Appeal (civil) 6527 of 2001; (2002) 4 SCC 105; AIR 2002 SC 1432, 13.3.2002.

1102 Delhi High Court, *Dominant Offset Pvt Ltd v Adamovske Strojirny,* 68 (1997) DLT 157; 1997 (2) Arb LR 335 (Delhi), 6.5.1997; Delhi High Court, *Suzuki Motor Corporation v Union of India,* 1997 (2) Arb LR 477 Delhi; 68 (1997) DLT 827, 22.9.1997; Delhi High Court, *Olex Focas Pvt Ltd & Anr v Skoda Export Company Ltd & Anr,* AIR 2000 Delhi 161, 5.11.1999; Andhra Pradesh High Court, *Cultor Food Science Inc v Nicholas Piramal India Limited,* 2001 (6) ALT 706; 2002 (2) ALD 149, 12.12.2001.

1103 Delhi High Court, *Marriott International Inc v Ansal Hotels Limited,* AIR 2000 Del 337; 2000 (3) Arb LR 369 (Delhi), 5.7.2000; Supreme Court, *Thyssen Stahlunion Gmbh Etc v Steel Authority of India Ltd,* Appeal (civil) 6036 of 1998; (1999) 9 SCC 334; AIR 1999 SC 3923, 7.10.1999; Bombay High Court, *Jindal Drugs Ltd, Mumbai v Noy Vallesina Engineering,* 2002 (3) BomCR 554; 2002 (2) MhLj 820, 6.2.2002.

b) Bhatia International v Bulk Trading SA (Bhatia)

aa) Entscheidung

Ein aus drei Richtern bestehender Senat des Supreme Courts nahm im Rechtsstreit *Bhatia International v Bulk Trading SA & ANR (Bhatia)*[1104] die beschriebene Rechtsunsicherheit unter Sec. 2 (2) SchiedsG a. F. hinsichtlich des Anwendungsbereiches von Teil I SchiedsG zum Anlass, eine Grundsatzentscheidung zu fällen.

Hintergrund dieser Entscheidung war, dass der Berufungskläger *Bhatia International* mit der ersten Berufungsbeklagten *Bulk Trading SA* (*Bulk)* im Mai 1997 einen Vertrag geschlossen hatte, der eine ICC-Schiedsklausel enthielt. Im Oktober 1997 legte *Bulk* Schiedsklage bei der ICC ein und die Schiedsparteien vereinbarten, dass das Schiedsverfahren in Paris durchgeführt werden sollte. *Bulk* beantragte ergänzend gem. Sec. 9 SchiedsG beim District Court in Indore (Madhya Pradesh) eine einstweilige Maßnahme, in der *Bhatia International* verboten werden sollte, über sein in Indien belegenes Betriebsvermögen zu verfügen. *Bhatia International* beantragte den Antrag zurückzuweisen, weil der erste Teil SchiedsG a. F. – der auch Sec. 9 SchiedsG enthält – nicht auf Schiedsverfahren anwendbar sei, die ihren Sitz im Ausland haben. Der District Court entschied im Februar 2000, dass er für die Anordnung der vorläufigen Maßnahme zuständig sei. Die dagegen eingelegte Berufung[1105] wies der Madhya Pradesh High Court im Oktober 2000 zurück.

Im zweiten Berufungsverfahren[1106] hatte der Supreme Court darüber zu entscheiden, ob die indischen Gerichte für ein in Paris (Frankreich) durchgeführtes ICC-Schiedsverfahren eine einstweilige Maßnahme gem. Sec. 9 SchiedsG erlassen können. Das oberste indische Gericht urteilte, dass der auf dem UNCITRAL Modellgesetz beruhende erste Teil SchiedsG a. F. den Gerichten die Zuständigkeit verleihe, vorläufige gerichtliche Maßnahmen für Schiedsverfahren mit ausländischem Sitz anzuordnen. Teil I SchiedsG a. F. sei auch auf Schiedsverfahren mit ausländischem Sitz anwendbar, sofern die Parteien dessen Anwendung auf ihr Schiedsverfahren nicht durch eine ausdrückliche oder konkludente Vereinbarung ausgeschlossen haben. Es sei die Intention des Gesetzgebers gewesen[1107], dass der erste Teil des SchiedsG a. F. auf alle Schiedsverfahren – unabhängig von ihrem Sitz – an-

---

1104 Appeal (civil) 6527 of 2001; (2002) 4 SCC 105; AIR 2002 SC 1432, 13.3.2002.

1105 *Bhatia International* hatte eine sog. „Write Petition" gegen die Entscheidung des District Courts eingelegt.

1106 In der Form einer „Special Leave Petition" gegen die Entscheidung des Madhya Pradesh High Courts, Malhotra, Indu, O. P. Malhotra on Arbitration, Sec. 2, S. 226.

1107 Dies schlussfolgert der Supreme Court aus dem Wortlaut von Sec. 2 (2) SchiedsG a. F.

wendbar sei. Als Begründung führte der Supreme Court an, dass der Gesetzgeber nicht unmissverständlich den Anwendungsbereich von Teil I SchiedsG a. F. für Schiedsverfahren mit ausländischem Sitz ausgeschlossen habe. Aus dem Umstand, dass in Sec. 2 (2) SchiedsG a. F. im Vergleich zum rezipierten Art. 2 (2) UNCITRAL Modellgesetz das englische Wort „only“ nicht übernommen worden war, schloss der Senat, dass es sich um eine deklaratorische Bestimmung handle und der Geltungsbereich von Teil I SchiedsG a. F. nicht auf Schiedsverfahren in Indien begrenzt sei. Den Anwendungsbereich von Teil I SchiedsG a. F. auf Schiedsverfahren mit Sitz im Ausland auszudehnen, sei geboten, da die Gerichte ansonsten den Parteien eines extraterritorialen Schiedsverfahrens keinen effektiven Rechtsschutz gewähren können.

Nach dem obersten Gericht Indiens ist das SchiedsG auf Schiedsverfahren mit inländischem Sitz zwingend anwendbar und die Schiedsparteien können lediglich die dispositiven Bestimmungen von Teil I SchiedsG abbedingen. Bei Schiedsverfahren mit ausländischem Sitz sei Teil I SchiedsG a. F. andererseits grundsätzlich auch immer anwendbar, die Parteien können jedoch hiervon explizit wie auch konkludent abweichen.[1108]

Der Supreme Court urteilte 2002, dass die Schiedsparteien Sec. 9 SchiedsG nicht durch ihr ICC-Schiedsverfahren abbedungen haben, weil Art. 23 ICC-Schiedsgerichtsordnung 1998 einstweiligem gerichtlichen Rechtsschutz nicht entgegenstehe. Das oberste indische Gericht bestätigte deshalb, dass in diesem Fall das zuständige indische Gericht eine einstweilige gerichtliche Maßnahme für ein im Ausland durchgeführtes Schiedsverfahren anordnen konnte und wies die Berufung zurück.

bb) Bewertung

Der Supreme Court setzte sich im *Bhatia*-Urteil über die Wortlautgrenze von Sec. 2 (2) SchiedsG a. F. hinweg[1109] und erweiterte den Anwendungsbereich von Teil I SchiedsG a. F. auch auf Schiedsverfahren mit Sitz im Ausland. Er

---

1108 Appeal (civil) 6527 of 2001, Rn. 21 ff.

1109 Kwatra, S. 6; Mohta/Mohta, Sec. 2, S. 88 f.; Chaterjee, Indian Journal of Arbitration Law 2015, Vol. IV, Ausg. 1, S. 19 (22); Rautray, Dispute Resolution Journal 2009, Vol. 64, Ausg. 1, S. 80 (83 f.); Rai, Journal of International Dispute Settlement 2012, Vol. 3, Ausg. 1, S. 169 (173 ff.). Im Schrifttum wird zudem kritisiert, dass der Supreme Court im Urteil zu Unrecht eine dem SchiedsG widersprechende, richterliche Rechtsfortbildung vornahm, Nariman, The George Washington International Law Review 2009–2010, Vol. 41, Ausg. 2, S. 367 (375); Nair, Arbitration International 2007, Vol. 23, Ausg. 4, S. 699 (718); Anchayil, Arbitration International 2013, Vol. 29, Ausg. 1, S. 105 (106); Parthasarathy/Visalakshi, Arbitration 2007, S. 394 ff.; Arvind, International & Comparative Law Quarterly 2010, S. 65 (75 f.); Jain, Alok, Arbitration International 2010, Vol. 26, Ausg. 2, S. 251 (257 ff.); Malhotra, Indu, O. P. Malhotra on Arbitration, Sec. 2 (2), S. 229; Mohta/Mohta, Sec. 2, S. 88 f.

verlieh dem SchiedsG hierdurch weltweite Geltung. Der Gesetzgeber war in Sec. 2 (2) SchiedsG a. F. allerdings bewusst von Art. 1 (2) UNCITRAL Modellgesetz abgewichen.[1110] Durch Sec. 2 (2) SchiedsG a. F. sollte den Parteien eines Schiedsverfahrens mit extraterritorialem Sitz der Zugriff auf einstweilige Maßnahmen der indischen Gerichte verwehrt bleiben, um die damit verbundenen gerichtlichen Interventionen[1111] zu verhindern.

Die Entscheidung des Supreme Courts bewirkte, dass für Schiedsverfahren mit Sitz im Ausland bei den indischen Gerichten vorläufige Maßnahmen (Sec. 9 SchiedsG) und die Unterstützung bei der Beweisaufnahme (Sec. 27 SchiedsG) beantragt werden konnten.[1112]

Diese beiden Unterstützungsmöglichkeiten der Gerichte zu Gunsten von Schiedsverfahren mit extraterritorialem Sitz können für ausländische Schiedsverfahren hilfreich sein.[1113] Andererseits gestattete der Supreme Court den indischen Gerichten aber auch, die Kontrolle über Schiedsverfahren mit ausländischem Sitz auszuüben. Die Gerichte konnten einen ausländischen Schiedsspruch wegen eines Verstoßes gegen die indische öffentliche Ordnung gem. Sec. 34 (2) (b) (ii) SchiedsG aufheben.[1114] Die Gerichte

---

1110 Parthasarathy/Visalakshi, Arbitration 2007, S. 394 (396 f.); Nair, Arbitration International 2007, Vol. 23, Ausg. 4, S. 699 (718); Rautray, Dispute Resolution Journal 2009, Vol. 64, Ausg. 1, S. 80 (83 f.); Jain, Alok, Arbitration International 2010, Vol. 26, Ausg. 2, S. 251 (257 ff.).

1111 Durch die Entscheidung *Bhatia* führte der Supreme Court durch die Hintertür wieder die Interventionsoption für staatliche indische Gerichte in Schiedsverfahren mit ausländischem Sitz ein, Dewan, Nakul, Asian International Arbitration Journal 2007, Vol. 3, Ausg. 1, S. 99 (113 f.); Sharma, Ajay, Indian Journal of Arbitration Law 2014, Vol. III, Ausg. 1, S. 6 (27 f.).

1112 Vgl. zudem Supreme Court, 1 Richter, *M/S Indtel Technical Services v W S Atkins Plc*, (2008) 10 SCC 308; AIR 2009 SC 1132; Arbitration Application No. 16 of 2006, 25.8.2008; Supreme Court, 1 Richter, *Citation Infowares Ltd v Equinox Corporation*, (2009) 7 SCC 220; [2009] 6 SCR 737; Arbitration Application No. 8 of 2008, 20.4.2009; Supreme Court, 1 Richter, *M/S Dozco India P Ltd v M/S Doosan Infracore Co Ltd*, (2011) 6 SCC 179; JT 2010 (12) SC 198; Arbitration Petition No. 5 of 2008, 8.10.2010.

1113 Thadikkaran, Journal of International Arbitration 2012, Vol. 29, Ausg. 6, S. 681; Sharma, Raghav, Journal of International Arbitration 2009, Vol. 26, Ausg. 3, S. 357 (362). Hinsichtlich der Vorteile von einstweiligen gerichtlichen Maßnahmen für Schiedsverfahren mit ausländischem Sitz, Parthasarathy/Visalakshi, Arbitration 2007, S. 394 (396 f.); Nair, Arbitration International 2007, Vol. 23, Ausg. 4, S. 699 (718); Mohta/Mohta, Sec. 2, S. 89; Sharma, Ajay, Indian Journal of Arbitration Law 2014, Vol. III, Ausg. 1, S. 6 (26).

1114 Sharma, Raghav, Journal of International Arbitration 2009, Vol. 26, Ausg. 3, S. 357 ff.; Gupta, Arpan, Indian Journal of Arbitration Law 2013, Vol. II, Ausg. 2, S. 1 ff.; Malhotra, Indu, O. P. Malhotra on Arbitration, Sec. 2 (2), S. 228 f.; Rai, Journal of International Dispute Settlement 2012, Vol. 3, Ausg. 1, S. 169 (191); Parthasarathy/Visalakshi, Arbitration 2007, S. 394 (396 f.); Nair, Arbitration International 2007, Vol. 23,

durften des Weiteren bei der Schiedsrichterbestellung und der Beendigung des Schiedsrichtermandats[1115] und bei der schiedsgerichtlichen Zuständigkeitsentscheidung[1116] in ausländische Schiedsverfahren intervenieren.[1117] Die Parteien konnten darüber hinaus die vom Schiedsgericht angeordneten vorläufigen Maßnahmen in Berufungsverfahren von den indischen Gerichten überprüfen lassen[1118].

Auf Grund der zuletzt genannten Gesichtspunkte betrachtete die internationale Schiedsbranche die *Bhatia*-Entscheidung als schiedsunfreundlich[1119] und internationale Investoren als Gefahr für zukünftige Handelsbeziehungen mit Indien[1120].[1121] Auch in der Literatur wird das Urteil wegen der geschaffenen Interventionsmöglichkeiten und der Gefahr von Verfahrensverzögerungen kritisiert und eine Gesetzesänderung gefordert.[1122]

Ausg. 4, S. 699 (719); Arvind, International & Comparative Law Quarterly 2010, S. 65 (74 f.); Rai, International Arbitration Law Review 2011, S. 138.

1115 Sec. 11 ff. SchiedsG.

1116 Sec. 16, 34 und 37 (2) (a) SchiedsG. Diese Bestimmungen umfassten die Entscheidung über die Zuständigkeit und die Unzuständigkeit, aber auch die Entscheidung über die Überschreitung der schiedsgerichtlichen Zuständigkeit.

1117 Zu Interventionen bei der Schiedsrichterbestellung, Supreme Court, *M/S Indtel Technical Services v W S Atkins Plc*, Arbitration Application No. 16 of 2006; AIR 2009 SC 1132; (2008) 10 SCC 308, 25.8.2008; Sharma, Raghav, Journal of International Arbitration 2009, Vol. 26, Ausg. 3, S. 357 ff.; Rai, Journal of International Dispute Settlement 2012, Vol. 3, Ausg. 1, S. 169 (176); Parthasarathy/Visalakshi, Arbitration 2007, S. 394 (396 f.); Nair, Arbitration International 2007, Vol. 23, Ausg. 4, S. 699 (719); Rai, International Arbitration Law Review 2011, S. 138.

1118 Sec. 37 (2) (b) SchiedsG.

1119 Mahajan/Anand, Arbitration 2013, S. 28 (33); Ray, Ashutosh, Journal of International Arbitration 2012, Vol. 29, Ausg. 3, S. 345 (345 ff.); Sindhu, Indian Journal of Arbitration Law 2014, Vol. III, Ausg. 2, S. 23 (36); Mahajan, Indian Journal of Arbitration Law 2014, Vol. III, Ausg. 2, S. 14 i. V. m. Fn. 1.

1120 Malhotra, Indu, O. P. Malhotra on Arbitration, Sec. 2 (2), S. 228; Anchayil, Arbitration International 2013, Vol. 29, Ausg. 1, S. 105 (107); Thadikkaran, Journal of International Arbitration 2012, Vol. 29, Ausg. 6, S. 681 (684).

1121 Thadikkaran, Journal of International Arbitration 2012, Vol. 29, Ausg. 6, S. 681 (681 ff.); Ray, Ashutosh, Journal of International Arbitration 2012, Vol. 29, Ausg. 3, S. 345 (353); Malhotra, Indu, O. P. Malhotra on Arbitration, Sec. 2 (2), S. 228 f.; Mahajan/Anand, Arbitration 2013, S. 28 ff.

1122 Zu den Interventionsmöglichkeiten, Mahajan/Anand, Arbitration 2013, S. 28 ff.; Sabharwal/Singh, Aditya, Global Arbitration Review 2012, Vol. 7, Ausg. 6, 22.10.2012; Sharma, Raghav, Journal of International Arbitration 2009, Vol. 26, Ausg. 3, S. 357 ff.; Gupta, Aditya/Das, Arbitration 2014, S. 466; Arvind, International & Comparative Law Quarterly 2010, S. 65 (75 ff.); Ray, Ashutosh, Journal of International Arbitration 2012, Vol. 29, Ausg. 3, S. 345 (346 ff.); Malhotra, Indu, O. P. Malhotra on Arbitration, Sec. 2, S. 229. Zu der Gefahr von Verfahrensverzögerungen, Mahajan/Anand, Arbitration 2013, S. 28 ff. Thadikkaran, Journal of International Arbitration 2012, Vol. 29, Ausg. 6, S. 681 (684); Sabharwal/Singh, Aditya, Global Arbitration Review

Die einzige Möglichkeit, Eingriffe der indischen Gerichte in Schiedsverfahren mit Sitz im Ausland zu verhindern, bestand darin, ausdrücklich oder konkludent die Anwendbarkeit von Teil I SchiedsG a. F. abzubedingen.

Die Auffassung des Supreme Courts, dass für Schiedsparteien ohne eine Ausdehnung des SchiedsG-Anwendungsbereichs auf ausländische Schiedsverfahren kein gerichtlicher einstweiliger Rechtsschutz besteht, ist zutreffend. Die Parteien können sich zwar an das Schiedsgericht und die Gerichte am Schiedssitz für den Erlass von einstweiligen Maßnahmen wenden. Wegen des Territorialitätsprinzips können die Gerichte im Sitzstaat den Parteien aber keinen effektiven Rechtsschutz in Indien gewähren. Die von Schiedsgerichten mit ausländischem Sitz[1123] angeordneten vorläufigen Maßnahmen können zudem in Indien nicht vollstreckt werden.[1124] Diese Verkürzung des Rechtsschutzes ist aber einer universellen Interventionszuständigkeit der indischen Gerichte auch gegenüber ausländischen Schiedsverfahren vorzuziehen.

An der Entscheidung ist ferner zu kritisieren, dass sich der Supreme Court nicht mit dem juristischen Sitz eines Schiedsverfahrens auseinandersetzte. Durch die Wahl des Sitzes eines Schiedsverfahrens in einem Land bestimmt dieses das auf das Schiedsverfahren anwendbare Schiedsrecht (*lex arbitri*), sofern die Parteien keine andere zulässige Schiedsrechtswahl getroffen haben.[1125] Das oberste Gericht Indiens spricht in seinem Urteil von ausländi-

---

2012, Vol. 7, Ausg. 6, 22.10.2012. Zu Kritik an der *Bhatia*-Entscheidung, Khanna, International Arbitration Law Review 2012, S. 203 ff.; Ray, Ashutosh, International Arbitration Law Review 2013, S. 97; Anchayil, Arbitration International 2013, Vol. 29, Ausg. 1, S. 105 ff.; Rewari, Asian International Arbitration Journal 2013, Vol. 9, Ausg. 2, S. 97 (117); Nariman, The George Washington International Law Review 2009–2010, Vol. 41, Ausg. 2, S. 367 (374 ff.); Jain, Alok, Arbitration International 2010, Vol. 26, Ausg. 2, S. 251 (257 ff.); Mahajan/Anand, Arbitration 2013, S. 28 ff.; Mahajan, International Arbitration Law Review 2013, S. N43; Agrawal, Divyanshu, International Arbitration Law Review 2014, S. N43; Prasad, Aakash, Arbitration 2009, S. 289 (290 f.); Rai, Journal of International Dispute Settlement 2012, Vol. 3, Ausg. 1, S. 169 (172 ff.); Gupta, Aditya/Das, Arbitration 2014, S. 466; Parthasarathy/Visalakshi, Arbitration 2007, S. 394 ff.; Nair, Arbitration International 2007, Vol. 23, Ausg. 4, S. 699 (718 f.); Arvind, International & Comparative Law Quarterly 2010, S. 65 (75 ff.); Sachdeva, International Arbitration Law Review 2010, S. 73 (76 ff.); Chaterjee, Indian Journal of Arbitration Law 2015, Vol. IV, Ausg. 1, S. 20 (22 ff.); Sathyapalan, Arbitration International 2016, S. 1 (5). Zu der geforderten Gesetzesänderung, Khanna, International Arbitration Law Review 2012, S. 203 (208); Rai, Journal of International Dispute Settlement 2012, Vol. 3, Ausg. 1, S. 169 (203); Parthasarathy/Visalakshi, Arbitration 2007, S. 394 (397); Mohta/Mohta, Sec. 2, S. 88 f.

1123 Der Sitz des Schiedsverfahrens befindet sich im Ausland.

1124 Sec. 17 (2), 2 (2) SchiedsG.

1125 Born, International Commercial Arbitration, Bd. 2, S. 1530 f., 1575 ff.; Blackaby/Partasides/Redfern/Hunter, International Arbitration, Rn. 3.37 ff., 3.53 ff.; Born, Law

schen Schiedsverfahren und von Schiedsverfahren, die im Ausland durchgeführt werden. Dabei lässt der Supreme Court außer Acht, dass nach der Sitztheorie bei Schiedsverfahren zwischen dem juristischen Sitz und dem Verhandlungsort[1126] differenziert werden muss. Der Sitz des Schiedsverfahrens bestimmt das anwendbare Schiedsverfahrensrecht, der Ort, an dem die Verhandlungen tatsächlich durchgeführt werden, ist unerheblich[1127]. Der Sitz ist demzufolge das „Herz" der gerichtlichen Kontrolle des Schiedsverfahrens.[1128] Nur die Gerichte des Sitzstaates dürfen die gerichtliche Kontrolle über das Schiedsverfahren ausüben. Der Verhandlungsort für das Schiedsverfahren wird hingegen meist danach ausgewählt, ob der Ort für die Parteien und Schiedsrichter bzw. die Beweisaufnahmen günstig gelegen ist.[1129] Hätte der Supreme Court in seinem Tatbestand festgestellt, dass Paris

---

and Practice, § 1.07 [B] [4], S. 37. Der Schiedssitz ist das juristische Zentrum des Schiedsverfahrens und das Schiedsrecht des Sitzstaates findet auf das Schiedsverfahren Anwendung. Die Bedeutung des Sitzes des Schiedsverfahrens ist in den nationalen Schiedsgesetzgebungen universell anerkannt, Born, International Commercial Arbitration, Bd. 2, S. 1530 ff.; Blackaby/Partasides/Redfern/Hunter, International Arbitration, Rn. 3.53 ff. Zur zulässigen Wahl des anwendbaren Schiedsrechts, siehe Art. 182 Schweizer Bundesgesetz über das Internationale Privatrecht und Art. 1505 französischer Code de procédure civile.

1126 Vgl. Art. 20 UNCITRAL Modellgesetz: Blackaby/Partasides/Redfern/Hunter, International Arbitration, Rn. 3.53 ff.; Born, International Commercial Arbitration, Bd. 2, S. 1538 ff., 1569 ff., 1596 f.; Lew/Mistelis/Kröll, Comparative International Commercial, Rn. 21-59 f.

1127 Der Sitz eines Schiedsverfahrens kann eine rechtliche Fiktion sein, die Verhandlungen des Schiedsverfahrens können an einem anderen Ort durchgeführt werden, auch die Parteien oder die Streitigkeit müssen keine Verbindung zum Sitz des Schiedsverfahrens aufweisen, Blackaby/Partasides/Redfern/Hunter, International Arbitration, Rn. 3.53 ff.; Born, International Commercial Arbitration, Bd. 2, S. 1538 ff., 1569 ff., 1596 f.; Lew/Mistelis/Kröll, Comparative International Commercial, Rn. 21-59 f.

1128 Auf Grund seiner zentralen Bedeutung ist der Sitz des Schiedsverfahrens als sein „Gravitationszentrum" (Blackaby/Partasides/Redfern/Hunter, International Arbitration, Rn. 3.56) oder seine „Heimat" (Born, International Commercial Arbitration, Bd. 2, S. 1530 ff.) anzusehen.

1129 Blackaby/Partasides/Redfern/Hunter, International Arbitration, Rn. 3.53 ff.; Born, International Commercial Arbitration, Bd. 2, S. 1538 ff., 1569 ff., 1596 f.; Lew/Mistelis/Kröll, Comparative International Commercial, Rn. 21-58 f. Die Delokalisierung (engl. delocalisation) des Schiedsverfahrens von staatlichem Schiedsrecht wird abgelehnt, Born, International Commercial Arbitration, Bd. 2, S. 1587 ff.; Blackaby/Partasides/Redfern/Hunter, International Arbitration, Rn. 3.79 ff. In Art. 20 UNCITRAL Modellgesetz kommt zudem zum Ausdruck, dass zwischen dem Schiedssitz und dem Ort der Verhandlungen zu differenzierten ist. Mit „place" ist in Art. 20 UNCITRAL Modellgesetz der Schiedssitz gemeint und unter „meet at any place it considers appropriate" ist der hiervon unabhängige Verhandlungsort des Schiedsverfahrens zu verstehen, der flexibel nach den Bedürfnissen des Schiedsverfahrens variiert werden kann. Der indische Gesetzgeber rezipierte Art. 20 UNCITRAL Modellgesetz in Sec. 20 SchiedsG, hierdurch brachte er zum Ausdruck, dass er die im UNCITRAL

nicht nur als der Verhandlungsort des Schiedsverfahrens anzusehen ist, sondern als Sitz des Schiedsverfahrens, hätte dies nach der Sitztheorie zu einem konkludenten Ausschluss von Teil I SchiedsG a. F. geführt. Eine vorläufige gerichtliche Maßnahme hätte dann für das ausländische Schiedsverfahren nicht ergehen dürfen. Klare Kriterien, wann von einer konkludenten Abbedingung von Teil I SchiedsG a. F. auszugehen ist, lassen sich der Entscheidung leider nicht entnehmen.

c) Gerichtliche Entscheidungen nach Bhatia

Ein mit zwei Richtern besetzter Senat des Supreme Courts entschied im Verfahren *Venture Global Engineering v Satyam Computer Services Ltd & Anr (Venture Global)*[1130], dass ein im Vereinigten Königreich ergangener Schiedsspruch in Indien gem. Sec. 34 SchiedsG, inklusive der extensiven Auslegung der öffentlichen Ordnung aus dem Urteil *Oil & Natural Gas Corporation Ltd v Saw Pipes Ltd (Saw Pipes)*[1131], aufgehoben werden kann.[1132]

Modellgesetz zu Grunde gelegte Sitztheorie für das indische SchiedsG übernahm, siehe UNCITRAL Sekretariat, Explanatory note, Rn. 13. Dies wird auch durch die vom 246. Report vorgeschlagenen Reformen der Law Commission deutlich. Nach dem 246. Report sollte in Sec. 20 das Wort „place“ mit „seat“ ersetzt werden und das Wort „place“ mit dem Wort „venue“ substituiert werden, um klar zum Ausdruck zu bringen, dass das SchiedsG der international anerkannten Sitztheorie folgt, Government of India, Law Commission of India, 246. Report, Amendments to the Arbitration and Conciliation Act 1996, 5.8.2014, S. 24, 52. Die Begriffe „seat“ und „place“ des Schiedsgerichts stellen Synonyme dar, Born, International Commercial Arbitration, Bd. 2, S. 1536 ff.; Blackaby/Partasides/Redfern/Hunter, International Arbitration, Rn. 3.53 ff.; Born, Law and Practice, § 1.07 [B] [4], S. 37.

1130 AIR 2008 SC 1061; (2008) 4 SCC 190; Appeal (civil) 309 of 2008 137, 10.1.2008.

1131 Siehe Besprechung des Urteils im Kapitel: Aufhebungsverfahren; Oil & Natural Gas v Saw Pipes (Saw Pipes) (C.VII.2.b)bb)).

1132 Rn. 21 f.; Die Entscheidung wird im Kapitel: Aufhebungsverfahren; Venture Global v Satyam (Venture Global) (C.VII.2.b)cc)) ausführlich dargestellt. Der Supreme Court verkennt in seinem Urteil, dass ausländische Schiedssprüche den engeren Nichtvollstreckungsgründen von Sec. 48 in Teil II SchiedsG (entspricht Art. V UNÜ) unterliegen, Rai, Journal of International Dispute Settlement 2012, Vol. 3, Ausg. 1, S. 169 (174 f.); Kachwaha, Asian International Arbitration Journal 2008, Vol. 4, Ausg. 1, S. 64 (78); Malhotra, Indu, O. P. Malhotra on Arbitration, Sec. 48, S. 1730; Mahajan/Anand, Arbitration 2013, S. 28 (31 ff.); Nariman, Journal of International Arbitration 2008, Vol. 25, Ausg. 6, S. 893 (898); Gupta, Arpan, Indian Journal of Arbitration Law 2013, Vol. II, Ausg. 2, S. 1 (7); Rewari, Asian International Arbitration Journal 2013, Vol. 9, Ausg. 2, S. 97 (120); Ritz, ASA Bulletin 2009, Vol. 27, Ausg. 4, S. 717 (727 ff.); Rautray, Dispute Resolution Journal 2009, Vol. 64, Ausg. 1, S. 80 (85); Khanna, International Arbitration Law Review 2012, S. 203 f.; Ray, Ashutosh, International Arbitration Law Review 2013, S. 97; Reynardson/Talbot-Garman, International Arbitration Law Review 2011, S. 90 (91); Rautray, International Arbitration Law Review 2008, S. N29 (N30 f.); Sharma, Raghav, Arbitration 2009, S. 148 ff. Differenziert

Diese Entscheidung beruhte auf dem *Bhatia*-Urteil, das den Anwendungsbereich von Teil I SchiedsG unter Sec. 2 (2) SchiedsG a. F. auch auf Schiedsverfahren mit ausländischem Sitz für anwendbar erklärt hatte.

Das *Venture Global*-Urteil wird aus der Perspektive der internationalen Schiedsbranche[1133], der ausländischen Investoren[1134] und auch mit Blick auf die Entwicklung ausländischer Handelsbeziehungen mit dem indischen Subkontinent[1135] zu Recht als hinderlich angesehen.[1136] An dem Urteil kriti-

---

Jain, der die Rechtsauffassung des Supreme Courts in der *Venture Global*-Entscheidung unter den gegebenen Umständen letztendlich teilt, Jain, Alok, Arbitration International 2010, Vol. 26, Ausg. 2, S. 251 (279 f.).

1133 Mahajan/Anand, Arbitration 2013, S. 28 (33); Rautray, Dispute Resolution Journal 2009, Vol. 64, Ausg. 1, S. 80 (86); Thadikkaran, Journal of International Arbitration 2012, Vol. 29, Ausg. 6, S. 681 (684 ff.); Sharma, Raghav, Arbitration 2009, S. 148 (157); Sattar, Journal of International Arbitration 2010, Vol. 27, Ausg. 1, S. 51 (63); Rebello, Cambridge Student Law Review 2010, S. 274 (283); Reynardson/Talbot-Garman, International Arbitration Law Review 2011, S. 90 (91).

1134 Thadikkaran, Journal of International Arbitration 2012, Vol. 29, Ausg. 6, S. 681 (684); Malhotra, Indu, O. P. Malhotra on Arbitration, Sec. 2, S. 228; Sharma, Raghav, Arbitration 2009, S. 148 (153); Anchayil, Arbitration International 2013, Vol. 29, Ausg. 1, S. 105 (107); Mahajan/Narayan, International Arbitration Law Review 2015, S. 63 (69).

1135 Sharma, Raghav, Arbitration 2009, S. 148 (153 ff.); Thadikkaran, Journal of International Arbitration 2012, Vol. 29, Ausg. 6, S. 681 (681 ff.); Rautray, Dispute Resolution Journal 2009, Vol. 64, Ausg. 1, S. 80 (85 f.); Rebello, Cambridge Student Law Review 2010, S. 274 (283).

1136 Thadikkaran, Journal of International Arbitration 2012, Vol. 29, Ausg. 6, S. 681 ff.; Nariman, Journal of International Arbitration 2008, Vol. 25, Ausg. 6, S. 893 (898); Nariman, The George Washington International Law Review 2009–2010, Vol. 41, Ausg. 2, S. 367 (375 f.); Rautray, Dispute Resolution Journal 2009, Vol. 64, Ausg. 1, S. 80 (84 ff.); Rai, Journal of International Dispute Settlement 2012, Vol. 3, Ausg. 1, S. 169 (174 ff.); Sabharwal/Singh, Aditya, Global Arbitration Review 2012, Vol. 7, Ausg. 6, 22.10.2012; Mainwaring-Taylor/Sullivan, Arbitration 2008, S. 133 ff.; Sattar, Journal of International Arbitration 2010, Vol. 27, Ausg. 1, S. 51 (63 ff.); Rebello, Cambridge Student Law Review 2010, S. 274 ff.; Schäfer, SchiedsVZ 2008, S. 299 f.; Kachwaha, Asian International Arbitration Journal 2008, Vol. 4, Ausg. 1, S. 64 (78 f.); Rewari, Asian International Arbitration Journal 2013, Vol. 9, Ausg. 2, S. 97 (120); Dunning, Arbitration 2008, S. 254 (258 ff.); Mahajan/Narayan, International Arbitration Law Review 2015, S. 63 (69 ff.); Rautray, International Arbitration Law Review 2008, S. N29 (N30 f.); Sharma, Raghav, Arbitration 2009, S. 148 ff.; Mistelis, Indian Journal of Arbitration Law 2015, Vol. IV, Ausg. 2, S. 1 (7 f.); Ray, Ashutosh, Journal of International Arbitration 2012, Vol. 29, Ausg. 3, S. 345 (348 ff.); Malhotra, Indu, O. P. Malhotra on Arbitration, Sec. 2, S. 228 f.; Sec. 34, S. 1364 f.; Sec. 44, S. 1581 ff., Sec. 48, S. 1730; Mahajan, Indian Journal of Arbitration Law 2014, Vol. III, Ausg. 2, S. 14 i. V. m. Fn. 1; Sharma, Raghav, Arbitration 2009, S. 148 ff.; Sharma, Ajay, Indian Journal of Arbitration Law 2014, Vol. III, Ausg. 1, S. 6 (27); Rautray, Dispute Resolution Journal 2009, Vol. 64, Ausg. 1, S. 80 (84 f.); Nariman, Arbitration International 2011, Vol. 27, Ausg. 2, S. 115 (125); Ritz, ASA Bulletin 2009, Vol. 27, Ausg. 4, S. 717

siert die Literatur, dass es zu gerichtlichen Interventionen[1137], zu Verfahrensverzögerungen[1138] und zu Kostenerhöhungen[1139] bei der Durchsetzung eines ausländischen Schiedsspruchs führe. Die *Venture Global*-Entscheidung spiegele ferner das fehlende Vertrauen der Gerichte in die Schiedsgerichtsbarkeit wider.[1140] *Ray* bezeichnet das *Venture Global*-Urteil sogar als gravierenderen Rückschlag für die Schiedsgerichtsbarkeit als die *Bhatia*-Entscheidung.[1141] Das Schriftum forderte demnach eine SchiedsG-Reform, um die Folgen der *Venture Global*-Entscheidung zu beseitigen.[1142]

Für die durch die *Bhatia*-Entscheidung geschaffene Möglichkeit, aus dem ersten Teil des SchiedsG a.F. heraus zu optieren, entwickelte die nachfolgende Rechtsprechung Kriterien, die für oder gegen ein Herausoptieren sprachen. Ein auf den Hauptvertrag[1143] anwendbares ausländisches Recht erachtete der Supreme Court für einen konkludenten Ausschluss von Teil I

(727 ff.); Mahajan/Bhatt, Journal of International Arbitration 2013, Vol. 30, Ausg. 6, S. 711 i. V. m. Fn. 1. Differenziert, Takahashi, The American Review of International Arbitration 2008, Vol. 19, Ausg. 1, S. 173 ff.; Jain, Devyani, Indian Journal of Arbitration Law 2012, Vol. I, Ausg. 1, S. 36 (41 ff.); Jain, Alok, Arbitration International 2010, Vol. 26, Ausg. 2, S. 251 (279 f.); Zaiwalla, Journal of International Arbitration 2008, Vol. 25, Ausg. 4, S. 507 (511). Zu Kritik an dem Urteil, Nariman, The George Washington International Law Review 2009–2010, Vol. 41, Ausg. 2, S. 367 (375 f.); Sharma, Raghav, Journal of International Arbitration 2009, Vol. 26, Ausg. 3, S. 357 (366 f.); Rai, Journal of International Dispute Settlement 2012, Vol. 3, Ausg. 1, S. 169 (174 f.); Nelson, Asian International Arbitration Journal 2014, Vol. 10, Ausg. 2, S. 105 (115 ff.); Ray, Ashutosh, International Arbitration Law Review 2013, S. 97; Anchayil, Arbitration International 2013, Vol. 29, Ausg. 1, S. 105 (106 f.).

1137 Khanna, International Arbitration Law Review 2012, S. 203 (204); Gupta, Arpan, Indian Journal of Arbitration Law 2013, Vol. II, Ausg. 2, S. 1 (8); Rautray, Dispute Resolution Journal 2009, Vol. 64, Ausg. 1, S. 80 (85); Mahajan/Anand, Arbitration 2013, S. 28 (31 ff.); Ray, Ashutosh, International Arbitration Law Review 2013, S. 97; Lawn/Virjee, Indian Finance Arbitration 2009, S. 52 f.; Mainwaring-Taylor/Sullivan, Arbitration 2008, S. 133; Rebello, Cambridge Student Law Review 2010, S. 274 (282 ff.); Dunning, Arbitration 2008, S. 254 (262); Arvind, International & Comparative Law Quarterly 2010, S. 65 (76 f.).

1138 Rautray, Dispute Resolution Journal 2009, Vol. 64, Ausg. 1, S. 80 (85); Kachwaha, Asian International Arbitration Journal 2008, Vol. 4, Ausg. 1, S. 64 (79); Mahajan/Narayan, International Arbitration Law Review 2015, S. 63 (69).

1139 Mahajan/Narayan, International Arbitration Law Review 2015, S. 63 (69).

1140 Sattar, Journal of International Arbitration 2010, Vol. 27, Ausg. 1, S. 51 (64); Rebello, Cambridge Student Law Review 2010, S. 274 (282).

1141 Ray, Ashutosh, Journal of International Arbitration 2012, Vol. 29, Ausg. 3, S. 345 (348 f.).

1142 Rai, Journal of International Dispute Settlement 2012, Vol. 3, Ausg. 1, S. 169 (203); Rebello, Cambridge Student Law Review 2010, S. 274 (287).

1143 Der Vertrag, der die Schiedsklausel enthält.

SchiedsG a. F. als nicht ausreichend.[1144] Ein auf die Schiedsvereinbarung anwendbares ausländisches Recht beurteilte das oberste indische Gericht hingegen als wirksamen konkludenten Ausschluss von Teil I SchiedsG a. F.[1145] Die Wahl eines ausländischen Schiedssitzes sah der Supreme Court gleichfalls als Abbedingung von Teil I SchiedsG a. F. an.[1146]

Die praktische Folge der Urteile *Bhatia* und *Venture Global*[1147] war, dass international agierende Anwaltskanzleien ihren Mandanten rieten, bei Schiedsklauseln mit Indienbezug Teil I SchiedsG abzubedingen.[1148]

1144 Supreme Court, 1 Richter, *M/S Indtel Technical Services v W S Atkins Plc*; (2008) 10 SCC 308; AIR 2009 SC 1132; Arbitration Application No. 16 of 2006, 25.8.2008; Supreme Court, 1 Richter, *Citation Infowares Ltd v Equinox Corporation*, (2009) 7 SCC 220; [2009] 6 SCR 737; Arbitration Application No. 8 of 2008, 20.4.2009.

1145 Supreme Court, 2 Richter, *Videocon Industries Ltd v Union of India & Anr*, AIR 2011 SC 2040; (2011) 6 SCC 161; Civil Appeal No. 4269 of 2011, 11.5.2011; Supreme Court, 1 Richter, *M/S Dozco India P Ltd v M/S Doosan Infracore Co Ltd*, (2011) 6 SCC 179; JT 2010 (12) SC 198; Arbitration Petition No. 5 of 2008, 8.10.2010; Supreme Court, 2 Richter, *Yograj Infras Ltd v Ssang Yong Engineering*, AIR 2011 SC 3517; (2011) 9 SCC 735; Civil Appeal No. 7562 of 2011, 1.9.2011; Supreme Court, 2 Richter, *Sakuma Exports Ltd v Louis Dreyfus Commodities Suisse SA*, (2015) 5 SCC 656; 2014 (2) Arb LR 14; Petition for Special Leave to Appeal (Civil) No. 27404 of 2013, 28.3.2014.

1146 Supreme Court, 2 Richter, *Sakuma Exports Ltd v Louis Dreyfus Commodities Suisse SA*, (2015) 5 SCC 656; 2014 (2) Arb LR 14; Petition for Special Leave to Appeal (Civil) No. 27404 of 2013, 28.3.2014; Supreme Court, 2 Richter, *Videocon Industries Ltd v Union of India & Anr,* AIR 2011 SC 2040; (2011) 6 SCC 161; Civil Appeal No. 4269 of 2011, 11.5.2011; Supreme Court, 2 Richter, *Eitzen Bulk A/S v Ashapura Minechem Limited & Anr*, AIR 2016 SC 2438; 2016 (3) Arb LR 98; Civil Appeal No. 5131–5133 of 2016, 13.5.2016.

1147 I.V.m. dem *Saw Pipes*-Urteil des Supreme Courts, siehe Besprechung des *Saw Pipes*-Urteils im Kapitel: Aufhebungsverfahren; Oil & Natural Gas v Saw Pipes (Saw Pipes) (C.VII.2.b)bb)).

1148 Aloke Ray/Dipen Sabharwal, India and Arbitration – Arbitration clauses for contracts with Indian parties, White & Case, Februar 2008, verfügbar unter https://international-arbitration-attorney.com/wp-content/uploads/arbitrationarbitrationlawArticle_India_and_Arbitration_Arbitration_Clauses_for_Contracts_With_Indian_Parties.pdf (zuletzt abgerufen am 28.4.2021); Herbert Smith, Dispute resolution and governing law clauses in India-related commercial contracts, S. 3 ff., verfügbar unter http://hsfnotes.com/arbitration/wp-content/uploads/sites/4/2011/04/2011-Dispute-resolution-and-governing-clauses-in-India-related-commercial-contracts.pdf (zuletzt abgerufen am 28.4.2021); Dipen Sabharwal, Another setback for Indian arbitration (and foreign investors), White & Case, India, 6.6.2008, verfügbar unter http://www.lexology.com/library/detail.aspx?g=4def9d16-1f37-4e2e-8843-a1faa3f47e93 (zuletzt abgerufen am 28.4.2021).

d) Bharat Aluminium v Kaiser Aluminium (Balco)

aa) Entscheidung

In der Rechtssache *Bharat Aluminium Co v Kaiser Aluminium Technical Service Inc (Balco)*[1149] sollte für mehrere Berufungsverfahren in einer Grundsatzentscheidung darüber geurteilt werden, ob der Supreme Court in der *Bhatia*-Entscheidung den Anwendungsbereich des SchiedsG a. F. zutreffend beurteilt hatte. Zuvor hatte der Supreme Court[1150] und die Literatur[1151] eine Änderung der *Bhatia*-Rechtsprechung angeregt.[1152]

Das *Balco*-Berufungsverfahren war seit 2005 beim obersten Gericht Indiens zunächst vor einem mit zwei Richtern besetzten Senat rechtshängig. Die Richter hatten im Januar 2008 unterschiedliche Auffassungen bezüglich der Auslegung von Sec. 2 (2) SchiedsG a. F. in den Urteilen *Bhatia* und *Venture Global*. Sie verwiesen daher die Berufung an den Chief Justice of India, der das Verfahren einem größeren Senat zuweisen sollte. Der Chief Justice betraute zunächst einen mit drei Richtern besetzten Senat mit der Rechtssache und verwies diese letztendlich an eine Constitutional Bench. Das Berufungsverfahren war seit dem 10. Januar 2012 vor einer mit fünf Richtern besetzten Constitutional Bench anhängig.

Nach dem Tatbestand des *Balco*-Verfahrens[1153] vereinbarte die Klägerin *Bharat Aluminium Co (Bharat)* 1993 mit der Beklagten *Kaiser Aluminium Technical Service Inc (Kaiser),* dass die Beklagte an *Bharat* zur Modernisierung ihres „Shelter" ein Computersystem liefern und installieren sollte. Der Vertrag enthielt eine Schiedsvereinbarung, nach der alle Vertragsstreitigkeiten von einem Schiedsgericht mit Sitz in London (England) nach englischem Schiedsrecht beigelegt werden sollten. Zwischen den Vertragsparteien kam es zu einer Streitigkeit. *Bharat* machte die Rückerstattung ihrer Investitionen für das Modernisierungsprogramm und Schadensersatz geltend. *Kaiser* forderte unbezahlte Ratenzahlungen, Zinsen und Schadensersatz wegen der Verletzung ihres geistigen Eigentums. *Kaiser* stellte im November 1997 *Bharat* ihre Schiedsklage zu. Nach dem in England durchgeführten Schieds-

---

1149 Constitutional Bench, 5 Richter, (2012) 9 SCC 552; 2012 (3) Arb LR 515 (SC); Civil Appeal No. 7019 of 2005, 6.9.2012.

1150 Supreme Court, 2 Richter, *M/S Centrotrade Minerals & Metal Inc v Hindustan Copper Ltd*, (2006) 11 SCC 245; 2006 (3) Arb LR 201 (SC); Civil Appeal 2562 of 2006, 9.5.2006; Supreme Court, 1 Richter, *Shreejee Traco Pvt Ltd v Paperline International Inc*, (2003) 9 SCC 79, 17.12.2002.

1151 Nariman, The George Washington International Law Review 2009–2010, Vol. 41, Ausg. 2, S. 367 (374 ff.); Nariman, Journal of International Arbitration 2008, Vol. 25, Ausg. 6, S. 893 (898); Parthasarathy/Visalakshi, Arbitration 2007, S. 394 ff.

1152 Rewari, Asian International Arbitration Journal 2013, Vol. 9, Ausg. 2, S. 97 (117).

1153 Die Constitutional Bench des Supreme Courts erachtete die ihm vorgelegte Berufung als Rechtsfrage, schilderte aber die essentiellen Fakten des Berufungsverfahrens.

verfahren erließ das Schiedsgericht im November 2002 zwei Schiedssprüche. *Bharat* beantragte daraufhin die Aufhebung der Schiedssprüche gem. Sec. 34 SchiedsG beim District Court Bilaspur (Chhattisgarh) in Indien. Der District Court erachtete das Aufhebungsverfahren für ausländische Schiedssprüche für unanwendbar und wies den Antrag auf Aufhebung der beiden Schiedssprüche im Juli 2004 zurück. Im August 2005 wies der Chhattisgarh High Court die Berufung zurück, weil eine Aufhebung von ausländischen Schiedssprüchen unter Sec. 34 SchiedsG nicht statthaft sei. Gegen diese Entscheidung richtete sich die beim Supreme Court eingelegte Berufung.[1154]

In seinem Urteil erörterte die Constitutional Bench des Supreme Courts zunächst die Geschichte der Schiedsgerichtsbarkeit in Indien. Die Constitutional Bench erläuterte daraufhin die Ziele, die der Gesetzgeber durch die Einführung des SchiedsG im Jahre 1996 verfolgte. Im *Balco*-Urteil gab die mit fünf Richtern besetzte Constitutional Bench des Supreme Courts sodann die Rechtsprechung der aus drei[1155] bzw. zwei[1156] Richtern bestehenden Senaten in den Entscheidungen *Bhatia* und *Venture Global* auf. Die Constitutional Bench war der Auffassung, dass nach dem Wortlaut von Sec. 2 (2) SchiedsG a. F. Teil I SchiedsG ausschließlich auf Schiedsverfahren mit Sitz in Indien anwendbar sei. Hierdurch habe der Gesetzgeber das Territorialitätsprinzip im SchiedsG verankert:

> „*In our opinion, a plain reading of Section 2(2) makes it clear that Part I is limited in its application to arbitrations which take place in India.* [...] *...Parliament by limiting the applicability of Part I to arbitrations which take place in India has expressed a legislative declaration. It has clearly given recognition to the territorial principle. Necessarily therefore, it has enacted that Part I of the Arbitration Act, 1996 applies to arbitrations having their place/seat in India.* “[1157]

1154 Von den weiteren, ebenfalls anhängigen Verfahren nahm der Supreme Court nur auf den Sachverhalt der „Special Leave Petition“ in der Rechtssache *Bharati Shipyard Ltd v Ferrostaal AG & Anr* Bezug. Die indische Berufungsklägerin *Bharati Shipyard Ltd* hatte mit der ersten Berufungsbeklagten *Ferrostaal AG (Ferrostaal)* die Herstellung von zwei Schiffen vereinbart. Die Parteien vereinbarten zur Beilegung ihre Streitigkeiten ein Schiedsverfahren nach den „Rules of London Maritime Arbitrators Association (LMAA)“ in London. Entsprechend legte *Ferrostaal* daraufhin zwei Schiedsklagen bei der LMAA ein. Während der Schiedsanhängigkeit vor der LMAA stellte *Ferrostaal* zwei Anträge auf einstweiligen Rechtsschutz gem. Sec. 9 SchiedsG in Indien. Der District Court Mangaluru (Karnataka) erließ den beantragten einstweiligen Rechtsschutz. Der hierauf folgenden Berufung der Gegenseite vor dem High Court Karnataka gab der High Court statt und hob den Beschluss des District Courts auf. Die „Special Leave Petition“ von *Ferrostaal* richtete sich gegen das Urteil des High Courts.

1155 *Bhatia.*

1156 *Venture Global.*

1157 Civil Appeal No. 7019 of 2005, Rn. 63.

Das UNCITRAL Modellgesetz habe nach dem Supreme Court das Territorialitätsprinzip übernommen, demzufolge die Gerichte mit der Ausnahme von Art. 8, 9, 35 und 36 UNCITRAL Modellgesetz nur zuständig sein sollten, sofern sich der Schiedssitz in deren Territorium befinde.[1158] Das englische Wort „only" sei in Art. 1 (2) UNCITRAL Modellgesetz notwendig, um klarzustellen, dass mit der Ausnahme von Art. 8, 9, 35 und 36 das UNCITRAL Modellgesetz ausschließlich auf Schiedsverfahren mit Sitz im Hoheitsgebiet des betreffenden Staates anwendbar sei. Mangels Übernahme dieser extraterritorialen Ausnahmen des Anwendungsbereiches im alten SchiedsG sei es überflüssig gewesen, das Wort „only" in Sec. 2 (2) SchiedsG a. F. zu rezipieren.[1159] Der Supreme Court wies die Rechtsauffassung desselben Gerichts in der *Bhatia*-Entscheidung zurück, weil aus einem Vergleich von Sec. 2 (2) SchiedsG a. F. mit Art. 1 (2) UNCITRAL Modellgesetz nicht abgeleitet werden könne, dass auf Grund des fehlenden Wortes „only" dem SchiedsG a. F. ein universeller Geltungsbereich zukomme.[1160] Der Supreme Court gab somit die vorherige, höchstrichterliche Rechtsprechung in den Verfahren *Bhatia* und *Venture Global* auf. Das oberste Gericht Indiens urteilte demzufolge, dass das SchiedsG auf dem „Territorialitätsprinzip" bzw. der „Sitztheorie" beruhe. Das SchiedsG komme deshalb nur zur Anwendung, wenn sich der Sitz des Schiedsverfahrens in Indien befinde.[1161]

Der Supreme Court entschied sich jedoch im *Balco*-Urteil dafür, seine vorherige *Bhatia*-Rechtsprechung lediglich für nach seiner *Balco*-Entscheidung am 6. September 2012 vereinbarte Schiedsvereinbarungen aufzugeben.[1162] Nach dieser sog. „Prospective Overruling"[1163] unterfallen vor dem 7. September 2012 vereinbarte Schiedsklauseln der alten *Bhatia*-Rechtsprechung.[1164] Nur auf Schiedsvereinbarungen, die Parteien seit dem 7. September 2012 trafen, fand die neue *Balco*-Rechtsprechung Anwendung.

1158 Der Supreme Court zitierte als Beleg die „Travaux Préparatoires" des UNCITRAL Modellgesetzes, UNCITRAL, 330. Sitzung, 19.6.1985.

1159 Civil Appeal No. 7019 of 2005, Rn. 68.

1160 Civil Appeal No. 7019 of 2005, Rn. 75.

1161 Malhotra, Indu, O. P. Malhotra on Arbitration, Sec. 2, S. 242.

1162 Civil Appeal No. 7019 of 2005, Rn. 201.

1163 Siehe mit weiteren Ausführungen hierzu, Malhotra, Indu, O. P. Malhotra on Arbitration, Sec. 2, S. 243 ff.

1164 Die Folge der Prospective Overruling war eine absurde Rechtslage. Die Gerichte mussten auf Schiedsverfahren mit bis einschließlich 6. September 2012 abgeschlossenen Schiedsvereinbarungen die *Bhatia*-Rechtsprechung anwenden, obwohl der Supreme Court das *Bhatia*-Urteil durch die *Balco*-Entscheidung zwischenzeitlich höchstrichterlich verworfen hatte, Government of India, Law Commission of India, 246. Report, Amendments to the Arbitration and Conciliation Act 1996, 5.8.2014, S. 25; Ray, Ashutosh, International Arbitration Law Review 2013, S. 97 (102).

Zusammengefasst fand das SchiedsG a.F. nach der Constitutional Bench des Supreme Courts Anwendung, wenn:

1. Das Schiedsverfahren seinen Sitz in Indien hat.
2. Die Schiedsvereinbarung seit dem 7. September 2012 vereinbart wurde („Prospective Overruling“).

bb) Bewertung

In der *Balco*-Entscheidung verlieh der Supreme Court dem gesetzgeberischen Willen in Sec. 2 (2) SchiedsG a.F. wieder Wirkung. Durch die Reduzierung der Interventionsmöglichkeiten in Schiedsverfahren mit ausländischem Sitz ist die Entscheidung als schiedsfördernd anzusehen.[1165] Das oberste indische Gericht entschied, dass sein Urteil ausschließlich nach dem 6. September 2012 abgeschlossene Schiedsvereinbarungen erfasst. Daher blieben sowohl die *Bhatia*-Entscheidung als auch das *Balco*-Urteil als höchstrichterliche Rechtsprechung nebeneinander bestehen. Dies bedrohte – trotz der Kritik[1166] an der „Prospective Overruling“ – die Rechtssicherheit nicht ernsthaft, da die *Bhatia*-Entscheidung in Verbindung mit der darauffolgenden Rechtsprechung den Anwendungsbereich des SchiedsG bei einem ausländischen Sitz des Schiedsverfahrens als abbedungen erachtete.[1167]

Dank des schiedsfreundlicheren *Balco*-Urteils verbesserte der Supreme Court die Rahmenbedingungen für Investitionen in Indien und Handelsbeziehungen mit Indien.[1168] Die Literatur bespricht die *Balco*-Entscheidung folglich positiv und sieht das Urteil als gerichtliche Interventionen unter-

---

1165 Constantin, International Business Law Journal 2015, S. 409. Zum Meinungsstand der Literatur betreffend der Schiedsfreundlichkeit und der Reduzierung der gerichtlichen Interventionen des Urteils, siehe ausführlich Fn. 1169 ff., S. 191.

1166 Diesen Aspekt der Entscheidung bemängelt die Literatur, Ray, Ashutosh, International Arbitration Law Review 2013, S. 97 (102); Mahajan/Anand, Arbitration 2013, S. 28 (33 f.); Rewari, Asian International Arbitration Journal 2013, Vol. 9, Ausg. 2, S. 97 (133); Malhotra, Indu, O. P. Malhotra on Arbitration, Sec. 44, S. 1586; Rautray, International Arbitration Law Review 2012, S. N48 (N50); Ashish Chugh, The Bharat Aluminium Case: The Indian Supreme Court Ushers In a New Era, Kluwer Arbitration Blog, 26.9.2012, verfügbar unter http://kluwerarbitrationblog.com/2012/09/26/the-bharat-aluminium-case-the-indian-supreme-court-ushers-in-a-new-era/ (zuletzt abgerufen am 28.4.2021). Differenziert, Born/Spears, Indian Journal of Arbitration Law 2012, Vol. I, Ausg. 1, S. 4 (7); Minn, in: Berg (Hrsg.), International Arbitration, The Coming of a New Age?, S. 235 (253); Perry, Global Arbitration Review 2013, Vol. 8, Ausg. 6, 24.10.2013.

1167 Vgl. o.

1168 Mahajan/Anand, Arbitration 2013, S. 28 (28, 36); Thadikkaran, Journal of International Arbitration 2012, Vol. 29, Ausg. 6, S. 681 (689 f.); Born/Spears, Indian Journal of Arbitration Law 2012, Vol. I, Ausg. 1, S. 4 (7 f.); Ross (Verweist auf die vorherrschende Auffassung von Professoren und Praktikern), Global Arbitration Review

bindend[1169], die Handelsbeziehungen mit Indien stärkend[1170] und damit als schiedsfreundlich[1171] an.[1172] Um einstweilige gerichtliche Maßnahmen und die gerichtliche Unterstützung bei der Beweisaufnahme für Schiedsverfah-

---

2012, Vol. 7, Ausg. 5, 7.11.2012; Mahajan, International Arbitration Law Review 2014, S. N9.

1169 Mahajan/Anand, Arbitration 2013, S. 28 (36); Khanna, International Arbitration Law Review 2012, S. 203 ff.; Constantin, International Business Law Journal 2015, S. 409; Rewari, Asian International Arbitration Journal 2013, Vol. 9, Ausg. 2, S. 97 ff. Prakash Pillai/Umer Chaudhry, Law Commission's Report Reinforces the Pro-Arbitration Trends in India, Kluwer Arbitration Blog, 9.10.2014, verfügbar unter http://kluwerarbitrationblog.com/2014/10/09/law-commissions-report-reinforces-the-pro-arbitration-trends-in-india/ (zuletzt abgerufen am 28.4.2021); Government of India, Law Commission of India, 246. Report, Amendments to the Arbitration and Conciliation Act 1996, 5.8.2014, S. 24.

1170 Karia/Mehra/Dhawan, The In-House Lawyer 2012, S. 20 (23).

1171 Mahajan, International Arbitration Law Review 2014 S. N9; Mahajan/Anand, Arbitration 2013, S. 28 ff.; Born, International Commercial Arbitration, Bd. 1, S. 107 i. V. m. Fn. 735; Prasad, Piyush/Parolia, International Arbitration Law Review 2014, S. N58; Constantin, International Business Law Journal 2015, S. 409; Allsop, Arbitration 2015, S. 169 (170 i. V. m. Fn. 5); Thadikkaran, Journal of International Arbitration 2012, Vol. 29, Ausg. 6, S. 681 (689 f.); Sathyapalan, Arbitration International 2016, S. 1 (13); Mahajan/Bhatt, Journal of International Arbitration 2013, Vol. 30, Ausg. 6, S. 711; Mahajan/Narayan, International Arbitration Law Review 2015, S. 63 (71); Gupta, Arpan, Indian Journal of Arbitration Law 2013, Vol. II, Ausg. 2, S. 1 ff.; Prakash Pillai/Umer Chaudhry, Law Commission's Report Reinforces the Pro-Arbitration Trends in India, Kluwer Arbitration Blog, 9.10.2014, verfügbar unter http://kluwerarbitrationblog.com/2014/10/09/law-commissions-report-reinforces-the-pro-arbitration-trends-in-india/ (zuletzt abgerufen am 28.4.2021); Minn, in: Berg (Hrsg.), International Arbitration, The Coming of a New Age?, S. 235 (251).

1172 Khanna, International Arbitration Law Review 2012, S. 203 ff.; Mahajan/Anand, Arbitration 2013, S. 28 ff.; Thej, International Arbitration Law Review 2014, S. 37 (41); Ray, Ashutosh, International Arbitration Law Review 2013, S. 97 ff.; Sabharwal/Singh, Aditya, Global Arbitration Review 2012, Vol. 7, Ausg. 6, 22.10.2012; Constantin, International Business Law Journal 2015, S. 409; Mahajan, Arbitration 2015, S. 48 i. V. m. Fn. 2; Constantin, International Business Law Journal 2016, S. 41 (42); Rautray, International Arbitration Law Review 2012, S. N48 (N50); Ashish Chugh, The Bharat Aluminium Case: The Indian Supreme Court Ushers In a New Era, Kluwer Arbitration Blog, 26.9.2012, verfügbar unter http://kluwerarbitrationblog.com/2012/09/26/the-bharat-aluminium-case-the-indian-supreme-court-ushers-in-a-new-era/ (zuletzt abgerufen am 28.4.2021); Rewari, Asian International Arbitration Journal 2013, Vol. 9, Ausg. 2, S. 97 ff.; Mahajan/Bhatt, Journal of International Arbitration 2013, Vol. 30, Ausg. 6, S. 711 ff.; Gupta, Arpan, Indian Journal of Arbitration Law 2013, Vol. II, Ausg. 2, S. 1 ff.; Minn, in: Berg (Hrsg.), International Arbitration, The Coming of a New Age?, S. 235 (251 ff.); Karia/Mehra/Dhawan, The In-House Lawyer 2012, S. 20 ff.

ren mit extraterritorialem Sitz in Zukunft zu ermöglichen, forderte die Literatur eine Novelle der Schiedsgesetzgebung.[1173]

Das *Balco*-Aufhebungsverfahren war bis zu seiner letztinstanzlichen Entscheidung über acht Jahre rechtshängig. Allein die Berufung vor dem Supreme Court dauerte mehr als sechs Jahre.

Neben der Rechtssache *Balco* sollte im gleichen Supreme Court-Verfahren über das Aufhebungsverfahren *M/s White Industries Australia Ltd v Coal India Ltd* entschieden werden, das wegen der überlangen Verfahrensdauer[1174] zum Investitionsschiedsspruch *White Industries Australia Limited v The Republic of India*[1175] führte.[1176] Beide Verfahren sind exemplarisch für die langsam mahlenden Mühlen des indischen Gerichtssystems.

e) Fazit

Die auf die *Bhatia*-Entscheidung folgende höchstrichterliche Rechtsprechung legte den konkludenten Ausschluss von Teil I SchiedsG a. F. großzügig aus, sodass bei einem ausländischen Schiedssitz der erste Teil des SchiedsG a. F. nicht anwendbar war. Mit dem *Balco*-Urteil verschaffte der Supreme Court dem gesetzgeberischen Willen wieder Geltung. Teil I SchiedsG a. F. war nach dem *Balco*-Urteil ausschließlich auf Schiedsverfahren mit Sitz in Indien anzuwenden. Festzuhalten ist somit, dass die Rechtsprechung im Endeffekt durch die *Bhatia*-Entscheidung in Verbindung mit den darauffolgenden Urteilen die gesetzgeberische Intention von Sec. 2 (2) SchiedsG a. F. honorierte. Bei dieser „Opt-Out"-Lösung des *Bhatia*-Urteils schlossen die Parteien den Anwendungsbereich von Teil I SchiedsG a. F. in ihrer Schiedsvereinbarung ausdrücklich oder konkludent – z. B. durch einen Schiedssitz im Ausland – aus, obwohl der Wortlaut des SchiedsG a. F. seinen Anwendungsbereich auf das indische Territorium begrenzte. Vor diesem Hintergrund ist die *Balco*-Entscheidung zu begrüßen, weil das oberste Ge-

---

1173 Born/Spears, Indian Journal of Arbitration Law 2012, Vol. I, Ausg. 1, S. 4 (8); Mahajan/Anand, Arbitration 2013, S. 28; Thadikkaran, Journal of International Arbitration 2012, Vol. 29, Ausg. 6, S. 681 (690); Biswas, S. 48 f. Teilweise wird an dem Urteil auch kritisiert, dass Parteien eines ausländischen Schiedsverfahrens kein einstweiliger gerichtlicher Rechtsschutz von den indischen Gerichten mehr zugesprochen werden kann, Ross (unter Verweis auf die Rechtsaufassung einer Minderheit von Praktikern), Global Arbitration Review 2012, Vol. 7, Ausg. 5, 7.11.2012; Karia/Mehra/Dhawan, The In-House Lawyer 2012, S. 20 (23).

1174 Der kurz nach dem Aufhebungsverfahren initiierte Vollstreckungsantrag wurde bis zur Entscheidung im Aufhebungsverfahren ausgesetzt.

1175 Schiedsspruch vom 30.11.2011, verfügbar unter http://www.italaw.com/sites/default/files/case-documents/ita0906.pdf (zuletzt abgerufen am 28.4.2021).

1176 Siehe Kapitel: Einleitung; Schiedsverfahren in Indien – ein Überblick (A. I. 2.).

richt Indiens in einfacher Fasson ausdrücklich der legislativen Entscheidung in Sec. 2 (2) SchiedsG a. F. entsprach und die Rechtssicherheit stärkte[1177].

Die Begrenzung des SchiedsG-Geltungsbereiches auf Schiedsverfahren mit Sitz in Indien bewirkte allerdings, dass für Schiedsverfahren mit ausländischem Sitz Beweise und Vermögen in Indien nicht durch vorläufige gerichtliche Maßnahmen gesichert werden konnten.[1178]

f) Arbitration Amendment Act

Die Law Commission empfahl 2014 in ihrem 246. Report, dass ein reformiertes SchiedsG im auf Indien beschränkten Anwendungsbereich Ausnahmen für den Erlass von einstweiligen gerichtlichen Maßnahmen und für die gerichtliche Beweisaufnahme zu Gunsten von Schiedsverfahren mit ausländischem Sitz eröffnen sollte[1179].[1180] In Sec. 2 (2) SchiedsG n. F. folgte der Gesetzgeber den Empfehlungen der Law Commission und erweiterte den Anwendungsbereich des SchiedsG für Sec. 9, 27 und 37[1181] SchiedsG auch auf Schiedsverfahren mit Sitz im Ausland. Durch diese gesetzliche Klarstellung ist das *Bhatia*-Urteil auch für vor 2012 abgeschlossene Schieds-

---

1177 Auf einen möglichen ausdrücklichen bzw. konkludenten Ausschluss des Anwendungsbereiches von Teil I SchiedsG a. F. war nicht mehr abzustellen.

1178 Born/Spears, Indian Journal of Arbitration Law 2012, Vol. I, Ausg. 1, S. 4 (8); Biswas, S. 48 f.; Mahajan/Anand, Arbitration 2013, S. 28 (35 f.); Rewari, Asian International Arbitration Journal 2013, Vol. 9, Ausg. 2, S. 97 (132 f.); Constantin, International Business Law Journal 2016, S. 41 (43); Government of India, Law Commission of India, 246. Report, Amendments to the Arbitration and Conciliation Act 1996, 5.8.2014, S. 24 f. Zur Verkürzung des Rechtsschutzes für die Parteien, vgl. Parthasarathy/Visalakshi, Arbitration 2007, S. 394 (396 f.); Nair, Arbitration International 2007, Vol. 23, Ausg. 4, S. 699 (718); Constantin, International Business Law Journal 2016, S. 41 (42 f.); Ministry of Law and Justice, Government of India, Proposed Amendments to the Arbitration & Conciliation Act, 1996, A Consultation Paper, S. 11, verfügbar unter http://lawmin.nic.in/la/consultationpaper.pdf (zuletzt abgerufen am 28.4.2021).

1179 Art. 1 (2) UNCITRAL Modellgesetz sieht eine extraterritoriale Ausnahme für gerichtlichen einstweiligen Rechtsschutz, nicht aber für eine gerichtliche Beweisaufnahme vor.

1180 Government of India, Law Commission of India, 246. Report, Amendments to the Arbitration and Conciliation Act 1996, 5.8.2014, S. 39.

1181 In Sec. 37 (1) (a) SchiedsG n. F. i. V. m. Sec. 2 (2) SchiedsG n. F. normierte der Gesetzgeber eine Berufung gegen die gerichtliche Nichtverweisungsentscheidung gem. Sec. 8 SchiedsG an ein schiedsgerichtliches Verfahren. Diese Berufungsmöglichkeit gewährleistet, dass die Gerichte Streitigkeiten an das vereinbarte ausländische Schiedsverfahren verweisen. Die Legislative folgte hierdurch dem Vorschlag für eine Schiedsgesetzesnovelle der Law Commission, Government of India, Law Commission of India, 246. Report, Amendments to the Arbitration and Conciliation Act 1996, 5.8.2014, S. 39, 57.

vereinbarungen, gegenstandslos geworden. Das Bedürfnis einer flexiblen Gestaltung des Schiedsverfahrens achtet das SchiedsG n.F. durch die Abbedingungsmöglichkeit des extraterritorialen Anwendungsbereiches.[1182] Der schiedsortunabhängige, die gerichtliche Beweisaufnahme und einstweilige gerichtliche Maßnahmen erfassende, Anwendungsbereich des SchiedsG n.F. ist als Schiedsverfahren unterstützend zu bewerten, weil hierdurch Rechtsschutzlücken der Schiedsparteien geschlossen werden.

Nicht einmal die schiedsfreundlichen asiatischen Rechtsordnungen von Singapur[1183] oder Hongkong[1184] und auch nicht die Ergänzungen des UNCITRAL Modellgesetzes 2006 billigen den Gerichten die Kompetenz zu, Schiedsverfahren mit ausländischem Schiedssitz bei der Beweisaufnahme behilflich zu sein. Im internationalen Vergleich eröffnen England[1185] und Frankreich[1186] eine gerichtliche Hilfestellung für Schiedsverfahren mit ausländischem Sitz bei der Beweisaufnahme. Die Schiedsgesetzgebung der Schweiz[1187] und der Vereinigten Staaten von Amerika[1188] gestatten eine solche gerichtliche Unterstützung von Schiedsverfahren mit ausländischem Sitz bei der Beweisaufnahme nicht. Die beschriebenen Erweiterungen des Anwendungsbereichs des SchiedsG n.F. übertreffen daher den internationalen Standard der Schiedsgerichtsbarkeit[1189] und gestatten in Schiedsverfahren fördernder Weise die Unterstützung von ausländischen Schiedsverfahren.

2. Anwendbares materielles Recht

Auf inländische Schiedsverfahren und internationale Nichthandelsschiedsverfahren (im Folgenden inländische Schiedsverfahren[1190]) ist nach Sec. 28 (1) (a) SchiedsG zwingend indisches Recht anzuwenden. Lediglich in internationalen Handelsschiedsverfahren billigt das SchiedsG eine freie materielle Rechtswahl.[1191] Durch die Verpflichtung für Schiedsgerichte in inländischen Schiedsverfahren indisches Recht anzuwenden, bringt der

---

1182 Sec. 2 (2) SchiedsG n.F.

1183 Siehe Kapitel: Singapur; Anwendungsbereich des Verfahrensrechts; Erweiterung des geographischen Anwendungsbereichs (B.I.1.b)).

1184 Siehe Sec. 5 i.V.m. Sec. 55 Hongkong Arbitration Law Ordinance.

1185 Sec. 2 (3) i.V.m. Sec. 43, 44 Arbitration Act 1996.

1186 Art. 1449 (1), 1469 (1) Code de procédure civile.

1187 Art. 184 und Art. 176 Bundesgesetz über das Internationale Privatrecht.

1188 Sec. 7 Federal Arbitration Act (Title 9, US Code).

1189 Zum internationalen Standard bezüglich einstweiliger gerichtlicher Maßnahmen für die Parteien eines ausländischen Schiedsverfahrens, vgl. Kapitel: Singapur; Einstweilige Maßnahmen; Gesetzesanpassung (B.VI.1.d)).

1190 Der Terminus inländische Schiedsverfahren wird verwendet, da die Anzahl der internationalen Nichthandelsschiedsverfahren gering ist.

1191 Sec. 28 (1) (b) SchiedsG.

Gesetzgeber sein Misstrauen gegenüber der schiedsgerichtlichen Streitbeilegung in Indien zum Ausdruck. Im Interesse der Parteiautonomie ist es wünschenswert, wenn im Zuge einer weiteren SchiedsG-Reform[1192] auch in inländischen Schiedsverfahren das für die Streitigkeit am besten geeignete materielle Recht frei gewählt werden darf. Die Parteien können dem Schiedsgericht[1193] allerdings nach Sec. 28 (2) SchiedsG ausdrücklich gestatten, ihre Streitigkeit *ex aequo et bono* oder als „Amiable Compositeur" zu entscheiden.

II. Kompetenz-Kompetenz

Im Unterschied zum Arbitration Act 1940[1194] räumt Sec. 16 (1) SchiedsG den Schiedsgerichten die „Kompetenz-Kompetenz" ein, über die eigene Zuständigkeit zu entscheiden.[1195] Dies entspricht dem internationalen Standard der Schiedsgerichtsbarkeit.[1196]

1. Überprüfung der Kompetenz-Kompetenz durch die Gerichte

a) Zuständigkeit des Schiedsgerichts

Im Unterschied zum UNCITRAL Modellgesetz[1197] ist gem. Sec. 16 (5), (6) i. V. m. 37 (2) (a) SchiedsG eine gerichtliche Kontrolle der positiven Zuständigkeitsentscheidung[1198] des Schiedsgerichts nicht eröffnet. Sec. 16

1192 Die Gesetzesnovelle des Jahres 2015 ließ Sec. 28 (1) SchiedsG unberührt.

1193 Dies gilt für internationale Handelsschiedsverfahren als auch für inländische und internationale nicht handelsrechtliche Schiedsverfahren gleichermaßen.

1194 Law Commission of India, 176. Report, The Arbitration and Conciliation (Amendment) Bill, 2001, 12.9.2001, S. 98, 262. 1984 entschied der Supreme Court im Verfahren Renusagar *Power Company Ltd v General Electric Company And Anr* (1985 AIR SC 1156; [1984] 4 SCC 679, 16.8.1984), dass die Schiedsparteien dem Schiedsgericht die Befugnis über ihre eigene Zuständigkeit zu entscheiden, vertraglich übertragen können.

1195 Nach Sec. 37 (2) SchiedsG entscheiden die Schiedsgerichte über ihre Kompetenz-Kompetenz durch Beschluss (engl. order).

1196 Das Prinzip der Kompetenz-Kompetenz ist universell anerkannt, siehe Art. 16 (1) UNCITRAL Modellgesetz; Gaillard/Savage, Fouchard Gaillard Goldman, Rn. 650 ff.; Born, International Commercial Arbitration, Bd. 1, S. 1046 ff.; Born, Law and Practice, § 2.05 [A], S. 56; Blackaby/Partasides/Redfern/Hunter, International Arbitration, Rn. 5.105 ff.

1197 Art. 16 (3) UNCITRAL Modellgesetz.

1198 Das Schiedstribunal weist die Einrede der Unzuständigkeit zurück, es erklärt sich für zuständig und eröffnet das Schiedsverfahren. Nach Sec. 37 (2) (a) i. V. m. Sec. 16 (3) SchiedsG ist auch gegen eine zurückgewiesene Einrede der Überschreitung der schiedsgerichtlichen Zuständigkeit durch das Schiedsgericht keine Berufung zu

SchiedsG enthält die gesetzgeberische Wertung, dass gerichtliche Interventionen in den Fortgang des Schiedsverfahrens durch parallele Gerichtsverfahren zu unterbinden sind. Eine Kontrolle der bejahenden Zuständigkeitsentscheidung der Schiedsgerichte wird erst im Aufhebungsverfahren[1199] gestattet, um rechtsmissbräuchliche Verschleppungstaktiken auszuschließen[1200]. Diese Entscheidung der Legislativen kritisieren Praktiker, weil die Fortführung des Schiedsverfahrens ohne sofortige gerichtliche Kontrolle der schiedsgerichtlichen Zuständigkeitsentscheidung bei einer späteren Aufhebung des Schiedsspruchs erhebliche Kosten verursache.[1201] Dieser Kritik muss aber entgegengehalten werden, dass eine sofortige gerichtliche Kontrolle der schiedsgerichtlichen Zuständigkeitsentscheidung – wie sie Art. 16 (3) UNCITRAL Modellgesetz vorsieht – im überlasteten und ineffizienten indischen Gerichtssystem zu langwierigen parallelen Gerichtsverfahren führen würde.

b) Unzuständigkeit des Schiedsgerichts

Gegen eine abweisende schiedsgerichtliche Zuständigkeitsentscheidung kann nach Sec. 37 (2) (a) i. V. m. Sec. 16 (2) SchiedsG Berufung bei den Gerichten eingelegt werden.[1202] Für die schiedsgerichtliche Unzuständigkeitsentscheidung enthält das UNCITRAL Modellgesetz in Art. 16 keine gerichtliche Überprüfungsmöglichkeit. Von *Born* wird vertreten, dass Art. 34 (2) (a) (iv) UNCITRAL Modellgesetz analog auch auf einen zu Unrecht die Zuständigkeit des Schiedsgerichts verneinenden Prozessschiedsspruch anwendbar sei.[1203] Durch die in Sec. 37 (2) (a) i. V. m. Sec. 16 (2) SchiedsG vorgesehene gerichtliche Berufung gegen den schiedsgerichtlichen Unzuständigkeitsbeschluss[1204] bedarf es jedoch eines solchen analogen

---

einem staatlichen Gericht statthaft. Die beschwerte Partei kann aber die Aufhebung (Sec. 34 SchiedsG) des ergangenen Schiedsspruchs gem. Sec. 16 (5), (6) SchiedsG beantragen.

1199 Sec. 34 SchiedsG.

1200 Vgl. Blackaby/Partasides/Redfern/Hunter, International Arbitration, Rn. 5.114; Law Commission of India 176. Report, The Arbitration and Conciliation (Amendment) Bill, 2001, 12.9.2001, S. 102 f.

1201 Law Commission of India, 176. Report, The Arbitration and Conciliation (Amendment) Bill, 2001, 12.9.2001, S. 13.

1202 Die Entscheidung das Schiedsgericht habe seine Zuständigkeit überschritten, kann gem. Sec. 37 (2) (a) i. V. m. Sec. 16 (3) SchiedsG ebenfalls einer gerichtlichen Überprüfung unterzogen werden. Ein zweites Berufungsverfahren ist nach Sec. 37 (3) SchiedsG nur zum Supreme Court eröffnet.

1203 Born, International Commercial Arbitration, Bd. 2, S. 1098 ff. Zur Anwendung des auf Art. 34 UNCITRAL Modellgesetz beruhenden § 1059 ZPO, BGH, III ZB 44/01, SchiedsVZ 2003, S. 39 f., 6.6.2002.

1204 Engl. order.

Rückgriffs auf Sec. 34 SchiedsG in Indien nicht. In Sec. 37 (2) (a) i. V. m. Sec. 16 (2) SchiedsG traf das SchiedsG eine Schiedsverfahren fördernde Regelung, durch die den Schiedsparteien die Frage der gerichtlichen Kontrollkompetenz des Unzuständigkeitsbeschlusses mit der erforderlichen Rechtsicherheit beantwortet wird.[1205]

Die Schiedsparteien können nach einer erstinstanzlichen gerichtlichen Überprüfung des schiedsgerichtlichen Unzuständigkeitsbeschlusses[1206] gem. Sec. 37 (3) SchiedsG eine zweite Berufung ausschließlich zum Supreme Court einlegen.

c) Bewertung

Die im SchiedsG vorgesehenen Überprüfungsmöglichkeiten der Zuständigkeits- bzw. Unzuständigkeits-Entscheidung der Schiedsgerichte offenbaren positive und negative Seiten. Negativ zu bewerten ist, dass die Entscheidung der Schiedsgerichte über ihre eigene Unzuständigkeit in zwei Instanzen von den Gerichten überprüft werden dürfen[1207], was zu langjährigen Gerichtsverfahren führen kann. Die Kontrollmöglichkeit der Unzuständigkeitsentscheidung weicht zwar vom UNCITRAL Modellgesetz ab, ist aber dennoch positiv hervorzuheben, da sie dem internationalen Standard der Schiedsgerichtsbarkeit[1208] entspricht und Rechtssicherheit schafft. Im Kontext des ineffizienten indischen Gerichtssystems ist es darüber hinaus als Schiedsverfahren fördernd zu bewerten, dass die Zuständigkeitsentscheidung des Schiedsgerichts – im Gegensatz zum UNCITRAL Modellgesetz – erst nach Erlass des Schiedsspruchs im Aufhebungsverfahren kontrolliert werden kann[1209]. Dies soll Interventionen der Gerichte in das Schiedsverfahren verhindern. Im Ergebnis überwiegt die Schiedsverfahren unterstützende Haltung der Schiedsgesetzgebung bei der gerichtlichen Überprüfung der Kompetenz-Kompetenz der Schiedsgerichte.

1205 Zu den negativen Konsequenzen einer fehlenden gerichtlichen Kontrollmöglichkeit der verneinenden schiedsgerichtlichen Zuständigkeitsentscheidung, siehe Kapitel: Singapur; Kompetenz-Kompetenz; Unzuständigkeitsentscheidung (B.II.3.).

1206 Sec. 37 (2) (a) i. V. m. Sec. 16 (2) SchiedsG.

1207 Das UNCITRAL Modellgesetz sieht in Art. 16 (3) bei der positiven Zuständigkeitsentscheidung lediglich eine gerichtliche Kontrollinstanz vor.

1208 Born, International Commercial Arbitration, Bd. 1, S. 1101 ff.

1209 Sec. 16 (5), (6) i. V. m. Sec. 34 SchiedsG. Gegen die gerichtliche Entscheidung im Aufhebungsverfahren nach Sec. 34 SchiedsG gestattet Sec. 37 (1) SchiedsG eine weitere Berufungsmöglichkeit.

2. Verletzung der Kompetenz-Kompetenz bei der Schiedsrichterbestellung

a) Konkan Railway v Rani Construction

Eine mit fünf Richtern besetzte Constitutional Bench des Supreme Courts hatte in der Rechtssache *Konkan Railway Corporation Ltd & Anr v Rani Construction Pvt Ltd*[1210] zu entscheiden, ob der Chief Justice des Supreme- oder des High Courts bzw. eine von ihm ernannte Stelle bei der Schiedsrichterbestellung streitige Rechtsfragen hinsichtlich der Schiedsvereinbarung überprüfen dürfen.[1211] Die Constitutional Bench erkannte in ihrer Entscheidung 2002 erstmals höchstrichterlich die in Sec. 16 (1) SchiedsG vorgesehene Kompetenz-Kompetenz ausdrücklich an:

> „*Section 16 provides for this. It states that the arbitral tribunal may rule on its own jurisdiction. That the arbitral tribunal may rule ‚on any objections with respect to the existence or validity of the arbitration agreement' shows that the arbitral tribunal's authority under Section 16 is not confined to the width of its jurisdiction* […] *but goes to the very root of its jurisdiction.*"[1212]

b) SBP v Patel Engineering (Patel Engineering)

2005 urteilte eine siebenköpfige Constitutional Bench des Supreme Courts in der Entscheidung *SBP & Co v Patel Engineering Ltd & Anr* (*Patel Engineering)*[1213] erneut über die Reichweite der Kompetenz-Kompetenz der Schiedsgerichte. Das oberste indische Gericht hatte zu beurteilen, ob bei der Schiedsrichterbestellung nach Sec. 11 SchiedsG a. F. durch den Chief Jus-

---

1210 AIR 2002 SC 778; (2002) 2 SCC 388; Appeal (civil) 5880–5889 of 1997, 30.1.2002. Die Entscheidung bewertet die Literatur positiv, Nair, Arbitration International 2007, Vol. 23, Ausg. 4, S. 699 (721 f.); Biswas, International Arbitration Law Review 2010, S. 42 (46).

1211 Die Constitutional Bench überprüfte ausschließlich die ihr gestellte Rechtsfrage, Tatsachen lagen dem Verfahren nicht zu Grunde. Die Constitutional Bench des Supreme Courts sah die Schiedsrichterbestellung als verwaltungsrechtlichen Beschluss des Chief Justice oder einer von ihm ernannten Stelle an. Sie entscheid, dass durch diese Ernennungspersonen lediglich die Schiedsrichterbestellung erfolgen solle und alle weiteren, zwischen den Parteien streitigen Rechtsfragen, vom Schiedsgericht entschieden werden sollten. Der Entscheidung beipflichtend, Biswas, International Arbitration Law Review 2010, S. 42 (46).

1212 Appeal (civil) 5880–5889 of 1997, S. 11 f.

1213 AIR 2006 SC 450; (2005) 8 SCC 618; Appeal (civil) 4168 of 2003, 26.10.2005. Der Supreme Court hatte lediglich eine Rechtsfrage zu entscheiden, einen Tatbestand enthält das Urteil nicht.

tice[1214] oder die stellvertretende ernennende Stelle diese die Wirksamkeit der Schiedsvereinbarung kontrollieren dürfen. In ihrem Urteil untergrub die Constitutional Bench wesentliche Teile der Kompetenz-Kompetenz der Schiedsgerichte. Im Rahmen der Verweisung der Streitigkeit nach Sec. 8 SchiedsG und bei der Schiedsrichterbestellung gem. Sec. 11 SchiedsG sei es den Gerichten gestattet, die Existenz und die Wirksamkeit der Schiedsvereinbarung verbindlich zu beurteilen. Dabei sei das Schiedsgericht an die Entscheidung des zuständigen Gerichts gebunden. Das Schiedsgericht könne seine in Sec. 16 (1) SchiedsG gesetzlich garantierte Kompetenz-Kompetenz nur vollumfänglich ausüben, wenn sich das Schiedsgericht ohne gerichtliche Verweisung i. S. d. Sec. 8 SchiedsG und ohne gerichtliche Schiedsrichterbestellung gem. Sec. 11 SchiedsG konstituieren konnte[1215]:

> „*Section 16 is said to be the recognition of the principle of Kompetenz-Kompetenz. The fact that the arbitral tribunal has the competence to rule on its own jurisdiction and to define the contours of its jurisdiction, only means that when such issues arise before it, the Tribunal can and possibly, ought to decide them. This can happen when the parties have gone to the arbitral tribunal without recourse to Section 8 or 11 of the Act. But where the jurisdictional issues are decided under these Sections, before a reference is made, Section 16 cannot be held to empower the arbitral tribunal to ignore the decision given by the judicial authority or the Chief Justice before the reference to it was made.*“[1216]

Durch diese Entscheidung gab die mit sieben Richtern besetzte Constitutional Bench des Supreme Courts die von der fünfköpfigen Constitutional Bench in der Rechtssache *Konkan Railway Corporation Ltd & Anr v Rani Construction Pvt Ltd* vertretene Rechtsauffassung auf und beschnitt die in Sec. 16 SchiedsG niedergeschriebene Kompetenz-Kompetenz erheblich.

c) Bewertung

Seit der im Jahre 2002 durch die mit fünf Richtern besetzte Constitutional Bench ergangenen Entscheidung *Konkan Railway Corporation Ltd & Anr v Rani Construction Pvt Ltd* war es gefestigte Rechtsprechung[1217] gewesen,

---

1214 Nach Sec. 11 SchiedsG a. F. war der Chief Justice des Supreme Courts bzw. des High Courts für die Schiedsrichterbestellung zuständig, siehe Kapitel: Schiedsrichter (C. V.).

1215 Siehe auch Rn. 43.

1216 Rn. 19.

1217 Supreme Court, *Narayan Prasad Lohia v Nikunj Kumar Lohia & Ors*, AIR 2002 SC 1139; (2002) 3 SCC 572; Appeal (civil) 1382 of 2002, 20.2.2002; Supreme Court, *Shree Subhlaxmi Fabrics Pvt Ltd v Chand Mal Baradia And Others*, AIR 2005 SC 2161; (2005) 10 SCC 704; Appeal (civil) 7653 of 2004, 29.3.2005.

dass die Kompetenz-Kompetenz der Schiedsgerichte anzuerkennen war.[1218] Diese Rechtsprechung stimmte mit dem internationalen Schiedsgerichtsstandard überein, wonach die Schiedsgerichte über ihre eigene Zuständigkeit selbst entscheiden sollten.[1219] Die von der siebenköpfigen Constitutional Bench getroffene *Patel Engineering*-Entscheidung eröffnete den Gerichten die Möglichkeit, die Kompetenz-Kompetenz der Schiedsgerichte signifikant einzuschränken. Die von Sec. 16 (1) SchiedsG vorgesehene Kompetenz-Kompetenz kam ausschließlich in Konstellationen zu ihrer vollen Geltung, in denen die Parteien direkt das Schiedsgericht anriefen, ohne dass zuvor eine Verweisung der Streitigkeit an das Schiedsgericht gem. Sec. 8 SchiedsG a. F. oder eine Schiedsrichterbestellung nach Sec. 11 SchiedsG a. F. stattgefunden hatte. Die Bindung der Schiedsgerichte an die gerichtliche Entscheidung über die Wirksamkeit der Schiedsvereinbarung schränkte die Autonomie der Schiedsgerichte ein. Sie konnten nicht unabhängig über die eigene Zuständigkeit befinden, da hierzu auch die Frage zählt, ob überhaupt eine wirksame Schiedsvereinbarung zwischen den Schiedsparteien besteht.

Das *Patel Engineering*-Urteil zeigt, dass die indischen Gerichte dem alternativen Streitbeilegungsmechanismus der Schiedsgerichtsbarkeit nicht vertrauen, sondern das letzte Wort bei der Entscheidung über die Wirksamkeit der Schiedsvereinbarung haben wollen.[1220] Die im Urteil geschaffene gerichtliche Kontrollkompetenz intervenierte in Schiedsverfahren und führte zu Verzögerungen bei der Durchführung von Schiedsverfahren.[1221] Die *Pa-*

1218 Die Anerkennung der Kompetenz-Kompetenz bewertet die Literatur positive, Biswas, S. 59; Kachwaha, Asian International Arbitration Journal 2005, Vol. 1, Ausg. 2, S. 105 (114 f.).

1219 Art. 16 (1) UNCITRAL Modellgesetz; Gaillard/Savage, Fouchard Gaillard Goldman, Rn. 650 ff.; Born, International Commercial Arbitration, Bd. 1, S. 1046 ff.; Born, Law and Practice, § 2.05 [A], S. 56; Blackaby/Partasides/Redfern/Hunter, International Arbitration, Rn. 5.105 ff.

1220 Sharma, Sidharth, Journal of International Arbitration 2006, Vol. 23, Ausg. 5, S. 467 (471 ff.); Dewan, Nakul, Asian International Arbitration Journal 2007, Vol. 3, Ausg. 1, S. 99 (110 ff.).

1221 Vgl. Dewan, Nakul, Asian International Arbitration Journal 2007, Vol. 3, Ausg. 1, S. 99 (101 ff.); Sharma, Sidharth, Journal of International Arbitration 2006, Vol. 23, Ausg. 5, S. 467 (471 ff.). Durch das ineffektive indische Gerichtssystem konnten im Schiedsverfahren unterliegende Parteien, aus prozesstaktischen Gründen, durch die umfassende Kontrolle der Schiedsvereinbarung, absichtlich das Schiedsverfahren sabotieren, um die Streitbeilegung zu verzögern, Ray, Aloke/Sabharwal, MEALEY'S International Arbitration Report 2007, Vol. 22, S. 26 (29); Dewan, Nakul, Asian International Arbitration Journal 2007, Vol. 3, Ausg. 1, S. 99 (110 ff.). Zu den Verzögerungen durch die Schiedsrichterbestellung unter dem *Patel Engineering*-Urteil, siehe ausführlich Srinivasan, Indian Journal of Arbitration Law 2012, Vol. I, Ausg. 1, S. 18 ff.; siehe hierzu auch Malhotra, O. P., Arbitration 2004, S. 177 (182). Zum Miss-

tel Engineering-Entscheidung verletzt auch das Gebot aus Sec. 5 SchiedsG, einzig in vom SchiedsG vorgesehenen Konstellationen in das Schiedsverfahren einzugreifen.[1222] Weder Sec. 8 noch Sec. 11 SchiedsG a. F. lässt sich eine Überprüfungskompetenz der Schiedsvereinbarung durch die Gerichte entnehmen. Vielmehr entschied sich der Gesetzgeber dafür, die in Art. 8 UNCITRAL Modellgesetz vorgesehene gerichtliche Kontrolle der Schiedsvereinbarung in Sec. 8 SchiedsG nicht zu übernehmen. Durch das *Patel Engineering*-Urteil verkehrte der Supreme Court diesen gesetzgeberischen Willen ins Gegenteil. Die Constitutional Bench hätte in der *Patel Engineering*-Entscheidung daher besser dem Urteil *Konkan Railway Corporation Ltd & Anr v Rani Construction Pvt Ltd* folgen und die Kompetenz-Kompetenz der Schiedsgerichte stärken sollen, anstatt deren Zuständigkeit auszuhöhlen. Der Supreme Court näherte sich zudem durch die schiedsunfreundliche Verletzung der Kompetenz-Kompetenz wieder der Rechtslage unter dem Arbitration Act 1940 an. Der Arbitration Act 1940 achtete die Kompetenz-Kompetenz des Schiedsgerichts ebenfalls nicht.[1223] Dies widerspricht dem Geiste des SchiedsG 1996. Ziel des SchiedsG 1996 war es, die mannigfaltigen Interventionsmöglichkeiten der Gerichte in Schiedsverfahren und die daraus resultierenden rechtsmissbräuchlichen, langwierigen und kostenintensiven parallelen gerichtlichen Verfahren unter dem Arbitration Act 1940 zu beenden.[1224] Unter der *Patel Engineering*-Rechtsprechung konnten die Schiedsparteien hingegen mittels eines Verfahrens vor staatlichen Gerichten (Sec. 8 SchiedsG) oder durch die Schiedsrichternichtbestellung (Sec. 11 SchiedsG) die Kompetenz-Kompetenz des Schiedsgerichts einseitig einschränken. Diese Interventionsoption für die Parteien ist mit dem parteiautonom vereinbarten Schiedsverfahren inkompatibel, weil die Parteien durch das Schiedsverfahren aus dem staatlichen Gerichtssystem weitgehend herausoptiert haben.

Auch in der Literatur wird das *Patel Engineering*-Urteil wegen der durch die gerichtliche Eingriffskompetenz verletzten Kompetenz-Kompetenz des Schiedsgerichts und der hiermit verbundenen Verzögerungsmöglichkeiten kritisiert.[1225]

---

trauen gegenüber der Schiedsgerichtsbarkeit, Kachwaha, International Arbitration Law Review 2007, S. 13 (16 f.).

1222 Malhotra, Indu, O. P. Malhotra on Arbitration, Sec. 11, S. 633; Sec. 16, S. 774; Panjwani/Pathak, Indian Journal of Arbitration Law 2013, Vol. II, Ausg. 2, S. 1 (13 ff.).

1223 Zur alten Rechtslage unter dem Arbitration Act 1940, Malhotra, Indu, O. P. Malhotra on Arbitration, Sec. 16, S. 761; Madhya Pradesh High Court, *M P Housing Board And Anr v Satish Kumar Raizada*, 2003 (2) Arb LR 553 (MP), 22.11.2002.

1224 Panjwani/Pathak, Indian Journal of Arbitration Law 2013, Vol. II, Ausg. 2, S. 1 (13 ff.).

1225 Dewan, Nakul, Asian International Arbitration Journal 2007, Vol. 3, Ausg. 1, S. 99 (110 ff.); Malhotra, O. P., Student Bar Review 2007, Vol. 19, Ausg. 2, S. 69 ff.; Malho-

Die Constitutional Bench wäre in der *Patel Engineering*-Entscheidung entsprechend besser beraten gewesen, der „Dissenting Opinion“ von Richter *C. K. Thakker*[1226] und *P. K. Balasubramanyan* zu folgen, die der Kompetenz-Kompetenz des Schiedsgerichts Wirkung verlieh. Nach der Dissenting Opinion obliege die Wirksamkeitskontrolle der Schiedsvereinbarung dem Schiedsgericht. Sofern das Schiedsgericht eine positive Zuständigkeitsentscheidung treffe, solle das Schiedsverfahren fortgeführt und diese Entscheidung erst im Aufhebungsverfahren[1227] gerichtlich überprüft werden können.[1228] Dies entspricht der Wertung des SchiedsG, das ausschließlich die nachträgliche Überprüfung der bejahten Kompetenz-Kompetenz vorsieht[1229], aber keine vorgreifende gerichtliche Kontrolle unter Sec. 16, 11, 8 SchiedsG gestattet.

Im Schrifttum wird die Akzeptanz der vom Gesetzgeber vorgesehenen Kompetenz-Kompetenz des Schiedsgerichts in der „Dissenting Opinion“ begrüßt und daraufhin gewiesen, dass dies den Anforderungen der Schiedsgerichtsbarkeit und den Bedürfnissen der Wirtschaft entspreche.[1230]

---

tra, Indu, O. P. Malhotra on Arbitration, Sec. 11, S. 633 f.; Sec. 16, S. 773 f.; Sen, Vindobona Journal of International Commercial Law & Arbitration 2006, S. 45 (50 ff.); Ray, Aloke/Sabharwal, MEALEY'S International Arbitration Report 2007, Vol. 22, S. 26 (29); Kachwaha, International Arbitration Law Review 2007, S. 13 (14 ff.); Srinivasan, Indian Journal of Arbitration Law 2012, Vol. I, Ausg. 1, S. 18 ff. Zu der Verletzung der Kompetenz-Kompetenz, Sathyapalan, Arbitration International 2016, S. 1 (6). Zu der Kritik an dem Urteil, Biswas, S. 31; Panjwani/Pathak, Indian Journal of Arbitration Law 2013, Vol. II, Ausg. 2, S. 1 (6 ff.); Sharma, Sidharth, Journal of International Arbitration 2006, Vol. 23, Ausg. 5, S. 467 (471 ff.). Zur Kritik an dem Urteil siehe auch Kapitel: Verweisung des gerichtlichen Verfahrens an das Schiedsverfahren; Bewertung (C.IV.1.e)) und Kapitel: Schiedsrichterbestellung; Bewertung (C.V.2.b)). Im Schrifttum wird kritisch angemerkt, dass Sec. 16 SchiedsG durch die *Patel Engineering*-Rechtsprechung in einer Weise modifiziert werde, die nicht dem gesetzgeberischen Willen entspreche, Parthasarathy/Visalakshi, Arbitration 2007, S. 394 ff.; Kachwaha, International Arbitration Law Review 2007, S. 13 (16 f.); Sharma, Avinash/Trivedi, International Arbitration Law Review 2010, S. 27 ff.; Bansal, Bharat's Commentary, Bd. 1, Sec. 16, S. 321.

1226 Zur Vorzugswürdigkeit des Minderheitsvotums, Sen, Vindobona Journal of International Commercial Law & Arbitration 2006, S. 45 (50 ff.); Sharma, Avinash/Trivedi, International Arbitration Law Review 2010, S. 27 (34); Biswas, International Company and Commercial Law Review 2011, S. 165 (170); Biswas, International Arbitration Law Review 2010, S. 42 (48).

1227 Sec. 34 SchiedsG.

1228 Rn. 44.

1229 Sec. 16 (5), (6), 34 SchiedsG.

1230 Biswas, S. 31, 63; vgl. Sen, Vindobona Journal of International Commercial Law & Arbitration 2006, S. 45 (50 ff.). *Ray/Sabharwal* erachten die „Dissenting Opinion“ als vorzugswürdig, Ray, Aloke/Sabharwal, MEALEY'S International Arbitration Report 2007, Vol. 22, S. 26 (29).

3. Arbitration Amendment Act

Nach dem 246. Report der Law Commission aus dem Jahr 2014 bedurfte das SchiedsG nach der Entscheidung *Patel Engineering* einer Korrektur, um wieder schiedsfreundliche Rahmenbedingungen in Indien herzustellen. Für eine Gesetzesreform von Sec. 8 und Sec. 11 SchiedsG schlug der 246. Report der Law Commission vor, dass die Gerichte nur noch *prima facie* die Existenz und die Wirksamkeit der Schiedsvereinbarung überprüfen dürfen und die letztendliche Entscheidung dem Schiedsgericht gem. Sec. 16 SchiedsG überlassen werden sollte.[1231]

Im Arbitration Amendment Act regelte der Gesetzgeber in Sec. 11 (6A) SchiedsG n. F. hingegen, dass die zuständigen Gerichte[1232] bei der Schiedsrichterbestellung nach Sec. 11 SchiedsG auf die Kontrolle beschränkt sind, ob zwischen den Parteien überhaupt eine Schiedsvereinbarung besteht. Eine inhaltliche Überprüfung der Schiedsvereinbarung ist nicht zulässig. Sec. 8 (1) SchiedsG n. F. erlaubt den Gerichten lediglich eine *prima facie*-Kontrolle der Schiedsvereinbarung.

Sec. 8 und 11 SchiedsG n. F. beseitigen die durch die *Patel Engineering*-Rechtsprechung geschaffene Interventionskompetenz der indischen Gerichte und die damit verbundenen langjährigen Gerichtsverfahren. Eine von einer Schiedsvereinbarung erfasste Streitigkeit soll von den Gerichten nur ausnahmsweise nicht an das einschlägige Schiedsverfahren verwiesen werden. Der Arbitration Amendment Act ist als schiedsfreundliche Gesetzesänderung anzusehen, weil er die Wirksamkeitskontrolle der Schiedsvereinbarung wieder den Schiedsgerichten übertrug. Es bleibt zu hoffen, dass sich die indische Gerichtsbarkeit in der Zukunft an diese gesetzlichen Schranken gerichtlicher Kontrolle hält und die Kompetenz-Kompetenz des Schiedsgerichts respektiert.

1231 Siehe Government of India, Law Commission of India, 246. Report, Amendments to the Arbitration and Conciliation Act 1996, 5.8.2014, S. 42 f., 45. In der Literatur wird ebenfalls lediglich eine *prima facie*-Kontrolle der Schiedsvereinbarung gefordert, Biswas, S. 31; Panjwani/Pathak, Indian Journal of Arbitration Law 2013, Vol. II, Ausg. 2, S. 1 (15 ff., 27); Sharma, Sidharth, Journal of International Arbitration 2006, Vol. 23, Ausg. 5, S. 467 (476 ff.); Malhotra, O. P., Student Bar Review 2007, Vol. 19, Ausg. 2, S. 69 (73); Sharma, Avinash/Trivedi, International Arbitration Law Review 2010, S. 27 (34).

1232 An Stelle des Chief Justice des High Courts und des Chief Justice des Supreme Courts ist seit der Schiedsgesetzgebungsreform aus dem Jahr 2015 gem. Sec. 11 SchiedsG n. F. der High Court und der Supreme Court zuständig. Das zuständige Gericht kann die Schiedsrichterbestellung gem. Sec. 11 SchiedsG n. F. auch an eine Person bzw. Institution weiter delegieren.

III. Unabhängigkeit der Schiedsvereinbarung

Die Schiedsvereinbarung ist in Sec. 7 SchiedsG geregelt und umfasst sowohl Schiedsklauseln als Teil eines Hauptvertrages sowie selbstständige Schiedsvereinbarungen[1233]. Die Wirksamkeit der Schiedsklausel und des sie enthaltenden Hauptvertrages werden gem. Sec. 16 (1) SchiedsG unabhängig voneinander beurteilt.[1234] Im alten Arbitration Act 1940 war diese Unabhängigkeit der Schiedsklausel vom Hauptvertrag noch nicht normiert.

1. Gerichtliche Entscheidungen

a) National Agricultural Co-Op v Gains Trading

Im Urteil *National Agricultural Co-Op v Gains Trading Ltd*[1235] entschied der Supreme Court im Jahr 2007 über einen Antrag auf Bestellung eines Einzelschiedsrichters gem. Sec. 11 (5) SchiedsG a. F.

Dem Tatbestand des Urteils lässt sich entnehmen, dass *National Agricultural Co-Op (National)* an *Gains Trading Ltd (Gains)* Eisenerz unter dem „FOB[1236]-Incoterm" verkauft hatte. Der FOB-Eisenerzvertrag enthielt eine Schiedsklausel.

National trug vor, dass *Gains* kein Schiff für den Eisenerz-Transport bestimmt und dadurch die Lieferung des Eisenerzes verhindert habe. Den hierdurch entstandenen Schaden wollte *National* im eingeleiteten Schiedsverfahren geltend machen. *National* übersandte *Gains* zudem eine Liste von Schiedsrichtervorschlägen für den zu bestellenden Einzelschiedsrichter. *Gains* plädierte, dass es sehr wohl ein Schiff für den Transport des Eisenerzes bestimmt habe, dass *National* dieses Schiff aber zu spät akzeptiert habe und der Hafen daraufhin wegen des einsetzenden Monsuns geschlossen gewesen sei. *Gains* trug darüber hinaus vor, dass eine Durchführung des Kaufvertrages nach dem „FOB-Incoterm" nicht mehr möglich gewesen sei. Die Parteien hätten sich daher auf den Abschluss eines neuen Vertrages geeinigt,

1233 Auch als Schiedsabrede bezeichnet.

1234 Dies steht im Einklang mit Art. 16 (1) UNCITRAL Modellgesetz.

1235 1 Richter, AIR 2007 SC 2327; (2007) 5 SCC 692; Arbitration Petition 15 of 2006, 22.5.2007.

1236 ICC Germany, Standards & Regelwerke, Incoterms 2010, FOB, „'Free On Board'/'Frei an Bord' bedeutet, dass der Verkäufer die Ware an Bord des vom Käufer benannten Schiffs im benannten Verschiffungshafen liefert oder die bereits so gelieferte Ware verschafft. Die Gefahr des Verlustes oder der Beschädigung der Ware geht über, wenn die Ware an Bord des Schiffs ist. Der Käufer trägt ab diesem Zeitpunkt alle Kosten." Verfügbar unter http://www.iccgermany.de/standards-regelwerke/incoterms/ (zuletzt abgerufen am 28.4.2021).

in dem sie die Lieferung des Eisenerzes nach dem „Incoterm CFR“[1237] vereinbarten. *Gains* berief sich deshalb auf die Unwirksamkeit der Schiedsklausel aus dem FOB-Vertrag und beteiligte sich nicht an der Schiedsrichterbestellung.

Im Rahmen der Schiedsrichterbestellung hatte der Supreme Court zu beurteilen, ob eine Schiedsklausel unwirksam wird, wenn die Parteien den sie enthaltenden Vertrag aufgehoben haben[1238]. Das oberste Gericht Indiens entschied, dass eine Schiedsklausel gem. Sec. 16 (1) SchiedsG in ihrer Wirksamkeit unabhängig von der Gültigkeit des Hauptvertrages sei. Die Ungültigkeit des Hauptvertrages führe entsprechend nicht *ipso jure* zur Unwirksamkeit der im Hauptvertrag enthaltenen Schiedsklausel.[1239]

b) World Sport Group v MSM Satellite

Im Verfahren *World Sport Group (Mauritius) Ltd v MSM Satellite (Singapore) Pte Ltd*[1240] hatte der Supreme Court darüber zu entscheiden, ob die rechtliche Würdigung der Schiedsvereinbarung unabhängig von dem sie enthaltenden Hauptvertrag erfolgt.

Der indische Cricketverband (engl. Board of Control for Cricket) vereinbarte mit *World Sport Group (World)* eine Lizenz für die Medienrechte an der „Indian Premier League“ – ein Wettbewerb indischer Cricket Mannschaften – für den indischen Subkontinent. Die Lizenzvereinbarung stand unter der Bedingung, dass *World* innerhalb von 72 Stunden einen Unterlizenznehmer[1241] findet. Diese Frist wurde zwei Mal verlängert, ohne dass *World* einen Unterlizenznehmer benennen konnte. Durch Vermittlung von *World* kam es später zu einem Lizenzvertrag für diese Medienrechte zwischen dem indischen Cricketverband und *MSM Satellite (MSM)*. In einem

1237 ICC Germany, Standards & Regelwerke, Incoterms 2010, CFR, „‚Cost and Freight‘/‚Kosten und Fracht‘ bedeutet, dass der Verkäufer die Ware an Bord des Schiffs liefert oder die bereits so gelieferte Ware verschafft. Die Gefahr des Verlustes oder der Beschädigung der Ware geht über, wenn die Ware an Bord des Schiffs ist. Der Verkäufer hat den Beförderungsvertrag abzuschließen und die Kosten und Fracht zu tragen, die für die Beförderung der Ware zum benannten Bestimmungshafen erforderlich sind.“ Verfügbar unter http://www.iccgermany.de/standards-regelwerke/incoterms/ (zuletzt abgerufen am 28.4.2021).

1238 Auf das Urteil war die Constitutional Bench Entscheidung *SBP v Patel Engineering (Patel Engineering)* aus dem Jahr 2005 anwendbar. Das *Patel Engineering*-Urteil eröffnete den Gerichten bei der Schiedsrichterbestellung die Kontrolle der Schiedsvereinbarung, vgl. Kapitel: Schiedsrichterbestellung; SBP v Patel Engineering (Patel Engineering) (C. V.2.a)).

1239 Rn. 6.

1240 2 Richter, AIR 2014 SC 968; (2014) 11 SCC 639; Civil Appeal No. 895 of 2014, 24.1.2014.

1241 Engl. sub-licensee.

Vermittlungsvertrag[1242] vereinbarte *World* mit *MSM*, dass dafür eine Vermittlungsgebühr[1243] an *World* zu entrichten war. Der Vermittlungsvertrag enthielt eine Schiedsklausel, nach der alle Vertragsstreitigkeiten in einem ICC-Schiedsverfahren mit Sitz in Singapur beigelegt werden sollten. *MSM* zahlte die Vermittlungsgebühr nur teilweise und focht den Vermittlungsvertrag wegen Falschdarstellung[1244] und Betrugs an. *World* behauptete, dass es ihre Medienrechte für den indischen Subkontinent erlöschen ließ, um später den Medienrechtsvertrag zwischen dem indischen Cricketverband und *MSM* zu vermitteln. *MSM* machte andererseits geltend, dass *World* durch den Bedingungsablauf bei Abschluss des Vermittlungsvertrags nicht mehr Inhaber der Medienrechte gewesen sei. *World* habe deshalb fälschlicherweise vorspiegelt, Inhaber der Medienrechte der „Indian Premier League" zu sein und auf diese Medienrechte zu Gunsten eines vermittelten Erwerbs der Medienrechte durch *MSM* verzichtet zu haben. *World* leitete im Juni 2010 das in der Schiedsklausel vorgesehene ICC-Schiedsverfahren ein. Neben einer Feststellungsklage[1245] beantragte *MSM* im Juni 2010 beim Bombay High Court eine einstweilige Maßnahme gegen das ICC-Schiedsverfahren.

Der zuständige Einzelrichter des High Courts wies den Antrag auf Erlass einer vorläufigen Maßnahme im August 2010 zurück. Ob der Vermittlungsvertrag unwirksam sei, müsse vom ICC-Schiedsgericht entschieden werden. Im September 2010 hob eine Division Bench des Bombay High Courts im Berufungsverfahren den Beschluss des Einzelrichters auf und erließ eine einstweilige Maßnahme, in der die Division Bench die Fortführung des ICC-Schiedsverfahrens untersagte.

Im Berufungsurteil vom 24.1.2014 überzeugte den Supreme Court die englische Entscheidung des House of Lords in der Rechtssache *Premium Nafta Products Ltd v Fili Shipping Company Ltd & Ors*[1246], nach der die Unwirksamkeit des Hauptvertrages nicht zwingend zur Ungültigkeit der im Hauptvertrag enthaltenen Schiedsklausel führe. Nach dem Supreme Court müsse die Schiedsklausel daher als gesonderter Vertrag angesehen werden, der nur aus Gründen unwirksam oder aufhebbar sei, die direkt mit der Schiedsklausel verknüpft sind.[1247] Für den vorliegenden Fall folgerte der Supreme Court, dass ein möglicherweise bestehendes Anfechtungsrecht des Vermittlungsvertrages von *MSM* und dessen Ausübung durch das Schreiben

---

1242 Engl. facilitation deed.

1243 Engl. facilitation fee.

1244 Engl. misrepresentation.

1245 *MSM* reichte beim Bombay High Court eine Klage ein, in der festgestellt werden sollte, dass der Vermittlungsvertrag nichtig sei und *World* sich nicht auf die Schiedsklausel im Vermittlungsvertrag berufen könne.

1246 House of Lords, [2007] UKHL 40; [2007] 4 All E. R. 951, 17.10.2007.

1247 Civil Appeal No. 895 of 2014, Rn. 24.

vom 25.6.2010 nicht die Unwirksamkeit der im Vermittlungsvertrag enthaltenen Schiedsklausel bewirke. Die Gültigkeit der Schiedsklausel sei demzufolge unabhängig und getrennt von der Wirksamkeit des Vermittlungsvertrages (engl. facilitation deed) zu beurteilen:

> „*This ground of challenge to the Facilitation Deed does not in any manner affect the arbitration agreement contained in Clause 9 of the Facilitation Deed, which is independent of and separate from the main Facilitation Deed and does not get rescinded as void by the letter dated 25.06.2010 of the respondent.*"[1248]

Das Schrifttum nahm das Urteil *World Sport Group (Mauritius) Ltd v MSM Satellite (Singapore) Pte Ltd* positiv auf und beurteilt es als schiedsfreundlich.[1249] Begrüßt werden an dem Urteil die verringerten Eingriffskompetenzen der Gerichte und die hiermit einhergehenden reduzierten Verzögerungen des Verfahrensablaufs. Durch das Urteil habe der Supreme Court Indiens Attraktivität für ausländische Investoren gesteigert.[1250]

In ständiger Rechtsprechung erkannte der Supreme Court auch im Übrigen die Unabhängigkeit der Schiedsklausel vom Hauptvertrag an.[1251]

2. Bewertung

Die in Sec. 16 (1) SchiedsG geregelte separate Wirksamkeitsbeurteilung von Schiedsklausel und Hauptvertrag entspricht dem rezipierten Art. 16 (1) UNCITRAL Modellgesetz und der globalen Norm des Schiedsgerichtswesens[1252]. Auch die Rechtsprechung erkennt die Unabhängigkeit der Schieds-

---

1248 Civil Appeal No. 895 of 2014, Rn. 25.

1249 Sindhu, Indian Journal of Arbitration Law 2014, Vol. III, Ausg. 2, S. 23 (42); Sharma, Ajay, Indian Journal of Arbitration Law 2014, Vol. III, Ausg. 1, S. 6 (25 f.); Malhotra, Indu, O. P. Malhotra on Arbitration, Anti-arbitration Injunctions, S. 1972; Sathyapalan, Arbitration International 2016, S. 1 (14); Mahajan, International Arbitration Law Review 2014, S. N9 ff.

1250 Mahajan, International Arbitration Law Review 2014, S. N9 ff.

1251 Supreme Court, *M/S P Manohar Reddy & Bros v Maharashtra Krishna Valley*, AIR 2009 SC 1776; Civil Appeal Nos. 7408–7409 of 2008, 18.12.2008; Supreme Court, *M/S Magma Leasing & Fin Ltd & Anr v Potluri Madhavilata & Anr*, (2009) 10 SCC 103; Civil Appeal No. 6399 of 2009, 18.9.2009; Supreme Court, *M/S Reva Electric Car Co P Ltd v M/S Green Mobil*, (2012) 2 SCC 93; Arbitration Petition No. 18 of 2010, 25.11.2011; Supreme Court, *Enercon (India) Ltd And Ors v Enercon Gmbh And Anr*, AIR 2014 SC 3152; Civil Appeal No. 2086 of 2014, 14.2.2014.

1252 Art. 178 (3) Schweizer Bundesgesetz über das Internationale Privatrecht; Art. 1447 (1) französischer Code de procédure civile; Sec. 6 (2) englischer Arbitration Act 1996; Sec. 34 (1) Hongkonger Arbitration Ordinance; Born, International Commercial Arbitration, Bd. 1, S. 349 ff.; Blackaby/Partasides/Redfern/Hunter, International Arbitration, Rn. 2.101 ff.; Schlosser, in Stein/Jonas, § 1040 ZPO Rn. 5, 11.

klausel von den übrigen Vertragsbestimmungen an. Die indische Rechtsordnung akzeptiert folglich die Unabhängigkeit der Schiedsklausel vom Hauptvertrag, der sie enthält und unterstützt hierdurch die Schiedsgerichtsbarkeit.

Der Arbitration Amendment Act 2015 änderte die Unabhängigkeit der Schiedsklausel in Sec. 16 (1) SchiedsG nicht.[1253] Auf Grund der schiedsfreundlichen Gesetzeslage und Rechtsprechung war dies nicht erforderlich.

IV. Verweisung des gerichtlichen Verfahrens an das Schiedsverfahren

1. Schiedssitz in Indien

Sec. 8 SchiedsG[1254] ordnet bei Vorliegen eines durch eine Schiedsvereinbarung erfassten gerichtlich rechtshängigen Streitgegenstandes und eines Verweisungsantrages für Schiedsverfahren mit Sitz in Indien die zwingende[1255] Verweisung des Streitgegenstandes an das schiedsrichterliche Verfahren an.[1256] Nach Art. 8 (1) UNCITRAL Modellgesetz ist eine vor einem Gericht in einer Angelegenheit erhobene Klage, die von einer Schiedsvereinbarung erfasst wird, auf Parteiantrag ebenfalls obligatorisch[1257] an das vereinbarte Schiedsverfahren zu verweisen. Das Gericht kann aber die Schiedsvereinbarung gem. Art. 8 (1) UNCITRAL Modellgesetz darauf überprüfen, ob sie nichtig, unwirksam oder undurchführbar ist. In Art. 8 (1) UNCITRAL Modellgesetz ist der „negative Effekt" einer Schiedsvereinbarung verankert, der besagt, dass ein Gericht eine denselben Streitgegenstand erfassende Schiedsvereinbarung durchzusetzen muss. Das Gericht muss das vor ihm

---

1253 Der Arbitration Amendment Act sieht für Sec. 16 SchiedsG keine Änderungen vor.

1254 Im Gegensatz hierzu sprach Sec. 34 Arbitration Act 1940 den Gerichten die Kompetenz zu, die Wirksamkeit der Schiedsvereinbarung überprüfen. Sec. 34 Arbitration Act 1940 gestand den Gerichten hierbei zudem einen weiten Entscheidungsspielraum bei der Frage zu, ob sie die Streitigkeit an ein schiedsgerichtliches Verfahren verweisen oder nicht („...such authority may make an order staying the proceedings."). Siehe auch Supreme Court, *I T C Limited v George Joseph Fernandes & Anr*, AIR 1989 SC 839; [1989] 1 SCR 469, 6.2.1989; Supreme Court, *Union of India v Birla Cotton Spinning & Weaving Mills Ltd*, AIR 1967 SC 688; [1964] 2 SCR 599, 27.3.1963; Supreme Court, *Anderson Wright Ltd v Moran And Company*, AIR 1955 SC 53; [1955] 1 SCR 862, 1.11.1951; siehe auch Malhotra, Indu, O. P. Malhotra on Arbitration, Sec. 8, S. 427.

1255 Dies ergibt sich aus der Verwendung des englischen Wortes „shall".

1256 Auf inländische Schiedsverfahren ist Sec. 8 SchiedsG anwendbar und auf ausländische Handelsschiedsverfahren ist Sec. 45 SchiedsG anwendbar. Sec. 45 SchiedsG setzt Art. II (3) UNÜ in das indische Schiedsrecht um.

1257 Dies wird durch die Verwendung des englischen Wortes „shall" deutlich gemacht.

rechtshängige Gerichtsverfahren aussetzen[1258], die Klage abweisen[1259] oder die Streitigkeit an das Schiedsgericht verweisen[1260].[1261] Das indische Parlament wich in Sec. 8 (1) SchiedsG bewusst vom UNCITRAL Modellgesetz ab und gestattete den Gerichten keine Überprüfung der Schiedsvereinbarung auf Nichtigkeit, Unwirksamkeit und Undurchführbarkeit. Hierdurch sollen Interventionen der Gerichte verhindert und Streitigkeiten „mechanisch" an das Schiedsgericht verwiesen werden. Das Schiedsgericht entscheidet daraufhin im Rahmen seiner „Kompetenz-Kompetenz"[1262] über die Wirksamkeit der Schiedsvereinbarung.[1263] Diese gesetzgeberische Wertung ist als Schiedsverfahren fördernd anzusehen, da den Schiedsgerichten die Autonomie eingeräumt wird, ihre Kompetenz-Kompetenz effektiv auszuüben.

a) P Anand Raju v Raju

Im Verfahren *P Anand Gajapathi Raju & Ors v P V G Raju (Died) & Ors (Raju)*[1264] hatte ein mit zwei Richtern besetzter Senat des Supreme Courts darüber zu entscheiden, ob eine im Berufungsverfahren rechtshängige Streitigkeit an das von den Parteien während der Berufung vereinbarte Schiedsverfahren verwiesen werden muss.

Das oberste indische Gericht urteilte, dass der Wortlaut von Sec. 8 SchiedsG a. F. die Gerichte bei Vorliegen einer Schiedsvereinbarung zwingend verpflichte, die Streitigkeit an das Schiedsgericht zu verweisen. Eine Kontrollkompetenz der Schiedsvereinbarung bestehe nicht. Der Supreme Court begründet dies insbesondere mit dem Nichtinterventionsgedanken von Sec. 5 SchiedsG, nach dem die Gerichte nur dann in das Schiedsverfahren eingrei-

1258 Siehe u. a. Sec. 9 englischer Arbitration Act 1996; Sec. 3 US Federal Arbitration Act (Title 9, US Code); Sec. 20 (1) und (5) Hongkonger Arbitration Ordinance.

1259 Siehe beispielsweise Art. 1448 (1) französischer Code de procédure civile; Art. 7 Schweizer Bundesgesetz über das Internationale Privatrecht.

1260 Art. 8 (1) UNCITRAL Modellgesetz; Art. II (3) UNÜ; Sec. 20 (1) und (5) Hongkonger Arbitration Ordinance; Sec. 8 (1) SchiedsG. Neben der Verweisung der Streitigkeit an das Schiedsverfahren kann vor indischen Gerichten die Aussetzung des Verfahrens beantragt werden, Rautray, Guide Arbitration, S. 136.

1261 Born, International Commercial Arbitration, Bd. 1, S. 1270 ff.; Born, Law and Practice, § 2.07 [B], S. 66 ff.; Gaillard/Savage, Fouchard Gaillard Goldman, Rn. 661 ff.; vgl. Lew/Mistelis/Kröll, Comparative International Commercial Arbitration, Rn. 7-81 ff.; Born, Cases and Materials, S. 327 ff.

1262 Zu der Kompetenz-Kompetenz, siehe ausführliche Erörterung im Kapitel: Kompetenz-Kompetenz (C.II.).

1263 Malhotra, Indu, O. P. Malhotra on Arbitration, Sec. 8, S. 429.

1264 AIR 2000 SC 1886; (2000) 4 SCC 539, 28.3.2000. *Parthasarathy/Visalakshi*, loben das Urteil, weil es den gesetzgeberischen Willen unter Sec. 8 SchiedsG wiedergebe, Parthasarathy/Visalakshi, Arbitration 2007, S. 394 (399).

fen dürfen, wenn dies gesetzlich vorgesehen ist. Der Supreme Court verwies die Parteien folgerichtig an das Schiedsverfahren.

b) Hindustan Petroleum v Pinkcity Midway Petroleums

Im Urteil *Hindustan Petroleum Corpn Ltd v M/S Pinkcity Midway Petroleums (Hindustan Petroleum)*[1265] ging es 2003 vor einem zweiköpfigen Senat des Supreme Courts um einen Antrag gem. Sec. 8 SchiedsG a. F. auf Verweisung einer Klage an das vereinbarte Schiedsverfahren.

Die Parteien hatten in einem sog. „Dealership Agreement" vereinbart, dass *Pinkcity Midway Petroleums (Pinkcity)* die Erdölprodukte des staatlichen Unternehmens *Hindustan Petroleum Corpn Ltd (Hindustan)* verkaufen sollte. Das Dealership Agreement enthielt eine Schiedsklausel, die einen Angestellten von *Hindustan* als Einzelschiedsrichter für die schiedsgerichtliche Streitbeilegung bestimmte.[1266] Wegen zu geringer Pumpleistung und der Manipulation von Zapfsäulen setzte *Hindustan* seine Erdöllieferungen an *Pinkcity* für 30 Tage aus und verhängte gegen *Pinkcity* eine Geldstrafe. *Pinkcity* legte gegen die unterbrochene Lieferung und gegen die Geldstrafe Klage auf Feststellung ein, dass diese Maßnahmen von *Hindustan* illegal und willkürlich seien. *Hindustan* beantragte die Verweisung der Streitigkeit gem. Sec. 8 a. F. und Sec. 5 SchiedsG an ein schiedsrichterliches Verfahren.

Im Februar 2002 lehnte der „Civil Judge"[1267] den Verweisungsantrag in der ersten Instanz ab. Da die gerichtlich anhängige Streitigkeit nicht von der Schiedsvereinbarung erfasst gewesen sei. Der High Court von Punjab und Haryana wies die eingelegte Revision sodann zurück.

Der Supreme Court urteilte im darauffolgenden Berufungsverfahren, dass die Parteien vereinbart hätten, alle Streitigkeiten aus dem Dealership Agreement der Schiedsgerichtsbarkeit zuzuweisen. Dem Wortlaut von Sec. 8 SchiedsG a. F. lasse sich entnehmen, dass die Gerichte bei Vorliegen einer Schiedsvereinbarung den rechtshängigen Streitgegenstand zwingend an ein Schiedsgericht verweisen müssen. Zuständigkeitsstreitigkeiten i. S. d.

1265 AIR 2003 SC 2881; (2003) 6 SCC 503; Appeal (civil) 5156 of 2003, 23.7.2003. *Parthasarathy/Visalakshi*, loben die Entscheidung, da sie dem gesetzgeberischen Willen unter Sec. 8 SchiedsG a. F. entspreche, Parthasarathy/Visalakshi, Arbitration 2007, S. 394 (399).

1266 Zur Bestellung von Parteischiedsrichtern, siehe ausführlich Kapitel: Mitarbeiter als Schiedsrichter (C. V. 1.).

1267 Ein „Civil Judge" ist ein dem District Court nachgeordnetes Gericht, District Court Rewari, Official Website of District Court, verfügbar unter http://ecourts.gov.in/rewari/history (zuletzt abgerufen am 28.4.2021); Indian Courts, District Courts, verfügbar unter http://indiancourts.nic.in/districtcourt.html# (zuletzt abgerufen am 28.4.2021); Robinson, in: Choudhry/Khosla/Mehta, The Oxford Handbook of the Indian Constitution, S. 330 (333).

Sec. 16 SchiedsG, die unter den Anwendungsbereich der Schiedsvereinbarung fallen, seien von dem zu konstituierenden Schiedsgericht unter dessen Kompetenz-Kompetenz zu entscheiden.[1268] In seinem Urteil hob der Supreme Court die Entscheidungen der nachgeordneten Instanzen auf und ordnete an, dass das Gericht der ersten Instanz, die Streitigkeit an das Schiedsverfahren zu verweisen habe.

c) Fazit

Die Urteile *Raju* und *Hindustan Petroleum* sind schiedsfreundlich, weil sie die Kompetenz-Kompetenz stärken und eine gerichtliche Kontrolle der Schiedsvereinbarung verhindern. Die Urteile korrespondieren deshalb mit dem Gesetzeswortlaut und dem Willen des Gesetzgebers bezüglich Sec. 8 a. F. und Sec. 16 SchiedsG[1269].

d) SBP v Patel Engineering (Patel Engineering)

Von der gesetzgeberischen Wertung der Sec. 8 SchiedsG a. F., dass die Gerichte die Schiedsvereinbarung nicht auf ihre Wirksamkeit überprüfen dürfen, ist eine mit sieben Richtern besetzte Constitutional Bench des Supreme Courts im Urteil *SBP & Co v Patel Engineering Ltd & Anr (Patel Engineering)*[1270] abgewichen. Die Constitutional Bench des Supreme Courts hatte zu beurteilen, welche Rechtsnatur die Schiedsrichterbestellung gem. Sec. 11 (6) SchiedsG hat. Bei der Erörterung dieser Fragestellung entschied die Constitutional Bench *obiter dicta*, dass die Gerichte nach Sec. 8 SchiedsG den rechtshängigen Streitgegenstand bei Vorliegen einer Schiedsvereinbarung nicht einfach mechanisch an das Schiedstribunal verweisen dürfen. Die Gerichte müssen vielmehr die Wirksamkeit der Schiedsvereinbarung und die Zuständigkeitsfrage, ob die Streitigkeit von der Schiedsvereinbarung erfasst werde, selbst verbindlich überprüfen, bevor eine Verweisung stattfinden könne.[1271] Die Constitutional Bench zitiert bei ihrer Erörterung zu Art. 8 SchiedsG a. F. die oben dargelegten Entscheidungen *Raju* und *Hindustan Petroleum* des Supreme Courts falsch. Denn diesen Entscheidungen ist gerade nicht zu entnehmen, dass ein Gericht vor der Verweisung einer Streitigkeit

1268 Appeal (civil) 5156 of 2003, Rn. k.

1269 Parthasarathy/Visalakshi, Arbitration 2007, S. 394 (399).

1270 Constitutional Bench, 7 Richter, AIR 2006 SC 450; (2005) 8 SCC 618; Appeal (civil) 4168 of 2003, 26.10.2005. Der Supreme Court hatte lediglich eine Rechtsfrage zu entscheiden, einen Tatbestand enthält das Urteil nicht.

1271 Die umfassende Kontrolle gem. Sec. 8 SchiedsG a. F. durch die *Patel Engineering*-Entscheidung wird kritisiert, Panjwani/Pathak, Indian Journal of Arbitration Law 2013, Vol. II, Ausg. 2, S. 1 ff.; Wadhwa/Krishnan/Bachawat/Bachawat, Bachawat's Arbitration, Bd. 1, Sec. 8, S. 434 f.

an das Schiedsgericht die Wirksamkeit der Schiedsvereinbarung überprüfen muss. Gleichwohl zitierte das oberste indische Gericht die Urteile *Raju* und *Hindustan Petroleum* und behauptete, diesen lasse sich entnehmen, dass die Gerichte eine Streitigkeit ausschließlich dann an das zu konstituierende Schiedsgericht verweisen müssen, wenn eine Schiedsvereinbarung bestehe und wirksam sei.[1272]

e) Bewertung

Den obligatorischen Charakter der Verweisung an das schiedsrichterliche Verfahren achtet die indische Rechtsordnung und stimmt hierdurch mit dem Standard der internationalen Schiedsgesetzgebung überein.[1273] Das Urteil *Patel Engineering* ist in Bezug auf die Schiedsfreundlichkeit der indischen Rechtsordnung als Rückschritt anzusehen. Die Entscheidung *Patel Engineering* der Constitutional Bench des Supreme Courts erschuf eine dem gesetzlichen Wortlaut nicht zu entnehmende umfassende Kontrolle der Schiedsvereinbarung bei der Verweisung einer gerichtlich rechtshängigen Streitigkeit an das Schiedstribunal (Sec. 8 SchiedsG a. F.) und bei der gerichtlichen Schiedsrichterbestellung (Sec. 11 SchiedsG a. F.). Durch die eröffnete Kontrollkompetenz führte die Constitutional Bench zudem die überholte Rechtslage des Arbitration Acts 1940[1274] wieder ein. Die durch diese „Rechtsfortbildung" des Supreme Courts etablierte gerichtliche Kontrollmöglichkeit unter Sec. 8 (1) SchiedsG a. F. widerspricht ferner dem Wortlaut von Sec. 8 (1) a. F. und Sec. 5 SchiedsG.[1275] Das Urteil *Patel Engineering* lässt des Weiteren außer Acht, dass der Gesetzgeber in Sec. 8 SchiedsG a. F. bewusst vom UNCITRAL Modellgesetz abgewichen war, das eine gerichtliche Kontrolle der Schiedsvereinbarung vorsieht.[1276] Durch die *Patel Engi-*

1272 Vgl. Appeal (civil) 4168 of 2003, Rn. 15.

1273 Dem Wortlaut von Art. 8 (1) UNCITRAL Modellgesetz und Art. II (3) UNÜ lässt sich durch die Verwendung des englischen Wortes „shall" der zwingende Charakter der Verweisung entnehmen, Born, International Commercial Arbitration, Bd. 1, S. 1273 ff. Siehe zum zwingenden Charakter der Aussetzung und der Klageabweisung auch Sec. 9 (4) englischer Arbitration Act 1996; Sec. 3 US Federal Arbitration Act (Title 9, US Code); Sec. 20 (1) und (5) Hongkonger Arbitration Ordinance; Art. 1448 (1) französischer Code de procédure civile; Art. 7 Schweizer Bundesgesetz über das Internationale Privatrecht.

1274 Nach Sec. 34 Arbitration Acts 1940 stand die Verweisung der rechtshängigen Streitigkeit an das Schiedsverfahren im Ermessen des Gerichts. Die Gerichte konnten unter Sec. 34 Arbitration Acts 1940 die Wirksamkeit der Schiedsvereinbarung kontrollieren, Richter Sabharwal, *Shin-Etsu Chemical Co Ltd v M/S Aksh Optifibre Ltd & Anr,* (2005) 7 SCC 234; AIR 2005 SC 3766; Appeal (civil) 5048 of 2005, 12.8.2005.

1275 Vgl. Panjwani/Pathak, Indian Journal of Arbitration Law 2013, Vol. II, Ausg. 2, S. 1 (14 ff.); Kachwaha, International Arbitration Law Review 2007, S. 13 (15 f.).

1276 Vgl. Panjwani/Pathak, Indian Journal of Arbitration Law 2013, Vol. II, Ausg. 2, S. 1 (14 ff.). Im Unterschied zu Sec. 45 SchiedsG, Art. II (3) UNÜ und Art. 8 UNCITRAL

neering-Entscheidung entspricht die Rechtslage unter Sec. 8 (1) SchiedsG a. F. betreffend der Kontrollmöglichkeiten der Schiedsvereinbarung Art. 8 (1) UNCITRAL Modellgesetz, das für ein das Schiedsverfahren unterstützendes und seine Integrität achtendes Schiedsrechtsregime steht[1277]. In Indien sind die Gerichte hingegen für Interventionstendenzen in schiedsgerichtliche Verfahren bekannt.[1278] Wegen der gerichtlichen Interventionen ist der Ausschluss der gerichtlichen Wirksamkeitskontrolle der Schiedsvereinbarung gem. Sec. 8 (1) SchiedsG a. F. – entgegen Art. 8 (1) UNCITRAL Modellgesetz – im indischen Kontext als Schiedsverfahren unterstützend zu bewerten. In Indien sollte es möglichst vermieden werden, dass unter Sec. 8 SchiedsG neben dem Schiedsverfahren langwierige parallele Verfahren vor Gerichten angestrengt werden können[1279]. Zumal es den Parteien auch ohne ein paralleles gerichtliches Verfahren freisteht, die Wirksamkeit der Schiedsvereinbarung im Aufhebungs- bzw. Vollstreckungsverfahren nachträglich gerichtlich überprüfen zu lassen.[1280] Durch eine Überprüfung nach Erlass des Schiedsspruchs wird auch die Kompetenz-Kompetenz des Schiedsgerichts geachtet.[1281] Die Verlagerung der Kontrolle der Schiedsvereinbarung auf die Ebene der Aufhebung bzw. Anerkennung und Vollstreckung des Schiedsspruchs führt im indischen Kontext zu einem stringenteren und ef-

---

Modellgesetz sah Sec. 8 SchiedsG a. F. keine gerichtliche Kontrolle der Schiedsvereinbarung vor, vgl. Wadhwa/Krishnan/Bachawat/Bachawat, Bachawat's Arbitration, Bd. 1, Sec. 8, S. 434; Biswas, S. 62 f.

1277 Art. 5 ff. UNCITRAL Modellgesetz; UNCITRAL Sekretariat, Explanatory note, Rn. 6 ff.

1278 Vgl. o. u. a. Kapitel: Einleitung; Schiedsverfahrensgesetz (SchiedsG) 1996 (A.III.7.b)).

1279 Sec. 8 (3) SchiedsG gestattet, dass ein Schiedsverfahren eingeleitet oder fortgesetzt wird. Born, Law and Practice, § 2.07, S. 62 ff.; Born, International Commercial Arbitration, Bd. 1, S. 1276 f., 1286; Art. 8 (2) UNCITRAL Modellgesetz.

1280 Vgl. Supreme Court, *Shin-Etsu Chemical Co Ltd v M/S Aksh Optifibre Ltd & Anr*, (2005) 7 SCC 234; AIR 2005 SC 3766; Appeal (civil) 5048 of 2005, 12.8.2005; Born, International Commercial Arbitration, Bd. 1, S. 1276 f.; Panjwani/Pathak, Indian Journal of Arbitration Law 2013, Vol. II, Ausg. 2, S. 1 (12).

1281 Born, International Commercial Arbitration, Bd. 1, S. 1276 f.; Gaillard/Savage, Fouchard Gaillard Goldman, Rn. 671. Die Hongkonger, die französische und die Schweizer Schiedsrechtsordnung sehen lediglich eine *prima facie*-Kontrolle der Schiedsvereinbarung vor, Born, International Commercial Arbitration, Bd. 1, S. 1091 f., 1110 ff., 1118 f.; Gaillard/Savage, Fouchard Gaillard Goldman, Rn. 672 ff. An der Rechtsauffassung der Constitutional Bench im *Patel Engineering*-Urteil wird in der indischen Literatur kritisiert, dass sie der dem Schiedsgericht zustehenden Kompetenz-Kompetenz widerspreche, Panjwani/Pathak, Indian Journal of Arbitration Law 2013, Vol. II, Ausg. 2, S. 1 (9); Wadhwa/Krishnan/Bachawat/Bachawat, Bachawat's Arbitration, Bd. 1, Sec. 8, S. 435.

fizienteren Schiedsverfahren ohne Verzögerungsmöglichkeiten[1282].[1283] Die höchstrichterliche *Patel Engineering*-Entscheidung ist dementsprechend als schiedsunfreundlich zu klassifizieren und wird auch in der Literatur kritisch besprochen[1284]. Es ist daher zu bedauern, dass die Constitutional Bench des Supreme Courts nicht den schiedsfördernden Entscheidungen desselben Gerichts in der Rechtssache *Raju* und *Hindustan Petroleum* folgte und auch nicht den progressiven und schiedsfreundlichen Gesetzeswortlaut von Sec. 8 (1) SchiedsG a. F. respektierte[1285].

f) Arbitration Amendment Act

Der neu eingeführte Sec. 8 (1) SchiedsG beschränkte den gerichtlichen Überprüfungsmaßstab der Schiedsvereinbarung auf eine *prima facie*-Kontrolle. Sec. 8 (1) SchiedsG n. F. ist ein Schritt nach vorne und gleichzeitig ein Schritt zurück. Positiv zu bewerten ist, dass der Gesetzgeber in Sec. 8 (1) SchiedsG n. F. die Rechtsprechung des Supreme Courts im *Patel Engineering*-Urteil gegenstandslos werden ließ und nur noch eine *prima facie*[1286]-Überprüfung der Schiedsvereinbarung durch die Gerichte zulässt. Andererseits gestand der Wortlaut von Sec. 8 (1) SchiedsG a. F. den Gerichten keine Kontrollkompetenz hinsichtlich der Wirksamkeit der Schiedsvereinbarung zu. Bei einem Verweisungsantrag und bei Vorliegen einer den gerichtlich rechtshängigen Streitgegenstand umfassenden Schiedsvereinbarung musste das Gericht die Streitigkeit an das Schiedsgericht verweisen. Einzig das Schiedsgericht entschied unter seiner ihm zukommenden Kompetenz-Kompetenz über die Wirksamkeit der Schiedsvereinbarung.[1287] Die gerichtliche *prima facie*-Überprüfung der Schiedsvereinbarung gem. Sec. 8

1282 Zu den Verzögerungsmöglichkeiten durch die Kontrolle der Schiedsvereinbarung, vgl. Gaillard/Savage, Fouchard Gaillard Goldman, Rn. 679 ff.

1283 In *Fouchard Gaillard Goldman* wird für eine Kontrolle der Schiedsvereinbarung auf der Ebene des Aufhebungsverfahrens plädiert, Gaillard/Savage, Fouchard Gaillard Goldman, Rn. 682 ff. Zur nachträglichen Kontrolle der Schiedsvereinbarung unter dem negativen Effekt der Schiedsvereinbarung, Schramm/Geisinger/Pinsolle, in: Kronke/Nacimiento/Otto/Port, Article II, S. 95.

1284 Wadhwa/Krishnan/Bachawat/Bachawat, Bachawat's Arbitration, Bd. 1, Sec. 8, S. 434 ff.; Panjwani/Pathak, Indian Journal of Arbitration Law 2013, Vol. II, Ausg. 2, S. 1 ff.; Sindhu, Indian Journal of Arbitration Law 2014, Vol. III, Ausg. 2, S. 23 (38); Ray, Aloke/Sabharwal, MEALEY'S International Arbitration Report 2007, Vol. 22, S. 26 (29); Sen, Vindobona Journal of International Commercial Law & Arbitration 2006, S. 45 (50 ff.); Kachwaha, International Arbitration Law Review 2007, S. 13 (15 ff.); Parthasarathy/Visalakshi, Arbitration 2007, S. 394 ff.

1285 Panjwani/Pathak, Indian Journal of Arbitration Law 2013, Vol. II, Ausg. 2, S. 1 (15 f.).

1286 *Wadhwa/Krishnan/Bachawat/Bachawat* forderten schon unter der *Patel Engineering*-Rechtsprechung die Einführung einer *prima facie*-Kontrolle, Wadhwa/Krishnan/Bachawat/Bachawat, Bachawat's Arbitration, Bd. 1, Sec. 8, S. 434 f.

1287 Sec. 8 (1) SchiedsG a. F.

SchiedsG n. F. kann im überlasteten indischen Gerichtssystem zu erheblichen Verzögerungen[1288] durch parallele Gerichtsverfahren führen[1289] und ist – verglichen mit der alten Gesetzeslage – als die Schiedsgerichtsbarkeit nicht unterstützend einzuordnen.

2. Entscheidungen unter dem UNÜ

In Sec. 45 SchiedsG setzte die Legislative Art. II (3) UNÜ in das indische Recht um. Durch Sec. 45 SchiedsG implementierte der Gesetzgeber für Schiedsverfahren mit ausländischem Sitz den „negativen Effekt" der Schiedsvereinbarung in das indische Schiedsrecht.[1290] Sec. 45 SchiedsG regelt – auf Antrag einer Partei – die zwingende Verweisung einer gerichtlich rechtshängigen Streitigkeit an ein Handelsschiedsverfahren mit Sitz in einem anderen Vertragsstaat des UNÜ.[1291] Sec. 45 a. E. SchiedsG gestattet den Gerichten hierbei – im Unterschied zu Sec. 8 SchiedsG – die Schiedsvereinbarung auf ihre Hinfälligkeit, Unwirksamkeit und Nichterfüllbarkeit zu überprüfen.

a) Shin-Etsu Chemical v Aksh Optifibre

In der Entscheidung *Shin-Etsu Chemical Co Ltd v M/S Aksh Optifibre Ltd & Anr (Shin-Etsu)*[1292] hatte ein aus drei Richtern bestehender Senat zu entscheiden, mit welcher Intensität die gerichtliche Kontrolle einer Schiedsver-

1288 S. o. u. a. Kapitel: Einleitung; Schiedsverfahrensgesetz 1996 (A.III.7.b)) und Kapitel: Einleitung; Strukturelle Probleme der indischen Gerichte (A.III.6.).

1289 Vgl. Parliament of India, Rajya Sabha, Department Related Parliamentary Standing Committee on Personnel, Public Grievance, Law and Justice, Ninth Report on the Arbitration and Conciliation (Amendment) Bill, 2003, in: Ministry of Law and Justice, Government of India, Proposed Amendments to the Arbitration & Conciliation Act, 1996, A Consultation Paper, Annex V, S. 141, verfügbar unter http://lawmin.nic.in/la/consultationpaper.pdf (zuletzt abgerufen am 28.4.2021).

1290 Zum negativen Effekt, Born, International Commercial Arbitration, Bd. 1, S. 1270 ff.; Born, Law and Practice, § 2.07 [B], S. 66 ff.; Gaillard/Savage, Fouchard Gaillard Goldman, Rn. 661 ff.; vgl. Lew/Mistelis/Kröll, Comparative International Commercial Arbitration, Rn. 7-81 ff.; Schramm/Geisinger/Pinsolle, in: Kronke/Nacimiento/Otto/Port, Article II, S. 95 f.; Born, Cases and Materials, S. 328 ff.; siehe hierzu auch vorherige Ausführungen im gleichen Kapitel (C.IV.1.).

1291 Sec. 44 SchiedsG. Zudem muss die indische Regierung die Sec. 44 ff. SchiedsG auf UNÜ Vertragsstaaten in der „Official Gazette" für anwendbar erklären (Sec. 44 [1] [b] SchiedsG), siehe hierzu Kapitel: Anerkennung und Vollstreckung (C.VIII.). Sec. 45 SchiedsG ist nicht auf Grund von Sec. 8 SchiedsG überflüssig, da Sec. 8 i. V. m. Sec. 2 (2) SchiedsG im Gegensatz zu Art. 8 i. V. m. Art. 1 (2) UNCITRAL Modellgesetz auf Schiedsverfahren mit Sitz in Indien beschränkt ist, zum UNCITRAL Modellgesetz, Born, International Commercial Arbitration, Bd. 1, S. 1271 f.

1292 (2005) 7 SCC 234; AIR 2005 SC 3766; Appeal (civil) 5048 of 2005, 12.8.2005.

einbarung gem. Sec. 45 SchiedsG bei einem Handelsschiedsverfahren mit ausländischem Sitz vorzunehmen ist.

Im zu Grunde liegenden Sachverhalt hatte die Berufungsklägerin einen Kaufvertrag gekündigt. Die im Kaufvertrag enthaltene Schiedsklausel sah für die Beilegung von Streitigkeiten ein Schiedsverfahren in Tokyo (Japan) nach der ICC-Schiedsgerichtsordnung vor. Im Jahr 2000 legte die erste Berufungsbeklagte neben einer einstweiligen Maßnahme eine Klage auf Feststellung ein, dass die Kündigung unwirksam gewesen sei. Hilfsweise beantragte die Beklagte festzustellen, dass der Kaufvertrag und die darin enthaltene Schiedsklausel *ex tunc* unwirksam seien. Die Berufungsklägerin beantragte die Verweisung der Streitigkeit gem. Sec. 8 SchiedsG an das vereinbarte Schiedsverfahren in Japan.[1293] Das Gericht erster Instanz gab dem Antrag der Berufungsklägerin 2003 statt und verwies die Parteien gem. Sec. 8 SchiedsG an das schiedsgerichtliche Verfahren. Der High Court[1294] hob den Beschluss der nachgeordneten Instanz auf und stellte richtig, dass nicht Sec. 8 SchiedsG, sondern Sec. 45 SchiedsG einschlägig sei.[1295]

Der Supreme Court hatte 2005 in der Berufung über die Rechtsfrage zu entscheiden, ob die Gerichte unter Sec. 45 SchiedsG die Wirksamkeit der Schiedsvereinbarung vollumfänglich und verbindlich oder nur *prima facie* überprüfen dürfen. Die Besonderheit dieses Urteils liegt darin, dass drei separate Urteile von den drei Richtern ergingen und die Rechtsauffassungen der Richter *Srikrishna* und *Dharmadhikari* nur teilweise übereinstimmten.

In seinem Minderheitsvotum war Richter *Sabharwal* der Ansicht, dass die Gerichte die Schiedsvereinbarung unter Sec. 45 SchiedsG nicht nur *prima facie*, sondern vollumfänglich auf ihre Wirksamkeit überprüfen dürfen. Richter *Sabharwal* stellte zwar fest, dass die schiedsfreundlichen Rechtordnungen der Schweiz, Frankreichs und Hongkongs einem liberalen Ansatz folgten und lediglich eine *prima facie*-Kontrolle der Schiedsvereinbarung durch die staatlichen Gerichte zuließen. Richter *Sabharwal* räumte den Gerichten unter Sec. 45 SchiedsG dennoch ein umfassendes Überprüfungsrecht der Schiedsvereinbarung ein. Nach Richter *Sabharwal* müssen die Gerichte nach dem Wortlaut von Sec. 45 SchiedsG letztinstanzlich und verbindlich über die Wirksamkeit der Schiedsvereinbarung entscheiden.

Richter *Srikrishna* war hingegen der Auffassung, dass sich eine *prima facie*-Kontrolle der Schiedsvereinbarung gem. Sec. 45 SchiedsG zwar nicht dessen Wortlaut entnehmen lasse. Mangels einer im SchiedsG vorgesehenen

---

1293 Zunächst beantragte die Berufungsklägerin die Verweisung nach Sec. 8 SchiedsG und später gem. Sec. 45 SchiedsG.

1294 Die Rechtssache gelangte als eine Petition gem. Art. 227 der indischen Verfassung vor den High Court.

1295 Der High Court verwies die Rechtssache an das Gericht erster Instanz zurück.

Möglichkeit für Schiedsverfahren mit ausländischem Sitz das Schiedsverfahren neben der gerichtlichen Kontrolle der Schiedsvereinbarung parallel weiterlaufen zu lassen – so wie dies in Sec. 8 (3) SchiedsG für Schiedsverfahren mit Sitz in Indien vorgesehen ist – sei aber eine *prima facie*-Überprüfung unabdingbar. Ein Schiedsverfahren müsse ansonsten bis zu einer verbindlichen gerichtlichen Kontrolle der Schiedsvereinbarung ausgesetzt werden. Dies wäre allerdings nicht mit der dem SchiedsG zu Grunde liegenden Maxime einer schnellen Streitbeilegung ohne gerichtliche Interventionen vereinbar.[1296] Die Gerichte dürften folglich die Schiedsvereinbarung nur *prima facie* auf ihre Wirksamkeit hin überprüfen. Die Schiedsvereinbarung könne aber vom Schiedsgericht und im Aufhebungs- und Vollstreckungsverfahren umfassend kontrolliert werden.

Richter *Dharmadhikari* stimmte Richter *Srikrishna* hinsichtlich der *prima facie*-Kontrolle der Schiedsvereinbarungen unter Sec. 45 SchiedsG zu.

In der Rechtssache *Shin-Etsu* entschied der Supreme Court somit mit zwei Stimmen zu einer[1297], dass die gerichtliche Kontrolle der Schiedsvereinbarung gem. Sec. 45 SchiedsG auf eine *prima facie*-Überprüfung beschränkt sei.

Durch dieses Urteil legte der Supreme Court die Kontrolle der Schiedsvereinbarung gem. Sec. 45 SchiedsG schiedsfreundlich[1298] und restriktiv aus und begrenzte gerichtliche Interventionen. Auch wird dem Schiedsgericht die „Kompetenz-Kompetenz“[1299] zugestanden, über die eigene Zuständigkeit inklusive der Wirksamkeit der Schiedsvereinbarungen zu entscheiden.

In der Literatur wird an dem Urteil *Shin-Etsu* gelobt, dass es dem Schiedsgericht die notwendige Kompetenz-Kompetenz zugestehe.[1300] Es schaffe eine ausgeglichene Balance zwischen gerichtlicher Kontrolle vor und nach dem Schiedsverfahren und unterbinde Verzögerungen bei der Durchführung des

1296 Diese Rechtsauffassung wird in der Literatur geteilt, Panjwani/Pathak, Indian Journal of Arbitration Law 2013, Vol. II, Ausg. 2, S. 1 (17); Ray, Aloke/Sabharwal, MEALEY'S International Arbitration Report 2007, Vol. 22, S. 26 (27).

1297 Ray, Aloke/Sabharwal, MEALEY'S International Arbitration Report 2007, Vol. 22, S. 26 (27).

1298 Vgl. Schramm/Geisinger/Pinsolle, in: Kronke/Nacimiento/Otto/Port, Article II, S. 109 f., Fn. 272; Kachwaha, Asian International Arbitration Journal 2005, Vol. 1, Ausg. 2, S. 105 (124); Gaillard, New York Law Journal 2005, S. 3, 7 f. *Ray/Sabharwal* bewerten das Urteil unter Verweis auf *Gaillard* als schiedsfreundlich, Ray, Aloke/Sabharwal, MEALEY'S International Arbitration Report 2007, Vol. 22, S. 26 (27).

1299 Siehe ausführlich hierzu Kapitel: Kompetenz-Kompetenz (C.II.).

1300 Gaillard, New York Law Journal 2005, S. 3, 7 f.; Ray, Aloke/Sabharwal, MEALEY'S International Arbitration Report 2007, Vol. 22, S. 26 (27).

Schiedsverfahrens.[1301] Das Urteil trage hierdurch dem Geiste des SchiedsG und des UNCITRAL Modellgesetzes Rechnung.[1302]

b) Chloro Controls v Severn Trent Water Purification

Im Urteil *Chloro Controls (I) P Ltd v Severn Trent Water Purification Inc & Ors (Chloro Controls)*[1303] hatte ein ebenfalls mit drei Richtern besetzter Senat des Supreme Courts erneut darüber zu urteilen, ob die Gerichte unter Sec. 45 SchiedsG verbindlich oder nur *prima facie* über die Wirksamkeit der Schiedsvereinbarung entscheiden dürfen.

Die Berufungsklägerin *Chloro Controls (I) P Ltd* beantragte 2004 beim Bombay High Court festzustellen, dass das u. a. mit der Berufungsbeklagten *Severn Trent Water Purification Inc (Severn)* geschlossene „Joint Venture Agreement" und das „Collaboration Agreement" wirksam seien. Die Berufungsbeklagte *Severn* beantragte *inter alia* die Verweisung der Streitigkeit gem. Sec. 8 und 5 SchiedsG an das schiedsgerichtliche Verfahren. In Vereinbarungen zwischen mehreren unterschiedlichen Parteien war eine Schiedsklausel für ein ICC-Schiedsverfahren mit Sitz in London enthalten. Ein Einzelrichter des Bombay High Courts lehnte den Antrag auf Verweisung an das schiedsgerichtliche Verfahren im April 2004 ab. Im Berufungsverfahren entschied eine Division Bench des Bombay High Courts 2010, dem Antrag auf Verweisung stattzugeben und die rechtshängige Streitigkeit gem. Sec. 45 SchiedsG an ein zu konstituierendes Schiedsgericht zu verweisen.

Im Berufungsverfahren[1304] folgte der Supreme Court dem Minderheitsvotum von Richter *Sabharwal* im Urteil *Shin-Etsu* und entschied, dass ein Gericht bei einer Verweisung einer Streitigkeit gem. Sec. 45 SchiedsG final über die Wirksamkeit der Schiedsvereinbarung entscheiden dürfe und nicht nur aus einem *prima facie*-Blickwinkel. Der Senat begründete dies mit dem *Patel Engineering*-Urteil der Constitutional Bench des obersten Gerichtshofs. Nach dem *Patel Engineering*-Urteil ist die gerichtliche Entscheidung über die Wirksamkeit der Schiedsvereinbarung gem. Sec. 8 SchiedsG für das Schiedsgericht bindend. Nach dem Supreme Court sei die Ratio des *Patel Engineering*-Urteils auf Sec. 45 SchiedsG übertragbar.[1305]

1301 Kachwaha, Asian International Arbitration Journal 2005, Vol. 1, Ausg. 2, S. 105 (124); Gaillard, New York Law Journal 2005, S. 3, 7 f.; Ray, Aloke/Sabharwal, MEALEY'S International Arbitration Report 2007, Vol. 22, S. 26 (27).

1302 Nair, Arbitration International 2007, Vol. 23, Ausg. 4, S. 699 (711).

1303 (2013) 1 SCC 641; 2012 (4) Arb LR 1 (SC); Civil Appeal No. 7134 of 2012, 28.9.2012.

1304 In der Form einer „Special Leave Petition".

1305 Civil Appeal No. 7134 of 2012, Rn. 124 ff.

Das Gericht entnahm dem Wortlaut von Sec. 45 SchiedsG ferner, dass durch die Verwendung des englischen Wortes „shall“ die Gerichte eine vor ihnen erhobene Streitigkeit zwingend an die Schiedsgerichtsbarkeit verweisen müssen, sofern die Schiedsvereinbarung wirksam sei.[1306] Der Supreme Court verwies die Streitigkeit im September 2012 – nach einer Verfahrensdauer von mehr als acht Jahren – an das verabredete ICC-Schiedsverfahren.

In der *Chloro Controls*-Entscheidung folgte der Supreme Court nicht seiner Schiedsverfahren unterstützenden *prima facie*-Rechtsprechung im Verfahren *Shin-Etsu*. Durch die wiedereröffnete Interventionskompetenz der indischen Gerichte unter Sec. 45 SchiedsG widerspricht das *Chloro Controls*-Urteil einer effizienten schiedsgerichtlichen Streitbeilegung. Die *Chloro Controls*-Entscheidung entspricht dennoch dem Wortlaut von Sec. 45 SchiedsG und dem diesem zu Grunde liegenden Art. II (3) UNÜ, die eine gerichtliche Kontrolle der Schiedsvereinbarung nicht auf eine *prima facie*-Überprüfung beschränken. Dieser Aspekt des *Chloro Controls*-Urteils ist zwar weniger schiedsfreundlich als die *Shin-Etsu*-Entscheidung, entspricht aber gleichwohl Art. II (3) UNÜ und erfüllt deshalb den internationalen Maßstab des Schiedsgerichtswesens.

Im Schrifttum wird das Urteil *Chloro Controls* wegen der Ausdehnung der durch die Entscheidung *Patel Engineering*[1307] eingeführten, verbindlichen gerichtlichen Kontrolle der Schiedsvereinbarung[1308] auf Sec. 45 SchiedsG kritisiert. [1309] Die Literatur moniert zudem, dass die Entscheidung *Chloro Controls* die Kompetenz-Kompetenz des Schiedsgerichts verletze.[1310] Die Entscheidung führe ferner zu gerichtlichen Interventionen und zu Verzögerungsmöglichkeiten, die dem gesetzgeberischen Willen widersprächen.[1311]

1306 Civil Appeal No. 7134 of 2012, Rn. 3, 64, 131.

1307 In der Literatur wird an der Entscheidung *Chloro Controls* der Rückgriff auf das Urteil *Patel Engineering* kritisiert, Mahajan/Bhatt, International Arbitration Law Review 2013, S. N25 (N26 f.); Sharma, Ajay, Indian Journal of Arbitration Law 2014, Vol. III, Ausg. 1, S. 6 (22); Mahajan/Bhatt, Journal of International Arbitration 2013, Vol. 30, Ausg. 6, S. 711 (725); Mahajan/Chatterjee, International Arbitration Law Review 2015, S. 114 (118).

1308 Diese finale Kontrolle der Schiedsvereinbarung hatte der Supreme Court für Sec. 11 SchiedsG kreiert.

1309 Mahajan/Bhatt, International Arbitration Law Review 2013, S. N25 (N26 ff.); Mahajan/Bhatt, Journal of International Arbitration 2013, Vol. 30, Ausg. 6, S. 711 ff.; Mahajan/Chatterjee, International Arbitration Law Review 2015, S. 114 (118 f.).

1310 Mahajan/Chatterjee, International Arbitration Law Review 2015, S. 114 (118 f.); Sharma, Ajay, Indian Journal of Arbitration Law 2014, Vol. III, Ausg. 1, S. 6 (22 f.).

1311 Mahajan/Bhatt, International Arbitration Law Review 2013, S. N25 (N26 ff.); Mahajan/Bhatt, Journal of International Arbitration 2013, Vol. 30, Ausg. 6, S. 711 ff.; Mahajan/Chatterjee, International Arbitration Law Review 2015, S. 114 (118 ff.); Sharma, Ajay, Indian Journal of Arbitration Law 2014, Vol. III, Ausg. 1, S. 6 (22 f.).

Im *Chloro Controls*-Urteil entschied – wie in der Rechtssache *Shin-Etsu* – ein mit drei Richtern besetzter Senat über die Kontrollintensität der Schiedsvereinbarung. Im Verfahren *Chloro Controls* stützte der Supreme Court seine Entscheidung auf das Urteil der mit sieben Richtern besetzten Constitutional Bench in der Entscheidung *Patel Engineering*. In letzterer Entscheidung urteilte die Constitutional Bench *obiter dicta*, dass das Schiedsgericht nur bei einer Verweisung nach Sec. 8 SchiedsG an die Entscheidung des verweisenden Gerichts hinsichtlich der Wirksamkeit der Schiedsvereinbarung gebunden sei. Sec. 45 SchiedsG erörterte die Constitutional Bench nicht. Das Parlament ließ darüber hinaus die *Patel Engineering*-Rechtsprechung durch den Arbitration Amendment Act 2015 obsolet werden.[1312]

In der Rechtssache *Chloro Controls* hätte der Supreme Court bei Zweifel an der Rechtmäßigkeit der Entscheidung des gleichgroßen Senats im Urteil *Shin-Etsu* beantragen können, die Rechtsstreitigkeit für eine Rechtsprechungsänderung an einen größeren Senat zu verweisen. Auf Grund der gleichen Anzahl an Richtern in den Gerichtsverfahren *Shin-Etsu* und *Chloro Controls* war der Senat in seiner *Chloro Controls*-Entscheidung an die zuvor ergangene Rechtsprechung im Urteil *Shin-Etsu* gebunden. Der Supreme Court hätte demgemäß im *Chloro Controls*-Urteil der *Shin-Etsu*-Entscheidung folgen müssen.[1313] Dieses Spannungsfeld zwischen den beiden sich widersprechenden Urteilen *Shin-Etsu* und *Chloro Controls* wird sich erst in der Zukunft auflösen.[1314] Die entstandene Rechtsunsicherheit über den Kontrollmaßstab der Schiedsvereinbarung gem. Sec. 45 SchiedsG bedarf somit einer Korrektur, entweder durch eine Gesetzesänderung[1315] oder durch eine Entscheidung eines größeren Senats des Supreme Courts.

c) Berufungsverfahren

Entscheidet ein Gericht, das rechtshängige Verfahren nicht gem. Sec. 45 SchiedsG an das vereinbarte Schiedsverfahren zu verweisen, können die

1312 Siehe Sec. 11 SchiedsG n. F. und Sec. 8 SchiedsG n. F. und Kapitel: Kompetenz-Kompetenz; Arbitration Amendment Act (C.II.3.).

1313 Lee, Michelle, Asian International Arbitration Journal 2014, Vol. 10, Ausg. 2, S. 67 (81); Mahajan/Bhatt, Journal of International Arbitration 2013, Vol. 30, Ausg. 6, S. 711 (724); Mahajan/Bhatt, International Arbitration Law Review 2013, S. N25 (N27); Mahajan/Chatterjee, International Arbitration Law Review 2015, S. 114 (118).

1314 Trotz der durch die beiden Entscheidungen kreierten Rechtsunsicherheit, bleibt das Urteil *Shin-Etsu* die höchstrichterliche Präzedenzentscheidung zu Sec. 45 SchiedsG, weil die *Chloro Controls*-Rechtsprechung die Entscheidung *Shin-Etsu* nicht verwerfen konnte (vgl. o.).

1315 Die Gesetzesreform von 2015 ließ Sec. 45 SchiedsG unberührt.

Parteien gegen diese Entscheidung Berufung gem. Sec. 50 SchiedsG[1316] einlegen.

d) Arbitration Amendment Act

Die Gesetzesreform des SchiedsG hatte keine Auswirkungen auf Sec. 45 und 50 SchiedsG.

e) Bewertung

Die zwingende Verweisung der Streitigkeit an das schiedsgerichtliche Verfahren gem. Sec. 45 SchiedsG steht im Einklang mit Art. III (3) UNÜ und dem internationalen Standard der Schiedsgerichtsbarkeit[1317].

Bei der Verweisung von UNÜ-Schiedsstreitigkeiten mit ausländischem Schiedssitz an das Schiedsverfahren beschränkte der Supreme Court in der *Shin-Etsu*-Entscheidung die gesetzlich vorgesehene Kontrollmöglichkeit der Schiedsvereinbarung durch die Gerichte schiedsfreundlich auf eine *prima facie*-Kontrolle. Die Hongkonger Rechtsordnung sieht ebenfalls nur eine *prima facie*-Überprüfung der Schiedsvereinbarung vor[1318]. Die Gerichte in Frankreich respektieren die Parteiautonomie der Schiedsgerichtsbarkeit, indem sie ausschließlich ihre Zuständigkeit annehmen, wenn die Schiedsvereinbarung offenkundig unwirksam ist oder die gerichtlich anhängige Streitigkeit offensichtlich nicht von der Schiedsvereinbarung erfasst wird.[1319] In der *Chloro Controls*-Entscheidung erweiterte das oberste Gericht Indiens die gerichtliche Kontrollkompetenz der Schiedsvereinbarung gem. Sec. 45 SchiedsG. Der Supreme Court gestand den Gerichten die Überprüfung der tatbestandlichen Nichtverweisungsgründe[1320] in Sec. 45 SchiedsG wieder zu. Diese Kontrollkompetenz der Schiedsvereinbarung bei der Verweisungsentscheidung lässt sich auch Art. II (3) UNÜ entnehmen. Das *Chloro Controls*-Urteil stimmt daher mit der internationalen Norm der Schiedsgerichtsbarkeit überein. Nach dem *Chloro Controls*-Urteil entscheiden die Gerichte bei der Verweisung gem. Sec. 45 SchiedsG zudem verbindlich, über die Wirksamkeit der Schiedsvereinbarung. Dies steht im Widerspruch zur Kompetenz-Kompetenz des Schiedsgerichts. Das Schiedsgericht kann hier-

---

1316 Unter Sec. 50 (1) (a) SchiedsG ist den Parteien eine Berufung zum zuständigen Berufungsgericht zugänglich. Eine zweite Berufungsinstanz zum Supreme Court bleibt unberührt, ansonsten ist eine zweite Berufungsinstanz ausgeschlossen (Sec. 50 [2] SchiedsG).

1317 Born, Law and Practice, § 2.07 [B], S. 66 f.

1318 Born, International Commercial Arbitration, Bd. 1, S. 1091 f.

1319 Art. 1448 (1) französischer Code de procédure civile.

1320 Hierzu zählt die Hinfälligkeit, die Unwirksamkeit oder die Nichterfüllbarkeit der Schiedsvereinbarung.

durch einzig über, von den Gerichten noch nicht beurteilte Zuständigkeitsfragen entscheiden. Die weite Auslegung des Überprüfungsmaßstabs der Schiedsvereinbarung der *Chloro Controls*-Rechtsprechung ist deshalb als für die schiedsgerichtliche Streitbeilegung hinderlich anzusehen. Im Sinne möglichst geringer gerichtlicher Eingriffe in das Schiedsverfahren ist das den Maßstab der gerichtlichen Kontrolle der Schiedsvereinbarung restriktiver fassende *Shin-Etsu*-Urteil vorzugswürdig. Nur durch eine restriktive und nicht verbindliche Überprüfung der Schiedsvereinbarung bei der Verweisungsentscheidung gem. Sec. 45 SchiedsG kann das Schiedsgericht seine ihm nach Sec. 16 SchiedsG zustehende Kompetenz-Kompetenz ausüben.

Im *Chloro Controls*-Urteil durfte der gleichgroße Senat des Supreme Courts nicht von der *Shin-Etsu*-Entscheidung abweichen. Die *Shin-Etsu*-Rechtsprechung besteht folglich als höchstrichterliche Präzedenzentscheidung zu Sec. 45 SchiedsG fort.

Es entspricht nicht dem UNÜ, die Entscheidung staatlicher Gerichte, eine rechtshängige Angelegenheit nicht an das Schiedsverfahren zu verweisen, einer Berufung i. S. v. Sec. 50 SchiedsG zu unterwerfen. Ein Berufungsverfahren gem. Sec. 50 SchiedsG führt allerdings nicht zu Verzögerungsmöglichkeiten und parallelen Verfahren. Vielmehr kann das zuständige Gericht im Berufungsverfahren i. S. d. Sec. 50 SchiedsG die Parteien auf das vereinbarte Schiedsverfahren verweisen. Die Berufung gem. Sec. 50 SchiedsG fördert demnach die Durchsetzung der Schiedsvereinbarung.

V. Schiedsrichter

Die Konstituierung des Schiedsgerichts erfolgt nach Sec. 10 ff. SchiedsG. Die Schiedsrichterbestellung gem. Sec. 11 SchiedsG soll primär nach dem von den Parteien vereinbarten Verfahren erfolgen.[1321] Für eine parteiautonome Schiedsrichterbestellung gibt es zwei Möglichkeiten. Die Parteien vereinbaren entweder ausdrücklich ein Bestellungsverfahren oder die auf das Schiedsverfahren anwendbare institutionelle Schiedsordnung führt konkludent zur Wahl der institutionellen Bestellungsregelungen.[1322]

Wenn keine Parteivereinbarung vorliegt, sieht Sec. 11 (3) SchiedsG als Auffangregelung bei einem sich aus drei Schiedsrichtern zusammensetzenden Schiedsgericht zunächst die Bestellung von zwei Schiedsrichtern durch die beiden Parteien vor. Die Bestellung des Vorsitzenden dritten Schiedsrich-

1321 Sec. 11 (2) SchiedsG.

1322 UNCITRAL Sekretariat, Explanatory note, Rn. 22; Born, Law and Practice, § 7.01, S. 129 ff.; Born, International Commercial Arbitration, Bd. 2, S. 1642 ff.; Art. 2 (e), 11 (2) UNCITRAL Modellgesetz.

ters erfolgt sodann durch die bestellten beiden Parteischiedsrichter.[1323] Die Auffangregelung für die Bestellung eines Einzelschiedsrichters sieht gem. Sec. 11 (5) SchiedsG eine einvernehmliche Bestellung durch die Schiedsparteien vor. Werden die Schiedsrichter nicht ordnungsgemäß bestellt, wird die Schiedsrichterbestellung von der zuständigen Stelle vorgenommen.

Die zuständige Stelle war gem. Sec. 11 (4), (5) und (6) SchiedsG a. F. der Chief Justice oder eine von ihm bestimmte Person oder Institution.[1324] Für Internationale Handelsschiedsverfahren war gem. Sec. 11 (12) (a) SchiedsG a. F. der Chief Justice des Supreme Courts, der auch als Chief Justice of India[1325] bezeichnet wird, zuständig. Die Schiedsrichterbestellung für die inländischen und die übrigen internationalen Schiedsverfahren (im Folgenden inländische Schiedsverfahren) oblag in Sec. 11 (12) (b) SchiedsG a. F. dem Chief Justice des zuständigen High Courts.

Durch den Arbitration Amendment Act 2015 übertrug der Gesetzgeber in Sec. 11 (12) SchiedsG n. F. die gerichtliche Schiedsrichterbestellung dem Supreme Court bei internationalen Handelsschiedsverfahren und dem zuständigen High Court für die inländischen Schiedsverfahren.

1. Mitarbeiter als Schiedsrichter

a) Indian Oil Corp v Raja Transport

Im Verfahren *Indian Oil Corp Ltd & Ors v M/S Raja Transport (P) Ltd (Indian Oil)*[1326] hatte der Supreme Court über die Wirksamkeit einer Schiedsklausel zu entscheiden, die die Bestellung eines Mitarbeiters von *Indian Oil Corp Ltd & Ors (Oil Corp)* als Einzelschiedsrichter vorsah. Bei Verträgen zwischen der Regierung[1327] oder öffentlich-rechtlichen Unternehmen bzw. Körperschaften[1328] und Privatunternehmen war es in Indien gängige Praxis, dass diese Verträge eine Schiedsklausel enthalten, nach der ein Mitarbeiter der Regierung oder der öffentlich-rechtlichen Unternehmen bzw. Körperschaften Streitigkeiten zwischen den Schiedsparteien entscheidet.[1329]

Oil Corp ist ein öffentlich-rechtliches Unternehmen, dessen Mehrheitseigentümer der indische Staat ist. *Oil Corp* vereinbarte mit *M/S Raja*

1323 Sec. 11 (3) SchiedsG.

1324 Sec. 11 SchiedsG.

1325 Chief Justice of India und Chief Justice des Supreme Courts werden als Synonyme verwandt, siehe Art. 124, 126 der indischen Verfassung.

1326 2 Richter, (2009) 8 SCC 520; [2009] 13 SCR 510; Civil Appeal No. 5760 of 2009, 24.8.2009.

1327 Der Zentralregierung und den Regierungen der Bundesstaaten.

1328 Engl. statutory corporations and public sector undertakings.

1329 Law Commission of India, 176. Report, The Arbitration and Conciliation (Amendment) Bill, 2001, 12.9.2001, S. 58, 298.

Transport (P) Ltd (Raja), dass *Raja* die Ölprodukte von *Oil Corp* verkaufen sollte. Die Vereinbarung enthielt eine Schiedsklausel, die regelte, dass alle Vertragsstreitigkeiten vom Direktor der Marketingabteilung oder einem vom Direktor ernannten Mitarbeiter von *Oil Corp* als Einzelschiedsrichter entschieden werden sollten. *Oil Corp* kündigte die Vereinbarung mit *Raja* 2005. Ende 2005 ordnete der „Court of Civil Judge“[1330] im Bezirk Dehradun (Uttarakhand) an, dass *Oil Corp* die Lieferung von Ölprodukten an *Raja* für zwei weitere Monate zu gewährleisten habe und verwies die Streitigkeit der Parteien an das vereinbarte Schiedsverfahren. Diese Entscheidung bestätigte der District Court in Dehradun im Januar 2006.

In diesem Kontext beantragte *Raja* im März 2006 beim Chief Justice des Uttarakhand High Courts gem. Sec. 11 (6) SchiedsG die Bestellung eines unabhängigen Schiedsrichters für ihre Kündigungsstreitigkeit mit *Oil Corp*. Der Chief Justice ernannte im September 2008 einen pensionierten High Court-Richter als Einzelschiedsrichter für das Schiedsverfahren und begründete dies mit der mangelnden Unabhängigkeit eines *Oil Corp*-Mitarbeiters.

Im August 2009 war der Supreme Court im Berufungsverfahren[1331] der Auffassung, dass es sich bei der Schiedsgerichtsbarkeit um eine bindende private Streitbeilegung handle. Es sei üblich für indische Regierungen[1332] und öffentlich-rechtliche Unternehmen bzw. Körperschaften[1333], ihre zukünftigen Streitigkeiten mit ihrem Vertragspartner in Schiedsvereinbarungen der Schiedsgerichtsbarkeit zu unterwerfen, die einen ihrer leitenden Angestellten als Einzelschiedsrichter vorsehen. Wenn ein Vertragspartner sehenden Auges beim Vertragsschluss mit einer indischen Regierung oder einem öffentlich-rechtlichen Unternehmen bzw. Körperschaft einer solchen Schiedsklausel zustimme, könne das Privatunternehmen später nicht geltend machen, einzig an die Schiedsklausel, aber nicht an den vereinbarten „Mitarbeiterschiedsrichter“ gebunden zu sein. Ein „Rosinenpicken“ solle dem privatwirtschaftlichen Vertragspartner nicht zugestanden werden. Das oberste indische Gericht begründete seine Entscheidung mit Verweis auf die

1330 Ein „Court of Civil Judge“ ist ein dem District Court nachgeordnetes Gericht, Indian Courts, District Courts, verfügbar unter http://indiancourts.nic.in/districtcourt.html# (zuletzt abgerufen am 28.4.2021).

1331 In der Form einer „Special Leave“.

1332 Engl. governments. Die indische Regierung und die Regierungen der Bundesstaaten.

1333 Engl. statutory corporations and public sector undertakings.

ständige Rechtsprechung[1334] des indischen Supreme Courts zu Mitarbeiterschiedsrichtern und mit einem englischen Urteil.[1335]

Diese Rechtsauffassung des Gerichts scheint jedoch nicht in Stein gemeißelt zu sein. Der Supreme Court weist zu Recht auf das Ungleichgewicht bei der Vertragsverhandlung und Vertragsgestaltung zwischen der Regierung oder öffentlich-rechtlichen Unternehmen bzw. Körperschaften und Privatunternehmen hin. Im Rahmen dieser Unausgewogenheit akzeptierten Privatunternehmen auch Schiedsvereinbarungen, die einen Mitarbeiter der kontrahierenden öffentlich-rechtlichen Rechtssubjekte als Schiedsrichter vorsehen. Das oberste Gericht Indiens riet den indischen Regierungen und den öffentlich-rechtlichen Unternehmen bzw. Körperschaften auf Grund dessen in Zukunft bei Verträgen mit Privatunternehmen auf einen Mitarbeiter als Schiedsrichter zu verzichten. Ein Verzicht auf „Mitarbeiterschiedsrichter" würde die Akzeptanz der Schiedsgerichtsbarkeit als gleichwertigen Streitbeilegungsmechanismus fördern.[1336]

b) Bewertung

In casu verletzt der Supreme Court *Rajas* Recht auf eine Entscheidung durch einen unabhängigen und unparteilichen Einzelschiedsrichter. Das *Indian Oil*-Urteil führte zu einem Schiedsverfahren, bei dem es dem von *Oil Corp* bestellten Mitarbeiterschiedsrichter an der notwendigen Unabhängigkeit und Unparteilichkeit mangelte.[1337] Der Mitarbeiter schwingt sich in einem solchen Fall zum Schiedsrichter über eine Rechtsstreitigkeit seines Arbeitgebers auf und verstößt gegen das Verbot *nemo iudex in sua causa*.[1338] Dies erkennt auch das indische Schiedsrecht in Sec. 12 (3) SchiedsG an, indem

---

1334 Supreme Court, *Executive Engineer, Irrigation Division, Puri v Gangaram Chhapolia*, AIR 1984 SC 234; (1984) 3 SCC 627, 24.10.1983; Supreme Court, *Secretary To The Government Transport Department, Madras v Munuswamy Mudaliar & Ors*, AIR 1988 SC 2232; 1988 SCR Suppl. (2) 673, 29.8.1988; Supreme Court, *S Rajan v State Of Kerala And Another*, AIR 1992 SC 1918; (1992) 3 SCC 608, 29.7.1992; Supreme Court, *Union of India v M P Gupta*, (2004) 10 SCC 504; 2005 (1) Arb LR 368, 5.2.2004; Supreme Court, *Ace Pipeline Contracts Private Limited v Bharat Petroleum Corporation*, 2007 (5) SCC 304; Appeal (civil) 1783 of 2007, 4.4.2007.

1335 Civil Appeal No. 5760 of 2009, Rn. 9 f.

1336 Civil Appeal No. 5760 of 2009, Rn. 17.

1337 Vgl. Lew/Mistelis/Kröll, Comparative International Commercial Arbitration, Rn. 11-29; Born, Law and Practice, § 7.01 [C] [1] [vi], S. 142; Biswas, S. 77 f.; Malhotra, Indu, O.P. Malhotra on Arbitration, Sec. 11, S. 669 f.; vgl. Gaillard/Savage, Fouchard Gaillard Goldman, Rn. 1030; Malhotra, Indu, O.P. Malhotra on Arbitration, Sec. 11, S. 669.

1338 Vgl. Biswas, S. 77; Malhotra, Indu, O.P. Malhotra on Arbitration, Sec. 11, S. 669; International Bar Association, IBA Guidelines on Conflicts of Interest in International Arbitration, 23.10.2014, S. 6, 17.; Jauernig/Hess, S. 376.

es die fehlende Unparteilichkeit und Unabhängigkeit eines Schiedsrichters als Ablehnungsgründe für einen Schiedsrichter vorsieht. Einen Mitarbeiter einer Partei als Schiedsrichter zu bestellen, verstößt auch gegen die nicht abdingbare rote Liste der international respektierten[1339] „IBA Guidelines on Conflicts of Interest in International Arbitration“. Die rote Liste sieht in einer solchen Konstellation einen nicht heilbaren Interessenskonflikt[1340], der mit dem internationalen Standard der Unabhängigkeit und Unparteilichkeit eines Schiedsrichters unvereinbar ist.[1341] Die Bestellung eines Mitarbeiters als Einzelschiedsrichter ist darüber hinaus nicht mit der in Sec. 18 SchiedsG verankerten Gleichbehandlung beider Schiedsparteien in Einklang zu bringen.[1342] Das Bestellen eines nicht unparteiischen „Mitarbeitereinzelschiedsrichters“ verstößt außerdem gegen den Grundsatz eines fairen Verfahrens[1343] gem. Art. V (1) (b) UNÜ[1344] und gegen die öffentliche Ordnung nach Art. V (2) (b) UNÜ[1345]. Sowohl die Anerkennung als auch die Vollstreckung eines solchen Mitarbeiterschiedsspruchs sind daher außerhalb von Indien problematisch.[1346]

1339 Siehe hierzu Born, International Arbitration Law: Law and Practice, § 7.01 [C.] [1] [iv], S. 140; International Bar Association, IBA Guidelines on Conflicts of Interest in International Arbitration, 23.10.2014, S. i; Blackaby/Partasides/Redfern/Hunter, International Arbitration, Rn. 4.85 ff.; Born, International Commercial Arbitration, Bd. 2, S. 1698, 1762, 1839.

1340 Part II, 1.1 (unverzichtbare Rote Liste), Part I: General Standards Regarding Impartiality, Independence and Disclosure, International Bar Association, IBA Guidelines on Conflicts of Interest in International Arbitration, 23.10.2014.

1341 Part I International Bar Association, IBA Guidelines on Conflicts of Interest in International Arbitration, 23.10.2014.

1342 Vgl. Konsultation von Praktikern, Law Commission of India, 176. Report, The Arbitration and Conciliation (Amendment) Bill, 2001, 12.9.2001, S. 2 f., 15, 58. Vgl. zudem zum internationalen Standard, Gaillard/Savage, Fouchard Gaillard Goldman, Rn. 785 f.

1343 Art. V (1) (b) UNÜ ist verletzt, wenn die Schiedsparteien ihre Angriffs- oder Verteidigungsmittel nicht geltend machen können.

1344 Born, Law and Practice, § 17.05 [C] [3], S. 396 f.; Born, International Commercial Arbitration, S. 1659, 1827 (Bd. 2), 3492 ff., 3586 ff. (Bd. 3); Gaillard/Savage, Fouchard Gaillard Goldman, Rn. 786 f.

1345 *Schlosser* ist der Ansicht, dass das Übergewicht einer Schiedspartei bei der Konstituierung des Schiedsgerichts eine Verletzung der öffentlichen Ordnung darstelle, Schlosser, in Stein/Jonas, Anhang zu § 1061 ZPO Rn. 356; Schlosser, Rn. 827 ff.; unter Verweis auf *Schlosser* auch Schwab/Walter, S. 472. Siehe hierzu auch Born, International Commercial Arbitration, S. 1659, 1827 f. (Bd. 2), 3586 ff., S. 3646 ff. (Bd. 3); Gaillard/Savage, Fouchard Gaillard Goldman, Rn. 786 f.; Berger, Klaus, S. 165 f.

1346 Nach *Malhotra* soll ein durch einen Mitarbeiter einer der Schiedsparteien ergangener Schiedsspruch zudem in Indien unter Sec. 34 (2) (a) (v) SchiedsG aufhebbar sein, Malhotra, Indu, O. P. Malhotra on Arbitration, Sec. 11, S. 669.

Die Praxis, Mitarbeiter einer Partei als Schiedsrichter zuzulassen, ist schiedsunfreundlich[1347] und beschädigt den Ruf der Schiedsgerichtsbarkeit als einen rechtsprechungsäquivalenten, unabhängigen Streitbeilegungsmechanismus. Der Supreme Court hätte im Urteil *Indian Oil* nicht nur den öffentlich-rechtlichen Rechtssubjekten empfehlen sollen, von der Praxis, Mitarbeiter als Schiedsrichter zu berufen, Abstand zu nehmen, sondern er hätte die Mitarbeiterschiedsrichterklausel für unwirksam erklären sollen.

Das *Indian Oil*-Urteil wird in der Literatur als für Schiedsverfahren hinderlich angesehen und zu Recht wegen des Verstoßes gegen den *nemo iudex in sua causa* Grundsatz kritisiert[1348].

c) Arbitration Amendment Act

Die Akzeptanz von Mitarbeitern der Regierung oder von öffentlich-rechtlichen Unternehmen bzw. Körperschaften als Schiedsrichter in Verträgen mit Privatunternehmen zeigte sich auch 2001 im 176. Report der Law Commission. Der Report empfahl weiterhin, Mitarbeiter der Regierung oder von öffentlich-rechtlichen Unternehmen bzw. Körperschaften, in Anbetracht ihrer Unabhängigkeit und Integrität gegenüber ihrem Arbeitgeber, als Parteischiedsrichter zu erlauben.[1349] In der Gesetzesnovelle des SchiedsG aus dem Jahre 2015 verwarf der Gesetzgeber erfreulicherweise die Empfehlungen des 176. Reports. Er folgte stattdessen dem im 246. Report der Law Commission aus dem Jahr 2014 vorgeschlagenen Verbot von Parteischiedsrichtern.[1350] Nach Sec. 12 (5) i. V. m. Seventh Schedule Nr. 1 SchiedsG n. F. ist die Bestellung eines Mitarbeiters einer der Schiedsparteien – unabhängig davon, ob es sich um einen öffentlich-rechtlichen oder einen privatrechtlichen Arbeitgeber handelt – als Schiedsrichter ausgeschlossen.[1351] Der neu eingefügte „Seventh Schedule" des SchiedsG, der auch das Verbot der Mitarbeiterbestellung enthält, beruht auf der roten Liste der IBA Guidelines on

---

1347 Der Minimalstandard der Unabhängigkeit eines Einzelschiedsrichters steht einem Mitarbeiter als Einzelschiedsrichter entgegen, Born, International Commercial Arbitration, Bd. 2, S. 1818, 1868 f.

1348 In der Literatur wird das Urteil kritisiert, Born, International Commercial Arbitration, Bd. 2, S. 1868 i. V. m. Fn. 1278; Biswas, S. 77 f.; Malhotra, Indu, O. P. Malhotra on Arbitration, Sec. 11, S. 664 f., 669 f.

1349 Sec. 10A der vorgeschlagenen Gesetzesänderungen des SchiedsG, Law Commission of India, 176. Report, The Arbitration and Conciliation (Amendment) Bill, 2001, 12.9.2001, S. 61 ff.

1350 Government of India, Law Commission of India, 246. Report, Amendments to the Arbitration and Conciliation Act 1996, 5.8.2014, S. 29 ff., 48 f., 63 ff.

1351 Nachdem eine Streitigkeit entstanden ist, kann Sec. 12 (5) SchiedsG n. F. gem. Sec. 12 (5) a. E. SchiedsG n. F. abbedungen werden.

Conflicts of Interest in International Arbitration.[1352] Durch diese Reform des SchiedsG soll im Sinne einer schiedsfreundlichen Gesetzgebung gewährleistet werden, dass ein unabhängiges und unparteiisches Schiedsgericht die der Schiedsgerichtsbarkeit unterworfenen Streitigkeiten entscheidet.[1353]

2. Schiedsrichterbestellung

Der mit drei Richtern besetzte Senat des Supreme Courts in der Rechtssache *Konkan Railway Corpn Ltd & Ors v M/S Mehul Construction Co*[1354] und die aus fünf Richtern bestehende Constitutional Bench in der Entscheidung *Konkan Railway Corporation Ltd & ANR v Rani Construction Pvt Ltd*[1355] urteilten, dass die Rechtsnatur der Schiedsrichterbestellung gem. Sec. 11 (6) SchiedsG a. F. durch den Chief Justice oder durch eine von ihm bestimmte Person bzw. Institution einen verwaltungsrechtlichen Beschluss darstelle.[1356] Diese Entscheidungen stimmen mit der Entstehungsgeschichte des UNCITRAL Modellgesetzes überein. Dieser ist zu entnehmen, dass die Schieds-

1352 Government of India, Law Commission of India, 246. Report, Amendments to the Arbitration and Conciliation Act 1996, 5.8.2014, S. 30 f., 49.

1353 Zum internationalen Standard der Unabhängigkeit und Unparteilichkeit des Schiedsgerichts, Blackaby/Partasides/Redfern/Hunter, International Arbitration, Rn. 4.75 ff.; Born, International Commercial Arbitration, Bd. 2, 1654 ff.; Lew/Mistelis/Kröll, Comparative International Commercial Arbitration, Rn. 11-4 ff.

1354 AIR 2000 SC 2821; (2000) 7 SCC 201, 21.8.2000. Der Senat hatte zu entscheiden, welche Rechtsnatur der Beschluss gem. Sec. 11 (6) SchiedsG hat. Kritisch zu dem Urteil, Krishan, International Arbitration Law Review 2001, S. 90 (93); Malhotra, O. P., Arbitration 2004, S. 177 (179).

1355 Supreme Court, AIR 2002 SC 778; (2002) 2 SCC 388; Appeal (civil) 5880–5889 of 1997, 30.1.2002. Die Rechtsfrage, welchen rechtlichen Charakter die Schiedsrichterbestellung hat, verwies ein sich aus zwei Richtern zusammensetzender Senat des Supreme Courts an einen größeren Senat des Supreme Courts. Grundlage der Verweisung war die Überprüfung der Rechtsauffassung des mit drei Richtern besetzten Senats im Urteil *Konkan Railway Corpn Ltd & Ors v M/S Mehul Construction Co*. Positiv zu dem Urteil, Biswas, International Arbitration Law Review 2010, S. 42 (46). Kritisch zu der Entscheidung, Malhotra, O. P., Arbitration 2004, S. 177 (179).

1356 Zustimmend, Panjwani/Pathak, Indian Journal of Arbitration Law 2013, Vol. II, Ausg. 2, S. 1 (6 f.). *Krishan* hält die Schiedsrichterbestellung für einen verwaltungsrechtlichen Rechtsakt ohne Berufungsmöglichkeit, Krishan, International Arbitration Law Review 2001, S. 90 (93). *Malhotra* ist der Auffassung, dass der Supreme Court in den Entscheidungen *Konkan Railway Corpn Ltd & Ors v M/S Mehul Construction Co* und *Konkan Railway Corporation Ltd & ANR v Rani Construction Pvt Ltd* in unzutreffender Weise davon ausgegangen sei, dass es sich bei der Schiedsrichterbestellung um eine „Verwaltungsfunktion" handle, Malhotra, Indu, O. P. Malhotra on Arbitration, Sec. 11, S. 627 ff. *Mohta/Mohta* lehnen ebenfalls die Qualifikation der Schiedsrichterbestellung als „Verwaltungsfunktion" ab, Mohta/Mohta, Sec. 11, S. 200 f. *Malhotra* erachtet die Schiedsrichterbestellung als privaten Rechtsakt, Malhotra, O. P., Arbitration 2004, S. 177 (180).

richterbestellung als Verwaltungshandlung des zuständigen Gerichts zu charakterisieren ist.[1357] In der Rechtssache *Konkan Railway Corporation Ltd & ANR v Rani Construction Pvt Ltd* urteilte der Supreme Court zudem, dass Zuständigkeitsfragen bei der Schiedsrichterbestellung vom Schiedsgericht im Rahmen von dessen „Kompetenz-Kompetenz“ zu entscheiden seien.[1358]

a) SBP v Patel Engineering (Patel Engineering)

Die mit sieben Richtern besetzte Constitutional Bench des Supreme Courts hatte im Verfahren *SBP & Co v Patel Engineering Ltd & Anr* (*Patel Engineering)*[1359] zu entscheiden, ob die Schiedsrichterbestellung nach Sec. 11 (6) SchiedsG eine Gerichts- oder eine Verwaltungshandlung darstellt.

Die Constitutional Bench des Supreme Courts urteilte zunächst, dass die Schiedsrichterbestellung durch den Chief Justice oder einen Richter (im Folgenden zuständige Richter) des Supreme Courts oder des High Courts erfolgen müsse. Der Chief Justice des High Courts könne die Schiedsrichterbestellung nur an einen Richter des High Courts, der Chief Justice of India nur an einen Richter des Supreme Courts delegieren. Es sei unzulässig, die Schiedsrichterbestellung an einen District Court oder an eine Schiedsinstitution zu delegieren. Das oberste indische Gericht begründete dies mit der Entscheidung des Gesetzgebers, abweichend vom UNCITRAL Modellgesetz[1360], die Kompetenz der Schiedsrichterbestellung nicht einem nachgeordneten Gericht oder einer sonstigen Behörde zu übertragen. Die Schiedsrichterbestellung habe der Gesetzgeber in Sec. 11 SchiedsG a.F. vielmehr exklusiv dem Chief Justice des High Courts bzw. des Supreme Courts anvertraut.

Die siebenköpfige Constitutional Bench erörterte die Entscheidung *Konkan Railway Corpn Ltd & Ors v M/S Mehul Construction Co* des mit drei Richtern besetzten Senats des Supreme Courts und die Entscheidung *Konkan Railway Corporation Ltd & ANR v Rani Construction Pvt Ltd* der mit fünf Richtern besetzten Constitutional Bench. Der Supreme Court lehnte diese beiden Entscheidungen letztlich ab und urteilte, dass der Chief Justice eine gerichtliche Funktion wahrnehme und es sich bei der Schiedsrichterbestel-

1357 UNCITRAL, 18. Sitzung, Report of the Secretary-General, Analytical Commentary on Draft Text of A Model Law on International Commercial Arbitration, A/CN.9/264, 25.3.1985, Art. 6, S. 20; Art. 11, S. 29. *Malhotra* erachtet die Schiedsrichterbestellung nicht als Verwaltungshandeln, weil sie keine Exekutivaufgabe darstelle, Malhotra, Indu, O. P. Malhotra on Arbitration, Sec. 11, S. 627 ff.

1358 Appeal (civil) 5880–5889 of 1997, Rn. 11.

1359 AIR 2006 SC 450; (2005) 8 SCC 618; Appeal (civil) 4168 of 2003, 26.10.2005. Der Supreme Court hatte lediglich eine Rechtsfrage zu entscheiden, einen Tatbestand enthält das Urteil nicht.

1360 Art. 11, 6 UNCITRAL Modellgesetz.

lung entsprechend nicht um eine verwaltungsrechtliche Aufgabe handle.[1361] Die Constitutional Bench übertrug den zuständigen Richtern des Supreme Courts und des High Courts[1362] die Kompetenz, über ihre eigene Zuständigkeit, die Wirksamkeit der Schiedsvereinbarung, das Vorliegen einer Streitigkeit, die tatbestandlichen Voraussetzungen der Schiedsrichterbestellung und die Qualifikationen der Schiedsrichter selbst verbindlich zu entscheiden:

> „*(iv) The Chief Justice or the designated judge will have the right to decide the preliminary aspects as indicated in the earlier part of this judgment. These will be, his own jurisdiction, to entertain the request, the existence of a valid arbitration agreement, the existence or otherwise of a live claim, the existence of the condition for the exercise of his power and on the qualifications of the arbitrator or arbitrators.*“[1363]

Eine Schiedsrichterbestellung könne gem. Sec. 11 SchiedsG a. F. durch die zuständigen Richter des Supreme Courts und des High Courts nur bei Vorliegen einer wirksamen Schiedsvereinbarung erfolgen. Der Supreme Court begründete die verbindliche Überprüfungskompetenz der Schiedsvereinbarung durch die zuständigen Richter des Supreme Courts und des High Courts insbesondere damit, dass ansonsten das Schiedsgericht nach seiner Bestellung als privater Spruchkörper die Unzulässigkeit der höchstrichterlichen Schiedsrichterbestellung feststellen könne. Dies sei mit der Verbindlichkeit der Schiedsrichterbestellung gem. Sec. 11 (7) SchiedsG a. F. nicht zu vereinbaren. Der Parallelvorschrift von Sec. 11 SchiedsG a. F. – Sec. 8 SchiedsG a. F. – lasse sich ferner entnehmen, dass der zuständige Richter unter Sec. 11 SchiedsG a. F. – wie das nach Sec. 8 SchiedsG a. F. zuständige Gericht, im Rahmen des Verweisungsantrags an ein Schiedsverfahren – über seine eigene Zuständigkeit umfassend entscheiden können müsse. Wenn der zuständige Richter des Supreme Courts und des High Courts verbindlich das Vorliegen einer wirksamen Schiedsvereinbarung feststelle und dann das Schiedsgericht bestelle, erspare der Richter den Parteien, dass in einer Konstellation, in der das Schiedsgericht seine Zuständigkeit zu Unrecht annehme, ein teures Schiedsverfahren angestrengt werde, dessen Schiedsspruch gem. Sec. 34 SchiedsG wieder aufgehoben werden könne.[1364]

Nach der Constitutional Bench kann das Schiedsgericht von der Kompetenz gem. Sec. 16 (1) SchiedsG über die eigene Zuständigkeit zu entscheiden, nur

1361 Appeal (civil) 4168 of 2003, Rn. 46. Zustimmend, Mohta/Mohta, Sec. 11, S. 200 f.

1362 Der Chief Justice des Supreme Courts bzw. des zuständigen High Courts als auch vom Chief Justice bestimmte Richter desselben Gerichts.

1363 Appeal (civil) 4168 of 2003, Rn. 46.

1364 Das SchiedsG gestattet gem. Sec. 16 SchiedsG während des Schiedsverfahrens keine gerichtliche Überprüfung der Zuständigkeitsentscheidung, vgl. hierzu Kapitel: Kompetenz-Kompetenz; Zuständigkeit des Schiedsgerichts (C.II.1.a)).

dann vollumfänglich Gebrauch machen, sofern die Rechtsstreitigkeit ohne Rückgriff auf Sec. 8 oder Sec. 11 SchiedsG von den Parteien direkt dem Schiedsgericht vorgelegt werde. Wenn die Zuständigkeitsfrage bereits durch ein Gericht oder einen zuständigen Richter geklärt worden sei, könne diese finale Zuständigkeitsentscheidung nicht mehr vom Schiedsgericht *de novo* aufgerollt und entschieden werden.

Die Constitutional Bench urteilte, die Schiedsrichterbestellung habe die Rechtsnatur eines gerichtlichen Beschlusses. Das Ziel einer möglichst geringen Intervention in das schiedsgerichtliche Verfahren führe nicht automatisch zur Qualifikation der Schiedsrichterbestellung als verwaltungsrechtliche Funktion. Bekanntlich seien den Parteien gegen einen verwaltungsrechtlichen Rechtsakt zwei Berufungen vor dem High Court unter Art. 226 der indischen Verfassung und eine dritte Berufungsinstanz gem. Art. 136 der indischen Verfassung zum Supreme Court eröffnet[1365]. Gegen die Einordnung der Schiedsrichterbestellung als verwaltungsrechtlichen Rechtsakt wandte die Constitutional Bench zudem ein, dass die Bestellung von Schiedsrichtern durch den Chief Justice des Supreme Courts in einem Berufungsverfahren von den High Courts oder im Schiedsverfahren durch das Schiedsgericht überprüft werden könne. Die Charakterisierung der Entscheidung unter Sec. 11 SchiedsG als gerichtlicher Beschluss führe hingegen zu einem einstufigen Berufungsverfahren[1366] vor dem Supreme Court. Das oberste indische Gericht beschränkte die einstufige Berufung zum Supreme Court gem. Art. 136 der indischen Verfassung schließlich auf Schiedsrichterbestellungen durch den Chief Justice des High Courts, bei denen es sich nicht um internationale Handelsschiedsverfahren[1367] handelte.

b) Bewertung

Im *Patel Engineering*-Urteil untergrub die siebenköpfige Constitutional Bench die gesetzgeberische Intention, das Schiedstribunal im Rahmen seiner Kompetenz-Kompetenz[1368] über die eigene Zuständigkeit selbst entscheiden zu lassen[1369]. Die Constitutional Bench ist hiermit zur alten Rechtslage unter dem Arbitration Act 1940 zurückgekehrt, der die Kompetenz-Kompetenz

---

1365 Vgl. zu den Berufungsverfahren, Law Commission of India, 176. Report, The Arbitration and Conciliation (Amendment) Bill, 2001, 12.9.2001, S. 74 ff.

1366 Gem. Art. 136 der indischen Verfassung.

1367 Bzw. einen von ihm ernannten Richter desselben Gerichts.

1368 Zur Kompetenz-Kompetenz siehe auch ausführlich Kapitel: Kompetenz-Kompetenz; Verletzung der Kompetenz-Kompetenz bei der Schiedsrichterbestellung; Bewertung (C.II.2.c)).

1369 Zur Verletzung des gesetzgeberischen Willens, Sen, Vindobona Journal of International Commercial Law & Arbitration 2006, S. 45 (51 ff.).

des Schiedsgerichts nicht respektierte[1370]. Die Constitutional Bench verkürzte die Kompetenz-Kompetenz des Schiedsgerichts auf Schiedsverfahren, bei denen keine gerichtliche Schiedsrichterbestellung (Sec. 11 SchiedsG) bzw. keine Verweisung (Sec. 8 SchiedsG) der Rechtsstreitigkeit an das Schiedsgericht erfolgt war. Das Urteil *Patel Engineering* degradierte dadurch die im SchiedsG[1371] vorgesehene Kompetenz-Kompetenz des Schiedsgerichts vom Regelfall zur Ausnahme.[1372] Diese Rechtsauffassung des Supreme Courts widerspricht dem internationalen Standard einer schiedsfreundlichen Schiedsrechtsordnung, in der die Gerichte die Kompetenz-Kompetenz des Schiedsgerichts bei der Schiedsrichterbestellung als Grundpfeiler der Schiedsgerichtsbarkeit achten.[1373]

Zu Recht wird ergänzend an dem Urteil kritisiert, dass das oberste indische Gericht Sec. 11 SchiedsG a. F. umgedeutet habe, indem es die Worte „any person or institution designated by him" dahingehend auslegte, dass die Schiedsrichterbestellung ausschließlich vom Chief Justice des High Courts bzw. des Supreme Courts an einen Richter desselben Gerichts delegiert werden kann.[1374] Auf Schiedsverfahren spezialisierte Schiedsinstitutionen verfügen über die notwendige Expertise für die Schiedsrichterbestellung und sind deshalb für die Schiedsrichterernennung unter Berücksichtigung der Bedürfnisse des internationalen Handels am besten geeignet.[1375]

Dem 246. Report der Law Commission aus dem Jahr 2014 lässt sich entnehmen, dass die nach Sec. 11 SchiedsG beantragten Schiedsrichterbestellungen jahrelang im indischen Gerichtssystem anhängig bleiben, bis eine

1370 Zur alten Rechtslage unter dem Arbitration Act 1940, Malhotra, Indu, O. P. Malhotra on Arbitration, Sec. 16, S. 761; Madhya Pradesh High Court, *M P Housing Board And Anr v Satish Kumar Raizada*, 2003 (2) Arb LR 553 (MP), 22.11.2002.

1371 Sec. 16 SchiedsG. Ausfluss der Kompetenz-Kompetenz ist auch Sec. 8 SchiedsG a. F., der die Gerichte verpflichtete eine rechtshängige Streitigkeit bei Vorliegen einer Schiedsvereinbarung an die Schiedsgerichtsbarkeit zu verweisen.

1372 *Ray/Sabharwal* kritisieren an der Entscheidung *Patel Engineering*, dass die gerichtliche Kontrolle der Schiedsvereinbarung die Kompetenz-Kompetenz verletzt, Ray, Aloke/Sabharwal, MEALEY'S International Arbitration Report 2007, Vol. 22, S. 26 (29).

1373 Art. 11, 16, 5 UNCITRAL Modellgesetz; vgl. Born, International Commercial Arbitration, S. 1221 ff. (Bd. 1), 1729 (Bd. 2); Lew/Mistelis/Kröll, Comparative International Commercial Arbitration, Rn. 10-58 ff.; Sen, Vindobona Journal of International Commercial Law & Arbitration 2006, S. 45 (52).

1374 Malhotra, Indu, O. P. Malhotra on Arbitration, Sec. 11, S. 633; Sec. 16, S. 774; Sen, Vindobona Journal of International Commercial Law & Arbitration 2006, S. 45 (51); Malhotra, O. P., Arbitration 2004, S. 177 (180 f.); Malhotra, O. P., Student Bar Review 2007, Vol. 19, Ausg. 2, S. 69 (72 ff.); Kachwaha, International Arbitration Law Review 2007, S. 13 (16 f.); Biswas, S. 32.

1375 Malhotra, O. P., Arbitration 2004, S. 177 (182); Sen, Vindobona Journal of International Commercial Law & Arbitration 2006, S. 45 (51).

Schiedsrichterbestellung erfolgt.[1376] In diesem Kontext ist es positiv zu bewerten, dass der Supreme Court Berufungen gegen eine Schiedsrichterbestellung des Chief Justice of India für internationale Handelsschiedsverfahren ausschloss. Dies entspricht dem internationalen Konsens, nach dem gegen die gerichtliche Schiedsrichterbestellung keine Berufung möglich ist und verhindert Verfahrensverzögerungen durch gerichtliche Berufungsverfahren.[1377] Für inländische Schiedsverfahren kann aber eine Berufung gegen die gerichtliche Schiedsrichterbestellung eingelegt werden. Eine solche Berufungsmöglichkeit ist mit dem Grundgedanken des UNCITRAL Modellgesetzes, gegen die gerichtliche Schiedsrichterbestellung keine Rechtsmittel zuzulassen, um Verzögerungstaktiken zu verhindern, nicht in Einklang zu bringen.[1378] Durch die Charakterisierung der Schiedsrichterbestellung als gerichtlichen Rechtsakt und der damit verbundenen umfassenden Kontrolle der Schiedsvereinbarung wird den Parteien ein langwieriges, zivilrechtliches Verfahren mit den ihm inhärenten Verschleppungsmöglichkeiten aufgezwungen.[1379] Die lange Verfahrensdauer bei der Schiedsrichterbestellung für inländische Schiedsverfahren durch die *Patel Engineering*-Rechtsprechung lässt sich auch empirisch belegen. Eine Studie von *Srinivasan* untersuchte 83 Schiedsrichterbestellungs-Berufungsverfahren vor dem Supreme Court seit dem *Patel Engineering*-Urteil. Die Untersuchung stellte fest, dass lediglich in 3 der 83 Berufungsverfahren (3,6%) die Schiedsrichter-Bestellung innerhalb des internationalen Standards von 12 Monaten erfolgte. Die Schiedsrichterbestellung mit einem darauffolgenden Berufungsverfahren

1376 Government of India, Law Commission of India, 246. Report, Amendments to the Arbitration and Conciliation Act 1996, 5.8.2014, S. 16.

1377 Vgl. Art. 11 (5) UNCITRAL Modellgesetz. Zu den verkürzten Berufungsmöglichkeiten gegenüber einer Charakterisierung der Schiedsrichterbestellung als Verwaltungshandeln und dem hiermit verbunden dreistufigen Berufungsverfahren, siehe ausführlich Law Commission of India, 176. Report, The Arbitration and Conciliation (Amendment) Bill, 2001, 12.9.2001, S. 74 f., 81. Auch für inländische Schiedsverfahren wurde durch die Einordnung der Schiedsrichterbestellung als gerichtliche Zuständigkeit des Chief Justice des zuständigen High Courts die Berufungsebene von drei auf eine Instanz verkürzt, Law Commission of India, 176. Report, The Arbitration and Conciliation (Amendment) Bill, 2001, 12.9.2001, S. 74 ff., 81.

1378 Art. 11 (5), 5 UNCITRAL Modellgesetz; UNCITRAL Sekretariat, Explanatory note, Rn. 23; Born, International Commercial Arbitration, Bd. 2, S. 1694, 1725 f. Dies entspricht auch der Schiedsgesetzgebung in Frankreich (siehe Art. 1460 [3] Code de procédure civile), Hongkong (Sec. 24 [1] Arbitration Ordinance) und den USA (Sec. 16 Federal Arbitration Act [Title 9, US Code]). Das englische Schiedsrecht gestattet andererseits nach Sec. 18 (5) Arbitration Act 1996 ein Berufungsverfahren gegen die gerichtliche Schiedsrichterbestellung.

1379 Die Literatur moniert die mit der *Patel Engineering*-Rechtsprechung einhergehenden Verzögerungen, Malhotra, Indu, O. P. Malhotra on Arbitration, Sec. 16, S. 773 f.; Kachwaha, International Arbitration Law Review 2007, S. 13 (14 ff.); Srinivasan, Indian Journal of Arbitration Law 2012, Vol. I, Ausg. 1, S. 18 (19).

dauerte in 40 Verfahren 13–36 Monate (48,2 %), in 17 Verfahren 37–60 Monate (20,5 %), in 15 Verfahren 61–84 Monate (18,1 %) und in 8 Verfahren über 84 Monate (9,6 %)[1380].[1381] Diese Verzögerungen bei der Schiedsrichterbestellung für inländische Schiedsverfahren durch Berufungsverfahren widerspricht dem UNCITRAL Modellgesetz und dem globalen Standard der Schiedsgerichtsbarkeit[1382] und ist als schiedsunfreundlich anzusehen. Eines Berufungsverfahrens bedarf es für die gerichtliche Schiedsrichterbestellung nicht, wenn das Schiedsgericht nicht an die Entscheidung der zuständigen Richter gebunden ist. Das Schiedsgericht kann die eigene Zuständigkeit – inklusive der Schiedsrichterbestellung und der Wirksamkeit der Schiedsvereinbarung – im Rahmen seiner Kompetenz-Kompetenz selbst kontrollieren. Eine weitere Überprüfung der Schiedsvereinbarung und der Zusammensetzung des Schiedsgerichts kann ferner im Aufhebungsverfahren[1383] und im Anerkennungs- und Vollstreckungsverfahren[1384] stattfinden.

Die Literatur unterzog die *Patel Engineering*-Rechtsprechung, insbesondere auf Grund der hierdurch geschaffenen Verzögerungs- und Interventionsmöglichkeiten, richtigerweise einer harten Kritik.[1385]

Vor diesem Hintergrund erarbeitete das indische „Ministry of Law and Justice“ ein „Consultation Paper“, in dem es angeregte, dass die Schiedsrichterbestellung vom Chief Justice an eine Schiedsinstitution übertragen

1380 In 71 Verfahren von den 83 untersuchten Berufungsverfahren (86,7 %) hob das oberste Gericht Indiens die Schiedsrichterbestellung auf und in 42 der 71 Verfahren (59,2 %) verwies der Supreme Court die Schiedsrichterbestellung an die zuständige Ernennungsstelle zurück. Nur in 3 Verfahren erfolgte eine Entscheidung über die Schiedsrichterbestellung ohne nachfolgende Gerichtsverfahren (3,6 %), Srinivasan, Indian Journal of Arbitration Law 2012, Vol. I, Ausg. 1, S. 18 ff.

1381 Srinivasan, Indian Journal of Arbitration Law 2012, Vol. I, Ausg. 1, S. 18 ff.

1382 Gaillard/Savage, Fouchard Gaillard Goldman, Rn. 901 ff.; Born, International Commercial Arbitration, Bd. 2, S. 1694; Berger, Klaus, S. 158 f.

1383 Sec. 34 SchiedsG.

1384 Art. V UNÜ.

1385 Malhotra, O. P., Student Bar Review 2007, Vol. 19, Ausg. 2, S. 69 ff.; Dewan, Nakul, Asian International Arbitration Journal 2007, Vol. 3, Ausg. 1, S. 99 (101 ff.); Srinivasan, Indian Journal of Arbitration Law 2012, Vol. I, Ausg. 1, S. 18 ff.; Sen, Vindobona Journal of International Commercial Law & Arbitration 2006, S. 45 (50 ff.); Panjwani/Pathak, Indian Journal of Arbitration Law 2013, Vol. II, Ausg. 2, S. 1 ff.; Ray, Aloke/Sabharwal, MEALEY'S International Arbitration Report 2007, Vol. 22, S. 26 (29); Sharma, Sidharth, Journal of International Arbitration 2006, Vol. 23, Ausg. 5, S. 467 ff. Siehe ausführlich zu den Verzögerungen bei der Schiedsrichterbestellung durch die Entscheidung *Patel Engineering*, Srinivasan, Indian Journal of Arbitration Law 2012, Vol. I, Ausg. 1, S. 18 ff.; Malhotra, O. P., Arbitration 2006, S. 201 (206); Kachwaha, International Arbitration Law Review 2007, S. 13 (14 ff.).

werden solle.[1386] Dem ist die Law Commission in ihrem 246. Report nicht gefolgt. Vielmehr schlug die Law Commission dem indischen Gesetzgeber lediglich vor, dass die Wirksamkeitskontrolle der Schiedsvereinbarungen entsprechend dem *Shin-Etsu*-Urteils des Supreme Courts auf eine *prima facie*-Überprüfung[1387] reduziert werden solle.[1388]

c) Arbitration Amendment Act

Eine Gesetzesänderung war nach der im Widerspruch zum SchiedsG stehenden *Patel Engineering*-Entscheidung überfällig.[1389] Die Kompetenz zur Schiedsrichterbestellung übertrug der Gesetzgeber vom Chief Justice des Supreme Courts und dem Chief Justice des High Courts auf den Supreme Court und den High Court.[1390] Im Arbitration Amendment Act 2015 hob das Parlament nochmals hervor, dass der Supreme Court bzw. die High Courts die Schiedsrichterbestellung an Personen oder Schiedsinstitutionen delegieren können.[1391] Eine sinnvolle, detailliert geregelte Delegation an die in Indien etablierten Schiedsinstitutionen nahm der Gesetzgeber allerdings nicht vor. Durch den neu eingefügten Absatz 6A von Sec. 11 SchiedsG n. F. stellte die Legislative klar, dass der Supreme Court und der High Court bei der Schiedsrichtestellung die Schiedsvereinbarung nicht mehr auf ihre Wirksamkeit kontrollieren dürfen, sondern lediglich prüfen sollen, ob eine Schiedsvereinbarung existiert. Die Überprüfung der Wirksamkeit der Schiedsvereinbarung soll daraufhin vom Schiedsgericht unter dessen Kompetenz-Kompetenz vorgenommen werden. Dem Vorschlag des 246. Reports der Law Commission, eine gerichtliche *prima facie*-Kontrolle der Schiedsvereinbarung zuzulassen, entsprach die Novelle des SchiedsG im Interesse einer schiedsfördernden gerichtlichen Schiedsrichterbestellung erfreulicherweise nicht.

1386 Ministry of Law and Justice, Government of India, Proposed Amendments to the Arbitration & Conciliation Act, 1996, A Consultation Paper, S. 15 ff., verfügbar unter http://lawmin.nic.in/la/consultationpaper.pdf (zuletzt abgerufen am 28.4.2021).

1387 Für eine *prima facie*-Kontrolle sprach sich ebenfalls aus, Sen, Vindobona Journal of International Commercial Law & Arbitration 2006, S. 45 (50 ff.); Bansal, Bharat's Commentary, Bd. 1, Sec. 11, S. 259, Sec. 16, S. 321. Nach der Law Commission soll die Schiedsrichterbestellung erfolgen, wenn das Gericht *prima facie* zu dem Schluss kommt, dass eine wirksame Schiedsvereinbarung bestehe. Das Gericht solle aber eine umfassende Prüfung der Schiedsvereinbarung vornehmen, wenn das Gericht im Rahmen einer *prima facie*-Kontrolle zu der Konklusion kommt, dass keine gültige Schiedsvereinbarung vorliege.

1388 Government of India, Law Commission of India, 246. Report, Amendments to the Arbitration and Conciliation Act 1996, 5.8.2014, S. 18 ff.

1389 Srinivasan, Indian Journal of Arbitration Law 2012, Vol. I, Ausg. 1, S. 18 (31).

1390 Sec. 11 SchiedsG n. F. Die gerichtliche interne Organisation obliegt dem Supreme Court bzw. den High Courts (Sec. 11 [10] SchiedsG n. F.).

1391 Sec. 11 (4), (5) und (6) SchiedsG n. F.

Die langjährigen Bestellungsverfahren unter Sec. 11 SchiedsG a. F. sollen durch die neue Sec. 11 (13) SchiedsG auf eine Dauer von 60 Tagen begrenzt werden, um Schiedsverfahren als schnellen Streitbeilegungsmechanismus zu stärken.[1392]

Die Gesetzesanpassung des SchiedsG bestätigt in Sec. 11 (7) SchiedsG n. F., dass die Schiedsrichterbestellung verbindlich sein soll und dagegen keine Rechtsmittel eröffnet sein sollen. Dies entspricht Art. 11 (5) UNCITRAL Modellgesetz, der ebenfalls keine Rechtsmittel gegen die Schiedsrichterbestellung gestattet.

Im Arbitration Amendment Act beseitigte der Gesetzgeber langwierige, gerichtliche Interventionen in Schiedsverfahren und stärkte die Kompetenz-Kompetenz der Schiedsgerichte. Zudem ließ er der Schiedsgesetzgebung wieder ihre, vom UNCITRAL Modellgesetz vorgesehene, Schiedsverfahren unterstützende Stellung zukommen.[1393] Der Arbitration Amendment Act passte somit das SchiedsG den Erfordernissen des modernen Schiedsgerichtswesens an.

VI. Einstweilige Maßnahmen

1. Gerichtlicher einstweiliger Rechtsschutz

Sec. 9 SchiedsG regelt gerichtliche Maßnahmen des einstweiligen[1394] Rechtsschutzes für Schiedsparteien. In dieser Vorschrift ist die Legislative von Art. 9 UNCITRAL Modellgesetz mit einer detaillierteren Norm abgewichen.[1395] Vor der Gesetzesänderung durch den Arbitration Amendment Act 2015 war der Anwendungsbereich von Teil I SchiedsG in Sec. 2 (2) SchiedsG a. F. – im Gegensatz zu Art. 1 (2) UNCITRAL Modellgesetz – auf Schiedsverfahren mit Sitz in Indien beschränkt. Die indischen Gerichte durften demzufolge gem. Sec. 2 (2) a. F. i. V. m. Sec. 9 SchiedsG keine vorläufigen gerichtlichen Maßnahmen für die Parteien eines Schiedsverfahrens

---

1392 Vgl. Government of India, Law Commission of India, 246. Report, Amendments to the Arbitration and Conciliation Act 1996, 5.8.2014, S. 16 f.

1393 Vgl. Government of India Law Commission of India, Amendments to the Arbitration and Conciliation Act 1996, 5.8.2014, S. 16 ff.

1394 Einstweilige und vorläufige Maßnahmen bzw. einstweiliger und vorläufiger Rechtsschutz werden als Synonyme verwandt, siehe §§ 1033, 1041 ZPO und Art. 9, 17 Deutsche Institution für Schiedsgerichtsbarkeit (DIS) Übersetzung des UNCITRAL Modellgesetzes, DIS, Materialien, UNCITRAL Modellgesetz für die internationale Handelsschiedsgerichtsbarkeit 85, verfügbar unter http://www.disarb.org/en/51/materials/uncitral-modellgesetz-f%C3%BCr-die-internationale-handelsschiedsgerichtsbarkeit-85-id31 (zuletzt abgerufen am 28.4.2021).

1395 Sec. 9 SchiedsG.

mit ausländischem Sitz anordnen. Im Urteil *Bhatia International v Bulk Trading SA & ANR (Bhatia)* erweiterte der Supreme Court zunächst den Geltungsbereich von Teil I SchiedsG – zu dem auch Sec. 9 SchiedsG zählt – im Jahr 2002 *contra legem* auch auf Schiedsverfahren mit Sitz außerhalb Indiens.[1396] Im Jahr 2012 entschied daraufhin aber eine Constitutional Bench des obersten indischen Gerichts in der Rechtssache *Bharat Aluminium Co v Kaiser Aluminium Technical Service Inc (Balco)*, dass der Anwendungsbereich von Teil I SchiedsG auf Schiedsverfahren mit Sitz in Indien beschränkt sei.[1397]

a) Videocon v Union of India

In der Entscheidung *Videocon Industries Ltd v Union of India & Anr (Videocon)*[1398] hatte der Supreme Court im Jahr 2011 – vor der Einführung des Arbitration Amendment Acts 2015 – darüber zu urteilen, ob ein indisches Gericht vorläufige gerichtliche Maßnahmen für die Parteien eines Schiedsverfahrens mit Sitz im Ausland erlassen kann.

Im Verfahren *Videocon* war der erste Berufungsbeklagte[1399] der Staat Indien, dem die Förderrechte für Erdölvorkommen in den indischen Hoheitsgewässern und in Indiens exklusiven Wirtschaftszonen zustehen. Die indische Regierung vereinbarte 1994 in einem „Production Sharing Contract (PSC)“ mit einem aus *Videocon Industries Ltd* und drei weiteren Vertragspartnern bestehenden Konsortium eine Erkundungslizenz[1400] und einen Förderpachtvertrag[1401], um Kohlenwasserstoffvorkommen zu erforschen und zu fördern. Die im PSC enthaltene Schiedsklausel sah als Verhandlungsort[1402] Kuala Lumpur in Malaysia vor. Auf die Schiedsklausel sollte englisches Recht angewendet werden. Im Jahr 2000 kam es zu Unstimmigkeiten über Kosten und Gewinne zwischen den Parteien. Über diese Streitigkeiten sollte in einem Schiedsverfahren entscheiden werden. Der erste Verhandlungstermin sollte im März 2003 in Kuala Lumpur stattfinden. Der Ausbruch der SARS-Epidemie bewog das Schiedsgericht, den Verhandlungsort zunächst nach Amsterdam und danach nach London zu verlegen. Im November 2003

1396 Siehe hierzu ausführlich Kapitel: Anwendungsbereich der Schiedsgesetzgebung; Bhatia International v Bulk Trading SA (Bhatia) (C. I.1.b)).

1397 Siehe hierzu ausführlich Kapitel: Anwendungsbereich der Schiedsgesetzgebung; Bharat Aluminium v Kaiser Aluminium (Balco) (C. I.1.d)).

1398 2 Richter, AIR 2011 SC 2040; (2011) 6 SCC 161; Civil Appeal No. 4269 of 2011, 11.5.2011.

1399 Der zweite Berufungsbeklagte war ein Referat (Engl. arm of the Ministry) des Ministeriums für Erdöl und Erdgas.

1400 Engl. exploration licence.

1401 Engl. mining lease.

1402 Engl. venue.

vereinbarten die Parteien den Schiedssitz London.[1403] Dessen ungeachtet beantragten die Beklagten, dass die verbleibenden Verhandlungstermine in Kuala Lumpur durchgeführt werden sollten. Das Schiedsgericht lehnte den Antrag im April 2006 ab und entschied, dass die verbleibenden Verhandlungen in London stattfinden. Die Berufungsbeklagten beantragten daraufhin beim Delhi High Court im Wege einer vorläufigen Maßnahme gem. Sec. 9 SchiedsG die Aussetzung des schiedsgerichtlichen Verfahrens. Der Delhi High Court erließ die einstweilige Maßnahme gem. Sec. 9 SchiedsG für das Schiedsverfahren mit Sitz in London.

Der Supreme Court folgte in seinem Urteil der derzeit höchstrichterlichen *Bhatia*-Entscheidung[1404], nach der Teil I SchiedsG – der Sec. 9 SchiedsG beinhaltet – auf Schiedsverfahren mit Sitz im Ausland anwendbar war, sofern die Schiedsparteien dessen Anwendbarkeit nicht abbedungen hatten.

Das oberste Gericht Indiens war jedoch der Ansicht, dass die Parteien durch die Unterwerfung der Schiedsklausel unter englisches Recht den Geltungsbereich von Teil I SchiedsG konkludent ausgeschlossen hätten. Der Delhi High Court hätte entsprechend keine vorläufige Maßnahme gem. Sec. 9 SchiedsG gewähren dürfen. Der Supreme Court hob deshalb die einstweilige Maßnahme des Delhi High Courts auf und wies die Berufung zurück.[1405]

Die Entscheidung *Videocon* wird in der Literatur kritisiert[1406], aber dennoch – auf Grund der reduzierten gerichtlichen Eingriffskompetenz – treffend als schiedsfreundlicher als die Urteile *Bhatia* und *Venture Global* des Supreme Courts angesehen.[1407] Die *Balco*-Grundsatzentscheidung der fünfköpfigen Constitutional Bench des Supreme Courts revidierte im Jahre 2012 die Urteile *Videocon* und *Bhatia*.[1408]

b) Arbitration Amendment Act

Der Arbitration Amendment Act 2015 erweiterte den Anwendungsbereich der indischen Schiedsgesetzgebung in Sec. 2 (2) SchiedsG n. F. für den

1403 Diese Vereinbarung hielt das Schiedsgericht in Beschluss Nummer 3 fest.

1404 Siehe ausführlich Kapitel: Anwendungsbereich der Schiedsgesetzgebung; Bhatia International v Bulk Trading SA (Bhatia) (C. I. 1. b)).

1405 Civil Appeal No. 4269 of 2011, Rn. 8 ff.

1406 Rai, International Arbitration Law Review 2011, S. 138 ff.; Malhotra, Indu, O. P. Malhotra on Arbitration, Sec. 2 (2), S. 232 ff., Sec. 9, S. 489 ff.

1407 Ray, Ashutosh, Journal of International Arbitration 2012, Vol. 29, Ausg. 3, S. 345 (353); Ray, Ashutosh, International Arbitration Law Review 2013, S. 97 i. V. m. Fn. 8 und 9; Anchayil, Arbitration International 2013, Vol. 29, Ausg. 1, S. 105 (113).

1408 Nach der *Balco*-Rechtsprechung konnte für nach dem 6. September 2012 abgeschlossene Schiedsvereinbarungen kein gerichtlicher einstweiliger Rechtsschutz mehr für Schiedsverfahren mit extraterritorialem Sitz gewährt werden, siehe Kapitel: Anwendungsbereich der Schiedsgesetzgebung (C. I. 1.).

gerichtlichen einstweiligen Rechtsschutz gem. Sec. 9 SchiedsG – neben Schiedsverfahren mit Sitz in Indien – auch auf Schiedsverfahren mit ausländischem Sitz. Der Gesetzgeber schloss hierdurch diese Rechtsschutzlücke[1409] für Parteien eines extraterritorialen Schiedsverfahrens. Die Gesetzesreform führte zum Gleichklang des SchiedsG mit dem Standard des UNCITRAL Modellgesetzes[1410] als auch mit der Schiedsgesetzgebung der internationalen Schiedszentren in England, Singapur und Hongkong[1411]. Die Novelle des SchiedsG ist folglich als Schiedsverfahren unterstützend zu charakterisieren, weil der Gesetzgeber den lückenhaften Rechtsschutz für Schiedsverfahren mit ausländischem Sitz behob, indem er für die Parteien dieser Schiedsverfahren vorläufige gerichtliche Maßnahmen eröffnete.

Nach Sec. 9 (3) SchiedsG n. F. sind die einstweiligen gerichtlichen Maßnahmen gegenüber den vorläufigen schiedsgerichtlichen Maßnahmen subsidiär und können nur angeordnet werden, wenn das Schiedsgericht den Parteien gem. Sec. 17 SchiedsG keinen effektiven einstweiligen Rechtsschutz gewähren kann.[1412] Um Missbrauch unter Sec. 9 SchiedsG zu verhindern, muss nach einer gerichtlich angeordneten vorläufigen Maßnahme gem. Sec. 9 (2) SchiedsG n. F., die betreffende Partei innerhalb von 90 Tagen[1413] Schiedsklage erheben.

c) Bewertung

Im Jahre 2015, ganze 30 Jahre nach der Verabschiedung des UNCITRAL Modellgesetzes 1985, übernahm Indien durch den Arbitration Amendment Act 2015 den Anwendungsbereich des UNCITRAL Modellgesetzes. Sec. 2 (2) SchiedsG n. F. gestattet den indischen Gerichten nunmehr auch, einstweilige Maßnahmen für Parteien eines Schiedsverfahrens mit ausländischem Sitz zu erlassen. Die indische Schiedsgesetzgebung entspricht hiermit der internationalen Norm des UNCITRAL Modellgesetzes. Mit der Subsidiarität von gerichtlichen gegenüber schiedsgerichtlichen vorläufigen

1409 Parthasarathy/Visalakshi, Arbitration 2007, S. 394 (396 f.); Nair, Arbitration International 2007, Vol. 23, Ausg. 4, S. 699 (718); Ministry of Law and Justice, Government of India, Proposed Amendments to the Arbitration & Conciliation Act, 1996, A Consultation Paper, S. 11, verfügbar unter http://lawmin.nic.in/la/consultationpaper.pdf (zuletzt abgerufen am 28.4.2021). Siehe auch Kapitel: Anwendungsbereich der Schiedsgesetzgebung (C. I. 1.).

1410 Das UNCITRAL Modellgesetz gestattet in Art. 1 (2) gerichtlichen einstweiligen Rechtsschutz auch für Schiedsverfahren mit ausländischem Schiedssitz.

1411 Sec. 2 (3) i. V. m. Sec. 44 englischer Arbitration Act 1996; Sec. 12A Singapurer IAA; Sec. 5 (2) i. V. m. Sec. 21 Hongkonger Arbitration Ordinance; Parthasarathy/Visalakshi, Arbitration 2007, S. 394 (399).

1412 Sec. 9 (3) SchiedsG n. F.

1413 Diese Frist kann das zuständige Gericht gem. Sec. 9 (2) a. E. SchiedsG n. F. verlängern.

Maßnahmen erkennt das SchiedsG n. F. Schiedsverfahren als gleichwertige Streitbeilegungsmechanismen an. Ein Missbrauch der vorläufigen gerichtlichen Maßnahmen unter Sec. 9 SchiedsG n. F. ist durch das innerhalb von 90 Tagen einzulegende Schiedsverfahren ausgeschlossen. In diesem Gesamtpaket soll durch einstweilige gerichtliche Maßnahmen lediglich dann in das Schiedsverfahren eingegriffen werden, wenn dies für einen effektiven einstweiligen Rechtschutz unabdingbar ist. Die durch den Arbitration Amendment Act eingefügten Neuerungen des SchiedsG unterstützen die schiedsgerichtliche Streitbeilegung durch subsidiären und effektiven vorläufigen gerichtlichen Rechtsschutz für die Schiedsparteien.

2. Einstweiliger Rechtsschutz durch Schiedsgerichte

a) Alte Rechtslage

Die durch ein Schiedsgericht gewährten Maßnahmen des einstweiligen Rechtsschutzes konnten nach Sec. 17 SchiedsG a. F. durch die Gerichte nicht vollstreckt werden,[1414] sodass Schiedsgerichte keine effektiven Eilverfahren anordnen konnten.[1415] Dieser lückenhafte Rechtsschutz für die Schiedsparteien war als schiedsunfreundlich zu bewerten.[1416]

b) Arbitration Amendment Act

Nach dem neuen Sec. 17 (2) SchiedsG können von Schiedsgerichten angeordnete, vorläufige Maßnahmen wie Beschlüsse eines Gerichts nach dem „Code of Civil Procedure 1908“ vollstreckt werden.[1417] Durch die

---

1414 Es fehlte eine gesetzliche Grundlage im SchiedsG a. F., Supreme Court, *M D Army Welfare Housing Organisation v Sumangal Services Pvt Ltd,* (2004) 9 SCC 619; Appeal (civil) 1725 of 1997, 8.10.2003; Supreme Court, *Sundaram Finance Ltd v Nepc India Ltd*, (1999) 2 SCC 479; Appeal (civil) 141–143 of 1999, 13.1.1999.

1415 Government of India, Law Commission of India, 246. Report, Amendments to the Arbitration and Conciliation Act 1996, 5.8.2014, S. 26; Law Commission of India, 176. Report, The Arbitration and Conciliation (Amendment) Bill, 2001, 12.9.2001, S. 215 f.

1416 Dies ergibt sich aus einem Vergleich mit dem Schiedsverfahren fördernden Art. 17 H Ergänzungen des UNCITRAL Modellgesetzes 2006, der die Vollstreckung von schiedsgerichtlichen vorläufigen Maßnahmen gestattet. Siehe auch United Nations General Assembly, 61. Sitzung, Resolutions adopted by the General Assembly, on the report of the Sixth Committee, A/61/453, 4.12.2006, S. 1; UNCITRAL Sekretariat, Explanatory Note by the UNCITRAL secretariat on the 1985 Model Law on International Commercial Arbitration as amended in 2006, Rn. 4, 27.

1417 Gegen die vom Schiedsgericht angeordneten bzw. nicht angeordneten vorläufigen Maßnahmen ist für die Parteien gem. Sec. 37 (2) (b) SchiedsG eine Berufung eröffnet. Sofern eine Partei ein Berufungsverfahren gem. Sec. 37 (2) (b) SchiedsG ein-

Schiedsrechtsreform von 2015 folgte die Legislative der Empfehlung des 246. Reports der Law Commission[1418] und räumte den schiedsgerichtlich angeordneten vorläufigen Maßnahmen gegenüber den, nur subsidiär zulässigen, einstweiligen gerichtlichen Maßnahmen den Vorrang[1419] ein. Dies stärkte den von den Parteien vereinbarten Streitbeilegungsmechanismus der Schiedsgerichtsbarkeit.

c) Bewertung

Der Gesetzgeber reagierte auf den „zahnlosen" schiedsgerichtlichen einstweiligen Rechtsschutz und regelte die Vollstreckung von schiedsgerichtlich angeordneten vorläufigen Maßnahmen im SchiedsG n.F. Das SchiedsG n.F. entspricht dadurch den Ergänzungen des UNCITRAL Modellgesetzes 2006,[1420] das in Art. 17 H gleichfalls die Durchsetzung von schiedsgerichtlich angeordneten vorläufigen Maßnahmen vorsieht. Auch die international bedeutenden Schiedsorte England[1421], Hongkong[1422] und die Schweiz[1423] gestatten die Vollstreckung von schiedsgerichtlich angeordneten einstweiligen Maßnahmen. Die Gesetzesänderung des Jahres 2015 entspricht daher dem internationalen Schiedsgerichtsstandard und ist somit als Schiedsverfahren fördernd einzuordnen. Für Schiedsverfahren noch unterstützender wäre es, wenn der Gesetzgeber die Ergänzungen des UNCITRAL Modellgesetzes 2006 *de lege ferenda* vollumfänglich umsetzt und für vorläufige Maßnah-

---

legt, kann die vorläufige schiedsgerichtliche Maßnahme nur unter Berücksichtigung dieser gerichtlichen Berufungsentscheidung vollstreckt werden, siehe Sec. 17 (2) SchiedsG n.F.

1418 Der 246. Report der Law Commission schlug vor, schiedsgerichtlich angeordneten einstweiligen Maßnahmen eine effektive gerichtliche Vollstreckung zu eröffnen, Government of India, Law Commission of India, 246. Report, Amendments to the Arbitration and Conciliation Act 1996, 5.8.2014, S. 27. Bereits in ihrem 176. Report empfahl die Law Commission, die Vollstreckung von schiedsgerichtlich angeordneten vorläufigen Maßnahmen zu gestatten, Law Commission of India, 176. Report, The Arbitration and Conciliation (Amendment) Bill, 2001, 12.9.2001, S. 114 f., 215 f.

1419 Sec. 9 (3) SchiedsG n.F. Nach Sec. 9 (3) SchiedsG n.F. ist es den Gerichten lediglich gestattet, einstweilige gerichtliche Maßnahmen zu erlassen, wenn ein effektiver Rechtsschutz durch das Schiedsgericht nicht gewährleistet ist.

1420 In der Schiedsrechtsreform übernahm die Legislative aber nicht alle in den Ergänzungen des UNCITRAL Modellgesetzes 2006 vorgesehen Bestimmungen für den schiedsgerichtlich angeordneten einstweiligen Rechtsschutz, Government of India, Law Commission of India, 246. Report, Amendments to the Arbitration and Conciliation Act 1996, 5.8.2014, S. 27.

1421 Sec. 42 Arbitration Act 1996.

1422 Sec. 61 Arbitration Ordinance.

1423 Art. 183 Bundesgesetz über das Internationale Privatrecht (IPRG); Kren Kostkiewicz, IPRG/LugÜ, Art. 183 IPRG Rn. 7; Mabillard, in: Honsell/Vogt/Schnyder/Berti, Basler Kommentar, Art. 183 IPRG Rn. 16.

men, die von Schiedsgerichten mit ausländischem Sitz[1424] und durch den „Emergency Arbitrator“[1425] erlassen werden, die Vollstreckung in Indien eröffnen würde.

VII. Aufhebungsverfahren

Schiedssprüche können bei tatbestandlicher Erfüllung eines der abschließend in Sec. 34 SchiedsG aufgeführten Gründe aufgehoben werden.[1426]

1. Formelle Aufhebungsgründe

Die formellen Aufhebungsgründe in Sec. 34 (2) (a) (i)–(v) SchiedsG stimmen mit Art. 34 (2) (a) (i)–(iv) UNCITRAL Modellgesetz[1427] überein und die Gerichte legen sie bislang schiedsfreundlich aus.[1428] Die zusätzlichen formellen Aufhebungsgründe in Sec. 13 (4), (5)[1429] und Sec. 16 (5), (6)[1430] SchiedsG sind Unterpunkte der formellen Annullierungsgründe in

---

1424 Art. 1 (2), Art. 17 H Ergänzungen des UNCITRAL Modellgesetzes 2006 erweitern den territorialen Anwendungsbereich des UNCITRAL Modellgesetzes für die Vollstreckung von durch Schiedsgerichte mit ausländischem Sitz angeordnete einstweilige Maßnahmen gem. Sec. 17 H Ergänzungen des UNCITRAL Modellgesetzes 2006. Die Hongkonger (Sec. 61 i. V. m. Sec. 5 [2] Arbitration Ordinance) und die Singapurer (Sec. 27 ff. IAA) Schiedsgesetzgebung gestatten ebenfalls die Vollstreckung vorläufiger Maßnahmen, die Schiedsgerichte mit ausländischem Sitz anordnen.

1425 Die Law Commission hatte empfohlen, die Definition eines Schiedsgerichts in Sec. 2 (1) (d) SchiedsG um den Emergency Arbitrator zu erweitern. Government of India, Law Commission of India, 246. Report, Amendments to the Arbitration and Conciliation Act 1996, 5.8.2014, S. 10, 37. Die vom Emergency Arbitrator angeordneten vorläufigen Maßnahmen wären hierdurch gem. Sec. 17 SchiedsG n. F. vollstreckbar gewesen. Diesem Vorschlag ist der Gesetzgeber in der neuen Fassung des SchiedsG 2015 nicht gefolgt. In Singapur und Hongkong ist eine Vollstreckung der vom Emergency Arbitrator erlassenen einstweiligen Maßnahmen möglich, siehe Sec. 22 B Hongkonger Arbitration Ordinance; Sec. 2 (1), 12 (6) Singapurer IAA und Sec. 2 (1), 28 (4) Singapurer AA. Die Ergänzungen des UNCITRAL Modellgesetzes 2006 sehen keine Vollstreckung der durch den Emergency Arbitrator angeordneten vorläufigen Maßnahmen vor.

1426 Sec. 34 (1) SchiedsG.

1427 Teilweise weicht der Wortlaut leicht ab, aber die Aufhebungstatbestände entsprechen dem UNCITRAL Modellgesetz.

1428 Bansal, Bharat's Commentary, Bd. 1, Sec. 34, S. 472 ff.; Wadhwa/Krishnan/Bachawat/Bachawat, Bachawat's Arbitration, Bd. 1, Sec. 34, 1529 ff.; Singh, Avtar, Arbitration, Sec. 34, S. 293 ff.

1429 Fehlerhafte Zusammensetzung des Schiedsgerichts gem. Sec. 34 (2) (a) (v) SchiedsG.

1430 Die positive Zuständigkeitsentscheidung des Schiedsgerichts im Rahmen der Kompetenz-Kompetenz gem. Sec. 16 SchiedsG kann erst im Aufhebungsverfahren nach Sec. 34 (2) (a) SchiedsG angefochten werden.

Sec. 34 (2) (a) SchiedsG. Ihre gerichtliche Kontrolle ist erst im Aufhebungsverfahrens zulässig[1431], um Intervention der Gerichte und langwierige Parallelverfahren während des Schiedsverfahrens zu verhindern.

2. Materielle Aufhebungsgründe

Die materiellen Aufhebungsgründe gem. Sec. 34 (2) (b) SchiedsG korrespondieren mit Art. 34 (2) (b) UNCITRAL Modellgesetz und sind vom zuständigen Gericht von Amts wegen zu prüfen.

a) Schiedsfähigkeit

Ein Schiedsspruch kann nach Sec. 34 (2) (b) (i) SchiedsG aufgehoben werden, wenn die entschiedene Streitigkeit nicht schiedsfähig ist.[1432]

b) Öffentliche Ordnung

Nach dem alten Arbitration Act 1940 konnte ein Schiedsspruch gem. Sec. 30[1433] bei einer Verfehlung des Schiedsgerichts oder fehlerhafter Verfahrensdurchführung, bei der Unvereinbarkeit mit einer gerichtlichen Entscheidung, wenn der Schiedsspruch auf unlautere Weise herbeigeführt wurde oder aus einem anderen Grund ungültig war, aufgehoben werden. Sec. 16[1434] Arbitration Act 1940 gestattete es den Gerichten, eine Streitigkeit an das Schiedsgericht zur nochmaligen Entscheidung zurück zu verweisen, sofern das Gericht dem Schiedsspruch dessen mangelnde Rechtmäßigkeit „auf den ersten Blick“ entnehmen konnte. Die indischen Gerichte

---

1431 Die positive Zuständigkeitsentscheidung gem. Sec. 16 SchiedsG des Schiedsgerichts als auch eine vom Schiedsgericht nach Sec. 13 SchiedsG zurückgewiesene Ablehnung eines Schiedsrichters kann nur im Aufhebungsverfahren von den staatlichen Gerichten kontrolliert werden.

1432 Zur Schiedsfähigkeit einer Streitigkeit, siehe Malhotra, Indu, O. P. Malhotra on Arbitration, Sec. 34, S. 1320 ff.; vgl. auch Singh, Avtar, Arbitration, Sec. 34, S. 355 ff. und Paranjape, Sec. 34, S. 284 f.

1433 30. Grounds for setting aside award
An award shall not be set aside except on one or more of the following grounds, namely: –
(a) that an arbitrator or umpire has misconducted himself or the proceedings
(b) that an award has been made after the issue of an order by the Court superseding the arbitration or after arbitration proceedings have become invalid under section 35;
(c) that an award has been improperly procured or is otherwise invalid.

1434 16. Power to remit award.
(1) The Court may from time to time remit the award or any matter referred to arbitration to the arbitrators or umpire for reconsideration upon such terms as it thinks fit -
[...]
(c) where an objection to the legality of the award is apparent upon the face of it.

und der Privy Council verwendeten Sec. 16 und Sec. 30 (c) des alten Arbitration Acts 1940, um Schiedssprüche, denen „auf den ersten Blick“ eine fehlerhafte Rechtsanwendung entnommen werden konnte, aufzuheben.[1435] Dadurch konnten Schiedssprüche auf ihre Übereinstimmung mit dem indischen Recht überprüft werden. Unter dem Arbitration Acts 1940 hatte der Supreme Court in der Rechtssache *National Thermal Power Corp v Singer Company And Ors*[1436] entschieden, dass auch ein aus einem ausländischen Schiedsverfahren[1437] entspringender Schiedsspruch in Indien aufgehoben werden könne, wenn auf den Hauptvertrag und die Schiedsklausel indisches Recht Anwendung finde.

Durch die Einführung des auf dem UNCITRAL Modellgesetz beruhenden Sec. 34 SchiedsG brachte der Gesetzgeber im Jahre 1996 zum Ausdruck, dass Schiedssprüche grundsätzlich nur bei formellen Fehlern des Schiedsverfahrens aufgehoben werden dürfen.[1438] Nur ausnahmsweise sollen Schiedssprüche auch wegen der materiellen Aufhebungsgründe der fehlenden Schiedsfähigkeit und der Verletzung der öffentlichen Ordnung (*ordre public*) aufgehoben werden können.[1439]

In Sec. 34 SchiedsG n. F. definierte die Legislative erstmals den Begriff der öffentlichen Ordnung. Der Begriff der öffentlichen Ordnung konnte unter Sec. 34 SchiedsG a. F. auf Grund seiner Unbestimmtheit mit einem nicht zu bändigenden Pferd verglichen werden, dessen Zügelung der Rechtsprechung obliegt. [1440] Die öffentliche Ordnung verändert sich ferner im Laufe der Zeit mit den gesellschaftlichen Entwicklungen eines Landes dynamisch. Diese Entwicklungen hat die Rechtsprechung bei der Konkretisierung des Begriffs der öffentlichen Ordnung zu berücksichtigen. Nachfolgend wird die gerichtliche Auslegung der öffentlichen Ordnung dargelegt, die 2015 zur Legaldefinition in Sec. 34 SchiedsG n. F. führte.

1435 Malhotra, Indu, O. P. Malhotra on Arbitration, Sec. 34, S. 1352 f.; Darwazeh/Linnane, International Arbitration Law Review 2004, S. 81 (82); Rai, Journal of International Dispute Settlement 2012, Vol. 3, Ausg. 1, S. 169 (189); Law Commission of India, 176. Report, The Arbitration and Conciliation (Amendment) Bill, 2001, Consultation paper on review of working of the Arbitration and Conciliation Act, 1996, 2001, 12.9.2001, S. 288 f.

1436 AIR 1993 SC 998; [1992] 3 SCR 106, 7.5.1992. Der Supreme Court hatte darüber zu entscheiden, ob ein vorläufiger Schiedsspruch (engl. interim award), der aus einem ICC-Schiedsverfahren in London entstammte, von einem indischen Gericht aufgehoben werden könne.

1437 Sitz des Schiedsverfahrens war London.

1438 Vgl. Sec. 34 UNCITRAL Modellgesetz; UNCITRAL Sekretariat, Explanatory note, Rn. 40 ff.

1439 Vgl. Sec. 34 UNCITRAL Modellgesetz; Sekretariat, Explanatory note, Rn. 40 ff.

1440 Vgl. Kapitel: Singapur; Aufhebungsverfahren; Öffentliche Ordnung (B.VII.2.a)).

aa) Renusagar Power v General Electric (Renusagar)

In der Rechtssache *Renusagar Power Co Ltd v General Electric Co (Renusagar)*[1441] hatte ein aus drei Richtern zusammengesetzter Senat des Supreme Courts 1993 über die Reichweite der öffentlichen Ordnung bei der Vollstreckung ausländischer Schiedssprüche gem. Sec. 7 (1) (b) (ii) „Foreign Awards (Recognition And Enforcement) Act 1961 (Foreign Award Act)" – der Sec. 48 SchiedsG entspricht[1442] – zu entscheiden. Das Gericht entschied nicht über die Aufhebung eines Schiedsspruchs, sondern urteilte über die Vollstreckbarkeit eines ausländischen Schiedsspruchs und konkretisierte hierbei den Begriff der indischen öffentlichen Ordnung. Den Terminus der öffentlichen Ordnung verwendete Sec. 34 (2) (b) (ii) SchiedsG a. F. deckungsgleich bei der Aufhebung von im Inland ergangenen Schiedssprüchen.[1443]

Nach dem Tatbestand des Berufungsverfahrens hatte das indische Energieunternehmen *Renusagar Power Co Ltd (Renusagar Power)* mit dem amerikanischen Unternehmen *General Electric Co (GE)* über die Lieferung und die Errichtung eines Wärmekraftwerks in Renukoot (Uttar Pradesh) verhandelt. Die indische Regierung gestattete das Projekt und die Parteien schlossen 1964 einen Vertrag über die Lieferung und Errichtung des Wärmekraftwerks für 13.195.000,00 US-Dollar. Nach einer Anzahlung von 10 Prozent des Kaufpreises waren der restliche Kaufpreis und die Zinsen in 16 Raten zu bezahlen (11.875.500,00 US-Dollar und 900.558,75 US-Dollar Zinsen). Der Vertrag enthielt eine Schiedsklausel und verpflichtete die Vertragsparteien, alle Vertragsstreitigkeiten durch ein ICC-Schiedsverfahren beizulegen. Während der Lieferung und der Errichtung des Wärmekraftwerks kam es zu Streitigkeiten zwischen den Parteien. Die Parteien legten diese Unstimmigkeiten 1968 in einem Vergleich bei. Sie vereinbarten, die ersten Kaufpreisraten zu verschieben und die Anzahl der Kaufpreisraten zu reduzieren. Mangels Ratentilgung erhöhten sich die Zinszahlungen. *Renusagar Power* bezahlte die ersten Raten nicht, wie im Kaufvertrag vereinbart, und beantragte bei der indischen Regierung die Genehmigung des geänderten Ratenplans. Die indische Regierung lehnte den geänderten Ratenplan 1969 mit der Begründung ab, dass dieser zu einer erhöhten Zinslast und damit zu einem höheren Abfluss ausländischer Devisen führe, dem die indische Regierung bei der ursprünglichen Genehmigung des Vertrages nicht zugestimmt habe. Die indische Regierung wies *Renusagar Power* an, ihre Raten entsprechend der ursprünglichen Vereinbarung zu bezahlen. *Renusagar Power* bezahlte die ersten Raten verspätet. *GE* legte daraufhin im März 1982 Schiedsklage gegen *Renusagar Power* bei der ICC ein. *Renusagar Power* wandte ein,

1441 AIR 1994 SC 860; (1994) Supp. 1 SCC 644; [1993] Supp. 3 SCR 22, 7.10.1993.

1442 Vor der Einführung von Sec. 48 SchiedsG im Jahre 1996, setzte Sec. 7 (1) (b) (ii) Foreign Award Act Art. V (2) (b) UNÜ in das indische Schiedsrecht um.

1443 Darwazeh/Linnane, International Arbitration Law Review 2004, S. 81 (83).

dass die Schiedsklage von *GE* nicht von der Schiedsvereinbarung erfasst sei und zudem der Streitgegenstand nicht schiedsfähig sei.

Parallel beantragte *Renusagar Power* im Juni 1982 beim Bombay High Court festzustellen, dass die vor der ICC anhängige Streitigkeit nicht von der Schiedsvereinbarung erfasst sei. Weiterhin begehrte *Renusagar Power* den Erlass einer einstweiligen Maßnahme gegen die Fortsetzung des ICC-Schiedsverfahrens und die Zahlung der ICC Verwaltungs- und Schiedsverfahrenskosten. Der Bombay High Court erließ *ex parte* die von *Renusagar Power* beantragte einstweilige Maßnahme[1444]. *GE* beantragte daraufhin die Aufhebung der angeordneten einstweiligen Maßnahme und die Aussetzung des gerichtlichen Verfahrens gem. Sec. 3[1445] Foreign Award Act. Ein Einzelrichter des Bombay High Courts hob die einstweilige Maßnahme auf und setzte das gerichtliche Verfahren aus. Diese Entscheidung bestätigte eine „Division Bench" des Bombay High Courts 1983 und letztinstanzlich der Supreme Court 1984. Ein weiteres Verfahren setze der Supreme Court 1987 ebenfalls gem. Sec. 3 Foreign Award Act aus.[1446]

Das ICC-Schiedsgericht erklärte sich für zuständig und entschied im September 1986, dass *Renusagar Power* an *GE* 12.215.622,14 US-Dollar zahlen müsse. Diese Summe setzte sich aus den nicht gezahlten Zinsen, Entschädigungszahlungen[1447], dem nicht bezahlten Kaufpreis für gelieferte Teile und aus Prozesskosten zusammen. Für die nicht beglichenen Zinsen ordnete das Schiedsgericht Zinseszinsen[1448] an.

Am 15.10.1986 beantragte *GE* beim Bombay High Court den Schiedsspruch für vollstreckbar zu erklären. *Renusagar Power* legte am 17.10.1986 eine Feststellungklage vor dem „Court of Civil Judge"[1449] Mirzapur (Uttar Pradesh) ein, in der die Unwirksamkeit des Schiedsspruchs festgestellt werden sollte. Auf Antrag von *GE* verwies der Court of Civil Judge die Rechtssache

1444 Engl. interim relief.

1445 In Sec. 3 Foreign Award Act setzte der indische Gesetzgeber Art. II (3) UNÜ in das indische Recht um. Sec. 3 Foreign Award Act entspricht Sec. 45 SchiedsG.

1446 1982 strengte *GE* ein Verfahren vor dem Kalkutta High Court gegen die *United Commercial Bank* an, um eine für *Renusagar Power* ausgestellte Bankgarantie zu vollstrecken. *Renusagar Power* war nach dem Vertrag verpflichtet, eine Bankgarantie der *United Commercial Bank* für die 16 Raten als Sicherheit zu leisten. *Renusagar Power* antworte auf dieses Verfahren mit einer Klage, in der festgestellt werden sollte, dass die Bankgarantie unwirksam sei. *GE* beantragte die Aussetzung des Verfahrens gem. Sec. 3 Foreign Award Act. Erst der Supreme Court gab diesem Antrag statt.

1447 Engl. compensatory damages.

1448 Darüber hinaus sprach das Schiedsgericht *GE* für den nicht bezahlten Kaufpreis Zinsen zu.

1449 Ein „Court of Civil Judge" ist ein dem District Court nachgeordnetes Gericht, Indian Courts, District Courts, verfügbar unter http://indiancourts.nic.in/districtcourt.html# (zuletzt abgerufen am 28.4.2021).

an den Bombay High Court, der die Feststellungsklage aussetzte. Im Vollstreckungsverfahren erklärte ein Einzelrichter des Bombay High Courts den Schiedsspruch 1988 nach dem Foreign Award Act für vollstreckbar. Eine Division Bench des Bombay High Courts bestätige 1989 die Vollstreckung des Schiedsspruchs.

Im Berufungsverfahren vor dem Supreme Court trug *Renusagar Power* vor, dass die Vollstreckung des Schiedsspruchs gegen die indische öffentliche Ordnung verstoße, weil sie Normen des „Foreign Exchange Regulation Acts 1973", des „Interest Acts 1978" und des „Indian Contract Acts 1872"[1450] verletze. Das oberste indische Gericht kam zu der Gesamtbewertung, dass der öffentlichen Ordnung enge Grenzen gesetzt werden müssen:[1451]

> *„Applying the said criteria it must be held that the enforcement of a foreign award would be refused on the ground that it is contrary to public policy if such enforcement would be contrary to (i) fundamental policy of Indian law; or (ii) the interests of India; or (iii) justice or morality."*[1452]

Entsprechend verletzt ein Schiedsspruch die öffentliche Ordnung, wenn er gegen

1. den grundlegenden Gesetzeszweck des indischen Rechts, oder
2. die Interessen Indiens, oder
3. Gerechtigkeit und Moral

verstößt.

Im Jahre 1993 entschied der Supreme Court, dass der Schiedsspruch nicht die öffentliche Ordnung in Indien tangiere. Der Supreme Court verneinte in seinem Urteil einen Verstoß des Schiedsspruchs gegen die einfachgesetzlichen Normen des Foreign Exchange Regulation Acts 1973, des Interest Acts 1978 und des Indian Contract Acts 1872.[1453]

Die enge Auslegung der öffentlichen Ordnung im *Renusagar*-Urteil lobt die Literatur als schiedsfreundlichen Schritt hin zu einer Schiedsverfahren unterstützenderen Rechtsordnung.[1454]

1450 Ungerechtfertigte Bereicherung.

1451 Ausführlich hierzu Kapitel: Anerkennung und Vollstreckung; Renusagar Power v General Electric (Renusagar) (C.VIII.2.b)aa)).

1452 [1993] Supp. 3 SCR, S. 22 (72 f.).

1453 Ausführlich hierzu Kapitel: Anerkennung und Vollstreckung; Renusagar Power v General Electric (Renusagar) (C.VIII.2.b)aa)).

1454 Mahajan/Narayan, International Arbitration Law Review 2015, S. 63 (68); Reddy/Nagaraj, Journal of International Arbitration 2002, Vol. 19, Ausg. 2, S. 117 (140 ff.); Sharma, Ajay, Indian Journal of Arbitration Law 2014, Vol. III, Ausg. 1, S. 6 (29 f.); Nariman, in: Bosman (Hrsg.), ICCA International Handbook on Commercial Arbitration, Bd. III, S. India 1 (India 55 Fn. 70); Thej, International Arbitration Law Review 2014, S. 37 (39); Kumar, Aakanksha, International Arbitration Law Review 2014,

Die Vollstreckbarerklärung des Schiedsspruchs dauerte wegen der langwierigen Verfahren vor dem High Court und dem Supreme Court sieben Jahre. Die verschiedenen, parallel zu dem vereinbarten schiedsgerichtlichen Verfahren eingelegten Gerichtsverfahren in der Causa *Renusagar* offenbaren zudem das zentrale Problem der indischen Schiedsrechtsordnung: Den Parteien ist eine Bandbreite an parallelen gerichtlichen Verfahren zugänglich, die eine effektive schiedsgerichtliche Streitbeilegung erschwert.

bb) Oil & Natural Gas v Saw Pipes (Saw Pipes)

In der Angelegenheit *Oil & Natural Gas Corporation Ltd v Saw Pipes Ltd* (*Saw Pipes*)[1455] hatte ein mit zwei Richtern besetzter Senat des Supreme Courts zu beurteilen, ob die Gerichte nach Sec. 34 SchiedsG a. F. einen Schiedsspruch unter dem Aufhebungsgrund der öffentlichen Ordnung annullieren können, wenn der Schiedsspruch gegen Vorschriften eines indischen Gesetzes verstößt.

Nach einer Ausschreibung vereinbarte das indische Staatsunternehmen *Oil and Natural Gas Corporation Limited (ONGC)* mit *Saw Pipes Ltd* 1995 die Lieferung von Rohren. Nach dem Kaufvertrag war *Saw Pipes Ltd* verpflichtet, für die Rohrherstellung Materialien eines bewährten Zulieferers zu verwenden und die Rohre im November 1996 zu liefern. Der Kaufvertrag sah für eine verspätete Lieferung der Rohre einen pauschalierten Schadensersatz[1456] vor und für strittige Forderungen[1457] sollte den Vertragsparteien kein Zins zustehen. *Saw Pipes Ltd* bestellte die für die Herstellung erforderlichen Stahlplatten bei einem italienischen Hersteller. Auf Grund eines Streiks konnte der italienische Hersteller die Stahlplatten nicht fristgemäß liefern. Die Parteien verständigten sich auf einen Liefertermin 45 Tage nach dem ursprünglichen. Unter Verweis auf den für die verspätete Lieferung vereinbarten pauschalierten Schadensersatz reduzierte *ONGC* den Kaufpreis. Ob *ONGC* berechtigt war, den Kaufpreis zu reduzieren, sollte ein Schiedsgericht entscheiden. Das Schiedstribunal entschied, dass der Streik der Arbeiter in Italien keine „höhere Gewalt“[1458] i. S. d. Kaufvertrages für *Saw Pipes Ltd* darstelle. Andererseits habe aber *ONGC* nicht beweisen können, dass es durch die verspätete Lieferung tatsächlich einen Schaden erlitten habe. *ONGC* habe deshalb zu Unrecht den pauschalierten Schadensersatz vom Kaufpreis abgezogen. Das Schiedsgericht sprach *Saw Pipes Ltd* den vom Kaufpreis abgezogenen Betrag inklusive Zinsen zu. *ONGC* beantragte die

S. 76 (79 f.). Differenziert Singhvi, Indian Journal of Arbitration Law 2015, Vol. IV, Ausg. 2, S. 14 (17); Malhotra, Indu, O. P. Malhotra on Arbitration, Sec. 48, S. 1717.

1455 AIR 2003 SC 2629; (2003) 5 SCC 705; Appeal (civil) 7419 2001 of 518, 17.4.2003.

1456 Engl. liquidated damages.

1457 Engl. disputed claims.

1458 Engl. force majeure.

Aufhebung des Schiedsspruchs vor dem Bombay High Court. Ein Einzelrichter des Bombay High Courts wies den Aufhebungsantrag zurück. Diese Entscheidung bestätigte eine Division Bench des Bombay High Courts.

In der Berufung vor dem Supreme Court machte *ONGC* geltend, dass der Schiedsspruch gegen Sec. 28 (3) SchiedsG a. F. verstoße, da der Kaufvertrag zwischen den Parteien für eine verzögerte Lieferung der Rohre einen pauschalierten Schadensersatz vorsehe, ohne dass der eingetretene Schaden bewiesen werden müsse. Auch die zugesprochenen Zinsen widersprächen dem Kaufvertrag, der für strittige Forderungen keine Zinsen vorsehe. *Saw Pipes Ltd* plädierte vor dem Supreme Court, dass unter Sec. 74 „Indian Contract Act 1872" ein Schadensersatz nur gefordert werden könne, wenn durch den Vertragsbruch ein Schaden auch tatsächlich entstanden sei. Ergänzend wies *Saw Pipes Ltd* das oberste indische Gericht darauf hin, dass es selbst bei einer falschen Rechtsanwendung des Schiedsgerichts im Aufhebungsverfahren gem. Sec. 34 SchiedsG nicht in den Schiedsspruch korrigierend intervenieren dürfe.[1459] Der Supreme Court berücksichtigte die von den Parteien referierte indische und englische Rechtsprechung und würdigte auch Sec. 68 f. des englischen „Arbitration Acts 1996", nach dem ein Schiedsspruch aus Rechtsgründen aufgehoben werden kann.

Der Supreme Court urteilte, dass der Begriff der öffentlichen Ordnung in Sec. 34 (2) (b) (ii) SchiedsG weiter als im *Renusagar*-Urteil auszulegen sei. Das Gericht führte aus, dass die öffentliche Ordnung das Gemeinwohl und das öffentliche Interesse beinhalte und dass sich diese Begriffe und die erforderliche Eingriffsintensität für deren Verletzung mit der Zeit veränderten. Das oberste indische Gericht orientierte sich bei seiner Konkretisierung der öffentlichen Ordnung an der Auslegung im Urteil *Renusagar*. Der Supreme Court fügte dieser Auslegung für Aufhebungsverfahren allerdings noch die „offensichtliche Rechtswidrigkeit" (engl. patent illegality) als viertes Auslegungskriterien hinzu.[1460] Die Öffentliche Ordnung umfasst nach dem Supreme Court für Aufhebungsverfahren

1. den grundlegenden Gesetzeszweck des indischen Rechts,
2. die Interessen Indiens,
3. Gerechtigkeit und Moral und
4. die offensichtliche Rechtswidrigkeit:

> *„Hence, in our view in addition to narrower meaning given to the term ‚public policy' in Renusagar's case (supra), it is required to be held that the award could be set aside if it is patently illegal. Result would be – award could be set aside if it is contrary to: -*
>
> *(a) fundamental policy of Indian law; or*

1459 Appeal (civil) 7419 2001 of 518, S. 16 f.
1460 Appeal (civil) 7419 2001 of 518, S. 7 ff.

(b) the interest of India; or

(c) justice or morality, or

(d) in addition, if it is patently illegal."[1461]

Folglich erachtete der Supreme Court die Konkretisierung der öffentlichen Ordnung desselben Gerichts im *Renusagar*-Urteil als zu eng. Er war der Auffassung, dass die Auslegung der öffentlichen Ordnung gem. Sec. 34 SchiedsG auch die „offensichtliche Rechtswidrigkeit" enthalten müsse. Unter einem offensichtlich rechtswidrigen Schiedsspruch sei ein Schiedsspruch zu verstehen, der gegen gesetzliche Bestimmungen des indischen Rechts verstoße. Der Supreme Court stellte allerdings klar, dass für die offensichtliche Rechtswidrigkeit eines Schiedsspruchs eine schwerwiegende Verletzung des indischen Rechts durch den Schiedsspruch erforderlich sei.[1462] Die erweiterte Auslegung der öffentlichen Ordnung im *Saw Pipes*-Urteil ermöglichte demnach die Annullierung eines Schiedsspruchs wegen eines Verstoßes gegen die indische Gesetzgebung.

In seiner Entscheidung unterzog das oberste indische Gericht die schiedsgerichtlichen Entscheidungsgründe deshalb einer umfassenden materiellrechtlichen Kontrolle.[1463] Nach einer ausführlichen Analyse der von den Parteien vorgetragenen indischen Rechtsprechung urteilte der Supreme Court, dass das Schiedsgericht im Schiedsspruch hinsichtlich des vertraglich vereinbarten pauschalierten Schadensersatzes und des Ausschlusses von Zinsen offensichtlich falsch entschieden habe. Der Schiedsspruch verletze dementsprechend das in Sec. 28 (3) SchiedsG a. F.[1464] gesetzlich verankerte Gebot, die Parteivereinbarung in der schiedsgerichtlichen Entscheidung zu achten[1465].[1466] Der Supreme Court hob den Schiedsspruch wegen eines Verstoßes gegen die zuvor geschaffene weite Konkretisierung der indischen öffentlichen Ordnung auf.

1461 Appeal (civil) 7419 2001 of 518, S. 15.

1462 Appeal (civil) 7419 2001 of 518, S. 15, 22 f.

1463 Appeal (civil) 7419 2001 of 518, S. 23 ff.

1464 Sec. 28 (3) SchiedsG a. F.: „In all cases, the arbitral tribunal shall decide in accordance with the terms of the contract and shall take into account the usages of the trade applicable to the transaction."

1465 Der Gesetzgeber änderte in der Schiedsgesetzesnovelle von 2015 Sec. 28 (3) SchiedsG, um die *Saw Pipes*-Rechtsprechung zu beseitigen. Nach Sec. 28 (3) SchiedsG n. F. soll das Schiedsgericht nur noch die vertraglichen Bestimmungen der Parteien berücksichtigen („...take into account the terms of the contract..."), aber nicht mehr zwingend nach den Vertragsbestimmungen entscheiden („...shall decide in accordance with the terms of the contract..."). Siehe auch Government of India, Law Commission of India, 246. Report, Amendments to the Arbitration and Conciliation Act 1996, 5.8.2014, S. 22.

1466 Appeal (civil) 7419 2001 of 518, S. 16 ff.

Am Urteil *Saw Pipes* des Supreme Courts kritisiert das Schrifttum zu Recht, dass es die in der Entscheidung *Renusagar* geschaffene Auslegung der öffentlichen Ordnung durch die „offensichtliche Rechtswidrigkeit" erweitert habe. Der Supreme Court habe dadurch die unter dem Arbitration Act 1940 vorherrschende Rechtslage wieder eingeführt, wonach ein Schiedsspruch wegen einer „fehlerhaften Rechtsanwendung, die sich dem Schiedsspruch auf den ersten Blick entnehmen lässt" (engl. error of law apparent on the face of the award) aufgehoben werden konnte.[1467] Darüber hinaus wird die Auffassung vertreten, dass die *Saw Pipes*-Entscheidung unzutreffend sei, weil sie nicht dem Geist und dem Gesetzeswortlaut des SchiedsG entspreche und das fehlende Vertrauen in die Schiedsgerichtsbarkeit als ebenbürtigen Streitbeilegungsmechanismus offenbare.[1468] Die weite Auslegung der öffentlichen Ordnung im Urteil *Saw Pipes* fördere ferner von unterlegenen Parteien initiierte Aufhebungsverfahren.[1469] Das *Saw Pipes*-Urteil führe zu-

1467 Malhotra (mit weiteren Nachweisen), O. P. Malhotra on Arbitration, Sec. 34, S. 1359; Nariman, Journal of International Arbitration 2008, Vol. 25, Ausg. 6, S. 893 (895 f.); Kachwaha, Asian International Arbitration Journal 2008, Vol. 4, Ausg. 1, S. 64 (68 ff.); Dewan, Nakul, Asian International Arbitration Journal 2007, Vol. 3, Ausg. 1, S. 99 (120 f.); Darwazeh/Linnane, International Arbitration Law Review 2004, S. 81 (82 ff.); Biswas (mit weiteren Nachweisen), S. 117 f.; Mody/Raghenth, International Arbitration Law Review 2003, S. N35 (N36); Kachwaha (unter Verweis auf eine Rede von Nariman), International Arbitration Law Review 2007, S. 13 (15); Rewari (mit weiteren Nachweisen), Asian International Arbitration Journal 2013, Vol. 9, Ausg. 2, S. 97 (111 ff.); Singhvi, Indian Journal of Arbitration Law 2015, Vol. IV, Ausg. 2, S. 14 (17 f.); Gaya, Law Quarterly Review 2004, S. 571 ff.; Rai, Journal of International Dispute Settlement 2012, Vol. 3, Ausg. 1, S. 169 (189); Kumar, Aakanksha, International Arbitration Law Review 2014, S. 76 (80). Zu Kritik an der weiten Auslegung der öffentlichen Ordnung im *Saw Pipes*-Urteil, Kröll, International Arbitration Law Review 2005, S. 170 (177 f.).

1468 Nair, Arbitration International 2007, Vol. 23, Ausg. 4, S. 699 (732 ff.); Kachwaha, International Arbitration Law Review 2007, S. 13 (14 ff.); Krishan, Journal of International Arbitration 2004, Vol. 21, Ausg. 3, S. 263 (274 ff.); Kachwaha, Asian International Arbitration Journal 2008, Vol. 4, Ausg. 1, S. 64 (68 ff.); Dewan, Nakul, Asian International Arbitration Journal 2007, Vol. 3, Ausg. 1, S. 99 (120 f.); Kachwaha (mit Verweis auf einen Vortrag von Nariman), Asian International Arbitration Journal 2005, Vol. 1, Ausg. 2, S. 105 (122 f.); Darwazeh/Linnane, International Arbitration Law Review 2004, S. 81 (85 ff.). Zur Verletzung des Geistes und des Gesetzeswortlaut, Nariman, Arbitration International 2011, Vol. 2, Ausg. 2, S. 115, (125); Thej, International Arbitration Law Review 2014, S. 37 ff.; Rai, Journal of International Dispute Settlement 2012, Vol. 3, Ausg. 1, S. 169 (189 ff.); Parekh, ICA Arbitration Quarterly 2005, Vol. XL, Ausg. 2, S. 11 (19). Zu dem fehlenden Vertrauen in die Schiedsgerichtsbarkeit als gleichwertigem Streitbeilegungsmechanismus, Rewari (mit weiteren Nachweisen), Asian International Arbitration Journal 2013, Vol. 9, Ausg. 2, S. 97 (137).

1469 Nair, Arbitration International 2007, Vol. 23, Ausg. 4, S. 699 (732 ff.); Kachwaha, International Arbitration Law Review 2007, S. 13 (14 ff.); Krishan, Journal of Interdem zu Verzögerungen bei der Durchsetzung eines Schiedsspruchs.[1470] Das Urteil sei auf Grund der genannten Aspekte insgesamt schlecht für den internationalen Handel und für ausländische Investitionen.[1471]

Vereinzelt verteidigen Stimmen in der Literatur die durch die *Saw Pipes*-Rechtsprechung geschaffene Kontrolle des Schiedsspruchs unter der erweiterten Auslegung der öffentlichen Ordnung.[1472] Der Kritik an der *Saw Pipes*-Rechtsprechung wird entgegengehalten, dass der Supreme Court der *Renusagar*-Auslegung der öffentlichen Ordnung im Urteil *Saw Pipes* nur einen weiteren, vierten Konkretisierungspunkt hinzugefügt habe. Zu Gunsten der *Saw Pipes*-Entscheidung wird ferner angeführt, dass die Schiedsgerichte gem. Sec. 28 (1) (a) SchiedsG in einem inländischen Schiedsverfahren Streitigkeiten nach indischem Recht entscheiden müssen.[1473]

Dem internationalen Standard der Schiedsgerichtsbarkeit ist zu entnehmen, dass der Begriff der öffentlichen Ordnung restriktiv auszulegen ist und Schiedssprüche nur ausnahmsweise aufgehoben werden sollen. Eine falsche Rechtsanwendung des nationalen Rechts des Aufhebungsstaates durch das Schiedsgericht reicht demnach für eine Verletzung der öffentlichen Ordnung nicht aus. Erforderlich ist vielmehr, dass der Schiedsspruch eindeutig gegen

national Arbitration 2004, Vol. 21, Ausg. 3, S. 263 (274 ff.); Kachwaha, Asian International Arbitration Journal 2008, Vol. 4, Ausg. 1, S. 64 (68 ff.); Dewan, Nakul, Asian International Arbitration Journal 2007, Vol. 3, Ausg. 1, S. 99 (120 f.); Kachwaha (mit Verweis auf einen Vortrag von Nariman), Asian International Arbitration Journal 2005, Vol. 1, Ausg. 2, S. 105 (122 f.); Darwazeh/Linnane, International Arbitration Law Review 2004, S. 81 (85 ff.). Zu gerichtlichen Interventionen in Schiedsverfahren, Gaya, Law Quarterly Review 2004, S. 571 ff.; Arvind, International & Comparative Law Quarterly 2010, S. 65 (75 f.); Ritz, ASA Bulletin 2009, Vol. 27, Ausg. 4, S. 717 (730 f.); Hilmer, International Arbitration Law Review 2007, S. 33 (37); Sattar, Journal of International Arbitration 2010, Vol. 27, Ausg. 1, S. 51 (62 ff.); Malhotra, Indu, O. P. Malhotra on Arbitration, Sec. 34, S. 1360; Parekh, ICA Arbitration Quarterly 2005, Vol. XL, Ausg. 2, S. 11 (19).

1470 Kachwaha, Asian International Arbitration Journal 2008, Vol. 4, Ausg. 1, S. 64 (70); Mody/Raghenth, International Arbitration Law Review 2003, S. N35 (N36); Darwazeh/Linnane, International Arbitration Law Review 2004, S. 81 (86 f.); Nair, Arbitration International 2007, Vol. 23, Ausg. 4, S. 699 (734).

1471 Dewan, Nakul (unter Verweis auf eine Rede des ehemaligen Chief Justice of India A.M. Ahmadi), Asian International Arbitration Journal 2007, Vol. 3, Ausg. 1, S. 99 (121); Reynardson/Talbot-Garman, International Arbitration Law Review 2011, S. 90 (92); Sabharwal/Singh, Aditya, Global Arbitration Review 2012, Vol. 7, Ausg. 6, 22.10.2012; Sattar, Journal of International Arbitration 2010, Vol. 27, Ausg. 1, S. 51 (64).

1472 Sharma, Sidharth, Journal of International Arbitration 2009, Vol. 26, Ausg. 1, S. 133 ff.; Malhotra, O. P., Arbitration 2005, S. 36 (42 ff.); Malhotra, Indu, O. P. Malhotra on Arbitration, Sec. 34, S. 1360 f. Zur positiven Bewertung in der indischen Wirtschaft, Arvind, International & Comparative Law Quarterly 2010, S. 65 (85 f.).

1473 Malhotra, Indu, O. P. Malhotra on Arbitration, Sec. 34, S. 1360.

die fundamentalen Gerechtigkeitsvorstellungen oder das elementare zwingende Recht[1474] des Aufhebungsstaates verstößt[1475].[1476] Auf Grund der Finalität des Schiedsspruchs lehnt die internationale Schiedsgerichtsnorm[1477] und das UNCITRAL Modellgesetz[1478] eine gerichtliche „révision au fond" des Schiedsspruchs ab.

Die erweiterte Auslegung der öffentlichen Ordnung im *Saw Pipes*-Urteil – die auch eine gerichtliche Kontrolle der schiedsgerichtlichen Entscheidung umfasst – widerspricht dem internationalen Standard des Schiedsgerichtswesens. Die *Saw Pipes*-Entscheidung stellt dementsprechend ein schiedsunfreundliches Urteil dar und wird zu Recht in der Literatur kritisiert.

Trotz Zweifel an der im *Saw Pipes*-Urteil vertretenen Rechtsauffassung folgten ihm die Senate des Supreme Courts.[1479]

cc) Venture Global v Satyam (Venture Global)

Die Rechtsfrage, ob ein ausländischer Schiedsspruch gem. Sec. 34 SchiedsG aufgehoben werden kann, beschäftigte in der Rechtssache *Venture Global Engineering v Satyam Computer Services Ltd & Anr (Venture Global)*[1480] einen aus zwei Richtern bestehenden Senat des Supreme Courts. Die Entscheidung des Gerichts erging nach der zu dieser Zeit höchstrichterlichen

1474 Eine Verletzung des abdingbaren einfachen Rechts des Aufhebungsstaates ist nicht ausreichend. Born, International Commercial Arbitration, Bd. 3, S. 3312 ff.; Born, Law and Practice, § 16.03 [B] [7], S. 333.

1475 Unterschiedlich wird beurteilt, ob der dem Schiedsspruch zu Grunde liegende materielle Anspruch oder die Durchsetzung des Schiedsspruchs gegen die öffentliche Ordnung des Aufhebungsstaates verstoßen muss. *Born* befürwortet, dass der im Schiedsspruch geltend gemachte Anspruch zunächst gegen die öffentliche Ordnung verstoßen müsse, Born, International Commercial Arbitration, Bd. 3, S. 3318 f. Erforderlich ist nach *Born* zudem, dass die konkrete Rechtsanwendung in einem Schiedsspruch die öffentliche Ordnung verletze. Ein abstrakter Verstoß eines im Schiedsspruch angewandten Gesetzes gegen die öffentliche Ordnung sei deshalb nicht ausreichend, siehe Born, International Commercial Arbitration, Bd. 3, S. 3320.

1476 Born, International Commercial Arbitration, Bd. 3, S. 3178 f., 3312 ff.; Born, Law and Practice, § 16.03 [B] [7], S. 333 f.; Blackaby/Partasides/Redfern/Hunter, International Arbitration, Rn. 10.81 ff.

1477 Born, International Commercial Arbitration, Bd. 3, S. 3323 ff.; Born, Law and Practice, § 16.03 [B] [7], S. 333; Berger, Klaus, S. 473 f.

1478 Art. 34 UNCITRAL Modellgesetz; Sekretariat, Explanatory note, Rn. 42 ff.

1479 Supreme Court, 2 Richter, M*cdermott International Inc v Burn Standard Co Ltd & Ors,* (2006) 11 SCC 181; Appeal (civil) 4492 of 1998, 12.5.2006; Supreme Court, 2 Richter, *Union of India v L S N Murthy & Anr*, (2012) 1 SCC 718; Civil Appeal No. 2755 of 2007, 23.11.2011; Supreme Court, 3 Richter, *Oil and Natural Gas Corporation v Western Geco International Ltd*, (2014) 9 SCC 263; Civil Appeal No. 3415 of 2007, 4.9.2014.

1480 AIR 2008 SC 1061; (2008) 4 SCC 190; Appeal (civil) 309 of 2008, 10.1.2008.

Bhatia International v Bulk Trading SA & ANR (Bhatia)-Rechtsprechung, die Teil I SchiedsG a. F. zwischenzeitlich auch auf Schiedsverfahren mit Sitz außerhalb von Indien für anwendbar erklärte.[1481]

Hintergrund dieses Verfahrens war, dass *Venture Global Engineering (Venture)* und *Satyam Computer Services Ltd (Satyam)* 1999 ein gemeinsames „Joint Venture" vereinbart hatten. Die Berufungsklägerin *Venture* war ein in den USA gegründetes Unternehmen. Die erste Berufungsbeklagte *Satyam* war ein im indischen Secunderabad registriertes Unternehmen. Das indische Joint Venture trug den Namen *Satyam Venture Engineering Services Ltd (Engineering)* und war zugleich die zweite Berufungsbeklagte. Beide Vertragspartner hielten 50 Prozent der Aktien von *Engineering.* Die Parteien vereinbarten zudem ein „Shareholder Agreement", das für die juristische Streitbeilegung eine Schiedsklausel enthielt. Das Shareholder Agreement war dem Recht des US-Bundesstaates Michigan unterstellt und verpflichtete die Aktieninhaber, indisches Recht einzuhalten. Im Februar 2005 kam es zu Streitigkeiten zwischen *Venture* und *Satyam. Satyam* war der Ansicht, *Venture* sei seinen Zahlungsverpflichtungen nach dem Shareholder Agreement nicht nachgekommen und machte von seinem Optionsrecht Gebrauch, die Aktien von *Venture* zu erwerben. Im Juli 2005 legte *Satyam* beim „London Court of International Arbitration" Schiedsklage ein. Der ernannte Einzelschiedsrichter ordnete im Schiedsspruch vom 3. April 2006 an, dass *Venture* seine *Engineering*-Aktien an *Satyam* transferieren müsse. *Satyam* beantragte am 14. April 2006 die Anerkennung und Vollstreckung des Schiedsspruchs in den USA. *Venture* wandte gegen die Anerkennung und Vollstreckung des Schiedsspruchs ein, dass die durch den Schiedsspruch angeordnete Aktientransaktion gegen indisches Recht[1482] verstoße. *Venture* beantragte am 28. April 2006 beim District Court im indischen Secunderabad die Aufhebung des Schiedsspruchs und eine einstweilige Maßnahme gegen den Aktientransfer. Im Juni 2006 erließ der District Court *ex parte* eine einstweilige Maßnahme gegen *Satyam* und verbot dieser, die *Engineering*-Aktien an sich zu transferieren. Im Berufungsverfahren hob der Andhra Pradesh High Court die einstweilige Maßnahme auf. Der District Court wies die Aufhebungsklage von *Venture* im Dezember 2006 ab. Im Berufungsverfahren urteilte der Andhra Pradesh High Court im Februar 2007, dass der ausländische Schiedsspruch auch nicht wegen eines Verstoßes gegen die indische öffentliche Ordnung oder gegen indische Gesetze aufgehoben werden könne und wies die Berufung zurück.

1481 Siehe Kapitel: Anwendungsbereich der Schiedsgesetzgebung (C.I.1.).
1482 „Foreign Exchange Management Act 1999".

Im Berufungsverfahren[1483] folgte der Supreme Court der *Bhatia*-Entscheidung[1484] und urteilte, dass Teil I SchiedsG – der auch die Aufhebungsklage gem. Sec. 34 SchiedsG beinhaltet – auch auf Schiedsverfahren mit ausländischem Sitz anwendbar sei.[1485] Das Gericht bestätigte zudem, dass die der *Saw Pipes*-Rechtsprechung entspringende, weite Auslegung der öffentlichen Ordnung[1486] auch auf ausländische Schiedssprüche – wie im vorliegenden Verfahren mit dem Schiedssitz in London – anzuwenden sei. Wenn ein Schiedsspruch in das in Indien befindliche Eigentum wegen eines Verstoßes gegen die indische öffentliche Ordnung nicht vollstreckt werden könne, dann dürfe er auch nicht gegenüber einem im Ausland wohnhaften Schiedsspruchschuldner mittels einer „Contempt of Court“[1487] durchgesetzt werden. In einer solchen Konstellation müsse sich der Schiedsspruchschuldner auf ein indisches Aufhebungsverfahren unter der weiten Auslegung der öffentlichen Ordnung aus der *Saw Pipes*-Entscheidung berufen können. Der Supreme Court war der Auffassung, dass *Satyam* den Schiedsspruch in den USA vollstrecken lassen wollte, um trotz des engen Nexus des indischen Unternehmens *Engineering* zu Indien die Voraussetzungen des „Foreign Exchange Management Acts 1999“ und des „Company Acts 1956“ zu umgehen.[1488] Das oberste Gericht Indiens entschied, dass Sec. 34 SchiedsG in einer solchen Konstellation auch auf ausländische Schiedssprüche anwendbar sei. Der Supreme Court hob deshalb die Entscheidungen des District Courts und des High Courts auf und verwies die Rechtssache zurück.

Dieses Urteil bedeutete schlussendlich, dass die indischen Gerichte vor der SchiedsG-Reform aus dem Jahr 2015 auch Schiedssprüche mit ausländischem Schiedssitz aufheben konnten.[1489] Dies widersprach der internationalen Schiedsgerichtsnorm, wonach Schiedssprüche ausschließlich von den Gerichten am Sitz des Schiedsverfahrens aufgehoben werden können.[1490]

1483 In der Form einer „Special Leave Petition“.

1484 Siehe Kapitel: Anwendungsbereich der Schiedsgesetzgebung; Bhatia International v Bulk Trading SA (Bhatia) (C.I.1.b)).

1485 Appeal (civil) 309 of 2008, Rn. 17 ff.

1486 Zur Unvereinbarkeit der Entscheidung *Saw Pipes* mit dem globalen Standard des Schiedsgerichtswesens, siehe Kapitel: Aufhebungsverfahren; Oil & Natural Gas v Saw Pipes (Saw Pipes) (C.VII.2.b)bb)).

1487 Ordnungsmittel, durch das ein Fehlverhalten im Gerichtsverfahren oder ein Nichtbefolgen eines Beschlusses des Gerichts durch Geldstrafen und Haft sanktioniert wird, siehe Law, Oxford Dictionary, S. 143; Garner, Black's Law Dictionary Pocket, S. 165.; Garner, Black's Law Dictionary, S. 385.

1488 Appeal (civil) 309 of 2008, Rn. 13 ff.

1489 Vgl. Kapitel: Anwendungsbereich der Schiedsgesetzgebung (C. I. 1.).

1490 Siehe Art. 1 (2) i. V. m. Art. 34 UNCITRAL Modellgesetz; Art. V (1) (e) UNÜ; Art. 176 (1) Schweizer Bundesgesetz über das Internationale Privatrecht (IPRG); Sec. 2 englischer Arbitration Act 1996; Sec. 5 Hongkonger Arbitration Ordinance; Sec. 10 US Federal Arbitration Act (Title 9, US Code); Born, International Commer-

Die den indischen Gerichten im Urteil *Venture Global* übertragene Kompetenz, im Ausland ergangene Schiedssprüche aufzuheben, war darüber hinaus für ausländische Schiedsverfahren nachteilhaft, weil dies die Vollstreckung von ausländischen Schiedssprüchen um mehrere Jahre verzögern konnte.[1491] In der Entscheidung *Venture Global* vertrat der Supreme Court nach der Einführung des SchiedsG 1996 ferner eine Rechtsauffassung, die an die Entscheidung *National Thermal Power Corp v Singer Company And Ors*[1492] des Supreme Courts unter dem Arbitration Act 1940 bezüglich der Aufhebung von im Ausland ergangenen Schiedssprüchen erinnert, obwohl der Gesetzgeber durch das SchiedsG 1996 das liberale UNCITRAL Modellgesetzes rezipiert hatte.

Die Literatur kritisiert an dem Urteil *Venture Global* die, im Widerspruch zu Art. V UNÜ stehende, Aufhebungsmöglichkeit ausländischer Schiedssprüche gem. Sec. 34 SchiedsG.[1493] Dem Urteil wird des Weiteren vorge-

---

cial Arbitration, Bd. 3, S. 3164 ff.; Born, Law and Practice, § 16, S. 311 ff.; Blackaby/Partasides/Redfern/Hunter, International Arbitration, Rn. 10.05 ff.; Schlosser, in: Stein/Jonas, Anhang zu § 1061 ZPO Rn. 146.

1491 Malhotra, Indu, O. P. Malhotra on Arbitration, Sec. 34, S. 1364 f.

1492 AIR 1993 SC 998; [1992] 3 SCR 106, 7.5.1992. Der Supreme Court hatte darüber zu entscheiden, ob ein vorläufiger Schiedsspruch, der aus einem ICC-Schiedsverfahren in London entstammte, von den indischen Gerichten aufgehoben werden könne.

1493 Thej, International Arbitration Law Review 2014, S. 37 (40); Malhotra, Indu, O. P. Malhotra on Arbitration, Sec. 34, S. 1365; Rautray, International Arbitration Law Review 2008, S. N29 (N30 f.); Sharma, Raghav, Arbitration 2009, S. 148 ff.; Schäfer, SchiedsVZ 2008, S. 299 f.; Kachwaha, Asian International Arbitration Journal 2008, Vol. 4, Ausg. 1, S. 64 (78 f.); Rewari, Asian International Arbitration Journal 2013, Vol. 9, Ausg. 2, S. 97 (120); Sharma, Raghav, Journal of International Arbitration 2009, Vol. 26, Ausg. 3, S. 357 (363 ff.); Nariman, Journal of International Arbitration 2008, Vol. 25, Ausg. 6, S. 893 (898); Sattar, Journal of International Arbitration 2010, Vol. 27, Ausg. 1, S. 51 (62 ff.). Kritisch zu der Entscheidung, Gupta, Arpan, Indian Journal of Arbitration Law 2013, Vol. II, Ausg. 2, S. 1 (8); Ritz, ASA Bulletin 2009, Vol. 27, Ausg. 4, S. 717 (727 ff.); Ray, Ashutosh, International Arbitration Law Review 2013, S. 97 ff.; Ray, Ashutosh, Journal of International Arbitration 2012, Vol. 29, Ausg. 3, S. 345 (348 f.); Mainwaring-Taylor/Sullivan, Arbitration 2008, S. 133 ff.; Rebello, Cambridge Student Law Review 2010, S. 274 ff.; Rai, Journal of International Dispute Settlement 2012, Vol. 3, Ausg. 1, S. 169 (174 ff.); Dunning, Arbitration 2008, S. 254 (258 ff.); Reynardson/Talbot-Garman, International Arbitration Law Review 2011, S. 90 (91 ff.); Mahajan/Narayan, International Arbitration Law Review 2015, S. 63 (69 ff.). *Rautray* kritisiert die Ausdehnung der weiten Auslegung der *Saw Pipes*-Rechtsprechung auf ausländische Schiedsverfahren, Rautray, Dispute Resolution Journal 2009, Vol. 64, Ausg. 1, S. 80 (84 ff.). Differenziert, Zaiwalla, Journal of International Arbitration 2008, Vol. 25, Ausg. 4, S. 507 ff.; Jain, Devyani, Indian Journal of Arbitration Law 2012, Vol. I, Ausg. 1, S. 36 (41 ff.). Zur Schiedsunfreundlichkeit des Urteils, Mahajan, Indian Journal of Arbitration Law 2014, Vol. III, Ausg. 2, S. 14 i. V. m. Fn. 1; Mahajan/Bhatt, Journal of International Arbitration 2013, Vol. 30, Ausg. 6, S. 711 i. V. m. Fn. 1; Gupta, Suvrajyot, International Arbitration Law

worfen, dass es zu Interventionen in ausländische Schiedsverfahren und zu Verfahrensverschleppungen führe.[1494] Dies beeinflusse den internationalen Handel mit Indien als auch Investitionen in Indien negativ.[1495] Das *Venture Global*-Urteil wird von einigen Autoren auf das fehlende Vertrauen der indischen Gerichte in die Schiedsgerichtsbarkeit als äquivalente Streitbeilegungsmethode zurückgeführt.[1496]

Klarzustellen ist, dass der Supreme Court in der Rechtssache *Venture Global* die Aufhebung eines ausländischen Schiedsspruchs für eine amerikanische Partei eröffnete, eine Begünstigung einer indischen Partei kann dem obersten Gericht Indiens *ergo* nicht vorgeworfen werden.

dd) Bewertung

Nach der internationalen Norm der Schiedsgerichtsbarkeit werden die materiellen Aufhebungsgründe restriktiv ausgelegt. Die Aufhebung eines Schiedsspruchs ist wegen Verletzung der öffentlichen Ordnung nur bei einem eindeutigen Verstoß des Schiedsspruchs gegen die fundamentalen Werte der öffentlichen Ordnung oder das elementare zwingende Recht des Aufhebungsstaates gerechtfertigt. Die gerichtliche Überprüfung der materiellen Entscheidungsgründe des Schiedsspruchs ist hingegen im Aufhebungsver-

---

Review 2013, S. 69 (71); Mahajan, Arbitration 2015, S. 48 i. V. m. Fn. 1. Zu differenzierter Kritik an dem Urteil, Takahashi, The American Review of International Arbitration 2008, Vol. 19, Ausg. 1, S. 173 ff. Zu Kritik an dem Urteil *Venture Global* siehe auch Kapitel: Anwendungsbereich der Schiedsgesetzgebung; Gerichtliche Entscheidungen nach Bhatia (C. I. 1. c)).

1494 Rautray, Dispute Resolution Journal 2009, Vol. 64, Ausg. 1, S. 80 (84 ff.); Thadikkaran, Journal of International Arbitration 2012, Vol. 29, Ausg. 6, S. 681 (681 ff.); Zaiwalla, Journal of International Arbitration 2008, Vol. 25, Ausg. 4, S. 507 ff.; Sharma, Raghav, Arbitration 2009, S. 148 (153 ff.); Sattar, Journal of International Arbitration 2010, Vol. 27, Ausg. 1, S. 51 (64); Mahajan/Narayan, International Arbitration Law Review 2015, S. 63 (69). Zu Interventionen in Schiedsverfahren, Lawn/Virjee, Indian Finance Arbitration 2009, S. 52 f.; Rebello, Cambridge Student Law Review 2010, S. 274 (282); Reynardson/Talbot-Garman, International Arbitration Law Review 2011, S. 90 (92); Arvind, International & Comparative Law Quarterly 2010, S. 65 (76 f.); Malhotra, Indu, O. P. Malhotra on Arbitration, Sec. 2, S. 228. Zu Interventionen und Verzögerungen durch die Entscheidung, Jain, Alok, Arbitration International 2010, Vol. 26, Ausg. 2, S. 251 (279). Siehe zudem Fn. 1136 ff., S. 184 f.

1495 Rautray, Dispute Resolution Journal 2009, Vol. 64, Ausg. 1, S. 80 (84 ff.); Thadikkaran, Journal of International Arbitration 2012, Vol. 29, Ausg. 6, S. 681 (681 ff.); Zaiwalla, Journal of International Arbitration 2008, Vol. 25, Ausg. 4, S. 507 ff.; Sharma, Raghav, Arbitration 2009, S. 148 (153 ff.); Sattar, Journal of International Arbitration 2010, Vol. 27, Ausg. 1, S. 51 (64); Mahajan/Narayan, International Arbitration Law Review 2015, S. 63 (69).

1496 Rebello, Cambridge Student Law Review 2010, S. 274 (282); Sattar, Journal of International Arbitration 2010, Vol. 27, Ausg. 1, S. 51 (64).

fahren nicht zulässig.[1497] Die Urteile *Saw Pipes* und *Venture Global* ließen eine materielle Kontrolle des Schiedsspruchs in Aufhebungsverfahren zu und widersprachen somit dem globalen Standard der Schiedsgerichtsbarkeit. Der indischen Rechtsprechung ist es entsprechend nicht gelungen, den mit einem nicht zu bändigenden Pferd verglichenen, unbestimmten Begriff der öffentlichen Ordnung die erforderliche enge Konkretisierung zu verleihen.[1498]

Die durch die *Venture Global*-Entscheidung mögliche Aufhebung von im Ausland ergangenen Schiedssprüchen und die hiermit verbundene universelle Interventionskompetenz der indischen Gerichte ist gleichfalls als Schiedsverfahren beeinträchtigend zu bewerten.

c) Betrug und Korruption

Eine Erklärung[1499] zu Sec. 34 (2) (b) (ii) SchiedsG – dem Aufhebungsgrund eines der öffentlichen Ordnung widersprechenden Schiedsspruches – stellt klar, dass Schiedssprüche gegen die öffentliche Ordnung in Indien verstoßen, wenn sie durch Betrug oder Korruption zustande gekommen sind. Der Aufhebungsgrund eines durch Betrug und Korruption tangierten Schiedsspruchs ist im internationalen Vergleich üblich.[1500] Aus der Entstehungsgeschichte des UNCITRAL Modellgesetzes lässt sich ableiten, dass ein durch Betrug bzw. Korruption beeinflusster Schiedsspruch unter dem Aufhebungsgrund der öffentlichen Ordnung anfechtbar sein soll.[1501] Nach der amerikanischen, englischen und Hongkonger Schiedsgesetzgebung kann ein durch Betrug oder Korruption zustande gekommener Schiedsspruch gleichfalls aufgehoben werden.[1502]

1497 Born, International Commercial Arbitration, Bd. 3, S. 3312 ff.; Born, Law and Practice, § 16.03 [B] [7], S. 333; Blackaby/Partasides/Redfern/Hunter, International Arbitration, Rn. 10.83 f.

1498 Vgl. Kapitel: Singapur; Aufhebungsverfahren; Öffentliche Ordnung (B.VII.2.a)).

1499 Engl. explanation.

1500 Born, Law and Practice, § 16.03 [B] [9], S. 335 f.; Born, International Commercial Arbitration, Bd. 3, S. 3318 ff.; Lew/Mistelis/Kröll, Comparative International Commercial Arbitration, Rn. 25-40; Sec. 10 (a) (1) US Federal Arbitration Act (Title 9, US Code); Sec. 68 (2) (g) englischer Arbitration Act 1996; Sec. 4 (2) (g) i. V. m. Schedule 2 Hongkonger Arbitration Ordinance; vgl. auch Art. 52 (1) (c) International Centre for Settlement of Investment Disputes (ICSID) Convention.

1501 UNCITRAL, 18. Sitzung, Report of the United Nations Commission on International Trade Law on the work of its eighteenth session, Supplement No. 17, A/40/17, 3.–21.6.1985, Rn. 297.

1502 Siehe Sec. 10 (a) (1) f. US Federal Arbitration Act (Title 9, US Code); Sec. 68 (2) (g) englischer Arbitration Act 1996; Sec. 4 (2) (g) i. V. m. Schedule 2 Hongkonger Arbitration Ordinance.

d) Arbitration Amendment Act

Durch den Arbitration Amendment Act 2015 stellte der Gesetzgeber in Sec. 2 (2) SchiedsG n. F. richtig, dass von Teil I SchiedsG ausschließlich Sec. 9, 27 und 37 SchiedsG auf Schiedsverfahren mit Sitz im Ausland angewendet werden dürfen. Der Arbitration Amendment Act beschränkte den ersten Teil des SchiedsG ansonsten auf Schiedsverfahren mit Sitz in Indien.[1503] Diese gesetzgeberische Entscheidung machte die Urteile *Venture Global* und *Bhatia* obsolet. Die indischen Gerichte können Schiedssprüche mit einem ausländischen Sitz des Verfahrens demzufolge unter Sec. 34 SchiedsG nicht mehr aufheben.[1504]

In den neuen Erklärungen 1 und 2 zu Sec. 34 (2) (b) (ii) SchiedsG n. F. definierte der Gesetzgeber den Begriff der öffentlichen Ordnung erstmals. Die neue Erklärung 1 orientiert sich an der Entscheidung *Renusagar*, komprimierte aber deren Auslegung der öffentlichen Ordnung weiter. Nach der Erklärung 1 kann ein Schiedsspruch auf Grund einer Verletzung des „grundlegenden Gesetzeszwecks des indischen Rechts“ oder wegen eines Verstoßes gegen die „grundlegendsten Gerechtigkeits- und Moralvorstellungen“ aufgehoben werden. Die Erklärung 1 verengte die *Renusagar*-Formel der öffentlichen Ordnung zunächst durch das Hinzufügen des Wortes „grundlegendst“ auf Verstöße eines Schiedsspruchs gegen die „grundlegendsten Gerechtigkeits- und Moralvorstellungen“.[1505] Die neue Erklärung 1 strich ferner die „Interessen Indiens“ aus der Auslegung der öffentlichen Ordnung der *Renusagar*-Entscheidung. Die Punkte „Interessen Indiens“ und „Gerechtigkeit und Moral“ in der *Renusagar*-Formel waren freilich ausufernd und eröffneten Fehlinterpretationen.[1506] Durch das Streichen des zweiten Punktes, der „Interessen Indiens“, und der restriktiveren Formulierung des dritten Konkretisierungspunktes „Gerechtigkeit und Moral“ der *Renusagar*-Formel gab der Gesetzgeber der öffentlichen Ordnung ein schärferes Profil.[1507] Die Definition der öffentlichen Ordnung in Sec. 34 SchiedsG n. F. umfasst:

1. den grundlegenden Gesetzeszweck des indischen Rechts und
2. die grundlegendsten Gerechtigkeits- und Moralvorstellungen.

Weiterhin stellte der Gesetzgeber in Erklärung 2 zu Sec. 34 (2) (b) (ii) SchiedsG n. F. klar, dass unter dem Begriff des grundlegenden Gesetzes-

---

1503 Sec. 2 (2) SchiedsG n. F.

1504 Siehe hierzu Kapitel: Anwendungsbereich der Schiedsgesetzgebung; Arbitration Amendment Act (C. I. 1. f)).

1505 Government of India, Law Commission of India, 246. Report, Amendments to the Arbitration and Conciliation Act 1996, 5.8.2014, S. 22.

1506 Vgl. Government of India, Law Commission of India, 246. Report, Amendments to the Arbitration and Conciliation Act 1996, 5.8.2014, S. 22.

1507 Vgl. Government of India, Law Commission of India, 246. Report, Amendments to the Arbitration and Conciliation Act 1996, 5.8.2014, S. 22.

zwecks des indischen Rechts keine „révision au fond“ des Schiedsspruchs durch das für das Aufhebungsverfahren zuständige Gericht erfolgen darf.

Die restriktivere Definition der öffentlichen Ordnung durch die Erklärung 1 und 2 zu Sec. 34 (2) (b) (ii) SchiedsG n. F. gewährleistet, dass die indischen Gerichte einen Schiedsspruch ausschließlich bei schwerwiegenden Verstößen gegen elementare Rechtsgrundsätze aufheben können. Dies entspricht dem Standard der Schiedsgerichtsbarkeit und ist als schiedsfreundlich anzusehen.

Der zusätzliche Aufhebungsgrund der offensichtlichen Rechtswidrigkeit differenziert in Sec. 34 (2A) SchiedsG n. F. zwischen Aufhebungsverfahren bei internationalen Handelsschiedssprüchen und inländischen und internationalen nicht handelsrechtlichen Schiedssprüchen (im Folgenden inländische Schiedssprüche[1508])[1509]. Auf diese Weise führte der Gesetzgeber eine zweigleisige Definition der öffentlichen Ordnung ein, mit einer geringeren gerichtlichen Kontrolle für inländische internationale Handelsschiedssprüche und einem intensiveren Überprüfungsmaßstab für inländische Schiedssprüche. In Anlehnung an das Urteil *Saw Pipes* des Supreme Courts können inländische Schiedssprüche auch aufgehoben werden, wenn sie „auf den ersten Blick offensichtlich rechtswidrig“[1510] sind.[1511] Zum Schutz von Parteien inländischer Schiedsverfahren empfahl das „Ministry of Law and Justice

1508 Der Begriff inländische Schiedssprüche umfasst Schiedssprüche, die in inländischen Schiedsverfahren und internationalen Nichthandelsschiedsverfahren ergingen. Der Terminus inländische Schiedssprüche wird verwendet, da die Anzahl der internationalen Nichthandelsschiedssprüche gering ist.

1509 Sec. 34 (2A) SchiedsG n. F. umfasst Schiedssprüche, die nicht in internationalen indischen Handelsschiedsverfahren ergingen. Internationale indische Handelsschiedsverfahren sind gem. Sec. 2 (1) (f) SchiedsG Handelsschiedsverfahren unter Beteiligung von mindestens einer nicht indischen Partei. Inländische Schiedsverfahren werden gem. Sec. 34 (2A) SchiedsG n. F. von internationalen Handelsschiedsverfahren negativ abgegrenzt und erfassen alle Schiedsverfahren, die nicht als internationale Handelsschiedsverfahren anzusehen sind.

1510 Engl. patent illegality appearing on the face of the award.

1511 Der durch den Arbitration Amendment Act 2015 eingeführte Sec. 34 (2A) lautet: „An arbitral award arising out of arbitrations other than international commercial arbitrations, may also be set aside by the Court, if the Court finds that the award is vitiated by patent illegality appearing on the face of the award:
Provided that an award shall not be set aside merely on the ground of an erroneous application of the law or by reappreciation of evidence.“

Government"[1512] und die Law Commission in ihrem 176. Report[1513] dem Gesetzgeber im reformierten SchiedsG eine Kontrolle von offensichtlich rechtswidrigen Schiedssprüchen zu ermöglichen. Die Law Commission begründete dies mit der Gefahr, dass in fehlerhaften Schiedssprüchen hohe Summen gegen den Staat oder öffentlich-rechtliche Unternehmen bzw. Körperschaften – wie im *Saw Pipes*-Urteil – verhängt werden können.[1514] Durch das Einfügen des restriktiveren Kriteriums „auf den ersten Blick"[1515] verengte Sec. 34 (2A) SchiedsG n. F. das aus der *Saw Pipes*-Entscheidung entspringende Kriterium der offensichtlichen Rechtswidrigkeit marginal. Sec. 34 (2A) a. E. SchiedsG n. F. stellte des Weiteren erfreulicherweise klar, dass letzteres Definitionskriterium der öffentlichen Ordnung weder die falsche Rechtsanwendung noch die falsche Beweiswürdigung durch das Schiedsgericht erfasst. Diese engere Definition der öffentlichen Ordnung und die begrenzte materielle Kontrolle des Schiedsspruchs sollen die Befürchtung der Schiedsbranche beschwichtigen, dass es in inländischen Schiedsverfahren zu einer uferlosen gerichtlichen Kontrolle kommen könne.[1516] Diese Bedenken sind nicht unbegründet. Ein inländischer Schiedsspruch kann im Rahmen der gerichtlichen Überprüfung auf seine offensichtliche Rechtswidrigkeit gem. Sec. 34 (2A) SchiedsG n. F. bei einer Verletzung des indischen Rechts weiterhin aufgehoben werden. Dies soll sicherstellen, dass auf inländische Schiedsverfahren indisches Recht Anwendung findet.[1517]

1512 Ministry of Law and Justice, Government of India, Proposed Amendments to the Arbitration & Conciliation Act, 1996, A Consultation Paper, S. 31 ff., verfügbar unter http://lawmin.nic.in/la/consultationpaper.pdf (zuletzt abgerufen am 28.4.2021). Siehe auch Summary of Recommendations of Justice Saraf Committee Report on implications of the recommendations of the Law Commission in its 176th Report regarding amendment of the Arbitration and Conciliation Act, 1996 and the amendments proposed by the Arbit[r]ation and Conciliation (Amendment) Bill, 2003 (As introduced in the Rajya Sabha on 22 December, 2003) and Suggestions and Recommendations, in: Ministry of Law and Justice, Government of India, Proposed Amendments to the Arbitration & Conciliation Act, 1996, A Consultation Paper, Annex IV, S. 128 f., verfügbar unter http://lawmin.nic.in/la/consultationpaper.pdf (zuletzt abgerufen am 28.4.2021).

1513 Law Commission of India, 176. Report, The Arbitration and Conciliation (Amendment) Bill, 2001, 12.9.2001, S. 137 ff.

1514 Law Commission of India, 176. Report, The Arbitration and Conciliation (Amendment) Bill, 2001, 12.9.2001, S. 137 ff.

1515 Das Kriterium „auf den ersten Blick" verwendete bereits der Arbitration Act 1940 in Sec. 16 (1) (c), vgl. Kapitel: Indien; Aufhebungsverfahren; Öffentliche Ordnung (C.VII.2.b)).

1516 Government of India, Law Commission of India, 246. Report, Amendments to the Arbitration and Conciliation Act 1996, 5.8.2014, S. 21.

1517 Nach Sec. 28 (1) SchiedsG ist auf inländische Schiedsverfahren zwingend indisches Recht anzuwenden. Nach der Law Commission erfordert Sec. 28 SchiedsG spiegelbildlich in Sec. 34 SchiedsG einen Aufhebungsgrund der offensichtlichen Rechtswid-

Nach der internationalen Norm der Schiedsgerichtsbarkeit kann ein Schiedsspruch einzig bei einem offensichtlichen Verstoß gegen die fundamentalen Gerechtigkeitsvorstellungen oder gegen das elementare zwingende Recht des Aufhebungsstaates annulliert werden.[1518] Die in Sec. 34 (2A) SchiedsG n. F. enger gefasste Formulierung der offensichtlichen Rechtswidrigkeit ist daher zwar ein Schritt in Richtung schiedsfreundlicherer Aufhebungsverfahren für inländische indische Schiedsverfahren. Es wird aber eine weitere Gesetzesreform oder eine höchstrichterliche Rechtsfortbildung erforderlich sein, um die indischen Aufhebungsverfahren in Einklang mit dem internationalen Standard des Schiedswesens zu bringen.

Vor der SchiedsG-Reform des Jahres 2015 zogen sich Aufhebungsverfahren über mehrere Jahre hin.[1519] Der Gesetzgeber reagierte durch Sec. 34 (6) SchiedsG n. F. auf die langjährigen Aufhebungsverfahren und begrenzte diese auf maximal ein Jahr.[1520]

e) Schlussbetrachtung

Durch die SchiedsG-Novelle des Jahres 2015 näherte der Gesetzgeber den Aufhebungsgrund der öffentlichen Ordnung wieder an den internationalen Standard des Schiedsgerichtswesens an. Lediglich Schiedssprüche eines indischen Schiedsverfahrens – mit Sitz in Indien – dürfen aufgehoben werden. Der Definition der öffentlichen Ordnung für internationale Handelsschiedssprüche steckte der Gesetzgeber durch zwei Kriterien einen restriktiven Rahmen. Für inländische Schiedssprüche erweiterte die Legislative 2015 den Begriff der öffentlichen Ordnung um die auf den „ersten Blick erkennbare offensichtliche Rechtswidrigkeit“ eines Schiedsspruches als drittes Definitionskriterium. Das Kriterium der offensichtlichen Rechtswidrigkeit ermöglicht eine „révision au fond“ des Schiedsspruches durch die Gerichte und bedarf der Korrektur.

Um zu einer schiedsfreundlicheren Rechtsordnung in Bezug auf Aufhebungsverfahren zu werden, müssen die indischen Gerichte das, die Verbindlichkeit des Schiedsspruchs fördernde, SchiedsG n. F. achten und dürfen dessen reduzierte gerichtliche Kontrollkompetenz nicht wieder durch gerichtliche Rechtsfortbildung ausdehnen.

---

rigkeit eines inländischen Schiedsspruchs, Law Commission of India, 176. Report, The Arbitration and Conciliation (Amendment) Bill, 2001, 12.9.2001, S. 14, 141 ff.

1518 Born, International Commercial Arbitration, Bd. 3, S. 3312 ff.; Born, Law and Practice, § 16.03 [B] [7], S. 333; Blackaby/Partasides/Redfern/Hunter, International Arbitration, Rn. 10.83 f.

1519 Government of India, Law Commission of India, 246. Report, Amendments to the Arbitration and Conciliation Act 1996, 5.8.2014, S. 8, 17.

1520 Sec. 34 (5 f.) SchiedsG n. F. Die Jahresfrist beginnt mit der Zustellung einer Benachrichtigung an die andere Partei.

VIII. Anerkennung und Vollstreckung

Art. V New Yorker UN-Übereinkommen über die Anerkennung und Vollstreckung ausländischer Schiedssprüche vom 10. Juni 1958 (UNÜ) regelt die Anerkennung und Vollstreckung von ausländischen Schiedssprüchen. Sec. 48 SchiedsG sieht hingegen einzig die Vollstreckung von ausländischen Schiedssprüchen vor. Die Vollstreckungsversagungsgründe in Sec. 48 SchiedsG entsprechen Art. V UNÜ. Nach Sec. 46 SchiedsG sind die Bestimmungen für die Vollstreckung von ausländischen Schiedssprüchen entsprechend auf die Anerkennung von ausländischen Schiedssprüchen anwendbar. Nach Sec. 44 ff. SchiedsG werden ausschließlich ausländische Handelsschiedssprüche anerkannt und vollstreckt.[1521]

1. Formelle Vollstreckungsversagungsgründe

Die formellen Vollstreckungsversagungsgründe gem. Sec. 48 (1) (a)–(e) SchiedsG sind identisch mit Art. V (1) (a)–(e) UNÜ und die Gerichte trafen hinsichtlich der formellen Nichtvollstreckungsgründe schiedsfreundliche Entscheidungen.[1522]

1521 In Indien können unter dem UNÜ nur Handelsschiedssprüche anerkannt und vollstreckt werden, die auf dem Territorium eines anderen Vertragsstaates des UNÜ ergingen (Territorialitätsvorbehalt; Sec. 44 [b] SchiedsG). Dass ein Vertragsstaat dem erforderlichen Gegenseitigkeitsvorbehalt genügt, muss von der indischen Regierung in der „Official Gazette" bekannt gemacht werden (qualifizierter Gegenseitigkeitsvorbehalt; Sec. 44 [b] SchiedsG). Diesen qualifizierten Gegenseitigkeitsvorbehalt erstreckte die indische Regierung auf 46 Staaten: die Arabische Republik Ägypten, die Arabische Republik Syrien, Belgien, Botswana, Bulgarien, die Bundesrepublik Deutschland, Chile, Dänemark, die Deutsche Demokratische Republik, Ecuador, Finnland, Frankreich, Ghana, Griechenland, Großbritannien, Italien, Irland, Japan, Kuba, Kuwait, Madagaskar, Malaysia, Marokko, Mexiko, die Niederlande, Nigeria, Norwegen, Österreich, die Philippinen, Polen, die Republik Korea, Rumänien, San Marino, Schweden, die Schweiz, Singapur, Spanien, Thailand, Trinidad und Tobago, die Tschechische Republik, Tunesien, die UdSSR, Ungarn, die Vereinigte Republik Tansania, die Vereinigte Staaten von Amerika und die Zentralafrikanische Republik, ICC, Digital Library, ICC Country Answers, India, verfügbar unter http://library.iccwbo.org/content/dr/COUNTRY_ANSWERS/CA_SUPP_0021_26.htm?l1=Supplements&l2=Guide+to+National+Rules+of+Procedure+for+Recognition+and+Enforcement+of+New+York+Convention+Awards (zuletzt abgerufen am 28.4.2021). Der qualifizierte Gegenseitigkeitsvorbehalt umfasst somit die wichtigsten internationalen Schiedsjurisdiktionen.

1522 Bansal, Bharat's Commentary, Bd. 1, Sec. 48, S. 623 ff.; Mohta/Mohta, Sec. 48, S. 452 ff.; Singh, Avtar, Arbitration, Sec. 48, S. 446 ff.; Paranjape, Sec. 48, S. 357 ff.

2. Materielle Vollstreckungsversagungsgründe

Das Vorliegen eines materiellen Nichtvollstreckungsgrundes wird vom zuständigen Gericht von Amts wegen überprüft.[1523]

a) Schiedsfähigkeit

Ein ausländischer Handelsschiedsspruch kann gem. Sec. 48 (2) (a) SchiedsG in Indien nicht vollstreckt werden, sofern der entschiedene Streitgegenstand nach indischem Recht nicht schiedsfähig ist.[1524] Schiedsunfreundliche Rechtsprechung existiert im Hinblick auf die Schiedsfähigkeit i. S. d. Sec. 48 (2) (a) SchiedsG nicht.

b) Öffentliche Ordnung

In Sec. 48 SchiedsG n. F. definierte der Gesetzgeber erstmals den Begriff der öffentlichen Ordnung (*ordre public*). Dem unbestimmten Rechtsbegriff der öffentlichen Ordnung konnte unter dem alten Sec. 48 (2) (b) SchiedsG a. F. nur eine klare gerichtliche Auslegung die erforderlichen Konturen verleihen.[1525]

aa) Renusagar Power v General Electric (Renusagar)

Im Urteil *Renusagar Power Co Ltd v General Electric Co (Renusagar)*[1526] hatte ein dreiköpfiger Senat des Supreme Courts über die Auslegung des Begriffs der öffentlichen Ordnung bei der Vollstreckung eines ausländischen Handelsschiedsspruchs gem. Sec. 7 (1) (b) (ii) „Foreign Awards (Recognition And Enforcement) Act 1961 (Foreign Award Act)" zu urteilen, durch den der Gesetzgeber Art. V (2) (b) UNÜ vor der Einführung von Sec. 48 SchiedsG in das indische Schiedsrecht umgesetzt hatte[1527].[1528]

1986 sprach das ICC-Schiedsgericht *General Electric Co (GE)* in seinem Schiedsspruch Entschädigungszahlungen, Zinsen und Zinseszins zu.[1529] Am

1523 Sec. 48 (2) SchiedsG.

1524 Zum Begriff der Schiedsfähigkeit, siehe Kapitel: Aufhebungsverfahren; Schiedsfähigkeit (C.VII.2.a)).

1525 Vgl. Kapitel: Singapur; Aufhebungsverfahren; Öffentliche Ordnung (B.VII.2.a)).

1526 AIR 1994 SC 860; (1994) Supp. 1 SCC 644; [1993] Supp. 3 SCR 22, 7.10.1993.

1527 Supreme Court, *Shri Lal Mahal Ltd v Progetto Grano Spa,* 2013 (3) Arb LR 1 (SC); Civil Appeal No. 5085 of 2013, 3.7.2013.

1528 Für den dem Verfahren zu Grunde liegenden Tatbestand, siehe ausführliche Darstellung im Kapitel: Aufhebungsverfahren; Renusagar Power v General Electric (Renusagar) (C.VII.2.b)aa)).

1529 Zur Höhe der im Schiedsverdikt zugesprochenen Summe und zu den weiteren im Schiedsspruch zugesprochenen Positionen, siehe Kapitel: Aufhebungsverfahren; Renusagar Power v General Electric (Renusagar) (C.VII.2.b)aa)).

15.10.1986 beantragte *GE* beim Bombay High Court den ausländischen Schiedsspruch unter Sec. 5[1530] Foreign Award Act für vollstreckbar zu erklären. *Renusagar Power Co Ltd (Renusagar Power)* antwortete am 17.10.1986 unverzüglich mit einer Feststellungklage vor dem „Court of Civil Judge“[1531] Mirzapur, in der die Unwirksamkeit des Schiedsspruchs festgestellt werden sollte. Auf Antrag von *GE* verwies das Gericht in Mirzapur die Rechtssache an den für die Vollstreckung des Schiedsverdikts zuständigen Bombay High Court, der die Feststellungsklage aussetzte. Ein Einzelrichter des Bombay High Courts erklärte den Schiedsspruch nach dem Foreign Award Act für vollstreckbar. Eine Division Bench des Bombay High Courts bestätige die Vollstreckbarkeit des Schiedsspruchs.

Im Berufungsverfahren vor dem Supreme Court trug *Renusagar Power* vor, die Vollstreckung des Schiedsspruchs verstoße gegen die indische öffentliche Ordnung, weil sie Normen des „Foreign Exchange Regulation Acts 1973“, des „Indian Contract Acts 1872“ (ungerechtfertigte Bereicherung) und des „Interest Acts 1978“ (Zinseszins) verletze. Der Supreme Court erörterte die Umsetzung des UNÜ im indischen Foreign Award Act und Gerichtsentscheidungen aus England und den USA zur öffentlichen Ordnung. Das oberste Gericht Indiens entschied anschließend, dass die öffentliche Ordnung eng auszulegen sei. Für die Vollstreckungsversagung eines ausländischen Schiedsspruchs sei eine Verletzung des indischen Rechts – im Gegensatz zu Sec. 1 (e) des „Genfer Abkommens zur Vollstreckung ausländischer Schiedssprüche 1927“ – für einen Verstoß gegen die öffentliche Ordnung i. S. v. Art. V (2) (b) UNÜ[1532] nicht ausreichend.[1533] Der Supreme Court verlieh dem Begriff der öffentlichen Ordnung 1993 die folgenden restriktiven Kriterien:

> *„Applying the said criteria it must be held that the enforcement of a foreign award would be refused on the ground that it is contrary to public policy if such enforcement would be contrary to (i) fundamental policy of Indian law; or (ii) the interests of India; or (iii) justice or morality.* “[1534]

Eine Verletzung der öffentlichen Ordnung liegt demnach vor, wenn die Vollstreckung eines ausländischen Schiedsspruchs unvereinbar ist mit:

1530 Sec. 5 regelte die Beantragung der Vollstreckung eines ausländischen Schiedsspruchs.

1531 Ein „Court of Civil Judge“ ist ein dem District Court nachgeordnetes Gericht, Indian Courts, District Courts, verfügbar unter http://indiancourts.nic.in/districtcourt.html# (zuletzt abgerufen am 28.4.2021).

1532 Zur Zeit der Entscheidung war Art. V (2) (b) UNÜ in Sec. 7 (1) (b) (ii) Foreign Award Act in das indische Recht umgesetzt. Im SchiedsG transformiert Sec. 48 (2) (b) SchiedsG Art. V (2) (b) UNÜ in das indische Recht.

1533 [1993] Supp. 3 SCR, S. 22 (63 ff.).

1534 [1993] Supp. 3 SCR, S. 22 (73).

1. dem grundlegenden Gesetzeszweck des indischen Rechts, oder
2. den Interessen Indiens, oder
3. Gerechtigkeit und Moral.

Der Supreme Court urteilte im vor ihm anhängigen Verfahren, dass der Schiedsspruch nicht die öffentliche Ordnung in Indien verletze. Einen Verstoß gegen die einfachgesetzlichen Bestimmungen des „Foreign Exchange Regulation Acts 1973“[1535] durch den Schiedsspruch verneinte das Gericht wegen einer möglichen Genehmigung des schiedsgerichtlich zugesprochenen Anspruchs.[1536] Die von *Renusagar Power* vorgetragene Verletzung der öffentlichen Ordnung durch eine ungerechtfertigte Bereicherung[1537] von *GE* lehnte das oberste indische Gericht ab, weil die ungerechtfertigte Bereicherung nicht die Vollstreckung des Schiedsspruchs betreffe.[1538] Den Verstoß gegen den Interest Act 1978[1539] erachtete das oberste Gericht Indiens als nicht ausreichend, um hierdurch zugleich die indische öffentliche Ordnung zu verletzten.[1540] Der Supreme Court bestätigte im Ergebnis die Vollstreckbarerklärung des Schiedsspruchs.

Zu begrüßen ist, dass der oberste Gerichtshof in dieser Entscheidung klar zwischen ausländischen Schiedssprüchen, die unter dem „Genfer Abkommen zur Vollstreckung ausländischer Schiedssprüche 1927“ und dem UNÜ ergingen, differenzierte. Der Supreme Court arbeitete folgerichtig heraus, dass der Gesetzgeber unter dem auf Art. V (2) (b) UNÜ beruhenden Sec. 7 (1) (b) (ii) Foreign Award Act einen Verstoß eines ausländischen Schiedsspruchs gegen das einfache indische Recht für eine Verletzung der öffentlichen Ordnung als nicht ausreichend erachtete.

Die Beschränkung der öffentlichen Ordnung in der Entscheidung *Renusagar* auf drei Kriterien verhinderte eine uferlose Auslegung der indischen öffentlichen Ordnung. Die Entscheidung steht im Einklang mit dem internationalen Standard unter dem UNÜ, nach dem der Nichtvollstreckungsgrund der öffentlichen Ordnung eng ausgelegt wird. Ein Schiedsspruch darf nach dem sog. „Pro-Enforcement Bias“ nur ausnahmsweise nicht vollstreckt werden. Die internationale Richtschnur des Schiedsgerichtswesens verbietet eine materielle Kontrolle eines ausländischen Schiedsspruchs durch das Vollstreckungsgericht. Für eine Verletzung der öffentlichen Ordnung des Vollstreckungsstaates fordert die internationale Norm, dass der ausländische Schiedsspruch[1541]

1535 Nach Ansicht des Gerichts lag keine Verletzung von Sec. 7, 9 und 47 vor.
1536 [1993] Supp. 3 SCR, S. 22 (82 f.).
1537 Nach Sec. 70, 72 Indian Contract Act 1872.
1538 [1993] Supp. 3 SCR, S. 22 (91).
1539 Sec. 3 (3) (c) verbietet es Gerichten Zinseszins zuzusprechen.
1540 [1993] Supp. 3 SCR, S. 22 (87 f.).
1541 Erforderlich ist, dass die im Schiedsspruch entschiedene, konkrete Rechtsfrage gegen die öffentliche Ordnung verstößt, Born, International Commercial Arbitration,

gegen die fundamentalsten zwingenden Normen bzw. die elementaren Gerechtigkeitsvorstellungen des Vollstreckungsstaates in gravierender Weise verstößt.[1542]

Auf Grund der Übereinstimmung mit dem Schiedsgerichtsstandard stößt das *Renusagar*-Urteil im Schrifttum auf positive Resonanz.[1543]

In den nachfolgenden Urteilen folgte der Supreme Court zunächst der *Renusagar*-Rechtsprechung.[1544]

bb) Phulchand Exports v Ooo Patriot

In der Entscheidung *Phulchand Exports Ltd v Ooo Patriot (Phulchand)*[1545] hatte ein aus zwei Richtern bestehender Senat des obersten indischen Gerichts 2011 über die Vollstreckbarkeit eines ausländischen Handelsschiedsspruchs zu urteilen.

Bd. 3, S. 3690; vgl. auch BGH, KZR 43/71, NJW 1972, S. 2180 (2181), 31.5.1972; Schlosser, in: Stein/Jonas, Anhang zu § 1061 ZPO Rn. 321 ff.

1542 Blackaby/Partasides/Redfern/Hunter, International Arbitration, Rn. 11.60 f., 11.105 ff.; Born, Law and Practice, § 17.03, S. 383, § 17.05 [H], S. 407 ff.; Gaillard/Savage, Fouchard Gaillard Goldman, Rn. 1711 ff.; Born, International Commercial Arbitration, Bd. 3, S. 3646 ff.; Born, Cases and Materials, S. 1198, 1250 ff.; Lew/Mistelis/Kröll, Comparative International Commercial Arbitration, Rn. 26-111 ff.; International Law Association, London Conference, 2000, Committee on International Commercial Arbitration, Interim Report on Public Policy as a Bar to Enforcement of International Arbitral Awards, S. 13 ff.; International Law Association, New Delhi Conference, 2002, Committee on International Commercial Arbitration, Final Report on Public Policy as a Bar to Enforcement of International Arbitral Awards, S. 2 ff.; Schlosser, in: Stein/Jonas, Anhang zu § 1061 ZPO Rn. 316 ff.

1543 Sharma, Ajay, Indian Journal of Arbitration Law 2014, Vol. III, Ausg. 1, S. 6 (29 f.); Mahajan/Narayan, International Arbitration Law Review 2015, S. 63 (68); Harisankar K. S., Second Look At The Foreign Award Forbidden On Enforcement – Indian Supreme Court, Kluwer Arbitration Blog, 1.8.2013, verfügbar unter http://arbitrationblog.kluwerarbitration.com/2013/08/01/second-look-at-the-foreign-award-forbidden-on-enforcement-indian-supreme-court/ (zuletzt abgerufen am 28.4.2021); Reddy/Nagaraj, Journal of International Arbitration 2002, Vol. 19, Ausg. 2, S. 117 (140 ff.); Nariman, in: Bosman (Hrsg.), ICCA International Handbook on Commercial Arbitration, Bd. III, S. India 1 (India 55 Fn. 70); Thej, International Arbitration Law Review 2014, S. 37 (39); Kumar, Aakanksha, International Arbitration Law Review 2014, S. 76 (79 f.). Differenziert Singhvi, Indian Journal of Arbitration Law 2015, Vol. IV, Ausg. 2, S. 14 (17); Malhotra, Indu, O. P. Malhotra on Arbitration, Sec. 48, S. 1717.

1544 Supreme Court, *Smita Conductors Ltd v Euro Alloys Ltd*; AIR 2001 SC 3730; Appeal (civil) 12930 of 1996, 31.8.2001; Supreme Court, *Technip Sa v Sms Holding Pvt Ltd*, 2005 5 SCC 465; Appeal (civil) 9258–9265 of 2003, 11.5.2005.

1545 (2011) 10 SCC 300; Civil Appeal No. 3343 of 2005, 12.10.2011.

1997 hatte das indische Unternehmen *Phulchand Exports Ltd (Phulchand Exports)* an den russischen Käufer *Ooo Patriot (Patriot)* 1.000 Tonnen Reis zum Preis von 12.450.000 Rupien (ca. 210.000 Euro) veräußert. Dem Kaufvertrag zufolge sollte der Reis gem. dem „Incoterm CIF“[1546] nach Noworossijsk in Russland geliefert werden. Die Verkäuferin war in diesem Kaufvertrag verpflichtet, den Reis nach der „Institute Cargo Clause (A)“ zu versichern und zu gewährleisten, dass das Frachtschiff den Hafen von Noworossijsk als ersten Verladehafen anläuft. Sollte der Reis Russland nicht innerhalb von 180 Tagen ab Kaufpreiszahlung erreichen, musste der Kaufpreis an den Käufer zurückerstattet werden.[1547] Die Verkäuferin verschiffte den Reis nicht rechtzeitig. Das den Reis transportierende Frachtschiff erlitt einen Motorschaden und die Seenotrettung schleppte das Schiff in einen türkischen Hafen. Das zuständige türkische Gericht nahm das Frachtschiff in Arrest und entschied, dass die Ladung des Frachtschiffs verkauft werden müsse, um die Rettungskosten zu begleichen. Der Transportversicherer wollte für den Schaden nicht aufkommen, weil er der Ansicht war, dass der Arrest des Schiffs nicht versichert gewesen sei. *Patriot* legte 1998 Schiedsklage auf Rückerstattung des Kaufpreises beim „Chamber of Commerce and Industry of the Russian Federation“ ein. *Phulchand Exports* entgegnete im Schiedsverfahren, dass das Risiko für das Transportgut nach dem Incoterm CIF beim Verschiffen bzw. mit Zugang der Transportdokumente an den Käufer *Patriot* übergegangen sei und entweder der Transportversicherer oder der Schiffseigentümer für den Schaden haften müsse.

Das Schiedsgericht entschied zunächst, dass die Verkäuferin *Phulchand Exports* die Waren verspätet verschifft und nicht sichergestellt habe, dass das Frachtschiff zuerst den Hafen in Noworossijsk ansteuerte. Die Verkäuferin sei nach dem Kaufvertrag verpflichtet, dem Käufer wegen der nicht erfolgten Lieferung der Waren den Kaufpreis zurückzuerstatten. Zudem zeige die Tatsache, dass die Verkäuferin einen Mitarbeiter in die Türkei entsandt habe, um sich nach dem Zustand der Lieferung zu erkundigen, dass die Verkäufe-

---

1546 ICC Germany, Standards & Regelwerke, Incoterms 2010, CIF, „‘Cost, Insurance and Freight‘/‘Kosten, Versicherung und Fracht‘ bedeutet, dass der Verkäufer die Ware an Bord des Schiffs liefert oder die bereits so gelieferte Ware verschafft. Die Gefahr des Verlustes oder der Beschädigung der Ware geht über, wenn die Ware an Bord des Schiffs ist. Der Verkäufer hat den Beförderungsvertrag abzuschließen sowie die Kosten und Fracht zu tragen, die für die Beförderung der Ware zum benannten Bestimmungshafen erforderlich sind. Zudem hat der Verkäufer auf eigene Kosten eine Transportversicherung abzuschließen, die zumindest der Mindestdeckung gemäß den Klauseln (C) der Institute Cargo Clauses (LMA/IUA) oder ähnlichen Klauseln entspricht.“ Verfügbar unter http://www.iccgermany.de/standards-regelwerke/incoterms/cif-kosten-versicherung-und-fracht-benannter-bestimmungshafen/ (zuletzt abgerufen am 28.4.2021).

1547 Dies ergab sich aus dem Kaufvertrag.

rin die Waren noch nicht als auf den Käufer übergegangen erachtete habe. Die Verkäuferin könne sich auch nicht durch „höhere Gewalt“ exkulpieren. Das Schiedsgericht stellte weiterhin fest, dass der Käufer *Patriot* der Verkäuferin Dokumente[1548] für die Reislieferung verspätet habe zukommen lassen und die Rückerstattung des Kaufpreises nicht sofort nach Ablauf der 180 Tage-Frist eingefordert habe. Das Schiedsgericht reduzierte deshalb den zu erstattenden Kaufpreis um die Hälfte, sodass nach dem Schiedsspruch die Verkäuferin die Hälfte des Kaufpreises[1549] an den Käufer zurückzahlen musste.

Der Käufer *Patriot* beantragte die Vollstreckung des Schiedsspruchs unter Sec. 48 f. SchiedsG. Die Verkäuferin *Phulchand Exports* war der Auffassung der Schiedsspruch sei wegen eines Verstoßes gegen die indische öffentliche Ordnung nicht vollstreckbar. Der Bombay High Court lehnte 2001 die Rechtsauffassung von *Phulchand Exports* ab und erklärte den Schiedsspruch für vollstreckbar. Die Berufung wies eine Division Bench des Bombay High Courts 2002 unter Verweis auf die *Renusagar*-Rechtsprechung zurück. Nach der Division Bench beruhe der Schiedsspruch auf durch das Schiedsgericht festgestellten Tatsachen und selbst unzutreffend festgestellte Tatsachen können die öffentliche Ordnung nicht verletzen.

Phulchand Exports machte in der Berufung vor dem Supreme Court geltend, dass der auf der Rückzahlungsklausel beruhende Schiedsspruch die öffentliche Ordnung verletze, weil die Rückzahlungsklausel indischem Recht[1550] widerspreche. In seiner Entscheidung folgte der Supreme Court dem *Saw Pipes*-Urteil desselben Gerichts zur erweiterten Auslegung der öffentlichen Ordnung in Aufhebungsverfahren gem. Sec. 34 SchiedsG. Das oberste indische Gericht dehnte daher die Konkretisierung der öffentlichen Ordnung gegenüber der *Renusagar*-Entscheidung ebenfalls um das Kriterium der „offensichtliche Rechtswidrigkeit“ (engl. patent illegality) eines Schiedsspruchs aus. Da der Begriff der öffentlichen Ordnung in Aufhebungsverfahren (Sec. 34 SchiedsG) und bei der Vollstreckung von ausländischen Handelsschiedssprüchen (Sec. 48 SchiedsG) miteinander übereinstimmen müsse. Nach dem Supreme Court umfasst der Begriff der öffentlichen Ordnung gem. Sec. 48 (2) (b) SchiedsG:

1. den grundlegenden Gesetzeszweck des indischen Rechts,
2. die Interessen Indiens,
3. Gerechtigkeit und Moral und
4. die offensichtliche Rechtswidrigkeit.[1551]

1548 Es handelte sich um das Versicherungs-Zertifikat und die Fracht-Dokumente.

1549 138.402,03 US-Dollar zuzüglich Zinsen und Kosten für das Schiedsverfahren.

1550 Sec. 74 und 23 Indian Contract Act 1872. Bei der Rückzahlungsklausel handle es sich nach *Phulchand Exports* um eine unzulässige Vertragsstrafe (Sec. 74 Indian Contract Act 1872), die nach Sec. 23 Indian Contract Act 1872 unwirksam sei.

1551 Civil Appeal No. 3343 of 2005, Rn. 12 f.

In seiner Entscheidung überprüfte der Supreme Court daraufhin den Schiedsspruch auf seine Vereinbarkeit mit dem indischen Recht[1552]. Er entschied, dass die Rückzahlungsklausel weder Sec. 23 noch Sec. 74 „Indian Contract Act 1872“ verletze. Der Schiedsspruch verstoße folglich auch nicht gegen die vom Supreme Court in dieser Entscheidung auf Vollstreckungsverfahren ausgedehnte weite Auslegung der indischen öffentlichen Ordnung aus dem *Saw Pipes*-Urteil.[1553] Das oberste indische Gericht erachtete den ausländischen Handelsschiedsspruch im Ergebnis demnach als für in Indien vollstreckbar.

Die gegenüber dem Urteil *Renusaga*r erweiterte Konkretisierung der öffentlichen Ordnung in der Entscheidung *Phulchand* widerspricht dem internationalen Standard der Schiedsgerichtsbarkeit, nach dem der Begriff der öffentlichen Ordnung eng ausgelegt wird. Ein ausländischer Schiedsspruch darf ausschließlich bei einer schwerwiegenden Verletzung der fundamentalsten, nicht dispositiven Normen bzw. der elementaren Gerechtigkeitsvorstellungen des Vollstreckungsstaates nicht vollstreckt werden.[1554]

Die Übertragung der weiten Auslegung der öffentlichen Ordnung aus dem Urteil *Saw Pipes* auf die Vollstreckung von ausländischen Handelsschiedssprüchen durch die Entscheidung *Phulchand* kommentierte die Literatur in zutreffender Weise kritisch.[1555] Es wird moniert, dass die Entscheidung zu

---

1552 Sec. 74 und 23 Indian Contract Act 1872.

1553 Civil Appeal No. 3343 of 2005, Rn. 15 ff.

1554 Blackaby/Partasides/Redfern/Hunter, International Arbitration, Rn. 11.60 f., 11.105 ff.; Born, Law and Practice, § 17.03, S. 383, § 17.05 [H], S. 407 ff.; Gaillard/Savage, Fouchard Gaillard Goldman, Rn. 1711 ff.; Born, International Commercial Arbitration, Bd. 3, S. 3646 ff.; Born, Cases and Materials, S. 1198, 1250 ff.; Lew/Mistelis/Kröll, Comparative International Commercial Arbitration, Rn. 26-111 ff.; International Law Association, London Conference, 2000, Committee on International Commercial Arbitration, Interim Report on Public Policy as a Bar to Enforcement of International Arbitral Awards, S. 13 ff.; International Law Association, New Delhi Conference, 2002, Committee on International Commercial Arbitration, Final Report on Public Policy as a Bar to Enforcement of International Arbitral Awards, S. 2 ff.; Schlosser, in: Stein/Jonas, Anhang zu § 1061 ZPO Rn. 316 ff.

1555 Gupta, Arpan, Indian Journal of Arbitration Law 2013, Vol. II, Ausg. 2, S. 1 (10); Mahajan/Narayan, International Arbitration Law Review 2015, S. 63 (69 ff.); Mahajan, International Arbitration Law Review 2013, S. N43 (N44); Somnath, Arbitration 2014, S. 217 f.; Dhruv Dewan/Mayank Pandey, Enforcing foreign awards: Supreme Court widens scope of „public policy“, International Law Office, 22.11.2011, verfügbar unter http://www.internationallawoffice.com/Newsletters/Litigation/India/Amarchand-Mangaldas-Suresh-A-Shroff-Co/Enforcing-foreign-awards-Supreme-Court-widens-scope-of-public-policy (zuletzt abgerufen am 28.4.2021); Herbert Smith, Arbitration e-bulletin, Indian Supreme Court expands public policy definition for enforcement of foreign awards, verfügbar unter http://sites.herbertsmithfreehills.vuturevx.com/33/537/landing-pages/indian-international-arbitration-e-bulletin---article-3.asp (zuletzt abgerufen am 28.4.2021). Kritisch zu der Entscheidung *Phul-*

Rechtsunsicherheit führe und Gerichte Schiedssprüche materiell kontrollieren können.[1556] Diese materielle Kontrolle verursache Verzögerungen und eröffne gerichtliche Interventionen bei der Vollstreckung von ausländischen Handelsschiedssprüchen.[1557]

cc) Shri Lal Mahal Ltd v Progetto Grano

Der Supreme Court hatte 2013 im Verfahren *Shri Lal Mahal Ltd v Progetto Grano Spa (Shri Lal Mahal)*[1558] in einer Besetzung von drei Richtern darüber zu urteilen, ob ein ausländischer Handelsschiedsspruch wegen eines Verstoßes gegen die öffentliche Ordnung Indiens nicht vollsteckbar ist.

Den Parteien des Berufungsverfahrens vor dem Supreme Court waren die Ansprüche der Käuferin und der Verkäuferin von Hartweizen[1559] abgetreten worden.[1560] Im Kaufvertrag aus dem Jahre 1994 vereinbarten die Verkäu-

---

chand, Khanna, International Arbitration Law Review 2012, S. 203 (204); Mahajan/Anand, Arbitration 2013, S. 28 (31 ff.); Timothy, International Arbitration Law Review 2016, S. 56 (57).

1556 Gupta, Arpan, Indian Journal of Arbitration Law 2013, Vol. II, Ausg. 2, S. 1 (10); Mahajan/Narayan, International Arbitration Law Review 2015, S. 63 (69 ff.); Mahajan, International Arbitration Law Review 2013, S. N43 (N44); Somnath, Arbitration 2014, S. 217 f.; Dhruv Dewan/Mayank Pandey, Enforcing foreign awards: Supreme Court widens scope of „public policy", International Law Office, 22.11.2011, verfügbar unter http://www.internationallawoffice.com/Newsletters/Litigation/India/Amarchand-Mangaldas-Suresh-A-Shroff-Co/Enforcing-foreign-awards-Supreme-Court-widens-scope-of-public-policy (zuletzt abgerufen am 28.4.2021); Herbert Smith, Arbitration e-bulletin, Indian Supreme Court expands public policy definition for enforcement of foreign awards, verfügbar unter http://sites.herbertsmithfreehills.vuturevx.com/33/537/landing-pages/indian-international-arbitration-e-bulletin---article-3.asp (zuletzt abgerufen am 28.4.2021).

1557 Gupta, Arpan, Indian Journal of Arbitration Law 2013, Vol. II, Ausg. 2, S. 1 (10); Mahajan/Narayan, International Arbitration Law Review 2015, S. 63 (69 ff.); Mahajan, International Arbitration Law Review 2013, S. N43 (N44); Somnath, Arbitration 2014, S. 217 f.; Dhruv Dewan/Mayank Pandey, Enforcing foreign awards: Supreme Court widens scope of „public policy", International Law Office, 22.11.2011, verfügbar unter http://www.internationallawoffice.com/Newsletters/Litigation/India/Amarchand-Mangaldas-Suresh-A-Shroff-Co/Enforcing-foreign-awards-Supreme-Court-widens-scope-of-public-policy (zuletzt abgerufen am 28.4.2021); Herbert Smith, Arbitration e-bulletin, Indian Supreme Court expands public policy definition for enforcement of foreign awards, verfügbar unter http://sites.herbertsmithfreehills.vuturevx.com/33/537/landing-pages/indian-international-arbitration-e-bulletin---article-3.asp (zuletzt abgerufen am 28.4.2021).

1558 2013 (3) Arb LR 1 (SC); Civil Appeal No. 5085 of 2013, 3.7.2013.

1559 Engl. durum wheat, bedeutet im Deutschen auch Durumweizen, Glasweizen und Gerstenweizen.

1560 Die Abtretung fand während der Rechtshängigkeit des Vollstreckungsverfahrens vor dem Delhi High Court statt.

ferin *Shiv Nath Rai Harnarain (India) Company* aus New Delhi und die Käuferin *Italgrani Spa* aus Neapel (Italien) den Erwerb von 20.000 Tonnen indischen Hartweizens zu 162 US-Dollar je Tonne. Die Waren sollten gem. dem „FOB-Incoterm“[1561] aus dem indischen Kandla zur Käuferin nach Italien verschifft werden.[1562] Der Kaufvertrag enthielt eine Schiedsklausel, nach der Streitigkeiten unter den „Grain and Feed Trade Association (GAFTA)“-Schiedsregeln beizulegen waren. Die „Société Générale de Surveillance (SGS)“ nach Wahl der Käuferin sollte die Durchschnittsqualität des Hartweizens überprüfen. Die „SGS Indien“ zertifizierte, dass Gewicht, Qualität und Verpackung des Hartweizens ordnungsgemäß seien. Nach der Ankunft des Hartweizens stellte die „SGS Genf“ fest, dass es sich bei dem gelieferten Weizen nicht um den vereinbarten Hartweizen, sondern um Weichweizen[1563] handelte. Im November 1994 legte die Käuferin Schiedsklage bei der GAFTA ein. Das Schiedsgericht sprach der Käuferin im Dezember 1997 Schadensersatz zu, weil es die SGS Genf als die von der Käuferin gewählte Überprüfungsstelle erachtete und nicht die SGS Indien, wie von der Verkäuferin vorgetragen.[1564]

Nachdem die Käuferin das GAFTA-Schiedsverfahren initiiert hatte, legte die Verkäuferin beim Delhi High Court eine Feststellungsklage[1565] ein und beantragte eine einstweilige Maßnahme[1566] gegen die Fortsetzung des GAFTA-Schiedsverfahrens. Der Delhi High Court erließ zunächst die einstweilige Maßnahme[1567], wies aber die Feststellungsklage ab. Auch eine Berufung[1568] zum Supreme Court war erfolglos.

1561 ICC Germany, Standards & Regelwerke, Incoterms 2010, FOB, „‘Free On Board‘/‘Frei an Bord‘ bedeutet, dass der Verkäufer die Ware an Bord des vom Käufer benannten Schiffs im benannten Verschiffungshafen liefert oder die bereits so gelieferte Ware verschafft. Die Gefahr des Verlustes oder der Beschädigung der Ware geht über, wenn die Ware an Bord des Schiffs ist. Der Käufer trägt ab diesem Zeitpunkt alle Kosten.“ Verfügbar unter http://www.iccgermany.de/standards-regelwerke/incoterms/ (zuletzt abgerufen am 28.4.2021).

1562 Dies besagte der Kaufvertrag.

1563 Engl. soft wheat, im Deutschen auch als Brotweizen und Saatweizen bezeichnet.

1564 Zudem initiierte die Käuferin am 5.2.1997 ein weiteres GAFTA Schiedsverfahren II gegen die Verkäuferin wegen der Verletzung der Schiedsvereinbarung durch das gerichtliche Verfahren in Indien. Im GAFTA Berufungsverfahren gegen den Schiedsspruch vor dem Board of Appeal sprach dieser der Käuferin am 21.9.1998 Schadensersatz und angemessene Gerichtskosten zu (Schiedsspruch II). Die Käuferin beantragte die Vollstreckung des Schiedsspruchs II vor dem Delhi High Court zusammen mit dem Schadensersatz-Schiedsspruch I.

1565 Es sollte festgestellt werden, dass zwischen den Parteien keine Schiedsvereinbarung bestehe.

1566 Engl. restraining order.

1567 Engl. interim order.

1568 Durch eine „Special Leave Petition“.

Im nach den GAFTA-Schiedsregeln vorgesehenen Berufungsverfahren[1569] vor dem „Board of Appeal“ bestätigte dieser im September 1998 den Schiedsspruch.[1570] Der High Court in London (England) wies daraufhin im Dezember 1998 die von der Verkäuferin beantragte Aufhebung des Schiedsspruchs zurück.

Im September 1998 beantragte die Käuferin (Berufungsbeklagte) beim Delhi High Court den ausländischen Schiedsspruch für vollstreckbar zu erklären.[1571] Die Verkäuferin (Berufungsklägerin) entgegnete dem Vollstreckungsantrag, dass der Berufungsschiedsspruch des GAFTA Board of Appeals wegen der Verletzung der Bestimmungen des Kaufvertrages gegen die öffentliche Ordnung in Indien verstoße. Nach Auffassung der Berufungsklägerin hätte der GAFTA Board of Appeal unter Berücksichtigung der Vereinbarung im Kaufvertrag nicht dem Testbericht von SGS Genf, sondern dem Testbericht von SGS Indien folgen müssen. Die Berufungsbeklagte war hingegen der Ansicht, dass die Entscheidung des GAFTA Board of Appeals bezüglich des SGS-Zertifikats die schiedsgerichtliche Beweiswürdigung betreffe, die nach Sec. 48 SchiedsG nicht kontrolliert werden könne. Der Delhi High Court folgte der Rechtsauffassung der Berufungsbeklagten und entschied, dass das Vollstreckungsgericht gem. Sec. 48 SchiedsG hinsichtlich der Qualität des Weizens keine Tatsachen neu bewerten dürfe und die Begründetheit eines ausländischen Schiedsspruchs nicht überprüft werden könne. Der High Court erklärte den Schiedsspruch für vollstreckbar.

In der Berufung vor dem Supreme Court machte die Berufungsklägerin (Verkäuferin) geltend, dass die weite Auslegung der öffentlichen Ordnung aus den Urteilen *Saw Pipes* und *Phulchand* auf die beantragte Vollstreckung gem. Sec. 48 SchiedsG anwendbar sei. Die Berufungsbeklagte (Käuferin) entgegnete, dass auf die Vollstreckung ausländischer Handelsschiedssprüche, im Gegensatz zur Aufhebung von Schiedssprüchen (Sec. 34 SchiedsG), die engeren Kriterien der öffentlichen Ordnung aus der *Renusagar*-Rechtsprechung angewendet werden müssen.

1569 Das GAFTA-Schiedsverfahren sieht ein zweistufiges Schiedsverfahren vor. Zunächst entscheidet das Schiedsgericht (1. Stufe) und dieser Schiedsspruch kann vom GAFTA „Board of Appeal“ (2. Stufe) überprüft werden, siehe GAFTA Arbitration Rules No. 125.

1570 Die Kosten für den Deckungskauf sollten im Unterschied zum Schiedsspruch aber nicht ersetzt werden. Zusätzlich sollte die Verkäuferin die Kosten für das Schiedsverfahren und das Berufungsverfahren tragen.

1571 Die Käuferin hatte zudem die Vollstreckung des Schiedsspruchs II vor dem Delhi High Court beantragt. Die indischen Gerichte haben insbesondere die Vollstreckung des Schadensersatz-Schiedsspruchs I erörtert, daher fokussiert sich die Darstellung auf die Vollstreckung des Schadensersatz-Schiedsspruchs I.

Der Supreme Court entschied, dass der Entscheidung *Saw Pipes* desselben Gerichts zur Reichweite der öffentlichen Ordnung in Aufhebungsverfahren nach Sec. 34 SchiedsG bei der Vollstreckung eines ausländischen Handelsschiedsspruchs gem. Sec. 48 SchiedsG nicht gefolgt werden könne. In seinem Urteil verwarf der dreiköpfige Senat des Supreme Courts daher die Rechtsauffassung des mit zwei Richtern besetzten Senats desselben Gerichts in der Rechtssache *Phulchand.* Mit diesem Urteil schränkte das oberste indische Gericht die Auslegung der öffentlichen Ordnung gem. Sec. 48 SchiedsG wieder auf die drei Kriterien aus der *Renusagar*-Entscheidung ein:

1. den grundlegenden Gesetzeszweck des indischen Rechts,
2. die Interessen Indiens und
3. Gerechtigkeit und Moral.[1572]

Die Konkretisierung des Rechtsbegriffs der öffentlichen Ordnung auf diese drei Auslegungspunkte ist positiv zu bewerten. Sie stimmt mit der internationalen Norm der Schiedsgerichtsbarkeit überein, wonach eine ausufernde Auslegung der öffentlichen Ordnung zu unterbinden ist.[1573] Die Rückbesinnung auf die dem *Renusagar*-Urteil entspringende restriktivere Auslegung der öffentlichen Ordnung in der Entscheidung *Shri Lal Mahal* ist demnach als Schiedsverfahren fördernd zu klassifizieren.

In dieser Entscheidung differenzierte der Supreme Court zwischen indischen und ausländischen Schiedssprüchen und begrenzte für ausländische Handelsschiedssprüche den Begriff der öffentlichen Ordnung auf die drei Kriterien der *Renusagar*-Auslegung. Für Aufhebungsverfahren i. S. v. Sec. 34 SchiedsG blieb es bei den in der Entscheidung *Saw Pipes* aufgestellten, weiter ausgestalteten vier Auslegungskriterien der öffentlichen Ordnung.[1574]

In concreto erachtete der Supreme Court den Schiedsspruch für vollstreckbar, da Sec. 48 SchiedsG keine Überprüfung der Begründetheit eines Schiedsspruchs zulasse. Die Entscheidung des GAFTA Board of Appeals über den maßgeblichen Testbericht der SGS könne demnach nicht von den

---

1572 Civil Appeal No. 5085 of 2013, Rn. 23 ff.

1573 Blackaby/Partasides/Redfern/Hunter, International Arbitration, Rn. 11.60 f., 11.105 ff.; Born, Law and Practice, § 17.03, S. 383, § 17.05 [H], S. 407 ff.; Gaillard/Savage, Fouchard Gaillard Goldman, Rn. 1711 ff.; Born, International Commercial Arbitration, Bd. 3, S. 3646 ff.; Born, Cases and Materials, S. 1198, 1250 ff.; Lew/Mistelis/Kröll, Comparative International Commercial Arbitration, Rn. 26-111 ff.; International Law Association, London Conference, 2000, Committee on International Commercial Arbitration, Interim Report on Public Policy as a Bar to Enforcement of International Arbitral Awards, S. 13 ff.; International Law Association, New Delhi Conference, 2002, Committee on International Commercial Arbitration, Final Report on Public Policy as a Bar to Enforcement of International Arbitral Awards, S. 2 ff.; Schlosser, in: Stein/Jonas, Anhang zu § 1061 ZPO Rn. 316 ff.

1574 Civil Appeal No. 5085 of 2013, Rn. 26 f.

Vollstreckungsgerichten kontrolliert werden und der Schiedsspruch verletze nicht die indische öffentliche Ordnung.[1575]

Dieser Beschränkung der öffentlichen Ordnung in Vollstreckungsverfahren auf die engen Auslegungskriterien aus dem *Renusagar*-Urteil ist zuzustimmen. Auch das Schriftum erachtet die reduzierte gerichtliche materielle Kontrolle von ausländischen Handelsschiedssprüchen und die Annäherung an die internationale Praxis der Schiedsgerichtsbarkeit[1576] durch das Urteil *Shri Lal Mahal* als schiedsfreundlich.[1577] Bedauert wird hingegen, dass die *Shri Lal Mahal*-Entscheidung, die im *Saw Pipes*-Urteil geschaffene, weite Auslegung der öffentlichen Ordnung für Aufhebungsverfahren i. S. v. Sec. 34 SchiedsG unberührt ließ.[1578]

dd) Bewertung

Das Vollstreckungsgericht hat im Rahmen der Überprüfung von Verstößen gegen die öffentliche Ordnung gem. Art. V (2) (b) UNÜ zwei Aspekte auszubalancieren. Das Interesse des Vollstreckungsstaates an der Nichtdurchsetzung von Schiedssprüchen, die seiner Rechtsordnung widersprechen, mit der grundsätzlichen Verbindlichkeit ausländischer Schiedssprüche. Bei aller Schwierigkeit, den Begriff der öffentlichen Ordnung im Rahmen der gebotenen Auslegung zu konkretisieren, entspricht in diesem Kontext die restriktive Auslegung der öffentlichen Ordnung in den Urteilen *Renusagar* und *Shri Lal* dem internationalen Schiedsgerichtstandard gem. Art. V (2) (b)

1575 Civil Appeal No. 5085 of 2013, Rn. 42 ff.

1576 Born, Law and Practice, § 17.05 [H] [3], S. 409; Gaillard/Savage, Fouchard Gaillard Goldman, Rn. 1711 ff.; Born, International Commercial Arbitration, Bd. 3, S. 3649 ff.; Born, Cases and Materials, S. 1198; Lew/Mistelis/Kröll, Comparative International Commercial Arbitration, Rn. 26-66, 26-114 ff.; International Law Association, New Delhi Conference, 2002, Committee on International Commercial Arbitration, Final Report on Public Policy as a Bar to Enforcement of International Arbitral Awards, S. 2 ff.

1577 Kumar, Aakanksha, International Arbitration Law Review 2014, S. 76 ff.; Sharma, Ajay, Indian Journal of Arbitration Law 2014, Vol. III, Ausg. 1, S. 6 (30); Somnath, Arbitration 2014, S. 217; Allsop, Arbitration 2015, S. 169 (170 i. V. m. Fn. 5); Mahajan/Narayan, International Arbitration Law Review 2015, S. 63 (71 ff.); Choudhary, Indian Journal of Arbitration Law, 2015, Vol. IV, Ausg. 2, S. 69 (85 f.); Thej, International Arbitration Law Review 2014, S. 37 ff.; Khambata, Arbitration 2013, S. 441 (443). *Kumar* weist darauf hin, dass die Entscheidung *Shri Lal Mahal* sowohl das Eingreifen der staatlichen Gerichte in Schiedsverfahren als auch die hiermit verbundenen Verzögerungen ausmerzt, Kumar, Aakanksha, International Arbitration Law Review 2014, S. 76 (83). Zu den durch das Urteil reduzierten Interventionen in Schiedsverfahren, Mahajan, International Arbitration Law Review 2013, S. N43 ff.; Sathyapalan, Arbitration International 2016, S. 1 (13).

1578 Thej, International Arbitration Law Review 2014, S. 37 (42); Mahajan, International Arbitration Law Review 2013, S. N43 (N45 f.).

UNÜ. Nach Letzterem ist die öffentliche Ordnung des Vollstreckungsstaates bei der Vollstreckung ausländischer Schiedssprüche[1579] enger auszulegen als die öffentliche Ordnung bei der Aufhebung von im Inland ergangenen Schiedssprüchen[1580]. In Vollstreckungsverfahren gem. Art. V (2) (b) UNÜ legen Gerichte in den meisten Rechtsordnungen die öffentliche Ordnung restriktiv aus und lehnen im Rahmen des „Pro-Enforcement Bias" nur ausnahmsweise die Vollstreckung eines ausländischen Schiedsspruchs ab. Nach der Norm der internationalen Schiedsgerichtsbarkeit darf die Vollstreckung einzig bei einer schwerwiegenden Verletzung der fundamentalsten zwingenden Bestimmungen bzw. der elementaren Gerechtigkeitsvorstellungen des Vollstreckungsstaates versagt werden. Die falsche Rechtsanwendung durch das Schiedsgericht ist nicht ausreichend, um einem ausländischen Schiedsspruch unter dem Deckmantel der nationalen öffentlichen Ordnung einer materiellen gerichtlichen Kontrolle zu unterziehen.[1581]

Der Supreme Court hatte in der Entscheidung *Renusagar* die indische öffentliche Ordnung für Vollstreckungsverfahren in schiedsfreundlicher Weise eng ausgelegt. Die im Urteil *Phulchand* mit Rückgriff auf die Entscheidung *Saw Pipes* erweiterte Konkretisierung der öffentlichen Ordnung führte das oberste Gericht Indiens in seinem *Shri Lal Mahal*-Urteil wieder zurück zu den engen Kriterien der öffentlichen Ordnung aus der Entscheidung *Renusagar*. Der höchstrichterlichen Rechtsprechung gelang es im Ergebnis, den mit einem nicht zu bändigenden Pferd verglichenen Begriff der öffentlichen Ordnung zu zügeln und ihm ein klares Profil zu geben.[1582] Diese enge, eine

1579 Erforderlich ist, dass die im Schiedsspruch entschiedene, konkrete Rechtsfrage gegen die öffentliche Ordnung verstößt, Born, International Commercial Arbitration, Bd. 3, S. 3690; vgl. auch BGH, KZR 43/71, NJW 1972, S. 2180 (2181), 31.5.1972; Schlosser, in: Stein/Jonas, Anhang zu § 1061 ZPO Rn. 321 ff.

1580 Zur engeren Auslegung der öffentlichen Ordnung in Vollstreckungsverfahren ausländischer Schiedssprüche, Born, International Commercial Arbitration, Bd. 3, S. 3317 f.; Born, Law and Practice, § 17.05 [H] [2] S. 408; Committee on International Commercial Arbitration, Interim Report on Public Policy as a Bar to Enforcement of International Arbitral Awards, S. 13.

1581 Blackaby/Partasides/Redfern/Hunter, International Arbitration, Rn. 11.60 f., 11.105 ff.; Born, Law and Practice, § 17.03, S. 383, § 17.05 [H], S. 407 ff.; Gaillard/Savage, Fouchard Gaillard Goldman, Rn. 1711 ff.; Born, International Commercial Arbitration, Bd. 3, S. 3646 ff.; Born, Cases and Materials, S. 1198, 1250 ff.; Lew/Mistelis/Kröll, Comparative International Commercial Arbitration, Rn. 26-111 ff.; International Law Association, London Conference, 2000, Committee on International Commercial Arbitration, Interim Report on Public Policy as a Bar to Enforcement of International Arbitral Awards, S. 13 ff.; International Law Association, New Delhi Conference, 2002, Committee on International Commercial Arbitration, Final Report on Public Policy as a Bar to Enforcement of International Arbitral Awards, S. 2 ff.; Schlosser, in: Stein/Jonas, Anhang zu § 1061 ZPO Rn. 316 ff.

1582 Vgl. Kapitel: Singapur; Aufhebungsverfahren; Öffentliche Ordnung (B.VII.2.a)) und Kapitel: Indien; Aufhebungsverfahren; Öffentliche Ordnung (C.VII.2.b)).

„révision au fond" ausschließende, Auslegung der öffentlichen Ordnung bei der Vollstreckung eines ausländischen Handelsschiedsspruchs ist als die Schiedsgerichtsbarkeit fördernd anzusehen.

c) Betrug und Korruption

Der Gesetzgeber stellte in einer Erklärung[1583] zum Begriff der öffentlichen Ordnung gem. Sec. 48 (2) (b) SchiedsG klar, dass ein ausländischer Handelsschiedsspruch, der durch Betrug oder Korruption beeinflusst wurde, gegen die indische öffentliche Ordnung verstößt. Nach dem internationalen Standard des Schiedsgerichtswesens werden Korruption und Betrug im Rahmen der öffentlichen Ordnung als legitime Vollstreckungsversagungsgründe angesehen.[1584]

3. Arbitration Amendment Act

In zwei Erklärungen zu Sec. 48 (2) (b) SchiedsG n. F. definierte der Gesetzgeber 2015 – wie in Sec. 34 SchiedsG n. F. – den Begriff der öffentlichen Ordnung. Die Erklärung 1 zu Sec. 48 (2) (b) SchiedsG n. F. beruht auf der Auslegung der öffentlichen Ordnung im Urteil *Renusagar*, verengt diese höchstrichterliche Konkretisierung der öffentlichen Ordnung jedoch entscheidend.[1585] Lediglich der Punkt des „grundlegenden Gesetzeszwecks des indischen Rechts" aus der *Renusagar*-Formel der öffentlichen Ordnung blieb semantisch unverändert. Der Gesetzgeber unterzog den Auslegungspunkt des grundlegenden Gesetzeszwecks des indischen Rechts allerdings in der Erklärung 2 zu Sec. 48 (2) (b) SchiedsG n. F. einer restriktiven Überarbeitung und stellte klar, dass unter diesem Auslegungspunkt eine materielle Kontrolle eines ausländischen Handelsschiedsspruchs nicht statthaft ist. Die „Gerechtigkeits- und Moralvorstellungen" der *Renusagar*-Auslegung beschränkte der Arbitration Amendment Act 2015 auf „grundlegendste Gerechtigkeits- und Moralvorstellungen".[1586] Die Formulierung der „grundlegendsten Gerechtigkeits- und Moralvorstellungen" (engl. most basic noti-

---

1583 Engl. explanation.

1584 Born, International Commercial Arbitration, Bd. 3, S. 3673 ff.; Lew/Mistelis/Kröll, Comparative International Commercial Arbitration, Rn. 26-118; International Law Association, London Conference, 2000, Committee on International Commercial Arbitration, Interim Report on Public Policy as a Bar to Enforcement of International Arbitral Awards, S. 24 f.; International Law Association, New Delhi Conference, 2002, Committee on International Commercial Arbitration, Final Report on Public Policy as a Bar to Enforcement of International Arbitral Awards, S. 7.

1585 Government of India, Law Commission of India, 246. Report, Amendments to the Arbitration and Conciliation Act 1996, 5.8.2014, S. 22.

1586 Erklärung 1 zu Sec. 48 SchiedsG.

ons of morality or justice) stimmt mit der Konkretisierung der öffentlichen Ordnung in der viel zitierten[1587] amerikanischen Entscheidung *Parsons & Whittemore Overseas Co v Societe Generale de l'Industrie du Papier (RAKTA)*[1588] überein. In der neuen Erklärung 1 strich der Gesetzgeber das Auslegungskriterium der „Interessen Indiens" aus der *Renusagar*-Formel, um den Begriff der öffentlichen Ordnung stärker zu konturieren und Fehlinterpretationen zu verhindern.[1589]

Durch diese Neuerungen definierte der Gesetzgeber die öffentliche Ordnung restriktiver. Die öffentliche Ordnung unter Sec. 48 (2) (b) SchiedsG n. F. umfasst:

1. den grundlegenden Gesetzeszweck des indischen Rechts und
2. die grundlegendsten Gerechtigkeits- und Moralvorstellungen.

Die weiter komprimierte Definition der öffentlichen Ordnung auf der Grundlage der *Renusagar*-Kriterien in den zwei Erklärungen zu Sec. 48 (2) (b) SchiedsG n. F. unterstützt Schiedsverfahren. Es wird gewährleistet, dass nur schwerwiegende Verstöße eines in Indien zu vollstreckenden ausländischen Handelsschiedsspruchs gegen elementare Rechtsgrundsätze zu einer Verletzung der öffentlichen Ordnung führen können. Der Gesetzgeber verleiht hiermit der öffentlichen Ordnung in Sec. 48 (2) (b) SchiedsG n. F. in Übereinstimmung mit dem Standard der internationalen Schiedsgerichtsbarkeit die notwendigen engen Konturen. Sec. 48 (2) (b) SchiedsG n. F. ist als schiedsfreundlich anzusehen, weil durch die restriktive Definition der öffentlichen Ordnung der „Pro-Enforcement Bias"[1590] gewährleistet wird.

Für die Definition der öffentlichen Ordnung fügte der Arbitration Amendment Act nach Sec. 34 (2) (b) (ii) SchiedsG und Sec. 48 (2) (b) SchiedsG zwei wortgleiche Erklärungen zum Begriff der öffentlichen Ordnung ins SchiedsG n. F. ein. Für inländische Schiedsverfahren erkennt Sec. 34 (2A) SchiedsG n. F. auch die offensichtliche Rechtswidrigkeit des Schiedsspruchs als zusätzliches Kriterium der öffentlichen Ordnung an. Die restriktive Definition der öffentlichen Ordnung für Vollstreckungsverfahren stimmt einzig mit der Definition für Aufhebungsverfahren von internationalen Handelsschiedssprüchen überein. Internationale Handelsschiedssprüche sollen demzufolge geringerer gerichtlicher Kontrolle ausgesetzt sein als inländische Schiedssprüche.

1587 International Law Association, New Delhi Conference, 2002, Committee on International Commercial Arbitration, Final Report on Public Policy as a Bar to Enforcement of International Arbitral Awards, S. 4.

1588 US Court of Appeals, Second Circuit, 508 F.2d 969 (2d Cir. 1974), 23.12.1974.

1589 Government of India, Law Commission of India, 246. Report, Amendments to the Arbitration and Conciliation Act 1996, 5.8.2014, S. 22.

1590 Vgl. o.

Die lange Verfahrensdauer bei der Vollstreckung von ausländischen Schiedssprüchen führte zu dem Investitionsschiedsspruch *White Industries Australia Limited v The Republic of India*[1591]. Um in der Zukunft durch stringentere Vollstreckungsverfahren eine weitere Haftung Indiens in Investitionsschiedsverfahren zu verhindern, schlug die Law Commission in ihrem 246. Report vor, eine neue Sec. 48 (4) in das SchiedsG einzuführen, in der die Verfahrensdauer von Vollstreckungsverfahren auf maximal ein Jahr beschränkt werden sollte.[1592] Diesem Vorschlag folgte der Gesetzgeber in der SchiedsG-Reform aus dem Jahr 2015 nicht. Gleichwohl übertrug der Gesetzgeber im SchiedsG n. F. dem High Court die erstinstanzliche Zuständigkeit für die Vollstreckung von ausländischen Handelsschiedssprüchen, um erfahrene und spezialisierte Richter mit der Vollstreckung ausländischer Handelsschiedssprüche zu betrauen.[1593] Der Verzicht des Parlaments, die Verfahrensdauer zu limitieren, birgt dennoch die Gefahr, dass es auf Grund des chronisch überlasteten indischen Gerichtswesens zu überlangen Vollstreckungsverfahren kommt, korrespondierend mit einer Schadenersatzpflicht in Investitionsschiedsverfahren.

4. Schlussbetrachtung

Die divergierende gerichtliche Auslegung der öffentlichen Ordnung in den Entscheidungen *Renusagar* (eng), *Phulchand* (weit) und *Shri Lal Mahal* (eng) unter Sec. 48 (2) (b) SchiedsG a. F. demonstriert, dass es einige Zeit in Anspruch nahm, bis sich die restriktiven Kriterien der öffentlichen Ordnung des *Renusagar*-Urteils als höchstrichterliche Rechtsprechung durchsetzten. Schlussendlich gelang es dem Supreme Court in den Grundsatzentscheidungen *Renusagar* und *Shri Lal Mahal*, den Begriff der öffentlichen Ordnung der internationalen Norm der Schiedsgerichtsbarkeit entsprechende restriktiv zu konkretisieren. Die SchiedsG-Reform aus dem Jahr 2015 fasste die Auslegung des Begriffs der öffentlichen Ordnung nochmals enger. Die gegenwärtige indische Rechtsordnung befindet sich im Einklang mit dem globalen Standard des Schiedsgerichtswesens und ist folglich als Schiedsverfahren unterstützend anzusehen.

1591 Schiedsspruch vom 30.11.2011, verfügbar unter http://www.italaw.com/sites/default/files/case-documents/ita0906.pdf (zuletzt abgerufen am 28.4.2021).

1592 Government of India, Law Commission of India, 246. Report, Amendments to the Arbitration and Conciliation Act 1996, 5.8.2014, S. 16 ff., 58.

1593 Sec. 2 (1) (e) (ii) SchiedsG n. F. Für Verfahren mit einem Streitwert von mindestens einem „Crore“ (10 Mio.) Rupien (ca. 135.000 Euro), sind die neu geschaffenen Handelssenate des High Courts zuständig, vgl. Commercial Court Act, siehe auch Kapitel: Einleitung; Reform des Gerichtssystems (A.III.6.b)).

D. Rechtsvergleich

I. Anwendungsbereich

1. Singapur

Zum Anwendungsbereich der Singapurer internationalen Schiedsgesetzgebung (IAA i.V.m. UNCITRAL Modellgesetz)[1594] ergingen zunächst Schiedsverfahren hinderliche Urteile. Der Singapurer High Court erachtete in den Entscheidungen *Coop International Pte Ltd v Ebel SA* und *John Holland Pty Ltd v Toyo Engineering Corp* die Vereinbarung einer institutionellen Schiedsordnung, die der internationalen Schiedsgesetzgebung widerspricht, als Abbedingung der internationalen Schiedsgesetzgebung zu Gunsten der inländischen Schiedslegislation (AA). Dem High Court zufolge wollten die Parteien konkludent das durch stärkere gerichtliche Kontrolle geprägte (AA) vereinbaren. Nach dem Urteil *Dermajaya Properties Sdn Bhd v Premium Properties Sdn Bhd and another* führt die Unvereinbarkeit einer institutionellen Schiedsordnung mit dem UNCITRAL Modellgesetz zur Unwirksamkeit der vereinbarten institutionellen Schiedsordnung. Die Urteile verletzten den fundamentalen Grundsatz der Parteiautonomie. Als Reaktion auf diese für Schiedsverfahren hinderlichen Entscheidungen novellierte der Singapurer Gesetzgeber zeitnah den Anwendungsbereich des IAA. Im IAA n.F. bedarf es einer ausdrücklichen Vereinbarung, um vom IAA in den AA zu wechseln. Weiterhin bleibt im IAA n.F. eine institutionelle Schiedsordnung auch bei Verstößen gegen zwingende Bestimmungen der Schiedsgesetzgebung im Übrigen wirksam. Die Legislative konnte dadurch die schiedsunfreundliche Rechtsprechung der Singapurer Gerichte aus der Welt schaffen. Der IAA n.F. passte die Singapurer Schiedsrechtsordnung dem internationalen Standard an und verlieh Singapur die erforderliche Rechtssicherheit, die für die weitere Entwicklung des Schiedsortes Singapur notwendig war.

Im Verfahren *Navigator Investment* entschied der Court of Appeal, entgegen dem Wortlaut des AA, dass die Parteien durch die Wahl der SIAC-Schiedsordnung 2007 mittelbar vom AA in den IAA gewechselt hätten. In Übereinstimmung mit der internationalen Norm beseitigten die reformierten SIAC-Schiedsordnungen die konkludente Abbedingung des AA.

Der Anwendungsbereich des IAA und des AA ist auf Schiedsverfahren mit Sitz in Singapur beschränkt. Das Singapurer Schiedsrecht sieht hiervon aber seit dem Jahr 2012 eine schiedsfreundliche Ausnahme vor. Der IAA unter-

---

1594 Der IAA erklärt neben den Bestimmungen des IAA das UNCITRAL Modellgesetz für anwendbar, vgl. Kapitel: Singapur; Anwendungsbereich des Verfahrensrechts (B.I.1.).

stützt auch die Parteien eines Schiedsverfahrens mit Sitz im Ausland durch einstweilige gerichtliche Maßnahmen. Um den schiedsfreundlichen Ruf des Singapurer Schiedszentrums zu erhalten, war es entscheidend, dass der Gesetzgeber die schiedsunfreundlichen Entscheidungen der Gerichte durch Gesetzesänderungen schnell revidierte und das SIAC seine Schiedsordnung anpasste.

2. Indien

2002 erweiterte der indische Supreme Court im Urteil *Bhatia,* entgegen der Wortlautgrenze von Sec. 2 (2) SchiedsG a. F., den Anwendungsbereich des SchiedsG auf Schiedsverfahren mit Sitz im Ausland. Die *Bhatia*-Entscheidung führte zu einer globalen Interventionskompetenz der indischen Gerichte in ausländische Schiedsverfahren. Eine Constitutional Bench des obersten Gerichts Indiens gab im Urteil *Balco* (2012) die bisherige Rechtsprechung in der Entscheidung *Bhatia* auf. Durch das *Balco*-Urteil begrenzte die Constitutional Bench für seit dem 7. September 2012 abgeschlossene Schiedsvereinbarungen den Geltungsbereich des SchiedsG ausschließlich auf Schiedsverfahren mit Sitz in Indien. Die Constitutional Bench entsprach hierdurch dem in Sec. 2 (2) SchiedsG a. F. zum Ausdruck gebrachten gesetzgeberischen Willen. Obwohl die Law Commission bereits 2001[1595] und 2014[1596] eine Gesetzesreform angeregt hatte, änderte der indische Gesetzgeber das SchiedsG erst im Jahr 2015. Die Legislative stellte im SchiedsG n. F. klar, dass dessen Anwendungsbereich auf Schiedsverfahren mit Sitz in Indien beschränkt ist. Die im Jahr 2015 ins SchiedsG n. F. eingefügten Ausnahmen des Anwendungsbereichs umfassen einstweilige gerichtliche Maßnahmen für die Parteien eines Schiedsverfahrens mit Sitz im Ausland sowie die gerichtliche Unterstützung bei Beweisaufnahmen für Schiedsverfahren mit ausländischem Sitz. Diese schiedsortunabhängigen Ausnahmen des SchiedsG-Anwendungsbereiches sind als Schiedsverfahren fördernd anzusehen.[1597] Es wäre allerdings erstrebenswert, wenn die indische Schiedsgesetzgebung anpassungsfähiger auf die zukünftigen Bedürfnisse der Schiedsgerichtsbarkeit und auf schiedsunfreundliche Urteile reagieren würde.

1595 Law Commission of India, 176. Report, The Arbitration and Conciliation (Amendment) Bill, 2001, 12.9.2001.

1596 Government of India, Law Commission of India, 246. Report, Amendments to the Arbitration and Conciliation Act 1996, 5.8.2014.

1597 Born, International Commercial Arbitration, Bd. 2, S. 1628 f.

3. Bewertung

Singapur gelang es, trotz anfänglich schiedsunfreundlicher Gerichtsentscheidungen, durch die Nachjustierung des IAA und der SIAC-Schiedsordnung ein den Anforderungen der Schiedsgerichtsbarkeit gerecht werdendes Regelungsregime zu schaffen.

Die Rechtsprechung des indischen Supreme Courts dehnte den Anwendungsbereich des SchiedsG zwischenzeitlich in schiedsunfreundlicher Weise weltweit aus. Erst die Reform des indischen SchiedsG aus dem Jahr 2015 ließ die zuvor ergangene Fehlentscheidung des Supreme Courts in der Rechtssache *Bhatia* durch die Schaffung eines universell anzuwendenden Geltungsbereiches des SchiedsG gegenstandslos werden.

Vom Schwellenland und Subkontinent Indien kann freilich nicht die gleiche Flexibilität der Schiedsgesetzgebung verlangt werden, wie sie im Industrie- und Stadtstaat Singapur möglich ist. Andererseits brauchte der indische Gesetzgeber nach der Verabschiedung des SchiedsG im Jahr 1996 zwei Jahrzehnte, bis er im Jahre 2015 das Schiedsrecht erstmals modernisierte. Ein Vergleich des Geltungsbereichs der Schiedsgesetzgebung in beiden Rechtsordnungen macht deutlich, dass das Singapurer Parlament Fehlurteile durch eine zügige gesetzliche Anpassung der Schiedsgesetzgebung behob und die Schiedsgesetzesnovellen von den Singapurer Gerichten respektiert werden. In Indien reagierte der Gesetzgeber dagegen lethargisch auf Fehlentscheidungen[1598] zum Anwendungsbereich des SchiedsG. Die Anpassungsfähigkeit der schiedsgesetzlichen Rahmenbedingungen des Stadtstaates Singapurs ist ein entscheidender Wettbewerbsvorteil gegenüber vielen anderen Schiedsjurisdiktionen weltweit.

Durch die Gesetzesnovelle aus dem Jahre 2015 enthält das indische verglichen mit dem Singapurer Schiedsrecht schiedsfreundlichere Ausnahmen des ansonsten auf Schiedsverfahren mit Sitz in Indien beschränkten SchiedsG. Die Singapurer Schiedslegislation wird allerdings in naher Zukunft ebenfalls eine schiedsortunabhängige Ausnahme für die gerichtliche Beweisaufnahme zu Gunsten von Schiedsverfahren vorsehen.

In den letzten Jahren schnitt die Singapurer Schiedsrechtsordnung folglich den Anwendungsbereich der Schiedsgesetzgebung im Vergleich zur indischen Rechtsordnung besser auf die Bedürfnisse des Schiedsgerichtswesens zu. Dies gilt auch für das anwendbare materielle Recht. Die materielle Rechtswahl ist für Singapurer Schiedsverfahren parteiautonom ausgestaltet. In Indien wird dem schiedsgerichtlichen Streitbeilegungsmechanismus immer noch Argwohn entgegengebracht. Die autonome Vereinbarung des materiellen Rechts wird nicht zugelassen. Stattdessen ist auf inländische und

1598 Die Urteile *Bhatia* und *Venture Global*.

internationale nicht handelsrechtliche Schiedsverfahren zwingend indisches Recht anwendbar.

II. Kompetenz-Kompetenz

1. Singapur

In Singapur konnte bis zur Gesetzesreform im Jahr 2012 nur die positive Zuständigkeitsentscheidung des Schiedsgerichts gerichtlich kontrolliert werden. Im Interesse der internationalen Schiedsbranche gestattet die Gesetzesreform aus dem Jahr 2012 den Gerichten, auch die negative Zuständigkeitsentscheidung der Schiedsgerichte zu überprüfen. Die Zuständigkeits- und Unzuständigkeits-Entscheidung kann in Singapur in zwei Instanzen gerichtlich überprüft werden. Die „Kompetenz-Kompetenz" des Schiedsgerichts wird von der Schiedsgesetzgebung und der Rechtsprechung beachtet.

2. Indien

Die indische Schiedsgesetzgebung zur Kompetenz-Kompetenz ist schiedsfreundlich. Seit seiner Verabschiedung im Jahre 1996 lässt das SchiedsG, abweichend vom UNCITRAL Modellgesetz, ein zweistufiges gerichtliches Überprüfungsverfahren der schiedsgerichtlichen Unzuständigkeitsentscheidung zu.[1599] Die positive Zuständigkeitsentscheidung des Schiedsgerichts darf von den Gerichten erst im Aufhebungsverfahren überprüft werden[1600], um gerichtliche Eingriffe in das laufende Schiedsverfahren zu verhindern. Im Urteil *Patel Engineering* verletzte eine Constitutional Bench des Supreme Courts aber bei der Schiedsrichterbestellung die Kompetenz-Kompetenz des Schiedsgerichts. Nach der Constitutional Bench dürfen die Gerichte vor einer Schiedsrichterbestellung gem. Sec. 11 SchiedsG a. F. die Schiedsvereinbarung auf ihre Wirksamkeit überprüfen. Das konstituierte Schiedsgericht sei – entgegen dem Wortlaut von Sec. 16 SchiedsG – insbesondere an die gerichtliche Entscheidung hinsichtlich der Wirksamkeit der Schiedsvereinbarung gebunden. Diese Beschränkung der Kompetenz-Kompetenz widerspricht dem in Art. 16 UNCITRAL Modellgesetz normierten Standard des Schiedsgerichtswesens und dem Willen des indischen Gesetzgebers. Es ist zu begrüßen, dass die Novelle des SchiedsG des Jahres 2015 die *Patel Engineering*-Rechtsprechung obsolet werden ließ. Nach Sec. 11 (6A) SchiedsG n. F. dürfen die Gerichte ausschließlich überprüfen, ob zwischen

---

1599 Sec. 16 (2), (3) i. V. m. Sec. 37 (2) (a) SchiedsG.
1600 Sec. 16 (5), (6) i. V. m. Sec. 34 SchiedsG.

den Parteien eine Schiedsvereinbarung besteht. Eine inhaltliche Kontrolle ist den Gerichten verwehrt.

3. Bewertung

Nach der schiedsunfreundlichen Einschränkung der Kompetenz-Kompetenz durch die *Patel Engineering*-Entscheidung stellte der indische Gesetzgeber durch die SchiedsG-Novelle die Kompetenz-Kompetenz der Schiedsgerichte wieder her. Die Singapurer Rechtsordnung stellte die Kompetenz-Kompetenz des Schiedsgerichts nie in Frage. Sowohl die indische als auch die Singapurer Gesetzgebung sehen Schiedsverfahren fördernde gerichtliche Kontrollmöglichkeiten gegen die Unzuständigkeitsentscheidung des Schiedsgerichts vor. Die nur in Singapur erlaubte Anfechtung der bejahenden Zuständigkeitsentscheidung des Schiedsgerichts in einem parallelen zweistufigen Gerichtsverfahren ist für Schiedsverfahren hinderlich.

Unter dem Vorbehalt, dass sich eine schiedsfeindliche Rechtsprechung wie in der *Patel Engineering*-Entscheidung nicht wiederholt, ist die indische Rechtsordnung bezüglich der Kompetenz-Kompetenz der Schiedsgerichte schiedsfreundlicher ausgestaltet als die Singapurer Schiedsrechtsordnung.

III. Unabhängigkeit der Schiedsvereinbarung

Die aktuelle Gesetzgebung und Rechtsprechung in Singapur und Indien erkennen die Unabhängigkeit der Schiedsvereinbarung vom Hauptvertrag an. Beide Rechtsordnungen entsprechen hierdurch dem internationalen Standard der Schiedsgerichtsbarkeit gem. Art. 16 (1) UNCITRAL Modellgesetz und unterstützen Schiedsverfahren.

IV. Aussetzung und Verweisung

1. Singapur

Die Wirksamkeitskontrolle der Schiedsvereinbarung bei der Aussetzungsentscheidung der gerichtlichen Streitigkeit gem. Sec. 6 IAA und Sec. 6 AA entspricht Art. 8 (1) UNCITRAL Modellgesetz und Art. II (3) UNÜ. Die Singapurer Rechtsprechung reduzierte für inländische und internationale Schiedsverfahren den Kontrollmaßstab der Schiedsvereinbarung auf eine *prima facie*-Überprüfung. Der Rechtsprechung gelang es dadurch, gerichtliche Interventionen in die schiedsgerichtliche Streitbeilegung zu unterbinden und die Kompetenz-Kompetenz des Schiedsgerichts zu stärken. Die durch Rechtsfortbildung etablierte *prima facie*-Kontrolle der Schiedsvereinbarung führt zu einem zeitgemäßen Kontrollmaßstab für inländische und internationale Schiedsverfahren.

Nach der internationalen Norm des Art. 8 (1) UNCITRAL Modellgesetz ist die gerichtliche Verweisung an das Schiedsverfahren zwingend ausgestaltet. In Singapur hat die Aussetzung des Gerichtsverfahrens gem. Sec. 6 IAA für internationale Schiedsverfahren gleichfalls zwingenden Charakter. Für inländische Schiedsverfahren räumt Sec. 6 AA und die einschlägige Rechtsprechung den Gerichten hingegen bei der Aussetzungsentscheidung einen Ermessenspielraum ein. Dieses gerichtliche Ermessen unter Sec. 6 AA führt zu einer schiedsunfreundlichen Gesamtbewertung der Aussetzung gerichtlicher Verfahren zu Gunsten von Schiedsverfahren.

2. Indien

Sec. 8 SchiedsG a. F. enthielt keine gerichtliche Kontrolle der Schiedsvereinbarung vor der Verweisung einer gerichtlich rechtshängigen Streitigkeit an das inländische[1601] Schiedsverfahren. Der Supreme Court respektierte zunächst diesen gesetzgeberischen Willen. Durch das Urteil *Patel Engineering* erlegte der Supreme Court den Gerichten sodann *obiter dicta* eine Wirksamkeitskontrolle der Schiedsvereinbarung entgegen dem Wortlaut von Sec. 8 SchiedsG a. F. auf, bevor eine gerichtliche Verweisung an das Schiedsverfahren stattfinden konnte. Diese Kontrolle der Schiedsvereinbarung entsprach zwar Art. 8 (1) UNCITRAL Modellgesetz. Auf Grund der Interventionstendenzen der indischen Gerichte und der langen gerichtlichen Verfahrensdauern stellte dieses Urteil aber eine schiedsunfreundliche „Rechtsfortbildung" dar. Der Supreme Court ließ hierdurch die alte Rechtslage unter dem Arbitration Act 1940 wiederaufleben. Problematisch an dem Urteil ist insbesondere, dass die Schiedsgerichte an die gerichtliche Entscheidung über die Wirksamkeit der Schiedsvereinbarung gebunden waren. Die vollumfängliche Kompetenz-Kompetenz des Schiedsgerichts war auf Konstellationen beschränkt, in denen die Parteien ohne gerichtliches Parallelverfahren ein Schiedsgericht konstituiert hatten. Die Beschränkung der Kompetenz-Kompetenz widerspricht dem internationalen Standard des Schiedsgerichtswesens. Sie ist zudem mit dem Willen der Parteien, ihre Streitigkeit durch ein außergerichtliches Schiedsverfahren beizulegen, nicht zu vereinbaren. Das SchiedsG n. F. beschränkte im Jahr 2015 die gerichtliche Kontrolle der Schiedsvereinbarung gem. Sec. 8 SchiedsG n. F. auf eine *prima facie*-Überprüfung ihrer Wirksamkeit. Gegenüber der alten Rechtslage unter Sec. 8 SchiedsG a. F. – das keine Kontrolle der Schiedsvereinbarung vorsah – ist die in der SchiedsG-Novelle eingeführte *prima facie*-Überprü-

1601 Der Sitz des Schiedsverfahrens ist in Indien.

fung im von Interventionen und Verzögerungen geprägten indischen Gerichtssystem als schiedsunfreundlicher Rückschritt anzusehen.

Für Handelsschiedsverfahren mit Sitz im Ausland begrenzte der Supreme Court 2005 im Urteil *Shin-Etsu*, bei der Entscheidung, ob eine gerichtliche Streitigkeit gem. Sec. 45 SchiedsG[1602] an das vereinbarte Schiedsverfahren zu verweisen ist, die Wirksamkeitskontrolle der Schiedsvereinbarung auf eine *prima facie*-Überprüfung. Die zeitgemäße *prima facie*-Kontrolle der Schiedsvereinbarung stärkt die Kompetenz-Kompetenz des Schiedsgerichts.

Im Einklang mit dem internationalen Standard müssen die Gerichte eine rechtshängige Streitigkeit gem. Sec. 8 und 45 SchiedsG – nach einer *prima facie*-Kontrolle der Schiedsvereinbarung – zwingend an das vereinbarte Schiedsverfahren verweisen.

3. Bewertung

Ein Vergleich zwischen der Singapurer und der indischen Schiedsrechtsordnung hinsichtlich der Aussetzung (Singapur) eines gerichtlichen Verfahrens bzw. der Verweisung (Indien) eines rechtshängigen Streitgegenstandes an das Schiedsverfahren ergibt, dass die Kontrolle der Schiedsvereinbarung in den beiden Rechtsordnungen auf eine schiedsfreundliche *prima facie*-Überprüfungskompetenz beschränkt ist. Die Verweisung einer gerichtlichen Streitigkeit an das Schiedsverfahren ist in der indischen Rechtsordnung zwingend. In Singapur besitzt die Aussetzung des gerichtlichen Verfahrens nur in internationalen Schiedsverfahren zwingenden Charakter. Eine Gesamtschau führt wegen des Ermessens der Singapurer Gerichte bei der Aussetzungsentscheidung für inländische Schiedsverfahren zu der Beurteilung, dass die indische Schiedsrechtsordnung bei der Aussetzung bzw. der Verweisung schiedsfreundlicher ausgestaltet ist als die Singapurer Rechtsordnung.

V. Schiedsrichterbestellung

1. Singapur

In Singapur erfolgt die Schiedsrichterbestellung durch das SIAC oder durch vom Chief Justice bestimmte Experten der Schiedsgerichtsbarkeit. Die Schiedsrichter werden dadurch von mit den Anforderungen des Schiedsgerichtswesens vertrauten Spezialisten bestellt.

1602 Durch Sec. 45 SchiedsG setzte der indische Gesetzgeber Art. II (3) UNÜ in das indische Recht um.

2. Indien

Vor der SchiedsG-Reform 2015 gestatteten die Gerichte den indischen Regierungen[1603] und öffentlich-rechtlichen Unternehmen bzw. Körperschaften, einen eigenen Mitarbeiter als Einzelschiedsrichter in Schiedsvereinbarungen einzusetzen. Ein solcher, nicht den Kriterien der Unparteilichkeit und der Unabhängigkeit entsprechender „Partei-Schiedsrichter", erschütterte die Neutralitätspflicht des Schiedsrichters. Das SchiedsG n. F. erklärt diese Praxis der „Mitarbeiterbestellung" entsprechend der internationalen Richtschnur des Schiedsgerichtswesens für unzulässig.[1604]

In der Entscheidung *Patel Engineering* eröffnete der Supreme Court den Gerichten bei der Schiedsrichterbestellung, *contra legem* zu Sec. 11 SchiedsG a. F., eine verbindliche Kontrolle der Schiedsvereinbarung. Der Supreme Court verkürzte hierdurch in für Schiedsverfahren hinderlicher Weise die Kompetenz-Kompetenz des Schiedsgerichts. Nach Sec. 11 SchiedsG n. F. dürfen die Gerichte bei der Schiedsrichterbestellung lediglich prüfen, ob eine Schiedsvereinbarung existiert. Weiterhin versagte die *Patel Engineering*-Entscheidung dem Chief Justice des Supreme Courts und des High Courts die in Sec. 11 SchiedsG vorgesehene Delegation der Schiedsrichterbestellung an sachkundige Schiedsinstitutionen.[1605] In der die Schiedsverfahren fördernden SchiedsG-Reform aus dem Jahr 2015 stellte das Parlament richtig, dass der Supreme Court und der High Court die Schiedsrichterbestellung an Schiedsinstitutionen oder an mit der Schiedsrichterbestellung vertraute Personen delegieren dürfen.[1606] Der Gesetzgeber ließ damit auch in diesem Punkt die Entscheidung *Patel Engineering* hinfällig werden.

3. Bewertung

In der indischen Rechtsordnung schaffte das SchiedsG n. F. erst kürzlich die Parteischiedsrichterbestellung ab. Insbesondere durch den Verzicht auf eine gerichtliche Kontrolle der Schiedsvereinbarung schuf die SchiedsG-Novelle aus dem Jahr 2015 zudem für die Schiedsrichterbestellung unter Sec. 11 SchiedsG schiedsfreundliche Rahmenbedingungen. Die Singapurer Schiedsrichterbestellung durch ausgewiesene Experten der Schiedsgerichtsbarkeit entspricht den Anforderungen des Schiedsgerichtswesens und unterstützt

---

1603 Der Zentralregierung und den Regierungen der Bundesstaaten.

1604 Sec. 12 (5) i. V. m. Fifth Schedule Nr. 1 SchiedsG n. F.

1605 Nach dem *Patel Engineering*-Urteil konnte die Schiedsrichterbestellung gem. Sec. 11 SchiedsG a. F. vom Chief Justice of India nur an Richter des Supreme Courts delegiert werden und vom Chief Justice des High Courts nur an Richter des High Courts weiter delegiert werden.

1606 Sec. 11 (4), (5) und (6) SchiedsG n. F.

Schiedsverfahren effektiver als der immer noch stark gerichtlich geprägte indische Bestellungsmechanismus.

VI. Einstweilige Maßnahmen

1. Singapur

In Singapur gewährleisten einstweilige Maßnahmen von staatlichen Gerichten und Schiedsgerichten einen effektiven Rechtsschutz für die Schiedsparteien. Die Rechtsunsicherheit durch die divergierende Rechtsprechung in den *Swift-Fortune Ltd v Magnifica Marine*-Entscheidungen und dem *Front Carriers v Atlantic*-Urteil beseitigte der Singapurer Gesetzgeber nach zwei Jahren durch eine Gesetzesänderung (2010)[1607]. Fortan erlaubt der neu eingefügte Sec. 12A IAA den Gerichten, auch für die Parteien eines Schiedsverfahrens mit Sitz im Ausland einstweilige gerichtliche Maßnahmen anzuordnen. Diese Gesetzesänderung erhielt dem Schiedsort Singapur seinen schiedsfreundlichen Ruf. In Singapur können seit Inkrafttreten des IAA (1995)[1608] und des AA (2002)[1609] von Schiedsgerichten angeordnete vorläufige Maßnahmen vollstreckt werden. Seit 2012 gestattet Singapur als eines der ersten internationalen Schiedszentren die Vollstreckung von vorläufigen Maßnahmen, die Schiedsgerichte mit ausländischem Sitz oder „Emergency Arbitrator" anordnen. Die Singapurer Rechtsordnung respektiert zudem die Parteiautonomie der Schiedsverfahren, indem sie dem schiedsgerichtlich angeordneten einstweiligen Rechtsschutz den Vorrang gegenüber von Gerichten erlassenen einstweiligen Maßnahmen einräumt. Hierdurch wird dem Willen der Parteien Rechnung getragen, ihre Streitigkeiten außerhalb des staatlichen Gerichtssystems mittels eines effektiv ausgestalteten Schiedsverfahrens beizulegen. Die Singapurer Schiedsgesetzgebung bringt *summa summarum* der Schiedsgerichtsbarkeit das erforderliche Vertrauen entgegen und behandelt Schiedsverfahren als äquivalenten Streitbeilegungsmechanismus.

2. Indien

Im Urteil *Videocon Industries Ltd v Union of India & Anr* hatte der Supreme Court, *contra legem* zu Sec. 2 (2) SchiedsG a. F., den indischen Gerichten die Kompetenz zugesprochen, einstweilige gerichtliche Maßnahmen für Parteien eines Schiedsverfahrens mit Sitz im Ausland anzuordnen. Das SchiedsG

1607 Die Gesetzesänderung trat am 1.1.2010 in Kraft.

1608 Den IAA verabschiedete das Parlament im Jahr 1994 und er trat am 27.1.1995 in Kraft.

1609 Den AA verabschiedete das Parlament im Jahr 2001 und er trat am 1.3.2002 in Kraft.

n. F.[1610] entspricht nunmehr Art. 1 (2) UNCITRAL Modellgesetz und gestattet einstweilige gerichtliche Maßnahmen auch für Schiedsverfahren mit Sitz im Ausland. Durch die Gesetzesänderung 2015 ist der vorläufige gerichtliche Rechtsschutz wie in Singapur gegenüber dem schiedsgerichtlich angeordneten einstweiligen Rechtsschutz subsidiär. Das SchiedsG n. F. erlaubte den Gerichten auch erstmals schiedsgerichtlich angeordnete vorläufige Maßnahmen in Indien zu vollstrecken. Einstweilige Maßnahmen eines Schiedsgerichts mit ausländischem Sitz und eines Emergency Arbitrators können auch nach der Gesetzesreform in Indien nicht vollstreckt werden.

3. Bewertung

Nach der anfänglichen Rechtsunsicherheit durch divergierende Gerichtsentscheidungen gewährt der IAA seit 2010 einstweilige gerichtliche Maßnahmen für die Parteien eines ausländischen Schiedsverfahrens. In Singapur werden schiedsgerichtlich angeordnete vorläufige Maßnahmen umfassend vollstreckt.

Seit 2015 eröffnet das indische SchiedsG n. F. einstweiligen gerichtlichen Rechtsschutz für Parteien eines ausländischen Schiedsverfahrens. Auch in Indien räumt der Gesetzgeber im SchiedsG n. F. den schiedsrichterlich angeordneten vorläufigen Maßnahmen Vorrang ein. Trotz dieser positiven Gesetzesänderung aus dem Jahre 2015 bedarf es in Indien einer weiteren Gesetzesreform zur Schließung der noch verbliebenen Rechtsschutzlücken. *De lege ferenda* sollte das SchiedsG – wie in Singapur – die Vollstreckung von Maßnahmen des vorläufigen Rechtsschutzes ermöglichen, die von Schiedsgerichten mit ausländischem Sitz und durch den Emergency Arbitrator angeordnete werden. Bei einer zukünftigen SchiedsG-Reform sollte sich Indien an der modernen und liberalen Singapurer Schiedsgesetzgebung orientieren.

1610 Sec. 2 (2) SchiedsG n. F. Die *Balco*-Entscheidung des Supreme Courts beschränkte den Anwendungsbereich von Teil I SchiedsG auf Schiedsverfahren mit Sitz in Indien. Sie galt allerdings nur für Schiedsvereinbarungen, die nach dem 6. September 2012 abgeschlossen wurden. Schiedsortunabhängige Ausnahmen des territorialen Anwendungsbereichs des SchiedsG a. F. ließ die *Balco*-Entscheidung nicht zu. Erst der Arbitration Amendment Act 2015 begrenzte den Anwendungsbereich des SchiedsG für alle Schiedsvereinbarungen auf Schiedsverfahren mit Sitz in Indien, erlaubt jedoch einstweiligen gerichtlichen Rechtsschutz und gerichtliche Beweisaufnahmen für Schiedsverfahren mit Sitz im Ausland, siehe ausführlich hierzu Kapitel: Indien; Anwendungsbereich der Schiedsgesetzgebung (C. I. 1.).

VII. Aufhebungsverfahren

1. Singapur

Im Urteil *PT Asuransi v Dexia Bank II* lehnte der Court of Appeal die weite Konkretisierung der öffentlichen Ordnung (*ordre public*) des indischen Supreme Courts in der Entscheidung *Saw Pipes* ab und legte den Begriff der öffentlichen Ordnung in schiedsfreundlicher Weise restriktiv aus. Im schiedsunfreundlichen Urteil *AJT v AJU* entschied der High Court, dass die Gerichte in bestimmten Konstellationen unter dem Aufhebungsgrund der öffentlichen Ordnung die Entscheidung des Schiedsgerichts nachkontrollieren dürfen. Im Berufungsverfahren *AJU v AJT* revidierte der Court of Appeal diese Entscheidung des High Court. Das oberste Singapurer Gericht betonte, dass Schiedssprüche verbindlich seien und die Gerichte im Aufhebungsverfahren keine materielle Kontrolle des Schiedsspruchs vornehmen dürfen. Die Aufhebung eines Schiedsspruchs erfordere vielmehr eine gravierende Unvereinbarkeit des Schiedsspruchs mit der öffentlichen Ordnung Singapurs. Der Begriff der öffentlichen Ordnung wird von den Singapurer Gerichten im Ergebnis – trotz der schiedsunfreundlichen High Court Entscheidung *AJT v AJU* – eng ausgelegt. Dies ist als Schiedsverfahren fördernd zu erachten. Der zusätzliche Aufhebungsgrund der „Natural Justice“ und die Berufungsmöglichkeit in inländischen Schiedsverfahren eröffnen hingegen eine dem internationalen Standard nicht entsprechende ergänzende Annullierungsmöglichkeit und sind deshalb als schiedsunfreundlich anzusehen. Auf Grund der restriktiven gerichtlichen Auslegung der öffentlichen Ordnung überwiegt gleichwohl der die Schiedsgerichtsbarkeit fördernde Charakter der Singapurer Rechtsordnung.

2. Indien

Der Supreme Court hatte in der Entscheidung *Renusagar* den Begriff der öffentlichen Ordnung für die Vollstreckung von ausländischen Schiedssprüchen[1611] durch drei Kriterien restriktiv ausgelegt. Im darauffolgenden *Saw Pipes*-Urteil erweiterte das oberste Gericht Indiens die drei *Renusagar*-Auslegungskriterien der öffentlichen Ordnung aber für die Aufhebung von Schiedssprüchen[1612] um ein viertes Kriterium, die „offensichtliche Rechtswidrigkeit“ eines Schiedsspruchs. Der Supreme Court führte hierdurch die Rechtslage unter dem alten Arbitration Act 1940 wieder ein. Unter diesem vierten Auslegungskriterium konnten die Gerichte den Schiedsspruch materiell überprüfen. Das Urteil *Venture Global* bestätigte die erweiterte Auslegung der öffentlichen Ordnung des *Saw Pipes*-Urteils und dehnte Auf-

1611 Für die Vollstreckung des Schiedsspruchs waren die das UNÜ umsetzenden indischen Bestimmungen einschlägig, siehe hierzu auch Fn. 1616.

1612 Sec. 34 SchiedsG.

hebungsverfahren auch auf Schiedsverfahren mit ausländischem Sitz aus. Durch die *Venture Global*-Entscheidung vertrat der Supreme Court ebenfalls eine Rechtsauffassung, die an die Ära unter dem Arbitration Act 1940 erinnert. Die Urteile *Saw Pipes* und *Venture Global* eröffneten den indischen Gerichten die „révision au fond" von inländischen und ausländischen Schiedssprüchen und führten zu erheblichen Verzögerungen bei der Vollstreckung.

Der Gesetzgeber reagierte im SchiedsG n. F. 2015 auf diese schiedsfeindliche Rechtsprechung. Die Gesetzesreform führte das SchiedsG wieder näher an die internationale Norm der Schiedsgerichtsbarkeit heran. Insbesondere die Aufhebung internationaler Handelsschiedssprüche unter der restriktiven und Schiedsverfahren unterstützenden Definition der öffentlichen Ordnung gem. Sec. 34 (2) (b) (ii) SchiedsG n. F., aber auch das zusätzliche Kriterium der offensichtlichen Rechtswidrigkeit[1613] inländischer Schiedssprüche[1614] formulierte der Gesetzgeber enger. Im SchiedsG n. F. können die Gerichte zudem ausschließlich in Indien abgesetzte Schiedssprüche[1615] aufheben. Für eine schiedsfreundlichere Ausrichtung der indischen Rechtsordnung ist es erforderlich, dass sich die Gerichte – dem Willen des Parlaments entsprechend – an das Verbot der materiellen Kontrolle von Schiedssprüchen im Aufhebungsverfahren halten.

3. Bewertung

Sowohl die Singapurer als auch die indische Rechtsordnung weisen bei der Aufhebung von Schiedssprüchen Schwächen auf. An der Singapurer Rechtsordnung ist zu kritisieren, dass der international nicht anerkannte, zusätzliche Aufhebungsgrund der „Natural Justice" verfügbar ist und für inländische Schiedsverfahren eine Berufung gegen die Rechtsanwendung des Schiedsgerichts eröffnet ist. Andererseits ist positiv hervorzuheben, dass es den Singapurer Gerichten gelungen ist, den als nicht zu bändigendes Pferd beschriebenen unbestimmten Rechtsbegriff der öffentlichen Ordnung zu zügeln, indem sie ihm in Übereinstimmung mit der globalen Schiedsgerichtsnorm enge Kriterien gaben.

In Indien führte die SchiedsG-Reform 2015 zu einer restriktiveren Definition der öffentlichen Ordnung für Aufhebungsverfahren. Der Gesetzgeber stellte im SchiedsG n. F. ferner klar, dass die indischen Gerichte ausländische Schiedssprüche nicht mehr aufheben dürfen.

Die in den Entscheidungen *Saw Pipes* und *Venture Global* eröffnete materiellen Kontrolle des Schiedsspruchs widersprach dem internationalen Stan-

1613 Sec. 34 (2A) SchiedsG n. F.

1614 Diese umfassen auch internationale nicht handelsrechtliche Schiedssprüche (im Folgenden inländische Schiedssprüche).

1615 Der Sitz des Schiedsverfahrens ist in Indien.

dard der Schiedsgerichtsbarkeit. In diesem Kontext ist es erforderlich, dass die indischen Gerichte die Integrität der abgesetzten Schiedssprüche respektieren und eine schiedsfreundliche Einstellung in Aufhebungsverfahren entwickeln, um die Attraktivität des Schiedsorts Indiens zu steigern.

Im Vergleich zu Indien setzt sich die Singapurer Rechtsordnung auf Grund ihrer restriktiven Auslegung der öffentlichen Ordnung auch gegenüber der reformierten indischen Rechtsordnung als Schiedsverfahren unterstützendere Rechtsordnung durch.

VIII. Anerkennung und Vollstreckung

1. Singapur

Aus Interesse an einer Anerkennung und Vollstreckung von Singapurer Schiedssprüchen im Ausland legte der High Court in der Entscheidungen *Re An Arbitration Between Hainan Machinery Import and Export Corp and Donald & McArthy Pte Ltd* und *Aloe Vera of America Inc v Asianic Food (S) Pte Ltd and another* den Begriff der öffentlichen Ordnung (*ordre public*) restriktiv aus. Der High Court urteilte in diesen Verfahren, dass ein ausländischer Schiedsspruch nur unter außergewöhnlichen Umständen nicht vollstreckt werden dürfe. Dies ist dem High Court zufolge nach dem „Comitas-Gedanken" erforderlich, um wiederum die Vollstreckung von Singapurer Schiedssprüchen im Ausland zu erleichtern und den Schiedsort Singapur international zu etablieren. Im Urteil *Strandore Invest A/S and others v Soh Kim Wat* fasste der High Court den Begriff der öffentlichen Ordnung noch enger. Die Singapurer Gerichte haben den Vollstreckungsversagungsgrund der öffentlichen Ordnung hierdurch im Einklang mit dem Standard des internationalen Schiedsgerichtswesens restriktiv ausgelegt. Wegen des „Pro-Enforcement Bias" wird es den Gerichten lediglich ausnahmsweise gestattet, einen ausländischen Schiedsspruch in Singapur nicht zu vollstrecken.

2. Indien

Im Urteil *Renusagar*[1616] legte der Supreme Court den Begriff der öffentlichen Ordnung in Übereinstimmung mit dem internationalen Standard der Schiedsgerichtsbarkeit eng aus. Es ist zu bedauern, dass der Supreme Court im *Phulchand*-Urteil die in der *Saw Pipes*-Entscheidung für die Aufhebung von inländischen Schiedssprüchen geschaffene weite Auslegung der öffent-

1616 Diese Entscheidung legte die öffentliche Ordnung gem. Sec. 7 (1) (b) (ii) Foreign Award Act aus. Vor der Einführung von Sec. 48 SchiedsG im Jahre 1996, setzte Sec. 7 (1) (b) (ii) Foreign Award Act Art. V (2) (b) UNÜ in das indische Schiedsrecht um.

lichen Ordnung auf die Vollstreckung von ausländischen Handelsschiedssprüchen übertrug. Durch die Entscheidung *Shri Lal Mahal* verwarf der Supreme Court das *Phulchand*-Urteil wieder und bestätigte die restriktive Konkretisierung der öffentlichen Ordnung aus der *Renusagar*-Rechtsprechung.

Eine Gesamtbetrachtung führt zu dem Ergebnis, dass die gerichtliche Auslegung der öffentlichen Ordnung für die Anerkennung und Vollstreckung ausländischer Handelsschiedssprüche – trotz der durch die *Phulchand*-Entscheidung entstandenen Rechtsunsicherheit – nach dem höchstrichterlichen *Shri Lal Mahal*-Urteil als schiedsfreundlich anzusehen ist.

Durch die SchiedsG-Reform im Jahr 2015 komprimierte der Gesetzgeber den Begriff der öffentlichen Ordnung in Sec. 48 SchiedsG n. F. auf der Grundlage der *Renusagar*-Formel weiter und verlieh ihr deutlichere Konturen. Die öffentliche Ordnung in der indischen Rechtsordnung entspricht der restriktiven internationalen Norm und stimmt mit dem „Pro-Enforcement Bias“ unter dem UNÜ überein. In der *Phulchand*-Entscheidung spiegelt sich allerdings die Tendenz der indischen Rechtsprechung, die Schiedsgerichtsbarkeit einer erhöhten gerichtlichen Kontrolle zu unterwerfen, wider. Um dauerhaft eine schiedsfreundliche Rechtsordnung zu etablieren, wird es entscheidend sein, dass die indischen Gerichte die Schiedsgerichtsverfahren als adäquaten Streitbeilegungsmechanismus respektieren und insbesondere ausländische Handelsschiedssprüche einer möglichst geringen gerichtlichen Überprüfung aussetzen.

3. Bewertung

In der Singapurer Rechtsordnung haben die Gerichte den Begriff der öffentlichen Ordnung bei der Anerkennung und Vollstreckung von ausländischen Schiedssprüchen eng ausgelegt. Die indische Rechtsordnung schwankte durch die Rechtsprechung des Supreme Courts zwischen einer restriktiven und einer weiteren Auslegung der öffentlichen Ordnung bei der Anerkennung und Vollstreckung von ausländischen Schiedssprüchen. Diese fehlende Kontinuität der Supreme Court-Rechtsprechung führte zu Rechtsunsicherheit und stellte die Schiedsfreundlichkeit der indischen Rechtsordnung bei der Anerkennung und Vollstreckung von ausländischen Schiedssprüchen in Frage. Erst die zukünftigen Entscheidungen der indischen Gerichte werden zeigen, ob sich die engere Legaldefinition der öffentlichen Ordnung der SchiedsG-Novelle dauerhaft durchsetzen kann. Die Singapurer Rechtsordnung fördert demzufolge die Anerkennung und Vollstreckung von ausländischen Schiedssprüchen durch die kontinuierlich enge Auslegung der öffentlichen Ordnung in höherem Maße als die indische Rechtsordnung.

E. Gesamtergebnis

Die untersuchten Schnittpunkte der Schiedsgerichtsbarkeit mit den nationalen Gerichten zeigen, dass die indische Rechtsordnung vor der Verabschiedung der SchiedsG-Novelle im Jahre 2015 im Vergleich zur Singapurer Rechtsordnung als schiedsunfreundlicher einzuordnen war. Mit seiner SchiedsG-Reform konnte Indien sein Schiedsrecht einen bedeutenden Schritt nach vorne bringen. Indien schuf durch das SchiedsG n.F. hinsichtlich des Anwendungsbereichs der Schiedsgesetzgebung, der Kompetenz-Kompetenz des Schiedsgerichts und der gerichtlichen Verweisung einer Streitigkeit an das vereinbarte Schiedsverfahren einen gesetzlichen Rahmen, der Schiedsverfahren stärker unterstützt, als es in der Singapurer Rechtsordnung der Fall ist. Die Singapurer Rechtsordnung ist aber auch nach der indischen SchiedsG-Novelle bei der materiellen Rechtswahl, bei der Schiedsrichterbestellung, bei einstweiligen Maßnahmen durch Schiedsgerichte und Gerichte, bei der Aufhebung von Schiedssprüchen und bei der Anerkennung und Vollstreckung von ausländischen Schiedssprüchen schiedsfreundlicher ausgestaltet als die indische Rechtsordnung. Die Unabhängigkeit der Schiedsvereinbarung vom Hauptvertrag respektieren beide Schiedsrechtsordnungen.

Die Rezeption des UNCITRAL Modellgesetzes war ein Meilenstein für die Schiedsgerichtsbarkeit in Indien. Das UNCITRAL Modellgesetz unterbindet gerichtliche Interventionen in die schiedsgerichtliche Streitbeilegung und gewährt den Schiedsparteien Parteiautonomie. Durch die Rezeption des UNCITRAL Modellgesetzes in das SchiedsG wollte die Legislative ein Schiedsverfahren unterstützendes Umfeld in Indien schaffen. Die indischen Gerichte respektierten hingegen in einer Vielzahl von Urteilen diesen Willen des Gesetzgebers nicht. Die Rechtsprechung missachtete die parteiautonome Streitbeilegung durch Schiedsverfahren und unterwarf die Schiedsgerichtsbarkeit umfassender gerichtlicher Kontrolle. Dies führte zu mannigfaltigen Interventionen der chronisch überlasteten indischen Gerichte und zu langen Verzögerungen bei der schiedsgerichtlichen Streitbeilegung. Renitente Schiedsbeklagte versuchten in diesem Kontext insbesondere durch Feststellungsklagen und einstweilige gerichtliche Maßnahmen das vereinbarte Schiedsverfahren zu torpedieren.

Die Entscheidungen der indischen Gerichte weisen insgesamt ein starkes Misstrauen gegenüber der Schiedsgerichtsbarkeit auf. Dies mag der Tatsache geschuldet sein, dass die außerhalb des Gerichtssystems angesiedelten Schiedsverfahren als fremdbestimmter Streitbeilegungsmechanismus betrachtet werden.[1617] Aber auch die koloniale Vergangenheit mag diese ablehnende Haltung gegenüber dem Schiedsgerichtswesen hervorgerufen haben.

1617 Vgl. Nariman, The George Washington International Law Review 2009–2010,

Es wird eine internationale Einmischung in innerindische Angelegenheiten befürchtet.

Für Schiedsverfahren unterstützendere Rahmenbedingungen ist – neben der Akzeptanz der schiedsfreundlichen SchiedsG-Änderungen des Jahres 2015 – eine die Schiedsgerichtsbarkeit fördernde Einstellung der indischen Gerichte essenziell. Auch weitere Anpassungen des SchiedsG werden Indien nicht zu einer schiedsfreundlicheren Rechtsordnung machen, wenn die indischen Gerichte nicht die Streitbeilegung durch Schiedsverfahren fördern. Die kommenden Jahre werden zeigen, ob die indischen Gerichte eine liberalere Haltung gegenüber Schiedsverfahren einnehmen werden.

Die SchiedsG-Reform im Jahre 2015 führte die indische Schiedsrechtsordnung wieder näher an den internationalen Standard der Schiedsgerichtsbarkeit heran. Bei der Beweisaufnahme zu Gunsten von Schiedsverfahren mit ausländischem Sitz traf das SchiedsG n.F. beispielsweise gegenüber dem Singapurer Schiedsgesetz und dem UNCITRAL Modellgesetz eine schiedsfreundlichere Regelung. Um eine permanent Schiedsverfahren unterstützende Schiedsgesetzgebung zu etablieren, wird es in Indien erforderlich sein, dass die Legislative gerichtliche Fehlurteile und Rechtsunsicherheit unter dem SchiedsG zeitnah beseitigt und das SchiedsG flexibel den Bedürfnissen des modernen Schiedswesens anpasst.

Indien kann darüber hinaus nur dann zu einer Schiedsverfahren unterstützenden Rechtsordnung werden, wenn sich die Dauer gerichtlicher Verfahren mit Schiedsbezug verringert. Die durch das SchiedsG n.F. eingeführte Begrenzung der Verfahrensdauer bei der Schiedsrichterbestellung und in Aufhebungsverfahren ist daher positiv zu vermerken. Es ist indessen zu bedauern, dass der Gesetzgeber in der SchiedsG-Novelle die Gerichte nicht durch die Delegation der Schiedsrichterbestellung an eine Schiedsinstitution – nach dem Vorbild Singapurs[1618] – entlastete. In der Zukunft sollte sich das indische Gerichtssystem weiterhin der Schiedsgerichtsbarkeit öffnen, um die große Anzahl der jedes Jahr anhängig gemachten Gerichtsverfahren zu reduzieren und so den Rückstau rechtshängiger Gerichtsverfahren abzubauen[1619].

Für internationale Handelsschiedsverfahren übertrug das SchiedsG n.F. die erstinstanzliche Zuständigkeit vom District Court auf den High Court.[1620] Der „Commercial Courts, Commercial Division and Commercial Appellate Division of High Courts Act 2015 (Commercial Court Act)“ verweist Han-

Vol. 41, Ausg. 2, S. 367 (369); Nelson, Asian International Arbitration Journal 2014, Vol. 10, Ausg. 2, S. 105 (114).

1618 Der Singapurer Gesetzgeber übertrug die Schiedsrichterbestellung auf Experten der Schiedsgerichtsbarkeit und die Schiedsinstitutionen SIAC.

1619 Vgl. About Us, Our Vision, verfügbar unter http://judicialacademy.nic.in/index.php?option=article&id=1&ItemId=5 (zuletzt abgerufen am 28.4.2021).

1620 Sec. 2 (1) (e) SchiedsG n.F.

delsstreitigkeiten mit einem hohen Streitwert[1621] an auf Handelsverfahren spezialisierte Kammern des District Courts bzw. Senate des High Courts. Der Commercial Court Act enthält Verfahrensmanagement-Vorschriften und strafft die Gerichtsverfahren durch klare zeitliche Vorgaben. Die Verfahrenskosten werden nach dem Commercial Court Act und dem SchiedsG n.F. der unterlegenen Partei auferlegt, um unbegründete Verfahren und Verzögerungstaktiken zu unterbinden. Diese Gesetzesreformen sind zu begrüßen. Die Reformen werden im überlasteten indischen Gerichtssystem allerdings nur vorübergehend eine Verkürzung der Verfahrensdauer für Gerichtsverfahren, auf die diese Gesetzesänderungen anwendbar sind, bewirken. In der Zukunft werden eine umfassende Reform des indischen Gerichtswesens und die Neueinstellung von tausenden von neuen Richtern erforderlich sein[1622], um mit dem anhaltenden Bevölkerungs- und Wirtschaftswachstum Indiens Schritt halten zu können und die hohe Anzahl an anhängigen Gerichtsverfahren auf allen gerichtlichen Ebenen abbauen zu können. Das indische Gerichtssystem sollte außerdem durch automatisierte Prozesse und ein „Case Management“[1623] effektiver organisiert werden und ein digitales Gerichts-

1621 Verfahren mit einem Streitwert von mindestens einem „Crore“ (10 Mio.) Rupien (ca. 135.000 Euro).

1622 Zur Unterbesetzung der indischen Gerichte, Robinson, in: Choudhry/Khosla/Mehta, The Oxford Handbook of the Indian Constitution, S. 330 (336); Nick Robinson, Too Many Cases, Frontline, Vol. 26, Ausg. 1, 3.–16. Januar 2009, verfügbar unter http://www.frontline.in/static/html/fl2601/stories/20090116260108100.htm (zuletzt abgerufen am 28.4.2021); Chief Justice Shri K. G. Balakrishnan, Address by Hon'ble Shri K. G. Balakrishnan, Chief Justice of India, at the Joint Conference of Chief Ministers and Chief Justices, at Vigyan Bhawan, 8.4.2007, verfügbar unter http://www.supremecourtofindia.nic.in/speeches/speeches_2007/8.4.2007.pdf (zuletzt abgerufen am 28.4.2021). Derzeit ist selbst der Supreme Court unterbesetzt, Baxi, in: Choudhry/Khosla/Mehta, The Oxford Handbook of the Indian Constitution, S. 94 (97). Teilweise wird vertreten, dass die angestauten Verfahren vor dem Supreme Court nur durch eine verschlankte Zuständigkeit des obersten indischen Gerichts reduziert werden können, Robinson, Too Many Cases, Frontline, Vol. 26, Ausg. 1, 3.–16. Januar 2009, verfügbar unter http://www.frontline.in/static/html/fl2601/stories/20090116260108100.htm (zuletzt abgerufen am 28.4.2021); George, Releasing India's Supreme Court from the Shadow of Delay, A Proposal for Policy Reform, S. 14 ff., verfügbar unter https://www.hks.harvard.edu/content/download/66823/1240102/version/1/file/SYPA_SimiGeorge_2014.pdf (zuletzt abgerufen am 28.4.2021).

1623 *Robinson* kritisiert ebenfalls das mangelhafte Verfahrens-Management in Indien, Robinson, in: Choudhry/Khosla/Mehta, The Oxford Handbook of the Indian Constitution, S. 330 (336).

verfahren[1624] sollte geschaffen werden.[1625] In der Zukunft wird auch eine schiedsrechtliche Ausbildung der Richter notwendig sein, damit die Richter den Stellenwert der Schiedsgerichtsbarkeit für das überlastete indische Gerichtssystem erkennen[1626] und eine schiedsfreundlichere Einstellung entwickeln. Nur wenn Indien effektive Gerichtsverfahren mit auf Schiedsverfahren spezialisierten Gerichten vorweisen kann, wird es zu einem attraktiven Sitz für Schiedsverfahren werden können.

Um der vorherrschenden Präferenz von *ad hoc*-Schiedsverfahren entgegen zu wirken, sollte Indien versuchen, durch die Etablierung und Förderung von modernen Schiedsinstitutionen den Parteien effektive institutionelle Schiedsverfahren als Alternative zu bieten. Eine höhere Anzahl an institutionell administrierten Schiedsverfahren würde das überforderte indische Gerichtssystem entlasten.[1627]

Durch die Kombination einer schiedsfreundlichen Gesetzgebung mit einer die Schiedsverfahren unterstützenden Judikativen und einem effizienten Gerichtsapparat kann Indien seinen Ruf als schiedsfeindliche Rechtsordnung revidieren. Bessere Rahmenbedingungen für die schiedsgerichtliche Streitbeilegung würden den internationalen Handel mit Indien begünstigen, Investitionen in Indien attraktiver machen und Indiens Aufstieg zu einer der führenden Wirtschaftsnationen katalysieren.

1624 Dies kann u. a. die elektronische Klageeinreichung, das elektronische Einreichen von Schriftsätzen, Anträgen und Beweisen umfassen und ermöglicht es dem zuständigen Gericht und den Anwälten im Idealfall auf die Gerichtsakte jederzeit elektronisch zuzugreifen und Gerichtstermine online zu vereinbaren, vgl. Kapitel: Einleitung; Entwicklung des effektiven Gerichtswesens (A.II.1.gg)). Lediglich beim Supreme Court können seit 2006 Klagen elektronisch eingereicht werden, Chief Justice Shri K. G. Balakrishnan, Address by Hon'ble Shri K. G. Balakrishnan, Chief Justice of India, at the Joint Conference of Chief Ministers and Chief Justices, at Vigyan Bhawan, 8. 4.2007, verfügbar unter http://www.supremecourtofindia.nic.in/speeches/speeches_2007/8.4.2007.pdf (zuletzt abgerufen am 28.4.2021).

1625 In diesem Kontext ist die Weiterbildung der Richter hinsichtlich Gerichtsorganisation und der Verwendung von modernen Technologien durch die „National Justice Academy" zu begrüßen.

1626 Die „Delhi Judicial Academy" verfolgt in der Richteraus- und Weiterbildung bereits das Ziel, durch die Schulung von Richtern die Verweisung von Streitigkeiten an alternative Streitbeilegungsmechanismen zu fördern, um den Rückstau der gerichtlich anhängigen Verfahren zu reduzieren, Delhi Judicial Academy, About Us, Our Vision, verfügbar unter http://judicialacademy.nic.in/index.php?option=article&id=1&ItemId=5 (zuletzt abgerufen am 28.4.2021).

1627 U. a. würde die Schiedsrichterbestellung und das Ablehnungsverfahren von einem oder mehreren Schiedsrichtern von Schiedsinstitutionen übernommen werden, Sec. 11 ff. SchiedsG; vgl. Born, Cases and Materials, S. 70 f.; Blackaby/Partasides/Redfern/Hunter, International Arbitration, Rn. 4.36 ff.; Gaillard/Savage, Fouchard Gaillard Goldman, Rn. 746 ff.; Born, Law and Practice, § 7, S. 129 ff.

Im Stadtstaat Singapur stellt die Schiedsgerichtsbarkeit einen wichtigen Wirtschaftszweig des Dienstleistungssektors dar. Die Singapurer Schiedsgesetzgebung rezipierte – wie das indische SchiedsG – das UNCITRAL Modellgesetz und entwickelte es Schiedsverfahren fördernd weiter. Die Schiedsverfahren begünstigende Haltung des Singapurer Gesetzgebers zeigt sich exemplarisch in der gesetzlich vorgesehenen Vollstreckungsmöglichkeit von vorläufigen Maßnahmen, die Schiedsgerichte mit ausländischem Sitz und der „Emergency Arbitrator" anordnen. Bei Rechtsunsicherheit, schiedsunfreundlichen Gerichtsentscheidungen und veränderten Anforderungen an die schiedsgesetzlichen Rahmenbedingungen passte Singapur die Gesetzgebung umgehend an.

Die Singapurer Rechtsordnung strebte seit der Verabschiedung des IAA an, das Land zu einem weltweit präferierten Schiedsort zu entwickeln. Dieser Prämisse entsprechend haben die Singapurer Gerichte die schiedsrechtlichen Bestimmungen in Schiedsverfahren fördernder Weise ausgelegt.

Singapur besitzt ferner ein effektives Gerichtssystem mit gut aus- und fortgebildeten Richtern[1628] und mit auf Schiedsverfahren spezialisierten Richtern am Supreme Court. Der Gerichtsapparat verfügt über ein modernes „State of the Art" „Case Management", automatisierte Verfahrensabläufe und über ein digitalisiertes Gerichtsverfahren. Die Schiedsrichterbestellung übertrug Singapur, um den High Court zu entlasten, an die international anerkannte Schiedsinstitution SIAC und an Experten der Schiedsgerichtsbarkeit.

Die flexible Anpassung der Schiedsgesetzgebung, seine Schiedsverfahren fördernde Gesetzgebung und Rechtsprechung und sein effizienter moderner Gerichtsapparat haben Singapur zu einer der führenden Schiedsjurisdiktionen in Asien und weltweit werden lassen. Auch bei indischen Parteien ist der Schiedsort Singapur beliebt. Indische Partien sind die am stärksten vertretene ausländische Nation in SIAC-Schiedsverfahren.[1629] Sie vereinbaren für

1628 Das Richteramt ist durch die weltweit höchste Vergütung für die besten Juristen attraktiv, vgl. Kapitel: Einleitung; Entwicklung des effektiven Gerichtswesens (A.II.1.gg)).

1629 Mit 85, 91 bzw. 153 eingelegten Schiedsverfahren waren indische Parteien 2013, 2015 und 2016 die am stärksten vertretene ausländische Nation in SIAC-Schiedsverfahren, SIAC Annual Report 2013, Nationality of Parties, verfügbar unter http://www.siac.org.sg/images/stories/articles/annual_report/SIAC_Annual_Report_2013.pdf (zuletzt abgerufen am 28.4.2021); SIAC Annual Report 2015, Nationality of Parties, verfügbar unter http://www.siac.org.sg/images/stories/articles/annual_report/SIAC_Annual_Report_2015.pdf (zuletzt abgerufen am 28.4.2021); SIAC Annual Report 2016, Nationality of Parties, verfügbar unter http://www.siac.org.sg/images/stories/articles/annual_report/SIAC_AR_2016_24pp_WEBversion_edited.pdf (zuletzt abgerufen am 28.4.2021). 2012 und 2014 waren indische Schiedsparteien mit 42 bzw. 37 SIAC-Verfahren die zweit- bzw. drittstärkste ausländische Nation, CEO's Annual Report 2012, Nationality of Parties, verfügbar unter http://www.siac.org.sg/

ihre inländischen Handelsstreitigkeiten SIAC-Schiedsverfahren mit Sitz in Singapur, um dem ineffizienten indischen Gerichtssystem zu entfliehen.[1630] Dies verdeutlicht, dass sich Indien bei der Modernisierung seines SchiedsG und seines Gerichtssystems an der progressiveren und effizienteren Singapurer Rechtsordnung orientieren sollte.

Singapur glich seine Schiedsgesetzgebung den Bedürfnissen der Schiedsverfahren an, um den Wirtschaftszweig der Schiedsgerichtsbarkeit zu erhalten und weiter auszubauen. Das Wirtschaftswachstum des BRIC-Staates Indien ist in den letzten Jahrzehnten trotz fehlender Reformen der Schiedsgesetzgebung rasant gestiegen. Dies zeigt, dass Indien im Vergleich zu Singapur wirtschaftliches Wachstum generierte, ohne dem Anforderungsprofil des internationalen Schiedsgerichtsstandards zu entsprechen. Als Schwellenland musste Indien seine Kräfte bündeln, um insbesondere die Armut zu bekämpfen[1631], Bildungschancen[1632] sowie die medizinische Versorgung[1633] zu verbessern und um die Infrastruktur weiter auszubauen[1634]. Reformen der Schiedslegislation waren bis zur Wahl der wirtschafsfreundlichen Regierung *Modi* (2014) nicht die erste Priorität auf der Agenda der indischen Regierungen. In diesem Kontext ist es nicht verwunderlich, dass Singapur seine Schiedsgesetzgebung im Vergleich zu Indien flexibler den Anforderungen der Schiedsgerichtsbarkeit anpasste.

Das Hauptproblem der indischen Schiedsrechtsordnung liegt gleichwohl in der abwehrenden Haltung der indischen Gerichte gegenüber der schiedsgerichtlichen Streitbeilegung. In Indien etablierte sich, trotz der Rezeption des liberalen UNCITRAL Modellgesetzes, durch richterliche „Rechtsfortbildung“[1635] eine Rechtsordnung, die mit der schiedsunfreundlichen Rechtslage vor Inkrafttreten des SchiedsG vergleichbar war. In der jüngeren Vergangenheit entwickelte die Rechtsprechung der obersten indischen Gerichte

images/stories/articles/annual_report/siac_annual_report_2012_new.pdf (zuletzt abgerufen am 28.4.2021); SIAC Annual Report 2014, Nationality of Parties, verfügbar unter http://www.siac.org.sg/images/stories/articles/annual_report/SIAC_Annual_Report_2014.pdf (zuletzt abgerufen am 28.4.2021).

1630 Mangan/Reed/Choong, S. 12.

1631 The World Bank, Who we are, India's Poverty Profile, 27.5.2016, verfügbar unter http://www.worldbank.org/en/news/infographic/2016/05/27/india-s-poverty-profile (zuletzt abgerufen am 28.4.2021).

1632 The World Bank, Who we are, Education in India, 20.9.2011, verfügbar unter http://www.worldbank.org/en/news/feature/2011/09/20/education-in-india (zuletzt abgerufen am 28.4.2021).

1633 The World Bank, Who we are, World Bank Support to the Health Sector in India, 6.4.2010, verfügbar unter http://www.worldbank.org/en/news/feature/2010/04/06/worldbank-india-health-support (zuletzt abgerufen am 28.4.2021).

1634 The World Bank, Global Rankings 2016, 2014, 2012, 2010, 2008, verfügbar unter http://lpi.worldbank.org/international/global/2016 (zuletzt abgerufen am 28.4.2021).

1635 Diese Rechtsprechung erging unter dem SchiedsG a. F.

zwar eine schiedsfreundlichere Haltung. Die Überlastung des Gerichtssystems und die wenig schiedsfreundliche Einstellung der Gerichte bleiben aber die zentralen Probleme der indischen Rechtsordnung. Die Singapurer Schiedsgesetzgebung und Rechtsprechung sind dagegen von einer kontinuierlich Schiedsverfahren fördernden und gerichtliche Interventionen unterbindenden Haltung geprägt. Singapur verfügt zudem über ein effektives und modernes Gerichtssystem.

Als Gesamtergebnis ist festzuhalten, dass Indien durch die Novelle des SchiedsG seit dem Jahr 2015 eine schiedsfreundliche Legislation besitzt, die mit den Singapurer Schiedsgesetzen auf Augenhöhe ist. Die Anpassung des SchiedsG an die Bedürfnisse des Schiedsgerichtswesens war in Indien, im Gegensatz zu den flexiblen Schiedsgesetzänderungen im Stadtstaat Singapur, ein 20 Jahre währender Prozess. Die indischen Gerichtsentscheidungen offenbarten eine schiedsunfreundliche Einstellung der Gerichte und Interventionstendenzen in den nicht als ebenbürtig angesehenen Streitbeilegungsmechanismus der Schiedsgerichtsbarkeit. Dies führte zu langen Verfahrensdauern im ineffizienten indischen Gerichtssystem. Ein Vergleich mit der Schiedsverfahren kontinuierlich fördernden Singapurer Rechtsordnung mit ihrem effektiven und modernen Gerichtswesen führt zu der Gesamtbewertung, dass die indische Schiedsrechtsordnung als schiedsunfreundlicher anzusehen ist. Damit Indien zu einer schiedsfreundlicheren Rechtsordnung wird, ist es erforderlich, dass Indien seine Schiedsgesetzgebung den Anforderungen der Schiedsgerichtsbarkeit flexibler anpasst und einen effektiven Gerichtsapparat schafft, der den Streitbeilegungsmechanismus der Schiedsgerichtsbarkeit als gleichwertig anerkennt und fördert.